CHILD AND ADOL
PSYCHOTHER.

Every day, millions of children experience serious mental health issues such as symptoms related to autism, psychosis, mania, depression, and anxiety. Moreover, many youth struggle with issues related to trauma, eating, sleep, disruptive behavior, and substance use. Most of these youth do not receive evidence-based treatments. Instead, they commonly receive untested, ineffective, and even harmful treatments. *Child and Adolescent Psychotherapy* presents the research-supported treatment packages and their individual components for every major mental health issue facing infants, children, and adolescents. Each chapter also identifies and analyzes other variables and resources that influence treatment: parents, assessment, comorbidity, demographics, and medication. Useful resources are included for each mental health issue covered in the book. The chapters are organized in the same order as they appear in the DSM-5.

STEPHEN HUPP is a professor of psychology in the Clinical Child and School Psychology program at Southern Illinois University, Edwardsville (SIUE). He is also a Licensed Clinical Psychologist and the Social-Emotional Consultant for the East St. Louis Head Start Program. He is the author of over 50 scholarly publications, including three other books – *Great Myths of Child Development*, *Great Myths of Adolescence*, and *Thinking Critically about Child Development*. In 2015, he won the Great Teacher Award from the SIUE Alumni Association, and he is an Executive Producer for the *Science Moms* documentary. You can find him on Twitter at @StephenHupp.

CHILD AND ADOLESCENT PSYCHOTHERAPY

Components of Evidence-Based Treatments for Youth and their Parents

Edited by

Stephen Hupp
Southern Illinois University, Edwardsville

CAMBRIDGE
UNIVERSITY PRESS

University Printing House, Cambridge CB2 8BS, United Kingdom

One Liberty Plaza, 20th Floor, New York, NY 10006, USA

477 Williamstown Road, Port Melbourne, VIC 3207, Australia

314–321, 3rd Floor, Plot 3, Splendor Forum, Jasola District Centre,
New Delhi – 110025, India

79 Anson Road, #06–04/06, Singapore 079906

Cambridge University Press is part of the University of Cambridge.

It furthers the University's mission by disseminating knowledge in the pursuit of
education, learning, and research at the highest international levels of excellence.

www.cambridge.org
Information on this title: www.cambridge.org/9781107168817
DOI:10.1017/9781316717615

First published 2018

Printed in the United States of America by Sheridan Books, Inc.

A catalogue record for this publication is available from the British Library.

Library of Congress Cataloging-in-Publication Data
Names: Hupp, Stephen, editor.
Title: Child & adolescent psychotherapy : components of evidence-based treatments for youth
    and their parents / edited by Stephen Hupp.
Other titles: Child and adolescent psychotherapy
Description: Cambridge, United Kingdom ; New York, NY : Cambridge University Press, 2019. |
    Includes bibliographical references and index.
Identifiers: LCCN 2018014388| ISBN 9781107168817 (hardback) | ISBN 9781316619759 (paperback)
Subjects: | MESH: Mental Disorders – therapy | Child | Adolescent | Psychotherapy – methods |
    Evidence-Based Medicine – methods
Classification: LCC RJ503 | NLM WS 350.2 | DDC 616.89/140835–dc23
LC record available at https://lccn.loc.gov/2018014388

ISBN 978-1-107-16881-7 Hardback
ISBN 978-1-316-61975-9 Paperback

To my mom, Deanna Hupp, for being my first and finest teacher.

Contents

viii   *Contents*

Contributors

Anca Alba, PhD, DClinPsy
Clinical Psychologist, South London and Maudsley NHS Foundation Trust, London, UK. National and Specialist CAMHS and CUES Trial Therapist.

Amy Altszuler, MS
Doctoral candidate, Department of Psychology and Center for Children and Families, Florida International University.

Michael I. Axelrod, PhD
Professor, Psychology Department, University of Wisconsin-Eau Claire. Author of *Behavior Analysis for School Psychologists* (2017).

Brittany Babycos, MA
Sr. Institutional Researcher, University of New Mexico-Gallup.

Brooke L. Bennett, MS
Doctoral candidate, Department of Psychology, University of Hawai'i at Mānoa.

Molly Bobek, LCSW
Director of Clinical Implementation, National Center on Addiction and Substance Abuse. Teaching Faculty, Ackerman Institute for the Family, New York.

John Borgen, PsyD, BCBA-D
Assistant Professor, Applied Psychology, Oregon Institute of Technology.

Deepika Bose, BA
Doctoral candidate, Department of Psychology, Florida International University.

Frances Bozsik, MS
Doctoral candidate, Department of Psychology, University of Missouri-Kansas City.

Karen Bracegirdle, PGDip
Research CBT therapist and Nurse Specialist, South London and Maudsley NHS Foundation Trust, and Clinical Tutor, King's College London (KCL), London, UK. National and Specialist CAMHS, CUES Team Lead Therapist and Supervisor.

Sophie Browning, PsychD, DClinPsy
Consultant Clinical Psychologist, South London and Maudsley NHS Foundation Trust, London, UK. National and Specialist CAMHS Inpatient Lead and CUES Team Clinical Lead.

Bruce F. Chorpita, PhD
Professor, University of California, Los Angeles. Lead author of the *MATCH-ADTC* protocol (2009) and 2019 President of the Association for Behavioral and Cognitive Therapies.

Andrea Chronis-Tuscano, PhD
Professor, University of Maryland. President-Elect of the International Society for Research in Child and Adolescent Psychopathology (ISRCAP).

Christina M. Danko, PhD
Assistant Research Professor, University of Maryland.

Susan Doyle, MS
Doctoral candidate, Department of Psychology, University of Toledo, Toledo. Graduate student member of the UT Child Anxiety and Stress Lab.

Jacqueline Horan Fisher, PhD
Research Scientist, Adolescent and Family Research, National Center on Addiction and Substance Abuse, New York.

Sarah E. Francis, PhD
Associate Professor, Department of Psychology, University of Toledo. Director of the UT Child Anxiety and Stress Lab.

Ann F. Garland, PhD
Professor and Founding Chair, Department of Counseling and Marital and Family Therapy, University of San Diego. Professor Emeritus in Psychiatry, UCSD.

Peter A. Girolami, PhD, BCBA-D
Program Director, Pediatric Feeding Disorders Program, Kennedy Krieger Institute, Baltimore, MD.

Michael B. Himle, PhD
Associate Professor, Department of Psychology, University of Utah. Co-Director of the Tourette Association of America Designated Center of Excellence for Tourette and Tic Disorders.

Aaron Hogue, PhD
Director of Adolescent and Family Research, National Center on Addiction and Substance Abuse, New York.

Sarah Morsbach Honaker, PhD, CBSM
Assistant Professor of Pediatrics at Indiana University School of Medicine, Director of Behavioral Sleep Medicine at Riley Children's Hospital, Indianapolis, Indiana.

Danae L. Hudson, PhD
Professor, Department of Psychology, Missouri State University. Co-author of *Revel Psychology, 1st edition* (2019).

Stephen Hupp, PhD
Professor, Department of Psychology, Southern Illinois University Edwardsville. Co-author of *Great Myths of Child Development* (2015).

Ashley Isaia, MA
Doctoral student in Clinical Psychology, Department of Psychology, University of Illinois at Chicago.

Tiffany John, LMSW
Research Associate, National Center on Addiction and Substance Abuse, New York.

Suzanne Jolley, PhD
Senior Lecturer and Honorary Consultant Clinical Psychologist, King's College London (KCL), Department of Psychology, Institute of Psychiatry Psychology and Neuroscience; and South London and Maudsley NHS Foundation Trust, London, UK. CUES Team Research Lead and Programme Leader for the KCL Cognitive Behavioural Therapy for Psychosis programmes.

Katherine A. Kennedy, BS
Doctoral candidate, Department of Psychology, Fordham University, Bronx, NY.

Elizabeth M. Kryszak, PhD
Psychologist, Child Development Center, Nationwide Children's Hospital, Columbus, OH.

Monique LeBlanc, PhD
Associate Professor, Department of Psychology, Southeastern Louisiana University.

Megan Lilly, PhD
Graduate from Louisiana State University.

Fiona L. Macphee, MS
Doctoral candidate, Center for Children and Families, Department of Psychology, Florida International University.

Shannon Manley, MA
Department of Psychology, University of Toledo. Graduate student member of the UT Child Anxiety and Stress Lab.

Michael C. Meinzer, PhD
Assistant Clinical Professor, University of Maryland.

Dean McKay, PhD
Professor, Department of Psychology, Fordham University. Past President of the Association for Behavioral and Cognitive Therapies, Bronx, NY.

James A. Mulick, PhD
Emeritus Professor of Pediatrics, The Ohio State University.

Danielle R. Novick, BA
Department of Psychology, University of Maryland.

William E. Pelham Jr., PhD, ABPP
Distinguished Professor of Psychology and Psychiatry, Director, Center for Children and Families, Department of Psychology, Florida International University and University of Buffalo; Distinguished Professor Emeritus of Psychology, State University of New York at Buffalo; Adjunct Professor of Psychiatry, Western Psychiatric Institute and Clinic, University of Pittsburgh School of Medicine.

Jeremy W. Pettit, PhD
Professor, Department of Psychology, Florida International University. Author of *Chronic Depression: Interpersonal Sources, Therapeutic Solutions* (2005).

Nicole Piazza, BA
Doctoral Fellow, Psychology Department, St. John's University. Research Associate at National Center on Addiction and Substance Abuse, New York.

Bieke D. Puncochar, PhD
Licensed Clinical Psychologist. Regional Clinical Director at Rogers Behavioral Health, Nashville, Tennessee.

Whitney Rostad, PhD
Postdoctoral Research Associate, Mark Chaffin Center for Healthy Development, Georgia State University, Atlanta, GA.

Jessica F. Scherr, PhD
Postdoctoral Psychology Fellow, Child Development Center, Nationwide Children's Hospital, Columbus, OH.

Stephen R. Shirk, PhD

Professor, Department of Psychology, University of Denver. Co-author of *Change Processes in Child Psychotherapy* (1996) and Past President (2005) of the Society of Clinical Child and Adolescent Psychology.

Mark D. Shriver, PhD, BCBA-D

Professor, Psychology, Munroe-Meyer Institute, University of Nebraska Medical Center.

Emily C. Stefano, MS

Doctoral candidate, Department of Psychology, University of Hawai'i at Mānoa.

John M. Vasko, MPS

Faculty Research Assistant, University of Maryland.

Sally M. Weinstein, PhD

Assistant Professor, Department of Psychiatry, University of Illinois at Chicago. Co-author of *RAINBOW: A Child- and Family-Focused Cognitive-Behavioral Treatment for Pediatric Bipolar Disorder, Clinician Guide, Programs that Work Series* (2017).

Brianna Wellen, BS

Graduate student, Department of Psychology, University of Utah.

Amy E. West, PhD

Associate Professor, Department of Pediatrics, Children's Hospital Los Angeles/University of Southern California. Co-author of *RAINBOW: A Child- and Family-Focused Cognitive-Behavioral Treatment for Pediatric Bipolar Disorder, Clinician Guide, Programs that Work Series* (2017).

Brooke L. Whisenhunt, PhD

Professor, Department of Psychology, Missouri State University. Co-author of *Revel Psychology, 1st edition* (2019).

Foreword

Bruce F. Chorpita

The study of mental health treatment for children is flourishing, with randomized clinical trials for childhood problems now numbering over 1,000, three-quarters of which have been published in the last 25 years. Most of these recent innovations were both inspired and bound by the evidence-based treatment (EBT) paradigm, which formalized a lexicon to characterize psychosocial treatments and the authenticity of their supporting evidence. What emerged was a proliferation of manualized treatments with empirical support meeting a defined standard of evidence.

Stephen Hupp offers a timely review of this literature with an innovative perspective. Hupp is not only a renowned educator in the realm of scientific approaches to assessment and treatment but also an authority on what constitutes a scientific approach to clinical psychology. For example, in addition to this book on science-based psychotherapy for children, he has compiled a companion volume, *Pseudoscience in Child and Adolescent Psychotherapy*, addressing pseudoscientific treatments. In the current book, Hupp has assembled a collection of expert and forward-thinking authors, whose analysis of psychotherapy goes beyond the specific treatment "brands" and "packages" that have come to characterize the EBT paradigm. In this regard, Hupp is to be commended for pushing the intellectual boundaries outward, encouraging a breadth of perspective, while carefully maintaining a grounding in the field's best science. The result is a wealth of new ideas and fresh perspectives on an evidence base that is now more than five decades old.

Aside from the diversity of problems addressed, ranging from common syndromes, to sleep, to feeding, and even to the therapeutic relationship, the particularly noteworthy aspect of this book is its organization and analysis of the treatments for those problems based on their clinical components or elements, which is a departure from the dominant EBT framework characterizing recent treatment development and research. As my colleagues and I have articulated elsewhere, despite remarkable benefits, the EBT paradigm has produced some challenges over time, such as (a) the difficulty aggregating knowledge across the empirical silos that have emerged over decades of replication within specific treatment packages, (b) the "big menu" problem of actually having too many suitable, evidence-based options for given problems, with limited means for adopters to choose among them, and (c) the "no option" scenarios that offer limited empirical guidance in contexts for which EBTs have not been identified, based on essentially all-or-nothing definitions of evidence.

Focusing on components or elements has its own limitations, but it does offer some direct solutions to these aforementioned challenges. Although often misinterpreted as a treatment toolkit, a common elements framework is certainly not meant to be construed as a formal treatment approach. Rather, it is a powerful analytic method that allows aggregation of treatment outcome research across any reported factors of interest (e.g., treatment targets or diagnosis, youth or family characteristics, contexts, and even combinations of these). This perspective is not a substitute for protocol building and testing, but identifying patterns of practices that are common among successful, evidence-based approaches shines considerable light on the process of protocol building and design in the laboratory context. In the practice world, a common elements perspective informs strategic adaptation and planning, whether in the context of EBTs that have hit roadblocks, or of "usual care" services in systems for which such treatments are unavailable. Element-level analysis of the treatment literature affords session-by-session responsivity if needed, as opposed to responsivity only at the level of selecting an entire course of treatment. This perspective holds considerable appeal for the clinical community, who face frequent emergent events, comorbidity, poor service engagement, and other sources of clinical interference. At the same time, this level of analysis has been characterized by occasional controversy among the academic community.

That controversy is moving to resolution – Hupp dispels the myth that there cannot be multiple valid lenses on a given body of knowledge. He has produced a milestone work whose elements-based view complements decades of traditional reviews, at last moving what was initially innovative and disruptive toward something mainstream, akin to Goodman, Bazerman, and Conlon's "social fact" (Institutionalization of planned organizational change. *Research in Organizational Behavior*, 2, 215–246). This book is perspective-altering, and it couldn't have come at a better time.

Bruce F. Chorpita, PhD, Professor, University of California, Los Angeles. Lead author of the *MATCH-ADTC* protocol and 2019 President of the Association for Behavioral and Cognitive Therapies.

Preface

There are a few important ways that this book is unique. First, it has a broader coverage than other similar books. Second, the chapters are organized in a manner that corresponds directly to the same topics in the latest edition of the *Diagnostic and Statistical Manual*. Finally, this book describes in detail both evidence-based treatments (EBTs) and their individual components while also identifying other important factors related to treatment for youth.

Unique Attributes

Broad Coverage

This book was developed in tandem with a companion book called *Pseudoscience in Child and Adolescent Psychotherapy*. Together, both books uniquely share the goal of helping readers distinguish between the science of EBTs and the pseudoscience of ineffective treatments. In addition to effective and ineffective treatments, both books include broad coverage of psychotherapy for youth in the following ways:

- *Types of psychosocial interventions*: The term "psychotherapy" is used in the broadest sense to represent different types of psychosocial interventions regardless of theoretical orientation.
- *Topic selection*: These books cover many topics that other similar books tend to give lighter coverage to or ignore (e.g., tics, psychosis, feeding).
- *Age range*: Chapters include interventions for infants, toddlers, children, and/or adolescents.
- *Other variables influencing treatment*: Several variables that influence treatment are discussed in every chapter, with an emphasis on the role of parents during psychotherapy for youth.

Although the companion book is useful for helping readers learn more about pseudoscience, the book you are now reading works just fine as a stand-alone text. All of the chapters are written by experts in their respective areas, and one distinguishing feature of this book is the emphasis on the specific *components* of EBTs instead of an emphasis on treatment *packages*. Early attempts at identifying EBTs often used treatment manuals as a major way to distinguish between different therapies. One strength of a focus on treatment manuals is the ability for others to replicate the therapies with relative ease. On the other hand, one limitation of focusing on manuals is that this approach results in lists of several very similar treatment packages. For example, several variations of behavioral parent training have individually been identified as being evidence-based (e.g., Parent Management Training, Parent–Child Interaction Therapy, Helping the Noncompliant Child, Incredible Years) even though they mostly share the same components.

An alternative method for identifying research-supported approaches has been starting to emerge, and this method identifies specific components of treatments (see Chorpita et al.'s 2011 article "Evidence-based treatments for children and adolescents" in *Clinical Psychology*). In the case of behavioral parent training, this method focuses on the components that are commonly used across many of the specific packages (e.g., parent attention, effective commands, praise, time-out). Moreover, some components are shared across EBTs for different disorders resulting in transdiagnostic interventions. This focus on EBT components is a complement to, not a replacement of, the earlier attempts at identifying comprehensive EBT packages. That is, it's useful for students, practitioners, and parents to have a sense of both components and packages.

This book can be used in graduate and undergraduate courses related to child and adolescent psychology. Specifically, it would fit well in *psychotherapy courses* as well as *psychopathology courses* where the one goal of the course is to link EBTs with disorders and related behaviors. This book has also been designed to be a useful starting point for practitioners in any field providing therapy with youth. To that end, each chapter also directs readers toward useful resources.

DSM-5 Compatible Organization

Overall, this book covers every major area in the *Diagnostic and Statistical Manual for Mental Disorders,* 5th edition (DSM-5) that is most pertinent to youth. The chapters are placed in the same order that the topics appear in the DSM-5 so that students can easily learn about treatments simultaneously as they learn about diagnoses. For example, after the introductory chapter, the next chapter covers intellectual and adaptive functioning, followed by chapters covering other topics consistent with the neurodevelopmental section of the DSM-5 (e.g., autism spectrum, inattention/hyperactivity, learning, tics). Chapter topics continue to correspond with the DSM-5 sections on psychosis, bipolar spectrum, and depression. Next, chapters cover anxiety, obsessions/compulsions, and trauma. Chapters also cover feeding, eating, toileting, and sleep with two of the last chapters on disruptive behavior and substance use.

Although the DSM-5 serves as the basis of the structure for both this book and the pseudoscience companion book, problematic diagnostic issues are also covered in these books. The companion book, in particular, discusses many diagnostic controversies. Additionally, authors in both books were encouraged to keep the discussion broader than just DSM-5 diagnostic categories, and this book emphasizes the value of linking assessment to intervention, with many authors describing how functional behavior assessment influences treatment.

The chapters begin with an introduction describing the disorders as well as other ways of conceptualizing related behaviors. Chapters discuss etiology as well as the theoretical underpinnings of EBTs. Usually with the aid of published reviews, chapters describe which treatment packages have been identified as being "well established" or "probably efficacious" using criteria set forth by the Divisions 12 and 53 of the American Psychological Association. The largest bulk of each chapter is comprised of describing the components of EBTs, and, when possible, evidence for the specific components is also included. Each chapter also includes additional variables influencing treatment.

The book wraps up with a chapter on common relational elements that cut across the different psychotherapies. In particular, the important roles of therapeutic alliance and active client involvement in therapy are described. The final chapter aims to highlight attempts to close the research to practice gap and also looks ahead to the future.

Subsections and Features

In addition to both EBT packages and components, this book identifies several other variables and resources related to treatment:

- *Parents*: The role of parents in their children's psychotherapy can vary widely. In some cases therapists spend more time working with parents than children, and in other cases therapists spend very little time with parents.

- *Assessment*: Minimal time is spent on assessment for the purpose of diagnosis, and instead each chapter describes how assessment procedures, such as functional behavioral assessment, specifically influence treatment selection.

- *Comorbidity*: Youth commonly meet the diagnostic criteria for more than one disorder, and this comorbidity can influence treatment decisions and progression.

- *Demographics*: Variables such as age, gender, and ethnicity can all affect treatment, and the most relevant demographic variables are discussed in every chapter.

- *Medication*: The role of pharmaceutical interventions is discussed throughout the book. In some cases medication may be a useful adjunct to psychotherapy, while in other cases medications do not provide any added benefit.

- *Side-Bars*: Each chapter provides a Side-Bar Box on a related topic. These boxes cover other promising treatments, other behaviors, other disorders, or other related issues.

- *Useful Resources*: Chapters end with a list of Useful Resources including organizations, websites, manuals, and other books.

Gratitude

A number of people have helped immensely in the development of this book. I am particularly thankful to Matt Bennett, who approached me with the idea for a new book about psychotherapy with youth. Other Cambridge staff have also helped make this book become a reality including Brianda Reyes, Stephen Acerra, Rosie Crawley, Emily Watton, and David Repetto. Additionally, Julene Knox deserves a lot of credit for giving the entire manuscript an immensely thorough edit. I am also grateful for the trailblazing writings of Bruce Chorpita and his colleagues on the topic of EBT components; without their work, this book would not exist. My advisor in graduate school, David Reitman, helped give me a passion for behaviorism and evidence-based practices. Other key mentors in my academic life include William Pelham Jr., C. Daniel Batson, C. R. Snyder, John Northup, Mary Lou Kelley, Keith D. Allen, Mark Shriver, and Emily Krohn. I probably should thank Jeremy Jewell for something, but I'm not exactly sure what. Additionally, for the last 15 years, the graduate students in the Clinical Child and School Psychology graduate program at Southern Illinois University Edwardsville have helped shape the focus of this book with their own insightful questions and even better answers.

I'm forever thankful for the support of the kids in my house, Henry, Vyla, and Evan (in the order I came to know them), and to my fabulous fiancée, Farrah, for helping me figure out how to best support them. I dedicated this book to my mom, Deanna Hupp, and the companion book to my dad, Dennis Hupp, to both of whom I simply owe everything.

Finally, I'd like to add that, upon turning down my request to write a chapter, a mentor of mine wished me luck but also told me, "You have a tiger by the tail." In the book we'll spend some time deciphering what he meant by this, but his friendly rejection also served to motivate me to put forward the best possible book. Luckily, I was able to round up some of the most influential scholars in their respective areas. We certainly haven't tamed the tiger yet, but it sure helped to have so many hands on the tail!

1

The Science of Psychotherapy with Youth

Stephen Hupp, Fiona L. Macphee, and William E. Pelham Jr.

Children and adolescents face a wide range of mental health challenges. Like many adults, youth often experience depression, phobias, and externalizing problems. In fact, many disorders first emerge in the early years of life, such as intellectual disability, autism spectrum disorder, and attention-deficit/hyperactivity disorder. Even infants and toddlers face challenges related to sleep, feeding, or toileting. Other mental health challenges may not emerge until later childhood or adolescence, such as eating disorders and substance use. As such, the focus of this book is far ranging, covering the time from infancy through adolescence, and we will commonly use the term *youth* in the broadest sense to include infants, children, and adolescents.

Complicating the mental health challenges of youth are the ever-changing definitions used to describe these challenges. For example, most disorders identified in youth went through mild to moderate changes in the latest revision of the *Diagnostic and Statistical Manual* (DSM-5; American Psychiatric Association, 2013). Even further complicating these mental health challenges is the large range of untested, ineffective, and sometimes harmful treatment approaches that have been used widely since the early roots of psychotherapy.

On the one hand, Sigmund Freud's psychodynamic approach deserves some credit for helping to popularize ideas such as: (a) biology is not the only factor influencing human behavior, (b) childhood experiences affect development, (c) parenting matters, and (d) therapy can help people cope with mental health challenges. On the other hand, Freud's approach was largely based on untested, and often untestable, ideas. Freud's case of Little Hans, a five-year-old with a fear of horses, is one good example (Freud et al., 1909/2001). In his psychoanalysis of Little Hans, Freud credited the boy's erotic feelings toward his mother, fear of his father, the birth of his sister, castration anxiety, masturbation, and a repressed libido (among other equally dubious causes) as all contributing to the boy's fear. Additionally, Freud concluded that the boy's fear of being bitten by a horse was related to having previously been frightened by a penis.

Freud's intervention was to help make the parents and child aware of the connection between the boy's repressed unconscious wishes and his fear of horses. Over a century later, there is no evidence that Freud's approach to treating Little Hans is an effective way to deal with childhood phobias, and alternative interpretations of the case of Little Hans are more parsimonious than Freud's (Wolpe & Rachman, 1960). Over that same century, many other pseudoscientific treatments have flourished and continue to proliferate today (see the *Pseudoscience and Questionable Ideas* Side-Bar Box for more information about untested, ineffective, and harmful treatments).

Pseudoscience and Questionable Ideas

Many practitioners rely on pseudoscience when they treat youth with mental health challenges (Hupp & Jewell, 2015; Jewell et al., in press; Mercer, Hupp, & Jewell, in press). One major type of pseudoscience involves using treatments that have research showing they are ineffective. In addition to pseudoscientific treatments, practitioners also commonly implement treatments based on questionable ideas that are implausible and that do not have supporting evidence. Although it's important to keep an open mind about new untested treatments that may potentially work, caution is typically warranted for treatments until well-designed studies examine their effectiveness. As members of the skeptical community often like to say, "it's important to keep an open mind but not so open that your brains fall out."

The major goal of this book is to provide information to students, scholars, and practitioners about EBTs. As worthy of a goal that this is, research shows that teaching about EBTs is not enough. That is, even after learning about EBTs, some learners continue to believe in the effectiveness of ineffective therapies (Hupp et al., 2012). The good news is that the belief in ineffective treatments can be diminished if the ineffective treatments are also overtly addressed (Hupp et al., 2013). To that end, this book also has a companion book called *Pseudoscience in Child and Adolescent Psychotherapy* (Hupp, 2019), which covers:

- diagnostic controversies
- questionable assessment practices
- myths that influence treatment
- implausible treatments
- ineffective treatments
- potentially harmful treatments
- and even attempts to bash evidence-based approaches.

It may be a long time before evidence-based approaches are used more frequently than pseudoscientific approaches. To get to that point, it's going to take persistent and effective science communication. Thus, the companion book also includes side-bars written by science communicators from a variety of fields.

Similar to Freud, John B. Watson (1924), argued against the prevailing view that heredity alone is the primary factor influencing human behavior. Contrary to Freud, however, Watson provided an alternative conceptualization. Instead of focusing on the unobservable world of the unconscious, Watson emphasized the study of how the environment affects observable phenomena such as overt actions and even thoughts (which are at least observable to the person experiencing them). Unlike Freud's largely untestable ideas, Watson's theories of development were testable and thus contributed to the *science* of psychology. For example, Watson's study of Little Albert directly demonstrated how a new fear could be developed in an 11-month-old infant (Watson & Watson, 1921). Specifically, Albert showed no signs of fear to a white rat until the researchers began making sudden loud sounds when the rat was near. Soon, Albert showed fear of the rat even when no sounds were being made, and this fear even generalized to other white furry stimuli, such as rabbits. With this early understanding of classical conditioning, Watson was also able to apply this research to the treatment of anxiety disorders in a manner consistent with evidence-based approaches today.

This behavioral science of psychology continued rapid development with help from B. F. Skinner in books such as *Science and Human Behavior* (Skinner, 1953) that summarized his groundbreaking research demonstrating the many ways the environment can be changed to influence behavior including both "public events" (e.g., physical actions, language) and "private events" (e.g., thoughts, feelings), largely through operant conditioning. Albert Bandura (1974) agreed with these early behavioral theories and offered up observational learning as another way to influence behavior. Moreover, Aaron T. Beck (1963) conducted influential research on the role of cognitions in the development of psychopathology in adults, and his research was quickly applied to youth as well.

Early Attempts at Evaluating Psychotherapies

Despite the early progress made in developing scientific theories of human behavior, research examining psychotherapies was limited until the second half of the twentieth century. In 1952, only 19 published studies were included in Eysenck's seminal review of the effects of psychotherapy, and each of these studies involved drastic limitations that called into question the validity of the findings (Eysenck, 1952). Moreover, the therapies studied were classified as either "psychoanalytic" or "eclectic," and they focused on adults. Eysenck concluded that the existing literature as a whole lacked the scientific rigor needed to study the efficacy of psychotherapy and, thus, that there was no existing evidence that psychotherapy ameliorated mental health problems.

Eysenck called for more stringent definitions of comparative control subjects, recovery, and therapy type, all of which he argued were not provided in the literature.

Similar conclusions were made by early reviews of the child and adolescent mental health treatment literature that served as extensions of Eysenck's pioneering work. Specifically, a review of 18 available studies concluded that psychotherapy was not more effective than the passage of time alone (Levitt, 1957). Six years later, a review of 22 additional studies of psychotherapy with youth reiterated the same findings (Levitt, 1963). Importantly, these conclusions were based on studies with weak methodology including lack of randomization, small sample sizes, and nonspecific treatment approaches.

The field of clinical psychology has made great strides in both the quantity and quality of empirical research since the early reviews. By the late 1970s, Smith and Glass (1977) published one of the first meta-analyses that demonstrated that specific treatments targeting mental health produced positive outcomes. Shortly after, a more rigorous meta-analysis also reached a similar conclusion, that psychotherapy was associated with ameliorative treatment effects (Shapiro & Shapiro, 1982). A meta-analysis on child-focused psychosocial treatment also found evidence for the benefits of psychotherapy (Casey & Berman, 1985). The field of clinical psychology was quickly moving toward identifying evidence-based approaches that maximized therapeutic gains.

In the beginning of the 1990s, McFall proposed his "Manifesto for A Science of Clinical Psychology" (1991). The cardinal principle of McFall's manifesto was that scientific clinical psychology was the only legitimate form of clinical psychology. Specifically, McFall proposed that the public should only receive psychological treatments that have scientifically supported benefits with possible negative side effects ruled out empirically. Around this time, the field was beginning to demonstrate that the effects of child and adolescent mental health treatment differed based on a number of factors including child problems and treatment type (Weisz et al., 1987; Weisz et al., 1995). As Paul (1967) famously called for, an understanding was beginning to form of "What treatment, by whom, is most effective for this individual with that specific problem, under which set of circumstances?"

Identifying Evidence-Based Treatment Packages

Members of the Clinical Psychology Division 12 Task Force on the Promotion and Dissemination of Psychological Procedures were the first to undertake a systematic, standardized annual review of more than 400 adult-focused treatment studies. Their goal was to create and maintain a list of efficacious psychotherapies that would be regularly updated when new studies became available. The initial criteria used by the Task Force were adapted from those used by the Federal Drug Administration (Beutler, 1998), and a small number of treatments were widely studied and deemed efficacious (Task Force on the Promotion and Dissemination of Psychological Procedures, 1995). Importantly, the Task Force made no claims that the interventions identified in the original review were the only effective treatments or should take precedence over other treatments (Beutler, 1998).

A more refined definition of empirically supported treatments (ESTs) was offered by Chambless and Hollon (1998). The authors defined ESTs as clearly specified treatments shown to be effective for a delineated population in a controlled setting. They also identified the randomized clinical trial as the gold standard for efficacy research. The article preceded a series of reviews for specific mental health problems in a special edition of the *Journal of Consulting and Clinical Psychology* (*JCCP*). A treatment was deemed *efficacious* if it: (1) led to statistically superior outcomes when compared to a control group; (2) was conducted with a treatment manual, specified population, reliable and valid outcome measures, and appropriate data analysis; and (3) showed superiority in at least two independent research settings. A treatment was classified as *possibly efficacious* if only one study demonstrated superiority and there was no conflicting evidence. Lastly, an intervention could be designated as *efficacious and specific* if the study met the same criteria as efficacious studies but had the additional benefit of having better comparison groups that included other interventions or placebos.

Efforts to define ESTs sparked a spirited discussion and debate among experts. Some researchers began to question the external validity of efficacy studies. For example, Seligman (1995) argued that *effectiveness* studies, conducted in the real world (e.g., community mental health settings), should be the mark of empirical support. He argued that *efficacy* studies were likely to give inflated results because they were conducted within highly controlled settings with narrow participant demographic characteristics. Seligman also called for treatment outcome researchers to consider that therapy is not typically of a fixed duration as it is in efficacy studies. Additionally, he argued that therapy is self-correcting in that if an approach is not leading to patient improvement another modality is tried, in part because many individuals seek therapy for multiple problems that may require multiple approaches. Lastly, Seligman said that treatment is focused on improving general functioning rather than symptom reduction. Chambless and colleagues contributed to the ongoing conversation by specifying that the intended focus of the preliminary list of ESTs was on efficacy rather than effectiveness trials. The subject of effectiveness would be broached once the initial list of treatments was identified (Chambless et al., 1998).

Since child-focused clinical psychologists had not been involved in the initial work on identifying ESTs, only treatment studies of adults were evaluated. Suzanne Bennett-Johnson, the President of Division 12 at the time, appointed a separate working group to extend the Division 12 Task Force's work to treatment of children and adolescents. Her appointees were the leadership of Section 1 of Division 12, the youth-focused members of the Division. As this youth Task Force was conducting the formal reviews, Section 1 was simultaneously in the process of moving from

Sectional status in Division 12 to Divisional status of the American Psychological Association.

The Society for Clinical Child and Adolescent Psychology (SCCAP; Division 53 of the American Psychological Association) was thus founded in 1999 and has been at the forefront of identifying treatments with research support for youth. The *Journal of Clinical Child & Adolescent Psychology* (*JCCAP* – the official journal of Section 1/ Division 53) introduced the first special issue on ESTs for child and adolescent mental health (Lonigan, Elbert, & Johnson, 1998). Two sets of criteria were put forth, one for *well-established* psychosocial interventions and one for *probably efficacious* psychosocial interventions. Similar to the initial Division 12 Task Force criteria (Chambless & Hollon, 1998), for a treatment to be well-established it had to be superior to a placebo or comparative treatments in at least two studies. To be probably efficacious a treatment had to be more effective than no treatment in two studies. Like before, the ideal study included random assignment, controlled conditions, manualized treatment, a fixed number of sessions, well-operationalized targets, blinded raters, clearly specified sample characteristics, and a follow-up assessment.

Ten years later, Division 53 released a second special issue with relevant updates (Silverman & Hinshaw, 2008). This second special issue replaced the term *empirically supported* with the term *evidence-based* and asked contributing researchers to discuss the effectiveness of treatments, which had not been emphasized in prior reviews. Another classification was also introduced – *experimental treatments* – which constituted treatments not yet tested in trials meeting Task Force criteria for methodology. This new category allowed for quick identification of treatments that may be widely implemented but not effective.

Rather than waiting another ten years before disseminating more updates, the *JCCAP* more recently started releasing follow-ups, called "Evidence Base Updates," as soon as five years later, across separate issues (Southam-Gerow & Prinstein, 2014). Review criteria used for Evidence Base Updates include five levels: well-established treatments; probably efficacious treatments; possibly efficacious treatments; experimental treatments; and treatments of questionable efficacy. In addition to having new authors update the previous reviews, some new topics (e.g., bipolar spectrum) have also been addressed for the first time.

Starting with the 1998 special issue, the SCCAP has emphasized the importance of manualized or operationalized interventions to ensure standardization of intervention procedures (see Barth et al., 2012). Using treatment manuals in this manner is necessary for other researchers and practitioners to readily replicate the specific components and procedures of the interventions employed. One side effect of emphasizing treatment manuals, however, is that several different "name-brand" therapeutic approaches can become identified as being evidence-based even though they are largely operating under the same principles of behavior change.

In the 1998 review, treatments for ADHD were evaluated as a group if they had comparable but not necessarily identical interventions – for example, behavioral parent training (Pelham, Wheeler, & Chronis, 1998). In contrast, however, the review of treatments for conduct problems (Brestan & Eyberg, 1998) identified specific published manuals as evidence-based. For example, Parent–Child Interaction Therapy, the Helping the Noncompliant Child program, the Positive Parenting Program, and the Incredible Years program were all identified separately as being probably efficacious for young children with disruptive behavior even though they were all derived from the same two-stage Hanf model of parent training (Reitman & McMahon, 2013), and they are very similar approaches. Thus, the use of manuals as a form of therapy differentiation in some (but not all) of the reviews led to some questions. Should therapists learn each manual or should they choose one? How should therapists decide which manual to choose? Is it the place of scholars to promote name-brand therapies or more generic, nonproprietary, therapeutic approaches?

Identifying Components of Evidence-Based Treatments

Most treatment packages are comprised of multiple distinguishable components, and analyzing treatments at the component level, rather than at the manualized treatment package level, is another way to identify evidence-based approaches. Bruce Chorpita and colleagues have been strong advocates for the component level of analysis (Barth et al., 2012; Bernstein et al., 2015; Boustani et al., 2017; Chorpita & Daleiden, 2009; Chorpita et al., 2011; Chorpita, Daleiden, & Weisz, 2005), and the multiple writings on this topic by these authors and others have led to the use of several terms.

Boustani et al. (2017) provide a helpful glossary of terms related to the component level of analysis. For example, they define the *common elements approach* as the identification of "specific practice techniques and strategies common across a defined set of selected treatments" and that occur within a specific context, such as treatment for a specific disorder (2017, p. 199). Although, the common elements approach aims to identify which elements are common across EBTs, there is generally not enough research to show which of the components are critically important to a treatment's success. However, occasionally research studies, such as those using dismantling designs, can help identify which elements are actually necessary.

Terms such "essential elements" or "effective ingredients" tend to denote either that the treatment element is necessary for the package to work or that the element can even work when used alone. This book, as reflected in the subtitle, uses the even broader term of "components" of EBTs. That is, most chapters discuss common elements as well as other elements that are used in EBTs even if they are not common across multiple EBTs. It would be reasonable to give more weight to elements that are used across EBTs, but it's still valuable to know about the other elements used in EBTs as well. Other variations of terms conveying similar ideas include "practice elements," "behavioral kernels," and "principles of behavior change."

In the above example of several name-brand variations of behavioral parent training, these interventions share several common elements, including parent attention, effective commands, praise, and time-out. More broadly, Chorpita et al. (2011) have identified 41 components that are commonly used in psychological treatments for a variety of mental health challenges in youth. A few of the other examples of components include problem-solving, relaxation, exposure, cognitive restructuring, and modeling. Thus, some of these components are used in EBTs across multiple disorders, such as cognitive restructuring, which is often used in the treatment of depression, anxiety, and anger.

It is important to note that the common elements approach is best thought of as a complement to the system of identifying treatments based on their manuals. In fact, *modular* treatments include manuals that emphasize some necessary core components while also including some additional supplemental components that may be selected based on the needs of the youth (e.g., Chorpita, 2007). These days, treatment manuals tend to provide more flexibility for therapists in terms of both which components are used and the order in which they are implemented. There has also been a similar move toward *transdiagnostic* treatments, which involves using the same packages and/or components for multiple related disorders (e.g., anorexia and bulimia).

Similar to the common elements approach, another framework seeks to identify *common factors*. Whereas common elements involve specific techniques and strategies, common factors include "nonspecific factors of therapy that characterize many psychosocial interventions" (Boustani et al., 2017, p. 199). One example of a common factor is therapeutic alliance, or the degree to which the therapist and client have a good bond with each other, agree about the therapeutic methods, and share the same therapeutic goals (Bordin, 1979). Another example is the degree of client involvement in therapy, such as active participation (O'Malley, Suh, & Strupp, 1983). These common factors are discussed in the penultimate chapter of this book.

Interestingly, the component-based approach emphasized in this book is not novel but is a return to the early days of behavior therapy, in which the emphasis was on operationally defining the environmental manipulations that were used to produce behavior change. As discussed above, this was in stark contrast to the nonspecific therapies that for so long dominated the field of psychotherapy. McFall's "Manifesto" presaged the current movement of common elements and common factors.

Conclusion

This book is largely focused on the components of EBTs for specific disorders and related behaviors in youth. Most of the book emphasizes the components of well-established treatments if they have been identified. When there are not yet

well-established treatments, this book reviews the components of probably efficacious treatments, and when no treatments meet the criteria for well-established or
probably efficacious, then the best available evidence was used to guide the selection
of components to be reviewed.

The component-based analysis is meant to be a complement to the manual-based
treatment package emphasis that has been dominant since Division 12 of the
American Psychological Association first commissioned a task force to identify
treatments that work. Beyond the components of EBTs, many other factors have the
potential to influence the success of a particular treatment for a particular youth.
The role of parents in the therapeutic process varies widely. Assessment before,
during, and after therapy typically shapes interventions in profound and invaluable
ways. Many clients present with more than one mental health challenge, and how well
specific therapies work can partially depend on demographic characteristics as well as
common factors that are shared across therapies. Many clients get medication in
addition to, or instead of, psychosocial interventions. Taken altogether, it's a wonder
that any therapist is ever able to deal with these interacting factors in a way that makes
meaningful change in anyone's life. The good news is that new research is published
every day to point therapists and their clients in a better direction, and this book has
been designed to help in this difficult, but hopefully rewarding, process.

References

American Psychiatric Association. (2013). *Diagnostic and statistical manual of mental disorders*. 5th edn. Washington, DC: American Psychiatric Association.

Bandura, A. (1974). Behavior theory and the models of man. *American Psychologist, 29*, 859–869.

Barth, R. P., Lee, B. R., Lindsey, M. A., Collins, K. S., Strieder, F., Chorpita, B. F., ... &
Sparks, J. A. (2012). Evidence-based practice at a crossroads: The timely emergence of
common elements and common factors. *Research on Social Work Practice, 22*(1), 108–119.

Beck, A. (1963). Thinking and depression: 1, Idiosyncratic content and cognitive distortions.
Archives of General Psychiatry, 9, 324–333.

Bernstein, A., Chorpita, B. F., Rosenblatt, A., Becker, K. D., Daleiden, E. L., &
Ebesutani, C. K. (2015). Fit of evidence-based treatment components to youths served by
wraparound process: A relevance mapping analysis. *Journal of Clinical Child & Adolescent
Psychology, 44*(1), 44–57.

Beutler, L. E. (1998). Identifying empirically supported treatments: What if we didn't?
Journal of Consulting and Clinical Psychology, 66(1), 113–120.

Bordin, E. S. (1979). The generalizability of the psychoanalytic concept of the working
alliance. *Psychotherapy: Theory, Research & Practice, 16*(3), 252–260.

Boustani, M. M., Gellatly, R., Westman, J. G., & Chorpita, B. F. (2017). Advances in cognitive
behavioral treatment design: Time for a glossary. *The Behavior Therapist, 40*(6), 199–208.

Brestan, E. V., & Eyberg, S. M. (1998). Effective psychosocial treatments of
conduct-disordered children and adolescents: 29 years, 82 studies, and 5,272
kids. *Journal of Clinical Child Psychology, 27*(2), 180–189.

Casey, R. J., & Berman, J. S. (1985). The outcome of psychotherapy with children. *Psychological Bulletin, 2*(98), 388.

Chambless, D. L., Baker, M. J., Baucom, D. H., Beutler, L. E., Calhoun, K. S., Crits-Christoph, P., . . . & Woody, S. R. (1998). Update on empirically validated therapies, II. *The Clinical Psychologist, 51*(1), 3–16.

Chambless, D. L., & Hollon, S. B. (1998). Defining empirically supported therapies. *Journal of Consulting and Clinical Psychology, 66*(1), 7–18.

Chorpita, B. F. (2007). *Modular cognitive-behavioral therapy for childhood anxiety disorders.* New York: Guilford Press.

Chorpita, B. F., & Daleiden, E. L. (2009). Mapping evidence-based treatments for children and adolescents: Application of the distillation and matching model to 615 treatments from 322 randomized trials. *Journal of Consulting and Clinical Psychology, 77*(3), 566–579.

Chorpita, B. F., Daleiden, E. L., Ebesutani, C., Young, J., Becker, K. D., Nakamura, B. J., . . . & Starace, N. (2011). Evidence-based treatments for children and adolescents: An updated review of indicators of efficacy and effectiveness. *Clinical Psychology: Science and Practice, 18*, 154–172.

Chorpita, B. F., Daleiden, E. L., & Weisz, J. R. (2005). Identifying and selecting the common elements of evidence based interventions: A distillation and matching model. *Mental Health Services Research, 7*(1), 5–20.

Eysenck, H. J. (1952). The effects of psychotherapy: An evaluation. *Journal of Consulting Psychology, 16*, 319–324.

Freud, S., Strachey, J., Freud, A., Strachey, A., & Tyson, A. (1909/republished in 2001). *The standard edition of the complete psychological works of Sigmund Freud: "Little Hans" and the "Rat Man."* London: Vintage.

Hupp, S. (2019). *Pseudoscience in child and adolescent psychotherapy: Skeptical guide for therapists and parents.* Cambridge, UK: Cambridge University Press.

Hupp, S., & Jewell, J. (2015). *Great myths of child development.* Malden, MA: Wiley.

Hupp, S. D. A., McKenney, E., Schmittel, M., McCobin, M., & Owens, S. A. (2013). Disseminate, debunk, differentiate: Teaching about evidence-based treatments in a child psychology course. *The Behavior Therapist, 36*, 14–16.

Hupp, S. D. A., Stary, A. K., Bradshaw, K. N., & Owens, S. (2012). Debunk, debunk, debunk: Some evidence for why dissemination is only half the battle. *The Behavior Therapist, 35*, 76–78.

Jewell, J., Axelrod, M., Prinstein, M., & Hupp, S. (in press). *Great myths of adolescence.* Malden, MA: Wiley.

Levitt, E. E. (1957). The results of psychotherapy with children: An evaluation. *Journal of Consulting Psychology, 21*(3), 189–196.

Levitt, E. E. (1963). Psychotherapy with children: A further evaluation. *Behavior Research and Therapy, 1*(1), 45–51.

Lonigan, C. J., Elbert, J. C., & Johnson, S. B. (1998). Empirically supported psychosocial interventions for children: An overview. *Journal of Clinical Child Psychology, 27*(2), 138–145. doi:10.1207/s15374424jccp2702_1

McFall, R. (1991). Manifesto for a science of clinical psychology. *The Clinical Psychologist, 44*(6), 75–88.

Mercer, J., Hupp, S., & Jewell, J. (in press). *Thinking critically about child development: Examining myths & misunderstandings.* 3rd edn. Washington, DC: Sage.

O'Malley, S. S., Suh, C. S., & Strupp, H. H. (1983). The Vanderbilt Psychotherapy Process Scale: A report on the scale development and a process-outcome study. *Journal of Consulting and Clinical Psychology*, *51*(4), 581–586.

Paul, G. L. (1967). Strategy of outcome research in psychotherapy. *Journal of Consulting Psychology*, *2*(31), 109.

Pelham Jr., W. E., Wheeler, T., & Chronis, A. (1998). Empirically supported psychosocial treatments for attention deficit hyperactivity disorder. *Journal of Clinical Child Psychology*, *27*(2), 190–205.

Reitman, D., & McMahon, R. J. (2013). Constance "Connie" Hanf (1917–2002): The mentor and the model. *Cognitive and Behavioral Practice*, *20*(1), 106–116. doi:10.1016/j.cbpra.2012.02.005

Seligman, M. E. P. (1995). The effectiveness of psychotherapy. The Consumer Report Study. *American Psychologist*, *50*(12), 965–974.

Shapiro, D. A., & Shapiro, D. (1982). Meta-analysis of comparative therapy outcome studies: A replication and refinement. *Psychological Bulletin*, *92*(3), 581–604.

Silverman, W. K., & Hinshaw, S. P. (2008). The second special issue on evidence-based psychosocial treatments for children and adolescents: A 10-year update. *Journal of Clinical Child & Adolescent Psychology*, *37*(1), 1–7. doi:10.1080/15374410701817725

Skinner, B. F. (1953). *Science and human behavior*. New York: The Free Press.

Smith, M. L., & Glass, G. V. (1977). Meta-analysis of psychotherapy outcome studies. *American Psychologist*, *9*(32), 752–760.

Southam-Gerow, M. A., & Prinstein, M. J. (2014). Evidence base updates: The evolution of the evaluation of psychological treatments for children and adolescents. *Journal of Clinical Child & Adolescent Psychology*, *43*(1), 1–6. doi:10.1080/15374416.2013.855128

Task Force on Promotion and Dissemination of Psychological Procedures. (1995). Training in and dissemination of empirically-validated psychological treatments: Report and recommendations. *The Clinical Psychologist*, *48*, 3–23.

Watson, J. B. (1924). *Behaviorism*. New York: The People's Institute Publishing Company Inc.

Watson, J. B., & Watson, R. R. (1921). Studies in infant psychology. *Scientific Monthly*, *13*, 493–515.

Weisz, J. R., Weiss, B., Alicke, M. D., & Klotz, M. L. (1987). Effectiveness of psychotherapy with children and adolescents: A meta-analysis for clinicians. *Journal of Consulting and Clinical Psychology*, *55*(4), 542–549.

Weisz, J. R., Weiss, B., Han, S. S., Granger, D. A., & Morton, T. (1995). Effects of psychotherapy with children and adolescents revisited: A meta-analysis of treatment outcome studies. *Psychological Bulletin*, *117*(3), 450–468. doi:10.1037/0033-2909.117.3.450

Wolpe, J., & Rachman, S. (1960). Psychoanalytic "evidence": A critique based on Freud's case of Little Hans. *Journal of Nervous and Mental Disease*, *131*, 135–148.

2

Intellectual and Adaptive Functioning

Jessica F. Scherr, Elizabeth M. Kryszak, and James A. Mulick

Intellectual disability (ID), previously known as mental retardation (American Association on Mental Retardation, 2002), is characterized by developmental impairment of general cognitive abilities and adaptive functioning. It is fundamentally a result of learning failure during early human development, varying in degree and type of learning affected depending on cause, the developmental stage when it begins, and the opportunities for learning provided in the environment. The criteria for diagnosis of ID have changed over the last several decades, shifting emphasis on a quantitative approach involving significant deficits in measured intelligence quotient (IQ) and adaptive behavior using standardized tests (Jacobson & Mulick, 1996), to the present where standardized measures are combined with more attention to qualitative impairment and an emphasis on support needs (Schalock et al., 2010). Deficits of adaptive behavior include the domains of conceptual functioning (e.g., language, reading, writing, math, reasoning, knowledge, memory), social functioning (e.g., empathy, social judgment, interpersonal skills), and practical skills (e.g., personal care, occupational responsibilities, leisure skills, and organization) in relation to both age expectation and culture in activities of daily living. Impairment in intellectual and adaptive functioning must begin during the developmental period and is further classified by the severity of impairment. In order to diagnose ID, as well as assess severity, clinical training and judgment are required. Standardized tests measure learning potential and generate IQ scores that help communicate level of impairment. Individuals with ID have IQ scores approximately two standard deviations or more below the population mean, with a small margin for measurement error. ID is categorized into levels of severity (e.g., mild to profound) depending on the amount of support required and adaptive functioning skills. The prevalence of ID occurs in 1–3% of the global population (Harris, 2006; Maulik et al., 2011) with about 85% of individuals meeting diagnostic criteria for mild ID (King et al., 2009).

Maladaptive behavior is common in children and adolescents with ID, and aggression is one of the leading reasons for behavioral treatment (Emerson et al., 2001;

Heyvaert, Maes, & Onghena, 2010). There is a positive relationship between level of impairment and maladaptive behavior, and individuals with severe to profound ID often demonstrate more behavioral difficulties (Janssen, Schuengel, & Stolk, 2002; Shogren et al., 2004). Maladaptive behavior can include a variety of behavioral responses such as physical or verbal aggression toward others, disruptive behavior, tantrums, stereotyped and/or repetitive behavior, and self-injurious behavior (Heyvaert, Maes, & Onghena, 2010).

Etiology and Theoretical Underpinnings of Treatment

ID is a lifelong disorder marked by variously impaired cognitive functioning that further impairs the ability to learn and function in daily life. Common causes of ID include genetic abnormalities (Gilissen et al., 2014; Ropers, 2008), infection or exposure to toxins such as alcohol or lead and other heavy metals in utero or later in development (Streissguth et al., 2004), malnutrition, and significant illnesses such as sequelae associated with whooping cough, meningitis, or measles, as well as a number of prenatal maternal infections and complications of birth and delivery (Harris, 2006). While both genetic and environmental factors influence symptom presentation and severity of ID, concentrated efforts have searched to explain *how* genes and individual experience contribute to intellectual impairment (Harris, 2006; van Bokhoven, 2011). Research has shown that the effects of environmental or experiential factors (e.g., social deprivation or marked sensory or motor deficits) are more likely to contribute to the development of mild and moderate ID, while severe and profound ID is more often associated with specific genetic causes such as chromosomal abnormalities or single gene defects and injury such as brain damage especially during the perinatal period (Gilissen et al., 2014; Switzky & Greenspan, 2006). Prevention efforts have focused on reduction of morbidity from disease and from injuries that contribute to impaired learning and central nervous system function during the developmental period. These include vaccination to prevent diseases associated with disability, good prenatal care and good maternal nutrition, and avoidance of toxins and teratogens during pregnancy and early childhood, among other public health strategies (Pueschel & Mulick, 1990). Despite efforts to under-stand etiological mechanisms associated with ID, the specific cause is never actually determined in as many as 80% of individuals with ID (Rauch et al., 2006).

Regardless of the etiological heterogeneity, theoretical principles related to behavior and learning guide evidence-based treatment aimed to remediate skill deficits and maladaptive behaviors in ID. *Applied behavior analysis* (ABA) is the systematic study and application of operant conditioning to solve socially significant problems, such as helping children with ID learn more efficiently. Skinner (1937; 1969; 1974) brilliantly described *operant conditioning* as behavior that is functionally affected by its consequences within the context in which the individual's actions have been perceived to produce those consequences. Behavioral consequences can be either positive (i.e., highly valued), which increase the probability of prior behavior occurring under similar circumstances in the future, or as negative (not desired or not valued), which decrease the probability of behavior. The smallest unit of analysis in operant conditioning is the "three term contingency": that is, actions (i.e., behavior) are understood to be "occasioned" (i.e., controlled) by a cue or stimulus than leads to a more or less valued consequence; generally shortened to Antecedent–Behavior–Consequence or the "ABC" of behavior. Once behavior began being conceptualized as a result of operant relations to the environment (Skinner, 1953, p. 35), and was understood to be maintained by specific consequences or contingencies, the field underwent a breakthrough in understanding, treating, and teaching individuals with ID.

Brief Overview of Evidence-Based Treatments

Currently in clinical practice, it is critical that professionals in the field deliver treatment and intervention services that have been empirically demonstrated to be efficacious so as to avoid haphazardly providing treatment that is not as effective or is even harmful (Anderson, 2006; Kazdin, 2008). In order to accomplish the goals of teaching skills and changing behavior in ID, there has to be a fundamental understanding of how learning takes place. The three term contingency (ABC of behavior) is a conceptual analytic tool that can be used in planning to change behavior and to teach new skills. Principles of reinforcement and punishment, as well as reinforcement schedules, encompass a major component of behavioral treatment of ID and are used to teach new behavior and modify existing behavior. Research has demonstrated that the timing of consequences and cues greatly influences performance, and the effect of such relations and their interaction are termed schedules of reinforcement. The schedule of reinforcement can be based on temporal (e.g., time-based) or ratio (e.g., quantity or frequency) aspects of behavior. Additionally, reinforcement can be variable or fixed, occurring only after a specific amount of time or number of responses. Given the tremendous complexity of the science of behavior, the most practical and effective way to pursue its application is by disciplined study and reliance on well-regarded ABA texts (Cooper, Heron, & Heward, 2007) and applied research periodicals (see the Useful Resources and References sections).

The focus of evidence-based treatment includes teaching children and adolescents with ID specific skills that enable greater independence and that enhance their ability to adapt to the demands and opportunities in their environment. Treatment programs are individualized and often targeted to decrease maladaptive behaviors, increase skills or adaptive behaviors, and promote the maintenance and generalization of skills through opportunities to perform them in varying contexts. Evidence-based treatments and interventions have been delivered across individuals with varying levels of impairment of ID across multiple contexts (home, school, etc.) and people (teacher, caregivers, etc.).

Components of Evidence-Based Treatments

Prevention and Antecedent Strategies

One way to avoid problem behavior is to prevent it from occurring. This can be achieved through behavioral strategies that manipulate identified antecedents or cues in the environment that "trigger" or control target behavior. Because antecedent strategies are implemented before a target behavior occurs, they have the potential to prevent problem behavior from occurring if the controlling triggers are not present. Radley and Dart (2016) highlight the appeal and acceptability of using antecedent strategies in parent-driven treatments especially in contexts in which consequence-based intervention cannot be consistently implemented. Prevention and antecedent strategies have been identified as partially effective treatment for increasing compliance, academic engagement, vocational or domestic activities, and leisure or social activities (Kern et al., 1998; Radley & Dart, 2016). Results from a recent meta-analysis identified the following evidence-based antecedent strategies that increase compliance in children: high-probability command sequences or encouraging positive "behavioral momentum," effective instruction delivery, and errorless compliance training (Radley & Dart, 2016). The following describes these and additional components of evidence-based antecedent strategies that prevent or reduce problem behavior in children and adolescents with ID.

Antecedent Environmental Control. One way to prevent problem behaviors from occurring is to adjust the environment or contextual cues so that problem behavior is less likely to occur and appropriate behavior is more likely to occur. This can be achieved by presenting or removing specific cues or discriminative stimuli that are associated with the behavior of interest or modifying the environment to increase or decrease the effort needed to exhibit desirable or undesirable behavior. An early study by Schroeder, Kanoy, and colleagues (1981) examined how specific antecedents in the environment influenced the management and maintenance of a treatment program for self-injurious behavior in residents at a state facility for individuals with ID. Results from this study indicated that self-injurious behavior increased in the presence of a disruptive client in the afternoon compared to the morning, and when toys were absent compared to being available. These findings highlight how ecological variables in the environment affect behavior and provide insight on how simply modifying the environment may cause a reduction in problem behavior. This work has been extended to decrease disruptive and aggressive behavior (Mace et al., 1986), increase compliance (Mace et al., 1988), and increase alternative and independent play behaviors (Mulick et al., 1978). Many examples abound in the ABA research journals.

Behavioral Momentum. Another antecedent strategy to decrease problem behavior is to modify the order of events. A strategy termed *behavioral momentum*, which involves delivering a sequence of requests that an individual is more likely to comply with (e.g., high-probability commands) immediately before delivering a request that has a lower probability of compliance, has been demonstrated to be particularly effective at managing noncompliance (Ducharme & Worling, 1994; Mace et al., 1988). Mace and Belfiore (1990) also found reductions in stereotypic behavior (e.g., pushing paper, kicking a chair, turning a light switch on and off, pushing staff, and kicking clients) in an individual with severe mental retardation when a high-probability request (e.g., "Give me five," "Give me a hug," and "Hold my hand") was delivered prior to a task-related request (e.g., "Hang up your coat," "Please take your plate to the sink"). These results suggest that other problem behaviors, in addition to noncompliance, can be reduced due to the collateral effects and functional incompatibility of competing behaviors when using behavioral momentum strategies and sequences. Additionally, breaking steps into smaller pieces while reinforcing successful completion or modifying the difficulty of a step are other antecedent strategies that can be effective. For example, Lalli and colleagues (1995) evaluated the effects of functional communication, extinction, and response chaining on individuals whose aberrant behavior (self-injury and aggression) was maintained by an escape function and found a reduction of problem behavior when escape from a task was contingent on the completion of a specified number of steps in a task (response chaining). The number of steps required to obtain a break was gradually increased over time with maintenance of the reduction of aberrant behavior. This study demonstrates the effectiveness of teaching an alternative escape response while chaining or adding components of a task, thus increasing appropriate behavior.

Providing Choices. Providing choice-making opportunities for children and adolescents with ID can decrease problem behavior in situations that involve transitions or demands. The modification of how a parent presents a demand or instruction can reduce opportunities for noncompliance. Research has studied how increasing the availability of choice-making opportunities can be incorporated into numerous areas of an individual's life (e.g., mealtime, leisure activities, vocational or occupational situations) and decrease problem behaviors (Kern et al., 1998). For example, giving individuals the opportunity to select their own reinforcers, rather than having others select reinforcers for them, results in increases in performance and a reduction of noncompliance (Kern et al., 1998). Problem behaviors can be prevented by allowing an individual to have control over what they can earn (e.g., reinforcement), as well as the task or task materials they are engaging with, by offering choices.

Addressing Setting Events. Setting events are complex antecedent conditions that can affect how an individual responds to the environment (Wahler & Fox, 1981). Setting events can include internal conditions in which the individual is hungry, tired, or sick. For example, disruption in an individual's internal physiological state, such as missing a dosage of medication, can negatively influence how an individual responds to stimuli and cues in the environment. Setting events can also include external factors, such as the presence or absence of a specific person. For example, a student may respond favorably to a teacher and become upset when the teacher is out sick and there is a substitute teacher. Temporal factors, such as time of day, can also influence behavioral responses. Collectively, it is important to consider and address setting events that may influence an individual's response to antecedent stimuli in their environment. Interventions that focus on removing or reducing the influence of setting events help decrease the frequency of problem behavior (Kennedy & Itkonen, 1993).

Using Visual or Auditory Cues. The use of visual and auditory cues, such as pictures, visual schedules, choice boards, first-then boards, and timers can be effective antecedent strategies to signal upcoming transitions or steps involved in completing an activity. The mode in which information is delivered is crucial to consider because individuals with ID often have communication difficulties (Bott, Farmer, & Rohde, 1997; Bradshaw, 2001), and failure to understand expectations can be distressing and lead to confusion and emotional arousal. A study conducted by Bradshaw (2001) examined the communication acts used by staff members when interacting with individuals with ID and found an average of 45% of communicative acts were above the understanding of the individual. Visual and auditory cues can help an individual understand signals or upcoming transitions in the environment. For example, a visual schedule can help children with intellectual disabilities keep track of steps to complete a routine task (e.g., washing hands). It is important to assure that a person with ID can see or hear the relevant cues for effective action, as well as allow enough time for a person with ID to begin an action. For example, allow perhaps five to ten seconds for compliance followed by praise or corrective feedback as appropriate (Radley & Dart, 2016).

Consequence-Based Strategies

One limitation of antecedent behavior-based interventions is that not all controlling relations are accessible or manipulable. Consequence-based strategies that incorporate behavioral principles of reinforcement and punishment are important components of intervention intended to reduce maladaptive behavior and increase appropriate behavior. The following are brief summaries of techniques used to reduce problem behavior in children and adolescents with ID.

Differential Reinforcement. The single most widely used nonaversive, behavioral strategy to reduce problem behavior in evidence-based treatments with children and adolescents with ID applies *differential reinforcement* procedures (Lennox et al., 1988). Differential reinforcement involves withholding reinforcers for undesirable behavior and presenting reinforcers contingent on some other (DRO) or incompatible (DRI) behavior. This strategy has been successful in reducing multiple sources of problem behavior in both profound to mildly delayed individuals (Frankel et al., 1976; Nolley et al., 1981; Petscher, Rey, & Bailey, 2009). Problem behaviors maintained by attention and escape contingencies have been demonstrated to be particularly responsive to DRO and DRI procedures

(Nolley et al., 1981; Petscher, Rey, & Bailey, 2009). In a review of empirical support conducted by Petscher, Rey, and Bailey (2009) for differential reinforcement of alternative (DRA) behavior the majority of problem behavior included destruction/combination of behavior topography (47.6%), self-injurious behavior (22.0%), and aggression (9.2%) with communication (85.4%) as a major target for alternative positively reinforced behavior. The effectiveness of treatment is greatly enhanced when the focus of teaching functional replacements for problem behavior is targeted (Gardner, 2007). Collectively, differential reinforcement procedures are an important component of evidence-based treatment in addressing a wide range of problem behaviors across levels of intellectual functioning, which can be used in addition to various antecedent and consequence-based strategies.

Token Reinforcement. Another reinforcement strategy that has evidence to support effectiveness across levels of intellectual functioning involves token reinforcement or a token economy. Children with ID and developmental delays have historically received extensive attention in using token reinforcement, particularly with a focus on improving communication, adaptive behavior, social behavior, and other skills that promote independence (Kazdin & Polster, 1973; Matson & Boisjoli, 2009; O'Leary & Drabman, 1971). Within a token economy, *tangible* conditioned reinforcers are used in the form of tokens (chips, points, stamps, etc.) for desirable behavior that can be exchanged for a reinforcer (food, activities, toys, etc.). Prior to implementing a token economy, the tokens should be established as conditioned reinforcers, or discriminative stimuli, for the back-up reinforcement (Kazdin & Bootzin, 1972). It is important to consider rules guiding the token economy by determining ahead of time how many tokens an individual has to earn to receive a reinforcer, the types of reinforcers available to the individual, and when the individual can trade in their tokens for reinforcement.

Token economies can be used in a variety of settings and can be easily and inexpensively administered by parents, caregivers, teachers, and therapists (Matson & Boisjoli, 2009). Also, token economies can be individualized to target idiosyncratic behavior of an individual or implemented with multiple individuals (e.g., classroom) with group contingencies (Birnbrauer et al., 1965; Jones & Kazdin, 1975; Matson & Boisjoli, 2009). In order to maintain and generalize improvements in behavior achieved with token reinforcement, it is sometimes desirable to pair "natural" reinforcers (e.g., social praise) when administering the token, so that these natural conditioned reinforcers can eventually be substituted for tokens (Kazdin & Bootzin, 1972; Kazdin & Polster, 1973). When shifting from token reinforcement to naturalistic reinforcement, token delivery can be gradually withdrawn with the amount of delay and schedule of the reinforcement adjusted (Kazdin, 1982; Stokes & Baer, 1977).

Time-Out. Punishment is an effective consequence-based strategy aimed at reducing problem behavior in both typically developing and developmentally delayed populations (Lerman & Vorndran, 2002). The limited use of punishment procedures over reinforcement-only based treatments has been demonstrated to be preferable in some situations where problem behavior must be suppressed quickly due to risk of physical harm (Schroeder et al., 1981). In a review conducted by Matson and Taras (1989) that examined punishment and alternative methods to treat problem behaviors in individuals with developmental disabilities, time-out procedures were among the most widely implemented treatments for disruptive and aggressive behavior. Time-out is a form of negative punishment that involves the temporary removal of positive reinforcement. There are a variety of ways to create time-out conditions including temporarily removing the child from the reinforcing environment (e.g., placing the child in the corner of the room or in a chair) or nonexclusionary time-out where scheduled reinforcement is interrupted (Foxx & Shapiro, 1978), or temporarily removing a reinforcing item (e.g., taking away a preferred toy, stopping an activity) or social attention (e.g., contingent brief planned ignoring).

Punishment contingencies are particularly effective when used in combination with differential reinforcement procedures, in which appropriate behavior and/or absence of problem behavior is strongly reinforced during the "time-in" period (Huguenin & Mulick, 1981; Gardner et al., 1986; Matson & DiLorenzo, 1984; Solnick, Rincover, & Peterson, 1977). Time-in programming has been present for over 40 years, and is an important factor of intervention to consider because the effectiveness of time-out procedures is dependent on how reinforcing the time-in conditions are to an individual (Schroeder et al., 1981). For example, Solnick and colleagues (1977) found that an "enriched" time-in environment that included novel toys and social attention, as well as reinforcement for on-task behavior, resulted in reductions in problem behavior. The use of a distinctive, wearable, discriminative cue (i.e., a badge or other easily seen accessory), as well as frequent reinforcement during time-in, when implementing nonexclusionary time-out procedures signals when time-out begins and ends and can be easily applied across settings in which there is no designated exclusionary time-out area (Foxx & Shapiro, 1978; Huguenin & Mulick, 1981). For example, Huguenin and Mulick (1981) used a discriminative cue (ribbon) and DRO reinforcement schedule (given an edible and social praise every ten minutes) to reduce inappropriate behaviors (inappropriate touching and disruptive behavior) in a 19-year-old male with severe mental retardation. When the student engaged in inappropriate behavior, the ribbon was removed from the student, and the reinforcement schedule was interrupted for five minutes. Improvement in behavior transferred across a different time of day and a different setting where the ribbon cue was used to signal the possibility of time-out, suggesting that appropriate behavior was under the control of the ribbon discriminative stimulus.

Role of Parents in Treatment

Parent involvement in treatment has been expanding and is recognized as a paramount component to help increase independence and improve the quality of life (Gavidia-Payne & Hudson, 2002; Matson, Mahan, & LoVullo, 2009). Parent training programs help aid in generalization of intervention and skills practiced in an educational or clinical setting to the home environment (Matson, Mahan, & LoVullo, 2009). In a study conducted by Clark and colleagues (1982), a mother's post-training program knowledge of behavioral principles was the single most important factor of positive outcomes. Parent training efforts often include instruction on behavioral principles with foundations in operant conditioning including reinforcement, antecedent modification, and discrete trial training (DTT) (Baker, Heifetz, & Murphy, 1980; Feldman & Werner, 2002; Matson, Mahan, & LoVullo, 2009). Research has also demonstrated the relationship of how increased parent stress negatively influences behavioral and adaptive outcomes (Floyd, Harter, & Costigan, 2004; Matson, Mahan, & LoVullo, 2009), which has led to interventions that focus on creating positive parent–child interactions when treating child behavior problems (Bagner & Eyber, 2007).

Other Variables That Influence Treatment

Assessment

Since behavior problems are often the focus of treatment, it is important to understand the function of the behavior, or *why* behavior is occurring. Given that almost all behavior is learned, it is important to assess and identify the associations between situations and events that predict and those that maintain behavior (Gresham, Watson, & Skinner, 2001). The ABC model is one method that is commonly used to identify specific antecedents (e.g., discriminant stimuli or events that occur prior to behavior) and consequences (e.g., what happens after the behavior) that are connected to a target behavior. Antecedents can be conceptualized as specific cue or "trigger" for a behavior to occur and can be characterized by many aspects of the environment, including events (e.g., demand being placed, change in routine), a person (e.g., parent, teacher, babysitter), or an object (e.g., preferred toy or food) in the environment (Bearss et al., 2015), or even an internal state such as a drug (Thompson & Pickens, 1971). Behavioral consequences increase or decrease behavior depending on whether the outcome is reinforcing or punishing. Behavior can serve multiple functions, such as (1) to obtain a preferred consequence (e.g., object, activity), (2) escape or avoid a nonpreferred consequence, (3) obtain social attention, and (4) self-stimulation (Durand & Carr, 1991; O'Neill et al., 1997).

One of the challenges in behavioral treatment is to accurately determine the function of behavior (Beavers, Iwata, & Lerman, 2013). Behavior is complex and an individual may display multiple behaviors (e.g., hitting, spitting, kicking) that all serve the same function (e.g., obtain attention) or the same behavior (e.g., crying) may have multiple functions (e.g., obtain preferred toy, escape homework, gain attention from parent). One way to better understand this is to collect data on the ABCs of behavior. Information can be collected through multiple modalities including interviews, direct observations, and behavioral charting to obtain information regarding specific antecedents, the topography of the behavior, consequences, and setting events (e.g., time of day). It is critical that the target behavior is defined in clear objective terminology that can be unmistakably identified by multiple people (e.g., teachers, parents, interventionists). For example, a target behavior defined as a "tantrum" can be characterized in multiple ways (e.g., screaming, hitting, head banging, verbal aggression) and differ across informants depending on their subjective interpretation of what a "tantrum" entails. This is important because behavioral data collected inform decisions about treatment programs and behavioral plans designed to change behavior. This information is sometimes then systematically used in what is called analog functional analysis, an experimental procedure in which antecedent conditions thought to have a role in controlling the behavior of clinical interest are systematically introduced and taken away to see if their presence actually does change the probability of the behavior. If a change in the condition is systematically related to the occurrence of the behavior, then a functional relation is said to have been supported.

Steps for Implementing Systematic Instruction

Treatment and educational programs for individuals with ID target teaching functional skills, such as communication, social skills, daily living skills, community and vocational skills (Browder & Spooner, 2011; Kauffman & Hung, 2009). The most effective approach to teaching children and adolescents with ID skills is systematic instruction, which is based on ABA principles (Kauffman & Hung, 2009). Browder and Spooner (2011) suggest the following steps for teachers and interventionists to implement systematic instruction:

a. **Define the Skills to be Acquired**. When identifying what skills should be taught, it is important to choose skills that can be objectively measured through behavioral responses. For individuals that are unable to complete an entire target response or skill independently, a task analysis should be completed in order to break down the task into smaller behaviors or steps (Alberto & Troutman, 2012). The sequence of each discrete step within a task analysis can be taught through forward or backward chaining procedures.

b. **Define the Methods to Use in Instructing the Skills**. Once the target response or skill has been objectively defined, it is critical to outline the methods involved in teaching the skills including the schedule of teaching trials or practice sessions, prompts, and procedures for reinforcement and error correction. DTT is an evidence-based strategy that applies methods of operant conditioning to individualized instruction and is delivered in a one-on-one setting and gives an opportunity for an individual to make a target response. (For a review of DTT, see Browder & Spooner, 2011 and Smith, 2001.)

c. **Implement the Systematic Instruction Plan**. It is important to consider how the systematic instruction plan will be implemented including determining individuals involved in teaching or instruction (e.g., parents, teachers), when instruction will be taught, where teaching will occur, and the amount of training or materials needed.

d. **Review Student Progress to Modify Instruction**. It is important to review progress regularly to determine if modifications need to be made to the systematic instruction plan as the individual gains mastery or if the individual is struggling to make progress.

Comorbidity

Given the etiological heterogeneity associated with ID, including both biological and environmental factors that influence the severity and presentation of cognitive and adaptive impairment, it is important to take an individualized approach to conceptualizing assessment and treatment practices with individuals with ID. ID is highly comorbid with genetic syndromes (Down syndrome, fragile X syndrome, Williams syndrome), autism spectrum disorder, anxiety disorder, attention-deficit/hyperactivity disorder (ADHD), and disruptive behavior disorders (Dekker & Koot, 2003; Matson & Shoemaker, 2009; McDermott et al., 2007; Rose et al., 2009). Individuals with ID who also have comorbid diagnoses may have a "double vulnerability" for increased impairment in both cognitive and adaptive functioning (Pearson et al., 1996). For example, in a study conducted by Dekker and Koot (2003), 37% percent of 474 children in a school for the intellectually disabled also had a comorbid disorder including disruptive disorder (25.1%), anxiety disorder (21.9%), and mood disorder (4.4%). Children who had multiple disorders also exhibited increased impairment across areas of daily living. It is important for clinicians and professionals working with children and adolescents with ID to engage in the practice of differential diagnosis, so treatment efforts can be individualized to all symptoms and factors that may be contributing to impairment.

Demographics

ID is a lifelong disability that affects how an individual learns and develops over time; therefore, targeted intervention aimed at modifying behavior and teaching fundamental skills early in development is critical to promote optimal outcomes (Guralnick, 2005; Ramey, Ramey, & Lanzi, 2007). Decades of research have demonstrated the benefits of early identification and treatment of children at risk for intellectual and developmental delays (Majnemer, 1998; Simeonsson, Cooper, & Scheiner, 1982). Children have the greatest capacity to adapt and learn from experiences early in development, which has led early intervention programs to target and provide services to children within the first five years of life. Populations that are particularly at risk for adverse developmental outcomes include children living in poverty (Emerson, 2007). Research has demonstrated that children from low resource families often benefit more from early intervention than children from higher resource families (Ramey & Ramey, 1999), which highlights the importance of also considering family environmental factors in treatment delivery.

Medication

The use of medication as a treatment option for individuals with ID has been a controversial topic, particularly in regard to using antipsychotic drugs (Tyrer et al., 2008). Although there is no medication that can directly "cure" the core cognitive impairments associated with ID, some medications, such as risperidone, may help improve severe problem behaviors (e.g., aggression, self-injury) in individuals with ID (Aman et al., 2002; Snyder et al., 2002). The use of psychotropic medication as a standard treatment option for individuals with ID is far from conclusive, which is worrisome because individuals with ID may represent one of the most overmedicated populations and many medications have adverse side effects (Deb & Unwin, 2007; Holden & Gitlesen, 2004).

Conclusion

In this chapter, we have attempted to outline the useful principles, procedures, and strategies used in evidence-based treatment for children and adolescents with ID. We have also tried to include useful examples that illustrate these concepts and strategies from the applied literature. It is safe to say empirically supported treatments have made life better for individuals with ID over the last half century well beyond the pre-scientific and socially isolating approaches of the past. Needless to say, we have only touched on the many areas of application that can help individuals with learning difficulties achieve new skills and a better life. For a more thorough review of these principles, please see the References below.

Useful Resources

- *Intellectual Disability: A Guide for Families and Professionals* by James C. Harris, M.D., Oxford University Press, 2010
- *Handbook of Intellectual and Development Disabilities* by John W. Jacobson, James A. Mulick, and Johannes Rojahn, Springer, 2007
- *Teaching Students with Moderate and Severe Disabilities* by Diane M. Browder and Fred Spooner, Guilford Press, 2011
- *Decreasing Behaviors of Persons with Severe Retardation and Autism* by Richard M. Foxx, Research Press, 1982
- *Living with Children: New Methods for Parents and Teachers* by Gerald R. Patterson, Research Press, revised edition, 2006
- *Parents Are Teachers: A Child Management Program* by Wesley C. Becker, Research Press, 1971
- *Steps to Independence: Teaching Everyday Skills to Children with Special Needs* by Alan Brightman and Bruce Baker, Paul H. Brookes Publishing Co., 4th edition, 2004
- *Crafting Connections* by Mitchell Taubman, Ron Leaf, and John McEachin, DRL Books, 2011
- *Friends Forever* by Fred Frankel, Jossey-Bass, 2010
- *Controversial Therapies for Autism and Intellectual Disabilities: Fad Fashion, and Science in Professional Practice* edited by Richard M. Foxx and James A. Mulick, Routledge, 2nd edition, 2016

References

Alberto, P. A., & Troutman, A. C. (2013). *Applied behavior analysis for teachers.* Boston: Pearson.

Aman, M. G., De Smedt, G., Derivan, A., Lyons, B., Findling, R. L., & Risperidone Disruptive Behavior Study Group. (2002). Double-blind, placebo-controlled study of risperidone for the treatment of disruptive behaviors in children with subaverage intelligence. *American Journal of Psychiatry, 159*(8), 1337–1346.

American Association on Mental Retardation. (2002). *Mental retardation: Definition, classification, and systems of supports.* 10th edn. Washington, DC: American Association on Mental Retardation.

Anderson, N. B. (2006). Evidence-based practice in psychology. *American Psychologist, 61*(4), 271–285.

Bagner, D. M., & Eyberg, S. M. (2007). Parent–child interaction therapy for disruptive behavior in children with mental retardation: A randomized controlled trial. *Journal of Clinical Child & Adolescent Psychology, 36*(3), 418–429.

Baker, B. L., Heifetz, L. J., & Murphy, D. M. (1980). Behavioral training for parents of mentally retarded children: One-year follow-up. *American Journal of Mental Deficiency, 85*(1), 31–38.

Bearss, K., Johnson, C., Smith, T., Lecavalier, L., Swiezy, N., Aman, M., . . . & Sukhodolsky, D. G. (2015). Effect of parent training vs parent education on behavioral problems in children with autism spectrum disorder: A randomized clinical trial. *Jama, 313*(15), 1524–1533.

Beavers, G. A., Iwata, B. A., & Lerman, D. C. (2013). Thirty years of research on the functional analysis of problem behavior. *Journal of Applied Behavior Analysis, 46*(1), 1–21.

Birnbrauer, J. S., Wolf, M. M., Kidder, J. D., & Tague, C. E. (1965). Classroom behavior of retarded pupils with token reinforcement. *Journal of Experimental Child Psychology, 2*(2), 219–235.

Bott, C., Farmer, R., & Rohde, J. (1997). Behaviour problems associated with lack of speech in people with learning disabilities. *Journal of Intellectual Disability Research, 41*(1), 3–7.

Bradshaw, J. (2001). Complexity of staff communication and reported level of understanding skills in adults with intellectual disability. *Journal of Intellectual Disability Research, 45*(3), 233–243.

Browder, D. M., Spooner, F., & Jimenez, B. (2011). Standards-based individualized education plans and progress monitoring. In D. M. Browder & F. Spooner (eds.), *Teaching students with moderate and severe disabilities* (pp. 42–91). New York: Guildford Press.

Clark, D. B., Baker, B. L., & Heifetz, L. J. (1982). Behavioral training for parents of mentally retarded children: Prediction of outcome. *American Journal of Mental Deficiency, 87*, 14–19.

Cooper, J. O., Heron, T. E., & Heward, W. L. (2007). *Applied Behavior Analysis.* 2nd edn. Saddle River, NJ: Prentice Hall.

Deb, S., & Unwin, G. L. (2007). Psychotropic medication for behaviour problems in people with intellectual disability: A review of the current literature. *Current Opinion in Psychiatry, 20*(5), 461–466.

Dekker, M. C., & Koot, H. M. (2003). DSM-IV disorders in children with borderline to moderate intellectual disability. I: Prevalence and impact. *Journal of the American Academy of Child & Adolescent Psychiatry, 42*(8), 915–922.

Ducharme, J. M., & Worling, D. E. (1994). Behavioral momentum and stimulus fading in the acquisition and maintenance of child compliance in the home. *Journal of Applied Behavior Analysis, 27*(4), 639–647.

Durand, V. M. & Carr, E. G. (1991). Functional communication training to reduce challenging behavior: Maintenance and application in new settings. *Journal of Applied Behavior Analysis, 24*, 251–264.

Emerson, E. (2007). Poverty and people with intellectual disabilities. *Mental Retardation and Developmental Disabilities Research Reviews, 13*(2), 107–113.

Emerson, E., Kiernan, C., Alborz, A., Reeves, D., Mason, H., Swarbrick, R., . . . & Hatton, C. (2001). The prevalence of challenging behaviors: A total population study. *Research in Developmental Disabilities, 22*(1), 77–93.

Feldman, M. A., & Werner, S. E. (2002). Collateral effects of behavioral parent training on families of children with developmental disabilities and behavior disorders. *Behavioral Interventions, 17*(2), 75–83.

Floyd, F. J., Harter, K. S., & Costigan, C. L. (2004). Family problem-solving with children who have mental retardation. *American Journal on Mental Retardation, 109*(6), 507–524.

Foxx, R. M., & Shapiro, S. T. (1978). The timeout ribbon: A nonexclusionary timeout procedure. *Journal of Applied Behavior Analysis, 11*(1), 125–136.

Frankel, F., Moss, D., Schofield, S., & Simmons III, J. Q. (1976). Case study: Use of differential reinforcement to suppress self-injurious and aggressive behavior. *Psychological Reports, 39*(3), 843–849.

Gardner, W. I. (2007). Aggression in persons with intellectual disabilities and mental disorders. In J. W. Jacobson, J. A. Mulick, & J. Rojahn (eds.), *Handbook of intellectual and developmental disabilities* (pp. 541–562). Boston, MA: Springer US.

Gardner, W. I., Cole, C. L., Davidson, D. P., & Karan, O. C. (1986). Reducing aggression in individuals with developmental disabilities: An expanded stimulus control, assessment, and intervention model. *Education and Training of the Mentally Retarded, 21*, 3–12.

Gavidia-Payne, S., & Hudson, A. (2002). Behavioural supports for parents of children with an intellectual disability and problem behaviours: An overview of the literature. *Journal of Intellectual & Developmental Disability, 27*(1), 31–55.

Gilissen, C., Hehir-Kwa, J. Y., Thung, D. T., van de Vorst, M., van Bon, B. W., Willemsen, M. H., . . . & Leach, R. (2014). Genome sequencing identifies major causes of severe intellectual disability. *Nature, 511*, 344–347.

Gresham, F. M., Watson, T. S., & Skinner, C. H. (2001). Functional behavioral assessment: Principles, procedures, and future direction. *School Psychology Review, 30*(2), 156.

Guralnick, M. J. (2005). Early intervention for children with intellectual disabilities: Current knowledge and future prospects. *Journal of Applied Research in Intellectual Disabilities, 18*(4), 313–324.

Harris, J. C. (2006). *Intellectual disability: Understanding its development, causes, classification, evaluation, and treatment.* New York: Oxford University Press.

Heyvaert, M., Maes, B., & Onghena, P. (2010). A meta-analysis of intervention effects on challenging behaviour among persons with intellectual disabilities. *Journal of Intellectual Disability Research, 54*, 634–649. doi:10.1111/j.1365–2788.2010.01291.x

Holden, B., & Gitlesen, J. P. (2004). Psychotropic medication in adults with mental retardation: Prevalence, and prescription practices. *Research in Developmental Disabilities, 25*(6), 509–521.

Huguenin, N. H., & Mulick, J. A. (1981). Nonexclusionary timeout: Maintenance of appropriate behavior across settings. *Applied Research in Mental Retardation, 2*(1), 55–67.

Jacobson, J. W., & Mulick, J. A. (eds.) (1996 [July]). *Manual of diagnosis and professional practice in mental retardation.* Washington, DC: American Psychological Association.

Janssen, C. G. C., Schuengel, C., & Stolk, J. (2002). Understanding challenging behaviour in people with severe and profound intellectual disability: A stress-attachment model. *Journal of Intellectual Disability Research, 46*(6), 445–453.

Jones, R. T., & Kazdin, A. E. (1975). Programming response maintenance after withdrawing token reinforcement. *Behavior Therapy, 6*(2), 153–164.

Kauffman, J. M., & Hung, L. Y. (2009). Special education for intellectual disability: Current trends and perspectives. *Current Opinion in Psychiatry, 22*(5), 452–456.

Kazdin, A. E. (1982). The token economy: A decade later. *Journal of Applied Behavior Analysis, 15*(3), 431–445.

Kazdin, A. E. (2008). Evidence-based treatment and practice: New opportunities to bridge clinical research and practice, enhance the knowledge base, and improve patient care. *American Psychologist, 63*(3), 146–159.

Kazdin, A. E., & Bootzin, R. R. (1972). The token economy: An evaluative review. *Journal of Applied Behavior Analysis, 5*(3), 343–372.

Kazdin, A. E., & Polster, R. (1973). Intermittent token reinforcement and response maintenance in extinction. *Behavior Therapy, 4*(3), 386–391.

Kennedy, C. H., & Itkonen, T. (1993). Effects of setting events on the problem behavior of students with severe disabilities. *Journal of Applied Behavior Analysis, 26*(3), 321–327.

Kern, L., Vorndran, C. M., Hilt, A., Ringdahl, J. E., Adelman, B. E., & Dunlap, G. (1998). Choice as an intervention to improve behavior: A review of the literature. *Journal of Behavioral Education, 8*(2), 151–169.

King, B. H., Toth, K. E., Hodapp, R. M., & Dykens, E. M. (2009). Intellectual disability. In B. J. Sadock, V. A. Sadock, P. Ruiz, & H. I. Kaplan (eds.), *Kaplan and Sadock's comprehensive textbook of psychiatry*, Philadelphia, PA: Lippincott Williams & Wilkins.

Lalli, J. S., Casey, S., & Kates, K. (1995). Reducing escape behavior and increasing task completion with functional communication training, extinction and response chaining. *Journal of Applied Behavior Analysis*, *28*(3), 261–268.

Lennox, D. B., Miltenberger, R. G., Spengler, P., & Erfanian, N. (1988). Five years of decelerative research for behavior problems by developmentally disabled persons: An annotated bibliography. *Mental Retardation & Learning Disability Bulletin*, *16*(1), 47–77.

Lerman, D. C., & Vorndran, C. M. (2002). On the status of knowledge for using punishment: Implications for treating behavior disorders. *Journal of Applied Behavior Analysis*, *35*(4), 431–464.

Mace, F. C., & Belfiore, P. (1990). Behavioral momentum in the treatment of escape-motivated stereotypy. *Journal of Applied Behavior Analysis*, *23*(4), 507–514.

Mace, F. C., Hock, M. L., Lalli, J. S., West, B. J., Belfiore, P., Pinter, E., & Brown, D. K. (1988). Behavioral momentum in the treatment of noncompliance. *Journal of Applied Behavior Analysis*, *21*(2), 123–141.

Mace, F. C., Page, T. J., Ivancic, M. T., & O'Brien, S. (1986). Analysis of environmental determinants of aggression and disruption in mentally retarded children. *Applied Research in Mental Retardation*, *7*(2), 203–221.

Majnemer, A. (1998). Benefits of early intervention for children with developmental disabilities. *Seminars in Pediatric Neurology*, *5*(1), 62–69.

Matson, J. L., & Boisjoli, J. A. (2009). The token economy for children with intellectual disability and/or autism: A review. *Research in Developmental Disabilities*, *30*(2), 240–248.

Matson, J. L., & DiLorenzo, T. M. (1984). *Punishment and its alternatives: A new perspective for behavior modification*. Vol. 13. New York: Springer Pub. Co.

Matson, J. L., Mahan, S., & LoVullo, S. V. (2009). Parent training: A review of methods for children with developmental disabilities. *Research in Developmental Disabilities*, *30*(5), 961–968.

Matson, J. L., & Shoemaker, M. (2009). Intellectual disability and its relationship to autism spectrum disorders. *Research in Developmental Disabilities*, *30*(6), 1107–1114.

Matson, J. L., & Taras, M. E. (1989). A 20 year review of punishment and alternative methods to treat problem behaviors in developmentally delayed persons. *Research in Developmental Disabilities*, *10*(1), 85–104.

Maulik, P. K., Mascarenhas, M. N., Mathers, C. D., Dua, T., & Saxena, S. (2011). Prevalence of intellectual disability: A meta-analysis of population-based studies. *Research in Developmental Disabilities*, *32*(2), 419–436.

McDermott, S., Durkin, M. S., Schupf, N., & Stein, Z. A. (2007). Epidemiology and etiology of mental retardation. In J. W. Jacobson, J. A. Mulick, & J. Rojahn (eds.), *Handbook of intellectual and developmental disabilities* (pp. 3–40). Boston, MA: Springer US.

Mulick, J. A., Hoyt, P., Rojahn, J., & Schroeder, S. R. (1978). Reduction of a "nervous habit" in a profoundly retarded youth by increasing toy play. *Journal of Behavior Therapy and Experimental Psychiatry*, *9*(4), 381–385.

Nolley, D., Butterfield, B., Fleming, A., & Muller, P. (1982). Nonaversive treatment of severe self-injurious behavior: Multiple replications with DRO and DRI. *Monographs of the American Association on Mental Deficiency 1982*(5), 161–189.

O'Leary, K. D., & Drabman, R. (1971). Token reinforcement programs in the classroom: A review. *Psychological Bulletin*, *75*(6), 379.

O'Neill, R. E., Horner, R. H., Albin, R. W., Storey, K. & Sprague, J. R. (1997). *Functional assessment and program development for problem behavior: A practical handbook.* 2nd edn. Pacific Grove, CA: Brooks/Cole.

Pearson, D. A., Yaffee, L. S., Loveland, K. A., & Lewis, K. R. (1996). Comparison of sustained and selective attention in children who have mental retardation with and without attention deficit hyperactivity disorder. *American Journal on Mental Retardation 100*(6), 592–607.

Petscher, E. S., Rey, C., & Bailey, J. S. (2009). A review of empirical support for differential reinforcement of alternative behavior. *Research in Developmental Disabilities, 30*(3), 409–425.

Pueschel, S. M., & Mulick, J. A. (1990). *Prevention of developmental disabilities.* Baltimore: Paul H. Brookes.

Radley, K. C., & Dart, E. H. (2016). Antecedent strategies to promote children's and adolescents' compliance with adult requests: A review of the literature. *Clinical Child and Family Psychology Review, 19*(1), 39–54.

Ramey, S. L., & Ramey, C. T. (1999). Early experience and early intervention for children "at risk" for developmental delay and mental retardation. *Developmental Disabilities Research Reviews, 5*(1),1–10.

Ramey, S. L., Ramey, C. T., & Lanzi, R. G. (2007). Early intervention. In J. W. Jacobson, J. A. Mulick, & J. Rojahn (eds.), *Handbook of intellectual and developmental disabilities* (pp. 445–463). Boston, MA: Springer US.

Rauch, A., Hoyer, J., Guth, S., Zweier, C., Kraus, C., Becker, C., ... & Nürnberg, P. (2006). Diagnostic yield of various genetic approaches in patients with unexplained developmental delay or mental retardation. *American Journal of Medical Genetics Part A, 140*(19), 2063–2074.

Ropers, H. H. (2008). Genetics of intellectual disability. *Current Opinion in Genetics & Development, 18*(3), 241–250.

Rose, E., Bramham, J., Young, S., Paliokostas, E., & Xenitidis, K. (2009). Neuropsychological characteristics of adults with comorbid ADHD and borderline/mild intellectual disability. *Research in Developmental Disabilities, 30*(3), 496–502.

Schalock, R. L., Borthwick-Duffy, S. A., Bradley, V. J., Buntinx, W. H., Coulter, D. L., Craig, E. M., ... & Shogren, K. A. (2010). *Intellectual disability: Definition, classification, and systems of supports.* Washington, DC: American Association on Intellectual and Developmental Disabilities.

Schroeder, S. R., Kanoy, R. C., Mulick, J. A., Rojahn, J., Thios, S. J., Stephens, M., & Hawk, B. (1982). Environmental antecedents which affect management and maintenance of programs for self-injurious behavior. *Monographs of the American Association on Mental Deficiency 1982*(5), 105–159.

Schroeder, S. R., Schroeder, C. S., Rojahn, J., & Mulick, J. A. (1981). Self-injurious behavior: An analysis of behavior management techniques. In J. L. Matson & J. R. McCartney (eds.), *Handbook of behavior modification with the mentally retarded.* New York: Plenum Press.

Shogren, K. A., Faggella-Luby, M. N., Bae, S. J., & Wehmeyer, M. L. (2004). The effect of choice-making as an intervention for problem behavior: A meta-analysis. *Journal of Positive Behavior Interventions, 6*(4), 228–237.

Simeonsson, R. J., Cooper, D. H., & Scheiner, A. P. (1982). A review and analysis of the effectiveness of early intervention programs. *Pediatrics, 69*(5), 635–641.

Skinner, B. F. (1937). Two types of conditioned reflex: A reply to Konorski and Miller. *Journal of General Psychology, 16*, 272–279.

Skinner, B. F. (1953). *Science and human behavior.* New York: The Free Press.

Skinner, B. F. (1969). *Contingencies of reinforcement.* New York: Appleton Century Crofts.

Skinner, B. F. (1974). *About behaviorism*. New York: Alfred A. Knopf.

Smith, T. (2001). Discrete trial training in the treatment of autism. *Focus on Autism and Other Developmental Disabilities*, *16*(2), 86–92.

Snyder, R., Turgay, A., Aman, M., Binder, C., Fisman, S., & Carroll, A. (2002). Effects of risperidone on conduct and disruptive behavior disorders in children with subaverage IQs. *Journal of the American Academy of Child & Adolescent Psychiatry*, *41*(9), 1026–1036.

Solnick, J. V., Rincover, A., & Peterson, C. R. (1977). Some determinants of the reinforcing and punishing effects of timeout. *Journal of Applied Behavior Analysis*, *10*(3), 415–424.

Stokes, T. F., & Baer, D. M. (1977). An implicit technology of generalization. *Journal of Applied Behavior Analysis*, *10*(2), 349–367.

Streissguth, A. P., Bookstein, F. L., Barr, H. M., Sampson, P. D., O'Malley Kieran, M. D., & Young, J. K. (2004). Risk factors for adverse life outcomes in fetal alcohol syndrome and fetal alcohol effects. *Journal of Developmental & Behavioral Pediatrics*, *25*(4), 228–238.

Switzky, H. N., & Greenspan, S. (2006). *What is mental retardation?: Ideas for an evolving disability in the 21st century*. Washington, DC: American Association on Mental Retardation.

Thompson, T., & Pickens, R. (eds.) (1971). *Stimulus properties of drugs*. New York:Plenum Press.

Tyrer, P., Oliver-Africano, P. C., Ahmed, Z., Bouras, N., Cooray, S., Deb, S., . . . & Kramo, K. (2008). Risperidone, haloperidol, and placebo in the treatment of aggressive challenging behaviour in patients with intellectual disability: A randomised controlled trial. *The Lancet*, *371*(9606), 57–63.

van Bokhoven, H. (2011). Genetic and epigenetic networks in intellectual disabilities. *Annual Review of Genetics*, *45*, 81–104.

Wahler, R. G., & Fox, J. J. (1981). Setting events in applied behavior analysis: Toward a conceptual and methodological expansion. *Journal of Applied Behavior Analysis*, *14*(3), 327–338.

3

Autism Spectrum

Elizabeth M. Kryszak, Jessica F. Scherr, and James A. Mulick

Autism spectrum disorder (ASD) is a neurodevelopmental disorder characterized by varying manifestations of significant developmental dysfunctions and delays in language, communication, and socialization skills, as well as restricted and repetitive language (when language is acquired at all) and behavior patterns including stereotyped movements or speech, rigid insistence on particular and sometimes nonfunctional routines, restricted interests, and unusual sensitivities (American Psychiatric Association, 2013). These symptoms appear during the first two or three years of life, although presentation varies greatly both between individuals and across a single individual's life span. Once thought to be relatively rare, prevalence based on current diagnostic standards has increased greatly with estimates of up to 1 in 68 individuals being affected by this disorder (Baio, 2012). The exact cause of ASD is still unknown, although recent research has suggested epigenetic etiological factors with roles for developmental, genetic, and environmental factors (Grafodatskaya et al., 2010). Symptoms of ASD can remain present across the life span, disrupting not only relationships with others but also the ability to learn effectively from the environment, often leading to significant cognitive and learning disabilities, deficits in adaptive functioning and ability to live independently, and severe behavior problems. Fortunately, it has been found that early identification followed by intensive behavior intervention can have significant corrective effects on development and learning, leading to increases in cognitive and adaptive functioning, decreases in behavior problems, and, in some, a return to typical functioning (Butter, Mulick, & Metz, 2006; Lovaas, 1987; Peters-Scheffer et al., 2011). In the 4th edition of the *Diagnostic and Statistical Manual of Mental Disorders* (DSM), what is now ASD was split into four diagnostic categories under the heading pervasive developmental disorders: *autistic disorder*, *Asperger disorder*, *pervasive developmental disorder not otherwise specified* (PDD-NOS), and *childhood disintegrative disorder*. These four disorders were collapsed under the single heading of ASD because research indicated that differential diagnosis between the categories was unreliable. *Rett's disorder* was also included in the DSM-IV under the PDD category, although the DSM-5 now considers this to be a separate diagnosis from ASD because of the specific genetic etiology.

Treatment for ASD can focus on several different targets depending on the level of functioning of the individual and the scope and intensity of the intervention employed. The most comprehensive treatments focus on improving skills across a variety of areas (e.g., language/communication, social/play skills, adaptive skills, cognitive/ academic skills, appropriate behavior) whereas more targeted interventions focus on improving specific problem areas or increasing a specific skill area (e.g., improving parent–child interactions; decreasing maladaptive behaviors; improving feeding skills). This chapter will focus primarily on early interventions for ASD (e.g., interventions typically started before age seven years) as these interventions have a stronger evidence base showing lasting change. Interventions for school-aged children and adolescents tend to vary based on the level of functioning of the child and co-occurring problems (discussed further in the Comorbidity section of this chapter). Interventions for higher functioning older children (i.e., typically average to above average language and cognitive skills) often focus on improving social skills. See Gates, Kang, and Lerner (2017) and Rao, Beidel, and Murray (2008) for an overview of social skills interventions with this population, including areas in need of further study.

Etiology and Theoretical Underpinnings of Treatment

The etiology underlying ASD is notably complex and appears to be multifactored. While a strong genetic link has been demonstrated through twin and familial studies, several pre- and postnatal environmental factors have also been linked to an increased risk for ASD including increased maternal stress, maternal age, infections, and exposure to neurotoxins (Landrigan, 2010). Outside of some specific toxic or viral perinatal causes (e.g., prenatal rubella syndrome), several medical and genetic conditions have been associated with ASD, including fragile X syndrome, Cornelia de Lange syndrome, Rett's syndrome, Prader-Willi syndrome, Angelman syndrome, Smith–Lemli–Opitz syndrome, CHARGE syndrome, and tuberous sclerosis (Grafodatskaya et al., 2010). Increasing evidence is accumulating to support an epigenetic etiology for ASD that affects neurodevelopmental processes as early as the prenatal period. It should be noted that there has been no credible evidence supporting the theory that vaccines cause ASD (Landrigan, 2010).

Theoretical underpinnings for ASD interventions currently fall into two broad categories as outlined fully in the American Psychological Association Task Force article in evidence-based treatments for ASD (Smith & Iadarola, 2015): those governing interventions based in principles of applied behavior analysis (ABA; also referred to as early intensive behavioral intervention [EIBI]) and those underlying developmental social-pragmatic (DSP) models (also called developmental, interactive, transactional, or interpersonal). As DSP-based interventions are still accumulating evidence needed to show that they have a long-term impact on functioning of children with ASD, they are summarized in the Side-Bar Box.

ABA is rooted in learning theory, the experimental analysis of behavior (Catania, 1992), and the scientific method. At its foundation, it is one of the only evidence-based interventions founded on a set of already research-based components, rather than the other way around of creating an intervention and then trying to figure out which pieces cause the change. ABA is based on the observation that symptoms of behavior in ASD cause significant difficulties in the child's ability to learn effectively from their environment. There may also be specific learning disabilities or dysfunctions associated with ASD. The core social-communication deficits lead to difficulties discriminating between what stimuli should be attended to, difficulties sustaining attention on relevant social stimuli (i.e., parents and teachers trying to teach them), and atypical communication skills that make it difficult to benefit from verbal teaching methods. This in turn disrupts typical development, in that development is fundamentally related to learning. Therefore, to restore a normal developmental trajectory to the extent possible, we must apply principles of behavior modification that have already been shown by research to result in more efficient learning to compensate for developmental delay. This can be by teaching in an intense, comprehensive, and systematic way in order to increase an individual's ability to learn effectively and function more independently. Treatment targets are chosen because they are prerequisite to restoring typical functioning (i.e., it is Applied) and they are observable so change can be measured (i.e., it is Behavioral). Teaching methods are then applied to these targets in a systematic manner that can be reliably replicated across teachers, and data are collected to demonstrate behavior change and indicate when a target is mastered (i.e., it is Analytic; Baer, Wolf, & Risley, 1968).

Brief Overview of Evidence-Based Treatments

There are several excellent data-driven ABA packages (see Useful Resources). These are traditionally delivered in a home-based setting. The individualized intervention program is designed by a psychologist or Board Certified Behavior Analyst (BCBA) therapist who also oversees implementation of the intervention by a team of "aides" or "tutors" (usually bachelor-level clinicians). Using discrete trial training, learning readiness skills (e.g., eye contact, sitting in a chair, imitation, following basic commands) are taught through compliance training. A comprehensive program is then developed to teach appropriate skills across a variety of settings, people, and variants: language (e.g., following commands, using words and gestures to request), social and play skills (e.g., appropriate object use, interactive play skills), basic self-care skills (e.g., feeding, bathing, dressing), fine motor skills (e.g., building with blocks, block imitation, drawing, writing, cutting with scissors), and cognitive and pre-academic skills (e.g., sizes, colors, shapes, letters, numbers, quantities). Once learned, skills are then generalized into a more natural environment through incidental teaching. Learned skills then continue to be maintained through repeated practice as new targets are built onto this foundation. This model is meant to be intensive, with intervention taking place 25–40 hours a week across a variety of settings and activities. ABA can also be delivered in a classroom-based setting. A data-driven, individualized program is implemented for each child. In such classroom-based settings, children may receive less one-on-one time but may have a greater opportunity to develop peer interaction skills. Learning Experiences: An Alternative Program for Preschoolers and Parents (LEAP) is one example of this type of program. More targeted programming focused on increasing a specific skill area may be employed, such as increasing communication abilities (e.g., teaching Picture Exchange Communication System [PECS]), decreasing negative behaviors (Smith, Groen, & Wynn, 2000), or decreasing restrictive eating patterns (Peterson, Piazza, & Volkert, 2016).

ABA is still the only intervention shown to be effective in increasing adaptive and cognitive skills in the long term, with a percentage of children achieving an optimal outcome of functioning similar to typically developing children. Seminal work completed by Ivar Lovaas (1987) found that 47% of the treatment group (i.e., 40 hours a week of one-on-one ABA) achieved cognitive functioning in the average range and were placed in regular education classrooms, as compared to 2% of the control group (i.e., 10 or fewer hours a week of ABA). While most children with ASD do not reach this optimal outcome, a large percentage of those who receive ABA do make large gains in skills. Over time these results have at least partially been replicated by several other studies, with one meta-analysis (Eldevik et al., 2009) comparing nine controlled ABA outcome studies finding a large effect size ($d = 1.10$) for changes in cognitive functioning and a moderate effect size ($d = 0.66$) for changes in adaptive functioning. No other intervention has been shown to have this large an impact on improving functioning in children with ASD. Similar meta-analysis indicated moderate to large effects for improvement in cognitive functioning, language, adaptive skills, and social-emotional functioning (Makrygianni & Reed, 2010; Matson, Hattier, & Belva, 2012; Peters-Scheffer et al., 2011; Virués-Ortega, 2010). Eldevik et al. (2010) compiled individual data from 309 participants collected over 16 studies to show significant increases in IQ and adaptive behavior compared to no treatment and alternative interventions. While some studies have shown that these effects last long term and are related to better outcomes as children age (Butter, Mulick, & Metz, 2006; Lovass, 1987), further long-term studies better characterizing outcomes into adolescence and adulthood are needed.

The Developmental Social-Pragmatic Model

Developmental social-pragmatic (DSP) models are based in developmental research exploring typical mother–child interactions during early communication and social skills acquisition (Ingersoll et al., 2005). DSP is based on the theory that language is developed through "affect-laden" interactions within strong relationships with caregivers, with a focus on the "function" of communication (e.g., requests, protests, sharing), rather than the "form" (e.g., eye contact, gestures, verbal language). Instead of deliberately focusing on teaching a set of skills, these interventions focus on "helping children develop various capacities related to social communication in a pragmatically appropriate social context" (Casenhiser, Shaner, & Stieben, 2013). For example instead of focusing on eye contact and pointing, DSP-based interventions focus on developing the "capacity" for joint attention. These models tend to be less intensive (i.e., one to three hours per week of clinician time, although parents are typically encouraged to engage in 15 hours a week of intervention with the child) and often include a larger parent-led component, as the focus is on improving parent–child interactions in order to improve language and social skills (Ingersoll et al., 2005). While a few randomized control trials and several other studies have shown differences between children receiving DSP-based interventions versus those receiving treatment-as-usual on highly specific parent report or observational measures of social/emotional abilities (often created specifically to measure the changes of DSP-based interventions), no changes on standardized measures of language, adaptive skills, or IQ/cognitive abilities have been found (see Smith & Iadarola 2015 for a more in-depth review). It should also be noted that no studies were found that compare DSP interventions to ABA interventions or that examine long-term outcomes. Such studies are needed to show that DSP-based interventions are meaningful evidence-based interventions worth diverting resources toward.

The Early Start Denver Model (ESDM) is a unique program integrating ABA and DSP elements in a model that can be applied to children as young as 12 months old (Dawson et al., 2010). The intervention is individualized and intensive (i.e., ~20 hours per week) and there is a strong parent training component to help generalize skills. Research indicates significant gains in both cognitive/early learning skills and adaptive behavior as measured by standardized assessments, a small decrease in symptoms of ASD (Dawson et al., 2010), and decreases in maladaptive behavior (Fulton et al., 2014). One significant gap in this research literature, however, is that we are aware of no studies comparing this model to more traditional ABA and DSP models to show that the combined program has added benefit beyond ABA alone.

Components of Evidence-Based Treatments

Developing Treatment Targets

The goal of ABA-based early intervention is to restore a typical developmental trajectory. Therefore the first step of successful intervention is to systematically assess the individual's current skills and develop treatment targets focused on teaching the next steps in a typical developmental sequence. Treatment targets are observable behaviors that can be measured to regularly assess progress. Since children with ASD vary significantly in their level of functioning and particular skill deficits, treatment programs will be highly individualized and progression will vary based on individual response. The following are common target areas.

Increasing Attention. Signs of attentional difficulties, particularly to social stimuli (e.g., low eye contact and response to human voices, lack of attention to social scenes) are among the earliest deficits seen in children with ASD (Chawarska, Macari, & Shic, 2013). This lack of attention to others severely impacts all learning; therefore increasing skills and capacities related to attention are often among the first targeted. These include underlying capacities such as joint attention and observable behaviors such as increasing eye contact, response to name, response to commands related to attending (e.g., come here, sit down, look), and ability to sit and focus attention on a particular task for increasing lengths of time. Intervention typically starts with training to follow simple commands in order to increase the child's ability to attend to a source of instruction, because learning can be accelerated with improved ability to focus as directed. Such compliance training increases attention and decreases inattention by continuously returning the child to the readiness position (i.e., sitting in a chair looking at the clinician) and then reinforcing this behavior (Lovaas, 2003).

Imitation. The ability to watch someone and replicate their actions is fundamental to all other learning, yet impaired imitation skills are another significant deficit seen in young children with ASD (Rogers et al., 2003). Imitation has been shown to be a key predictor of verbal language development (Stone & Yoder, 2001; Thurm et al., 2007) making it a key target for all early intervention programs. Unlike other skills sets, imitation is not a defined set of responses, but rather an ability to reproduce observed behavior. It has been shown that while initial imitation often requires significant time and effort, as an individual learns to imitate an initial set of behaviors, imitation of novel behavior is acquired much faster and becomes generalized, such that new behaviors are imitated without direct teaching (Baer, Peterson, & Sherman, 1967). It should be noted though that generalization happens most effectively within response class (e.g., actions with objects; gross motor actions; fine motor actions; oral motor actions; vocalizations), indicating that direct instruction will be needed for the first set of responses in each class (Garcia, Baer, & Firestone, 1971).

Social/Play Skills. Play is the typical mode of learning for many early skills including those related to social and communication skills. Goals to increase play skills include increasing functional play with toys (e.g., pushing a car, banging a drum), turn-taking, participating in social songs, and playing imaginatively with toys (see Leaf & McEachin, 1999, Chapter 11).

Verbal Behavior. Verbal behavior is the primary goal of early intervention as learning in all other areas is facilitated by strong receptive and expressive language skills. The goal areas discussed so far are considered precursors for language development, as are matching and concept formation. Initial language goals will focus on teaching the child how to request what they want because these are skills children will be particularly motivated to learn. Interventions will focus on teaching specific developmentally appropriate behaviors starting with gestures (e.g., reaching and pointing), specific signs, picture exchanges, and then verbal labels. Intervention will then move to a series of receptive language (i.e., following commands to engage in actions or point to specific items and pictures) and expressive language (i.e., labeling targets, answering questions, identifying early academic concepts such as letters and numbers) targets leading up to social-communication goals (see Sundberg & Pardington, 1998 for an overview of teaching language).

Teaching Techniques

Behavior exhibited by an individual is dependent both on their knowledge or skills as well as on their motivation. We must know how to do something *and* want to do it. This section focuses on techniques that allow us to most effectively teach an individual how to do something as well as on how to increase motivation to engage in that behavior.

Differential Reinforcement. Reinforcement is a broad term referring to any behavioral consequence that increases the likelihood a behavior will occur again in the future. Obtaining reinforcement elaborates and maintains behavior, positive or negative. Differential reinforcement refers to providing a reinforcer after a targeted response (e.g., presenting a piece of fruit if a child sits in a chair following the command "sit down") in order to increase the likelihood that the response will occur again as opposed to other behavior. There are several factors to consider when using reinforcement as a teaching tool. The first is what to use as a reinforcer. Reinforcers can include edibles (e.g., small pieces of preferred foods), tangibles (e.g., access to a preferred toy or item), activities (e.g., listening to music, popping bubbles), physical (e.g., tickles, swinging in the air), and social (e.g., praise, attention), as well as any combination of these. While certain reinforcers tend to be desired by most children, preference will vary based on the individual. A child with ASD may be particularly attached to unusual items (e.g., pieces of string or paper) or find enjoyment in an activity other children may not (e.g., running the vacuum). It is important to be observant and creative in finding ways to use atypical reinforcers to teach adaptive behavior. Children with ASD may also find social reinforcers aversive at first, although repeatedly pairing these social behaviors with items the child does like (e.g., pairing praise with tickles) will make social interaction on its own reinforcing over time. It is also important to keep in mind that reinforcers change over time so regular preference assessments should be completed with the child to determine what is currently most reinforcing. Having multiple reinforcers available and giving the child a choice can reduce satiation (North & Iwata, 2005). Finally it is necessary that the reinforcers chosen are those that can be given frequently and easily. A trip to a theme park might be highly preferred but will likely not be feasible for the average family to give often enough to use it as a successful reinforcer for teaching most skills. The most successful reinforcers are those that can be delivered immediately upon completion of the target behavior, as this will increase the likelihood that the child will associate that behavior with obtaining the reinforcer. As children become better at verbal communication, language can be used as a mediator to better bridge gaps between behavior and reinforcer (e.g., "you cleaned up all your toys so you can get a snack when we go upstairs"; see Lovaas, 2003, pp. 11–15, for an overview).

After determining what reinforcers will be used, one must then determine the schedule of when the reinforcer will be given. Schedules are typically based on a *ratio* (reinforcement is given after every X response) or *interval* (reinforcement is given after every X interval). Schedules can also be *fixed* (reinforcement is given after every X response or minute) or *variable* (reinforcement is given an average of every X response or minute but this varies). There are advantages and disadvantages to using different types of schedules depending on the target behavior, how quickly a response is learned, and how quickly a response decreases after reinforcement is stopped. For teaching a new behavior, frequent reinforcement, often after every correct response or at very short intervals, leads to quicker learning. It should be noted that children with ASD often need many repetitions to learn a completely new behavior, although similar responses in the same category of behavior may then be learned more quickly. As the child learns the behavior, longer or more variable intervals and ratios will be used, as these types of schedules tend to maintain the behavior longer after reinforcement is decreased or stopped.

Establishing Operations. Establishing operations (EOs) set the stage for learning by "momentarily altering (a) the reinforcing effectiveness of other events and (b) the frequency of occurrence of the type of behavior that has been consequated by those events" (Michael, 2004, p. 136). In other words, EOs increase an individual's perceived value of a reinforcer. Many of the most common EOs are unconditioned and typically involve some sort of deprivation (e.g., limited access to stimulation or activity, lack of social attention), although motivation can also be sparked by stimuli associated with desirable events, and these are called conditioned EOs. When a particular EO is present it can mean that a certain type of reinforcer will be more effective (e.g., if a child is hungry, working to obtain food will be more motivating) and the individual will be more likely to engage in any behavior that leads to that reinforcer. An EO can also determine when a reinforcer will be less effective (e.g., if a person is full, they will be less likely to work to obtain food, even if food is available). Clinicians use EOs to maximize the power of the reinforcers they are presenting in order to increase the child's motivation to learn a new behavior (see Micheal, 2004 for an in-depth review of EOs and their applications).

Discriminative Stimuli. A stimulus is a change of energy in the environment that affects an organism's response (Michael, 2004, p. 7). These connections can either be unlearned (e.g., loud sound causes one to startle, food in mouth causes salivation) or learned (e.g., the command "sit down" results in the child sitting down). Teaching any behavior involves establishing stimulus control by teaching the child how the signals indicate which response will lead to the desired reinforcer. Accordingly, the child is taught to discriminate between different stimuli. For example, a child can be taught that if they sit down after the stimulus "sit down" they may receive praise or a small treat, but they receive nothing if they sit down after the stimulus "clap your hands." ABA-based interventions deliberately seek to teach the relationship between a particular discriminative stimulus (typically abbreviated as S^d) and a particular response (e.g., the only response after the S^d "sit down" that leads to reinforcement is sitting) or set of responses (e.g., several responses will lead to reinforcement after the S^d "What do you want?").

Prompting and Prompt Fading. Prompting is used to help the individual respond correctly to an S^d in order to provide more opportunity to earn the reinforcer and therefore learn the new behavior (see MacDuff, Krantz, & McClannahan, 2001 for a more in-depth review). If the child is not prompted, the clinician has to wait for the child to accidently stumble on the correct response, which creates far fewer opportunities to provide reinforcement and slows down the process of learning. Prompts vary by level of intensity and often a variety of prompts will be employed to help the child learn most effectively. Common prompts include verbal, modeled, and physical. For example, if the S^d was "touch the picture of a fruit," a verbal prompt could be "touch apple," pointing to the apple picture would be a modeled prompt, and a physical prompt would be taking the child's hand and guiding them to touch the apple picture.

The clinician often goes through a hierarchy of prompts when teaching. Common hierarchies include Most to Least (MTL) prompting and Least to Most (LTM) prompting. MTL prompting involves using the most intensive prompt level when initially teaching a response and then fading through less intense prompts until the child can do the behavior independently. In the previous example the clinician would start using a physical prompt immediately to help the child touch the fruit without giving any opportunity to touch anything else. This would be repeated several times and then the clinician would move back a step on the response hierarchy (e.g., lightly pushing the child's hand to the apple picture), and then as the child was correctly responding at that level continue to fade to less intense prompts. Alternatively, an LTM hierarchy starts with the least intensive prompt and moves up the hierarchy until a correct response is shown. The benefit of MTL prompting is that it can be used in "errorless learning" procedures by reducing the errors the child makes and therefore preventing practice of incorrect responses, while the downside can be an overreliance on prompting by the child. The costs and benefits would be reversed for LTM prompting (Libby et al., 2008).

Other types of prompting include flexible prompting, where the clinician chooses the level of prompting needed rather than moving step by step up or down a hierarchy, and simultaneous prompting, where multiple prompts may be used at one time to gain a correct response. Several factors should be considered when choosing the most effective type of prompting including the skill being taught, cognitive level of the child, and their current ability level with the particular skill (MacDuff, Krantz, & McClannahan, 2001).

Shaping and Chaining. Shaping and chaining are two strategies that can be used to break down responses that are too complex to teach directly (Neidert et al., 2010). Shaping is the reinforcement of successive approximations toward the desired behavior, while decreasing reinforcement for previously learned steps toward the desired behavior. For example, when teaching a child to say "ball," the clinician may first reward any vocalization in response to "What's this?"; then they may reward the child saying "buh" but no other consonant sounds; and then finally reward the child only when they say "ball" but no other word approximations. Chaining is used to teach sequences of behavior by teaching one new behavior at a time and then linking the new behavior onto a chain of already learned responses. For example, to teach a child to put on pants, a clinician may start with having them hold the pants up, then teach putting one leg in, then the other, then pulling the pants up to the knees, then pulling them all the way up. Chains can be taught in either direction, starting with teaching the child to do the first step while the clinician does the rest of the task, then the first two steps while the clinician does the rest, and so on. Alternatively the clinician may do all the steps up to the last, which they have the child do, then the clinician does all the steps except for the last two, which the child does, and so on (see Spooner & Spooner, 1984 for a comparison of chaining procedures). Task analyses are used to break a task down into its component parts. How many steps a task is broken into for either shaping or chaining depends again on multiple factors, including the complexity of the task and the cognitive level of the child.

Discrete Trial Training. Discrete Trial training (DTT) is the primary instructional method used to teach skills in an ABA program, particularly in early skill acquisition (see Lerman, Valentino, & LeBlanc, 2016 for a comprehensive review). By combining several of the components discussed previously, this teaching method can be used to teach skills across developmental areas. DTT involves breaking skills into smaller parts, identifying where the individual is in the mastery of these different subparts, then teaching the remain subparts one at a time, allowing repeated practice in a concentrated period of time, providing prompting and then fading prompts as necessary, and employing reinforcement procedures. Learning sessions are broken down into "trials." Trials begin with an S^d, followed immediately by a desired reinforcer. Then after a short interval, this sequence will be repeated. Repeatedly pairing the S^d with the reinforcer over several trials will allow the child to learn more efficiently. As stimulus control is established, the prompts are faded, until the S^d can independently control the target behavior. For example to teach a child the meaning of the word "ball," the clinician would place a ball and a distractor item in front of the child. The clinician would give the S^d of "touch ball." She would then prompt the child by taking their hand and placing it on the ball, and then reinforcing the child by saying "good job, that's the ball!" while giving them a piece of candy. This would be one trial. The clinician would repeat several trials of this sequence, slowly fading prompts, until the child was reliably touching the ball after hearing the S^d. The clinician would take data on each trial to know when to reduce the level of prompting and when to switch to a new target.

Promoting Generalization. Generalization is often mistakenly thought of as a passive process, in that, after teaching a child to engage in a specific behavior (saying "hi") in response to a specific stimuli (the clinician saying "hi" first) to obtain a specific reinforcer (a piece of fruit), the child will naturally (i.e., without any specific intervention) begin to engage in similar behaviors (waving, saying "hello/what's up/ hey") in response to similar stimuli (across different people, settings, and times) to obtain more natural reinforcers (getting someone to smile or start a conversation). Generalization, however, often does not occur "naturally," particularly to children with ASD, as they are more prone to stimulus overselectivity (i.e., pairing very specific stimuli with very specific responses). Instead generalization must be actively promoted within teaching methods (see Stokes & Baer, 1977 for a more in-depth overview of these methods and the supporting research). One option is teaching each behavior in response to every possible stimuli combination, although this would be time consuming and unnecessary. Often one must only train *sufficient* exemplars of the behavior to produce generalization. For example often teaching children using discrete trial training to imitate a few behaviors in response to the S^d "do this" will lead to them imitating many behaviors not specifically taught. As discussed previously, fading reinforcement by moving to more intermittent reinforcement schedules is also a way to generalize behavior by helping it continue even as reinforcement is lessened. This is often paired with the generalization technique of moving to using more natural consequences as reinforcers. For example toilet training may initially be maintained by receiving a preferred treat after each successful attempt but then continues to be maintained by avoiding the discomfort of having an accident. "Training loosely" refers to teaching in a way that is purposefully less structured, using a variety of similar stimuli (e.g., using a mix of "touch/point to/show me") and/ or allowing for a number of similar responses to count as correct. This technique immediately begins to build in generalization. Generalization can also occur by rewarding a child only when they use a new version of a behavior or apply a behavior under a new set of conditions (e.g., rewarding a child for each different person they greet or for each different question they ask in a conversation). Planning for generalization within a teaching program is extremely important to developing verbal and social behaviors that are more natural and not "robotic." Some programs attempt to use more naturalistic teaching methods from the beginning to avoid stimulus overselectivity and encourage generalization. The only difficulty with this method is that, without direct instruction of certain behaviors, children with ASD will likely learn these behaviors more slowly, if at all. If natural teaching methods alone worked to teach children with ASD verbal and social behaviors, there would not be a need for intervention in the first place.

Role of Parents in Treatment

Parents are expected to play a large role in early intervention programs for ASD. Setting up a full time ABA program is a significant amount of work for families, which includes finding a qualified agency or professional to design and oversee the program, helping to recruit a team of aides to run the program, securing the large amount of funding needed to pay for the program, and organizing schedules to allow for as many intervention hours as possible each week. As ABA is based on teaching skills within a developmental framework, it is well recognized that parents are the primary teacher of young children. Therefore most ABA-based interventions also include a parent training component, in order to integrate the teaching skills discussed above into how parents interact with their child every day. This increases the amount of practice a child receives and how quickly skills generalize into the home environment. Specific intervention packages vary on how integral the parent training component is, varying from using parents primarily to generalize skills after they have been learned, to using parents as the primary teachers within the intervention. It should be noted that while there is support for the effectiveness of parent-led (i.e., clinicians provide parent training but no direct intervention) interventions, purely parent-led interventions have often been shown to be less effective than clinician-led models (Rogers et al., 2012; Smith, Groen, & Wynn, 2000; Vismara et al., 2016). This is likely due to the significant burden of being both therapist and parent interfering with successful implementation without a trained treatment team to shoulder some of this burden.

Other Variables Influencing Treatment

Assessment

The comprehensive assessment of ASD includes a complete developmental history, direct observation, and standardized assessment of symptoms specific to ASD (e.g., Autism Diagnostic Observational Schedule – Second Edition). It is also very important to fully assess the child's current functioning level (i.e., cognitive, academic, language, and adaptive skills) as this will guide initial treatment targets and provide a baseline against which to measure progress. The assessment also includes a thorough consideration of common comorbid conditions and problems including attention-deficit/hyperactivity disorder, anxiety disorders, feeding difficulties, pica, sleep problems, and behavior problems (e.g., aggression, self-injury, severe tantrums), as these concerns can affect targets for ABA-based intervention, the effectiveness of intervention, as well as the need for additional types of treatment.

Comorbidity

While ABA-based interventions are recommended for all young children with ASD, comorbid conditions can affect the success of treatment, as well as treatment targets. Several conditions which often occur in children with ASD can be included as target areas for ABA-based interventions, including feeding problems, pica, behavior problems (e.g., aggression, tantrums, self-injury), and sleep difficulties. Although the prevalence of intellectual disability (ID) in those with ASD has recently been reported to occur at a much lower estimated rate (approximately 31% of those with ASD, down from 70%; Wingate et al., 2014) following the changes in early detection methods and diagnostic criteria, ID remains the most difficult aspect of ASD to ameliorate, and those with both diagnoses have the poorest prognosis in treatment (Eldevik et al., 2010). ABA-based intervention is still strongly recommended for this group, as primary treatment targets are increasing cognitive abilities and daily living skills. Interventions for older children who continue to have comorbid ID often focus on decreasing maladaptive behavior and increasing functional living skills through the use of behavioral interventions, which are discussed in detail in Chapter 2 of this book, which is focused on intellectual disabilities.

Anxiety, attention-deficit/hyperactivity disorder (ADHD), and ASD have several overlapping symptoms and differential diagnosis between these three disorders is often difficult (Grzadzinski et al., 2016; Kerns et al., 2016). Children with ASD often have high levels of anxiety, frequently associated with social interactions and/or disruptions to rigid behavior or routines. Evidence-based interventions such as cognitive-behavioral therapy can be used with this population to treat high anxiety with some modifications (Ung et al., 2015; see Chapter 10 in this book on intervention for anxiety). Evidence-based behavioral treatments for ADHD share many of the components of ABA, particularly considering that increasing attention is typically one of the first goals of many comprehensive programs (see Chapter 4 in this book for an overview of ADHD interventions). Medications used to treat inattention and hyperactivity are also often prescribed to those with ASD and co-occurring ADHD. Stimulant medications are most often prescribed as the first-line choice for treating comorbid ADHD, although initial research has indicated a poorer therapeutic response and a higher rate of side effects, particularly significant irritability in those with comorbid ASD and ADHD, compared to those with only ADHD (Mahajan et al., 2012).

Demographics

Improvements in assessment techniques now allow for accurate diagnoses of children as young as 12 months of age (Guthrie et al., 2013) and studies indicating deficits related to ASD present at six months promise possibilities of detection at an even younger age (Chawarska, Macari, & Shic, 2013). Early diagnosis is important as it opens the path to early intervention, and research indicates that the earlier intervention begins the greater the effects of treatment (Harris & Handleman, 2000; Itzchak & Zachor, 2011). This follows the logic that the gap tends to be smaller between typical and delayed development at younger ages and grows as the child gets older as delays in early skills compound into larger delays in more advanced skill. Also certain developmental abilities, such as language development, are bound by critical and sensitive periods, such that if a skill is not learned within a certain period (e.g., functional language by age five), it is unlikely to develop. Indeed, it has been shown that the rate of significant outcomes gained through ABA-based interventions decreases significantly in children receiving intervention over seven years of age (Granpeesheh et al., 2009).

Medication

There are no medications currently approved which address the core symptoms of ASD (i.e., social-communication deficits and restricted and repetitive behaviors). To date, only risperidone and aripipazole, both atypical antipsychotic medications, have been approved by the US Food and Drug Administration to help treat behavior problems in ASD (McPheeters et al., 2011). While both medications have been shown to be effective in reducing irritability, aggression, self-injury, stereotypy, and hyper-activity in some children with ASD, they are also associated with several significant side effects including increased weight gain, sedation, and risk of extrapyramidal symptoms, and should therefore be used with extreme caution in the context of a full range of effective therapies.

Intensity

The developmental delays accompanying ASD are pervasive. Therefore any treatment focusing on restoring a typical developmental trajectory must span across all areas. Such a treatment will naturally be quite intensive. The average recommended intensity for a comprehensive ABA program is 40 hours a week with a minimum recommendation of at least 20 hours a week. Less than 20 hours a week has not been associated with large gains, with studies often using 10 hours a week of ABA as a control group (Lovaas, 1987). Higher intensity of treatment has been shown to be a significant moderator of treatment gains across several studies (Eldevik et al., 2010; Granpeesheh et al., 2009; Makrygianni & Reed, 2010; Virués-Ortega, 2010).

Severity of Symptoms

As its name implies, ASD encompasses a spectrum of symptoms that can vary significantly in their severity and impact on a child's level of functioning. The severity of symptoms at the start of treatment, particularly lower cognitive abilities, has been shown to be a predictor of response to treatment, with a better response to treatment seen in those with higher IQ (Eldevik et al., 2010; Harris & Handleman, 2000), higher adaptive skills (Makrygianni & Reed, 2010), and better verbal skills (Itzchak & Zachor, 2011) at the start of treatment.

Access to Intervention

Despite demonstrated effectiveness, many children with ASD do not receive early intensive intervention. Several possible barriers to setting up intervention have been identified including financial cost, problems with accessing services, and family resource constraints (i.e., the time and energy needed; Grindle et al., 2009; Johnson & Hastings, 2002; Trudgeon & Carr, 2007). These factors are understandable as the cost of an intensive treatment ABA program can range from $20,000 to $80,000 a year and waitlists are often several months to several years long. While these costs are high, the benefits to the individuals, families, and society as a whole from successfully improving an individual with ASD's quality of life and ability to successfully contribute to society are even greater (Buescher et al., 2014; Jacobson, Mulick, & Green, 1998). This speaks to the continued importance of advocating for expanded support for intensive interventions already shown to be successful, rather than putting already precious resources into creating watered-down, less-expensive interventions that are unable to achieve meaningful long-term outcomes.

Conclusion

While the impacts of ASD are typically lifelong, ABA-based interventions offer the opportunity of a significantly brighter future for young children with this disorder. These behaviorally based interventions tackle the underlying roots of ASD by providing the learning experiences needed to restore a typical developmental trajectory. While it is the hope that future research in epigenetics will illuminate better prevention strategies along with interventions to treat the underlying neurobiological causes of this disorder, ABA-based interventions will continue to help children with ASD reach their highest potential.

Useful Resources

Websites

- Cambridge Center for Behavioral Studies (CCBS) at www.behavior.org/
- Learning ABA! – an online, interactive course developed by UMass Medical School and the E. K. Shriver Center on the basics of ABA. www.udiscovering.org/products/learning-aba/product-preview
- Organization for Autism Research (OAR) – the OAR provides resources for families, educators, and providers to aid in understanding the large body of research on ASD and related interventions. www.researchautism.org
- Rethink – Rethink is an ABA-based online service for families and ABA providers, which uses video modeling strategies as a way to train family and tutors on how to deliver different ABA programs to the child. www.rethinkfirst.com/
- The UC Davis MIND Institute UCEDD – this group has developed a set of free videos that allow parents and teachers to learn strategies for teaching functional skills. http://media.mindinstitute.org/education/ADEPT/Module1Menu.html.

Treatment Manuals

- *Behavioral Intervention for Young Children with Autism* by Catherine Maurice, Gina Green, and Stephen C. Luce, PRO-ED, 1996
- *Crafting Connections: Contemporary Applied Behavioral Analysis for Enriching the Social Lives of Persons with Autism Spectrum Disorder* by Mitchell Taubman, Ron Leaf, and John McEachin, DRL Books, 2011
- *Defying Autism: Keeping Your Sanity and Taking Control* by Stephanie B. Lockshin, Jennifer M. Gillis, and Raymond G. Romanczyk, DRL Books, 2004
- *Teaching Individuals with Developmental Delays: Basic Intervention Techniques* by O. Ivar Lovass, PRO-ED, 2003
- *Teaching Language to Children with Autism or Other Developmental Disabilities* by Mark L. Sundberg and James W. Partington, Behavior Analysts, 1998
- *A Work in Progress: Behavior Management Strategies and a Curriculum for Intensive Behavioral Treatment of Autism*, by Ron Leaf and John McEachin, DRL Books, 1999
- *The Early Start Denver Model for Young Children with Autism: Promoting Language, Learning, and Engagement*, by Sally J. Rogers and Geraldine Dawson, Guilford Press, 2010

References

American Psychiatric Association. (2013). *Diagnostic and statistical manual of mental disorders.* 5th edn. Washington, DC: American Psychiatric Association.

Baer, D. M., Peterson, R. F., & Sherman, J. A. (1967). The development of imitation by reinforcing behavioral similarity to a model. *Journal of the Experimental Analysis of Behavior*, *10*(5), 405–416.

Baer, D. M., Wolf, M. M., & Risley, T. R. (1968). Some current dimensions of applied behavior analysis. *Journal of Applied Behavior Analysis*, *1*(1), 91–97.

Baio, J. (2012). Prevalence of Autism Spectrum Disorders: Autism and Developmental Disabilities Monitoring Network, 14 Sites, United States, 2008. Morbidity and Mortality Weekly Report. Surveillance Summaries. Volume 61, Number 3. Centers for Disease Control and Prevention.

Buescher, A. V., Cidav, Z., Knapp, M., & Mandell, D. S. (2014). Costs of autism spectrum disorders in the United Kingdom and the United States. *JAMA Pediatrics*, *168*(8), 721–728.

Butter, E. M., Mulick, J. A., & Metz, B. (2006). Eight case reports of learning recovery in children with pervasive developmental disorders after early intervention. *Behavioral Interventions*, *21*(4), 227–243.

Casenhiser, D. M., Shanker, S. G., & Stieben, J. (2013). Learning through interaction in children with autism: Preliminary data from a social-communication-based intervention. *Autism*, *17*(2), 220–241.

Catania, A. C. (1992). *Learning*. 3rd edn. Englewood Cliffs, NJ: Prentice-Hall.

Chawarska, K., Macari, S., & Shic, F. (2013). Decreased spontaneous attention to social scenes in 6-month-old infants later diagnosed with autism spectrum disorders. *Biological Psychiatry*, *74*(3), 195–203.

Dawson, G., Rogers, S., Munson, J., Smith, M., Winter, J., Greenson, J., . . . & Varley, J. (2010). Randomized, controlled trial of an intervention for toddlers with autism: The Early Start Denver Model. *Pediatrics*, *125*(1), e17–e23.

Eldevik, S., Hastings, R. P., Hughes, J. C., Jahr, E., Eikeseth, S., & Cross, S. (2009). Meta-analysis of early intensive behavioral intervention for children with autism. *Journal of Clinical Child & Adolescent Psychology*, *38*(3), 439–450.

Eldevik, S., Hastings, R. P., Hughes, J. C., Jahr, E., Eikeseth, S., & Cross, S. (2010). Using participant data to extend the evidence base for intensive behavioral intervention for children with autism. *American Journal on Intellectual and Developmental Disabilities*, *115*(5), 381–405.

Fulton, E., Eapen, V., Črnčec, R., Walter, A., & Rogers, S. (2014). Reducing maladaptive behaviors in preschool-aged children with autism spectrum disorder using the Early Start Denver Model. *Frontiers in Pediatrics*, *2*, 40.

Garcia, E., Baer, D. M., & Firestone, I. (1971). The development of generalized imitation within topographically determined boundaries. *Journal of Applied Behavior Analysis*, *4*(2), 101–112.

Gates, J. A., Kang, E., & Lerner, M. D. (2017). Efficacy of group social skills interventions for youth with autism spectrum disorder: A systematic review and meta-analysis. *Clinical Psychology Review*, *52*, 164–181.

Grafodatskaya, D., Chung, B., Szatmari, P., & Weksberg, R. (2010). Autism spectrum disorders and epigenetics. *Journal of the American Academy of Child & Adolescent Psychiatry*, *49*(8), 794–809.

Granpeesheh, D., Dixon, D. R., Tarbox, J., Kaplan, A. M., & Wilke, A. E. (2009). The effects of age and treatment intensity on behavioral intervention outcomes for children with autism spectrum disorders. *Research in Autism Spectrum Disorders*, *3*(4), 1014–1022.

Grindle, C. F., Kovshoff, H., Hastings, R. P., & Remington, B. (2009). Parents' experiences of home-based applied behavior analysis programs for young children with autism. *Journal of Autism and Developmental Disorders*, *39*(1), 42–56.

Grzadzinski, R., Dick, C., Lord, C., & Bishop, S. (2016). Parent-reported and clinician-observed autism spectrum disorder (ASD) symptoms in children with attention deficit/hyperactivity disorder (ADHD): Implications for practice under DSM-5. *Molecular Autism*, *7*(1), 7.

Guthrie, W., Swineford, L. B., Nottke, C., & Wetherby, A. M. (2013). Early diagnosis of autism spectrum disorder: Stability and change in clinical diagnosis and symptom presentation. *Journal of Child Psychology and Psychiatry*, *54*(5), 582–590.

Harris, S. L., & Handleman, J. S. (2000). Age and IQ at intake as predictors of placement for young children with autism: A four- to six-year follow-up. *Journal of Autism and Developmental Disorders*, *30*(2), 137–142.

Ingersoll, B., Dvortcsak, A., Whalen, C., & Sikora, D. (2005). The effects of a developmental, social-pragmatic language intervention on rate of expressive language production in young children with autistic spectrum disorders. *Focus on Autism and Other Developmental Disabilities*, *20*(4), 213–222.

Itzchak, E. B., & Zachor, D. A. (2011). Who benefits from early intervention in autism spectrum disorders? *Research in Autism Spectrum Disorders*, *5*(1), 345–350.

Jacobson, J. W., Mulick, J. A., & Green, G. (1998). Cost–benefit estimates for early intensive behavioral intervention for young children with autism – general model and single state case. *Behavioral Interventions*, *13*(4), 201–226.

Johnson, E., & Hastings, R. P. (2002). Facilitating factors and barriers to the implementation of intensive home based behavioural intervention for young children with autism. *Child: Care, Health and Development*, *28*(2), 123–129.

Kerns, C. M., Rump, K., Worley, J., Kratz, H., McVey, A., Herrington, J., & Miller, J. (2016). The differential diagnosis of anxiety disorders in cognitively-able youth with autism. *Cognitive and Behavioral Practice*, *23*(4), 530–547.

Landrigan, P. J. (2010). What causes autism? Exploring the environmental contribution. *Current Opinion in Pediatrics*, *22*(2), 219–225.

Leaf, R., & McEachin, J. (1999). *A work in progress: Behavior management strategies and a curriculum for intensive behavioral treatment of autism*. New York: DRL Books.

Lerman, D. C., Valentino, A. L., & LeBlanc, L. A. (2016). Discrete trial training. In R. Lang, T. B. Hancock, and N. N. Singh (eds.), *Early Intervention for Young Children with Autism Spectrum Disorder* (pp. 47–83). Cham: Springer International Publishing.

Libby, M. E., Weiss, J. S., Bancroft, S., & Ahearn, W. H. (2008). A comparison of most-to-least and least-to-most prompting on the acquisition of solitary play skills. *Behavior Analysis in Practice*, *1*, 37–43.

Lovaas, O. I. (1987). Behavioral treatment and normal educational and intellectual functioning in young autistic children. *Journal of Consulting and Clinical Psychology*, *55*(1), 3.

Lovaas, O. I. (2003). *Teaching individuals with developmental delays: Basic intervention techniques*. Austin, TX: PRO-ED.

MacDuff, G. S., Krantz, P. J., & McClannahan, L. E. (2001). Prompts and prompt-fading strategies for people with autism. In G. Maurice, G. Green, & R. Foxx (eds.), *Making a difference: Behavioral intervention for autism* (pp. 37–50). Austin, TX: PRO-ED.

Mahajan, R., Bernal, M. P., Panzer, R., Whitaker, A., Roberts, W., Handen, B., ... & Veenstra-VanderWeele, J. (2012). Clinical practice pathways for evaluation and medication choice for attention-deficit/hyperactivity disorder symptoms in autism spectrum disorders. *Pediatrics*, *130* (Supplement 2), S125–S138.

Makrygianni, M. K., & Reed, P. (2010). A meta-analytic review of the effectiveness of behavioural early intervention programs for children with autistic spectrum disorders. *Research in Autism Spectrum Disorders*, *4*(4), 577–593.

Matson, J. L., Hattier, M. A., & Belva, B. (2012). Treating adaptive living skills of persons with autism using applied behavior analysis: A review. *Research in Autism Spectrum Disorders*, 6(1), 271–276.

McPheeters, M. L., Warren, Z., Sathe, N., Bruzek, J. L., Krishnaswami, S., Jerome, R. N., & Veenstra-VanderWeele, J. (2011). A systematic review of medical treatments for children with autism spectrum disorders. *Pediatrics*, 127(5), e1312–e1321.

Michael, J. L. (2004). *Concepts and principles of behavior analysis*. Kalamazoo, MI: Western Michigan University, Association for Behavior Analysis International.

Neidert, P. L., Dozier, C. L., Iwata, B. A., & Hafen, M. (2010). Behavior analysis in intellectual and developmental disabilities. *Psychological Services*, 7(2), 103.

North, S. T., & Iwata, B. A. (2005). Motivational influences on performance maintained by food reinforcement. *Journal of Applied Behavior Analysis*, 38, 317–333.

Peters-Scheffer, N., Didden, R., Korzilius, H., & Sturmey, P. (2011). A meta-analytic study on the effectiveness of comprehensive ABA-based early intervention programs for children with autism spectrum disorders. *Research in Autism Spectrum Disorders*, 5(1), 60–69.

Peterson, K. M., Piazza, C. C., & Volkert, V. M. (2016). A comparison of a modified sequential oral sensory approach to an applied behavior-analytic approach in the treatment of food selectivity in children with autism spectrum disorder. *Journal of Applied Behavior Analysis*, 49(3), 485–511.

Rao, P. A., Beidel, D. C., & Murray, M. J. (2008). Social skills interventions for children with Asperger's syndrome or high-functioning autism: A review and recommendations. *Journal of Autism and Developmental Disorders*, 38(2), 353–361.

Rogers, S. J., Estes, A., Lord, C., Vismara, L., Winter, J., Fitzpatrick, A., . . . & Dawson, G. (2012). Effects of a brief Early Start Denver Model (ESDM)-based parent intervention on toddlers at risk for autism spectrum disorders: A randomized controlled trial. *Journal of the American Academy of Child & Adolescent Psychiatry*, 51(10), 1052–1065.

Rogers, S. J., Hepburn, S. L., Stackhouse, T., & Wehner, E. (2003). Imitation performance in toddlers with autism and those with other developmental disorders. *Journal of Child Psychology and Psychiatry*, 44(5), 763-781.

Smith, T., Groen, A. D., & Wynn, J. W. (2000). Randomized trial of intensive early intervention for children with pervasive developmental disorder. *American Journal on Mental Retardation*, 105(4), 269–285.

Smith, T., & Iadarola, S. (2015). Evidence base update for autism spectrum disorder. *Journal of Clinical Child & Adolescent Psychology*, 44(6), 897-922.

Spooner, F., & Spooner, D. (1984). A review of chaining techniques: Implications for future research and practice. *Education and Training of the Mentally Retarded*, 19(2), 114-124.

Stokes, T. F., & Baer, D. M. (1977). An implicit technology of generalization. *Journal of Applied Behavior Analysis*, 10(2), 349–367.

Stone, W. L., & Yoder, P. J. (2001). Predicting spoken language level in children with autism spectrum disorders. *Autism*, 5(4), 341–361.

Sundberg, M. L., & Partington, J. W. (1998). *Teaching language to children with autism and other developmental disabilities*. Pleasant Hill, CA: Behavior Analysts.

Thurm, A., Lord, C., Lee, L. C., & Newschaffer, C. (2007). Predictors of language acquisition in preschool children with autism spectrum disorders. *Journal of Autism and Developmental Disorders*, 37(9), 1721–1734.

Trudgeon, C., & Carr, D. (2007). The impacts of home-based early behavioural intervention programmes on families of children with autism. *Journal of Applied Research in Intellectual Disabilities*, 20(4), 285–296.

Ung, D., Selles, R., Small, B. J., & Storch, E. A. (2015). A systematic review and meta-analysis of cognitive-behavioral therapy for anxiety in youth with high-functioning autism spectrum disorders. *Child Psychiatry & Human Development, 46*(4), 533–547.

Virués-Ortega, J. (2010). Applied behavior analytic intervention for autism in early childhood: Meta-analysis, meta-regression and dose–response meta-analysis of multiple outcomes. *Clinical Psychology Review, 30*(4), 387–399.

Vismara, L. A., McCormick, C. E., Wagner, A. L., Monlux, K., Nadhan, A., & Young, G. S. (2016). Telehealth parent training in the Early Start Denver Model results from a randomized controlled study. *Focus on Autism and Other Developmental Disabilities*, 1–13. doi:1088357616651064.

Wingate, M., Kirby, R. S., Pettygrove, S., Cunniff, C., Schulz, E., Ghosh, T., . . . & Fitzgerald, R. (2014). Prevalence of autism spectrum disorder among children aged 8 years – autism and developmental disabilities monitoring network, 11 sites, United States, 2010. *MMWR Surveillance Summaries, 63*(2), 1–21.

4

Inattention and Hyperactivity

*Michael C. Meinzer, Christina M. Danko, Danielle R. Novick,
John M. Vasko, and Andrea Chronis-Tuscano*

Attention-deficit/hyperactivity disorder (ADHD) is a highly prevalent childhood disorder present in 5–11% of youth (CDC, 2016). The *Diagnostic and Statistical Manual for Mental Disorders* (DSM-5; American Psychiatric Association, 2013) requires that symptoms be present and cause impairment in at least two settings prior to age 12. Approximately 50–80% of children with ADHD continue to display symptoms into adolescence and 10–50% continue into adulthood (Barkley, Murphy, & Kwasnik, 1996; Klassen, Katzman, & Chokka, 2010), making ADHD a chronic disorder in the majority of cases.

The DSM-5 (American Psychiatric Association, 2013) divides symptoms of ADHD into two clusters: inattention and hyperactivity/impulsivity. Inattentive symptoms include difficulties paying close attention to details, sustaining attention in tasks or play activities, listening when spoken to directly, following through on instructions, and organizing tasks and activities. The hyperactive-impulsive symptom cluster is characterized by excessive motor activity (e.g., fidgeting, running or climbing in inappropriate situations), talking excessively, and interrupting or intruding on others. In order to meet diagnostic criteria, six symptoms (five symptoms if the person is 17 years old or older) within a given symptom domain must be present for six months or more and cause impairment in at least two domains.

Typical impairment resulting from ADHD symptoms appears in academic, social, and home contexts. Within the school context, children and adolescents with ADHD tend to exhibit off-task behavior, difficulty listening to instructions and completing tasks, and losing assignments or materials necessary for class (Raggi & Chronis, 2006). They may also create classroom disruption due to difficulties remaining seated and staying on task, fidgeting, and playing noisily (Raggi & Chronis, 2006). Thus, children with ADHD are more likely to display lower academic achievement (Kent et al., 2011). Further, students with ADHD continue to face academic difficulties as they progress through future stages of development. For example, youth with ADHD are at a higher risk for dropping out of high school relative to youth without the disorder (Barbaresi et al., 2007).

According to the developmental-transactional model of ADHD (Johnston & Chronis-Tuscano, 2014), family members' interactions with a child with ADHD are reciprocally influential. Within the family context, children with ADHD display higher rates of disruptive behavior, less compliance to parents' directions, and less on-task behavior compared to their peers without ADHD (Johnston & Mash, 2001). Therefore, it is not surprising that parenting a child with ADHD is a stress-generating experience. The negative behaviors of children with ADHD can result in negative parental cognitive, behavioral, and emotional functioning which can subsequently influence children's behavior (Johnston & Chronis-Tuscano, 2014).

Socially, children with ADHD often exhibit difficulties with their peer relations including greater deficits in social skills, fewer close friendships, and greater levels of peer rejection potentially due to difficulties with behavioral inhibition and perspective-taking (Mikami, 2010).

Etiology and Theoretical Underpinnings of Treatment

Though the etiology of ADHD is neurobiological and genetic in nature (Tripp & Wickens, 2009) with heritability estimates at 76% (Faraone et al., 2005), the quality of the environment can predict the persistence of ADHD and the development of comorbidity (Johnston & Chronis-Tuscano, 2014). The risk for associated impairment and co-occurring disorders in youth with ADHD include but are not limited to significantly higher rates of delinquency (Sibley et al., 2011b), substance abuse (Lee et al., 2011), anxiety (Jarrett & Ollendick, 2008), and depression (Meinzer, Pettit, & Viswesvaran, 2014) compared to youth without ADHD.

It follows that evidence-based treatments for ADHD target altering children's environments to reduce the above-mentioned impairment associated with ADHD through behavioral intervention. Barkley's theoretical model of ADHD (1997) posits that symptoms of ADHD arise due to difficulties in response inhibition and self-regulation as well as poor self-motivation to persist at challenging tasks. Therefore, behavioral interventions in which parents and teachers modify antecedents and consequences within the youth's environment as well as provide feedback and extrinsic motivation for desired behaviors have been the cornerstone for EBTs for ADHD. Components of these treatments will be described in detail in the coming sections.

Brief Overview of Evidence-Based Treatments

The two categories of evidence-based psychosocial treatments for ADHD are behavioral interventions and training interventions (Evans, Owens, & Bunford, 2014). The first, behavioral interventions, seek to modify the antecedents and consequences of inattentive, disruptive, and oppositional behavior in home, school, and peer domains by providing contingencies in a child's environment. The treatments classified under the behavioral intervention category include: behavioral parent training (BPT), behavioral classroom management (BCM), and also behavioral peer interventions (BPIs), in addition to combined behavioral interventions that use aspects of BPT, BCM, and/or BPIs. These behavioral interventions are well established according to American Psychological Association Task Force criteria (Evans, Owens, & Bunford, 2014) which indicates the intervention has very strong research support.

Training interventions, including organizational skills training, is the second evidence-based psychosocial treatment category for children and adolescents with ADHD. Training interventions focus on a different mechanism of action in comparison to the previously described behavioral interventions. Behavior change occurs through enhancing a child's skill set instead of modifying behavioral contingencies in the child's environment. Improvement in a child's skill set may lead to behavior change through generalization of the enhanced skills or through training using reinforcement and punishment that may occur within a child's daily life (Stokes & Baer, 1977). Organizational skills training also meets well-established American Psychological Association Task Force criteria (Evans, Owens, & Bunford, 2014).

Components of Evidence-Based Psychosocial Treatments

Behavioral Interventions

Behavioral interventions for ADHD can be broken down into two categories: behavioral parent training programs (BPTs) and behavior classroom management (BCM). BPTs have been found to be an extremely effective method of reducing impairments associated with ADHD in youth (Evans, Owens, & Bunford, 2014). The disruptive behaviors exhibited by children with ADHD contribute to heightened levels of stress in parents of children with ADHD as well as strains on the parent–child relationship (Johnston & Chronis-Tuscano, 2014). Consequently, parents may form maladaptive patterns of parenting strategies that may worsen child problem behaviors (Patterson, DeBaryshe, & Ramsey, 1989). Such patterns of behavior have become targets of treatments for parents, as poor parenting practices have been identified as predictors of negative outcomes in children with ADHD (Johnston & Chronis-Tuscano, 2014). As such, BPT, an evidence-based treatment for ADHD, aims to modify counterproductive parenting strategies to decrease child problem-behaviors associated with ADHD, and, therefore, ameliorate child outcomes (Pelham & Fabiano, 2008). These evidence-based interventions are derived from the Hanf parent management training model (Hanf & Kling, 1973) and include, but are not limited to, *Defiant Children: A Clinician's Manual for Assessment and Parent Training* (Barkley, 2013), *Defiant Teens: A Clinician's Manual for Assessment and Family Intervention* (Barkley & Robin, 2014),

Parent–Child Interaction Therapy (Eyberg, Boggs, & Algina, 1995), Incredible Years (Webster-Stratton, 2001), and Triple P (Sanders, Mazzucchelli, & Studman, 2004). These interventions contain a combination of the following behavioral strategies.

Given that academic and behavioral difficulties for children with ADHD are maintained or can worsen over the course of development, early intervention within the school setting is of utmost importance in order to prevent negative long-term outcomes. Similar to BPT, BCM instructs teachers to utilize behavior management techniques to address the maladaptive behaviors exhibited by children with ADHD in the school setting. After a psychoeducation portion that covers an overview of ADHD and identification of target behaviors, teachers are taught antecedent- and conse-quence-based strategies (Pfiffner & DuPaul, 2014). Components of these behavioral interventions will be described in more detail below.

Praise. Based on social learning and operant conditioning principles, one of the most common components of behavioral interventions for youth with ADHD is the use of praise in response to specific target behaviors (Chronis, Jones, & Raggi, 2006). Praise is a consequence-based strategy, as it is implemented following a behavior in order to elicit more of that specific behavior. Such reinforcement should be administered as frequently as possible and immediately after the behavior being reinforced (DuPaul, Weyandt, & Janusis, 2011). Therefore, in addition to mental health providers using praise to reinforce beha-vior during treatment, teaching parents how to properly praise target behaviors and ignore unwanted behaviors is an important aspect of treatment.

Praise is also a central component of many BCM interventions. BCM instructs teachers to utilize behavioral management techniques to address the maladaptive behaviors exhibited by children with ADHD in the school setting. For example, teachers are taught to provide frequent praise to children with ADHD who adhere to the rules of the classroom and follow through with assignments (Pfiffner, Barkley, & DuPaul, 2006).

Time-Out. Another strategy is the removal of a child from positive reinforcement in order to reduce unwanted behaviors (Pfiffner, Barkley, & DuPaul, 2006). However, the implementation of this technique is contingent upon the child being in a positive situation or environment. For example, if a child is removed from a situation that they find more aversive than the time-out itself, time-out could actually reinforce disruptive behaviors (DuPaul, Weyandt, & Janusis, 2011). Parents and/or teachers need to develop a list of specific rules (Anastopoulos, Rhoads, & Farley, 2006) that, if broken, should result in an immediate consequence such as a time-out (e.g., hitting a sibling/peer, destruction of property). For older children, response cost procedures in which a privilege is removed (e.g., cell phone, screen time) are also highly effective.

Tangible Rewards. This technique is another consequence-based strategy which consists of providing a reward following a behavior in order to elicit more or less of that specific behavior. Rewards should be individualized for each child based on their specific interests. Additionally, the reinforcements given to children should vary over time to ensure that children remain motivated and do not become disinterested by such rewards (DuPaul, Weyandt, & Janusis, 2011).

Token Reinforcement. Parents and teachers can also employ contingent positive reinforcement in the form of token reinforcement such that students are provided with token reinforcers (e.g., poker chips or stickers) when they display certain desired behaviors. These token reinforcers can eventually be exchanged for tangible prizes after a predetermined amount have been earned (DuPaul, Weyandt, & Janusis, 2011). Team contingencies can also be used where students are divided into teams and compete against each other for points where positive behaviors result in points earned and negative behaviors result in points lost (Pfiffner & DuPaul, 2014).

Commands. Verbal commands are antecedent-based strategies used to redirect a child's attention to a specific activity or to elicit an appropriate behavior. Research has shown that commands must be executed in a certain manner in order to attain desired behaviors. These statements should be delivered in a calm and neutral fashion while maintaining eye contact with the child (DuPaul & Weyandt, 2006). Further, commands should be reduced in length to match a child's attention span and should be phrased in a positive manner by telling the child what to do rather than what not to do. Over time, the length and complexity of the command can be increased as the child becomes more comfortable following shorter commands (DuPaul, Weyandt, & Janusis, 2011).

Routines. Establishing clear and consistent routines in both the home and class-room settings is another antecedent-based strategy to reduce child misbehavior. Disruptive behavior is often linked with family chaos (Valiente, Lemery-Chalfant, & Reiser, 2007) or an environment low in structural and temporal routine (Mokrova et al., 2010). Further, levels of family routine moderated the relationship between ADHD symptoms and oppositional behavior (Lanza & Drabick, 2010). Therefore, it is important to establish a consistent routine so children know what is expected of them. Routines can be created for throughout the child's day (e.g., getting ready for school, in the classroom, completing homework, getting ready for bed). It will be important for adults in the child's life to consistently abide by the routine and provide reinforcement for following it.

Psychoeducation. A component of various interventions targeting childhood ADHD, psychoeducation aims to strengthen parents' understanding of their child's diagnosis and associated problem behaviors. This may involve incorporating a didactic portion to provide information about ADHD, supporting parents' sense of self-efficacy, or teaching parents conflict management among other skills (McCleary & Ridley, 1999). Further, it has been shown that this treatment component increases knowledge about ADHD as well as positive attitudes and behaviors toward family members with ADHD (Nussey, Pistrang, & Murphy, 2013).

Daily Report Card. Many of the antecedent- and consequence-based strategies mentioned above are incorporated in the daily report card (DRC), a school-based intervention in which children are rewarded at home and/or school for reaching goals associated with problem behaviors displayed in the classroom (Fabiano et al., 2010). Individualized behavioral goals are set at a developmentally appropriate and attainable level, and are made progressively more difficult until the child's behavior has been shaped to match classroom norms. Younger children's goals may need to be fewer in number and met with more frequent positive reinforcement than for older children (McGoey, Eckert, & DuPaul, 2002). The DRC also allows teachers to provide parents with daily feedback concerning their child's classroom behavior upon which children are rewarded if they meet daily goals (Chronis, Jones, & Raggi, 2006). Overall, many studies have demonstrated improvements in classroom behavior, measures of attention, hyperactivity, impulsivity, academic productivity and success, and improved student–teacher relationships when implementing the DRC (Moore, Whittaker, & Ford, 2016).

Organizational Skills Training (OST) Interventions

Executive functioning, or the ability to plan and organize actions to aid in decision making and goal-directed processes, is often deficient in youth with ADHD (Biederman et al., 2004). More specifically, deficits in executive functioning consist of difficulties in temporal and materials organization throughout childhood and adolescence (Langberg, Epstein, & Graham, 2008). These deficits often manifest as trouble planning for the completion of tasks and assignments, procrastinating, and trouble keeping class materials organized (Evans et al., 2009; Langberg, Epstein, & Graham, 2008), which may result in poor test performance or lost assignments. Several evidence-based treatments have been developed to address these organizational shortcomings and have received empirical support through conducting randomized controlled trials. For children, these interventions include The Child Life and Attention Skills Program for children with the inattentive presentation (CLAS; Pfiffner et al., 2007); Family-School Success (FSS; Power et al., 2012); self-management/monitoring (Blicha & Belfiore, 2013; Gureasko-Moore, DuPaul, & White, 2006); and Parents and Teachers Helping Kids Organize (PATHKO; Abikoff et al., 2013). Evidence-based organizational interventions for adolescents consist of The Challenging Horizons Program (CHP; Evans et al., 2011); Supporting Teens' Academic Needs Daily (STAND; Sibley et al., 2016); Adolescent Summer Treatment Program (STP-A; Sibley et al., 2011a); and Homework Organization, and Planning Skills Intervention (HOPS; Langberg et al., 2012).

Each intervention is unique in terms of the age group it was developed for, the number and length of sessions, treatment providers (clinical psychologists versus teachers versus paraprofessionals), use of technology, and the setting in which the treatment is delivered (clinic-based versus school-based). However, every program consists of a combination of the following behavioral organization components in combination with contingency management strategies (e.g., use of rewards, behavioral intervention strategies) and the use of motivational interviewing (unique to STAND; Sibley et al., 2016). The following components have collectively resulted in higher levels of homework completion, organization of materials, and decreases in parent-reported homework problems and inattentive symptoms (Langberg, Epstein, & Graham, 2008). Though findings are somewhat inconsistent, some interventions resulted in small improvements in grade point average as well (Langberg, Epstein, & Graham, 2008).

Preparation for Class and Homework. One area targeted among organizational training interventions for ADHD focuses on ensuring youth come prepared to class as well as ensuring homework completion when they leave school. Students with ADHD tend to have difficulties keeping academic materials organized, forgetting to complete or losing homework assignments, and planning for the completion of long-term assignments (Langberg, Epstein, & Graham, 2008). OST interventions address this concern through the use of checklists to outline goals and token economies to reinforce behavior (e.g., Pfiffner et al., 2007).

One way to ensure preparedness for completing assigned tasks at home is having students' backpacks checked for the necessary materials prior to leaving school. Teachers make note of whether the backpack was packed acceptably in order to communicate to parents whether the child should receive a reward for meeting the organizational goal. However, this may not always be feasible to implement given the number of responsibilities and minimal resources teachers face. Alternatively, if school staff cannot commit to monitoring the student's backpack at the end of each day, parents check their child's backpack when they return home and reward them for bringing home the necessary materials to complete homework. With either procedure, parents reward preparedness to shape behavior.

Organization of School Materials. In addition to forgetting classroom materials and assignments, not being able to find homework or belongings can also result in missed assignments. Therefore, OST interventions focus on helping students organize their backpacks, binders, and lockers to ensure that all academic materials have a "home" and only relevant academic materials are present in backpacks and lockers (e.g., Sibley et al., 2011a).

In terms of binder/notebook organization, OST interventions aim to help students keep notes in chronological order to aid in studying as well as having binders or sections for each class so the student knows exactly where each subject's materials belong (e.g., Langberg et al., 2012; Sibley et al., 2011a). Additionally, having a certain folder for homework helps make sure that the student knows where homework is when it comes time to turn in an assignment (e.g., Sibley et al., 2011a). Rewards are administered for meeting organizational goals.

Some OST interventions also target note-taking and writing organization. For example, within the STP-A (Sibley et al., 2011a) and CHP (Evans et al., 2011), students learn how to structure lecture notes capturing the main points and supporting information, how to construct efficient flashcards (keeping the definitions concise), and how to properly structure writing assignments. These components have resulted in improvements in creative writing assignments and higher accuracy recording notes (Sibley et al., 2011a).

Homework Management. Youth with ADHD tend to struggle with forgetfulness (Loe & Feldman, 2007), which can result in difficulties remembering assignments especially when they may not be due for several days or weeks. Classroom teachers can initial a student's planner at the end of each class to communicate to parents that homework was correctly recorded. This has also been accomplished electronically through the use of personal digital assistants (Currie, Lee, & Scheeler, 2005). An alternative and arguably more feasible method, if available, is through parents' use of online portals where teachers post daily homework assignments. However, this amenity is not available in all school districts. Like other organizational strategies, rewards are used to reinforce proper planner usage.

In addition to not recording homework, youth with ADHD often struggle with time management in the completion of their homework, particularly with regard to longer-term assignments (Loe & Feldman, 2007). OST interventions seek to remedy this difficulty by first teaching students to create an outline or schedule to complete homework (e.g., Langberg et al., 2012). Schedules include when they will begin homework and how much time they estimate the assignment will take. Parents or school staff (if homework is being completed during study hall or afterschool care) should assist with the creation of each day's schedule and taper their involvement as students learn to estimate how long assignments will take. Subsequently, parents, school staff, or treatment providers monitor progress to ensure the student is remaining on task (Sibley et al., 2011a). This ensures that students are making progress on all assignments and not spending an entire evening completing only one subject. This method can also be used to schedule time for the student to work on portions of larger long-term assignments. As with other organizational components, rewards should be used to reinforce meeting homework completion goals.

Behavioral Peer Intervention

Behavioral peer interventions (BPIs) have been developed to help integrate children with ADHD into social settings and reinforce prosocial behavior. Traditional office-based social skills training produces minimal effects (Pelham & Fabiano, 2008) perhaps due to lack of generalization to the actual settings where children with ADHD are socially impaired. Three interventions have been developed and subsequently empirically supported: Parent Friendship Coaching (PFC; Mikami et al., 2010), Making Socially Accepting Inclusive Classrooms (MOSAIC; Mikami et al., 2013), and The Summer Treatment Program (STP; Pelham et al., 2010).

PFC focuses on teaching parents how to encourage positive peer interaction between their child with ADHD and their peers. Components include instructing parents to teach their child good dyadic play skills through modeling, choosing the right peers to foster relationships with their child, organizing play dates, preparing their child for successful play dates (e.g., preventing boredom and minimizing conflict), and providing constructive feedback following peer interactions (Mikami et al., 2010).

MOSAIC provides classroom teachers with specific skills to decrease social de-valuation of ADHD, exclusionary peer behavior, and reputational bias (Mikami et al., 2013). Teachers set up explicit rules for social inclusion in the classroom, emphasizing the need to work together to succeed. Also, teachers publicly provide children in their classroom with daily awards ensuring those for children with ADHD focus on their genuine strengths (e.g., creativity, talent) rather than on behavioral compliance.

The *STP* intensively targets social skills deficits within recreational camp and academic settings daily over a period of eight weeks. Within the STP, points are awarded to children for displaying positive behaviors (e.g., helping, sharing, good sportsmanship, and ignoring provocation) and points are taken for negative behavior (e.g., negative verbalizations, aggression; Pelham et al., 2010). In addition to behavior modification efforts to shape prosocial behavior, direct social skills training is administered in the form of daily brief group discussion sessions followed by feedback and reinforcement for the use of prosocial behavior throughout the day. This model has been developmentally modified for use in the adolescent STP (Sibley et al., 2011a).

Role of Parents in Treatment

Parents are typically viewed as integral to treatment success for children with ADHD, but depending on the treatment utilized, parents may be more (e.g., BPT) or less involved (e.g., BCM). Several parent factors have been shown to affect treatment response, including parental psychopathology, the marital or co-parenting relationship, and parent treatment expectations (e.g., Johnston & Chronis-Tuscano, 2014).

Parents of children with ADHD have higher rates of psychopathology than parents of children without ADHD. Rates of depression among mothers of children with ADHD are approximately 40–50%, and up to 50% of children with ADHD have a parent with high levels of ADHD symptoms (Johnston & Chronis-Tuscano, 2014). Research indicates a negative effect of parental psychopathology on treatment response in BPT (e.g., Owens et al., 2003; Wang, Mazursky-Horowitz, & Chronis-Tuscano, 2014), pointing to the importance of addressing parental psychopathology when treating children with ADHD. There is early evidence that integrated treatments that address both parent psychopathology and child ADHD can improve both parental symptoms and child externalizing symptoms (Chronis-Tuscano et al., 2013; Jans et al., 2015). For example, The Integrated Parenting Intervention for ADHD (IPI-A; Chronis-Tuscano & Clarke, 2008) was developed to simultaneously address maternal depression and their child's behavior problems through a combined approach of cognitive-behavioral therapy and parent training.

Interparental conflict is experienced more frequently by parents of children with ADHD compared to parents of children without ADHD (Johnston & Chronis-Tuscano, 2014). Marital conflict is associated with negative parenting behavior and can impact treatment progress and outcomes (Chronis et al., 2004). Research has also found marital dissatisfaction to predict child BPT treatment outcome for children with disruptive behaviors. Therefore, assessing and addressing the interaction between interparental conflict and marital dissatisfaction and child variables is recommended when treating children with ADHD (Wymbs et al., 2008).

Given the importance placed on parental involvement in the treatment of ADHD (Chacko et al., 2014), researchers have modified existing evidence-based interventions to enhance the access of parent training to families. For example, Chacko and colleagues (2012) developed a modified BPT, Strategies to Enhance Positive Parenting (STEPP), for children with ADHD that included additional components designed to address maladaptive parent expectations and other factors that impact treatment engagement. To attract fathers to parent training, Fabiano and colleagues (2012) developed Coaching Our Acting-Out Children: Heightening Essential Skills (COACHES), a modified model of BPT tailored to teach parents behavior management through coaching their children in soccer. These heterogeneous designs of BPT have been proven to be effective treatments for parents of children with ADHD, including populations that may not usually participate in such services (Chacko et al., 2012; Chronis-Tuscano et al., 2013; Fabiano et al., 2012).

Other Variables Influencing Treatment

Assessment

Evidence-based assessment is crucial for effective treatment planning for ADHD. The primary mission of ADHD assessment is to evaluate impairments in adaptive functioning and to develop specific goals for treatment. Targets can consist of addressing the core symptoms of ADHD (i.e., inattention, hyperactivity, impulsivity) defined behaviorally and/or difficulties with functional domains such as peer relationships, parenting, or academic achievement (Pelham, Fabiano, & Massetti, 2005). Further, a functional analysis (i.e., identifying antecedents and consequences of behavior) to better understand the context of the behavior is essential to appreciating the unique strengths and difficulties experienced by each family. A thorough assessment is important in establishing explicit behaviors to target in treatment.

Given symptoms and impairment associated with ADHD occur in both the home and school settings, combining parent report with teacher report of behavior is useful during the assessment process. Parents may not be aware of all the behavioral difficulties teachers experience in the classroom and children and adolescents with ADHD tend to be poor reporters of their own impairment (Sibley et al., 2012). Teacher report of behavior problems allows for treatment planning and implementation of classroom-based behavior management strategies.

Comorbidity

Children with ADHD often present with co-occurring externalizing, internalizing, and/or learning disorders that can impact the course of treatment (Pliszka, 2014). Approximately three-quarters of clinic-referred children with ADHD have at least one additional co-occurring disorder (Barkley, Murphy, & Fischer, 2008). When ADHD co-occurs with additional psychopathology, children are placed at higher risk for worse developmental trajectories and outcomes (e.g., Chronis-Tuscano et al., 2010). Children with ADHD and multiple co-occurring disorders have been shown to have a less optimal treatment response compared to children with ADHD only or ADHD and one co-occurring disorder (Jensen et al., 2001). A careful assessment of childhood behavioral or emotional disorders that can co-occur with ADHD is important before beginning treatment. Additionally, a psychoeducational evaluation is recommended to determine if a learning disorder or an intellectual disability is present and requires attention due to the frequency of these issues in children with ADHD and the need for educational accommodations/services (DuPaul & Langberg, 2014).

Demographics

Research has investigated the influence of several demographic variables on the effects of treatment for youth with ADHD. Differential rates of ADHD are present across gender with two to nine times as many males receiving a diagnosis of ADHD compared to females (Rucklidge, 2010). Additionally, teachers tend to make more referrals of boys even when presented with a girl with comparable symptoms (Sciutto, Nolfi, & Bluhm, 2004).

Effectiveness of treatments for ADHD among ethnic minority youth is a rather understudied area. Results from the Multimodal Treatment Study of Children with ADHD (MTA) indicate that among African-American and Latino youth with ADHD combined behavioral treatment and stimulant medication should be the frontline treatment (Arnold et al., 2003). However, stimulant medication alone has also been identified as an effective treatment for African-American youth (Huey & Polo, 2008). The prevalence of stimulant usage significantly differs between Caucasian youth and racial/ethnic minority youth with one potential explanation being cultural differences (Hudson, Miller, & Kirby, 2007). Research needs to continue examining effectiveness for delivering evidence-based practices (e.g., parent training) in a culturally sensitive manner (Baumann et al., 2015).

Medication

Stimulant medications are frequently used treatments for children with ADHD, and approximately 85% of children with ADHD receive stimulant medications (Visser et al., 2015). Stimulant medications are effective in reducing the core ADHD symptoms of hyperactivity, impulsivity, and inattention, but are less effective in reducing the impairments associated with ADHD (Connor, 2014; Epstein et al., 2010). Since behavioral treatments target child impairment, multi-modal treatment approaches that combine evidence-based behavioral treatments and medication often result in better functional impairment outcomes and may also demonstrate a lower dosage of medication for children with ADHD (MTA Cooperative Group, 1999). Pelham and colleagues (2016) more recently investigated the optimal sequence of behavior therapy and stimulant medication to treat children with ADHD. Children with ADHD exhibited the best response to the specific treatment protocol which began with the behavioral intervention and then initiated stimulant medication if children demonstrated insufficient response (Pelham et al., 2016).

Conclusion

ADHD is a highly heritable disorder, affecting both males and females regardless of race or ethnicity. Several EBTs for children and adolescents with ADHD have been empirically identified; these include stimulant medication, behavioral interventions, and organizational skills training interventions. The core components of behavioral interventions include psychoeducation, the use of rewards (i.e., praise, token rewards, tangible rewards), time-out, and antecedent controls (i.e., structure/routines, clear and simple commands, and daily report cards outlining expectations and behavioral goals). Organizational skills training (OST) interventions include teaching children and adolescents how to organize school materials, prepare for class, use a planner, and create and follow an outline for completing homework. Additionally, comorbidity needs to be taken into account when implementing these evidence-based strategies, given the high prevalence of co-occurring internalizing or externalizing psychopathology. Further, across all treatment modalities, parents' and/or teachers' consistent participation in treatment is crucial to successful outcomes.

Useful Resources

Organizations

- Children and Adults with Attention-Deficit/Hyperactivity Disorder (CHADD) is a nonprofit organization for individuals with ADHD that provides support, education, advocacy, and resources. www.chadd.org
- The American Professional Society of ADHD and Related Disorders (APSARD) is an organization for professionals interested in ADHD that offers resources to stay current on best clinical practices and scientific research on ADHD. apsard.org
- Understood.org is an online informational resource for parents created by 15 nonprofit organizations focused on helping children with learning and attention problems. This resource provides personalized support and information about a variety of topics, including 504 plans and individualized education plans (IEPs).

Books

- *Taking Charge of ADHD, Third Edition: The Complete, Authoritative Guide for Parents* by Russell Barkley (Guilford Press, 2013) provides parents with information about ADHD as well as a behavior management plan for school-aged children with ADHD.
- *ADHD in the Schools: Assessment and Intervention Strategies* by George J. DuPaul and Gary Stoner (Guilford Press, 2014) contains information for school-based professionals working with students who have ADHD.
- *Attention-Deficit Hyperactivity Disorder, Fourth Edition: A Handbook for Diagnosis and Treatment* by Russell Barkley (Guilford Press, 2015) contains a broad range of information about ADHD in children, adolescents, and adults.

Other Resources

- *Know Your Rights: Students with ADHD*, and *Students with ADHD and Section 504: A Resource Guide*, released by the US Department of Education, detail the federal laws protecting youth with ADHD and the testing and services they are entitled to.
- The Effective Child Therapy website (effectivechildtherapy.org) contains resources for parents and professionals on the treatment of child and adolescent psychopathology, including ADHD.

References

Abikoff, H., Gallagher, R., Wells, K. C., Murray, D. W., Huang, L., Lu, F., & Petkova, E. (2013). Remediating organizational functioning in children with ADHD: Immediate and long-term effects from a randomized controlled trial. *Journal of Consulting and Clinical Psychology*, *81*(1), 113–128.

American Psychiatric Association. (2013). *Diagnostic and statistical manual of mental disorders.* 5th edn. Washington, DC: American Psychiatric Association.

Anastopoulos, A. D., Rhoads, L. H., & Farley, S. E. (2006). Counseling and training parents. In R. A. Barkley (ed.), *Attention-deficit/hyperactivity disorder: A handbook for diagnosis and treatment.* 3rd edn. (pp. 453–479). New York: Guilford Press.

Arnold, L. E., Elliott, M., Sachs, L., Kraemer, Abikoff, H. B., ... & Wigal, T. (2003). Effects of ethnicity on treatment attendance, stimulant response/dose, and 14-month outcome in ADHD. *Journal of Consulting and Clinical Psychology*, *71*(4), 713–727.

Barbaresi, W. J., Katusic, S. K., Colligan, R. C., Weaver, A. L., & Jacobsen, S. J. (2007). Long-term school outcomes for children with attention-deficit/hyperactivity disorder: A population-based perspective. *Journal of Developmental & Behavioral Pediatrics*, *28*, 265–273.

Barkley, R. A. (1997). Behavioral inhibition, sustained attention, and executive functions: Constructing a unifying theory of ADHD. *Psychological Bulletin*, *121*(1), 65–94.

Barkley, R. A. (2013). *Defiant children: A clinician's manual for assessment and parent training, third edition.* New York: Guilford Press.

Barkley, R. A., Murphy, K. R., & Fischer, M. (2008). *Adult ADHD: What the science says.* New York: Guilford Press.

Barkley, R. A., Murphy, K., & Kwasnik, D. (1996). Psychological adjustment and adaptive impairments in young adults with ADHD. *Journal of Attention Disorders*, *1*(1), 41–54. doi:10.1177/108705479600100104

Barkley, R. A., & Robin, A. L. (2014). *Defiant children: A clinician's manual for assessment and family intervention.* 2nd edn. New York: Guilford Press.

Baumann, A. A., Powell, B. J., Kohl, P. L., Tabak, R. G., Penalba, V., ... & Cabassa, L. J. (2015). Cultural adaptation and implementation of evidence-based parent-training: A systematic review and critique of guiding evidence. *Child Youth Services Review*, *53*, 113–120.

Biederman, J., Monuteaux, M. C., Doyle, A. E., Seidman, L. J., Wilens, T. E., ... & Faraone, S. V. (2004). Impact of executive function deficits and attention-deficit/hyperactivity disorder (ADHD) on academic outcomes in children. *Journal of Consulting and Clinical Psychology*, *72*(5), 767–766.

Blicha, A., & Belfiore, P. J. (2013). The effects of automated prompting and self-monitoring on homework completion for a student with attention deficit hyperactivity disorder. *Journal of Education and Learning*, *2*(3), 51–60.

Centers for Disease Control (CDC). (2016). Attention-deficit hyperactivity disorder: Data & statistics. www.cdc.gov/ncbddd/adhd/data.html

Chacko, A., Allan, C. C., Uderman, J., Cornwell, M., Anderson, L., & Chimiklis, A. (2014). Training parents of youth with ADHD. In R. A. Barkley (ed.), *Attention-deficit hyperactivity disorder: A handbook for diagnosis and treatment* (pp. 513–536). New York: Guilford Press.

Chacko, A., Wymbs, B. T., Chimiklis, A., Wymbs, F. A., & Pelham, W. E. (2012). Evaluating a comprehensive strategy to improve engagement to group-based behavioral parent training for high-risk families of children with ADHD. *Journal of Abnormal Child Psychology*, *40*(8), 1351–1362.

Chronis, A. M., Chacko, A., Fabiano, G. A., Wymbs, B. T., & Pelham, W. J. (2004). Enhancements to the behavioral parent training paradigm for families of children with ADHD: Review and future directions. *Clinical Child and Family Psychology Review*, *7*(1), 1–27.

Chronis, A., Jones, H. A., & Raggi, V. L. (2006). Evidence-based treatments for children and adolescents with attention-deficit/hyperactivity disorder. *Clinical Psychology Review*, *26*(4), 486–502.

Chronis-Tuscano, A., & Clarke, T. L. (2008). Integrated behavioral treatment for depressed mothers of children with ADHD. In L. L'Abate (ed.), *Toward a science of clinical psychology: Laboratory evaluations and interventions* (pp. 57–77). Hauppagauge, NY: Nova Science.

Chronis-Tuscano, A., Clarke, T. L., O'Brien, K. A., Raggi, V. L., Diaz, Y., Mintz, A. D., . . . & Seeley, J. (2013). Development and preliminary evaluation of an integrated treatment targeting parenting and depressive symptoms in mothers of children with attention-deficit/hyperactivity disorder. *Journal of Consulting and Clinical Psychology*, *81*(5), 918.

Chronis-Tuscano, A., Molina, B. G., Pelham, W. E., Applegate, B., Dahlke, A., Overmyer, M., & Lahey, B. B. (2010). Very early predictors of adolescent depression and suicide attempts in children with attention-deficit/hyperactivity disorder. *Archives of General Psychiatry*, *67*, 1044–1051.

Connor, D. F. (2014). Stimulant and non-stimulant medications for childhood ADHD. In R. A. Barkley (ed.), *Attention-deficit/hyperactivity disorder: A handbook for diagnosis and treatment*. 4th edn. (pp. 666–685). New York: Guilford Press.

Currie, D., Lee, D. L., & Scheeler, M. C. (2005). Using PDAs to increase the homework completion of students with ADHD. *Journal of Evidence-Based Practices for Schools*, *6*(2), 151–162.

DuPaul, G. J., & Langberg, J. M. (2014). Educational impairments in children with ADHD. In R. A. Barkley (ed.), *Attention-deficit/hyperactivity disorder: A handbook for diagnosis and treatment*. 4th edn. (pp. 169–190). New York: Guilford Press.

DuPaul, G. J., & Weyandt, L. L. (2006). School-based intervention for children with attention deficit hyperactivity disorder: Effects on academic, social, and behavioural functioning. *International Journal of Disability, Development and Education*, *53*(2), 161–176.

DuPaul, G. J., Weyandt, L. L., & Janusis, G. M. (2011). ADHD in the classroom: Effective intervention strategies. *Theory into Practice*, *50*(1), 35–42.

Epstein, J. N., Langberg, J. M., Lichtenstein, P. K., Altaye, M., Brinkman, W. B., House, K., & Stark, L. J. (2010). Attention-deficit/hyperactivity disorder outcomes for children treated in community-based pediatric settings. *Archives of Pediatrics & Adolescent Medicine*, *164*, 160–165. doi:10.1001/archpediatrics.2009.263

Evans, S. W., Owens, J. S., & Bunford, N. (2014). Evidence-based psychosocial treatments for children and adolescents with attention-deficit/hyperactivity disorder. *Journal of Clinical Child & Adolescent Psychology*, *43*(4), 527–551.

Evans, S. W., Schultz, B. K., DeMars, C. E., & Davis, H. (2011). Effectiveness of the Challenging Horizons after school program for young adolescents with ADHD. *Behavior Therapy*, *42*(3), 462–474.

Evans, S. W., Schultz, B. K., White, C., Brady, C., Sibley, M. H., & Van Eck, K. (2009). A school-based organization intervention for young adolescents with attention-deficit/hyperactivity disorder. *School Mental Health*, *1*(2), 78–88.

Eyberg, S. M., Boggs, S. R., & Algina, J. (1995). Parent–child interaction therapy: A psychosocial model for the treatment of young children with conduct problem behavior and their families. *Psychopharmacology Bulletin*, *31*(1), 83–91.

Fabiano, G. A., Pelham, W. E., Cunningham, C., Yu, J., Gangloff, B., Buck, M., . . . & Gera, S. (2012). A waitlist-controlled trial of behavioral parent training for fathers of children with ADHD. *Journal of Clinical Child & Adolescent Psychology, 41*, 337–345.

Fabiano, G. A., Vujnovic, R. K., Pelham, W. E., Waschbusch, D. A., Massetti, G. M., Pariseau, M. E., . . . & Volker, M. (2010). Enhancing effectiveness of special education programming for children with attention-deficit hyperactivity disorder using a report card. *School Psychology Review, 39*(2), 219–239.

Faraone, S. V., Perlis, R. H., Doyle, A. E., Smoller, J. W., Goralnick, J. J., Holmgren, M. A., & Skylar, P. (2005). Molecular genetics of attention-deficit/hyperactivity disorder. *Biological Psychiatry, 57*, 1313–1323.

Gureasko-Moore, S., DuPaul, G. J., & White, G. P. (2006). The effects of self-management in general education classrooms on the organizational skills of adolescents with ADHD. *Behavior Modification, 30*(2), 159–183.

Hanf, C., & Kling, J. (1973). "Facilitating parent–child interaction: A two-stage training model." Unpublished manuscript.

Hudson, J. L., Miller, G. E., & Kirby, J. B. (2007). Explaining racial ethnic differences in children's use of stimulant medications. *Medical Care, 45*(11), 1068–1075.

Huey, S. J., & Polo, A. J. (2008). Evidence-based psychosocial treatments for ethnic minority youth. *Journal of Clinical Child & Adolescent Psychology, 37*(1), 262–301.

Jans, T., Jacob, C., Warnke, A., Zwanzger, U., Groß-Lesch, S., Matthies, S., . . . & Retz, W. (2015). Does intensive multimodal treatment for maternal ADHD improve the efficacy of parent training for children with ADHD? A randomized controlled multicenter trial. *Journal of Child Psychology and Psychiatry, 56*(12), 1298–1313.

Jarrett, M. A., & Ollendick, T. H. (2008). A conceptual review of the comorbidity of attention-deficit/hyperactivity disorder and anxiety: Implications for future research and practice. *Clinical Psychology Review, 28*(7), 1266–1280.

Jensen, P. S., Hinshaw, S. P., Kraemer, H. C., Lenora, N., Newcorn, J. H., Abikoff, H. B., . . . & Elliott, G. R. (2001). ADHD comorbidity findings from the MTA study: Comparing comorbid subgroups. *Journal of the American Academy of Child & Adolescent Psychiatry, 40*(2), 147–158.

Johnston, C., & Chronis-Tuscano, A. M. (2014). Families and ADHD. In R. A. Barkley (ed.), *Attention-deficit hyperactivity disorder: A handbook for diagnosis and treatment* (pp. 191–209). New York: Guilford Press.

Johnston, C., & Mash, E. J. (2001). Families of children with attention-deficit/hyperactivity disorder: Review and recommendations for future research. *Clinical Child and Family Psychology Review, 4*(3), 183–207.

Kent, K. M., Pelham, W. E., Molina, B. S. G., Sibley, M. H., Waschbusch, D. A., Yu, J., . . . & Karch, K. M. (2011). The academic experience of male high school students with ADHD. *Journal of Abnormal Child Psychology, 39*(3), 451–462.

Klassen, L. J., Katzman, M. A., & Chokka, P. (2010). Adult ADHD and its comorbidities, with a focus on bipolar disorder. *Journal of Affective Disorders, 124*(1–2), 1–8.

Langberg, J. M., Epstein, J. N., Becker, S. P., Girio-Herrera, E., & Vaughn, A. J. (2012). Evaluation of the Homework, Organization, and Planning Skills (HOPS) Intervention for middle school students with ADHD as implemented by school mental health providers. *School Psychology Review, 41*(3), 342–364.

Langberg, J. M., Epstein, J. N., & Graham, A. J. (2008). Organizational-skills interventions in the treatment of ADHD. *Expert Reviews in Neurotherapeutics, 8*(10), 1549–1561.

Lanza, H. I., & Drabick, D. A. G. (2010). Family routine moderates the relation between child impulsivity and oppositional defiant disorder symptoms. *Journal of Abnormal Child Psychology*, *39*(1), 83–94.

Lee, S. S., Humphreys, K. L., Flory, K., Liu, R., & Glass, K. (2011). Prospective association of childhood attention-deficit/hyperactivity disorder (ADHD) and substance use and abuse/dependence: A meta-analytic review. *Clinical Psychology Review*, *31*(3), 328–341.

Loe, I. M., & Feldman, H. M. (2007). Academic and educational outcomes of children with ADHD. *Journal of Pediatric Psychology*, *52*(6), 643–654.

McCleary, L., & Ridley, T. (1999). Parenting adolescents with ADHD: Evaluation of a psychoeducation group. *Patient Education and Counseling*, *38*(1), 3–10.

McGoey, K. E., Eckert, T. L., & DuPaul, G. J. (2002). Early intervention for preschool-age children with ADHD: A literature review. *Journal of Emotional and Behavioral Disorders*, *10*(1), 14–28.

Meinzer, M. C., Pettit, J. W., & Viswesvaran, C. (2014). The co-occurrence of attention-deficit/hyperactivity disorder and unipolar depression in children and adolescents: A meta-analytic review. *Clinical Psychology Review*, *34*(8), 569–607.

Mikami, A. Y. (2010). The importance of friendship for youth with attention-deficit/hyperactivity disorder. *Clinical Child and Family Psychology Review*, *13*(2), 181–198.

Mikami, A. Y., Lerner, M. D., Griggs, M. S., McGrath, A., & Calhoun, C. D. (2010). Parent influence on children with attention-deficit/hyperactivity disorder: II. Results of pilot intervention training parents as friendship coaches for children. *Journal of Abnormal Child Psychology*, *38*, 737–749.

Mikami, A. Y., Griggs, M. S., Lerner, M. D., Emeh, C. C., Reuland, M. M., Jack, A., & Anthony, M. R. (2013). A randomized trial of a classroom intervention to increase peers' social inclusion of children with attention-deficit/hyperactivity disorder. *Journal of Consulting and Clinical Psychology*, *81*(1), 100–112.

Mokrova, I., O'Brien, M., Calkins, S., & Keane, S. (2010). Parental ADHD symptomology and ineffective parenting: The connecting link of home chaos. *Parenting*, *10*(2), 119–135.

Moore, D. A., Whittaker, S., & Ford, T. J. (2016). Daily report cards as a school-based intervention for children with attention-deficit/hyperactivity disorder. *Support for Learning*, *31*(1), 71–83.

MTA Cooperative Group. (1999). A 14-month randomized clinical trial of treatment strategies for attention-deficit/hyperactivity disorder. *Archives of General Psychiatry*, *56*(12), 1073–1086.

Nussey, C., Pistrang, N., & Murphy, T. (2013). How does psychoeducation help? A review of the effects of providing information about Tourette syndrome and attention-deficit/hyperactivity disorder. *Child: Care, Health and Development*, *39*(5), 617–627.

Owens, E. B., Hinshaw, S. P., Arnold, L. E., Cantwell, D. P., Elliot, G., . . . & Wigal, T. (2003). Which treatment for whom for ADHD? Moderators of treatment response in the MTA. *Journal of Consulting and Clinical Psychology*, *71*(3), 540–552.

Patterson, G. R., DeBaryshe, B. D., & Ramsey, E. (1989). A developmental perspective on anti-social behavior. *American Psychologist*, *44*, 329–335.

Pelham, W. J., & Fabiano, G. A. (2008). Evidence-based psychosocial treatments for attention-deficit/hyperactivity disorder. *Journal of Clinical Child & Adolescent Psychology*, *37*(1), 184–214.

Pelham, W. E., Fabiano, G. A., & Massetti, G. M. (2005). Evidence-based assessment of attention deficit hyperactivity disorder in children and adolescents. *Journal of Clinical Child & Adolescent Psychology*, *34*(3), 449–476.

Pelham, W. E., Fabiano, G. A., Waxmonsky, J. G., Greiner, A. R., Gnagy, E. M., Pelham, W. E., . . . & Karch, K. (2016). Treatment sequencing for childhood ADHD: A multiple-randomization study of adaptive medication and behavioral interventions. *Journal of Clinical Child & Adolescent Psychology*, *45*(4), 396–415.

Pelham, W. E., Gnagy, E. M., Greiner, A. R., Washcbusch, D. W., Fabiano, G. A., & Burrows-MacLean, L. (2010). Summer Treatment Programs for attention-deficit/hyperactivity disorder. In J. R. Weisz & A. E. Kazdin (eds.), *Evidence-based psychotherapies for children and adolescents* (pp. 277–292). New York: Guildford Press.

Pfiffner, L. J., Barkley, R. A., & DuPaul, G. J. (2006). Treatment of ADHD in school settings. In R. A. Barkley (ed.), *Attention-deficit hyperactivity disorder: A handbook for diagnosis and treatment*. 3rd edn. (pp. 547–589). New York: Guilford Press.

Pfiffner, L. J., & DuPaul, G. J. (2014). Treatment of ADHD in school settings. Training parents of youth with ADHD. In R. A. Barkley (ed.), *Attention-deficit hyperactivity disorder: A handbook for diagnosis and treatment* (pp. 596–629). New York: Guilford Press.

Pfiffner, L. J., Mikami, A. Y., Huang-Pollock, C., Easterlin, B., Zalecki, C., & McBurnett, K. (2007). A randomized, controlled trial of integrated home–school behavioral treatment for ADHD, predominantly inattentive type. *Journal of the American Academy of Child & Adolescent Psychiatry*, *46*(8), 1041–1050.

Pliszka, S. R. (2014). Comorbid psychiatric disorders in children with ADHD. In R. A. Barkley (ed.), *Attention-deficit/hyperactivity disorder: A handbook for diagnosis and treatment*. 4th edn. (pp. 140–168). New York: Guilford Press.

Power, T. J., Mautone, J. A., Soffer, S. L., Clarke, A. T., Marshall, S. A., Sharman, J., . . . & Jawad, A. F. (2012). Family–school intervention for children with ADHD: Results of randomized clinical trial. *Journal of Consulting and Clinical Psychology*, *80*(4), 611–623.

Raggi, V. L., & Chronis A. M. (2006) Interventions to address the academic impairment of children and adolescents with ADHD. *Clinical Child and Family Psychology Review*, *9*(2), 85–111.

Rucklidge, J. J. (2010). Gender differences in attention-deficit/ hyperactivity disorder. *Psychiatric Clinics of North America*, *33*, 643–655.

Sanders, M. R., Mazzucchelli, T. G., & Studman, L. (2004). Stepping Stones Triple P – an evidence-based positive parenting program for families with a child who has a disability: Its theoretical basis and development. *Journal of Intellectual & Developmental Disability*, *29*, 1–19.

Sciutto, M. J., Nolfi, C. J., & Bluhm, C. (2004). Effects of child gender and symptom type on referrals for ADHD by elementary school teachers. *Journal of Emotional and Behavioral Disorders*, *12*(4), 247–253.

Sibley, M. H., Graziano, P. A., Kuriyan, A. B., Coxe, S., Pelham, W. E., Rodriguez, L., . . . & Ward, A. (2016). Parent–teen behavior therapy + motivational interviewing adolescents with ADHD. *Journal of Consulting and Clinical Psychology*, *84*(8), 699–712.

Sibley, M. H., Pelham, W. E., Evans, S. W., Gnagy, E. M., Ross, J. M., & Greiner, A. R. (2011a). An evaluation of a summer treatment program for adolescents with ADHD. *Cognitive Behavioral Practice*, *18*, 530–544.

Sibley, M. H., Pelham, W. E., Molina, B. S., G., Gnagy, E. M., Waschbusch, D. A., Biswas, A., . . . & Karch, K. M. (2011b). The delinquency outcomes of boys with ADHD with and without comorbidity. *Journal of Abnormal Child Psychology*, *39*, 21–32.

Sibley, M. H., Pelham, W. E., Molina, B. S. G., Gnagy, E. M., Waschbush, D. A., Garefino, A. C., . . . & Karch, K. M. (2012). Diagnosing ADHD in adolescence. *Journal of Consulting and Clinical Psychology*, *80*(1), 139–150.

Stokes, T. F., & Baer, D. M. (1977). An implicit technology of generalization. *Journal of Applied Behavior Analysis*, *10*(2), 349–367.

Tripp, G., & Wickens, J. R. (2009). Neurobiology of ADHD. *Neuropharmacology, 57,* 579–589.

Valiente, C., Lemery-Chalfant, K., & Reiser, M. (2007). Pathways to problem behaviors: Chaotic homes, parent and child effortful control, and parenting. *Social Development, 16*(2), 249–267.

Visser, S. N., Bitsko, R. H., Danielson, M. L., Ghandour, R. M., Blumberg, S. J., Schieve, L. A., . . . & Cuffe, S. P. (2015). Treatment of attention deficit/hyperactivity disorder among children with special health care needs. *The Journal of Pediatrics, 166*(6), 1423–1430.

Wang, C. H., Mazursky-Horowitz, H., & Chronis-Tuscano, A. (2014). Delivering evidence-based treatments for child attention-deficit/hyperactivity disorder (ADHD) in the context of parental ADHD. *Current Psychiatry Reports, 16*(10), 474–486.

Webster-Stratton, C. (2001). The incredible years: Parents, teachers, and child training series. *Residential Treatment for Children & Youth, 18*(3), 31–45.

Wymbs, B. T., Pellham, W. E., Molina, B. S. G., Gnagy, E. M., Wilson, T. K., & Greenhouse, J. B. (2008). Rate and predictors of divorce among parents of youth with ADHD. *Journal of Consulting and Clinical Psychology, 76*(5), 735–744.

5

Learning

Mark D. Shriver

Learning disabilities are one of the most prevalent disorders affecting children and adolescents. It is estimated that anywhere from 5 to 15% of school-aged children exhibit a specific learning disability in reading, math, writing, or some combination of these academic areas (American Psychiatric Association [APA], 2013). The primary feature of learning disabilities is that these deficits in academic skills are unexpected given the child's age, sensory capabilities, educational history, and intellectual functioning.

The *Diagnostic and Statistical Manual of Mental Disorders* (DSM-5; American Psychiatric Association, 2013) uses the term specific learning disorder (SLD) with an emphasis on the specific academic area or skill which is impaired. Diagnosis may be made for an SLD with impairment in reading, specifically word reading accuracy, reading fluency, reading comprehension, or some combination. Diagnosis may be made for an SLD with impairment in mathematics, specifically number sense, memorization of arithmetic facts, accurate or fluent calculation, accurate math reasoning, or some combination. Diagnosis may also be made for an SLD with impairment in written expression, specifically spelling accuracy, grammar and punctuation accuracy, clarity or organization of written expression, or some combination. Finally, similar to other diagnoses in the DSM-5, an impression of severity (mild, moderate, severe) is determined as part of the diagnosis respective to the degree to which the child is impaired in one or more of the academic areas and the level of support or accommodations needed to function in expected daily activities.

Dyslexia is a common term often used to describe a learning disability in reading. Dyslexia refers to an SLD in reading that includes a pattern of deficits in word level decoding, fluent word recognition, and spelling. Likewise, dyscalculia may be used to refer to an SLD in math that includes a pattern of deficits in processing numerical information, learning math facts, and completing accurate or fluent math calculations. Finally, dysgraphia may sometimes be used to refer to an SLD in writing.

The Individuals with Disabilities Education Act (IDEA, 2004) classification system for eligibility for special education services utilizes a similar definition for specific learning disabilities as the DSM-5. In short, if a child is experiencing unexpected deficits in academic skill areas relative to the child's age, intellectual development, sensory capabilities, and learning history, then the child may be eligible for special education services under a classification of a specific learning disability. The academic skill areas in IDEA classification in which an SLD may occur include oral expression, listening comprehension, written expression, basic reading skills, reading fluency, reading comprehension, mathematics calculation, mathematics problem-solving, or some combination of academic skill area deficits (IDEA, 2004). Oral expression and listening comprehension are areas typically addressed by speech and language pathologists/therapists. This chapter will focus primarily on treatment related to academic skill areas in reading, math, and writing.

Sometimes, particularly in the popular press, but also in educational settings historically, the term "learning disabilities" is used to refer to any diagnosis that may negatively affect academic progress, such as intellectual disability, autism spectrum disorder (ASD), or attention-deficit/hyperactivity disorder (ADHD; e.g., MacMillan, Gresham, & Bocian, 1998). The diagnosis of an intellectual disability typically would rule out diagnosis of SLD; however, since academic skill deficits would be likely to occur for a child with intellectual disability (i.e., not unexpected), a child with SLD may have comorbid ADHD or ASD. In fact, ADHD tends to be a highly comorbid diagnosis with SLD (Denckla et al., 2013; Mayes, Calhoun, & Crowell, 2000). These are exclusively determined diagnoses, however, and this chapter will focus solely on interventions that address the academic skill area deficits associated with SLD and not areas of deficit common in ADHD (inattention, impulsivity, hyperactivity) or ASD (social interactions, restricted patterns of interest or behavior).

There are students who exhibit low academic achievement but who, for various reasons, may not be diagnosed with an SLD (e.g., lack of large enough discrepancy between intelligence and academic achievement scores). Students with SLD are generally considered to be a distinct population relative to students who exhibit low academic achievement. Specifically, students with a diagnosis of SLD tend to have more severe academic skill deficits (Fuchs et al., 2002). However, the same evidence-based treatments used with students with SLD may be used effectively with students with low academic achievement or at risk for SLD and may help prevent diagnosis of SLD (Gresham, 2002). As such, this chapter will focus on interventions for students with SLD and/or at risk (i.e., low academic achievers) for academic skill deficits commonly associated with SLD.

Etiology and Theoretical Underpinnings of Treatment

Specific learning disabilities are largely considered to be a neurological impairment (e.g., APA, 2013; IDEA, 2004). For samples of children with reading SLD, previous research has indicated that there appear to be differences in neurological structure and processing compared to children without reading SLD (Shaywitz & Shaywitz, 2013). In addition, evidence-based intensive reading intervention appears to change neurological functioning for children with reading SLD (Richards et al., 2002; Shaywitz et al., 2004; Simos et al., 2005). However, there are no evidence-based neurologically focused treatments. Neurological changes may occur in response to treatment, but evidence-based treatments are not neurologically based. In fact, Fletcher et al. (2007, p. 130) note, "if there is one cardinal intervention principle for students with LDs, it is that training in motor, visual, neural, or cognitive processes without academic content does not lead to better academic outcomes."

Treatment for SLD typically occurs in educational settings. This makes sense, since the primary deficits are in academic areas and effective interventions need to include academic content. Intervention in schools typically takes place within one or more contexts including general education, response to intervention (RTI), or as part of special education. These are all contexts, settings, or processes within which intervention may be delivered. They are not, in and of themselves, intervention. These contexts may help specify the level of resources that are allocated toward intervention for a student or group of students, but they do not necessarily prescribe whether or not an evidence-based intervention is delivered. An evidence-based intervention may be delivered in any one or more of these educational contexts. In short, the content or deficits addressed by evidence-based interventions for SLD are academically focused and the setting in which intervention takes place is typically an educational (i.e., school) setting. The theoretical foundation of evidence-based interventions is largely founded on learning theory.

The educational treatments that have the best evidence for effectiveness are largely based on principles of learning derived from the science of behavior analysis (Catania, 2013; Gardner et. al., 1994; Skinner, 1953). Basic learning principles such as operationally defining the response to be learned, stimulus control, reinforcement, and generalization (to name a few) are combined strategically to demonstrably facilitate student learning of targeted academic skills. These basic learning principles will be further described below when discussing the components of evidence-based treatments for SLD.

Brief Overview of Evidence-Based Treatments

Given the expansive array of academic skills any individual needs to learn, treatments for an SLD range along a continuum that on one end focuses on a specific, targeted academic skill and on the other end addresses multiple, related academic skills within a particular academic area or perhaps across academic areas. For example, a treatment for an SLD may be comprised of a single targeted intervention for a particular academic skill deficit (e.g., constant time delay flashcard drill for math fact acquisition). A treatment may consist of a program targeting an academic skill with multiple components (e.g., planning and organization strategies for written expression).

Treatment may also consist of a curriculum that includes a broader scope and sequence of targeted academic skills (e.g., reading decoding, fluency, comprehension) and/or a curriculum that includes a scope and sequence of targeted academic skills and explicitly describes teaching techniques for those skills (e.g., Reading Mastery curriculum). For shorthand purposes, and to remain consistent with the book's emphasis, this chapter will utilize the term "treatments" to refer to all of these types of possible interventions, programs, and curricula unless otherwise specifically stated.

There is a vast research literature base in education and education-related psychology fields on treatments for improving the academic skills of students with SLD. Education-focused treatments, however, have not been reviewed using the standards of the evidence-based treatment paradigm advanced by the American Psychological Association (Southam-Gerow & Prinstein, 2014). Of course, this is not surprising, since the research on treatments for SLD is largely educational not psychological.

The US Department of Education Institute for Educational Science (IES) has developed a research review criteria paradigm and process for reviewing and disseminating evidence-based treatments in education published on a website called the What Works Clearinghouse (WWC). The WWC has developed an extensive review process and detailed criteria guidelines for reviewing educational treatments that are being updated regularly and which can be found online at the Institute of Education Sciences (www.ies.ed.gov). Unfortunately, to date, few educational treatments reviewed meet the WWC criteria for research standards. Because the WWC review process sets such high standards and is subsequently so limiting in the research examined in support of educational treatments, some researchers have questioned the validity of the WWC review process and product (e.g., Stockard & Wood, 2016). The WWC has examined research related to treatments for students with disabilities including students with learning disabilities. At this time, there are only a few treatments with positive or potentially positive evidence listed on the WWC website for students with learning disabilities.

More recently the Council for Exceptional Children (CEC) has developed standards for evidence-based practices in special education (CEC, 2014). These standards may be more easily accessible for individual practitioners and scholars to utilize when evaluating the research support for a particular treatment for students with SLD. One example using CEC standards is provided by Cook and colleagues, who evaluated the evidence support for class wide peer tutoring (CWPT) for students with high-incidence disabilities (including SLD). They found that while some studies indicated positive findings or support for the effectiveness of CWPT for students with SLD, particularly for teaching spelling, no study met standards for research that would allow for examination or classification of CWPT as an evidence-based practice at this time (Cothren Cook, Cook, & Cook, 2016).

Given that there are not yet an agreed upon set of standards for reviewing educational research to identify evidence-based treatments, identifying effective treatments for SLD largely rests on the educator or clinician scanning the relevant literature for treatments with the best available evidence. This process requires the individual practitioner to seek out trusted sources of information to identify treatments for students with SLD with the best available evidence. In essence, the clinician is not necessarily seeking treatments that have met a priori standards for identification as evidence-based, but rather the clinician is seeking treatments identified as having the best evidence available. As always, when conducting searches of the literature it is also important that the clinician be aware of and acknowledge the philosophical assumptions one holds regarding human behavior and learning that act to filter the journals, texts, and other sources (i.e., experts, websites) searched and utilized.

The primary goal of any treatment for SLD is to facilitate learning. Given the range of types and focuses of treatments available for treating SLD and the vast amount of research available, it is important that the clinician understand the essential components necessary for learning to occur. Treatments for students with SLD that have the strongest evidence support have readily identifiable components in common that facilitate learning. Treatments that do not include these basic components are generally not effective. As noted earlier, these components are largely derived from principles of learning based on the science of behavior analysis. Note that these components are also typically components of evidence-based treatments for most other diagnoses. A primary point a clinician needs to keep in mind is that learning is behavior and subsequently the clinician should examine treatments to determine if basic behavior or learning principles are in effect. These learning principles constitute the components of evidence-based treatments for SLD.

Interventions Identified by the What Works Clearinghouse

Phonological Awareness Training had four studies which met review criteria. The study samples were preschool children with disabilities. Review showed positive evidence in the area of communication and language.

Dialogic Reading had two studies which met review criteria. The study samples were preschool students with disabilities. Review showed the intervention is potentially positive evidence in the area of communication and language.

Peer Assisted Learning Strategies had five studies which met review criteria. The study samples were students with learning disabilities in grades 2–6. Two studies showed potentially positive effects for reading comprehension and two studies showed potentially positive effects for reading fluency. One study had mixed effects for mathematics achievement.

Lindamood Phoneme Sequencing® (LiPS®) had five studies that met review criteria. The study samples were all fourth grade students with learning disabilities. There was one study for alphabetics, one study for mathematics achievement, and one study for reading fluency, all demonstrating potentially positive effects. There was one study for reading comprehension demonstrating mixed effects and one study for writing achievement demonstrating no discernable effect.

Read Naturally® had two studies which met review criteria. Study samples were students with learning disabilities in grades 4–6. One study showed positive effect for writing achievement and the other study demonstrated mixed effects for reading fluency.

Repeated Reading had five studies which met review criteria. Study samples were students with learning disabilities in grades 5–12. Two studies demonstrated positive effects for reading comprehension while the other three studies demonstrated mixed effects for alphabetics, reading achievement, and reading fluency respectively.

Spelling Mastery had two studies which met review criteria. Study samples were students with learning disabilities in grades 2–4. The studies showed positive effects for writing achievement.

Components of Evidence-Based Treatments

Identification of a Well-Defined Academic Skill Response

While SLD is widely considered to be a neurologically based disorder, the focus of effective treatment is not on neurological processes, but rather is directly on the academic skills to be learned. As noted above, the term *academic skills* is quite inclusive of a wide range of behaviors. Academic skills may consist of basic skills such as math facts, historical dates or names, letter sounds, sight words, etc. Academic skills may also consist of learning strategies to solve problems such as steps for mathematically based word problems, or steps in comprehending a reading passage, or how to plan and organize writing an essay, etc. Finally, academic skills may consist of even larger behavioral repertoires such as learning how to research a topic for a paper, asking critical questions about a topic, or creating algorithms to solve coding problems. In many cases, the primary academic skill area deficits for students with SLD are in basic or foundational skills (see common definitions of SLD above) which subsequently impedes effective learning of larger repertoires of academic behaviors.

Most academic skills include multiple components and all are multidimensional. For example, multiplication requires skill components such as counting and addition. Multiplication also has dimensions such as accuracy (i.e., responding with correct or accurate answer to problem, such as $2 \times 2 = $ ___), or fluency (i.e., responding quickly and accurately to the problem statement) or generalization (i.e., able to respond to the problem statement provided on a flashcard or orally or as part of a larger problem). Choosing the particular component or dimension to target for intervention is largely determined through individualized evaluation of a student's academic skill strengths and deficits (Shapiro, 2010). A key component of any evidence-based intervention for SLD is that it specifically targets an observable and measurable academic skill.

Any academic skill deficit may serve as a target for intervention, but some academic skills are more important than others for targeted intervention as mastery of these skills may facilitate learning of other related academic skills. These types of behaviors are termed "behavioral cusps" (Rosales-Ruiz & Baer, 1997). A behavioral cusp is defined as a behavior that meets at least one of the following criteria "(a) access to new reinforcers, contingencies, and environments; (b) social validity (both proposed by Rosales-Ruiz and Baer); (c) generativeness; (d) competition with inappropriate responses; and (e) number and the relative importance of people affected" (Bosch & Fuqua, 2001, p. 123). An example of an academic behavioral cusp may be acquisition of one-to-one correspondence when counting which allows for learning to count by groups (i.e., by 2s, 5s, 10s) and adding, subtracting, multiplication, and so on.

Likewise, when considering targets for intervention, there is hierarchy of dimensions to consider also. Accuracy of the skill is required prior to working on fluency. For example, if a child cannot accurately state the answer to a math fact, then the child will not be able to state it fluently (accurately and quickly). If a child cannot state the math fact fluently, then it is less likely that the child will be able to generalize answering or using the math fact in other contexts (Binder, 1996). Finally, if the child cannot generalize the math fact to other contexts, then it is unlikely the child will learn to adapt use of the math fact creatively. This learning hierarchy is a useful heuristic for determining the focus of intervention (Haring et al., 1978).

Setting Modifications

Since, by definition, individuals with SLD are not learning as expected within the typical general education large group classroom environment, treatments for SLD are usually delivered in small group or individualized settings (Slavin et al., 2009). Small groups or individualized instruction increases the opportunities for a teacher to implement the evidence-based treatment components described further below. Other setting factors may include specialized training of the teacher or paraprofessionals in the classroom in the delivery of the intervention. Finally, setting factors may also include the provision of additional adults in the classroom environment to assist with the delivery of the intervention. Note that these setting factors are consistent with what is often described as special education, but these factors themselves are not interventions, but rather factors that may be essential to the effective implementation of intervention for SLD (e.g., Slavin et al., 2009). These setting factors help facilitate delivery of other evidence-based treatment components.

Stimulus Control

Like any behavior, learning is largely about establishing a particular functional relation between a stimulus and a response, termed "stimulus control." As such, particular attention needs to be addressed to the environmental stimuli present when a child is learning an academic skill and the environmental stimuli that will be present when the child is expected to exhibit the academic skill. Evidence-based treatments for SLD are specifically designed with careful consideration of the type of stimulus materials needed to successfully match with learner factors and teach the academic skills targeted.

Instructional Match. Identification of the specific academic skills to be learned and of the learner's current strengths and needs leads to identification and development of instructional materials that best lead to the desired stimulus control of the targeted academic response. Materials may include curricula, textbooks, worksheets, manipulatives, computer software, or any other item that presents the stimulus targeted to establish control of the academic response. Effective intervention for SLD must include close attention to the scope and sequence of the curriculum and intervention. For example, direct instruction is carefully and empirically designed to present stimuli in such a way to evoke and control accurate responding, fluency, and generalization (Kame'enui, Fien, & Korgesaar, 2013). Direct instruction has garnered much empirical support since the 1960s (Watkins, 1995) and has curriculum programs for many academic areas including reading, math, and writing (Marchand-Martella, Slocum, & Martella, 2004) designed to address typical learners as well as learners at risk for and exhibiting learning difficulties.

Opportunities to Respond

It may appear that individuals with SLD need more time with academic material in order to learn the material. Time is important, but time is probably not the most relevant variable. Instead, it is imperative that individuals with SLD have more opportunities to respond to material relative to typical peers in order to learn academic skills. Learning cannot take place unless the individual is responding, and individuals with SLD need more responses to learn material compared to typical learners (Greenwood et al., 1994). Evidence-based treatments for individuals with SLD provide many more opportunities to respond to stimulus materials compared to typical teaching that occurs in general education classrooms. If the intervention does not include more opportunities for student responding, then it will not be effective.

Positive Reinforcement and Corrective Feedback

All learning requires reinforcement. If reinforcement does not occur, then the response is not repeated and learning does not occur (Catania, 2013). Likewise, corrective feedback is needed to decrease the probability of inaccurate responding occurring again and to provide a model of the correct response that will lead to reinforcement. Evidence-based treatments for SLD include explicit delineation of reinforcement and reinforcement schedules and corrective feedback. There should be a higher ratio of reinforcement relative to corrective feedback in an effective program. If reinforcement and/or corrective feedback are not explicitly addressed as part of the intervention, then it is unlikely to be effective.

Progress Monitoring

Close continual contact with relevant outcome data (Bushell & Baer, 1994) is essential to effective teaching generally and particularly for treatment for individuals with SLD. There is substantial research indicating progress monitoring improves intervention outcomes (Deno et al., 2001; Fuchs, Fuchs, & Hamlett, 1989a, 1989b; Fuchs et al., 1991). Effective decision making regarding changes in instructional strategies cannot be made without reliable and valid data. An evidence-based treatment for SLD will explicitly prescribe not only the academic skill to be learned, but also how progress regarding learning of the skill will be monitored. Frequent, direct measurement of the academic skill is typically preferred (Shapiro, 2010).

Behavioral Skills Training

All of the evidence-based components described above are utilized in the teaching process that follows a model described as behavioral skills training (Miltenberger, 2008). Essentially, there are four steps in the teaching sequence: instructions, modeling, practice, and feedback. The instructions step is what many may think of when they think about teaching. In this step, the teacher typically may orally explain or instruct the skill to be learned (e.g., lecture). It is also at this step that written materials are used to explain the skill to be learned. If teaching only includes this step, however, learning is not likely to occur. The entire sequence of behavioral skills training or teaching is needed for learning to successfully happen.

The next step is modeling. Here the teacher may orally or physically model the response to be learned, or the materials used may provide models for the response to be learned. Positive and negative examples of the response to be learned may be presented, with emphasis on the positive or accurate response. Next, the response or academic skill to be learned is practiced. As noted above, it is best that there are multiple opportunities to respond to or practice the academic skill to be learned, particularly for individuals with SLD. Finally, feedback in the form of reinforcement or corrective feedback is required contingent on the practiced academic skill response demonstrated. If any of the steps of this teaching sequence are missing in an intervention, then it is unlikely that learning will occur.

Role of Parents in Treatment

Parent involvement in education has long been considered to be an important factor in student learning (Booth & Dunn, 1996; Kim & Hill, 2015; Lilly, 2014). Parent involvement may occur anywhere along a continuum of activities from visiting the school or attending parent–teacher conferences, to volunteering in the classroom, helping a student with homework, or implementing an academic intervention in the home to help facilitate academic progress. This last type of activity of parent involvement has been termed "parent tutoring."

Parent tutoring, which has a specific focus on implementing academic interventions to improve children's reading, writing, and mathematics skills, also has a long history in clinical practice (e.g., Duvall, Delquadri, & Hall, 1996; Erion, 2006; Patterson et al., 1975). Parent tutoring has been demonstrated to be effective in improving reading skills of diverse students at risk for reading problems (Kupzyk, Daly, & Anderson, 2012; Kupzyk et al., 2011; Mitchell & Begeny, 2014; Powell-Smith et al., 2000; Resetar, Noell, & Pellegrin, 2006; Sénéchal & Young, 2008; Valleley, Begeny, & Shriver, 2005) as well as students identified with learning disabilities (Duvall et al., 1992; Gortmaker et al., 2007; Persampieri et al., 2006). Parent tutoring typically requires explicit training of the parent (Shriver & Allen, 2008), and requires resources that many parents may not possess, such as time, materials, and teaching skill or knowledge base. However, when parents have these resources, and are trained, parent tutoring can be effective in improving the academic performance of students with SLD.

Other Variables Influencing Treatment

Assessment

A diagnosis or educational verification of SLD helps to provide access to treatment within educational settings, but the diagnosis does not directly prescribe the treatment to be implemented. The most effective assessment processes to inform evidence-based treatment are typically referred to as direct skills assessment and include curriculum-based assessment and measurement processes (Shapiro, 2010). In addition, brief experimental analysis methods have been used successfully to identify effective treatments and treatment components for students with learning disabilities (Burns, Ganuza, & London, 2009; Codding et al., 2009; Daly & Martens, 1999).

In addition, the evaluation must also take into account particular factors of the learner which may affect treatment efficacy and learning of the academic skill. Evaluation of learner factors may include assessment of sensory capabilities (e.g., vision, hearing), physical capabilities (e.g., gross motor, fine motor, oral motor), comorbid diagnoses (ADHD, ASD, mood disorders, etc.), and neurological capabilities (particularly if there is evidence of brain injury). Evaluation of these learner factors is not meant to delineate limits of the learner's capabilities, but rather the adjustments that must be made to tailor the treatment to best meet the learner's needs and facilitate the learning of the targeted academic skills.

Comorbidity

As noted earlier, ADHD is a common comorbid diagnosis with SLD. Evidence-based treatment for ADHD (see Chapter 4, this volume) may help students attend to and engage with academic materials more effectively, which subsequently increases opportunities to respond and may help facilitate learning of academic skills. While there are no specific medications to address SLD, medication to address the inattentive characteristics of ADHD may also help students attend to and engage with academic materials more effectively. It is important as part of evaluation of learner factors and SLD to consider ADHD as a rule-out diagnosis.

Demographics

Age is one primary demographic variable known to differentially affect treatment outcomes for individuals with SLD. Older children with SLD make slower progress with treatment than younger children with SLD (Fletcher et al., 2007). This may be due to the fact that older children have had fewer opportunities to respond to relevant academic material in their past and are generally more substantially delayed over time. This fact makes it essential that students at risk for learning difficulties or SLD be identified at younger ages so that evidence-based treatments can be applied to reduce further academic delay.

Medication

As noted above, except for the treatment of comorbid conditions associated with SLD, such as ADHD, there are no medications demonstrated to be effective for the treatment of SLD.

Special Education

In addition, while many students are subsequently placed in a special education setting following a diagnosis of SLD, special education is not treatment. Special education services might help students access evidence-based treatment, however, if the right learning components are in place. Unfortunately, this model of educational service delivery (i.e., access to special education required in order to possibly access treatment for SLD) may make it more difficult for students with low academic achievement without SLD to access effective treatment to improve academic progress unless they are also identified with SLD. This type of service delivery model seems to set up students with low academic achievement for failure in order to contact possible treatment at school.

Response to Intervention

A response to intervention service delivery model is an alternative model designed to help prevent further academic failure for students at risk for academic delays by providing evidence-based treatment in a general education setting prior to identification for special education (Gresham, 2002). Such a model requires that the school team identify evidence-based treatments and implement those treatments with integrity in the general education environment. Knowledge of learning theory and the principles of learning that need to be included in any intervention for learning problems is essential for an education team to make effective decisions about treatment implementation for a student at risk for learning problems or SLD.

Conclusion

By definition, a specific learning disability is a *learning* disorder. Therefore, evidence-based treatment must include the implementation of basic learning principles derived from learning theory and research in behavior analysis. While SLD may be considered a neurologically based disorder, evidence-based treatment for SLD targets well-defined, measurable academic skills, not neurological processes. Evidence-based treatments for SLD include explicit consideration of setting factors, stimulus control, response opportunities, reinforcement and corrective feedback, teaching process (i.e., behavioral skills training steps), and frequent progress monitoring of learning. When searching for and/or examining possible treatments for an individual with SLD, the clinician should evaluate the treatment to assess if these EBT components are included. Hopefully, as WWC, CEC, and other organizations continue to review the psychological and educational research related to the treatment of SLD, additional treatments with strong evidence for the treatment of SLD will be identified and disseminated.

Useful Resources

- Best Evidence Encyclopedia at www.bestevidence.org/
- Colorado Learning Disabilities Research Center at ibgwww.colorado.edu/cldrc/
- Council for Exceptional Children at www.cec.sped.org/Standards/Evidence-Based-Practice-Resources-Original
- Florida Learning Disabilities Research Center at fcrr.org/projects/projects_fldrc.html
- Intervention Central at www.interventioncentral.org/home

- Missouri Evidence-Based Intervention at ebi.missouri.edu/?page_id=807
- National Institute for Direct Instruction at www.nifdi.org/
- Texas Center for Learning Disabilities at www.texasldcenter.org/
- What Works Clearinghouse at ies.ed.gov/ncee/wwc/
- Wing Institute for Evidence-Based Intervention at www.winginstitute.org/

References

American Psychiatric Association (APA). (2013). *Diagnostic and statistical manual of mental disorders*. 5th edn.Washington, DC: American Psychiatric Association.

Binder, C. (1996). Behavioral fluency: Evolution of a new paradigm. *The Behavior Analyst, 19*, 163–197.

Booth, A., & Dunn, J. (eds.) (1996). *Family–school links*. Mahwah, NJ: Lawrence Erlbaum.

Bosch, S., & Fuqua, R. W. (2001). Behavioral cusps: A model for selecting target behaviors. *Journal of Applied Behavior Analysis, 34*, 123–125.

Burns, M. K., Ganuza, Z., & London, R. (2009). Brief experimental analysis of written letter formation: Single-case demonstration. *Journal of Behavioral Education, 18*, 20–34. doi:10.1007/s10864-008-9076-z

Bushell, D., & Baer, D. M. (1994). Measurably superior instruction means close, continual contact with the relevant outcome data. Revolutionary! In R. Gardner III, D. M. Sainato, J. O. Cooper, T. E. Heron, W. L. Heward, J. Eshleman, & T. A. Grossi (eds.), *Behavior analysis in education: Focus on measurably superior instruction* (pp. 3–10). Pacific Grove, CA: Brooks/Cole Publishing Company.

Catania, A. C. (2013). *Learning*. 5th edn. Cornwall on Hudson, NY: Sloan Publishing.

Codding, R. S., Baglici, S., Gottesman, D., Johnson, M., Kert, A. S., & Lebeouf, P. (2009). Selecting intervention strategies: Using brief experimental analysis for mathematics problems. *Journal of Applied School Psychology, 25*, 146–168. doi:10.1177/0145445510391242

Cothren Cook, S., Cook, B. G., & Cook, L. (2016). Classifying the evidence base of classwide peer tutoring for students with high incidence disabilities. *Exceptionality, 25*(1). http://dx.doi.org/10.1080/09362835.2016.1196448

Council for Exceptional Children (CEC). (2014). *Council for Exceptional Children standards for evidence-based practices in special education*. Arlington, VA: Council for Exceptional Children.

Daly, E. J., III, & Martens, B. K. (1999). A brief experimental analysis for identifying instructional components needed to improve oral reading fluency. *Journal of Applied Behavior Analysis, 32*, 83–95. doi:10.1901/jaba.1999.32-83

Denckla, M. B., Barquiero, L. A., Lindstrom, E. R., Benedict, S. L., Wilson, L. M., & Cutting, L. E. (2013). Attention-deficit/hyperactivity disorder, executive function, and reading comprehension: Different but related. In H. L. Swanson, K. R. Harris, & S. Graham (eds.), *Handbook of learning disabilities*. 2nd edn. New York: Guilford Press.

Deno, S. L., Fuchs, L. S., Marston, D., & Shin, J. (2001). Using curriculum-based measurement to establish growth standards for students with learning disabilities. *School Psychology Review, 30*, 507–524.

Duvall, S. F., Delquadri, J. C., Elliott, M., & Hall, R. V. (1992). Parent tutoring procedures: Experimental analysis and validation of generalization in oral reading across passages, settings, and time. *Journal of Behavior Education, 2,* 281–303. doi:10.1007/BF00948819

Duvall, S. F., Delquadri, J. C., & Hall, R. V. (1996). *Parents as reading tutors.* Longmont, CO: Sopris West.

Erion, R. J. (2006). Parent tutoring: A meta-analysis. *Education & Treatment of Children, 29*(1), 79–106. www.educationandtreatmentofchildren.net/

Fletcher, J. M., Lyon, G. R., Fuchs, L. S., & Barnes, M. A. (2007). *Learning disabilities: From identification to intervention.* New York: Guilford Press.

Fuchs, D., Fuchs, L. S., Mathes, P. G., Lipsey, M. W., & Roberts, P. H. (2002). Is "Learning Disabilities" just a fancy term for low achievement? A meta-analysis of reading differences between low achievers with and without the label. In R. Bradley, L. Danielson, & D. P. Hallahan (eds.), *Identification of learning disabilities: Research to practice.* Mahwah, NJ: Lawrence Erlbaum Associates.

Fuchs, L. S., Fuchs, D., & Hamlett, C. L. (1989a). Effects of alternative goal structures within curriculum-based measurement. *Exceptional Children, 55,* 429–438.

Fuchs, L. S., Fuchs, D., & Hamlett, C. L. (1989b). Effects of instructional use of curriculum-based measurement to enhance instructional programs. *Remedial and Special Education, 10*(2), 43–52.

Fuchs, L. S., Fuchs, D., Hamlett, C. L., & Stecker, P. M. (1991). Effects of curriculum-based measurement and consultation on teacher planning and student achievement in mathematics operations. *American Educational Research Journal, 28,* 27–48.

Gardner, R., Sainato, D. M., Cooper, J. O., Heron, T. E., Heward, W. L., Eshleman, J., & Grossi, T. A. (1994). *Behavior analysis in education: Focus on measurably superior instruction.* Pacific Grove, CA: Brooks/Cole Publishing Company.

Gortmaker, V. J., Daly, E. J., III, McCurdy, M., Persampieri, M. J., & Hergenrader, M. (2007). Improving reading outcomes for children with learning disabilities: Using brief experimental analysis to develop parent tutoring interventions. *Journal of Applied Behavior Analysis, 40,* 203–222. doi:10.1901/jaba.2007.105–05

Greenwood, C. R., Hart, B., Walker, D., & Risley, T. (1994). The opportunity to respond and academic performance revisited: A behavioral theory of developmental retardation and its prevention. In R. Gardner III, D. M. Sainato, J. O. Cooper, T. E. Heron, W. L. Heward, J. Eshleman, & T. A. Grossi (eds.), *Behavior analysis in education: Focus on measurably superior instruction* (pp. 213–223). Pacific Grove, CA: Brooks/Cole Publishing Company.

Gresham, F. M. (2002). Responsiveness to intervention: An alternative approach to the identification of learning disabilities. In R. Bradley, L. Danielson, & D. P. Hallahan (eds.), *Identification of learning disabilities: Research to practice.* Mahwah, NJ: Lawrence Erlbaum Associates.

Haring, N. G., Lovitt, T. C, Eaton, M. D., & Hansen, C. L. (1978). *The fourth R: Research in the classroom.* Columbus, OH: Merrill.

Individuals with Disabilities Act Reauthorization (IDEA). (2004). Office of Special Education Programs, US Department of Education.

Kame'enui, E. J., Fien, H., & Korgesaar, J. (2013). Direct instruction as eo nomine and contronym: Why the right words and details matter. In H. L. Swanson, K. R. Harris, & S. Graham (eds.). *Handbook of learning disabilities.* 2nd edn. New York: Guilford Press.

Kim, S., & Hill, N. E. (2015). Including fathers in the picture: A meta-analysis of parental involvement and students' academic achievement. *Journal of Educational Psychology* (no pagination specified).

Kupzyk, S., Daly, E. J., & Andersen, M. N. (2012). Preparing teachers to train parents to use evidence-based strategies for oral reading fluency with their children. *Contemporary School Psychology*, *16*(1), 129–140.

Kupzyk, S., McCurdy, M., Hofstadter, K. L., & Berger, L. (2011). Recorded readings: A taped parent-tutoring intervention. *Journal of Behavioral Education*, *20*, 87–102. doi:10.1007/s10864-011-9123-z

Lilly, S. (2014). A family literacy intervention to support parents in children's early literacy learning. *Reading Psychology*, *35*, 703–735.

MacMillan, D. L., Gresham, F. M., & Bocian, K. M. (1998). Discrepancy between definitions of learning disabilities and school practices: An empirical investigation. *Journal of Learning Disabilities*, *31*, 314–326.

Marchand-Martella, N. E., Slocum, T. A., & Martella, R. C. (2004). *Introduction to direct instruction*. Boston, MA: Pearson.

Mayes, S. D., Calhoun, S. L., & Crowell, E. W. (2000). Learning disabilities and ADHD: Overlapping spectrum disorders. *Journal of Learning Disabilities*, *33*, 417–424.

Miltenberger, R. G. (2008). *Behavior modification: Principles and procedures*. 4th edn. Belmont, CA: Wadworth/Thomas Learning.

Mitchell, C., & Begeny, J. C. (2014). Research into practice: Improving student reading through parents' implementation of a structured reading program. *School Psychology Review*, *43*, 41–58.

Patterson, G. R., Reid, J. B., Jones, R. R., & Conger, R. E. (1975). *A social learning approach to family intervention. I. Families with aggressive children*. Eugene, OR: Castalia.

Persampieri, M., Gortmaker, V., Daly, E. J., III, Sheridan, S. M., & McCurdy, M. (2006). Promoting parent use of empirically supported reading interventions: Two experimental investigations of child outcomes. *Journal of Behavioral Interventions*, *21*, 31–57. doi:10.1002/bin.210

Powell-Smith, K. A., Shinn, M. R., Stoner, G. & Good, R. H., III (2000). Parent tutoring using literature and curriculum materials: Impact on student reading achievement. *School Psychology Review*, *29*(1), 5–27.

Resetar, J. L., Noell, G. H., & Pellegrin, A. L. (2006). Teaching parents to use research supported systematic strategies to tutor their children in reading. *School Psychology Quarterly*, *21*, 241–261. doi:10.1521/scpq.2006.21.3.241

Richards, T. L., Berninger, V., Sylward, E., Richards, A., Thomson, J., Nagy, W., et al. (2002). Reproducibility of proton MR spectroscopic imaging (PEPSI): Comparison of dyslexic and normal reading children and effects of treatment on brain lactate levels during language tasks. *American Journal of Neuroradiology*, *23*, 1678–1685.

Rosales-Ruiz, J., & Baer, D. M. (1997). Behavioral cusps: A developmental and pragmatic concept for behavior analysis. *Journal of Applied Behavior Analysis*, *30*, 533–544.

Sénéchal, M., & Young, L. (2008). The effect of family literacy interventions on children's acquisition of reading from kindergarten to grade 3: A meta-analytic review. *Review of Educational Research*, *78*(4), 880–907. doi:10.3102/0034654308320319

Shapiro, E. S. (2010). *Academic skills problems: Direct assessment and intervention*. 4th edn. New York: Guilford Press.

Shaywitz, B. A., Shaywitz, S. E., Blachman, B., Pugh, K. R., Fulbright, R. K., Skudlarski, P., et al. (2004). Development of left occipitotemporal systems for skilled reading in children after a phonologically based intervention. *Biological Psychiatry*, *55*, 926–933.

Shaywitz, S. E., & Shaywitz, B. A. (2013). Making a hidden disability visible: What has been learned from neurobiological studies of dyslexia. In H. L. Swanson, K. R. Harris, & S. Graham (eds.), *Handbook of learning disabilities*. 2nd edn. New York: Guilford Press.

Shriver, M. D., & Allen, K. D. (2008). *Working with parents of noncompliant children: A guide to evidence-based parent training for practitioners and students.* Washington, DC: American Psychological Association.

Simos, P. G., Fletcher, J. M., Sarkari, S., Billingsley, R. L., Francis, D. J., Castillow, E. M., et al. (2005). Early development of neurophysiological processes involved in normal reading and reading disability. *Neuropsychology, 19,* 787–798.

Skinner, B. F. (1953). *Science and human behavior.* New York: Macmillan.

Slavin, R. E., Lake, C., Davis, S., & Madden, N. (2009). *Effective programs for struggling readers: A best evidence synthesis.* Baltimore, MD: Johns Hopkins University, Center for Data-Driven Reform in Education. www.bestevidence.org/reading/strug/strug_read.htm

Southam-Gerow, M. A., & Prinstein, M. J. (2014). Evidence base updates: The evolution of the evaluation of psychological treatments for children and adolescents. *Journal of Clinical Child & Adolescent Psychology, 43,* 1–6.

Stockard, J., & Wood, T. W. (2016).The threshold and inclusive approaches to determining "best available evidence": An empirical analysis. *American Journal of Evaluation,* 1–22. doi:10.1177/1098214016662338

Valleley, R. J., Begeny J. C., & Shriver, M. D. (2005). Collaborating with parents to improve children's reading. *Journal of Evidence Based Practices for Schools, 6,* 19–41.

Watkins, C. L. (1995). Follow through: Why didn't we? *Effective School Practices, 15.* http://darkwing.uoregon.edu/~adiep/ft/watkins.htm

6

Tics

Brianna Wellen and Michael B. Himle

Tic disorders are a class of childhood onset neuropsychiatric disorders characterized by sudden, rapid, recurrent, nonrhythmic, involuntary motor movements (i.e., motor tics) and/or vocalizations (i.e., vocal or phonic tics). The *Diagnostic and Statistical Manual of Mental Disorders*, 5th edition (American Psychiatric Association [APA], 2013) specifies three primary tic disorders that are differentiated only by the duration of symptoms and the type of tic(s) present (motor, vocal, or both). Tourette's disorder (TD) involves the presence of multiple motor tics and at least one vocal tic that have been present at some point during the illness (though not necessarily concurrently) whereas persistent motor/vocal tic disorder (PMVTD) involves the presence of one or more motor *or* vocal tics, but not both. For both TD and PMVTD, tics may fluctuate in frequency over the course of the disorder, but must have been present in some form for at least one year. Provisional tic disorder involves single or multiple motor and/or vocal tics that have been present for less than one year. All three tic disorders require that initial tic onset occur prior to 18 years of age and that tics not be attributable to the physiological effects of a substance or another medical condition (APA, 2013).

Epidemiological studies have shown that transient tics are quite common, occurring in 4–24% of school-aged children (Robertson, 2008). For many children, tics are transient and spontaneously remit without clinical intervention or are mild enough that they go undetected and/or undiagnosed (Snider et al., 2002). Best estimates for persistent tic disorders, including TD, suggest a lifetime prevalence of 0.5–1% in school-aged children and tic disorders have been shown to be four to six times more common in males than females (Robertson, 2008).

The clinical course of tic disorders is highly variable, but some common patterns have been identified (Bloch & Leckman, 2009). Tics typically first emerge between four and six years of age. For most children, tics wax and wane in severity and change in topography over the course of the disorder, increasing in number, frequency, intensity, and complexity through adolescence. Early in the course of the disorder, tics are typically simple in appearance and involve brief contractions of single muscle groups, usually in the face and/or head and neck. Over time, tics tend to progress in a cephalocaudal pattern to involve orchestrated movements of the torso and limbs and become more complex and purposeful in appearance. Most individuals experience a gradual decrease in tic severity by young adulthood (Bloch & Leckman, 2009). Although some children experience little or no functional impairment due to their tics, many report substantial problems in social, academic, and/or family functioning as well as decreased self-esteem and diminished quality of life (Eddy et al., 2011; Storch et al., 2007).

Etiology and Theoretical Underpinnings of Treatment

Although the exact cause of tics remains unclear, there is converging evidence that they are the direct result of dysfunction within cortical-striato-thalamo-cortical pathways that are known to be involved in the selection, execution, and inhibition of movement (Shprecher, Schrock, & Himle, 2014). Despite having a neurobiological origin, however, there is also evidence that tics, once executed, are influenced by dynamic environmental factors (Himle et al., 2014). Rather than trying to explain or correct the underlying cause of tics, a behavioral approach to tic management aims to identify learning processes that function to increase the frequency, intensity, and complexity of tics.

The behavioral model of tics is based on four well-established phenomena. First, although tics are involuntary, they can be brought under voluntary control (i.e., suppressed), at least temporarily (Himle & Woods, 2005). Second, most individuals' tics fluctuate (increase or decrease) in response to contextual cues (Himle et al., 2014), which is not easily explained by biological models. For example, most individuals report that their tics are worsened by certain activities, mood states, in specific settings, and/or in the presence of specific individuals (Silva et al., 1995). Third, research has shown that tic-contingent consequences (e.g., reinforcement and punishment) can increase or decrease the frequency and intensity of tics in the short term (Himle et al., 2014). Finally, most individuals report that their tics are preceded by unpleasant somatic sensations, referred to as "premonitory urges," that worsen when tics are suppressed and are alleviated by performance of the tic (Himle et al., 2007; Woods et al., 2005).

Based on these findings, the behavioral model conceptualizes tics from an Antecedent–Behavior–Consequence (ABC) framework that aims to understand how contextual factors shape the frequency, intensity, and topography of tics over time (Himle et al., 2014; Woods et al., 2008). Antecedents (As) are stimuli that precede tics and, because they have been paired with tic-contingent consequences (Cs), make tics more likely to occur within a given context. Importantly, antecedents can be internal or external to the individual. External antecedents are specific settings in which the tics occur regularly or with high frequency. Internal antecedents include mood states, premonitory urges, or other internal states (e.g., muscle tension) that immediately precede tics. Consequences (Cs) are events or stimuli that immediately follow tics and occur contingent upon tics. Like antecedents, these can also be internal or external to the individual. Examples of external consequences include tic-contingent social reactions (e.g., attention) and escape or avoidance of aversive tasks (i.e., social positive and negative reinforcement). Internal consequences include relief from premonitory urges or muscle tension (i.e., automatic negative reinforcement). When consequences are delivered contingent upon tic performance, they can serve to increase (reinforce) tic performance within a particular antecedent context.

The ABC model provides a useful conceptual framework for understanding and treating tic disorders using a behavioral approach. First, within the ABC model, tics are conceptualized as reflexive reactions that function to reduce an aversive internal state (e.g., a premonitory urge, muscle tension) and thus are strengthened through automatic negative reinforcement. Because they are performed with high frequency and are automatically reinforced, they become overlearned (automatic) and occur outside the individual's awareness. Thus, if an individual can learn to recognize when a tic is about to occur and can inhibit the tic, the automatic negative reinforcement contingency will be interrupted and the urge to tic will decrease, theoretically through habituation learning. In addition, the ABC model posits that some of the situational fluctuations commonly observed in children with tics are the result of tic-contingent positive and negative reinforcement (e.g., attention, escape from demanding tasks) contingencies that can be systematically identified and altered to decrease the frequency and severity of tics.

Brief Overview of Evidence-Based Treatments

Habit Reversal Training (HRT)

HRT is a multicomponent treatment package designed to alter the automatic negative reinforcement function of tics (Azrin & Nunn, 1973). The original HRT treatment package consisted of 12 different therapeutic activities; however, component analysis studies have concluded that only three components are necessary: awareness training, competing response training, and social support (Miltenberger, Fuqua, & McKinley, 1985). Awareness training involves a set of techniques to teach the individual to recognize each time a particular tic has occurred or is about to occur. After sufficient tic awareness is achieved, competing response training is used to teach the individual to interrupt or prevent the tic from occurring by engaging in a behavior that is incompatible with the tic. Finally, a social support person (usually a parent) is taught to supportively prompt and reinforce correct use of the competing response outside of sessions. Treatment is typically conducted during weekly 60-minute sessions with one tic targeted at each session and HRT practice is assigned between sessions. The total number of sessions required depends upon the number of tics targeted in treatment as well as the client's mastery of HRT skills. HRT has been extensively studied and is considered a well-established treatment for reducing tics (Himle et al., 2007).

Comprehensive Behavioral Intervention for Tics (CBIT)

Like HRT, CBIT is a multicomponent treatment package designed to teach a collection of tic management skills (Woods et al., 2008). It includes HRT as one of the primary treatment components. In addition to HRT, the CBIT protocol includes relaxation training and a systematic function-based assessment and intervention (FBAI) protocol (Himle et al., 2014). FBAI is an individualized, function-based approach designed to systematically identify contextual factors (i.e., antecedents) associated with tic-worsening and alter potential tic-exacerbating consequences. The CBIT treatment package is typically delivered over 10–12 weekly sessions, each lasting 60–90 minutes, with one tic targeted each week. As a package, CBIT has been shown to be more effective than supportive psychotherapy for reducing tics with treatment gains maintained three and six months post treatment (Piacentini et al., 2010). CBIT is now recommended as a first-line intervention for tics disorders according to the best-practice guidelines published by several interdisciplinary bodies (Murphy et al., 2013; Verdellen et al., 2011).

Exposure with Response Prevention (ERP)

ERP for tics is an adapted version of exposure-based interventions that have been shown to be efficacious for treating obsessive-compulsive disorder (OCD; Hoogduin, Verdellen, & Cath, 1997). Like HRT, the underlying premise of ERP is that tics are strengthened through automatic negative reinforcement because they function to remove aversive premonitory urges (in the same way that compulsions are reinforced because they reduce anxiety arising from obsessions). Similar to HRT, it is posited that if individuals prevent themselves from performing a tic, and therefore are "exposed" to the premonitory sensations, they will habituate to the urge and tics will reduce in frequency and intensity. While the underlying rationale for ERP is similar to HRT, there are several important procedural differences. In contrast to HRT, ERP involves instructing the client to suppress all tics simultaneously for increasing durations of time. In addition, there are no formal procedures for increasing tic awareness, the client is not taught specific tic-suppressing strategies such as competing responses, and sessions typically last 120 minutes (versus 60 minutes for HRT). While more empirical studies are needed, preliminary research has shown ERP to be a promising treatment for reducing tics. For example, Hoogduin et al. (1997) treated four individuals with tics using ERP and found that tics were significantly reduced for three of the participants and all three responders reported a reduction in the urge to tic during the session. In addition, at least one randomized controlled trial comparing ERP to HRT found both were effective for reducing tics with no differences between the two treatment modalities (Verdellen et al., 2004).

Components of Evidence-Based Treatments

The EBTs described above share several theoretically driven treatment components, including increasing tic awareness, teaching and reinforcing tic inhibition, and function-based assessment and intervention techniques to identify external antecedents and consequences that maintain and worsen tics. In addition, each of the EBTs share several nonspecific components that are considered important for improving treatment engagement and maximizing and maintaining treatment gains, including psychoeducation, the use of positive reinforcement and reward programs, and maintenance/relapse prevention. Each of these components is described below.

Increasing Tic Awareness

Upon entering treatment, most children know *that* they have tics, but are not particularly proficient at knowing exactly *when* specific tics have occurred or are about to occur (Muller-Vahl, Riemann, & Bokemeyer, 2014). As such, a prerequisite for interrupting tics (which is central to all EBTs for tics) is teaching the child to recognize when a tic is occurring or is about to occur. This process is generally referred to as awareness training (Azrin & Nunn, 1973; Woods et al., 2008). Awareness training involves several steps that are repeated for each tic targeted in treatment. First, the child is asked to describe the targeted tic in considerable detail, noting all of the muscle movements involved in producing the tic, the progression or sequence of movements involved in the tic, and to describe any premonitory sensations that precede tics. During this process, the child is asked to simulate the tic several times and is prompted by the clinician to pay particular attention to specific muscle groups involved in producing the tic. When necessary, the clinician points out observed movements that the child does not recognize. In doing so, the therapist and child generate a detailed operational definition (often referred to as a "tic chain") of the targeted tic. Second, the child practices response detection. Response detection involves asking the child to self-monitor tics and to indicate each time a tic occurs (usually by raising a finger) while engaged in a mildly distracting activity, such as playing a game or conversing with the therapist. When the child successfully detects a tic, the therapist delivers descriptive praise. When the child misses a tic, the therapist points this out and encourages the child to attend carefully to the first movements in the tic chain. Finally, the therapist uses shaping to reinforce the child's detection of the tic as early in the tic chain as possible, ideally upon recognizing a premonitory urge. Within the shaping procedure, the child initially receives praise for detecting tics after they occur. Once the child has mastered this task (usually defined as the detection of 80% of tics), the therapist withholds praise for detecting tics after they occur, and instead reinforces detection of tics as they are occurring or, ideally, before they occur (i.e., when the child recognizes a premonitory urge). Self-monitoring and tic detection are assigned to be practiced at home between sessions with a parent's assistance. Although awareness training has not been shown to be sufficient for reducing tics in the long term for most children with tics, component analysis research does suggest that awareness training alone can result in a modest reduction in tics for some individuals (Woods, Miltenberger, & Lumley, 1996).

Teaching and Reinforcing Tic Inhibition

Teaching children to inhibit tics is a primary component of all EBTs for tic disorders. Within HRT, tic inhibition involves teaching the child to inhibit tics using a procedure referred to as competing response (CR) training (Azrin & Nunn, 1973; Woods et al., 2008). CR training involves teaching the child to engage in a tic-incompatible behavior whenever they perform a tic or, preferably, when they recognize that a tic is about to occur. The "rules" for CR training are that the CR used to interrupt the tic should (1) be physically incompatible with performing the tic, (2) be less noticeable than the tic and socially inconspicuous, (3) be a response that can be performed easily and maintained for several minutes, and (4) is a behavior they can perform while engaged in other normal activities. Selection of the CR is a collaborative process between the clinician and the client. The specific topography of the CR is highly dependent upon the nature of the tic, and each tic will likely require a different CR. Ideally, the CR will interrupt the tic as early in the tic chain as possible, emphasizing the importance of generating a detailed description of the tic during awareness training. Once the CR is selected, the therapist and the child practice using the CR in session to interrupt the target tic, and child and parent are instructed to practice using the CR regularly between sessions. Specifically, the child is instructed to initiate the CR contingent upon tic "warning signs" (e.g., a premonitory urge or the earliest movement involved in the tics) and actively maintain the CR for at least one minute or until the tic subsides, whichever is longer. It is important to note that engaging in the CR *contingent upon* tic warning signs is essential as research has shown that simply practicing use of the CR noncontingently is ineffective (Miltenberger & Fuqua, 1985). Within the ERP protocol, the child is not taught a specific CR, but rather is simply asked to suppress all tics for as long as possible (which most children can do for at least several minutes; Himle et al., 2007) while periodically monitoring and rating the subjective severity of premonitory urges. The clinician records the length of time that the child can suppress their tics and the child is challenged to do so for increasing lengths of time. Whether the CR or ERP approach to tic inhibition is more efficacious remains an empirical question.

Prompting and reinforcement are also used in both HRT and ERP to reinforce tic-inhibition skills. Prompting involves the issuing of a verbal cue to increase the probability that a desired behavior will occur within a particular context. Positive reinforcement refers to the delivery of a reward, usually in the form of verbal praise or access to a preferred item or activity, contingent upon performance of the desired behavior and serves to establish and strengthen skill acquisition. Prompting and positive reinforcement are used extensively in HRT. Specifically, a social support person, such as a parent or teacher, is taught to supportively remind (i.e., prompt) the child to use the competing response whenever a tic is observed for which the child did not engage in a tic-incompatible CR. When the child engages in the CR, either in response to being prompted or independently, positive reinforcement, usually in the form of verbal praise, is delivered to strengthen learning and increase the likelihood that the CR will be used in the future. Likewise, in ERP, positive reinforcement is used to encourage the child to suppress tics for increasing durations of time (Verdellen et al., 2004). Importantly, in both of these treatments, prompting and positive reinforcement are used to establish and reinforce the use of specific tic management skills rather than to simply draw attention to tics or reward tic reduction per se. In other words, simply pointing out when a child has ticced or providing reward for periods in which tics have not occurred are not likely to be effective because such procedures do not strengthen a specific tic management skill.

Function-Based Assessment and Intervention

The rationale for including the FBAI component in CBIT is based on research showing that tics often increase in severity in particular contexts (settings, activities, presence of specific people; Himle et al., 2014). As noted above, FBAI is a structured, individualized, function-based approach designed to systematically identify contextual factors (i.e., antecedents) associated with tic worsening and alter potential tic-exacerbating consequences. To conduct an FBAI, the clinician first interviews the patient and their family about common antecedent and consequence variables shown in research to be associated with tic worsening. After assessing for common tic-exacerbating antecedents, the clinician interviews the family about possible consequences that may follow tics in each of the antecedent situations endorsed. Families are then asked to monitor tic exacerbations on a daily basis and record antecedents (setting, activity, people present) and consequences (reactions to the tics) associated with the increase in tics. These daily observations are reviewed at the beginning of each weekly therapy session and are used to derive individualized function-based intervention strategies and therapeutic recommendations. The specific intervention strategies recommended depend entirely on the antecedents and consequences identified for any particular individual, but generally involve altering antecedents (e.g., minimizing tic-exacerbating activities, such as watching television, or scheduling them for a time when tic exacerbations will be less problematic) and eliminating tic-exacerbating consequences (e.g., ignoring tics that are worsened by attention, not allowing escape from nonpreferred tasks in response to tics). The overarching goal of FBAI is to create a "tic-neutral" environment in which tics do not receive any particular attention or accommodation. Studies have shown FBAI to be effective for reducing tics in some children as a stand-alone intervention (Watson & Sterling, 1998) and it is included as a primary component in some EBTs treatment packages (e.g., CBIT; Himle et al., 2014; Woods et al., 2008); however, the extent to which FBAI will reduce tics depends entirely upon the degree to which the child's tics are influenced by contextual factors.

Relaxation Training

The rationale for including relaxation training in the treatment of tics is based on studies showing that most individuals report that their tics are exacerbated by stress and anxiety (Silva et al., 1995). It is perhaps best conceptualized as a function-based intervention because it aims to alter a tic-exacerbating internal antecedent. However, given that virtually all children experience at least some level of stress and anxiety, along with the fact that these have been shown to exacerbate tics in most children, most EBTs include relaxation training for all children (as compared to the highly individualized functional interventions applied in the FBAI approach described above). The most common relaxation training exercises included in EBTs for tics are developmentally tailored diaphragmatic breathing and progressive muscle relaxation exercises (Woods et al., 2008). These skills are taught and practiced both during sessions and between sessions as therapy homework. While relaxation training has not been shown to be an effective monotherapy for long-term tic reduction in most individuals (Peterson & Azrin, 1992), the rationale for including relaxation training in the treatment of tics is that reducing autonomic arousal and stress can indirectly reduce or prevent tic exacerbations in the short term and can therefore reduce tic-related interferences and distress in anxiety-provoking and stressful situations (e.g., when taking an exam).

Reward Programs

Research has shown that lack of treatment compliance and adherence can undermine the effectiveness of behavioral interventions for tic disorders (Carr et al., 1996). Like most skills-based, self-management interventions, behavioral tic management techniques require considerable effort and consistent practice from the child, both within and between sessions, in order to be effective. In addition, when children are asked/taught to inhibit their tics, for example when using a competing response during HRT, they often experience a short-term worsening of unpleasant premonitory urges that they must be willing to tolerate in the service of longer-term tic reduction (as opposed to ticcing, which requires less effort and results in an immediate decrease in premonitory urges). Relatedly, research has also shown that children, especially younger and/or impulsive children, tend to choose immediate small rewards (e.g., ticcing to immediately remove the urge) over those that are delayed or less certain (e.g., long-term tic reduction), even if the delayed reward is more valuable (i.e., delay discounting; Wilson et al., 2011). To increase motivation and compliance with tic management techniques, positive reinforcement programs are commonly used to motivate and reward the child for active participation and treatment compliance. Such reward programs usually involve token economies in which secondary reinforcers, such as points or stickers, can be earned and exchanged for preferred items. It is important to note that because tics are viewed as involuntary and not all children benefit from treatment (even when they are compliant), rewards are not delivered contingent upon tic reduction, but rather for attending sessions, attempting therapeutic tasks, and completion of homework assignments such as regular tic management practice between sessions (Woods et al., 2008).

Psychoeducation

Psychoeducation is a common component of all EBTs for tics and serves several purposes. First, it has been shown to promote positive attitudes and healthy interactions toward youth with tics and to increase treatment engagement and adherence (Nussey, Pistrang, & Murphy, 2013). Second, psychoeducation can be used as a tool to help the family accurately conceptualize their child's tics and non-tic behaviors, as parents often enter treatment confused about which of the child's behaviors are, and are not, tics. Third, psychoeducation can help to reduce guilt and stigma surrounding a tic disorder diagnosis and create optimism for the future by helping parents understand that tics can be effectively managed. Finally, and perhaps most importantly, psychoeducation can help to set the stage for treatment by providing a conceptual rationale and expectations for the intervention, which is important for treatment engagement and success. Although the bulk of psychoeducation occurs in the first few sessions, it is an ongoing process that is infused throughout all aspects of EBT for tic disorders. Common topics covered as part of psychoeducation include diagnostic criteria for tic disorders, differentiating tics from non-tic behavior (such as comorbid symptoms and normal behavior), phenomenology and clinical course of tics, difficulties commonly experienced by children with tics, and underlying causes and prevalence of tic disorders (Woods et al., 2008). Most importantly, it is essential that the parents and child understand the rational for a behavioral approach to tic management.

Maintenance/Relapse Prevention

Although behavioral interventions have been shown to reduce the overall severity of tics, few children experience complete tic remission following treatment (Piacentini et al., 2010). In addition, tics are known to wax and wane over time and it is not uncommon for new tics to emerge following treatment (Bloch & Leckman, 2009; Peterson et al., 2016). As such, it is important to plan carefully to ensure that children continue to use the tic management skills taught in therapy after treatment has ended. For example, most EBTs include specific instructions for the child to practice tic management skills in as many situations and contexts as possible (referred to as public mastery; Azrin & Nunn, 1973). In addition, behavior therapy is a skill-based approach to tic management. As such, the goal of treatment is to teach the child specific skills they can use if a new tic emerges after treatment has ended. To address this, most EBTs focus the final session (or two) on assessing the child's (and their parents') knowledge and skills taught in treatment by, for example, conducting a role-play for how they might address a hypothetical tic that could emerge in the future (Woods et al., 2008).

Applying HRT to Other Repetitive Behavior Disorders

In addition to treating tics, the components of EBTs reviewed in this chapter have been shown to be efficacious for treating a variety of other repetitive behavior problems in children, including thumb-sucking, hair-pulling, and nail-biting (referred to informally as body-focused repetitive behavior disorders, BFRBs). In fact, several of the underlying theoretical assumptions outlined for tics have been applied to BFRBs (Azrin & Nunn, 1973; Woods & Miltenberger, 1995). Although the underlying etiology of BFRBs likely differs from that of tics, from a behavioral perspective, BFRBs share several functional similarities to tics. For example, BFRBs, like tics, are performed repetitively and with high frequency. As a result, it is posited that they become overlearned (automatic) and are performed largely outside the individual's awareness. Furthermore, research has shown that these behaviors are influenced by both automatic and social reinforcement and occur with higher frequency during periods of negative emotion (Teng et al., 2004). The assumption is that if the individual can learn to recognize when a BFRB is about to occur and can inhibit the behavior, the automatic negative reinforcement contingency will be interrupted and the behavior will decrease. Procedurally, HRT looks almost identical when used to treat BFRBs and tics (Woods & Miltenberger, 1995). Awareness training and CR training are used to teach the individual to recognize discrete instances of the BFRB and interrupt its performance; prompting and social reinforcement are used to reinforce use of the CR; and social reactions reinforcing BFRB are systematically identified and modified. However, although HRT has been shown to be effective for reducing BFRBs in children (Miltenberger, Fuqua, & Woods, 1998), additional therapeutic strategies are sometimes necessary. For example, for some children, especially adolescents, BFRBs can function to reduce strong negative emotions. In such cases, simply blocking the BFRB and reinforcing a competing behavior may be insufficient and additional therapeutic strategies such as cognitive restructuring, mindfulness, or teaching emotional regulation skills might be necessary (Woods & Houghton, 2014).

Role of Parents in Treatment

Although behavioral treatments for tics are considered "self-management" interventions, parents are heavily involved in treatment. In addition to bringing the child to sessions and assisting the child with between-session therapy assignments, the parents are directly involved in treatment in several ways. First, during awareness training, parents, like the child, are taught to monitor their child's tics between sessions. Parent–child agreement regarding when and how many tics occurred provides important information about the child's level of tic awareness. Second, and perhaps most importantly, treatment involves teaching parents to appropriately respond to their child's tics. For example, parents are taught to supportively prompt and reinforce the child's use of the CR between sessions. Doing so is essential to the success of HRT, especially for young children. Likewise, as part of FBAI, parents assist with monitoring and identifying tic-exacerbating antecedents and consequences. Studies have shown that parental reactions to tics are among the most common tic-exacerbating consequences (Himle et al., 2014), so parent involvement in reducing these reactions is essential. This typically involves teaching parents to selectively ignore tics, decreasing tic-related accommodation (e.g., allowing the child to skip homework because they are ticcing), managing other tic-exacerbating variables (e.g., decreasing teasing from siblings, and reducing unnecessary stressors). Finally, parents are largely responsible for managing the child's reward program, including monitoring homework completion, delivering secondary reinforcers, and ensuring that the reward exchange takes place as agreed.

Other Variables Influencing Treatment

Assessment

A thorough assessment is essential prior to beginning EBTs for tics. Assessment typically begins with a consideration of common comorbid conditions that might take precedence in treatment and/or might interfere with EBTs for tics (see below). A thorough assessment of tic symptoms is also important and serves several purposes. First, it can help to differentiate tics from non-tic symptoms that are commonly confused with tics, including normal childhood rituals, body-focused repetitive behaviors, motor stereotypies, noncompliance, and compulsions associated with OCD. Second, tic severity rating scales can be used to quantify tic severity. The gold standard measure for assessing tic severity is the Yale-Global Tic Severity Scale (YGTSS; Leckman et al., 1989). The YGTSS is a semi-structured clinical interview designed to assess for the presence of common motor and vocal tics and rate their severity along several dimensions (frequency, intensity, complexity, interference, and impairment). Information provided by measures such as the YGTSS can be useful for creating a list of all of the tics that will be targeted in treatment as well as to monitor treatment progress. In addition, it is often useful to have the parent and child create a "tic hierarchy" in which they rank-order their tics from most to least bothersome. This can help to prioritize which tics to target first in treatment. It is generally recommended that the most bothersome tics be targeted first.

Comorbidity

Internalizing and externalizing comorbidity are exceptionally common with tic disorders. Large international samples have found that up to 85% of children with a tic disorder meet diagnostic criteria for at least one comorbid internalizing and/or externalizing psychiatric disorder, including attention-deficit/hyperactivity disorder (ADHD), obsessive-compulsive disorder/behaviors (OCD/OCB), anxiety and mood disorders, and oppositional defiant disorder (ODD; Freeman et al., 2000). Numerous studies have shown that comorbidity, especially ADHD, is associated with additional functional impairment and interference beyond that directly associated with tics (Storch et al., 2007). Although additional research is needed, clinical experience suggests that comorbidity can complicate treatment in several ways. For example, the awareness training component of HRT involves teaching the child to pay attention to fleeting premonitory urges so that they can better recognize when tics are about to occur. Children with ADHD often struggle with this aspect of treatment due to difficulties shifting, allocating, and sustaining attention. Likewise, children who are impulsive and inattentive can have difficulty engaging in, and maintaining, tic-suppression strategies. Finally, anxiety, depression, and oppositional behavior, all of which are relatively common in children with tic disorders, can decrease motivation and treatment compliance. When comorbid problems are present, they often need to be addressed, to the extent possible, prior to beginning behavioral treatment for tics.

Demographics

To our knowledge, no studies have examined the association between relevant demographic variables and treatment outcomes when using EBTs to treat tics. One demographic variable that is almost certainly related to treatment outcome, however, is the child's age. To date, most studies examining EBTs in children have included those nine years of age and older because it is assumed that younger children do not have the cognitive abilities to master HRT (however, a study examining an adapted version of CBIT for children ages four to eight is currently underway). Studies have also shown that the time and cost associated with treatment, as well as lack of trained providers (especially in underserved areas), are among the most frequently cited barriers that prevent families from receiving EBTs for tics (Woods, Conelea, & Himle, 2010).

Medication

Effective medications for treating tics are available. However, the most efficacious agents (e.g., typical and atypical neuroleptics) are usually only recommended for the most severe and treatment-resistant cases due to the potential for serious side effects (Scahill et al., 2006). No studies have directly compared behavioral and psychopharmacological interventions, or their combination. However, follow-up analyses of a large randomized controlled trial comparing CBIT to supportive psychotherapy found that medication status did not predict response to CBIT, suggesting that behavioral interventions and medication can be effectively combined without impacting treatment response (Sukhodolsky et al., 2017).

Conclusion

Efficacious, evidence-based treatments for tic disorders are available. The treatments with the most research support are HRT and the expanded CBIT treatment package that includes HRT as a primary component. An adapted version of exposure with response prevention has also shown promise. Procedures for increasing tic awareness and teaching and reinforcing tic inhibition are common across each of these interventions. Relaxation training and procedures for identifying and altering tic-exacerbating antecedents and consequences have also been shown to be effective and are included in most EBTs. Nonspecific elements, including psychoeducation, reward programs, and maintenance/relapse prevention are also commonly included and are important for improving treatment engagement and maximizing and maintaining treatment gains. Comorbidity is common in tic disorders and can complicate treatment, emphasizing the need for careful treatment planning.

Useful Resources

- Tourette Association of America's website at www.tourette.org
- Tourette's Action website at www.tourettes-action.org.uk
- Centers for Disease Control and Prevention website at www.cdc.gov/ncbddd/tourette/freematerials.html
- Comprehensive behavioral intervention for tics treatment manual: *Managing Tourette Syndrome: A Behavioral Intervention for Children and Adults: Therapist Guide* by Woods et al., Oxford University Press, 2008

References

American Psychiatric Association. (2013). *Diagnostic and statistical manual of mental disorders.* 5th edn. Washington, DC: American Psychiatric Association.

Azrin, N. H., & Nunn, R. G. (1973). Habit-reversal: A method of eliminating nervous habits and tics. *Behaviour Research and Therapy, 11*, 619–628.

Bloch, M. H., & Leckman, J. F. (2009). Clinical course of Tourette syndrome. *Journal of Psychosomatic Research, 6*, 497–501.

Carr, J., Bailey, J., Carr, C., & Coggin, A. (1996). The role of independent variable integrity in the behavioral management of Tourette syndrome. *Behavioral Interventions, 11*, 35–45.

Eddy, C. M., Rizzo, R., Gulisano, M., Agodi, A., Barchitta, M., Cali, P., . . . & Cavanna, A. E. (2011). Quality of life in young people with Tourette syndrome: A controlled study. *Journal of Neurology, 258*, 291–301.

Freeman, R. D., Fast, D. K., Burd, L., Kerbeshian, J., Robertson, M. M., & Sandor, P. (2000). An international perspective on Tourette syndrome: Selected findings from 3,500 individuals in 22 countries. *Developmental Medicine and Child Neurology, 42*(7), 436–447.

Himle, M. B., Capriotti, M. R., Hayes, L. P., Ramanujam, K., Scahill, L., Sukhodolsky, D. G., . . . & Piacentini, J. (2014). Variables associated with tic exacerbation in children with tic disorders. *Behavior Modification, 38*, 163–183.

Himle, M. B., & Woods, D. W. (2005). An experimental evaluation of tic suppression and the tic rebound effect. *Behaviour Research and Therapy, 43*(11), 1443–1451.

Himle, M. B., Woods, D. W., Conelea, C. A., Bauer, C. C., & Rice, K. A. (2007). Investigating the effects of tic suppression on premonitory urge ratings in children and adolescents with Tourette's syndrome, *Behaviour Research and Therapy, 45*, 2964–2976.

Hoogduin, K., Verdellen, C., & Cath, D. (1997). Exposure and response prevention in the treatment of Gilles de la Tourette's syndrome: Four case studies. *Clinical Psychology & Psychotherapy, 4*, 125–137.

Leckman, J. F., Riddle, M. A., Hardin, M. T., Ort, S. I., Swartz, K. L., Stevenson, J., & Cohen, D. J. (1989). The Yale Global Tic Severity Scale: Initial testing of a clinician-rated scale of tic severity. *Journal of the American Academy of Child & Adolescent Psychiatry, 28*, 566–573.

Miltenberger, R. G., & Fuqua, R.W. (1985). A comparison of contingent vs non-contingent competing response practice in the treatment of nervous habits. *Journal of Behavior Therapy and Experimental Psychiatry, 3*, 195–200.

Miltenberger, R. G., Fuqua, R. W., & McKinley, T. (1985). Habit reversal with muscle tics: Replication and component analysis. *Behavior Therapy, 16*, 39–50.

Miltenberger, R. G., Fuqua, R. W., & Woods, D. W. (1998). Applying behavior analysis to clinical problems: Review and analysis of habit reversal. *Journal of Applied Behavior Analysis, 31*, 447–469.

Muller-Vahl, K. R., Riemann, L., & Bokemeyer, S. (2014). Tourette patients' misbelief of a tic rebound is due to overall difficulties in reliable tic rating. *Journal of Psychosomatic Research, 76*, 472–476.

Murphy, T. K., Lewin, A. B., Storch, E. A., Stock, S., and the American Academy of Child & Adolescent Psychiatry. (2013). Practice parameters for the assessment and treatment of children and adolescents with tic disorders. *Journal of the American Academy of Child & Adolescent Psychiatry, 52*, 1341–1359.

Nussey, C., Pistrang, N., & Murphy, T. (2013). How does psychoeducation help? A review of the effects of providing information about Tourette syndrome and attention-deficit/hyperactivity disorder. *Child: Care, Health and Development, 39*, 617–627.

Peterson, A. L., & Azrin, N. H. (1992). An evaluation of behavioral treatments for Tourette syndrome. *Behaviour Research and Therapy, 30*, 167–174.

Peterson, A. L., McGuire, J. F., Wilhelm, S., Piacentini, J., Woods, D. W., Walkup, J. T., ... & Scahill, L. (2016). An empirical examination of symptom substitution associated with behavior therapy for Tourette's disorder. *Behavior Therapy, 47,* 29–41.

Piacentini, J. C., Woods, D. W., Scahill, L. D., Wilhelm, S., Peterson, A., Chang, S., ... & Walkup, J. T. (2010). Behavior therapy for children with Tourette syndrome: A randomized controlled trial. *Journal of the American Medical Association, 303,* 1929–1937.

Robertson, M. M. (2008). The prevalence and epidemiology of Gilles de la Tourette syndrome: Part 1: The epidemiological and prevalence studies. *Journal of Psychosomatic Research, 65,* 461–472.

Scahill, L., Erenberg, G., Berlin, C. M., Budman, C., Coffey, B. J., Jankovic, J., ... & Walkup, J. (2006). Contemporary assessment and pharmacotherapy of Tourette syndrome. *NeuroRX, 3,* 192–206.

Shprecher, D. R., Schrock, L., & Himle, M. B. (2014). Neurobehavioral aspects, pathophysiology, and management of Tourette syndrome. *Current Opinion in Neurology, 4,* 484–492.

Silva, R. R., Munoz, D. M., Barickman, J., & Friedhoff, A. J. (1995). Environmental factors and related fluctuation of symptoms in children and adolescents with Tourette's disorder. *Journal of Child Psychology and Psychiatry, 36,* 305–312.

Snider, L. A., Seligman, L. D., Ketchen, B. R., Levitt, S. J., Bates, L. R., Garvey, M. A., & Swedo, S. E. (2002). Tics and problem behaviors in schoolchildren: Prevalence, characterization, and associations. *Pediatrics, 110,* 331–336.

Storch, E. A., Lack, C. W., Simons, L. E., Goodman, W. K., Murphy, T. K., & Geffken, G. R. (2007). A measure of functional impairment in youth with tics. *Journal of Pediatric Psychology, 32,* 950–959.

Sukhodolsky, D. G., Woods, D. W., Piacentini, J., Wilhelm, S., Peterson, A. L., Katsovich, L., ... & Scahill, L. (2017). Moderators and predictors of response to behavior therapy for tics in Tourette syndrome. *Neurology, 88,* 1029–1036.

Teng, E. J., Woods, D. W., Marcks, B. A., & Twohig, M. P. (2004). Body-focused repetitive behaviors: The proximal and distal effects of affective variables on behavioral expression. *Journal of Psychopathology and Behavioral Assessment, 26,* 55–64.

Verdellen, C. W. J., Keijsers, G. P. J., Cath, D. C., & Hoogduin, C. A. L. (2004). Exposure with response prevention versus habit reversal in Tourette's syndrome: A controlled study. *Behaviour Research and Therapy, 42,* 501–511.

Verdellen, C., van de Griendt, J., Murphy, T., & the ESSTS Guidelines Group. (2011). European clinical guidelines for Tourette syndrome and other tic disorders. Part III: Behavioural and psychosocial interventions. *European Child & Adolescent Psychiatry, 4,* 197–207.

Watson, T. S., & Sterling, H. E. (1998). Brief functional analysis and treatment of a vocal tic. *Journal of Applied Behavior Analysis, 31,* 471–474.

Wilson, V. B., Mitchell, S. H., Musser, E. D., Schmitt, C. F., & Nigg, J. T. (2011). Delay discounting of reward in ADHD: Application in young children. *Journal of Child Psychology and Psychiatry, 52,* 256–264.

Woods, D. W., Conelea, C. A., & Himle, M. B. (2010). Behavior therapy for Tourette's disorder: Utilization in a community sample and an emerging area of practice. *Professional Psychology: Research and Practice, 41,* 518–525.

Woods, D. W., & Houghton, D. C. (2014). Evidence-based psychosocial treatments for pediatric body-focused repetitive behavior disorders. *Journal of Clinical Child & Adolescent Psychology, 45,* 227–240.

Woods, D. W., & Miltenberger, R. G. (1995). Habit reversal: A review of applications and variations. *Journal of Behavior Therapy and Experimental Psychiatry, 26,* 123–131.

Woods, D. W., Miltenberger, R. G., & Lumley, V. A. (1996). Sequential application of major habit-reversal components to treat motor tics in children. *Journal of Applied Behavior Analysis, 29,* 483–493.

Woods, D. W., Piacentini, J. C., Chang, S. W., Deckersbach, T., Ginsburg, G. S., Peterson, A. L., . . . & Wilhelm, S. (2008). *Managing Tourette Syndrome: A behavioral intervention for children and adults: Therapist Guide.* New York: Oxford University Press.

Woods, D. W., Piacentini, J., Himle, M. B., & Chang, S. (2005). Premonitory urge for tics scale (PUTS): Initial psychometric results and examination of the premonitory urge phenomenon in youths with tic disorders. *Journal of Developmental & Behavioral Pediatrics, 26,* 397–403.

7

Psychosis

Sophie Browning, Anca Alba, Karen Bracegirdle, and Suzanne Jolley

Psychosis is an umbrella term for changes in thoughts, feelings, and behaviors that occur in affective, neurocognitive, and personality disorders, but are most characteristic of schizophrenia spectrum diagnoses, including schizophrenia, schizoaffective, and delusional disorders (American Psychiatric Association, 2013; World Health Organisation [WHO], 1993). Symptoms cluster into positive (perceptions and beliefs that appear unusual or unfounded to others); negative (lack of motivation and emotional blunting); disorganized (disrupted cognitive and emotional processes); and affective (high and low mood, affective dysregulation) (Liddle, 1987; Reininghaus et al., 2016). Adult prevalence and incidence rates are 1% and 0.1 to 0.4 per 1,000 population per year, respectively (Kirkbride et al., 2012). Childhood onset is rare, but is associated with poor outcome and medical comorbidity (Chan, 2017; Giannitelli et al., 2017). Incidence peaks during late adolescence and early adulthood; overall prevalence in under 18s is 0.4% (United Kingdom National Institute for Health and Care Excellence [NICE], 2013). The global personal (physical morbidity, early death, poor quality of life) and societal (cost of formal and informal care, lost productivity) burden of schizophrenia spectrum psychosis is high (Charlson et al., 2016; Jin & Mosweu, 2017).

Psychotic symptoms also occur in the general population with prevalence rates of 8% (range 2–40%) in adults, and 15% (range 5–95%) in children, and are considered to be a phenotypic expression of the range of biopsychosocial risk factors for psychosis (Kelleher et al., 2012; van Os & Reininghaus, 2016). Methodology influences reported prevalence: multi-item self-report measures suggest higher rates than clinical interviews and diagnostically based brief screening assessments (Kelleher et al., 2011; Kline et al., 2015). Psychotic symptoms are persistent and associated with distress, emotional and behavioral problems, and functional impairment in around 20% of cases, becoming increasingly specific predictors of progression to an "at-risk mental state" (ARMS; increased likelihood of developing clinical psychosis), and future psychosis from around 14 years (Addington et al., 2011; NICE, 2013; Schimmelmann et al., 2015; Schmidt et al., 2015; van Os & Murray, 2013).

Etiology and Theoretical Underpinnings of Treatment

Service Context

Adverse social and functional outcomes associated with psychosis are evident from first episode, may precede ARMS presentations, and are not restricted to those who go on to develop psychosis (Díaz-Caneja et al., 2015; Fusar-Poli et al., 2015; Laurens & Cullen, 2016; Woodberry et al., 2016). Treatment guidelines in Europe and the UK therefore recommend cognitive-behavioral individual and family-based interventions at any stage of presentation, to reduce current distress and impairment associated with psychotic symptoms, and to treat comorbid conditions (cognitive-behavioral therapy for psychosis [CBTp]; and family intervention for psychosis, FIp; NICE, 2013, 2014; Schmidt et al., 2015). Similar psychological therapy recommendations are made for the treatment of psychosis in adults in the United States and across the world (Dixon et al., 2010; Gaebel, Riesbeck, & Wobrock, 2011; WHO, 2015). Psychotherapy is usually offered as part of a broad biopsychosocial care plan, and, from mid-adolescence, should be in specialized psychosis services. Early intervention psychosis (EIP) services work intensively with people for the first two to three years following a first episode of psychosis, which is thought to be a "critical period" in determining future outcome (Breitborde et al., 2017).

Earlier intervention for help-seeking ARMS presentations, identified by standardized assessments, aims to reduce transition to psychosis (Fusar-Poli & Schulze-Lutter, 2016; Thompson et al., 2015). Children under 14 years are usually treated in Child and Adolescent Mental Health Services (CAMHS), sometimes with a specialist psychosis worker, but the interface between CAMHS and EIP is often problematic, resulting in longer durations of untreated psychosis for younger presentations (Joa et al., 2009; Tiffin & Welsh, 2013). As shorter duration of untreated psychosis is linked to better outcome, assertive identification and treatment have been advocated (Sommer et al., 2016). As younger children tend not to seek help themselves, and may not report their experiences unless directly asked, routine screening in CAMHS has been suggested (Laurens & Cullen, 2016). A brief nine-item screen for "unusual experiences" (UEs; the term preferred to "psychotic" by many young people and families in consultations), which includes ratings for associated distress/functional impairment, has shown good acceptability to young people, families, and staff (Ames et al., 2014; Gin et al., 2017; Laurens et al., 2007, 2011, 2012).

Individual Cognitive-Behavioral Models of Psychosis

In adults, the development, maintenance, and remission of psychosis has been linked to a range of psychosocial factors which may interact with genetic and neurodevelopmental vulnerabilities (Howes et al., 2017; Owen, Sawa, & Mortensen, 2016). These include social factors (adverse events, interpersonal relationships); cognitive and emotional processes, including thinking style, beliefs about the self, the world and other people; difficulties with attention and working memory; and behaviors such as avoidance (Bebbington, 2015). Importantly, many psychosocial mechanisms are common between nonclinical unusual experiences and clinical psychosis, supporting a central tenet of cognitive models: that psychosis can be understood, and treated, by applying normal psychological processes (Peters et al., 2016). Cognitive models highlight external, personal, and threatening appraisals of experiences, influenced by cognitive and emotional processes, as causal in the development of clinical disorder (Garety & Hardy, 2017). CBTp aims to promote flexibility in appraisals, to reduce distress and disability (Johns et al., 2014). Research is limited in under 18s, but early studies support the extension of adult therapy recommendations, including to presentations of unusual experiences accompanied by distress or adverse life impact (UEDs; Laurens & Cullen, 2016).

Family- and Caregiver-Focused Cognitive-Behavioral Models in Psychosis

Family interventions in adults with psychosis draw on a psychosis-specific cognitive model of caregiving (Kuipers, Onwumere, & Bebbington, 2010). Caregivers' appraisals of psychosis influence their emotional and behavioral reactions toward the person with psychosis. Blaming appraisals are linked with critical and hostile communication. Assuming no control can lead to undermining by overcaring and limiting independence. Such interactions are classified as "expressed emotion." Research reliably demonstrates better outcomes for people with psychosis who remain in contact with families, especially if expressed emotion is low, though this varies with culture (Jansen, Gleeson, & Cotton, 2015; Kuipers, Jolley, & Onwumere, 2016; Onwumere & Kuipers, 2017). FIp aims to change appraisals of psychosis, by offering psychoeducation with individually tailored discussion, and promoting active problem-solving and independent activity (Claxton, Onwumere, & Fornells-Ambrojo, 2017). When the individual with psychosis is unable or unwilling to engage, caregivers may be offered intervention alone (Yesufu-Udechuku et al., 2015). Similar family factors are linked with UEs in the general population and increasing psychosis risk (O'Brien, Miklowitz, & Cannon, 2015; Premkumar et al., 2015; Wüsten & Lincoln, 2017). In earlier childhood, however, aspects of expressed emotion may represent closer involvement and parental care, and have less adverse impact (Tobin, 2013). Cognitive-behavioral family intervention models have yet to be systematically tested in CAMHS, and family therapy, unadapted for the specific difficulties of psychosis, is often the main provision.

Brief Overview of Evidence-Based Treatments

There are no large-scale studies of child-specific psychological interventions for psychosis or unusual experiences. Studies of the at-risk mental state may include a small proportion of young people, rarely below mid-adolescence. Treatment recommendations for under 18s rely on the adult and youth (up to 35 years) evidence base. For CBTp, current evidence suggests that interventions are cost-effective, with small but consistent improvements across a range of psychotic symptoms, affective and functioning outcomes, and, from mid-adolescence, reduced transition from an at-risk presentation to clinical psychosis (NICE, 2014, 2013). Improvements are found for both delusions and hallucinations, including in people not taking medication, or with medication-resistant symptoms (Burns, Erickson, & Brenner, 2014; Morrison et al., 2014; Thomas et al., 2014; van der Gaag, Valmaggia, & Smit, 2014). Recent reviews indicate a need to improve interventions for negative symptoms (Remington et al., 2016) and for trauma in the context of psychosis (Swan et al., 2017). Groups may confer additional nonspecific benefits, but evidence is stronger for individual interventions (NICE, 2014). Interventions targeting particular psychological mechanisms, identified in pre-therapy research, may be briefer with greater treatment effects than heterogeneous approaches (Birchwood et al., 2014; Hazell et al., 2016; Mehl, Werner, & Lincoln, 2015), but often require a carefully selected subgroup, limiting routine implementation. "Third-wave" cognitive-behavioral approaches (such as acceptance and commitment therapy), which focus on the relationship the person has with their distressing symptoms/experiences, rather than the experiences themselves, are broadly applicable across presentations, and may effect change in fewer sessions than traditional CBTp (Dindo, Van Liew, & Arch, 2017; Louise et al., 2017).

UK guidance also recommends routinely offered arts therapies (Attard & Larkin, 2016), with supportive psychotherapy and counselling available if preferred. Cognitive remediation therapy (CRT) is recommended to improve vocational outcomes, may improve negative symptoms, and, as cognitive difficulties are a key predictor of transition from an at-risk state, may play a particular role in ARMS services (Bora et al., 2014; Cella et al., 2017; Chan, Hirai, & Tsoi, 2015). FIp has a strong evidence base, particularly for reducing relapse, including in early psychosis, and may contribute to reducing transition in adolescents and young adults with ARMS presentations (Calvo et al., 2014, 2015; Claxton, Onwumere, & Fornells-Ambrojo, 2017; Kuipers, Jolley, & Onwumere, 2016; NICE, 2013, 2014; Miklowitz et al., 2014). FIp may require fewer developmental adaptations than CBTp, where effects may be no better than supportive interventions if treatment is not developmentally tailored (Browning et al., 2013; Haddock et al., 2006; Okuzawa et al., 2014; Stain et al., 2016; Thompson et al., 2015).

Adapting Interventions to a Public Health Context

There has been increasing interest internationally in school-based programs to improve mental health resilience and promote wellbeing (WHO, 2013). To date, interventions have shown little impact, particularly for the most vulnerable, and no program has yet incorporated work on unusual experiences, despite their importance as a transdiagnostic vulnerability factor (Fazel et al., 2014). CUES-Ed is an eight-session, manualized cognitive-behavioral mental health promotion intervention for seven- to ten-year-olds, designed for whole-class delivery in schools by mental health clinicians (teachers are strongly encouraged to participate). Sessions comprise games, puzzles, illusions, videos, and discussion, with between-session workbooks and diaries (e.g., recording sleep, mood, or activity). Engaging characters, high-specification graphics, and developmentally tailored language, with repetition, summaries, and links to real-life situations, promote engagement and retention. Key messages include promoting physical wellbeing to "keep our brains amazing"; recognizing signs ("cues") about feeling upset and responding appropriately; understanding the links between thoughts, feelings, and behaviors; and learning how, through senses and thoughts, our brains can nevertheless make mistakes and play tricks on us. All children complete measures of wellbeing and emotional and behavioral difficulties before and after the intervention: the service aim is to improve outcomes for children scoring in the problem range on these measures (i.e., those most in need). Reaching the most vulnerable young people, without singling out or labeling, but rather by teaching skills to the whole class, is inherently normalizing and destigmatizing. Recent in-service evaluation suggests pre–post improvement of small to medium effect size, and improvement in comparison to a naturalistic waiting list (a class due to receive the intervention shortly) of small effect size, in those children most in need. Qualitative feedback from over 700 children and 27 teachers highlights improvements in coping, behavior, attention, and emotional regulation, using a wider range of strategies including more cognitive strategies. Controlled evaluation is planned.

Components of Evidence-Based Treatments

With adults, therapy adherence rating scales, competence frameworks, and a Delphi study of experts have been used to identify common components of CBTp and FIp (Fowler, Rollinson, & French, 2011; Johns et al., 2014; Kuipers, Jolley, & Onwumere, 2016; Morrison & Barrett, 2010; Onwumere et al., 2009; Roth & Pilling, 2013). Engagement and developing a trusting, collaborative, therapeutic relationship are central. Communicating warmth, empathy, and positive regard, respecting and validating different perspectives, and explicitly acknowledging strengths and successes supports rapport building. Therapists offer intervention assertively, being flexible about difficulties with attendance and time-keeping, going to lengths to tailor interventions to the particular needs of service users and caregivers, which may change within and between sessions. The pace, complexity, and duration of sessions, and the use of prompts and materials, may need adjusting to accommodate difficulties with memory, attention, and coherence of thought and speech, often alongside adjustments for comorbid autism spectrum presentations, or learning disability. Therapists establish structure through a collaborative focus on goals, maintained through agenda-setting and adherence, frequent "checking in," between-session activities, "bridging" from session to session and across the course of therapy, and, in FIp, managing communication between family members. Assessment aims to understand the day-to-day impact of difficulties, within a framework of normal psychological processes, formulating specific examples of experience—appraisal–reaction links. Formulations can be extended to overarching difficulties as much as is helpful or acceptable. Change focuses on modifying appraisals of and reactions to difficulties, facilitating movement toward identified goals. Perceived risks of change can be weighed against potential gains, using motivational approaches. The aim is to develop strategies for considering new information and trying out new responses, which can be generalized beyond therapy. Predictors of positive outcome in treatment trials include therapist competence and genuineness, a more behavioral than cognitive focus to the work, and, in an at-risk group, individualized formulation and homework setting (Flach et al., 2015; Jung et al., 2015; Wykes et al., 2008).

There are, as yet, no studies of effective therapy components for exclusively adolescent populations. The remainder of the chapter details recent work, highlighting adaptations to adult work, drawing on clinical experience with adolescents with psychosis or unusual experiences. Evaluation to date, through the CUES (Coping with Unusual ExperienceS) clinical research group, comprises a case series, uncontrolled and controlled pilot studies, and a randomized controlled trial underway (Browning et al., 2013; Maddox et al., 2013).

Facilitating Identity Development

Establishing a coherent sense of self and identity is a key developmental task in adolescence (Erikson, 1963). The less opportunity to develop an adaptive sense of self, to draw on in adjusting to the health threat of psychosis, the greater the potential impact. Therapy often focuses explicitly on understanding the developing self in relation to the experience of psychosis (Jackson et al., 1998); addressing meaning about "me, who I am, and how I fit in the world," hopes, goals, and future aspirations; and repairing and promoting peer relationships, as these play an important role in the developing sense of self (Harter, 1999).

Psychoeducation to Reduce Stigma

Young people commonly have misconceptions about psychosis, drawn from portrayals in the media, or experience of an unwell family member. Psychoeducation with the child's network may reduce stigma from others. Internalized stigma impacts more on individual outcomes; resilience-building work with the young person may help (Schnyder et al., 2017; Wood, Byrne, & Morrison, 2017; Wood et al., 2016).

Facilitating Cognitive Development

Cognitive development is ongoing during adolescence: abstract, hypothetical thinking, metacognition (thinking about thinking), perspective-taking (another person, oneself in another context), and judging potential outcomes may all be particularly difficult (Piaget & Inhelder, 1958). Concrete tasks can scaffold formal operational thinking, alongside a greater (but not exclusive) emphasis on behavioral, rather than cognitive components ("big B, little c"). Schemas develop during adolescence, so are less likely to play a causal role, but their consequent amenability to change may make them a good target of therapy to reduce persistence and future vulnerability (Noone et al., 2015). Hasty and inflexible reasoning, associated with delusions, is characteristic of earlier childhood, but comparable to adults by adolescence (Hassanali et al., 2015).

Operationalizing Emotion Language

Therapists need to adjust the content and complexity of language (e.g., word length, frequency of use, sentence complexity, degree of abstraction) to the individual child (Stallard, 2005). Further idiosyncratic adjustment may be needed to accommodate changes in mental state, or particular therapy topics (e.g., preferences for simpler or more formal language to discuss distressing events). Children may use stock phrases to mask poor comprehension, and therapists can use open questioning and nonverbal cues to gauge understanding. Emotional literacy (recognizing and describing feelings) may be poorly developed. Operationalizing emotion language with visual aids, such as cartoon strips with speech and thought bubbles, can be useful. Therapists need to be sensitive to adolescent mores. For example, "practice task" is better than "homework"; something "bothering" or "getting to you" are better than being "scared." Preferences are best established by directly asking the young person.

Promoting Engagement and Establishing Goals

Young people are often unused to collaborative relationships with adults, and may need explicit socializing and time to adjust to the focus on their own views and wishes, and to therapists clarifying, summarizing, checking out, and eliciting feedback. Therapists may need to work harder to hold young people's attention, adjust the cognitive load accordingly, and maintain a productive balance of work and play. Talking through a typical day, identifying areas of impact, current explanations of experiences, and reactions establishes a focus of the work.

Treatment goals should involve realistic, manageable, day-to-day changes to improve wellbeing or functioning. More substantial life goals are validated and supported, while explaining the need for an immediate focus that could be achieved over the next few weeks. Goals are designed to be SMART (specific, measurable, achievable, realistic, and time limited; Doran, 1981), while accommodating the changing preoccupations often characteristic of adolescence (e.g., "having 30 minutes each day to do something nice for me, instead of listening to the voices," "something nice" can change each week). Help is often sought by parents or teachers, rather than the adolescent themselves. Differences in perspective on the problem are explicitly discussed, and extra time may be needed to identify goals that make sense for the young person. Session check-ins and between-session tasks include reference to the young person's home, school, and peer context, and to liaison appropriate to developmental context (e.g., for younger children, regular discussion with parental responsibility holders).

Developing a Shared Formulation

Assessment informs the development of a shared understanding of difficulties to drive intervention. In early presentations, when the problem history is accessible and adjustment is key, emotional processing and developing a helpful narrative may be a useful start. For more entrenched or harder-to-talk-about problems, an initial focus on a specific goal – bringing in narrative and processing work over time, as relevant – may be more productive. "Stress buckets" are useful tools to map day-to-day examples, and the development and maintenance of the overarching difficulties, using taps above the bucket to represent factors building stress, and letting water out of the bucket as coping mechanisms. Hoses can be used to show water returning to the bucket for short-term strategies increasing stress in the longer term (like avoidance or substance misuse). Too high a water level in the bucket makes us feel bad and gets in the way of what we want to do. Detail and complexity (schematic beliefs, traumatic events, unusual experiences) can be added gradually over time: initial formulations should not be cognitively or emotionally overwhelming.

Four key questions (Browning et al., 2013) provide structure to map out vulnerability factors ("Why me?"), triggers ("Why now?"), maintaining factors ("Why still?"), and protective factors ('What helps?'). The model is matched to the young person's perspective, and draws on normal psychological processes. Care is taken not to invalidate strongly held beliefs. For example, therapists may talk about how having scary things happen to us makes us look out for scary things in the future, and treat the world, or other people, as scary or threatening, to keep ourselves safe, but can also mean missing out on things we want to do. Checking out if something we would like to do is always as dangerous as we might think, or if there are ways to make ourselves feel, or be, safer, so we could take a step toward doing it, will form the intervention strategy. Pie charts, showing the relative contributions of different explanatory factors, can facilitate understanding and discussion of alternative perspectives. Multiple charts can be compared to facilitate communication about areas of common ground and difference in family work. Standardized and individually tailored psychoeducational materials, about psychosis, medication and other treatment, unusual experiences, substance use, or any other aspects of the young person's presentation can also be reviewed for potentially helpful new information in developing different pie charts, and elaborating the stress bucket formulation.

Behavioral Change Techniques

A functional analysis of the setting conditions, triggers, and maintaining factors for unusual experiences or associated problems can help identify potentially effective coping strategies. These may include attentional strategies (e.g., distraction, mindfulness, grounding), physiological strategies (e.g., relaxation, exercise), cognitive strategies (e.g., coping or positive self-talk), or behavioral strategies (e.g., confronting or briefly avoiding). Often strategies have been tried before, but not systematically, or may need modification to be more effective. Behavioral activation (gradually increasing pleasurable or achievement-oriented activity to improve mood) and graded exposure (gradually approaching a feared stimulus to overcome anxious avoidance) are commonly used early in therapy to manage comorbid depression and anxiety. Assertiveness or other social skills training can help reduce stress and build positive interactions with peers. Problem-solving can be a simple strategy for dealing with difficult situations, particularly social situations, and can be linked with a "stop, think, do" traffic light cue card. For example, noticing an unpleasant feeling, we can stop, then think of two or three things to reduce the unpleasant feeling, then do (or not do) one of these, see what happens, and use this information for next time (e.g., to build a list of what helps and what doesn't in different situations). Creativity (e.g., using video clips, photo-strip stories, and illustrative tasks and games) is needed to make the work appealing, engaging, and memorable for each child (Browning et al., 2013; Maddox et al., 2013).

Identifying Cognitive Biases

Complex cognitive work is often difficult for younger adolescents, and may consequently be avoided by therapists, in favor of behavioral interventions. One example is "Top Brain Training" to introduce cognitive biases as something all people have, influencing thoughts, interpretation of the world around us, and decision making. Biases may be part of everyday human reasoning, or linked with our own particular experiences or reasoning processes. They can be, or might once have been, helpful, but sometimes trip us up, so that we make unhelpful appraisals and react in unhelpful ways. Biases particularly associated with psychosis include: jumping to conclusions (making probabilistic decisions on the basis of minimal evidence); belief inflexibility (not considering the possibility of being mistaken, rejecting or accommodating contradictory evidence, rather than changing beliefs, and difficulty generating plausible alternative explanations); externalizing biases (a tendency to blame others, rather than oneself or circumstances for bad outcomes); and difficulty identifying the intentions of others (Garety & Freeman, 2013). The few studies investigating these biases in childhood suggest that they are broadly similar in adolescence, but further research is needed (Ames et al., 2014; Hassanali et al., 2015). Visual illusions are used to illustrate how our "amazing brains" can play tricks on us. This may be a helpful reframe for unusual experiences. Slowing down, and gathering more evidence/information helps us compensate for our reasoning biases, and makes us less likely to miss useful information or make a hasty decision, especially when we are trying to make sense of complex or unclear information (Moritz, Woodward, & Balzan, 2016). Behavioral experiments are used to check out old or new ideas, and gather evidence/new information, but careful planning and a graded approach may be needed to avoid overarousal and retriggering of psychotic symptoms (Bennett-Levy et al., 2004).

Cognitive Change Methods

Cognitive strategies (finding, catching, and changing negative thoughts, schemas, and cognitive biases) often need to be presented concretely. For example, a strategy could include discussing a scene from a popular television show and asking the young person about each character's thoughts, thinking "traps," what will happen next and what they could do, then moving to imagine themselves in the character's shoes and how they would think, feel, and react, before asking about specific examples to identify the thoughts, images, and beliefs underlying their own difficulties. Modeling and live role-play are usually more productive than abstract discussion. Alternative ways of thinking, to help the young person move closer to their goals, can be accessed using cognitive restructuring techniques, asking "magic questions" (e.g., What's the evidence? Am I jumping to conclusions? Do I know the whole truth? Even if it is like that, am I overreacting? What would a friend think?). Therapists will likely need to suggest possible alternatives for consideration, because young people may struggle to generate them (Browning et al., 2013; Maddox et al., 2013).

Relapse Prevention and Staying Well Plans

Adolescents often need extra help to think back to when things were difficult, or forward to potential future difficulties, and to identify the nuances of early, middle, and late signs of difficulty, who may spot these, and what could be done (Birchwood et al., 1989). Again, concrete scenarios and specific perspective-taking exercises are more effective than discussion alone, and the young person's network (e.g., family, school, and CAMHS) should be involved as much as possible, in both developing and implementing the plan.

Role of Parents in Treatment

Young people usually live with family members or other caregivers, and, according to developmental stage, rely on family for a range of needs. Establishing helpful, developmentally appropriate involvement of parental figures is prioritized, accommodating the likely differences in familial appraisals of and responses to psychosis according to age and family context (Landa et al., 2015).

Direct parental involvement in therapy is common for younger children, and parents may be enlisted as informal co-therapists in individual work. Family sessions, directed toward improved parental understanding of the child's difficulties, with a view to changing unhelpful appraisals and promoting more adaptive problem-solving and coping strategies, are an important adjunct to individual therapy (Maddox et al., 2013). FIp principles can also inform liaison with schools to facilitate understanding and management of a child's condition and needs, ensuring the young person keeps up with educational and other opportunities to successfully reintegrate.

Other Variables Influencing Treatment

Assessment

Assessment is often in the context of a wider CAMHS structure, and it includes aspects of development, and home/school/peer functioning as well as likes and dislikes, hobbies and interests. Standardized assessments of childhood psychopathology are often suitable for use throughout adolescence, and can be supplemented by screening measures of unusual experiences. Assessments designed for adults may be considered for older adolescents (16–18 years) but their length, linguistic complexity, and focus (prioritizing emotional over behavioral problems) limit applicability (Law & Wolpert, 2014).

Comorbidity

Unusual experiences are transdiagnostic and may occur across a wide range of clinical and neurodevelopmental conditions, as well as forming a focus of treatment in their own right. Anxiety, mood, attachment, and spectrum disorder are common comorbidities, alongside emerging personality disorders, self-harming behavior, and suicidality (Kelleher, Cederlöf, & Lichtenstein, 2014). Clinical psychosis is characterized by similar comorbidity, with a third to half of presentations co-occurring with each of anxiety, depression, and personality disorders (NICE, 2013, 2014).

Demographics

General population surveys indicate increased incidence of unusual experiences with emotional, behavioral, and neurodevelopmental problems in boys and in Black African and Caribbean ethnic groups, in line with increased psychosis incidence, as well as in younger children (Laurens et al., 2011). However, girls are more likely to self-report distressing unusual experiences (Gin et al., 2017). Routine screening may therefore need adjustment to identify those who could potentially benefit from earlier interventions to reduce psychosis risk.

Medication

Treatment with medication is not recommended for unusual experiences occurring in the absence of a clinical psychosis, but may be used to treat a comorbid condition. Medical recommendations for the treatment of childhood psychosis are summarized in the UK NICE guidance and its updates (NICE, 2013).

Conclusion

While evidence-based interventions for psychosis with adults are well established, effects remain small for CBTp, implementation difficulties are long-standing (Ince, Haddock, & Tai, 2015), and research to refine interventions and models of delivery is ongoing. The evidence base for adapting adult work to adolescents remains limited: child-specific studies are needed to explicitly test the applicability of models and therapy approaches, identifying areas of difference for further investigation, and appropriate service structures to effectively manage early, pre-ARMS, interventions between CAMHS and specialist psychosis services. Advanced therapist skills are needed to work effectively with this group: training for practitioners and supervisors needs significant development, with implications for the CAMHS workforce. Notwithstanding the substantial scale of the work ahead, current interest in this area is high, and the synergy between epidemiological, early intervention, therapy development, and implementation research offers exciting opportunities to make real changes to improve the lives of these vulnerable young people over the coming years.

Useful Resources

- *Headspace*: National Youth Mental Health Foundation in Australia, providing early intervention mental health services to 12–25 year-olds. www.headspace.org.au
- *Metacognitive training (MCT)*: interactive resources suitable for "Top Brain Training," developed by Steffen Moritz and colleagues and generously made available in several languages for research and clinical use. https://clinical-neuropsychology.de/metacognitive_training-psychosis/
- *Voice Collective*: Support children and young people who hear voices, see visions, or have other unusual sensory experiences. voicecollective.co.uk
- *Young Minds*: UK charity for young people's mental health. (Free booklet: Browning, Corrigall, Blair, & Wragg, 2003. *Want to know more about psychosis? A Young Minds Booklet*). www.youngminds.org.uk
- *MindEd*: free advice and information on managing mental health issues in children and young people. www.minded.org.uk

References

Addington, J., Cornblatt, B. A., Cadenhead, K. S., Cannon, T. D., McGlashan, T. H., Perkins, D. O., . . . & Heinssen, R. (2011). At clinical high risk for psychosis: Outcome for nonconverters. *American Journal of Psychiatry*, *168*(8), 800–805.

American Psychiatric Association. (2013). *Diagnostic and statistical manual of mental disorders*. 5th edn. Washington, DC: American Psychiatric Association.

Ames, C. S., Jolley, S., Laurens, K. R., Maddox, L., Corrigall, R., Browning, S., . . . & Kuipers, E.. (2014). Modelling psychosocial influences on the distress and impairment caused by psychotic-like experiences in children and adolescents. *European Child & Adolescent Psychiatry*, *23*(8), 715–722.

Attard, A., & Larkin, M. (2016). Art therapy for people with psychosis: A narrative review of the literature. *The Lancet Psychiatry*, *3*(11), 1067–1078.

Bebbington, P. E. (2015). Unravelling psychosis: Psychosocial epidemiology, mechanism and meaning. *Shanghai Archives of Psychiatry*, *27*(2), 70–81.

Bennett-Levy, J. E., Butler, G. E., Fennell, M. E., Hackman, A. E., Mueller, M. E., & Westbrook, D. E. (2004). *Oxford guide to behavioural experiments in cognitive therapy*. Oxford: Oxford University Press.

Birchwood, M., Michail, M., Meaden, A., Tarrier, N., Lewis, S., Wykes, T., . . . & Peters, E. (2014). Cognitive behaviour therapy to prevent harmful compliance with command hallucinations (COMMAND): A randomised controlled trial. *The Lancet Psychiatry*, *1*(1), 23–33.

Birchwood, M., Smith, J., Macmillan, F., Hogg, B., Prasad, R., Harvey, C., & Bering, S. (1989). Predicting relapse in schizophrenia: The development and implementation of an early signs monitoring system using patients and families as observers. *Psychological Medicine*, *19*, 649–656.

Bora, E., Lin, A., Wood, S. J., Yung, A. R., McGorry, P. D., & Pantelis, C. (2014). Cognitive deficits in youth with familial and clinical high risk to psychosis: A systematic review and meta-analysis. *Acta Psychiatrica Scandinavica*, *130*(1), 1–15.

Breitborde, N. J., Moe, A. M., Ered, A., Ellman, L. M., & Bell, E. K. (2017). Optimizing psychosocial interventions in first-episode psychosis: Current perspectives and future directions. *Psychology Research and Behavior Management*, *10*, 119.

Browning, S., Corrigall, R., Garety, P., Emsley, R., & Jolley, S. (2013). Psychological interventions for adolescent psychosis: A pilot controlled trial in routine care. *European Psychiatry, 28*(7), 423–426.

Burns, A. M., Erickson, D. H., & Brenner, C. A. (2014). Cognitive-behavioral therapy for medication-resistant psychosis: A meta-analytic review. *Psychiatric Services, 65*(7), 874–880.

Calvo, A., Moreno, M., Ruiz-Sancho, A., Rapado-Castro, M., Moreno, C., Sánchez-Gutiérrez, T., ... & Mayoral, M. (2014). Intervention for adolescents with early-onset psychosis and their families: A randomized controlled trial. *Journal of the American Academy of Child & Adolescent Psychiatry, 53*(6), 688–696.

Calvo, A., Moreno, M., Ruiz-Sancho, A., Rapado-Castro, M., Moreno, C., Sánchez-Gutiérrez, T., ... & Mayoral, M. (2015). Psychoeducational group intervention for adolescents with psychosis and their families: A two-year follow-up. *Journal of the American Academy of Child & Adolescent Psychiatry, 54*(12), 984–990.

Cella, M., Preti, A., Edwards, C., Dow, T., & Wykes, T. (2017). Cognitive remediation for negative symptoms of schizophrenia: A network meta-analysis. *Clinical Psychology Review, 52*, 43–51.

Chan, J. Y., Hirai, H. W., & Tsoi, K. K. (2015). Can computer-assisted cognitive remediation improve employment and productivity outcomes of patients with severe mental illness? A meta-analysis of prospective controlled trials. *Journal of Psychiatric Research, 68*, 293–300.

Chan, V. (2017). Schizophrenia and psychosis: Diagnosis, current research trends, and model treatment approaches with implications for transitional age youth. *Child and Adolescent Psychiatric Clinics of North America, 26*(2), 341–366.

Charlson, F. J., Baxter, A. J., Dua, T., Degenhardt, L., Whiteford, H. A., & Vos, T. (2016). Excess mortality from mental, neurological, and substance use disorders in the global burden of disease study 2010. *Mental, Neurological, and Substance Use Disorders, 41*.

Claxton, M., Onwumere, J., & Fornells-Ambrojo, M. (2017). Do family interventions improve outcomes in early psychosis? A systematic review and meta-analysis. *Frontiers in Psychology, 8*, 371. doi:10.3389/fpsyg.2017.00371

Díaz-Caneja, C. M., Pina-Camacho, L., Rodríguez-Quiroga, A., Fraguas, D., Parellada, M., & Arango, C. (2015). Predictors of outcome in early-onset psychosis: A systematic review. *npj Schizophrenia, 1*, 14005. doi:10.1038/npjschz.2014.5

Dindo, L., Van Liew, J. R., & Arch, J. J. (2017). Acceptance and commitment therapy: A transdiagnostic behavioral intervention for mental health and medical conditions. *Neurotherapeutics, 14*, 1–8. doi:10.1007/s13311-017-0521-3

Dixon, L. B., Dickerson, F., Bellack, A. S., Bennett, M., Dickinson, D., Goldberg, R. W., ... & Peer, J. (2010). The 2009 schizophrenia PORT psychosocial treatment recommendations and summary statements. *Schizophrenia Bulletin, 36*(1), 48–70.

Doran, G. T. (1981). There's a SMART way to write management's goals and objectives. *Management Review, 70*(11), 35–36.

Erikson, E. H. (1963). *Childhood and Society*. 2nd edn. New York: Norton.

Fazel, M., Hoagwood, K., Stephan, S., & Ford, T. (2014). Mental health interventions in schools 1: Mental health interventions in schools in high-income countries. *Lancet Psychiatry. 2014 October; 1*(5), 377–387. doi:10.1016/S2215-0366(14)70312–8

Flach, C., French, P., Dunn, G., Fowler, D., Gumley, A. I., Birchwood, M., ... & Morrison, A. P. (2015). Components of therapy as mechanisms of change in cognitive therapy for people at risk of psychosis: Analysis of the EDIE-2 trial. *The British Journal of Psychiatry, 207*(2), 123–129.

Fowler, D., Rollinson, R., & French, P. (2011). Adherence and competence assessment in studies of CBT for psychosis: Current status and future directions. *Epidemiology and Psychiatric Sciences, 20*(2), 121–126.

Fusar-Poli, P., Rocchetti, M., Sardella, A., Avila, A., Brandizzi, M., Caverzasi, E., ... & McGuire, P. (2015). Disorder, not just state of risk: Meta-analysis of functioning and quality of life in people at high risk of psychosis. *The British Journal of Psychiatry*, *207*(3), 198–206.

Fusar-Poli, P., & Schultze-Lutter, F. (2016). Predicting the onset of psychosis in patients at clinical high risk: Practical guide to probabilistic prognostic reasoning. *Evidence Based Mental Health*, *19*(1), 10–15.

Gaebel, W., Riesbeck, M., & Wobrock, T. (2011). Schizophrenia guidelines across the world: A selective review and comparison. *International Review of Psychiatry*, *23*(4), 379–387.

Garety, P. A., & Freeman, D. (2013). The past and future of delusions research: From the inexplicable to the treatable. *The British Journal of Psychiatry*, *203*(5), 327–333.

Garety, P. A., & Hardy, A. (2017). The clinical relevance of appraisals of psychotic experiences. *World Psychiatry*, *16*(2), 140–141.

Giannitelli, M., Consoli, A., Raffin, M., Jardri, R., Levinson, D. F., Cohen, D., & Laurent-Levinson, C. (2017). An overview of medical risk factors for childhood psychosis: Implications for research and treatment. *Schizophrenia Research*.

Gin, K., Banerjea, P., Abbott, C., Browning, S., Bracegirdle, K., Corrigall, R., & Jolley, S. (2017). Childhood unusual experiences in community Child and Adolescent Mental Health Services in South East London: Prevalence and impact. *Schizophrenia Research*.

Haddock, G., Lewis, S., Bentall, R., Dunn, G., Drake, R., & Tarrier, N. (2006). Influence of age on outcome of psychological treatments in first episode psychosis. *British Journal of Psychiatry*, *188*, 250–254.

Harter, S. (1999). *The construction of the self: A developmental perspective*. New York: Guilford Press.

Hassanali, N., Ruffell, T., Browning, S., Bracegirdle, K., Ames, C., Corrigall, R., ... & Jolley, S. (2015). Cognitive bias and unusual experiences in childhood. *European Child & Adolescent Psychiatry*, *24*(8), 949–957.

Hazell, C. M., Hayward, M., Cavanagh, K., & Strauss, C. (2016). A systematic review and meta-analysis of low intensity CBT for psychosis. *Clinical Psychology Review*, *45*, 183–192.

Howes, O. D., McCutcheon, R., Owen, M. J., & Murray, R. M. (2017). The role of genes, stress, and dopamine in the development of schizophrenia. *Biological Psychiatry*, *81*(1), 9–20.

Ince, P., Haddock, G., & Tai, S. (2015). A systematic review of the implementation of recommended psychological interventions for schizophrenia: Rates, barriers, and improvement strategies. *Psychology and Psychotherapy: Theory, Research and Practice*, *89*, 324–350.

Jackson, H., McGorry, J. E., Hulbert, C., & Francey, S. (1998). Cognitive-oriented psychotherapy for early psychosis (COPE): Preliminary results. *British Journal of Psychiatry*, *172*(33), 93–100.

Jansen, J. E., Gleeson, J., & Cotton, S. (2015). Towards a better understanding of caregiver distress in early psychosis: A systematic review of the psychological factors involved. *Clinical Psychology Review*, *35*, 56–66.

Jin, H., & Mosweu, I. (2017). The societal cost of schizophrenia: A systematic review. *PharmacoEconomics*, *35*(1), 25–42.

Joa, I., Johannessen, J. O., Langeveld, J., Friis, S., Melle, I., Opjordsmoen, S., ... & Larsen, T. K. (2009). Baseline profiles of adolescent vs. adult-onset first-episode psychosis in an early detection program. *Acta Psychiatrica Scandinavica*, *119*(6), 494–500.

Johns, L., Jolley, S, Keen, N., & Peters, E. (2014). CBT for people with psychosis. In A. Whittington & N. Grey (eds.), *How to become a more effective CBT therapist: Mastering metacompetence in clinical practice*. Chichester: Wiley.

Jung, E., Wiesjahn, M., Rief, W., & Lincoln, T. M. (2015). Perceived therapist genuineness predicts therapeutic alliance in cognitive behavioural therapy for psychosis. *British Journal of Clinical Psychology, 54*(1), 34–48.

Kelleher, I., Cederlöf, M., & Lichtenstein, P. (2014). Psychotic experiences as a predictor of the natural course of suicidal ideation: A Swedish cohort study. *World Psychiatry, 13*(2), 184–188. http://doi.org/10.1002/wps.20131

Kelleher, I., Connor, D., Clarke, M. C., Devlin, N., Harley, M., & Cannon, M. (2012). Prevalence of psychotic symptoms in childhood and adolescence: A systematic review and meta-analysis of population-based studies. *Psychological Medicine, 42*(09), 1857–1863.

Kelleher, I., Harley, M., Murtagh, A., & Cannon, M. (2011). Are screening instruments valid for psychotic-like experiences? A validation study of screening questions for psychotic-like experiences using in-depth clinical interview. *Schizophrenia Bulletin, 37*(2), 362–369.

Kirkbride, J. B., Errazuriz, A., Croudace, T. J., Morgan, C., Jackson, D., Boydell, J., . . . & Jones, P. B. (2012). Incidence of schizophrenia and other psychoses in England, 1950–2009: A systematic review and meta-analyses. *PloS One, 7*(3), e31660. doi:10.1371/journal.pone.0031660

Kline, E., Thompson, E., Demro, C., Bussell, K., Reeves, G., & Schiffman, J. (2015). Longitudinal validation of psychosis risk screening tools. *Schizophrenia Research, 165*(2), 116–122.

Kuipers, E., Jolley, S., & Onwumere, J. (2016). Cognitive behavioral interventions in psychosis. In C. M. Nezu & A. M. Nezu (eds.), *The Oxford handbook of cognitive behavioral therapies.* Oxford: Oxford University Press.

Kuipers, E., Onwumere, J., & Bebbington, P. (2010). Cognitive model of caregiving in psychosis. *The British Journal of Psychiatry, 196*(4), 259–265.

Landa, Y., Mueser, K., Wyka, K., Shreck, E., Jespersen, R., Jacobs, M., . . . & Silbersweig, D. (2015). Development of a group and family-based cognitive behavioral therapy program for youth at risk for psychosis. *Early Intervention in Psychiatry, 6,* 511–521.

Laurens, K. R., & Cullen, A. E. (2016). Toward earlier identification and preventative intervention in schizophrenia: Evidence from the London Child Health and Development Study. *Social Psychiatry and Psychiatric Epidemiology, 51*(4), 475–491.

Laurens, K. R., Hobbs, M. J., Sunderland, M., Green, M. J., & Mould, G. L. (2012). Psychotic-like experiences in a community sample of 8000 children aged 9 to 11 years: An item response theory analysis. *Psychological Medicine, 42*(7), 1495–1506.

Laurens, K. R., Hodgins, S., Taylor, E. A., & Murray, R. M. (2011). Is earlier intervention for schizophrenia possible? Identifying antecedents of schizophrenia in children aged 9–12 years. In A. S. David, P. McGuffin, & S. Kapur (eds.) *Schizophrenia: The final frontier.* London: Psychology Press.

Laurens, K. R., Hodgins, S., West, S. A., & Murray, R. M. (2007). Prevalence and correlates of psychotic-like experiences and other developmental antecedents of schizophrenia in children aged 9–12 years. *Schizophrenia Bulletin, 33,* 239–239.

Law D., & Wolpert, M. (2014) *Guide to using outcomes and feedback tools with children, young people and families. Vol. 2: Children and young peoples' improving access to psychological therapies.* London: CAMHS Outcomes Research Consortium.

Liddle, P. F. (1987) The symptoms of chronic schizophrenia. A re-examination of the positive–negative dichotomy. *British Journal of Psychiatry, 151,* 145–151.

Louise, S., Fitzpatrick, M., Strauss, C., Rossell, S. L., & Thomas, N. (2017). Mindfulness- and acceptance-based interventions for psychosis: Our current understanding and a meta-analysis. *Schizophrenia Research.* doi:10.1016/j.schres.2017.05.023

Maddox, L., Jolley, S., Laurens, K. R., Hirsch, C., Hodgins, S., Browning, S., . . . & Kuipers, E. (2013). Cognitive behavioural therapy for unusual experiences in children: A case series. *Behavioural and Cognitive Psychotherapy, 41*(3), 344–358.

Mehl, S., Werner, D., & Lincoln, T. M. (2015). Does Cognitive Behavior Therapy for psychosis (CBTp) show a sustainable effect on delusions? A meta-analysis. *Frontiers in Psychology, 6*, 1450. doi:10.3389/fpsyg.2015.01450

Miklowitz, D. J., O'Brien, M. P., Schlosser, D. A., Addington, J., Candan, K. A., Marshall, C., . . . & Friedman-Yakoobian, M. (2014). Family-focused treatment for adolescents and young adults at high risk for psychosis: Results of a randomized trial. *Journal of the American Academy of Child & Adolescent Psychiatry, 53*(8), 848–858.

Moritz, S., Woodward, T. S., & Balzan, R. (2016). Is metacognitive training for psychosis effective? *Expert Review of Neurotherapeutics, 16*(2), 105–107.

Morrison, A. P., & Barratt, S. (2010). What are the components of CBT for psychosis? A Delphi study. *Schizophrenia Bulletin, 36*(1), 136–142.

Morrison, A. P., Turkington, D., Pyle, M., Spencer, H., Brabban, A., Dunn, G., . . . & Grace, T. (2014). Cognitive therapy for people with schizophrenia spectrum disorders not taking antipsychotic drugs: A single-blind randomised controlled trial. *The Lancet, 383*(9926), 1395–1403.

National Institute for Health and Care Excellence (NICE). (2013) *Psychosis and schizophrenia in children and young people: Recognition and management (CG155).* London: National Collaborating Centre for Mental Health.

National Institute for Health and Care Excellence (NICE). (2014). *Psychosis and schizophrenia in adults: Treatment and management (CG178).* London: National Institute for Health and Care Excellence.

Noone, D., Ames, C., Hassanali, N., Browning, S., Bracegirdle, K., Corrigall, R., . . . & Fowler, D. (2015). A preliminary investigation of schematic beliefs and unusual experiences in children. *European Psychiatry, 30*(5), 569–575.

O'Brien, M. P., Miklowitz, D. J., & Cannon, T. D. (2015). Decreases in perceived maternal criticism predict improvement in subthreshold psychotic symptoms in a randomized trial of family-focused therapy for individuals at clinical high risk for psychosis. *Journal of Family Psychology, 29*(6), 945–951.

Okuzawa, N., Kline, E., Fuertes, J., Negi, S., Reeves, G., Himelhoch, S., & Schiffman, J. (2014). Psychotherapy for adolescents and young adults at high risk for psychosis: A systematic review. *Early Intervention in Psychiatry, 8*(4), 307–322.

Onwumere, J., & Kuipers, E. (2017). Caregiving roles: When will they be routinely recognized and supported? *Journal of Mental Health, 26*(2), 95–97.

Onwumere, J., Kuipers, E., Gamble, C., Jolley, S., Smith, B., Rollinson, R., Steel., C., Fowler, D., Bebbington, P., Dunn, G., Freeman, D., & Garety, P. (2009). Family interventions in psychosis: A scale to measure therapist adherence. *Journal of Family Therapy, 31*, 270–283.

Owen, M. J., Sawa, A., & Mortensen, P. B., (2016). Schizophrenia. *Lancet, 38*, 86–97.

Peters, E., Ward, T., Jackson, M., Morgan, C., Charalambides, M., McGuire, P., . . . & Garety, P. A. (2016). Clinical, socio-demographic and psychological characteristics in individuals with persistent psychotic experiences with and without a "need for care." *World Psychiatry, 15*(1), 41–52.

Piaget, J., & Inhelder, B. (1958). *The growth of logical thinking from childhood to adolescence: An essay on the construction of formal operational structures (developmental psychology).* Oxford: Routledge.

Premkumar, P., Onwumere, J., Albert, J., Kessel, D., Kumari, V., Kuipers, E., & Carretié, L. (2015). The relation between schizotypy and early attention to rejecting interactions: The influence of neuroticism. *The World Journal of Biological Psychiatry*, *16*(8), 587–601.

Reininghaus, U., Böhnke, J. R., Hosang, G., Farmer, A., Burns, T., McGuffin, P., & Bentall, R. P. (2016). Evaluation of the validity and utility of a transdiagnostic psychosis dimension encompassing schizophrenia and bipolar disorder. *The British Journal of Psychiatry*, *209*, 107–113.

Remington, G., Foussias, G., Fervaha, G., Agid, O., Takeuchi, H., Lee, J., & Hahn, M. (2016). Treating negative symptoms in schizophrenia: An update. *Current Treatment Options in Psychiatry*, *3*(2), 133–150.

Roth, A. D., & Pilling, S. (2013). A competence framework for psychological interventions with people with psychosis and bipolar disorder. www.ucl.ac.uk/clinical-psychology/CORE/compe tence_mentalillness_psychosisandbipolar.html

Schimmelmann, B. G., Michel, C., Martz-Irngartinger, A., Linder, C., & Schultze-Lutter, F. (2015). Age matters in the prevalence and clinical significance of ultra-high-risk for psychosis symptoms and criteria in the general population: Findings from the BEAR and BEARS-kid studies. *World Psychiatry*, *14*(2), 189–197.

Schmidt, S. J., Schultze-Lutter, F., Schimmelmann, B. G., Maric, N. P., Salokangas, R. K. R., Riecher-Rössler, A., ... & Morrison, A. (2015). European Psychiatric Association guidance on the early intervention in clinical high risk states of psychoses. *European Psychiatry*, *30*(3), 388–404.

Schnyder, N., Panczak, R., Groth, N., & Schultze-Lutter, F. (2017). Association between mental health-related stigma and active help-seeking: Systematic review and meta-analysis. *The British Journal of Psychiatry*, *210*(4), 261–268.

Sommer, I. E., Bearden, C. E., Van Dellen, E., Breetvelt, E. J., Duijff, S. N., Maijer, K., ... & Díaz-Caneja, C. M. (2016). Early interventions in risk groups for schizophrenia: What are we waiting for? *npj Schizophrenia*, *2*, 16003. doi:10.1038/npjschz.2016.3

Stain, H. J., Bucci, S., Baker, A. L., Carr, V., Emsley, R., Halpin, S., ... & Startup, M. (2016). A randomised controlled trial of cognitive behaviour therapy versus non-directive reflective listening for young people at ultra high risk of developing psychosis: The detection and evaluation of psychological therapy (DEPTh) trial. *Schizophrenia Research*, *176*(2), 212–219.

Stallard, P. (2005). *A clinician's guide to think good-feel good: Using CBT with children and young people*. Chichester: Wiley.

Swan, S., Keen, N., Reynolds, N., & Onwumere, J. (2017). Psychological interventions for post-traumatic stress symptoms in psychosis: A systematic review of outcomes. *Frontiers in Psychology*, *8*, 341. doi:10.3389/fpsyg.2017.00341

Thomas, N., Hayward, M., Peters, E., van der Gaag, M., Bentall, R. P., Jenner, J., ... & García-Montes, J. M. (2014). Psychological therapies for auditory hallucinations (voices): Current status and key directions for future research. *Schizophrenia Bulletin*, *40*(Supplement 4), S202–S212.

Thompson, E., Millman, Z. B., Okuzawa, N., Mittal, V., DeVylder, J., Skadberg, T., ... & Schiffman, J. (2015). Evidence-based early interventions for individuals at clinical high risk for psychosis: A review of treatment components. *The Journal of Nervous and Mental Disease*, *203*(5), 342–351.

Tiffin, P. A., & Welsh, P. (2013). Practitioner review: Schizophrenia spectrum disorders and the at-risk mental state for psychosis in children and adolescents – evidence-based management approaches. *Journal of Child Psychology and Psychiatry*, *54*(11), 1155–1175.

Tobin, C. (2013). Parents of children and adolescents with psychotic-like experiences. Unpublished DClinPsy thesis. King's College, London.

van der Gaag, M., Valmaggia, L. R., & Smit, F. (2014). The effects of individually tailored formulation-based cognitive behavioural therapy in auditory hallucinations and delusions: A meta-analysis. *Schizophrenia Research*, *156*(1), 30–37.

van Os, J., & Murray, R. M. (2013). Can we identify and treat "schizophrenia light" to prevent true psychotic illness. *British Medical Journal*, *346*, f304–f304. doi:10.1136/bmj.f304

van Os, J., & Reininghaus, U. (2016). Psychosis as a transdiagnostic and extended phenotype in the general population. *World Psychiatry*, *15*(2), 118–124.

Wood, L., Byrne, R., & Morrison, A. P. (2017). An integrative cognitive model of internalized stigma in psychosis. *Behavioural and Cognitive Psychotherapy*, 1–16. doi:10.1017/S1352465817000224

Wood, L., Byrne, R., Varese, F., & Morrison, A. P. (2016). Psychosocial interventions for internalised stigma in people with a schizophrenia-spectrum diagnosis: A systematic narrative synthesis and meta-analysis. *Schizophrenia Research*, *176*(2), 291–303.

Woodberry, K. A., Shapiro, D. I., Bryant, C., & Seidman, L. J. (2016). Progress and future directions in research on the psychosis prodrome: A review for clinicians. *Harvard Review of Psychiatry*, *24*(2), 87–103.

World Health Organization (WHO). (1993). *The ICD-10 classification of mental and behavioural disorders: Diagnostic criteria for research*. Vol. 2. Geneva: World Health Organization.

World Health Organisation (WHO). (2013). *Comprehensive mental health action plan 2013–2020*. Geneva: WHO. www.who.int/mental_health/maternal-child/child_adolescent/en/

World Health Organization (WHO). (2015). *Update of the Mental Health Gap Action Programme (mhGAP) guidelines for mental, neurological and substance use disorders, 2015*. Geneva: World Health Organization.

Wüsten, C., & Lincoln, T. M. (2017). The association of family functioning and psychosis proneness in five countries that differ in cultural values and family structures. *Psychiatry Research*, *253*, 158–164.

Wykes, T., Steel, C., Everitt, B., & Tarrier, N. (2008). Cognitive behavior therapy for schizophrenia: Effect sizes, clinical models, and methodological rigor. *Schizophrenia Bulletin*, *34*(3), 523–537.

Yesufu-Udechuku, A., Harrison, B., Mayo-Wilson, E., Young, N., Woodhams, P., Shiers, D., . . . & Kendall, T. (2015). Interventions to improve the experience of caring for people with severe mental illness: Systematic review and meta-analysis. *The British Journal of Psychiatry*, *206*(4), 268–274.

8

Bipolar Spectrum

Sally M. Weinstein, Ashley Isaia, and Amy E. West

Bipolar disorder (BD) in children and adolescents is a serious and debilitating illness that is characterized by mood lability and is associated with significant psychiatric burden, including functional impairments at home, at school, and with peers (Geller et al., 2000; Goldstein et al., 2009; Lewinsohn, Seeley, & Klein, 2003). Compared to adults, youth with bipolar disorder are more likely to experience rapid fluctuations in their mood, with fluctuations between poles that occur daily (ultradian cycling) or every few days (ultrarapid cycling) (Tillman & Geller, 2003). Additionally, mixed mood episodes, in which depressive and manic symptoms occur simultaneously, are more common in pediatric BD (Birmaher et al., 2006; Findling et al., 2001; Geller et al., 2002). Moreover, youth with BD often present with prominent irritability or "rage episodes" (i.e., extreme mood changes, outbursts, and tantrums) (Findling et al., 2001; Wozniak et al., 2005). Currently, the diagnosis of BD in youth is determined via DSM-5 diagnostic criteria (American Psychiatric Association, 2013) for bipolar spectrum disorders, including Bipolar I, Bipolar II, cyclothymia, and unspecified bipolar disorder. The presence of a manic episode is required for a diagnosis of Bipolar I, defined as prominent irritability or elevated mood for one week, in addition to three accompanying symptoms (or four if mood is predominately irritable): inflated self-esteem, decreased need for sleep, pressured speech, racing thoughts, distractibility, increased goal-directed activity or psychomotor agitation, and impulsivity (which may manifest as hypersexuality in youth). While individuals with Bipolar I often experience depressive episodes, they are not required for a diagnosis. For Bipolar II disorder, youth are required to meet criteria for a past or current hypomanic episode (duration of manic symptoms occurs for four days) along with one or more past or current major depressive episodes. In children and adolescents, cyclothymia is defined by a period of one year or more in which the individual experiences hypomanic symptoms alternating with depressive symptoms, but symptoms do not meet full diagnostic criteria for a hypomanic or major depressive episode. Finally, unspecified bipolar disorder is diagnosed when symptoms do not meet criteria for a full threshold diagnosis due to reduced number, intensity, duration, or frequency.

Etiology and Theoretical Underpinnings of Treatment

The burgeoning research literature on BD in pediatric populations has shaped our understanding of this disorder and offers key targets for effective intervention. In particular, psychosocial treatments for BD are informed by the evidence on developmentally specific symptoms of the disorder. As aforementioned, early onset bipolar disorder is characterized by several unique symptom characteristics, including rapid cycling, mixed mood episodes, and predominately irritable mood. Findings from functional neuroimaging studies have also accumulated evidence of affective circuitry brain dysfunction that underlies the emotion dysregulation experienced by youth with BD, and offer important mechanisms for treatment efficacy. Specifically, findings indicate that in response to negative emotional stimuli (e.g., viewing words or faces with positive, negative, or neutral valence), youth with BD demonstrate increased activation in the limbic centers of the brain, including the amygdala, anterior cingulate cortex, and paralimbic cortex, and decreased activation in the ventrolateral prefrontal cortex (VLPFC) and dorsolateral prefrontal cortex (DLPFC) as compared to healthy controls (Garrett et al., 2012; Pavuluri et al., 2007; Pavuluri et al., 2008). These areas are responsible for emotional and cognitive control functions in healthy individuals, including emotion processing and regulation, decision making, and problem-solving, thus suggesting that youth with BD demonstrate greater reactivity to negative emotions and difficulties recruiting the cognitive control centers to problem-solve responses to these negative emotions. Finally, due to the complex symptom presentation and difficulties regulating emotional responses, youth with BD experience psychosocial stress across family, peer, and academic domains. The family environments of youth with BD are characterized by significant tension and hostility (Geller et al., 2000). Elevated levels of conflict and poor family cohesion may exacerbate and maintain difficult family interactions in this population (Esposito-Smythers et al., 2006). Interpersonal difficulties among youth with BD extend to peer relationships as well, including limited social networks and impaired social skills (Geller et al., 2000; Goldstein, Miklowitz, & Mullen, 2006; Wilens et al., 2003). Further, neurocognitive deficits may interfere with learning and contribute to poor academic performance (Pavuluri et al., 2006). The accumulation of difficulties at home, at school, and with peers has negative consequences for the child's view of the self. Not surprisingly, these children are more likely to suffer from low self-esteem, feelings of hopelessness, an external locus of control, and ineffective coping skills (Rucklidge, 2006). Guided by these lines of research, psychosocial interventions for pediatric BD address the range of cognitive, social, and interpersonal impairments that are typical of this disorder and supply families with a set of tools and skills to

Disruptive Mood Dysregulation Disorder

Disruptive mood dysregulation disorder (DMDD) was recently added as a diagnostic category in the DSM-5. DMDD refers to marked and persistent periods of severe irritability co-occurring with emotional (e.g., explosive anger, rage attacks) and behavioral outbursts (e.g., physical aggression, temper tantrums). To meet criteria for the diagnosis of DMDD, these features must have lasted for at least one year and become apparent before the age of ten years. The inclusion of DMDD in the DSM-5 was driven by evidence suggesting that youth experiencing *chronic* rather than *episodic* irritability are more likely to develop subsequent depressive or anxiety disorders than bipolar disorder (e.g., Brotman et al., 2006; Stringaris et al., 2009). As research on DMDD accumulates, additional light will be shed on the diagnostic features of this disorder. In turn, this information is likely to have significant implications for the development and dissemination of evidence-based psychosocial treatments designed to address the specific needs of this population.

Given the paucity of research on DMDD and the lack of established psychosocial treatment guidelines, the literature on psychosocial treatments for pediatric BD serves as the foundation for the treatment of mood dysregulation. We anticipate that many of the components of evidence-based treatments for youth with BD will be relevant for families affected by DMDD. However, given preliminary evidence indicating distinct patterns of neural activity in response to negative emotional stimuli between youth with chronic, severe irritability and those with BD (Rich et al., 2011), DMDD may require specific treatment modifications. Future research may elucidate the pathophysiology underlying chronic mood dysregulation and also inform the development of targeted intervention strategies for DMDD.

bolster them against the negative impact of symptoms and improve their quality of life.

Brief Overview of Evidence-Based Treatments

The psychosocial impairments and high rates of morbidity and mortality associated with BD have led to consensus that high-quality, evidence-based psychosocial treatment as an adjunct to pharmacotherapy is essential to improve the prognosis and course of the disorder in children and adolescents (McClellan, Kowatch, & Findling, 2007). Indeed, although pharmacotherapy is considered the frontline treatment for BD, medications rarely can address the full range of social, family, and academic difficulties these youth and families face; further, findings indicating negative side effect profiles and high rates of nonresponse to medication (Birmaher et al., 2009; Emslie et al., 2003; Geller et al., 2008) underscore the need for adjunctive psychosocial treatment. The following section provides an overview of evidence-based psychosocial interventions designed for adjunctive use with pharmacotherapy to target pediatric BD, following guidelines provided by the Task Force on the Promotion and Dissemination of Psychological Procedures (Chambless et al., 1996; Chambless et al., 1998; Chambless & Hollon, 1998; Chambless & Ollendick, 2001; Southam-Gerow & Prinstein, 2014). Currently, no specific treatment package for BD in children and adolescents has been identified as *well-established*. However, several existing interventions meet criteria for *probably efficacious* treatments. Given their shared foci on family psychoeducation and skills training, these treatments together reflect a class of interventions that are supported by research (Fristad, 2016): family-focused therapy (FFT) for adolescents, psychoeducational psychotherapy (PEP), and child- and family-focused cognitive-behavioral therapy (CFF-CBT). These intervention packages are discussed briefly below.

Family-focused Treatment for Adolescents

Miklowitz and colleagues adapted family-focused treatment (FFT) for adults with bipolar disorder to adolescents (FFT-A; Miklowitz et al., 2004). The goal of FFT-A is to reduce symptoms and increase psychosocial functioning through a greater understanding about the disorder, decreased family conflict, and improved family communication, coping, and problem-solving. FFT-A is delivered via 21 individual sessions over the course of nine months and is organized into three components: psychoeducation, communication enhancement training, and problem-solving. The efficacy of FFT-A as an adjunct to pharmacotherapy was examined in a two-site randomized controlled trial with 58 adolescents (aged 12–17) with bipolar spectrum disorders and their families (Miklowitz et al., 2008) assigned to receive either FFT-A or "Enhanced Care" (three weekly family sessions focused on psychoeducation and relapse prevention). Results indicated that FFT-A youth experienced shorter time to recovery from depression, less time in depressive episodes, and lower depression severity scores over the two-year study period as compared to those in the control condition. A second randomized controlled trial of FFT-A conducted with a larger sample of adolescents with bipolar disorder (N = 145) demonstrated that those who participated in FFT-A had less severe manic symptoms during year two (follow-up period) than those in control (Miklowitz et al., 2008), although they did not differ from control on time to recovery or recurrence, or weeks ill during follow-up. FFT-A was also recently adapted to younger patients who may be at risk for bipolar disorder. Data from a small randomized trial for at-risk youth (N = 40, aged 9–17, mean = 12.3 years) indicated more rapid recovery from their initial mood symptoms, more weeks in remission, and a more favorable trajectory of mania symptoms over one year compared to youth in enhanced care (Miklowitz et al., 2013).

Psychoeducational Psychotherapy

Fristad and colleagues developed an adjunctive psychoeducational psychotherapy treatment (PEP) for children aged 8–12 with bipolar or depressive spectrum disorders and their parents (Fristad, Goldberg-Arnold, & Gavazzi, 2002; Fristad et al., 2009). This treatment combines psychoeducational components with elements from cognitive-behavioral, family systems, and interpersonal approaches. Similar to FFT, PEP is designed to increase knowledge of BD, improve symptom management, improve communication and problem-solving, and increase the family's sense of support in dealing with the disorder; moreover, parents are guided in ways to advocate for their child's needs (Fristad, Goldberg-Arnold, & Gavazzi, 2002). Originally developed as an eight-session multi-family psychoeducation psychotherapy group (MF-PEP) for children and parents, the treatment has subsequently been adapted as a 24-session individual family format (IF-PEP; Fristad, Arnold, & Leffler, 2011). A randomized clinical trial (N = 165) of adjunctive MF-PEP in youth aged 8–12 with unipolar depression or bipolar disorder demonstrated efficacy in reducing mood symptoms (Fristad et al., 2009) compared to a waitlist control group. Additionally IF-PEP demonstrated preliminary efficacy versus waitlist control in a small randomized controlled trial (Fristad, 2006). The dissemination of MF-PEP to real-world settings was also recently examined in a small open trial; findings indicated that MF-PEP was acceptable and feasible in community clinic settings (MacPherson, Leffler, & Fristad, 2014).

Child- and Family-Focused Cognitive-Behavioral Therapy:
The RAINBOW Program

Child- and family-focused cognitive-behavioral therapy (CFF-CBT) is a family-based adjunctive psychosocial intervention developed by our research group for children ages 7–13 with bipolar spectrum disorders and their families (Pavuluri, Graczyk, et al., 2004; West, Henry, & Pavuluri, 2007; West et al., 2009; West & Weinstein, 2012). CFF-CBT integrates psychoeducation and cognitive-behavioral therapy (CBT) with complementary techniques from mindfulness-based intervention, positive psychology, and interpersonal therapy to augment the traditional CBT framework and address the range of therapeutic needs of families affected by BD. The CFF-CBT format is a 12-session protocol-driven treatment program, alternating between child-, parent-, and family-focused sessions. CFF-CBT has also been adapted to a 12-week group format that consists of weekly 60-minute parallel parent and child groups and a 15-minute multi-family child/parent combined component. In both formats, treatment is structured around seven core components that form the acronym RAINBOW: **R**outine, **A**ffect Regulation, **I** can do it (self-efficacy boosting), **N**o negative thoughts and live in the now,

Be a good friend and balanced lifestyles for parents, **O**h, how can we solve this problem?, and **W**ays to get social support. A recent randomized controlled trial (N = 69) of youth with bipolar disorder (aged 7–13) indicated efficacy for CFF-CBT in improving mania, depression, and global functioning compared to a control group receiving dose-matched psychotherapy-as-usual (West et al., 2014).

Components of Evidence-Based Treatments

Although the interventions for BD in youth have traditionally been examined as "stand-alone" packages, efficacious treatment for youth and families affected by bipolar disorder comprises several common elements. In particular, existing treatments are similar in their adjunctive approach; the incorporation of psychoeducation about the nature and symptoms of pediatric onset BD; the intensive involvement of the family; and a focus on developing cognitive and behavioral skills for coping with mood dysregulation and interpersonal functioning. We describe each of these components, along with available research evidence, below.

Psychoeducation

A primary component across treatments is psychoeducation, an intervention that combines psychotherapy with education to enhance the family's knowledge of a problem and foster self-efficacy and skill building (Lukens & McFarlane, 2004). A major objective of psychoeducational approaches for BD is to build the family's understanding of the symptoms, etiology, and course of the disorder, which is typically accomplished through didactic methods and engaging handouts and worksheets to help youth and caregivers internalize the information. This shared understanding can enhance self-efficacy to cope with and manage the disorder, and improve communication about symptoms and patterns among family members, treatment providers, and school staff. Psychoeducational methods also aid relapse prevention efforts by recognizing early warning signs of recurrence; for example, in FFT, families complete a "mania prevention contract" that lists prodromal signs of mania, triggers, and how the youth, family, and treatment team can respond. Across treatments, families are provided with education regarding the neurobiological underpinnings of mood disorders to decrease the negative interactions and blame surrounding the child's mood dysregulation. An important goal is to help the family differentiate the child from the disorder. Families are encouraged to develop a common language of symptoms and triggers (e.g., in CFF-CBT, youth may refer to emotional dysregulation and rage episodes as "volcanoes," and triggers are "bugs") to increase comfort and familiarity with common symptoms and patterns experienced by the child, as well as distance these experiences from the child. Last, information is provided about medication, and barriers to adherence are addressed.

   Psychoeducational approaches were initially developed for use with families of
adults with schizophrenia (Goldstein & Miklowitz, 1995), and later adapted for
families affected by mood disorders (e.g., Brent et al., 1993; Holder & Anderson,
1990; Miklowitz & Goldstein, 1990). Specific to pediatric BD, research suggests
strong support for treatments that include psychoeducation as a primary target (Fristad
et al., 2009; Miklowitz et al., 2008, 2013; West et al., 2014). Findings also indicate
that psychoeducation components of treatment packages may specifically relate to
treatment improvement. Research examining the mechanisms of MF-PEP suggested
that treatment may teach parents how to advocate for and access better health services,
which may, in turn, result in symptom improvement in the child (Fristad et al., 2009;
Mendenhall, Fristad, & Early, 2009).

Affect Regulation and Coping Strategies

A major goal of effective treatment for BD is the development of strategies to
address the documented impairments in affect regulation in children with bipolar
disorder. Affect regulation strategies encompass several different treatment methods, including recognizing and labeling feelings, self-monitoring of mood states,
and developing cognitive and behavioral coping skills with child and parent to
manage expansive, negative, and irritable moods. Such techniques are ideally
employed sequentially. Youth and caregivers are first engaged in *affect education*
to improve their ability to identify and label various mood states, through direct
instruction, use of visual aids (e.g., feelings posters), and play techniques (e.g., in
CFF-CBT, youth and therapist play "feelings charades"). The child and parents
are then encouraged to *monitor mood states* daily to better understand the youth's
mood patterns and triggers of different emotional states. Although specific methods may differ between treatment packages, monitoring typically involves rating
or labeling mood states several times daily using colorful and engaging worksheets. Such monitoring is a necessary foundation for skills work focused on
prevention and management of negative emotional states and their triggers, as
described below. Affective education and mood monitoring have been shown to
enhance awareness of mood patterns and triggers in children with depression
(Rohde et al., 2005) and adults with bipolar disorder (Leahy, 2005), and thus are
integral components of evidence-based treatments for BD.
   Coping skills training incorporates cognitive and behavioral methods targeting
both youth and caregiver. Youth and parents may be instructed in the connections
between thoughts, feelings, and behavior, and taught cognitive restructuring techniques to reduce negative thought patterns (e.g., thought stopping, reframing situations positively, modifying thoughts, and use of positive self-talk/mantras during
difficult situations). In PEP, youth are taught the "Thinking–Feeling–Doing" connection and develop a "toolkit" of positive and calming activities in each of four domains

(creative, active, relaxing, and social) to manage negative moods (Fristad, 2006; Fristad, Gavazzi, & Soldano, 1998). Similarly in CFF-CBT (West et al., 2014), youth develop "think and do" skills and apply both cognitive restructuring techniques and behavioral strategies (positive, soothing, and release activities) to cope with their identified "bugs," which are rehearsed via game-play (e.g., "Coping Baseball," where youth identify both maladaptive and then adaptive ways to respond to triggers by running the Mind, Feelings, and Behavior/Body bases). The parent and child are also encouraged to identify the child's strengths, and to engage in activities that promote these strengths to enhance positive affect and mastery.

Additionally, parents are trained in skills to help their youth cope with affect dysregulation. Specifically, *parent training* in behavioral management strategies that are specific to the rage episodes common in BD can help families prevent and cope with these affective storms. For example, many parents use behavioral management systems developed for children with disruptive behavior disorders, which emphasize immediate contingency enforcement, redirection, and the implementation of consequences (Barkley, 1997). Unfortunately, in the case of BD, this method can sometimes backfire. Children whose rage is rooted in a loss of control over emotional responses (rather than a purposeful, manipulative behavior) will not respond to limit-setting in the moment; in fact, this often tends to exacerbate their negative emotions. Rather, parents are instructed to use calming tones and modulate their own responses so as not to model emotional reactivity, and focus on defusing the situation, keeping everyone safe, and using an empathic, collaborative problem-solving approach. Consequences and limits, if necessary, can be implemented at a later time when the child is calm. A common analogy used in CFF-CBT is "putting out the fire" in the management of rage episodes to illustrate the importance of immediate stabilization and establishing safety, only later to be followed by discussion and consequences when the "fire is out." Evidence suggests that the incorporation of behavioral management techniques can help parents find effective ways of coping with their child's affective outbursts and behavioral difficulties (Stark et al., 1996). Other parenting strategies for regulating mood include establishing simple and predictable routines, minimizing transitions, emphasizing the timing and tone of interactions during mood episodes, and using positive reinforcement.

Cognitive and behavioral coping skill-focused treatments have garnered significant empirical support in the youth mood literature, and effective use of cognitive and behavioral coping skills has been shown to relate to youth symptom improvement in treatment for youth depression (Jacobs et al., 2014; Kaufman et al., 2005). Specific to BD, research has shown that improvement in parenting skills and parent coping via CFF-CBT contributed to youth improvement in mania symptoms and global functioning across treatment (MacPherson et al., 2016). Thus, findings suggest that improving affect regulation via the development of both parent and child coping skills may be necessary for youth with BD.

Communication Skills

Treatment for BD seeks to target family and social functioning by enhancing the youth's and caregivers' communication skills via instruction, role-playing, and between-session practice. In FFT, PEP, and CFF-CBT, youth and caregivers are taught active listening, such as nonverbal skills (e.g., looking at the speaker, nodding head) and verbal skills (e.g., asking clarifying questions and summarizing what you heard to assess understanding, speaking clearly). In CFF-CBT, we use the acronym "BEME" (Back Straight, Eye Contact, Mouth to Speak Clearly, Ears to Listen) to help children remember key listening skills. Training also includes positive ways to request change in others' behaviors and ways to express feelings respectfully, termed "I Statements" in CFF-CBT (e.g., *I feel* frustrated, *because I* do not like doing my homework, and *I would like it* if you would help me do my homework). To promote positive peer relationships, treatment focuses on ways to initiate and maintain conversations, "be a good friend" to others via respectful communication, and be included in social interactions. Parents are also encouraged to seek opportunities for children to practice newly developed skills and develop friendships.

Problem-Solving

Youth and parents are also engaged in *problem-solving skills training* to target interpersonal and family difficulties, as well as to enhance self-efficacy related to coping with the disorder. Families practice defining problems in simple and clear ways, brainstorming solutions, discussing pros and cons of possible solutions, implementing solutions, and reviewing and rewarding their efforts. Parents are encouraged to view their children as collaborative partners in the problem-solving process and to use preventative, empathic, and creative approaches to problem-solving to minimize reactivity. For example, therapists using CFF-CBT sometimes discuss using a "Bug Box" in the home as a way for families to discuss grievances or "bugs" from the week using problem-solving and communication skills at a predetermined time when all family members are present, calm, and have time to discuss solutions. Problem-solving is a component of all three effective treatments for BD; indeed, findings suggest that family flexibility and reframing of problems may be mechanisms via which CFF-CBT improves youth symptomology (MacPherson et al., 2016).

Parent Self-Care

A vital, but often overlooked, component of treatment for BD targets parental wellbeing and coping. Parents of children with bipolar disorder often suffer from physical and emotional exhaustion, frustration, guilt, and feelings of isolation (Fristad & Goldberg-Arnold, 2003). Therefore, treatment encourages parents to develop a more balanced lifestyle that involves finding ways to rest, replenish their energy, and enjoy life. In CFF-CBT, parents complete a "Balanced Lifestyle" activity where they draw a pie diagram that depicts the percentages of time they currently invest in their own self-care versus being a spouse, worker, or parent. Then, the therapist and parent together explore ways to "recarve the pie" to allow for greater balance between the demands of caring for a child with BD and taking care of themselves. The techniques used in this component also emphasize identifying and accessing those in their social support network who can help the child and the parents through difficult situations. Additionally, parents are instructed in cognitive restructuring and mindfulness techniques to help manage their own negative thoughts and to increase a focus on coping in the present moment, rather than dwelling on past failures or anticipating future failures. Research highlights the importance of parent-focused treatment components, particularly for parents with depressive symptoms. Specifically, CFF-CBT was more effective for youth of parents with subclinical depressive symptoms as compared to the psychotherapy-as-usual control, suggesting that CFF-CBT may be a better match for families with parental distress than traditional psychotherapy approaches (Weinstein et al., 2015).

Role of Parents in Treatment

Families affected by BD often experience difficulties managing and coping with the child's illness, and thus all empirically supported treatments for youth with BD incorporate parents and family members in the treatment process as described above. Negative family dynamics have significant implications for treatment outcomes in BD. For example, parental expressed emotion (i.e., critical, hostile, or emotionally over-involved interactions among caregivers and family members) moderated treatment outcomes in the randomized clinical trial (RCT) of FFT-A. Families demonstrating high expressed emotion required an intensive family-based intervention to achieve reductions in manic and depressive symptoms, compared to families low in expressed emotion who benefited equally from FFT-A and a brief psychoeducational intervention (Miklowitz et al., 2009). Parental expressed emotion was not a significant predictor or moderator of treatment response in MF-PEP (MacPherson, Algorta et al., 2014). Additionally, the incorporation of parents into the treatment process may be essential for positive treatment gains in CFF-CBT; increases in parents' ability to cope with their child's illness and improvements in their parenting skills were identified as mechanisms by which children experienced decreases in manic symptoms and increases in psychosocial functioning (MacPherson et al., 2016). Additionally, parent depressive symptomology and family income were moderators of child symptom response in the RCT of CFF-CBT such that youth with parents with higher levels of depressive symptoms, and those with lower family income, experienced greater reductions in their own depressive symptoms in CFF-CBT compared to the control treatment (Weinstein et al., 2015).

Other Variables Influencing Treatment

Assessment

Although we have made significant progress in the development and dissemination of empirically supported treatments, additional work is required to ensure existing treatments are delivered to the right families. Recent findings indicate that a diagnosis of bipolar disorder may not be sufficient for determining appropriate treatment services due to heterogeneity in symptom presentation among youth with BD. Using a cluster analytic approach, Peters and colleagues (2016) explored patterns of symptoms in a sample of 7–13-year-olds with bipolar spectrum diagnoses. Two unique clusters of symptoms emerged – a "classic presentation" and a "dysregulated/defiant" presentation – and were associated with distinct patterns of functional impairment and treatment outcomes (Peters et al., 2016). These findings suggest that careful assessment of symptoms may be warranted for matching individuals with specific treatment packages or components in order to optimize youth and family outcomes.

Comorbidity

Diagnosis and treatment of BD in youth is often complicated by high rates of comorbid conditions, including attention-deficit/hyperactivity disorder (ADHD), oppositional defiant disorder (ODD), and anxiety disorders (Biederman, 1995; Geller et al., 2002; Leibenluft et al., 2003; Tillman et al., 2003; Wozniak et al., 1995).

Demographics

Several studies have examined factors that may influence psychosocial treatment outcomes for youth with bipolar disorder. Fortunately, the empirically supported interventions for bipolar disorder in children and adolescents appear to be fairly robust regardless of demographic variables such as age, sex, and race.

Medication

As noted above, practice parameters for BD in youth identify pharmacotherapy as a frontline treatment, in conjunction with psychotherapy (McClellan, Kowatch, & Findling, 2007). Increasingly, pharmacologic interventions used to treat BD in adults are being applied to the treatment of BD in youth. For a review of the evidence base for these medications in pediatric populations, as well as leading treatment algorithms to guide pharmacologic decisions in BD, the reader is referred to Washburn, West, and Heil (2011) and Pavuluri, Henry, et al. (2004).

Severity

Findings from the RCT of MF-PEP indicated that the treatment was actually most effective for children with the greatest functional impairments at baseline, but was less effective for children who presented to treatment with moderately impaired functioning (MacPherson, Algorta, et al., 2014).

Therapeutic Format

Prior research indicates that therapeutic format may also play a role in treatment outcomes. PEP was originally delivered in multi-family group format (Fristad, Goldberg-Arnold, & Gavazzi, 2002; Fristad et al., 2009), but was subsequently tested with individual families (Fristad, Arnold, & Leffler, 2011). CFF-CBT has also been tested in individual (West et al., 2014) and multi-family group format (West et al., 2009). Thus far, there have been no head-to-head comparisons of individual versus group psychotherapy for BD in youth. However, for families affected by BD, group psychotherapy may offer valuable opportunities for child socialization and parent social support. In addition, novel treatment formats such as internet-/mobile-based therapy services are gaining traction. Future research may explore these alternatives to traditional treatment delivery as a means of disseminating empirically supported treatments to hard-to-reach families.

Conclusion

Children with BD evidence substantial difficulties in social, emotional, and academic functioning, highlighting the need for psychosocial treatment as an essential part of a comprehensive treatment approach for BD. Several effective, evidence-based interventions have been developed to improve symptoms and psychosocial functioning among youth affected by BD and their families. Empirically supported interventions share key elements to address the range of needs in the BD population, including an adjunctive approach to pharmacother-apy; psychoeducation about BD; development and implementation of coping skills for mood dysregulation; communication and social skills training to improve interpersonal functioning; and the intensive involvement of parents and the family. Research suggests that the incorporation of parents and family is vital to treatment success, given the findings that improvement in child BD symptoms and global functioning is mediated by changes in parenting and family variables. As the field evolves, research aims to identify symptom, psychosocial, and neurocognitive predictors of intervention response to guide the selection of optimal evidence-based treatment for a particular patient as well as for improving treatment outcomes in youth with BD.

Useful Resources

- The National Alliance on Mental Illness (NAMI; www.nami.org) provides families with infor-mational content about mental health conditions, programs, and support groups, and information regarding available treatment options.
- The Balanced Mind Parent Network (BMPN; www.dbsalliance.org) is tailored for families struggling with the challenges of having a child with a mood disorder, offering online and local community support, treatment search tools, and research opportunities.
- For clinicians, treatment manuals for PEP, FFT, and CFF-CBT are all available for purchase. Clinicians are also encouraged to access online tools available on the BMPN website and from the American Academy of Child & Adolescent Psychiatry to stay current on empirically supported treatments.

References

American Psychiatric Association. (2013). *Diagnostic and statistical manual of mental disorders*. 5th edn. Washington, DC: American Psychiatric Association.

Barkley, R. A. (1997). *Defiant children: A clinician's manual for assessment and parent training*. 2nd edn. New York: Guilford Press.

Biederman, J. (1995). Developmental subtypes of juvenile bipolar disorder. *Harvard Review of Psychiatry*, *3*(4), 227–230.

Birmaher, B., Axelson, D., Goldstein, B., Strober, M., Gill, M. K., Hunt, J., . . . & Keller, M. (2009). Four-year longitudinal course of children and adolescents with bipolar spectrum disorders: The Course and Outcome of Bipolar Youth (COBY) study. *American Journal of Psychiatry*, *166*(7), 795–804. doi:10.1176/appi.ajp.2009.08101569

Birmaher, B., Axelson, D., Strober, M., Gill, M. K., Valeri, S., Chiappetta, L., . . . & Keller, M. (2006). Clinical course of children and adolescents with bipolar spectrum disorders. *Archives of General Psychiatry*, *63*(2), 175–183. doi:10.1001/archpsyc.63.2.175

Brent, D. A., Poling, K., McKain, B., & Baugher, M. (1993). A psychoeducational program for families of affectively ill children and adolescents. *Journal of the American Academy of Child & Adolescent Psychiatry*, *32*(4), 770–774.

Brotman, M. A., Schmajuk, M., Rich, B. A., Dickstein, D. P., Guyer, A. E., Costello, E. J., ... & Leibenluft, E. (2006). Prevalence, clinical correlates, and longitudinal course of severe mood dysregulation in children. *Biological Psychiatry*, *60*(9), 991–997. doi:10.1016/j.biopsych.2006.08.042

Chambless, D., Sanderson, W., Shoham, V., Bennett Johnson, S., Pope, K., Crits-Christoph, P., ... & McCurry, S. (1996). An update on empirically validated therapies. *The Clinical Psychologist*, *49*, 5–18.

Chambless, D. L., Baker, M. J., Baucom, D. H., Beutler, L. E., Calhoun, K. S., Crits-Christoph, P., ... & Haaga, D. A. (1998). Update on empirically validated therapies, II. *The Clinical Psychologist*, *51*(1), 3–16.

Chambless, D. L., & Hollon, S. D. (1998). Defining empirically supported therapies. *Journal of Consulting and Clinical Psychology*, *66*(1), 7–18.

Chambless, D. L., & Ollendick, T. H. (2001). Empirically supported psychological interventions: Controversies and evidence. *Annual Review of Psychology*, *52*(1), 685–716. doi:10.1146/annurev.psych.52.1.685

Emslie, G. J., Mayes, T. L., Laptook, R. S., & Batt, M. (2003). Predictors of response to treatment in children and adolescents with mood disorders. *Psychiatric Clinics of North America*, *26*(2), 435–456. doi:http://dx.doi.org/10.1016/S0193-953X(02)00110-7

Esposito-Smythers, C., Birmaher, B., Valeri, S., Chiappetta, L., Hunt, J., Ryan, N., ... & Keller, M. (2006). Child comorbidity, maternal mood disorder, and perceptions of family functioning among bipolar youth. *Journal of the American Academy of Child & Adolescent Psychiatry*, *45*(8), 955–964. doi:10.1097/01.chi.0000222785.11359.04

Findling, R. L., Gracious, B. L., McNamara, N. K., Youngstrom, E. A., Demeter, C. A., Branicky, L. A., & Calabrese, J. R. (2001). Rapid, continuous cycling and psychiatric co-morbidity in pediatric bipolar I disorder. *Bipolar Disorders*, *3*(4), 202–210.

Fristad, M. A. (2006). Psychoeducational treatment for school-aged children with bipolar disorder. *Development and Psychopathology*, *18*(4), 1289–1306. doi:10.1017/S0954579406060627

Fristad, M. A. (2016). Evidence-based psychotherapies and nutritional interventions for children with bipolar spectrum disorders and their families. *The Journal of Clinical Psychiatry*, *77*(Supplement E1), e4. doi:10.4088/JCP.15017su1 c.04

Fristad, M. A., Arnold, J. S. G., & Leffler, J. M. (2011). *Psychotherapy for children with bipolar and depressive disorders*. New York: Guilford Press.

Fristad, M. A., Gavazzi, S. M., & Soldano, K. W. (1998). Multi-family psychoeducation groups for childhood mood disorders: A program description and preliminary efficacy data. *Contemporary Family Therapy*, *20*(3), 385–402. doi:10.1023/a:1022477215195

Fristad, M. A., & Goldberg-Arnold, J. S. (2003). Family interventions for early-onset bipolar disorder. In B. G. Geller & M. P. DelBello (eds.), *Bipolar disorder in childhood and early adolescence* (pp. 295–313). New York: Guilford Press.

Fristad, M. A., Goldberg-Arnold, J. S., & Gavazzi, S. M. (2002). Multifamily psychoeducation groups (MFPG) for families of children with bipolar disorder. *Bipolar Disorders*, *4*(4), 254–262.

Fristad, M. A., Verducci, J. S., Walters, K., & Young, M. E. (2009). Impact of multifamily psychoeducational psychotherapy in treating children aged 8 to 12 years with mood disorders. *Archives of General Psychiatry*, *66*(9), 1013–1021. doi:10.1001/archgenpsychiatry.2009.112

Garrett, A. S., Reiss, A. L., Howe, M. E., Kelley, R. G., Singh, M. K., Adleman, N. E., ... & Chang, K. D. (2012). Abnormal amygdala and prefrontal cortex activation to facial expressions in pediatric bipolar disorder. *Journal of the American Academy of Child & Adolescent Psychiatry*, *51*(8), 821–831. doi:http://dx.doi.org/10.1016/j.jaac.2012.06.005

Geller, B., Bolhofner, K., Craney, J. L., Williams, M., DelBello, M. P., & Gundersen, K. (2000). Psychosocial functioning in a prepubertal and early adolescent bipolar disorder phenotype. *Journal of the American Academy of Child & Adolescent Psychiatry, 39*(12), 1543–1548.

Geller, B., Craney, J. L., Bolhofner, K., Nickelsburg, M. J., Williams, M., & Zimerman, B. (2002). Two-year prospective follow-up of children with a prepubertal and early adolescent bipolar disorder phenotype. *American Journal of Psychiatry, 159*(6), 927–933. doi:10.1176/appi.ajp.159.6.927

Geller, B., Tillman, R., Bolhofner, K., & Zimerman, B. (2008). Child bipolar I disorder: Prospective continuity with adult bipolar I disorder; characteristics of second and third episodes; predictors of 8-year outcome. *Archives of General Psychiatry, 65*(10), 1125–1133. doi:10.1001/archpsyc.65.10.1125

Goldstein, M. J., & Miklowitz, D. J. (1995). The effectiveness of psychoeducational family therapy in the treatment of schizophrenic disorders. *Journal of Marital and Family Therapy, 21*(4), 361–376.

Goldstein, T. R., Birmaher, B., Axelson, D., Goldstein, B. I., Gill, M. K., Esposito-Smythers, C., . . . & Keller, M. (2009). Psychosocial functioning among bipolar youth. *Journal of Affective Disorders, 114*(1–3), 174–183. doi:10.1016/j.jad.2008.07.001

Goldstein, T. R., Miklowitz, D. J., & Mullen, K. L. (2006). Social skills knowledge and performance among adolescents with bipolar disorder. *Bipolar Disorders, 8*(4), 350–361.

Holder, D., & Anderson, C. (1990). Psychoeducational family intervention for depressed patients and their families. In G. I. Keitner (ed.), *Depression and families: Impact and treatment* (pp. 159–184). Washington, DC: American Psychiatric Press.

Jacobs, R. H., Becker, S. J., Curry, J. F., Silva, S. G., Ginsburg, G. S., Henry, D. B., & Reinecke, M. A. (2014). Increasing positive outlook partially mediates the effect of empirically supported treatments on depression symptoms among adolescents. *Journal of Cognitive Psychotherapy, 28*(1), 3–19. doi:10.1891/0889–8391.28.1.3

Kaufman, N. K., Rohde, P., Seeley, J. R., Clarke, G. N., & Stice, E. (2005). Potential mediators of cognitive-behavioral therapy for adolescents with comorbid major depression and conduct disorder. *Journal of Consulting and Clinical Psychology, 73*(1), 38–46. doi:10.1037/0022-006x.73.1.38

Leahy, R. L. (2005). Special series: Cognitive therapy of bipolar disorder: Introduction. *Cognitive and Behavioral Practice, 12*(1), 64–65. doi:http://dx.doi.org/10.1016/S1077-7229(05)80040-9

Leibenluft, E., Charney, D. S., Towbin, K. E., Bhangoo, R. K., & Pine, D. S. (2003). Defining clinical phenotypes of juvenile mania. *American Journal of Psychiatry, 160*(3), 430–437.

Lewinsohn, P. M., Seeley, J. R., & Klein, D. N. (2003). Bipolar disorders during adolescence. *Acta Psychiatrica Scandinavica*, Supplement 418, 47–50.

Lukens, E. P., & McFarlane, W. R. (2004). Psychoeducation as evidence-based practice: Considerations for practice, research, and policy. *Brief Treatment and Crisis Intervention, 4*(3), 205–225.

MacPherson, H. A., Algorta, G. P., Mendenhall, A. N., Fields, B. W., & Fristad, M. A. (2014). Predictors and moderators in the randomized trial of multifamily psychoeducational psychotherapy for childhood mood disorders. *Journal of Clinical Child & Adolescent Psychology, 43*(3), 459–472. doi:10.1080/15374416.2013.807735

MacPherson, H. A., Leffler, J. M., & Fristad, M. A. (2014). Implementation of multi-family psychoeducational psychotherapy for childhood mood disorders in an outpatient community setting. *Journal of Marital and Family Therapy, 40*(2), 193–211. doi:10.1111/jmft.12013

MacPherson, H. A., Weinstein, S. M., Henry, D. B., & West, A. E. (2016). Mediators in the randomized trial of Child- and Family-Focused Cognitive-Behavioral Therapy for pediatric bipolar disorder. *Behaviour Research and Therapy*, 85, 60–71. doi:http://dx.doi.org/10.1016/j.brat.2016.08.014

McClellan, J., Kowatch, R., & Findling, R. L. (2007). Practice parameter for the assessment and treatment of children and adolescents with bipolar disorder. *Journal of the American Academy of Child & Adolescent Psychiatry*, 46(1), 107–125. doi:http://dx.doi.org/10.1097/01.chi.0000242240.69678.c4

Mendenhall, A. N., Fristad, M. A., & Early, T. J. (2009). Factors influencing service utilization and mood symptom severity in children with mood disorders: Effects of multifamily psychoeducation groups (MFPGs). *Journal of Consulting and Clinical Psychology*, 77(3), 463–473. doi:10.1037/a0014527

Miklowitz, D. J., Axelson, D. A., Birmaher, B., George, E. L., Taylor, D. O., Schneck, C. D., ... & Brent, D. A. (2008). Family-focused treatment for adolescents with bipolar disorder: Results of a 2-year randomized trial. *Archives of General Psychiatry*, 65(9), 1053–1061. doi:10.1001/archpsyc.65.9.1053

Miklowitz, D. J., Axelson, D. A., George, E. L., Taylor, D. O., Schneck, C. D., Sullivan, A. E., ... & Birmaher, B. (2009). Expressed emotion moderates the effects of family-focused treatment for bipolar adolescents. *Journal of the American Academy of Child & Adolescent Psychiatry*, 48(6), 643–651. doi:http://dx.doi.org/10.1097/CHI.0b013e3181a0ab9d

Miklowitz, D. J., George, E. L., Axelson, D. A., Kim, E. Y., Birmaher, B., Schneck, C., ... & Brent, D. A. (2004). Family-focused treatment for adolescents with bipolar disorder. *Journal of Affective Disorders*, 82(Supplement 1), S113–128. doi:10.1016/j.jad.2004.05.020

Miklowitz, D. J., & Goldstein, M. J. (1990). Behavioral family treatment for patients with bipolar affective disorder. *Behavior Modification*, 14(4), 457–489.

Miklowitz, D. J., Schneck, C. D., Singh, M. K., Taylor, D. O., George, E. L., Cosgrove, V. E., ... & Chang, K. D. (2013). Early intervention for symptomatic youth at risk for bipolar disorder: A randomized trial of family-focused therapy. *Journal of the American Academy of Child & Adolescent Psychiatry*, 52(2), 121–131. doi:10.1016/j.jaac.2012.10.007

Pavuluri, M. N., Graczyk, P. A., Henry, D. B., Carbray, J. A., Heidenreich, J., & Miklowitz, D. J. (2004). Child- and family-focused cognitive-behavioral therapy for pediatric bipolar disorder: Development and preliminary results. *Journal of the American Academy of Child & Adolescent Psychiatry*, 43(5), 528–537. doi:10.1097/00004583–200405000-00006

Pavuluri, M. N., Henry, D. B., Devineni, B., Carbray, J. A., Naylor, M. W., & Janicak, P. G. (2004). A pharmacotherapy algorithm for stabilization and maintenance of pediatric bipolar disorder. *Journal of the American Academy of Child & Adolescent Psychiatry*, 43(7), 859–867.

Pavuluri, M. N., O'Connor, M. M., Harral, E. M., Moss, M., & Sweeney, J. A. (2006). Impact of neurocognitive function on academic difficulties in pediatric bipolar disorder: A clinical translation. *Biological Psychiatry*, 60(9), 951–956. doi:http://dx.doi.org/10.1016/j.biopsych.2006.03.027

Pavuluri, M. N., O'Connor, M. M., Harral, E., & Sweeney, J. A. (2007). Affective neural circuitry during facial emotion processing in pediatric bipolar disorder. *Biological Psychiatry*, 62(2), 158–167. doi:10.1016/j.biopsych.2006.07.011

Pavuluri, M. N., O'Connor, M. M., Harral, E. M., & Sweeney, J. A. (2008). An fMRI study of the interface between affective and cognitive neural circuitry in pediatric bipolar disorder. *Psychiatry Research: Neuroimaging*, 162(3), 244–255. doi:http://dx.doi.org/10.1016/j.pscychresns.2007.10.003

Peters, A. T., Weinstein, S. M., Isaia, A., Van Meter, A., Henry, D. B., & West, A. E. (2016). Symptom dimensions and trajectories of functioning among bipolar youth: A cluster analysis. Paper presented at the 2016 Meeting of the International Society for Bipolar Disorders, Amsterdam, the Netherlands.

Rich, B. A., Carver, F. W., Holroyd, T., Rosen, H. R., Mendoza, J. K., Cornwell, B. R., ... & Leibenluft, E. (2011). Different neural pathways to negative affect in youth with pediatric bipolar disorder and severe mood dysregulation. *Journal of Psychiatric Research*, *45*(10), 1283–1294. doi:http://dx.doi.org/10.1016/j.jpsychires.2011.04.006

Rohde, P., Lewinsohn, P. M., Clarke, G. N., Hops, H., & Seeley, J. R. (2005). The Adolescent Coping with Depression Course: A cognitive-behavioral approach to the treatment of adolescent depression. In E. D. Hibbs & P. S. Jensen (eds.), *Psychosocial treatments for child and adolescent disorders: Empirically based strategies for clinical practice.* 2nd edn (pp. 219–237). Washington, DC: American Psychological Association.

Rucklidge, J. J. (2006). Psychosocial functioning of adolescents with and without paediatric bipolar disorder. *Journal of Affective Disorders*, *91*(2–3), 181–188. doi:http://dx.doi.org/10.1016/j.jad.2006.01.001

Southam-Gerow, M. A., & Prinstein, M. J. (2014). Evidence base updates: The evolution of the evaluation of psychological treatments for children and adolescents. *Journal of Clinical Child & Adolescent Psychology*, *43*(1), 1–6. doi:10.1080/15374416.2013.855128

Stark, K. D., Swearer, S., Kurowski, C., Sommer, D., & Bowen, B. (1996). Targeting the child and family: A holistic approach to treating child and adolescent depressive disorders. In E. D. Hibbs & P. S. Jensen (eds.), *Psychosocial treatments for child and adolescent disorders: Empirically based strategies for clinical practice* (pp. 207–238). Washington, DC: American Psychological Association.

Stringaris, A., Cohen, P., Pine, D. S., & Leibenluft, E. (2009). Adult outcomes of youth irritability: A 20-year prospective community-based study. *American Journal of Psychiatry*, *166*(9), 1048–1054. doi:10.1176/appi.ajp.2009.08121849

Tillman, R., & Geller, B. (2003). Definitions of rapid, ultrarapid, and ultradian cycling and of episode duration in pediatric and adult bipolar disorders: A proposal to distinguish episodes from cycles. *Journal of Child and Adolescent Psychopharmacology*, *13*(3), 267–271.

Tillman, R., Geller, B., Bolhofner, K., Craney, J. L., Williams, M., & Zimerman, B. (2003). Ages of onset and rates of syndromal and subsyndromal comorbid DSM-IV diagnoses in a prepubertal and early adolescent bipolar disorder phenotype. *Journal of the American Academy of Child & Adolescent Psychiatry*, *42*(12), 1486–1493. doi:http://dx.doi.org/10.1097/00004583-200312000-00016

Washburn, J. J., West, A. E., & Heil, J. A. (2011). Treatment of pediatric bipolar disorder: A review. *Minerva Psichiatrica*, *52*(1), 21.

Weinstein, S. M., Henry, D. B., Katz, A. C., Peters, A. T., & West, A. E. (2015). Treatment moderators of child- and family-focused cognitive-behavioral therapy for pediatric bipolar disorder. *Journal of the American Academy of Child & Adolescent Psychiatry*, *54*(2), 116–125. doi:http://dx.doi.org/10.1016/j.jaac.2014.11.007

West, A. E., Henry, D. B., & Pavuluri, M. N. (2007). Maintenance model of integrated psychosocial treatment in pediatric bipolar disorder: A pilot feasibility study. *Journal of the American Academy of Child & Adolescent Psychiatry*, *46*(2), 205–212. doi:10.1097/01.chi.0000246068.85577.d7

West, A. E., Jacobs, R. H., Westerholm, R., Lee, A., Carbray, J., Heidenreich, J., & Pavuluri, M. N. (2009). Child- and family-focused cognitive-behavioral therapy for pediatric bipolar disorder:

Pilot study of group treatment format. *Journal of the Canadian Academy of Child and Adolescent Psychiatry, 18*(3), 239–246.

West, A. E., & Weinstein, S. M. (2012). A family-based psychosocial treatment model. *Israel Journal of Psychiatry and Related Sciences, 49*(2), 86–93.

West, A. E., Weinstein, S. M., Peters, A. T., Katz, A., Henry, D., Cruz, R., & Pavuluri, M. (2014). Child- and family-focused cognitive-behavioral therapy for pediatric bipolar disorder: A randomized clinical trial. *Journal of the American Academy of Child & Adolescent Psychiatry, 53*(11), 1168–1178.e11. doi:10.1016/j.jaac.2014.08.013

Wilens, T. E., Biederman, J., Forkner, P., Ditterline, J., Morris, M., Moore, H., . . . & Wozniak, J. (2003). Patterns of comorbidity and dysfunction in clinically referred preschool and school-age children with bipolar disorder. *Journal of Child and Adolescent Psychopharmacology, 13*(4), 495–505. doi:10.1089/104454603322724887

Wozniak, J., Biederman, J., Kiely, K., Ablon, J. S., Faraone, S. V., Mundy, E., & Mennin, D. (1995). Mania-like symptoms suggestive of childhood-onset bipolar disorder in clinically referred children. *Journal of the American Academy of Child & Adolescent Psychiatry, 34*(7), 867–876. doi:http://dx.doi.org/10.1097/00004583–199507000-00010

Wozniak, J., Biederman, J., Kwon, A., Mick, E., Faraone, S., Orlovsky, K., . . . & van Grondelle, A. (2005). How cardinal are cardinal symptoms in pediatric bipolar disorder? An examination of clinical correlates. *Biological Psychiatry, 58*(7), 583–588. doi:http://dx.doi.org/10.1016/j.biopsych.2005.08.014

9

Depression

Deepika Bose and Jeremy W. Pettit

Depression in children and adolescents (hereon referred to as youth) is characterized primarily by emotional disturbances, including sadness, irritability, or loss of interest in activities that were once pleasurable. Depression often includes disturbances in cognition (e.g., trouble concentrating, indecisiveness), sleep, appetite, and self-evaluation (e.g., feelings of guilt, worthlessness). Recurrent thoughts of death and suicide also are common. According to the *Diagnostic and Statistical Manual of Mental Disorders*, 5th edition (American Psychiatric Association [APA], 2013), a major depressive episode (MDE) occurs when youth experience at least five symptoms of depression, including sadness or irritability or anhedonia, nearly every day for at least two weeks. A diagnosis of major depressive disorder is made when youth experience one or more MDEs. A more chronic presentation of symptoms yields a diagnosis of persistent depressive disorder. Persistent depressive disorder is diagnosed when youth experience depressed or irritable mood plus at least two other depressive symptoms for at least one year, with symptoms present most of the day, most days of the year (APA, 2013).

Depressive disorders are among the most common and impairing psychiatric conditions experienced by youth, especially adolescents. The lifetime prevalence of depressive disorders in childhood is approximately 2% (Birmaher et al., 1996; Keenan et al., 2004), and increases rapidly following puberty and reaches 15–20% by age 18 (Lewinsohn et al., 2003; Merikangas et al., 2010). Depression is associated with significant impairment across social and academic domains (Birmaher, Brent, & AACAP Work Group on Quality Issues, 2007; Rao et al., 1995), and, once present, tends to follow a recurrent, chronic course, with over 70% of adolescents experiencing recurrent episodes when followed for a decade or more (Pettit et al., 2013). Furthermore, early onset of depression is a predictor of a more chronic course through adolescence and adulthood (Pettit, Lewinsohn, et al., 2009). Based on the distress and impairment associated with depression, as well as the chronic and recurrent nature of the disorder, theorists and researchers have sought to identify variables that contribute to and maintain depression, and then develop treatments designed to target these variables to reduce the burden of depression.

Etiology and Theoretical Underpinnings of Treatment

Treatment approaches for depression are largely based on cognitive, behavioral, interpersonal, and biological theories. Cognitive theories of depression emphasize the roles of cognitive distortions or irrational thinking patterns (e.g., overgeneralization, catastrophizing), and negative views of one's self, past, present, and future in the development and maintenance of depressive symptoms (Beck, 1976; Verduyn, 2000). According to cognitive theories, treatment should help clients identify negative cognitive distortions and thought patterns, and then generate alternative, more realistic cognitions that will lead to more positive moods.

Behavioral theories of depression assert that depressive symptoms develop and are maintained by a low frequency of positively reinforcing events or behaviors (e.g., positive social interaction) and/or a high frequency of aversive events or behaviors (e.g., social rejection; Lewinsohn, 1974). Subsequently, the main goals of behavioral treatments are to help clients increase the frequency of engaging in pleasant activities such as going to a movie with friends and decrease the frequency of aversive activities such as arguing with parents (Dimidjian et al., 2011), which in turn will lead to more positive and less negative moods, respectively.

Interpersonal theories of depression emphasize the roles of interpersonal stress and poor interpersonal relationships in the development and maintenance of depression (Pettit & Joiner, 2006; Young & Mufson, 2008). According to interpersonal theories, treatments should help clients improve familial and other interpersonal relationships, which in turn will lead to reductions in depressive symptoms (e.g., Mufson et al., 1999).

Biological theories of depression highlight genetic and biological contributions to the etiology of depression. Depression is moderately heritable, with heritability estimates ranging from 0.3 to 0.4 (Sullivan, Neale, & Kendler, 2000). Biological theories emphasize perturbations in neural circuitry involved in stress reactivity and reward responsivity (Bogdan, Nikolova, & Pizzagalli, 2013). According to these theories, treatment should modulate these perturbations in neural circuitry to facilitate reductions in depressive symptoms, either directly through techniques such as neuromodulation (Cook, Espinoza, & Leuchter, 2014) or indirectly through medications that act on neurotransmitters including serotonin and dopamine.

Brief Overview of Evidence-Based Treatments

The theoretical models described above served as the impetus for the development of evidence-based treatments (EBTs) for depression in youth, including cognitive-

Suicide Risk Assessment and Safety Planning

Although suicide risk assessment and management has not been identified as a common component in EBTs for depression, we briefly present recommendations for suicide risk assessment and safety planning given the elevated risk of suicidal behaviors in youth who are depressed (for more details, see Pettit, Buitron, & Green, in press). For a review of treatments specifically targeting self-harm behaviors in youth, we refer readers to Glenn, Franklin, and Nock (2015).

In assessing risk, information should be obtained from as many sources as possible (at least youth and parent) and priority should be given to the strongest predictors of suicide attempt and suicide: a past history of suicide attempt or nonsuicidal self-injury (e.g., Asarnow et al., 2011; Shaffer et al., 1996) and plans for suicide (Pettit, Lewinsohn, et al., 2009; Posner et al., 2011). When specific plans for suicide are present, especially among youth with a history of self-harm, immediate steps need to be taken to ensure the youth's short-term safety, including continuous monitoring and evaluation for hospitalization.

When suicidal ideation is present but youth do not have specific plans for suicide, safety planning is an efficient approach to managing suicide risk (Stanley & Brown, 2012; Pettit, Buitron, & Green, in press). Safety planning involves collaboration between therapists and youth (and ideally parents) to develop a detailed, sequential, and written plan of action for staying safe in the event suicidal thoughts emerge or intensify. Step 1 involves identifying and listing specific, personal warning signs that prompt youth to use the safety plan. Step 2 involves identifying and listing specific strategies youth can do by themselves to distract themselves from the crisis or suicidal thoughts. Step 3 involves identifying and listing social contacts that youth can seek out to distract themselves from the crisis or suicidal thoughts. Step 4 involves identifying and listing social contacts (i.e., trusted adults) that youth can seek out to help with the suicidal crisis. Step 5 involves identifying and listing professional resources that youth can contact for help. Finally, Step 6 involves developing plans to restrict access to potentially lethal means of self-injury. When developing a safety plan, therapists should assess potential barriers to implementing a step and help youth problem-solve to remove those barriers.

behavioral therapies (CBTs) and interpersonal therapy (IPT). Below, we review the current status of psychosocial EBTs for youth depression.

Cognitive-Behavioral Therapy (CBT)

CBT is a structured, goal-oriented treatment that seeks to identify and change maladaptive cognitions and behaviors associated with depression. The underlying premise of CBT is that thoughts, emotions, and behaviors are interrelated and influence each other, such that changes in thoughts and/or behaviors lead to changes in emotions. Cognitive and behavioral skills are initially taught in-session (through didactics and role-play), and then are applied to real-life contexts in the form of homework assignments. Treatment duration typically ranges from 12 to 16 weekly sessions, and treatment can be delivered in individual youth format, group format, parent-involved format, or via computer (e.g., Asarnow, Scott, & Mintz, 2002; Kahn et al., 1990; Nelson, Barnard, & Cain, 2003; Roberts et al., 2003; Stasiak et al., 2014). As a general family of treatments, CBT is the most extensively studied and supported treatment model for youth depression (Weersing et al., 2017). The most well-known CBTs for youth depression are the Coping with Depression Course and Self-Control Therapy.

Adolescent Coping with Depression Course (CWD-A). The original CWD-A (Clarke & Lewinsohn, 1986) was designed to be delivered in a group, classroom-based format over 14 two-hour sessions. Since its inception, CWD-A has served as a template for several adaptations and delivery formats, including youth-only delivery, parent-involved delivery, and prevention of depression in at-risk youth (e.g., Clarke et al., 1995). Large-scale, multisite trials for adolescent depression, including the Treatment for Adolescents with Depression study (TADS Team, 2004) and the Treatment of SSRI-Resistant Depression in Adolescents study (TORDIA; Brent et al., 2008), used modular CBTs based largely on CWD-A and the Pittsburgh Cognitive Therapy protocol for adolescents (Brent et al., 1997), the latter of which emphasized monitoring and modification of negative cognitions and development of problem-solving skills.

CWD-A and its adaptations target cognitive skills such as identifying and modifying irrational or negative thoughts, and behavioral skills such as relaxation, increasing pleasant activities, and improving social skills (Lewinsohn et al., 1990).

Self-Control Therapy (SCT). SCT (Stark, Reynolds, & Kaslow, 1987) was developed around the same time as CWD-A, and, like CWD-A, SCT was designed to be delivered in a group format in school settings over twelve 45–50-minute sessions. SCT targets both cognitions and behaviors and emphasizes the development of self-management skills, including self-monitoring, setting realistic standards, and drawing accurate causal interpretations of positive and negative events.

Interpersonal Therapy for Adolescents (IPT-A)

IPT-A (Mufson et al., 1993) is a structured, goal-oriented treatment that seeks to reduce depressive symptoms and improve interpersonal functioning. In treatment, the therapist and youth identify a specific problem area in interpersonal functioning, such as grief or loss, role transition, interpersonal disputes, or interpersonal skills deficits. In identifying a problem area, emphasis is placed on developmentally relevant topics such as peer pressure, parental relationships, dyadic interpersonal relationships, and initial experiences with the death of a relative or friend (Mufson et al., 1993, 1999). In the context of the specific problem area, the therapist and client discuss and practice communication and problem-solving techniques. IPT-A is typically delivered over twelve 45-minute sessions, either in adolescent individual format or in group format (e.g., Mufson et al., 1999; Young, Mufson, & Davies, 2006). IPT-A is considered a well-established treatment for adolescents (Weersing et al., 2017).

Components of Evidence-Based Treatments

Despite differences in underlying theory and delivery formats, the EBTs described above share common practices, or components. In recent years, researchers have advocated evaluating EBTs on a component level of analysis, with the goal of identifying specific components that are commonly used and contribute to successful treatment outcomes. In the context of youth depression, researchers have identified 24 separate components used in treatments (Chorpita & Daleiden, 2009). The most commonly used components are psychoeducation (youth), cognitive restructuring, activity scheduling, problem-solving, self-monitoring, and maintenance/relapse prevention (Chorpita & Daleiden, 2009; McCarty & Weisz, 2007; Weersing, Rozenman, & Gonzalez, 2009). Each of these six components has been used in a majority of treatments examined in clinical trials for youth depression.

Psychoeducation

Psychoeducation refers to sharing information with youth regarding the development, course, and symptoms of depression, and how treatment aims to target the youth's symptoms (Birmaher, Brent, & AACAP Work Group on Quality Issues, 2007). Psychoeducation is typically provided to youth orally at the beginning of treatment, and sometimes is supplemented with the distribution of written materials such as handouts. CBTs often include a brief description of the treatment rationale, goal-setting, and the development of a behavioral contract between the therapist and youth (Lewinsohn, Clarke, & Hoberman, 1989). In IPT, the therapist typically reviews the adolescent's depressive symptoms, discusses the underlying principles of IPT, and may also establish goals and set a contract as a commitment to therapy (Mufson et al., 2011).

Although a relatively common practice, individual treatments differ in terms of which and how many treatment sessions explicitly include psychoeducation (Weersing, Rozenman, & Gonzalez, 2009). For example, the manual for CWD-A includes psychoeducational components during the first session only, the manual for the Pittsburgh Cognitive Therapy protocol includes psychoeducational components during the first three sessions, and the manual for the Treatment for Adolescent Depression Study (TADS) includes psychoeducational components during sessions 1, 3, 5, and 12 (Weersing, Rozenman, & Gonzalez, 2009). Additionally, although typically delivered to youth only, several treatments provide psychoeducation to parents, either together with youth or separately (Lewinsohn et al., 1990; Mufson et al., 1999; Rosselló & Bernall, 1999). Overall, psychoeducation is a practice common to EBTs for youth depression, and its use has been associated with improvements in depressive symptoms and treatment adherence (Brent et al., 1993).

Cognitive Restructuring

Cognitive components involve a collaborative approach between therapists and youth to identify negative thoughts, beliefs, and interpretations that maintain depressed mood. After identifying these negative thoughts, beliefs, and interpretations, therapists help youth develop skills in cognitive restructuring. Cognitive restructuring involves challenging negative thoughts, beliefs, and interpretations by generating realistic alternatives and positive statements (Verduyn, 2000). Cognitive restructuring is common to CBTs for youth depression, and there is some evidence that its use leads to improvements in depressive symptoms: cognitive change mediated depression reduction effects in a trial of CWD-A (Kaufman et al., 2005). However, cognitive techniques are unlikely to be an *essential* treatment component because similar effect sizes have been found for treatments that include cognitive components and treatments that do not include cognitive components (Weisz, McCarty, & Valeri, 2006).

Activity Scheduling

Activity scheduling, also referred to as behavioral activation (BA), involves working collaboratively with youth to identity activities that provide a sense of pleasure or achievement, and then scheduling specific times for youth to participate in these identified activities (Dimidjian et al., 2011). Activity scheduling is based on the premise that participation in pleasant activities will induce positive emotions, which in turn will serve as positive reinforcement to increase the likelihood of future participation in pleasant activities, leading to an upward spiral of positive mood. Activity scheduling also may be used to target avoidance, or escape behaviors, that are commonly seen in youth depression (Chu et al., 2009). Although avoidance behaviors (e.g., staying home from school) provide short-term relief from negative emotions, they can maintain depressed mood and result in a number of secondary problems with negative long-term consequences (e.g., poor school attendance, falling grades, limited social interaction; Jacobson, Martell, & Dimidjian, 2001). Activity scheduling directly targets avoidant behaviors by encouraging the youth to actively engage in approach behaviors.

Preliminary studies suggest that activity scheduling produces depression reduction effects in youth (Chu et al., 2009; Ruggerio et al., 2007). For example, a pilot study testing the preliminary efficacy of a group BA program for anxiety and depression in youth demonstrated that most participants experienced a moderate benefit from the intervention (Chu et al., 2009). Nevertheless, further evaluation of the efficacy of this component is necessary before firm conclusions are drawn.

Problem-Solving

Problem-solving involves training youth on skills to generate and implement solutions for a given problem. Although specific problem-solving protocols differ across EBTs, protocols consistently emphasize problem recognition, brainstorming/identifying potential solutions, evaluating potential solutions, and then choosing and implementing a solution. Problem-solving is an active coping skill that may reduce stress and enhance interpersonal relationships, and may be particularly helpful for adolescents who engage in rumination (Waller et al., 2014). The use of problem-solving has been associated with a higher rate of response to treatment (Kennard et al., 2009).

Self-Monitoring

Self-monitoring involves the repeated measurement of the youth's behavior (by the youth), with most self-monitoring focusing on daily mood and/or activities (e.g., Kauer et al., 2012; Stark, Reynolds, & Kaslow, 1987). For example, youth may be asked to rate their mood prior to and following a target activity, or document the number of times they complete a target activity in the course of a week. The purpose of self-monitoring is to enhance youths' awareness of their moods and to help them identify connections between specific events/activities and mood states. Self-monitoring is one of the more common practices used in youth depression treatment, as approximately 90% of the most successful treatments (i.e., treatments demonstrating an effect size of 0.50 or greater) used some form of self-monitoring (McCarty & Weisz, 2007). The use of self-monitoring techniques in depression treatment also has been associated with increased levels of emotional self-awareness and social behaviors (Gangestad & Snyder, 2000; Kauer et al., 2012).

Maintenance/Relapse Prevention

Maintenance/relapse prevention techniques are designed to review learned skills, anticipate challenges that may arise after treatment, and plan how to use the acquired skills to address those challenges (Curry, 2014). The goal of relapse prevention is to ensure that treatment gains are maintained, and that relapse is prevented. Maintenance/relapse prevention is an important component of depression treatment because youth who respond to treatment remain at a high risk for relapse (a re-emergence of symptoms after a period of remission) and recurrence (a new episode of depression after a period of recovery; Kennard, Hughes, & Foxwell, 2016). Specific techniques can range from "booster" sessions following treatment termination or, in the case of internet-delivered treatments, emails sent to youth reminding them to practice the skills they learned during treatment. For example, during the last sessions of CBT, youth are encouraged to continue using self-monitoring techniques, partake in permanent lifestyle changes that will equip them to handle stressful situations, and actively engage in social support. Additionally, youth may return for booster sessions to review concepts tailored to their specific concerns (Clarke et al., 1999). In IPT, the therapist concludes the acute phase of treatment with a discussion of the positive treatment gains and potential problems that may arise in the future. The maintenance phase of treatment is distinct from the acute phase, and may consist of shorter sessions (e.g., 20–30 minutes) during which the therapist plays a less active role, allowing youth to apply the problem-solving skills learned during the acute phase of treatment (Stuart & Robertson, 2012).

Role of Parents in Treatment

Researchers have proposed that parent involvement in youth depression treatment may lead to enhanced treatment outcomes compared with youth-only treatment (e.g., Birmaher, Brent, & AACAP Work Group on Quality Issues, 2007). There are a number of potentially positive outcomes of parent-involved treatments (e.g., improving parent–child interactions, parenting skills, family problem-solving strategies; Birmaher, Brent, & AACAP Work Group on Quality Issues, 2007; Restifo & Bogels, 2009). Nevertheless, questions remain about the optimal level of parental involvement and the treatment-enhancing effects of parental involvement beyond youth-only treatments (Restifo & Bögels, 2009; Sander & McCarty, 2005). Effect sizes for parent-involved treatments range from small to large (Weisz, McCarty, & Valeri, 2006) and overall are similar to effect sizes for youth-only treatments (Sander & McCarty, 2005). Possible reasons for the failure to clearly demonstrate treatment-enhancing effects of parental involvement include wide variability in the level of parental involvement and the specific parenting variables targeted in treatment (Restifo & Bögels, 2009). Further, as research on parent-involved treatments progresses, it will be important to examine not only treatment-enhancing effects but also specificity and mediation of parenting variables targeted in treatment (Silverman et al., 2018). That is, it will be important to investigate whether parent-involved treatments lead to changes in the specific parenting variables that are targeted in treatment, and whether changes in these specific parenting variables mediate youth depressive symptom reductions.

In contrast to CBTs and IPT, which can involve parents but often do not, recently developed treatment approaches such as attachment-based family therapy (ABFT; Diamond et al., 2002) and family-focused treatment for child depression (FFT-CD; Tompson et al., 2007, in press) explicitly involve parents in treatment. These treatments are rooted in theory and show promise in reducing depression in youth, but further empirical evaluation will be necessary to establish their efficacy for youth depression.

Other Variables Influencing Treatment

Assessment

The assessment of depression is useful for diagnosis, treatment planning, treatment monitoring, and outcome evaluation (Klein, Dougherty, & Olino, 2005). Optimal assessment of depression includes administration of clinical interviews (e.g., *Schedule for Affective Disorders and Schizophrenia in School-Age Children*; Puig-Antich & Chambers, 1978) and rating scales (e.g., Children's Depression Inventory; Kovacs, 1992), and involves the collection of data from both parents and youth. The assessment of variables such as current psychosocial functioning and comorbidities can also inform treatment decisions (Klein, Dougherty, & Olino, 2005). For example, if the greatest level of depression-related impairment occurs in academics (e.g., youth is too depressed to attend school), then the therapist may focus the application of behavioral, cognitive, and interpersonal techniques specifically on improving academic functioning. The assessment of comorbidities is useful for determining whether depression is the most impairing condition experienced by the youth, and ensuring that treatment for depression is prioritized over treatments for other conditions (e.g., anxiety disorders). Furthermore, due to the episodic and cyclical nature of depression, it is important to regularly monitor key symptoms (e.g., suicidal ideation) that may warrant immediate action.

Comorbidity

Common comorbidities include anxiety disorders, attention-deficit/hyperactivity disorder, disruptive behavior disorders (e.g., oppositional defiant disorder, conduct disorder), and substance use disorders (Avenevoli et al., 2015; Cummings, Caporino, & Kendall, 2014; Meinzer, Pettit, & Viswesvaran, 2014). Typically, the onset of these disorders temporally precedes the onset of depression, with the exception of substance use disorders. The presence of comorbid disorders, especially anxiety disorders, predicts poorer treatment response (e.g., Curry et al., 2006; Weersing et al., 2017). Given the high rates of comorbidities and their association with poorer depression treatment response, researchers have designed and begun to evaluate interventions that directly target depression and its comorbidities. Examples include transdiagnostic approaches for comorbid anxiety and depression (Chu et al., 2016), sequenced/coordinated approaches for comorbid substance use disorders and depression (Rohde et al., 2014), and modularized approaches for anxiety, depression, trauma, and conduct disorders (Weisz et al., 2012).

Demographics

Overall, demographic variables (e.g., age, sex, ethnicity) do not consistently predict or moderate response to treatment (Weersing et al., 2017). However, there is some evidence that CBT and IPT may be more efficacious among older relative to younger youth (Asarnow et al., 2009; Mufson et al., 2004). Further research is needed on age as a moderator of youth depression treatment response. Regarding youth race and ethnicity, ethnic minority youth with depression tend to underutilize services and may not receive adequate services compared to Non-Hispanic White individuals (Stewart, Simmons, & Habibpour, 2012). Developing and evaluating strategies for enhancing mental health service utilization for racial and ethnic minority youth represents a priority.

Medication

Antidepressant medications are widely used and efficacious for the treatment of depression in youth (Bachmann et al., 2016). Of most direct relevance to this chapter is the use of antidepressant medications as an adjuvant to psychotherapy. To our knowledge, adjunctive medication has been evaluated in the context of CBT but not other psychosocial interventions for youth depression. Results from clinical trials largely provide evidence of a treatment-enhancing effect of adjuvant antidepressant medication. For example, in the TADS study (TADS Team, 2004), researchers compared the effects of CBT alone, fluoxetine alone, a combination of CBT and fluoxetine, and a pill placebo (with clinical management) on depressive symptoms in youth. The combination of CBT and fluoxetine was superior to pill placebo and each treatment condition alone. In the TORDIA study (Brent et al., 2008), adolescents who had not responded to an SSRI switched medications (either to a different SSRI or venlafaxine) with or without adjunctive CBT. Combined medication plus CBT led to superior depression reduction effects compared with medication-only groups (Brent et al., 2008). Overall, data support the use of antidepressant medication as an adjuvant to enhance the effects of CBT for youth depression. Additional research is needed to evaluate the potential enhancing effects of antidepressant medications as an adjuvant to other psychotherapies.

Conclusion

A number of treatments for youth depression have been developed and established as evidence-based, with CBTs and IPT considered well-established for adolescent depression and CBTs considered possibly efficacious for child depression. Across treatments, the most common components are psychoeducation, cognitive restructuring, activity scheduling, problem-solving, self-monitoring, and maintenance/relapse prevention. Suicide risk assessment and safety planning also is an important component of depression treatment. Future research will be necessary to identify which components are the most efficacious in the reduction of depression, and for which youth. Such research will set the stage for streamlined treatments that are more efficient and efficacious in the treatment of depression in youth.

Useful Resources

- Society of Clinical Child & Adolescent Psychology's Effective Child Therapy Depression site: http://effectivechildtherapy.org/content/depression
- National Institute of Mental Health's Teen Depression site: www.nimh.nih.gov/health/publications/teen-depression/index.shtml
- American Academy of Child & Adolescent Psychiatry's Depression Resource Center: www.aacap.org/aacap/families_and_youth/resource_centers/depression_resource_center/Home.aspx
- Association for Behavioral and Cognitive Therapies' Clinical Resources site: www.abct.org/Resources/?m=mResources&fa=ClinicalResources
- Kaiser Permanente Center for Health Research's listing of Youth Depression Treatment and Prevention Programs site: https://research.kpchr.org/Research/Research-Areas/Mental-Health/Youth-Depression-Programs#Downloads

References

American Psychiatric Association (APA). (2013). *Diagnostic and statistical manual of mental disorders*. 5th edn. Washington, DC: American Psychiatric Association.

Asarnow, J. R., Emslie, G., Clarke, G., Wagner, K. D., Spirito, A., Vitiello, B., . . . & Ryan, N. (2009). Treatment of selective serotonin reuptake inhibitor-resistant depression in adolescents: Predictors and moderators of treatment response. *Journal of the American Academy of Child & Adolescent Psychiatry*, *48*(3), 330–339.

Asarnow, J. R., Porta, G., Spirito, A., Emslie, G., Clarke, G., Wagner, K. D., . . . & Mayes, T. (2011). Suicide attempts and nonsuicidal self-injury in the treatment of resistant depression in adolescents: Findings from the TORDIA study. *Journal of the American Academy of Child & Adolescent Psychiatry*, *50*(8), 772–781.

Asarnow, J. R., Scott, C. V., & Mintz, J. (2002). A combined cognitive-behavioral family education intervention for depression in children: A treatment development study. *Cognitive Therapy and Research*, *26*(2), 221–229.

Avenevoli, S., Swendsen, J., He, J. P., Burstein, M., & Merikangas, K. R. (2015). Major depression in the National Comorbidity Survey – Adolescent Supplement: Prevalence, correlates, and treatment. *Journal of the American Academy of Child & Adolescent Psychiatry*, *54*(1), 37–44.

Bachmann, C. J., Aagaard, L., Burcu, M., Glaeske, G., Kalverdijk, L. J., Petersen, I., . . . & Hoffmann, F. (2016). Trends and patterns of antidepressant use in children and adolescents from five western countries, 2005–2012. *European Neuropsychopharmacology*, *26*(3), 411–419.

Beck, A. T. (1976). *Cognitive therapy and the emotional disorder*. New York: International University Press.

Birmaher, B., Brent, D., & AACAP Work Group on Quality Issues. (2007). Practice parameter for the assessment and treatment of children and adolescents with depressive disorders. *Journal of the American Academy of Child & Adolescent Psychiatry, 46*(11), 1503–1526.

Birmaher, B., Ryan, N. D., Williamson, D. E., Brent, D. A., Kaufman, J., Dahl, R. E., . . . & Nelson, B. (1996). Childhood and adolescent depression: A review of the past 10 years. Part I. *Journal of the American Academy of Child & Adolescent Psychiatry, 35*(11), 1427–1439.

Bogdan, R., Nikolova, Y. S., & Pizzagalli, D. A. (2013). Neurogenetics of depression: A focus on reward processing and stress sensitivity. *Neurobiology of Disease, 52,* 12–23.

Brent, D., Emslie, G., Clarke, G., Wagner, K., Asarnow, J., Keller, M., . . . & Birmaher, B. (2008). The Treatment of Adolescents with SSRI-Resistant Depression (TORDIA): A comparison of switch to venlafaxine or to another SSRI, with or without additional cognitive behavioral therapy. *Journal of the American Medical Association, 299*(8), 901–913.

Brent, D. A., Holder, D., Kolko, D., Birmaher, B., Baugher, M., Roth, C., . . . & Johnson, B. A. (1997). A clinical psychotherapy trial for adolescent depression comparing cognitive, family, and supportive therapy. *Archives of General Psychiatry, 54*(9), 877–885.

Brent, D. A., Poling, K., McKain, B., & Baugher, M. (1993). A psychoeducational program for families of affectively ill children and adolescents. *Journal of the American Academy of Child & Adolescent Psychiatry, 32*(4), 770–774.

Chorpita, B. F., & Daleiden, E. L. (2009). Mapping evidence-based treatments for children and adolescents: Application of the distillation and matching model to 615 treatments from 322 randomized trials. *Journal of Consulting and Clinical Psychology, 77*(3), 566–579.

Chu, B. C., Colognori, D., Weissman, A. S., & Bannon, K. (2009). An initial description and pilot of group behavioral activation therapy for anxious and depressed youth. *Cognitive and Behavioral Practice, 16*(4), 408–419.

Chu, B. C., Crocco, S. T., Esseling, P., Areizaga, M. J., Lindner, A. M., & Skriner, L. C. (2016). Transdiagnostic group behavioral activation and exposure therapy for youth anxiety and depression: Initial randomized controlled trial. *Behaviour Research and Therapy, 76,* 65–75.

Clarke, G. N., Hawkins, W., Murphy, M., Sheeber, L. B., Lewinsohn, P. M., & Seeley, J. R. (1995). Targeted prevention of unipolar depressive disorder in an at-risk sample of high school adolescents: A randomized trial of a group cognitive intervention. *Journal of the American Academy of Child & Adolescent Psychiatry, 34*(3), 312–321.

Clarke, G. N., & Lewinsohn, P. M. (1986). Leader manual for the Adolescent Coping with Depression Course. Unpublished manuscript, Oregon Research Institute.

Clarke, G. N., Rohde, P., Lewinsohn, P. M., Hops, H., & Seeley, J. R. (1999). Cognitive-behavioral treatment of adolescent depression: Efficacy of acute group treatment and booster sessions. *Journal of the American Academy of Child & Adolescent Psychiatry, 38*(3), 272–279.

Cook, I. A., Espinoza, R., & Leuchter, A. F. (2014). Neuromodulation for depression: Invasive and noninvasive (deep brain stimulation, transcranial magnetic stimulation, trigeminal nerve stimulation). *Neurosurgery Clinics of North America, 25*(1), 103–116.

Cummings, C. M., Caporino, N. E., & Kendall, P. C. (2014). Comorbidity of anxiety and depression in children and adolescents: 20 years after. *Psychological Bulletin, 140*(3), 816.

Curry, J., Rohde, P., Simons, A., Silva, S., Vitiello, B., Kratochvil, C., . . . & Weller, E. (2006). Predictors and moderators of acute outcome in the Treatment for Adolescents with Depression Study (TADS). *Journal of the American Academy of Child & Adolescent Psychiatry, 45*(12), 1427–1439.

Curry, J. F. (2014). Future directions in research on psychotherapy for adolescent depression. *Journal of Clinical Child & Adolescent Psychology, 43*(3), 510–526.

Diamond, G. S., Reis, B. F., Diamond, G. M., Siqueland, L., & Isaacs, L. (2002). Attachment-based family therapy for depressed adolescents: A treatment development study. *Journal of the American Academy of Child & Adolescent Psychiatry*, *41*(10), 1190–1196.

Dimidjian, S., Barrera Jr., M., Martell, C., Muñoz, R. F., & Lewinsohn, P. M. (2011). The origins and current status of behavioral activation treatments for depression. *Annual Review of Clinical Psychology*, *7*, 1–38.

Gangestad, S. W., & Snyder, M. (2000). Self-monitoring: Appraisal and reappraisal. *Psychological Bulletin*, *126*(4), 530–555.

Glenn, C. R., Franklin, J. C., & Nock, M. K. (2015). Evidence-based psychosocial treatments for self-injurious thoughts and behaviors in youth. *Journal of Clinical Child & Adolescent Psychology*, *44*(1), 1–29.

Jacobson, N. S., Martell, C. R., & Dimidjian, S. (2001). Behavioral activation treatment for depression: Returning to contextual roots. *Clinical Psychology: Science and Practice*, *8*(3), 255–270.

Kahn, J. S., Kehle, T. J., Jenson, W. R., & Clark, E. (1990). Comparison of cognitive-behavioral, relaxation, and self-modeling interventions for depression among middle-school students. *School Psychology Review*, *19*(2), 196–211.

Kauer, S. D., Reid, S. C., Crooke, A. H. D., Khor, A., Hearps, S. J. C., Jorm, A. F., . . . & Patton, G. (2012). Self-monitoring using mobile phones in the early stages of adolescent depression: Randomized controlled trial. *Journal of Medical Internet Research*, *14*(3), e67.

Kaufman, N. K., Rohde, P., Seeley, J. R., Clarke, G. N., & Stice, E. (2005). Potential mediators of cognitive-behavioral therapy for adolescents with comorbid major depression and conduct disorder. *Journal of Consulting and Clinical Psychology*, *73*(1), 38–46.

Keenan, K., Hipwell, A., Duax, J., Stouthamer-Loeber, M., & Loeber, R. (2004). Phenomenology of depression in young girls. *Journal of the American Academy of Child & Adolescent Psychiatry*, *43*(9), 1098–1106.

Kennard, B. D., Clarke, G. N., Weersing, V. R., Asarnow, J. R., Shamseddeen, W., Porta, G., . . . & Keller, M. B. (2009). Effective components of TORDIA cognitive-behavioral therapy for adolescent depression: Preliminary findings. *Journal of Consulting and Clinical Psychology*, *77*(6), 1033–1041.

Kennard, B. D., Hughes, J. L., & Foxwell, A. A. (2016). *CBT for depression in children and adolescents: A guide to relapse prevention*. New York: Guilford Publications.

Klein, D. N., Dougherty, L. R., & Olino, T. M. (2005). Toward guidelines for evidence-based assessment of depression in children and adolescents. *Journal of Clinical Child & Adolescent Psychology*, *34*(3), 412–432.

Kovacs, M. (1992). *Children's depression inventory*. North Tonawanda, NY: Multi-Health System.

Lewinsohn, P. M. (1974). A behavior approach to depression. In R. J. Friedman & M. M. Katz (eds.), *The psychology of depression: Contemporary theory and research* (pp. 157–185). New York: Wiley.

Lewinsohn, P. M., Clarke, G. N., & Hoberman, H. M. (1989). The Coping With Depression Course: Review and future directions. *Canadian Journal of Behavioural Science*, *21*(4), 470–493.

Lewinsohn, P. M., Clarke, G. N., Hops, H., & Andrews, J. (1990). Cognitive-behavioral treatment for depressed adolescents. *Behavior Therapy*, *21*(4), 385–401.

Lewinsohn, P. M., Pettit, J. W., Joiner Jr., T. E., & Seeley, J. R. (2003). The symptomatic expression of major depressive disorder in adolescents and young adults. *Journal of Abnormal Psychology*, *112*(2), 244–252.

McCarty, C. A., & Weisz, J. R. (2007). Effects of psychotherapy for depression in children and adolescents: What we can (and can't) learn from meta-analysis and component profiling. *Journal of the American Academy of Child & Adolescent Psychiatry, 46*(7), 879–886.

Meinzer, M. C., Pettit, J. W., & Viswesvaran, C. (2014). The co-occurrence of attention-deficit/hyperactivity disorder and unipolar depression in children and adolescents: A meta-analytic review. *Clinical Psychology Review, 34*(8), 595–607.

Merikangas, K. R., He, J. P., Burstein, M., Swanson, S. A., Avenevoli, S., Cui, L., . . . & Swendsen, J. (2010). Lifetime prevalence of mental disorders in US adolescents: Results from the National Comorbidity Survey Replication–Adolescent Supplement (NCS-A). *Journal of the American Academy of Child & Adolescent Psychiatry, 49*(10), 980–989.

Mufson, L., Dorta, K. P., Moreau, D., & Weissman, M. M. (2011). *Interpersonal psychotherapy for depressed adolescents*. New York: Guilford Press.

Mufson, L., Dorta, K. P., Wickramaratne, P., Nomura, Y., Olfson, M., & Weissman, M. M. (2004). A randomized effectiveness trial of interpersonal psychotherapy for depressed adolescents. *Archives of General Psychiatry, 61*(6), 577–584.

Mufson, L., Moreau, D., Weissman, M. M., & Klerman, G. L. (1993). *Interpersonal psychotherapy for depressed adolescents*. New York: Guilford Press.

Mufson, L., Weissman, M. M., Moreau, D., & Garfinkel, R. (1999). Efficacy of interpersonal psychotherapy for depressed adolescents. *Archives of General Psychiatry, 56*(6), 573–579.

Nelson, E. L., Barnard, M., & Cain, S. (2003). Treating childhood depression over videoconferencing. *Telemedicine Journal and e-Health, 9*(1), 49–55.

Pettit, J. W., Buitron, V., & Green, K. L. (in press). Assessment and management of suicide risk in children and adolescents, *Cognitive and Behavioral Practice*.

Pettit, J. W., Hartley, C., Lewinsohn, P. M., Seeley, J. R., & Klein, D. N. (2013). Is liability to recurrent major depressive disorder present before first episode onset in adolescence or acquired after the initial episode? *Journal of Abnormal Psychology, 122*(2), 353–358.

Pettit, J. W., & Joiner, T. E. (2006). *Chronic depression: Interpersonal sources, therapeutic solutions*. Washington, DC: American Psychological Association.

Pettit, J. W., Lewinsohn, P. M., Roberts, R. E., Seeley, J. R., & Monteith, L. (2009). The long-term course of depression: Development of an empirical index and identification of early adult outcomes. *Psychological Medicine, 39*(3), 403–412.

Posner, K., Brown, G. K., Stanley, B., Brent, D. A., Yershova, K. V., Oquendo, M. A., . . . & Mann, J. J. (2011). The Columbia-Suicide Severity Rating Scale: Initial validity and internal consistency findings from three multisite studies with adolescents and adults. *American Journal of Psychiatry, 168*(12), 1266–1277.

Puig-Antich, J., & Chambers, W. (1978). *The schedule for affective disorders and schizophrenia for school-age children (Kiddie-SADS)*. New York: New York State Psychiatric Institute.

Rao, U. M. A., Ryan, N. D., Birmaher, B., Dahl, R. E., Williamson, D. E., Kaufman, J., . . . & Nelson, B. (1995). Unipolar depression in adolescents: Clinical outcome in adulthood. *Journal of the American Academy of Child & Adolescent Psychiatry, 34*(5), 566–578.

Restifo, K., & Bögels, S. (2009). Family processes in the development of youth depression: Translating the evidence to treatment. *Clinical Psychology Review, 29*(4), 294–316.

Roberts, C., Kane, R., Thomson, H., Bishop, B., & Hart, B. (2003). The prevention of depressive symptoms in rural school children: A randomized controlled trial. *Journal of Consulting and Clinical Psychology, 71*(3), 622–628.

Rohde, P., Waldron, H. B., Turner, C. W., Brody, J., & Jorgensen, J. (2014). Sequenced versus coordinated treatment for adolescents with comorbid depressive and substance use disorders. *Journal of Consulting and Clinical Psychology, 82*(2), 342–348.

Rosselló, J., & Bernal, G. (1999). The efficacy of cognitive-behavioral and interpersonal treatments for depression in Puerto Rican adolescents. *Journal of Consulting and Clinical Psychology, 67*(5), 734–745.

Ruggiero, K. J., Morris, T. L., Hopko, D. R., & Lejuez, C. W. (2007). Application of behavioral activation treatment for depression to an adolescent with a history of child maltreatment. *Clinical Case Studies, 6*(1), 64–78.

Sander, J. B., & McCarty, C. A. (2005). Youth depression in the family context: Familial risk factors and models of treatment. *Clinical Child and Family Psychology Review, 8*(3), 203–219.

Shaffer, D., Gould, M. S., Fisher, P., Trautman, P., Moreau, D., Kleinman, M., & Flory, M. (1996). Psychiatric diagnosis in child and adolescent suicide. *Archives of General Psychiatry, 53*(4), 339–348.

Silverman, W. K., Marin, C. E., Rey, Y., Jaccard, J., & Pettit, J.W. (2018). Group cognitive behavior therapy (CBT) and CBT with parent involvement for anxiety disorders in youth: Treatment specificity, mediation, and directionality. Unpublished manuscript.

Stanley, B., & Brown, G. K. (2012). Safety planning intervention: A brief intervention to mitigate suicide risk. *Cognitive and Behavioral Practice, 19*(2), 256–264.

Stark, K. D., Reynolds, W. M., & Kaslow, N. J. (1987). A comparison of the relative efficacy of self-control therapy and a behavioral problem-solving therapy for depression in children. *Journal of Abnormal Child Psychology, 15*(1), 91–113.

Stasiak, K., Hatcher, S., Frampton, C., & Merry, S. N. (2014). A pilot double blind randomized placebo controlled trial of a prototype computer-based cognitive behavioural therapy program for adolescents with symptoms of depression. *Behavioral and Cognitive Psychotherapy, 42*(4), 385–401.

Stewart, S. M., Simmons, A., & Habibpour, E. (2012). Treatment of culturally diverse children and adolescents with depression. *Journal of Child and Adolescent Psychopharmacology, 22*(1), 72–79.

Stuart, S., & Robertson, M. (2012). *Interpersonal psychotherapy: A clinician's guide*. London: Hodder Arnold Press.

Sullivan, P. F., Neale, M. C., & Kendler, K. S. (2000). Genetic epidemiology of major depression: Review and meta-analysis. *American Journal of Psychiatry, 157*(10), 1552–1562.

Tompson, M. C., Langer, D. A., Hughes, J. L., & Asarnow, J. R. (in press). Family-focused treatment for childhood depression: Model and case illustrations. *Cognitive and Behavioral Practice*.

Tompson, M. C., Pierre, C. B., Haber, F. M., Fogler, J. M., Groff, A. R., & Asarnow, J. R. (2007). Family-focused treatment for childhood-onset depressive disorders: Results of an open trial. *Clinical Child Psychology and Psychiatry, 12*(3), 403–420.

Treatment for Adolescents with Depression Study (TADS) Team. (2004). The treatment for adolescents with depression study (TADS): Demographic and clinical characteristics. *Journal of the American Academy of Child & Adolescent Psychiatry, 44*(1), 28–40.

Verduyn, C. (2000). Cognitive behaviour therapy in childhood depression. *Child Psychology and Psychiatry Review, 5*(4), 176–180.

Waller, J. M., Silk, J. S., Stone, L. B., & Dahl, R. E. (2014). Co-rumination and co-problem solving in the daily lives of adolescents with major depressive disorder. *Journal of the American Academy of Child & Adolescent Psychiatry, 53*(8), 869–878.

Weersing, V. R., Jeffreys, M., Do, M., Schwartz, K. G., & Bolano, C. (2017). Evidence base update of psychosocial treatments for child and adolescent depression. *Journal of Clinical Child & Adolescent Psychology*, *46*(1), 11–43.

Weersing, V. R., Rozenman, M., & Gonzalez, A. (2009). Core components of therapy in youth: Do we know what to disseminate? *Behavior Modification*, *33*(1), 24–47.

Weisz, J. R., Chorpita, B. F., Palinkas, L. A., Schoenwald, S. K., Miranda, J., Bearman, S. K., ... & Gray, J. (2012). Testing standard and modular designs for psychotherapy treating depression, anxiety, and conduct problems in youth: A randomized effectiveness trial. *Archives of General Psychiatry*, *69*(3), 274–282.

Weisz, J. R., McCarty, C. A., & Valeri, S. M. (2006). Effects of psychotherapy for depression in children and adolescents: A meta-analysis. *Psychological Bulletin*, *132*(1), 132–149.

Young, J. F., & Mufson, L. (2008). Interpersonal psychotherapy for treatment and prevention of adolescent depression. In J. R. Z. Abela & B. L. Hankin (eds.), *Handbook of depression in children and adolescents* (pp. 288–306). New York: Guilford Press.

Young, J. F., Mufson, L., & Davies, M. (2006). Efficacy of Interpersonal Psychotherapy-Adolescent Skills Training: An indicated preventive intervention for depression. *Journal of Child Psychology and Psychiatry*, *47*(12), 1254–1262.

10

Anxiety

Sarah E. Francis, Susan Doyle, and Shannon Manley

Anxiety in childhood is an emotion characterized by feelings of tension, worried thoughts, and fear. Anxiety exists on a continuum of severity, which ranges from normative and protective fears to those that cause significant impairment in the individual's daily functioning (American Psychological Association, 2013). Childhood anxiety can present itself through multiple pathways: behaviorally, cognitively, and physiologically (Weems, 2007). Behaviorally, children who are highly anxious typically exhibit avoidance behaviors, such as school refusal. Cognitively, they often engage in negative self-talk and pessimistic predictions about the future (worry). Physiologically, they often experience anxiety through bodily symptoms such as an upset stomach, a pounding heart, sweatiness, or shaking (Weems, 2007). These symptoms can create significant functional impairment across the child's domains of activity, including home, school, and peers (Higa-McMillan et al., 2016).

Temperamental, environmental, and biological or genetic influences contribute to the development of an anxiety disorder in childhood (Affrunti, Geronimi, & Woodruff-Borden, 2014; Wood et al., 2003). Temperamental traits, such as high negative affect and behavioral inhibition, have been repeatedly shown to contribute to an individual's anxiety and have been identified as risk factors for emotional disorders (Affruniti et al., 2014). In addition to temperamental influences, environmental influences, such as parenting styles, living situations, and school environments, have also been shown to contribute to the development of anxiety in children (Affrunti, Geronimi, & Woodruff-Borden, 2014). Previous research has also demonstrated support for biological influences of childhood anxiety. For example, serotonin and dopamine genes have been linked to anxiety development; genes of different effect sizes impact the development of anxiety in individuals through interactions with the child's environment (Gregory & Eley, 2007). Anxiety moves from normative worry to a diagnosable disorder when it becomes excessive and uncontrollable, occurs in response to no specific threat, and is associated with a varied and intense range of both physical and affective symptoms such as changes in behavior and normative cognitive functioning (Rodgers & Dunsmuir, 2013).

Presently, anxiety disorders are the most frequently diagnosed group of psychological disorders in children (Higa-McMillan et al., 2016; Stopa, Barrett, & Golingi, 2010). Prevalence rates indicate that up to 24.9% of all children will develop an anxiety disorder during their childhood lasting at least one year (Kessler et al., 2012), and that 26.1–38.0% of those children will live with an anxiety disorder (and/or comorbid internalizing disorder) for the rest of their lives (Beesdo, Knappe, & Pine, 2009). Longitudinal research has shown that anxiety disorders are chronic in nature, and the development of an anxiety disorder in childhood may significantly predict the presence of an anxiety disorder in adolescence and adulthood (Pine et al., 1998). In both nonclinical and clinical samples of youth, anxiety has been associated with a poor self-perceived quality of life (Bastiaansen et al., 2004; Stevanovic et al., 2015), and can lead to the onset of subsequent forms of psychopathology including depression (e.g., Kessler et al., 1996) and substance abuse (e.g., Buckner et al., 2012).

The *Diagnostic and Statistical Manual of Mental Disorders* (DSM-5; American Psychiatric Association [APA], 2013) has defined seven anxiety disorders that are distinguished from each other by their associated behaviors and cognitions (APA, 2013; Zinbarg et al., 2015). Each disorder is also marked by functional impairment (APA, 2013). These anxiety disorders are: separation anxiety disorder (SAD), marked by a developmentally inappropriate fear of separation from major attachment figures (such as parents or primary caregivers) or the home; specific phobia (SP), characterized by an intense, extreme fear of specific stimuli that induces an immediate fear response; social anxiety disorder (social phobia), marked by a persistent fear of social situations where the child may be judged or evaluated; panic disorder (PD), characterized by recurrent, unexpected panic attacks, and a persistent fear of panic attacks; agoraphobia, characterized by fear or distress in situations where escape might be difficult or help not easily available should symptoms of panic occur; selective mutism (SM), characterized by the absence of speech in situations in which it is expected of the child with no evidence of speech difficulties in other situations; and generalized anxiety disorder (GAD), characterized by excessive, uncontrollable worry about different facets of life (e.g., schoolwork, friendships, and parents all at the same time). Given the low prevalence of SM, most treatment efficacy review studies do not include this disorder in their analyses; we have presented information on SM in the Side-Bar Box.

Etiology and Theoretical Underpinnings of Treatment

Cognitive-behavioral treatments (CBTs) are the most commonly employed interventions for child and adolescent anxiety. CBTs are hypothesized to be effective by targeting maladaptive cognitions *and* behaviors of youth with anxiety disorders. Treatment from a CBT model assumes that anxiety is an adaptive and normal emotion that consists of behavioral, biological, and psychological components. In its adaptive form, anxiety is functional and plays a protective role (Albano & Kendall, 2002). Anxiety is part of normal development, and anxieties change through development. For example, a young child may fear the dark, while a junior high student may fear social situations. These normative fears become problematic when developmental levels are exceeded and cause functional impairment (Kendall, Furr, & Podell, 2010).

CBTs for childhood anxiety typically consist of five components: (1) psychoeducation, (2) somatic management skills training, (3) cognitive restructuring, (4) exposure practices, and (5) relapse prevention plans (Albano & Kendall, 2002; Kendall, Furr, & Podell, 2010). Psychoeducation provides corrective information about anxiety and feared stimuli, which normalizes the experience of anxiety. Somatic management techniques address physiological responses by teaching the child to recognize and cope with physical symptoms that accompany their anxieties; techniques such as relaxation may be introduced. Cognitive restructuring skills focus on identifying and challenging maladaptive cognitions while introducing adaptive and coping-focused thinking that is developmentally appropriate (Kendall et al., 2010).

After the skill-building portion of treatment, exposure techniques are implemented through systematic exposures to the feared situations/stimuli. Lastly, relapse prevention methods that focus on consolidating and generalizing treatment gains are incorporated to promote a long-lasting impact (Albano & Kendall, 2002; Kendall et al., 2010). Overall, the CBT model of treatment targets all facets of childhood anxiety by addressing the biological, behavioral, and psychological components of anxiety in a single course of treatment. By emphasizing the relationship between thoughts, feelings, and behaviors, CBT is theorized to help youth better understand, master, and manage distressing anxiety (Kendall, Gosch et al., 2008).

Selective Mutism

Selective mutism (SM) is marked by a lack of expected speech in certain social situations despite an ability and willingness to speak in other situations (APA, 2013). Initially termed elective mutism (APA, 1980), SM was renamed to emphasize that children with this diagnosis may not willfully refuse to speak in these specific circumstances (APA, 2000). Although previously considered to be related to oppositional behavior, recent research suggests that SM is more closely related to anxiety. SM is highly comorbid with other anxiety disorders (especially social anxiety disorder) and anxiety-related symptoms (Muris & Ollendick, 2015), and is related to temperamental risk factors of anxiety (e.g., behavioral inhibition; Ford et al., 1998). Indeed, the DSM-5 now includes SM as an Anxiety Disorder (APA, 2013).

Still considered a relatively rare disorder (Pionek Stone et al., 2002), SM's prevalence has been estimated by clinician polling methods to be between 0.11% and 0.54% (Carlson, Kratochwill, & Johnston, 1994; Steinhausen & Juzi, 1996). Teacher sampling methods have estimated the prevalence to be higher, as they include children who have neither sought treatment nor been diagnosed (e.g., Bergman, Piacentini, & McCracken, 2002; Elizur & Perednik, 2003). However, even more inclusive studies suggest between 0.18% and 1.9% of children meet criteria for SM (Muris & Ollendick, 2015). Because of SM's low prevalence rate, the existing SM treatment literature has primarily relied upon case studies and SM is not typically included in major treatment efficacy reviews (e.g., Higa-McMillan et al., 2016). Cohan, Chavira, and Stein (2006) did find, however, that the majority of studies they reviewed used behavioral or cognitive-behavioral approaches to treat SM. In a recent randomized control study, Bergman and colleagues (2013) found that children with SM who were treated with integrative behavior therapy significantly increased their functional speech in comparison to a control group. This suggests that common SM treatment components include behavioral techniques such as exposure, modeling, contingency management, and shaping (Muris & Ollendick, 2015). More research is needed to determine the effectiveness of these various components, but larger sample sizes are needed to accomplish this. One avenue that may prove promising for this is use of online treatments for SM (e.g., Ooi et al., 2012).

Brief Overview of Evidence-Based Treatments

In 1998, the first systematic review of the treatment literature for childhood phobias and anxiety was conducted (Ollendick & King, 1998). This review identified multiple specific therapeutic procedures for which empirical support had been observed, including systematic desensitization, emotive imagery, modeling, reinforced practice, verbal self-instruction, cognitive-behavioral interventions, and integrated cognitive-behavioral plus family-based procedures. Between this initial review and its subsequent update one decade later (Silverman, Pina, & Viswesvaran, 2008), a key change was made in the criteria for a treatment to be considered well-established or probably efficacious such that the inclusion of a treatment manual in the outcome study was required. Accordingly, *treatment packages* rather than *therapeutic techniques* became the focus of lists of empirically supported treatments. One result of this change was for specific treatment manuals for specific disorders to be evaluated and disseminated rather than individual or grouped treatment components.

In a review of the treatment literature for childhood emotional and behavioral disorders in 2011, Chorpita et al. put forth the term *treatment families* to facilitate the shift back to identifying specific therapeutic techniques that work and away from "naming" specific treatment packages, protocols, and manuals. This shift allowed for two things. First, it elucidated the parallels between generic and "name-brand" treatments. Focusing on similarities allowed for increased inclusivity in the evaluation of treatment validity, as it actively sought to equally assess the efficacy of well-established manualized treatments and less commonly employed interventions. Second, the validity of specific therapeutic components could now be tested (e.g., Rogers & Vismara, 2008). While the effects of these therapeutic practices had been intertwined with the packaged programs, the focus on treatment families enabled researchers and practitioners to move toward evaluating the effectiveness of their foundational elements.

A subsequent update of empirically supported treatments for childhood anxiety disorders not only presented these treatments at the level of treatment families, but also introduced the concept of *practice elements* whereby the specific "clinical ingredients" of treatment protocols can be identified (Higa-McMillan et al., 2016, p. 94). This 2016 review for the first time allowed researchers and practitioners to understand the extent to which specific practice elements were represented in supported protocols. Consistent with the goals of this chapter, recent decades have witnessed the full circle from the identification of specific therapeutic techniques to the identification of practice elements that are helpful to youth experiencing clinical levels of anxiety.

In the most recent review of treatment family efficacy for child and adolescent anxiety disorders, Higa-McMillan et al. (2016) used a five-level classification system to identify six Level 1 (best supported/well-established treatments) treatment families. These primarily comprised CBT and its iterations, including CBT with parents, CBT plus medication, and traditional CBT. *Exposure* – a behavioral component of CBT – was also classified in Level 1. In addition to these, *modeling* – an intervention in which the therapist demonstrates a nonfearful response to an anxious child – and *education*, which includes academic support and skills training for children with test anxiety and school phobia, were also found to be well-established families (e.g., Bandura & Menlove, 1968; Sanghvi, 1995).

Components of Evidence-Based Treatments

Of primary interest here are the specific practice elements that form these Level 1 treatments. To assist in the review of these practice elements, the Practice Wise Evidence-Based Services (PWEBS) Database was consulted (PracticeWise, 2016). This searchable database contains summaries of hundreds of randomized clinical trials of treatments for disorders of childhood (Chorpita & Daleiden, 2014) and can be used by clinicians and clinical researchers to match diagnostic profiles, child demographic characteristics, level of evidence, and treatment protocols and components. Using the Higa-McMillan et al. (2016) review as a starting point, these authors, using *practice element profiles*, or frequency graphs, reported on the frequency with which each practice element identified in these Level 1 treatments occurred across treatment protocols. Five practice elements were identified as occurring most frequently in the Level 1 treatment families: *exposure* (occurring in 87.9% of Level 1 treatments), *cognitive techniques* (61.8%), *relaxation* (53.9%), *psychoeducation for child* (42%), and *modeling* (33.9%).

Exposure Techniques

Exposure techniques involve systematic and repeated practices in which the child is placed in direct (in vivo exposure) or imagined (imaginal exposure) contact with the feared stimulus. Exposure exercises can be gradual or sudden and can involve the therapist engaging in discussion with the child about the feared stimulus. Included under the broad heading of exposure practices are flooding, implosion, and desensitization. Exposure therapy is theorized to work by directing attention toward the feared object or situation and then incorporating new information that challenges existing schemas: specifically, existing fear schemas will predict that something bad is going to happen when in contact with the feared stimulus or situation. New information acquired during the course of the exposure exercise (and attentional allocation to the feared stimulus) is hypothesized to challenge these existing fears by demonstrating that the feared outcome does not occur (e.g., Peris et al., 2015; Waters et al., 2015). Interestingly, pre-treatment bias toward threat has been significantly associated with treatment outcome, such that greater allocation of attentional resources toward threat before treatment predicts higher levels of pre–post-treatment improvement (Waters et al., 2015). Such findings suggest that efforts to ensure that the child's attentional resources are directed toward the threat cues relevant in the exposure exercises might directly enhance the effects of these practices on symptom reduction (Waters et al., 2015).

Exposure as a practice element has been used in all of the study groups comprising the Level 1 treatments for agoraphobia, generalized anxiety disorder, panic disorder, separation anxiety disorder, social phobia, and specific phobia (PracticeWise, 2016). This means that all of the study groups contributing to the evidence base for each of these disorders included protocols in which exposure was a practice element. As a component of the CBT treatment family, exposure practices are typically combined with other treatment practices, such as cognitive techniques, relaxation, self-monitoring, modeling, psychoeducation, and social skills training. As a component of the modeling treatment family, exposure and modeling procedures are often combined, sometimes also in the context of other practice elements such as relaxation and praise and rewards (PracticeWise, 2016).

Exposure as a treatment family has also garnered Level 1 support for childhood anxiety disorders (Higa-McMillan et al., 2016). Several of the treatment outcome studies contributing to the evidence base for exposure therapy pre-date the empirically supported treatment movement and involve the use of exposure in the context of systematic desensitization for specific fears (e.g., Johnson et al., 1971; Kuroda, 1969). More recent applications of exposure therapy have been in the context of specific phobias (e.g., Ollendick et al., 2009) or exposure with response prevention for obsessive-compulsive disorder (e.g., Bolton & Perrin, 2008). That is, as a stand-alone treatment component, exposure practices have not been evaluated in the context of a randomized controlled trial in the treatment of various childhood anxiety disorders.

With respect to indirect evidence to examine the individual contribution of exposure to the treatment of child anxiety, there is the oft-cited data from early studies of the Coping Cat manual to suggest that evidence of symptom improvement was observed after, but not before, the introduction of exposure exercises, which are introduced approximately halfway through this treatment program (e.g., Kendall et al., 1997). The flip side of this observation has been that cognitive restructuring techniques alone do not appear to be associated with symptom improvement and that these techniques might not yield added benefit to the improvements associated with exposure exercises (e.g., Muris, Meesters, & Gobel, 2002; Muris, Meesters, & Melick, 2002; Ollendick & King, 1998).

In a more direct examination of the question of the "active" components of CBT treatments for child anxiety, Ale and colleagues (2015) used meta-analytic techniques to compare RCTs of CBT for childhood anxiety and RCTs of exposure with response prevention (ERP) for obsessive-compulsive disorder (OCD). Their findings suggested that the literature to date does not support the hypothesis that the introduction of cognitive techniques and relaxation is required to prepare children to benefit from exposure exercises as these techniques were not associated with improved outcomes; in contrast, ERP for OCD relies much more heavily on exposure exercises and is associated with better outcomes than CBT for childhood anxiety (Ale et al., 2015). Similarly, a study by Gryczkowski and colleagues (2013) confirmed that successful treatment outcomes are observed with treatments of shorter duration than most typical manuals, with an earlier introduction of exposure exercises, and with a larger propor-tion of the treatment devoted to exposure practices, observations that have been confirmed elsewhere as well (e.g., Chorpita et al., 2004; Vande Voort et al., 2010). Such findings are particularly compelling when considering that a significant minority of youth participating in CBT trials do not receive the full treatment package and thus do not participate in the exposure component of these treatments (e.g., Chorpita & Southam-Gerow, 2006).

The findings of Gryczkowski and colleagues (2013) indicated that by delivering exposure practices earlier in treatment, more children received this component of treatment and attrition rates were not adversely affected. Whiteside and colleagues (2015) similarly introduced parent-coached exposure practices without first introdu-cing cognitive techniques and observed increased rates of improvement in the context of a briefer treatment duration relative to the standard practice of cognitive techniques first followed by exposure, again without negatively impacting attrition rates. Finally, in an adaptation of Parent–Child Interaction Therapy (PCIT) for very young anxious children (the CALM – Coaching Approach behavior and Leading by Modeling – program), the amount of time families devoted to engaging in exposure-based exercises was maximized with favorable treatment outcomes maintained at post-treatment (Comer et al., 2012). Taken together, these findings reinforce the notion that exposure practices are the "active" component of CBT treatment packages and that exposure-based techniques can be effectively implemented without the preparatory work of cognitive techniques or relaxation.

Cognitive Techniques

Cognitive techniques include any therapeutic practice that is focused on changing the child's interpretation of events by examining self-reported thoughts and subsequently working with the child to identify realistic and alternative self-statements. Some variants of cognitive techniques also have the child test the veracity of the existing and alternative thoughts by collecting and then examining evidence from the child's experiences. Cognitive techniques, as a component of treatment, should assist the child in not only identifying but also challenging thoughts that lead to maladaptive functioning (e.g., Peris et al., 2015). Cognitive techniques have been used in all of the Level 1 treatments for agoraphobia and panic disorder, and in the vast majority (over 75%) of the Level 1 treatments for separation anxiety disorder, generalized anxiety disorder, social phobia, and specific phobia. As a component of the CBT treatment family, cognitive techniques are typically combined with other practice elements, such as exposure, modeling, psychoeducation, and relaxation (PracticeWise, 2016).

Relaxation Techniques

Relaxation techniques include those exercises that are intended to induce a sense of physical calm often through activities such as muscle relaxation, guided breathing, imagery, and meditation. In theory, relaxation should assist in the amelioration of anxiety by lessening physiological reactivity often associated with fear and worry (e.g., Peris et al., 2015). Relaxation has been included as a component of all of the Level 1 treatments for agoraphobia, the majority (over 50%) of the Level 1 treatments for panic disorder, separation anxiety disorder, generalized anxiety disorder, social phobia, and specific phobia. As a component of the CBT treatment family, relaxation techniques are typically combined with other practice elements such as exposure, cognitive techniques, psychoeducation, self-monitoring, and problem-solving (PracticeWise, 2016).

Psychoeducation

The practice of *psychoeducation with the child* includes the formal review of information about the nature and development of the child's anxiety and its symptoms (e.g., increased heart rate, upset stomach) and the relationship of this information to the proposed treatment. In theory, psychoeducation should assist the child in formulating less harmful interpretations of the physiological cues that are associated with anxiety (e.g., Peris et al., 2015). Psychoeducation with the child has been used in all of the Level 1 treatments for agoraphobia and panic disorder, and in the vast majority (over 80%) of the Level 1 treatments for separation anxiety disorder, generalized anxiety disorder, social phobia, and specific phobia. As a component of the CBT treatment family, psychoeducation is typically combined with other practice elements such as cognitive techniques, exposure, relaxation, self-monitoring, and psychoeducation for the parent (PracticeWise, 2016).

Modeling

Modeling practices entail the therapist or another individual, such as a confederate or peer, demonstrating to the child the target behavior. This demonstration is intended to prompt the child to imitate and then spontaneously perform this behavior independently. Modeling, in contrast to the other practice elements listed here, has been used in less than half of all study groups comprising Level 1 treatment protocols for agoraphobia, panic, separation anxiety disorder, generalized anxiety disorder, social phobia, and specific phobia. As a component of the CBT treatment family, modeling is typically combined with other practice elements such as cognitive techniques, exposure, relaxation, problem-solving, and psychoeducation for the caregiver (PracticeWise, 2016).

Role of Parents in Treatment

The contribution of parental involvement to the child's treatment outcome has been a topic of investigation of numerous studies; yet, conclusions about the effects of parental involvement in the child's treatment for anxiety disorders are anything but clear, which might be due in part to methodological differences across studies that are challenging to make sense of when reading one study in isolation (Pereira et al., 2016). Overall, multiple studies have failed to find any added benefit of parental involvement with respect to treatment outcome (Cobham, Dadds, & Spence, 1998; Kendall, Hudson, et al., 2008; Mendlowitz et al., 1999; Nauta et al., 2001, 2003; Öst, Cederlund, & Reuterskiold, 2015; Silverman et al., 2009; Spence, Donovan, & Brechman-Toussaint, 2000), with some finding superior effects of child-only treatment conditions when compared to parental involvement conditions (Öst et al., 2001; Bodden et al., 2008), and others observing improved outcomes when parents are involved (Barrett, 1998; Barrett, Dadds, & Rapee, 1996; Cobham, Dadds, & Spence, 1998; Wood et al., 2006). Although cognitive-behavioral interventions that include a family or parent component might be efficacious in the treatment of childhood anxiety, evidence does seem to suggest that there are no differences in outcome when parents are involved (e.g., Wei & Kendall, 2014). Attempts to examine this question via meta-analysis, examining 16 studies which included direct comparisons of child-only and parent-involvement treatments, suggested a small and nonsignificant benefit associated with child-only conditions (Hedges' $g = -0.10$) when compared to parental involvement conditions (Thulin et al., 2014).

One way to achieve perhaps greater clarity with respect to the contribution of parental involvement to cognitive-behavioral interventions for child anxiety (consistent with suggestions made by Öst, Cederlund, & Reuterskiold, 2015 and Thulin et al., 2014) might be to match parents exhibiting certain risk factors (such as parental psychopathology, parental negative beliefs about the child's anxiety, low socioeconomic status; e.g., Pereira et al., 2016) with targeted intervention components designed specifically to assist in facilitating the child's benefit from exposure exercises. The case may be that many parents are not in need of such additional treatment components and the effect of these additive components is diminished when examined in a heterogeneous parent sample. Conversely, it might also be the case that when parents are included in the child's treatment, too many treatment components are attempted without sufficient time devoted to any specific practice or set of practices that might work (e.g., Spence, Donovan, & Brechman-Toussaint, 2000; Thulin et al., 2014). Given the numerous studies that have accumulated examining interactions between anxious parents and anxious children and how these interactions differ from those of nonanxious parent–child dyads (e.g., Hudson, Comer, & Kendall, 2008; Hudson & Rapee, 2001), it might be time to target these specific behaviors in the context of treatment in order to observe treatment gains associated with parental involvement.

Interestingly, recent evidence has provided some support for the direction of change during treatment to be from child to parent, given that improvements in child anxiety predicted decreases in maternal anxiety (Settipani, O'Neil, Podell, Beidas, & Kendall, 2013). These results were specific to mother reports of child anxiety suggesting that maternal *perceptions* might be of particular relevance to mothers' own anxiety. These results also suggest that intervention approaches that focus solely on the child might also lead to benefits for the parent and warrant further investigation.

Findings regarding the contribution of parental psychopathology to the child's treatment outcome are also mixed (e.g., Bodden et al., 2008; Knight et al., 2014; Lundkvist-Houndoumadi, Hougaard, & Thastum, 2014), but Hudson, Keers, et al. (2015) observed some support for poorer outcomes at follow-up for children whose parents endorsed elevated levels of anxiety, depression, or stress. These authors hypothesized that the influence of parental psychopathology on the post-treatment phase might be due to children's increased reliance on parents to assist in challenging activities once the child–therapist relationship has concluded. These findings also suggest the importance of continuing to assess parental psychopathology as a variable potentially influencing treatment outcome not just during treatment but during follow-up assessment points as well.

Other Variables Influencing Treatment

Assessment

A comprehensive diagnostic assessment is an essential first step in appropriately matching specific treatment components to the child's presenting anxiety concerns. Assessment is particularly important in the context of child anxiety given that it assists in discriminating normal childhood anxiety from that which is clinically interfering, identifies not only symptoms of anxiety but also their severity and functional impact, allows for the differential diagnosis of the specific anxiety disorders, and provides valuable information as to the existing comorbid conditions of the child including not only other anxiety disorders but also other mental health disorders and physiological presentations that could impact the anxiety disorder (Creswell, Waite, & Cooper, 2014).

Comorbidity

A comorbid diagnosis of depression seems to be quite consistently linked to worse post-treatment outcomes, even when factors such as age and gender are controlled for (Rapee et al., 2013). Comorbid mood disorders, as discussed below, tend to be associated with higher levels of impairment, which mean that even in the context of successful treatment, these children remain significantly impaired at post-treatment given their severity starting point (Rapee et al., 2013). Importantly, although youth with comorbid diagnoses are significantly less likely to be diagnosis free at the conclusion of treatment for their anxiety disorder, comorbidity does not negatively impact the rate of change for these youth (e.g., Rapee et al., 2013). Thus, although children with comorbid diagnoses will remain more impaired at post-treatment, this is likely an artifact of having started treatment with higher levels of impairment. Although more time in treatment might help to ameliorate these effects, the findings of Hudson, Rapee, et al. (2015) suggest that different treatment components might instead be needed to assist this group of youth.

Demographics

In addition to efforts striving to identify those practice elements that are most efficacious in the treatment of childhood anxiety, significant efforts have also been aimed at identifying individual demographic predictors of treatment outcome, such as age, gender, and problem severity. Such studies have revealed little support for any systematic differences in treatment outcome as a function of age, gender, or pre-treatment severity (e.g., Berman et al., 2000; Hudson, Keers, et al., 2015; Knight et al., 2014; Lundkvist-Houndoumadi, Hougaard, & Thastum, 2014; Wergeland et al., 2016).

Medication

Psychopharmacological treatments for child and adolescent anxiety disorders can assist with symptom reduction, but are most effective when used in conjunction with psychotherapy (e.g., when used to complement manualized CBT-based treatments; Kodish et al., 2011). Previous research has shown support for the use of selective serotonin reuptake inhibitors (SSRIs) and short-term benzodiazepines in cases where anxiety symptoms are particularly debilitating for the child (i.e., for OCD-related anxieties). As is the case for all indications, the use of psychiatric medications for child anxiety must be closely monitored for possible negative side effects (Kodish et al., 2011).

Conclusion

In sum, recent years have brought about many favorable advances not only in the treatment of youth with anxiety disorders, but also in our understanding of the "active ingredients" of the treatment programs that work (e.g., Higa-McMillan et al., 2016). As a field, although we now have considerable evidence to suggest that CBT treatments for childhood anxiety are a first-line intervention, we are only beginning to conclusively elucidate the specific elements of these treatment packages that are most effective and the way in which these components can be most efficiently delivered (Higa-McMillan et al., 2016). Realizations that significant minorities of youth are still not diagnosis free at the conclusion of treatment (e.g., Wei & Kendall, 2014), in concert with the fact that many youth leave treatment before having access to all treatment components (e.g., Chorpita & Southam-Gerow, 2006), will continue to serve as powerful motivators to more rigorous evaluations of specific treatment components and their optimal sequencing in the context of treatment.

One approach to navigating the gap between the existing efficacy data on treatment packages and the relative absence of knowledge about specific practice elements is perhaps the modular approach to treatment (e.g., Chorpita et al., 2004; Southam-Gerow et al., 2013; Weisz et al., 2012). This approach, outlined in *Match-ADTC: Modular Approach to Therapy for Children with Anxiety, Depression, or Conduct Problems* (Chorpita & Weisz, 2009), takes individual practice elements from empirically supported treatment packages and presents them in stand-alone modules. Decision flowcharts are used to assist therapists in understanding when to apply specific modules to best meet the client's presenting concerns. When compared with both standard manualized approaches and treatment-as-usual conditions, the modular approach to treatment has been associated with faster rates of response to treatment and with fewer diagnoses at post-treatment (Weisz et al., 2012). Further study of efforts to match youths' clinical presentations with specific practice elements will not only move toward building the evidence base for specific treatment components but will also help elucidate those common factors of existing treatment manuals that warrant further study, refinement, and development as supported treatments for anxiety in youth.

At this time, the evidence suggests that exposure practices are the primary element of change for anxious youth and that cognitive techniques and relaxation, while part of efficacious treatment packages, are not associated with benefits to outcome beyond those associated with exposure (e.g., Ale et al., 2015; Whiteside et al., 2015). Similarly, parental involvement in treatment, while efficacious when compared to no-treatment conditions, also does not appear to have additive benefits to treatment outcome (e.g., Thulin et al., 2014), suggesting either a refinement of the parental components to treatment that are implemented, or a more systematic matching of youth and parent presentations to the parental interventions applied. Finally, the evidence to date suggests that youth diagnosed with social phobia require further study to identify those practice elements that are most strongly linked with favorable treatment outcomes (e.g., Lundkvist-Houndoumadi & Thastum, 2015), and, in particular, youth with comorbid diagnoses of depression warrant this same attention (e.g., Rapee et al., 2013). Further investigation along all of these lines has the great potential of advancing our treatment and understanding of childhood anxiety disorders into the coming decades.

Useful Resources

- AnxietyBC at www.anxietybc.com
- Child F.I.R.S.T. Focus on Innovation and Redesign in Systems and Treatment at www.childfirst .ucla.edu
- Bruce F. Chorpita, Jon R. Weisz, Eric L. Daleiden, Sonja K. Schoenwald, Lawrence A. Palinkas, Jeanne Miranda, et al. (2013). Long term outcomes for the Child STEPs randomized effectiveness trial: A comparison of modular and standard treatment designs with usual care. *Journal of Consulting and Clinical Psychology, 81*, 999–1009. doi:10.1037/a0034200
- *MATCH-ADTC: Modular Approach to Therapy for Children with Anxiety, Depression, Trauma, or Conduct Problems*, by Bruce F. Chorpita and John R. Weisz, PracticeWise, 2009
- PracticeWise. www.practicewise.com
- Society of Clinical Child and Adolescent Psychology (Division 53). www.clinicalchildpsychology .org/
- WorryWiseKids.org

References

Affrunti, N. W., Geronimi, E. M. C., & Woodruff-Borden, J. (2014). Temperament, peer victimization, and nurturing parenting in child anxiety: A moderated mediation model. *Child Psychiatry & Human Development*, *45*, 483–492. doi:10.1007/s10578-013-0418-2

Albano, A. M., & Kendall, P. C. (2002). Cognitive behavioral therapy for children and adolescents with anxiety disorders: Clinical research advances. *International Review of Psychiatry*, *14*(2), 129–134. doi:10.1080/09540260220132644

Ale, C. M., McCarthy, D. M., Rothschild, L. M., & Whiteside, S. P. (2015). Components of cognitive behavioral therapy related to outcome in childhood anxiety disorders. *Clinical Child and Family Psychology Review*, *18*(3), 240–251.

American Psychological Association. (2013). Anxiety. www.apa.org/topics/anxiety/

American Psychiatric Association (APA). (1980). *Diagnostic and statistical manual of mental disorders*. 3rd edn. Washington, DC: American Psychiatric Association.

American Psychiatric Association (APA). (2000). *Diagnostic and statistical manual of mental disorders*. 4th edn, text rev. Washington, DC: American Psychiatric Association.

American Psychiatric Association (APA). (2013). *Diagnostic and statistical manual of mental disorders*. 5th edn. Washington, DC: American Psychiatric Association.

Bandura, A., & Menlove, F. L. (1968). Factors determining vicarious extinction of avoidance behavior through symbolic modeling. *Journal of Personality and Social Psychology*, *8*(2p1), 99.

Barrett, P. M. (1998). Evaluation of cognitive-behavioral group treatments for childhood anxiety disorders. *Journal of Clinical Child & Adolescent Psychology*, *27*, 459–468.

Barrett, P. M., Dadds, M. R., & Rapee, R. M. (1996). Family treatment of childhood anxiety: A controlled trial. *Journal of Consulting and Clinical Psychology*, *64*, 333–342.

Bastiaansen, D., Koot, H. M., Ferdinand, R. F., & Verhulst, F. C. (2004). Quality of life in children with psychiatric disorders: Self-, parent, and clinician report. *Journal of the American Academy of Child & Adolescent Psychiatry*, *43*, 221–230. doi:10.1097/00004583-200402000-00019

Beesdo, K., Knappe, S., & Pine, D. S. (2009). Anxiety and anxiety disorders in children and adolescents: Developmental issues and implications for DSM-V. *The Psychiatric Clinics of North America*, *32*, 483–524. doi:10.1016/j.psc.2009.06.002

Bergman, R. L., Gonzalez, A., Piacentini, J., & Keller, M. L. (2013). Integrated behavior therapy for selective mutism: A randomized controlled pilot study. *Behaviour Research and Therapy*, *51*(10), 680–689.

Bergman, R. L., Piacentini, J., & McCracken, J. T. (2002). Prevalence and description of selective mutism in a school-based sample. *Journal of the American Academy of Child & Adolescent Psychiatry*, *41*(8), 938–946.

Berman, S. L., Weems, C. F., Silverman, W. K., & Kurtines, W. M. (2000). Predictors of outcome in exposure-based cognitive and behavioral treatments for phobic and anxiety disorders in children. *Behavior Therapy*, *31*(4), 713–731.

Bodden, D., Bogels, S., Nauta, M., De Haan, E., Ringrose, J., Appelboom, C., . . . & Appelboom-Geerts, K. (2008). Child versus family cognitive-behavioral therapy in clinically anxious youth: An efficacy and partial effectiveness study. *Journal of the American Academy of Child & Adolescent Psychiatry*, *47*, 1384–1394.

Bolton, D., & Perrin, S. (2008). Evaluation of exposure with response-prevention for obsessive compulsive disorder in childhood and adolescence. *Journal of Behavior Therapy and Experimental Psychiatry*, *39*, 11–22.

Buckner, J. D., Heimberg, R. G., Matthews, R. A., & Silgado, J. (2012). Marijuana-related problems and social anxiety: The role of marijuana behaviours in social situations. *Psychology of Addictive Behaviours*, *26*, 151–156. doi:10.1037/a0025822

Carlson, J. S., Kratochwill, T. R., & Johnston, H. (1994). Prevalence and treatment of selective mutism in clinical practice: A survey of child and adolescent psychiatrists. *Journal of Child and Adolescent Psychopharmacology*, *4*(4), 281–291.

Chorpita, B., & Daleiden, E. (2014). Structuring the collaboration of science and service in pursuit of a shared vision. *Journal of Clinical Child & Adolescent Psychology*, *43*, 323–338.

Chorpita, B. F., Daleiden, E. L., Ebesutani, C., Young, J., Becker, K. D., Nakamura, B. J., & Smith, R. L. (2011). Evidence based treatments for children and adolescents: An updated review of indicators of efficacy and effectiveness. *Clinical Psychology: Science and Practice*, *18*(2), 154–172.

Chorpita, B. F., & Southam-Gerow, M. A. (2006). Fears and anxieties. In E. J. Mash & R. A. Barkley (eds.), *Treatment of child disorders*. 3rd edn (pp. 271–335). New York: Guilford Press.

Chorpita, B. F., Taylor, A. A., Francis, S. E., Moffitt, C. E., & Austin, A. A. (2004). Efficacy of modular cognitive behavior therapy for childhood anxiety disorders. *Behavior Therapy*, *35*, 263–287.

Cobham, V. E., Dadds, M. R., & Spence, S. H. (1998). The role of parental anxiety in the treatment of childhood anxiety. *Journal of Consulting and Clinical Psychology*, *66*, 893–905.

Cohan, S. L., Chavira, D. A., & Stein, M. B. (2006). Practitioner review: Psychosocial interventions for children with selective mutism: A critical evaluation of the literature from 1990–2005. *Journal of Child Psychology and Psychiatry*, *47*(11), 1085–1097.

Comer, J. S., Puliafico, A. C., Aschenbrand, S. G., McKnight, K., Robin, J. A., Goldfine, M. E., & Albano, A. M. (2012). A pilot feasibility evaluation of the CALM Program for anxiety disorders in early childhood. *Journal of Anxiety Disorders*, *26*(1), 40–49.

Creswell, C., Waite, P., & Cooper, P. J. (2014). Assessment and management of anxiety disorders in children and adolescents. *Archives of Disease in Childhood*, *99*, 674–678.

Elizur, Y., & Perednik, R. (2003). Prevalence and description of selective mutism in immigrant and native families: A controlled study. *Journal of the American Academy of Child & Adolescent Psychiatry*, *42*(12), 1451–1459.

Ford, M. A., Sladeczek, I. E., Carlson, J., & Kratochwill, T. R. (1998). Selective mutism: Phenomenological characteristics. *School Psychology Quarterly*, *13*(3), 192.

Gregory, A. M., & Eley, T. C. (2007). Genetic influences on anxiety in children: What we've learned and where we're heading. *Clinical Child and Family Psychology Review*, *10*(3), 199–212.

Gryczkowski, M. R., Tiede, M. S., Dammann, J. E., Jacobsen, A. B., Hale, L. R., & Whiteside, S. P. H. (2013). The timing of exposure in clinic-based treatment for childhood anxiety disorders. *Behavior Modification*, *37*, 211–225.

Higa-McMillan, C. K., Francis, S. E., Rith-Najarian, L., & Chorpita, B. F. (2016). Evidence base update: 50 years of research on treatment for child and adolescent anxiety. *Journal of Clinical Child & Adolescent Psychology*, *45*(2), 91–113. doi:10.1080/15374416.2015.1046177

Hudson, J. L., Comer, J. S., & Kendall, P. C. (2008). Parental responses to positive and negative emotions in anxious and nonanxious children. *Journal of Clinical Child & Adolescent Psychology*, *37*, 303–313.

Hudson, J. L., Keers, R., Roberts, S, Coleman, J. R. I., Breen, G., Arendt, K., . . . & Eley, T. C. (2015). Clinical predictors of response to cognitive-behavioral therapy in pediatric anxiety disorders: The genes for treatment (GxT) study. *Journal of the American Academy of Child & Adolescent Psychiatry, 54*, 454–463.

Hudson, J. L., & Rapee, R. M. (2001). Parent–child interactions and anxiety disorders: An observational study. *Behaviour Research and Therapy, 39*(12), 1411–1427.

Hudson, J. L., Rapee, R. M., Lyneham, H. J., McLellan, L. F., Wuthrich, V. M., & Schniering, C. A. (2015). Comparing outcomes for children with different anxiety disorders following cognitive behavioral therapy. *Behaviour Research and Therapy, 72*, 30–37.

Johnson, T., Tyler, V., Thompson, R., & Jones, E. (1971). Systematic desensitization and assertive training in the treatment of speech anxiety in middle-school students. *Psychology in the Schools, 8*, 263–267.

Kendall, P. C., Flannery-Schroeder, E., Panichelli-Mindel, S. M., Southam-Gerow, M., Henin, A., & Warman, M. (1997). Therapy for youths with anxiety disorders: A second randomized clinical trial. *Journal of Consulting and Clinical Psychology, 65*, 366–380.

Kendall, P. C., Furr, J. M., & Podell, J. L. (2010) Child focused treatment of anxiety. In J. R. Weisz & A. E. Kazdin (eds.) *Evidence-based psychotherapies for children and adolescents* (pp. 45–60). New York: Guilford Press.

Kendall, P. C., Gosch, E., Furr, J. M., & Sood, E. (2008). Flexibility within fidelity. *Journal of the American Academy of Child & Adolescent Psychiatry, 47*(9), 987–993. doi:10.1097/ CHI.0b013e31817eed2f

Kendall, P. C., Hudson, J. L., Gosch, E., Flannery-Schroeder, E., & Suveg, C. (2008). Cognitive-behavioral therapy for anxiety disordered youth: A randomized clinical trial evaluating child and family modalities. *Journal of Consulting and Clinical Psychology, 76*(2), 282.

Kessler, R. C., Avenevoli, S., Costello, E. J., Georgiades, K., Green, J. G., Gruber, M. J., & Sampson, N. A. (2012). Prevalence, persistence, and sociodemographic correlates of DSM-IV disorders in the National Comorbidity Survey Replication–Adolescent Supplement. *Archives of General Psychiatry, 69*(4), 372–380.

Kessler, R. C., Nelson, C. B., McGonagle, K. A., & Liu, J. (1996). Comorbidity of DSM-III-R major depressive disorder in the general population: Results from the US national comorbidity survey. *The British Journal of Psychiatry, 168*, 17–30.

Knight, A., McLellen, L., Jones, M., & Hudson, J. (2014). Pre-treatment predictors of outcome in childhood anxiety disorders: A systematic review. *Psychopathology Review, 1*, 77–129.

Kodish, I., Rockhill, C., Ryan, S., & Varley, C. (2011). Pharmacotherapy for anxiety disorders in children and adolescents. *Pediatric Clinics of North America, 58*(1), 55–72.

Kuroda, J. (1969). Elimination of children's fears of animals by the method of experimental desensitization: An application of learning theory to child psychology. *Psychologia: An International Journal of Psychology in the Orient, 12*, 161–165.

Lundkvist-Houndoumadi, I., Hougaard, E., & Thastum, M. (2014). Pre-treatment child and family characteristics as predictors of outcome in cognitive behavioral therapy for youth anxiety disorders. *Nordic Journal of Psychiatry, 68*(8), 524–535.

Lundkvist-Houndoumadi, I., & Thastum, M. (2015). Anxious children and adolescents non-responding to CBT: Clinical predictors and families' experiences of therapy. *Clinical Psychology & Psychotherapy*.

Mendlowitz, S., Manassis, K., Bradley, S., Scapillato, D., Miezitis, S., & Shaw, B. E. (1999). Cognitive-behavioral group treatments in childhood anxiety: The role of parental involvement. *Journal of the American Academy of Child & Adolescent Psychiatry, 38*, 1223–1229.

Muris, P., Meesters, C., & Gobel, M. (2002). Cognitive coping versus emotional disclosure in the treatment of anxious children: A pilot-study. *Cognitive Behaviour Therapy, 31*, 59–67.

Muris, P., Meesters, C., & van Melick, M. (2002). Treatment of childhood anxiety disorders: A preliminary comparison between cognitive-behavioral group therapy and a psychological placebo intervention. *Journal of Behavior Therapy and Experimental Psychiatry, 33*, 143–158.

Muris, P., & Ollendick, T. H. (2015). Children who are anxious in silence: A review on selective mutism, the new anxiety disorder in DSM-5. *Clinical Child and Family Psychology Review, 18* (2), 151–169.

Nauta, M. H., Scholing, A., Emmelkamp, P. M., & Minderaa, R. B. (2001). Cognitive-behavioral therapy for anxiety disordered children in a clinical setting: Does additional cognitive parent training enhance treatment effectiveness? *Clinical Psychology & Psychotherapy, 8*, 330–340.

Nauta, M. H., Scholing, A., Emmelkamp, P. M., & Minderaa, R. B. (2003). Cognitive-behavioral therapy for children with anxiety disorders in a clinical setting: No additional effect of a cognitive parent training. *Journal of the American Academy of Child & Adolescent Psychiatry, 42*(11), 1270–1278.

Ollendick, T. H., & King, N. J. (1998). Empirically supported treatments for children with phobic and anxiety disorders: Current status. *Journal of Clinical Child Psychology, 27*(2), 156–167.

Ollendick, T. H., Öst, L., Reuterskiold, L., Costa, N., Cederlund, R., Sirbu, C., Davis, T. E., & Jarrett, M. A. (2009). One-session treatment of specific phobias in youth: A randomized clinical trial in the United States and Sweden. *Journal of Consulting and Clinical Psychology, 77*, 504–516.

Ooi, Y. P., Raja, M., Sung, S. C., Fung, D. S., & Koh, J. B. (2012). Application of a web-based cognitive-behavioural therapy programme for the treatment of selective mutism in Singapore: A case series study. *Singapore Medical Journal, 53*(7), 446–450.

Öst, L.-G., Cederlund, R., & Reuterskiöld, L. (2015). Behavioral treatment of social phobia in youth: Does parent education training improve the outcome? *Behaviour Research and Therapy, 67*, 19–29.

Öst, L.-G., Svensson, L., Hellstrom, K., & Lindwall, R. (2001). One-session treatment of specific phobias in youths: A randomized clinical trial. *Journal of Consulting and Clinical Psychology, 69*, 814–824.

Pereira, A. I., Muris, P., Mendonça, D., Barros, L., Goes, A. R., & Marques, T. (2016). Parental involvement in cognitive-behavioral intervention for anxious children: Parents' in-session and out-session activities and their relationship with treatment outcome. *Child Psychiatry & Human Development, 47*(1), 113–123.

Peris, T. S., Compton, S. N., Kendall, P. C., Birmaher, B., Sherrill, J., March, J., . . . & Piacentini, J. (2015). Trajectories of change in youth anxiety during cognitive-behavior therapy. *Journal of Consulting and Clinical Psychology, 83*, 239–252.

Pine, D. S., Cohen, P., Gurley, D., Brook, J., & Ma, Y. (1998). The risk for early-adulthood anxiety and depressive disorders in adolescents with anxiety and depressive disorders. *Archives of General Psychiatry, 55*, 56–64. doi:10.1001/archpsyc.55.1.56

Pionek Stone, B., Kratochwill, T. R., Sladezcek, I., & Serlin, R. C. (2002). Treatment of selective mutism: A best-evidence synthesis. *School Psychology Quarterly, 17*(2), 168.

PracticeWise. (2016). PracticeWise evidence-based services database. Satellite Beach, FL: PracticeWise.

Rapee, R. M., Lyneham, H. J., Hudson, J. L., Kangas, M., Wuthrich, V. M., & Schniering, C. A. (2013). Effect of comorbidity on treatment of anxious children and adolescents: Results from a large, combined sample. *Journal of the American Academy of Child & Adolescent Psychiatry, 52*(1), 47–56.

Rodgers, A., & Dunsmuir, S. (2013). A controlled evaluation of the "friends for life" emotional resiliency programme on overall anxiety levels, anxiety subtype levels and school adjustment. *Child and Adolescent Mental Health, 20*, 13–19. doi:10.1111/camh.12030

Rogers, S. J., & Vismara, L. A. (2008). Evidence-based comprehensive treatments for early autism. *Journal of Clinical Child & Adolescent Psychology, 37*(1), 8–38.

Sanghvi, C. (1995). Efficacy of study skills training in managing study habits and test anxiety of high test anxious students. *Journal of the Indian Academy of Applied Psychology, 21*(1), 71–75.

Settipani, C. A., O'Neil, K. A., Podell, J. L., Beidas, R. S., & Kendall, P. C. (2013). Youth anxiety and parent factors over time: Directionality of change among youth treated for anxiety. *Journal of Clinical Child & Adolescent Psychology, 42*(1), 9–21.

Silverman, W. K., Kurtines, W. M., Jaccard, J., & Pina, A. A. (2009). Directionality of change in youth anxiety treatment involving parents: An initial examination. *Journal of Consulting and Clinical Psychology, 77*(3), 474.

Silverman, W. K., Pina, A. A., & Viswesvaran, C. (2008). Evidence-based psychosocial treatments for phobic and anxiety disorders in children and adolescents. *Journal of Clinical Child & Adolescent Psychology, 37*(1), 105–130.

Southam-Gerow, M. A., Daleiden, E. L., Chorpita, B. F., Bae, C., Mitchell, C., Faye, M., & Alba, M. (2013). MAPping Los Angeles County: Taking an evidence-informed model of mental health care to scale. *Journal of Clinical Child & Adolescent Psychology, 43*, 190–200.

Spence, S. H., Donovan, C., & Brechman-Toussaint, M. (2000). The treatment of childhood social phobia: The effectiveness of a social skills training-based, cognitive-behavioral intervention, with and without parental involvement. *Journal of Child Psychology and Psychiatry, 41*(6), 713–726.

Steinhausen, H.-C., & Juzi, C. (1996). Elective mutism: An analysis of 100 cases. *Journal of the American Academy of Child & Adolescent Psychiatry, 35*(5), 606–614.

Stevanovic, D., Atilola, O., Balhara, Y. P. S., Avicenna, M., Kandemir, H., Vostanis, P., & Petrov, P. (2015). The relationships between alcohol/drug use and quality of life among adolescents: An international, cross-sectional study. *Journal of Child & Adolescent Substance Abuse, 24*, 177–185. doi:10.1080/1067828X.2013.773864

Stopa, J. E., Barrett, P. M., & Golingi, F. (2010). The prevention of childhood anxiety in socioeconomically disadvantaged communities: A universal school-based trial. *Advances in School Mental Health Promotion, 3*, 5–24. doi:10.1080/1754730X.2010.971568

Thulin, U., Svirsky, L., Serlachius, E., Andersson, G., & Öst, L.-G. (2014). The effect of parent involvement in the treatment of anxiety disorders in children: A meta-analysis. *Cognitive Behavior Therapy, 43*(3), 185–200.

Vande Voort, J. L., Svecova, J., Brown Jacobsen, A., & Whiteside, S. P. (2010). A retrospective examination of the similarity between clinical practice and manualized treatment of childhood anxiety disorders. *Cognitive and Behavioral Practice, 17*, 322–328.

Waters, A. M., Potter, A., Jamesion, L., Bradley, B. P., & Mogg, K. (2015). Predictors of treatment outcomes in anxious children receiving group cognitive-behavioral therapy: Pretreatment attention bias to threat and emotional variability during exposure tasks. *Behaviour Change, 32*, 143–158.

Weems, C. F. (2007). Development trajectories of childhood anxiety: Identifying continuity and change in anxious emotion. *Developmental Review, 28*, 488–502. doi:10.1016/j.dr.2008.01.001

Wei, C., & Kendall, P. C. (2014). Parental involvement: Contribution to childhood anxiety and its treatment. *Clinical Child and Family Psychology Review, 17*(4), 319–339.

Weisz, J. R., Chorpita, B. F., Palinkas, L. A., Schoenwald, S. K., Miranda, J., Bearman, S. K., . . . & the Research Network on Youth Mental Health. (2012). Testing standard and modular designs for psychotherapy with youth depression, anxiety, and conduct problems: A randomized effectiveness trial. *Archives of General Psychiatry*, *69*, 274–282.

Wergeland, G. J. H., Fjermestad, K. W., Marin, C. E., Bjelland, I., Haugland, B. S. M., Silverman, W. K., . . . & Havik, O. E. (2016). Predictors of treatment outcome in an effectiveness trial of cognitive behavioral therapy for children with anxiety disorders. *Behaviour Research and Therapy*, *76*, 1–12.

Whiteside, S. P., Ale, C. M., Young, B., Dammann, J. E., Tiede, M. S., & Biggs, B. K. (2015). The feasibility of improving CBT for childhood anxiety disorders through a dismantling study. *Behaviour Research and Therapy*, *73*, 83–89.

Wood, J. J., McLeod, B. D., Sigman, M., Hwang, W., & Chu, B. C. (2003). Parenting and childhood anxiety: Theory, empirical findings, and future directions. *Journal of Child Psychology and Psychiatry*, *44*, 134–151. doi:10.1111/1469-7610.00106

Wood, J. J., Piacentini, J. C., Southam-Gerow, M., Chu, B. C., & Sigman, M. (2006). Family cognitive behavioral therapy for child anxiety disorders. *Journal of the American Academy of Child & Adolescent Psychiatry*, *45*(3), 314–321.

Zinbarg, R. E., Anand, D., Lee, J. K., Kendall, A. D., & Nunez, M. (2015). Generalized anxiety disorder, panic disorder, social anxiety disorder, and specific phobias. In P. H. Blaney, R. F. Krueger, & T. Millon (eds.) *Oxford textbook of psychopathology* (pp. 133–162). New York: Oxford University Press.

11

Obsessions and Compulsions

Dean McKay and Katherine A. Kennedy

Obsessive-compulsive disorder (OCD) has a lifetime prevalence of about 1–3% worldwide (Horwath & Weissman, 2000; Karno et al., 1988; Ruscio et al., 2010), affects approximately 1% of children and adolescents (Flament et al., 1988; Valleni-Basile et al., 1994), and is considered a leading cause of global disability by the World Health Organization (WHO, 2005). The disorder typically begins in childhood, interfering with academic and social functioning, and persisting through the life span (Markarian et al., 2010), causing significant impairment and distress (Gryczkowski & Whiteside, 2014; Micali et al., 2010). The defining characteristics of OCD are recurrent and persistent obsessions (i.e., intrusive and unwanted thoughts) and compulsions (i.e., behaviors performed in response to obsessions to reduce anxiety) (American Psychiatric Association [APA], 2013). According to the *Diagnostic and Statistical Manual of Mental Disorders* (DSM-5; APA, 2013), to meet the criteria for the diagnosis obsessions and compulsions would need to be time consuming (e.g., more than an hour per day), or cause significant distress or impairment. Childhood OCD is typically a heterogeneous condition with varied clinical presentations and associated symptoms (McKay et al., 2004).

Children with OCD often have limited insight and communication skills compared to adults, causing pediatric OCD to be underdiagnosed and undertreated (Heyman et al., 2001). OCD symptoms are more common in male youths than female youths; moreover, males more frequently experience early onset symptoms compared to females (Fireman et al., 2001; Geller et al., 1998). Males, and females with an earlier age of onset tend to present with comorbid psychological disorders, greater symptom severity, and chronic impairment (Taylor, 2011). Children may exhibit compulsions without endorsing obsessions and atypical blinking and breathing rituals instead of typical checking or cleaning rituals (Hanna, 1995; Rettew et al., 1992). Obsessions in children often focus on a distressing family event (Rettew et al., 1992) and many parents participate in these obsessions by assuring their children of safety.

As noted above, childhood OCD is highly heterogeneous, and recent research has described it as comprised of subtypes. Factor analyses of symptom checklists, most often derived from the Children's Yale Brown Obsessive Compulsive Scale checklist (Scahill et al., 1997), have revealed several dimensions. In one large study of children with OCD spanning five countries, three symptom factors were identified: harming and sexual obsessions, symmetry obsessions/hoarding behavior, and contamination obsessions and cleaning compulsions (Højgaard et al., 2017). It is important to note that hoarding is no longer part of the diagnosis of OCD, but instead is a separate disorder in the current edition of the DSM (APA, 2013). Harming and sexual obsessions encompass checking related compulsions, which are behaviors primarily completed to prevent harm to oneself and others. At the present time, while it has been asserted that treatment outcome varies based on major presenting symptom, it remains a clinical hypothesis. Indeed, recent research has suggested no difference in outcome for different symptom manifestations (Storch et al., 2008). Further, there remain questions as to what subtypes may be valid in characterizing the disorder (Roswell & Francis, 2015). In light of these observations, the remainder of this chapter will focus on treatment protocols for OCD generally rather than for any specific symptom presentation of the condition.

Trichotillomania and Excoriation

In addition to tics, two other problems can co-occur that deserve specific clinical attention, namely trichotillomania (compulsive hair-pulling) and excoriation disorder (compulsive skin-picking) (Snorrason, Belleau, & Woods, 2012). In the context of OCD, evidence-based treatment entails habit reversal, but the emotional concomitants set these apart from tic disorders. These significant variations from the manifestation of OCD have led to critical commentary on the suitability of disorders characterized by habit and pleasurable response for the broader class of obsessive-compulsive related disorders (OCRD) (Abramowitz & Jacoby, 2015; Abramowitz, Storch, et al., 2009; Ferrão, Euripedes, & Stein, 2009). Further, while repetitive behavior problems have been considered potential OCRDs, it has not been shown that there is an especially high association with OCD for these conditions as compared to other psychopathology, such as anxiety and mood disorders (Houghton et al., 2016).

Trichotillomania tends to have a chronic course, and is also recalcitrant to intervention. Therefore, while there is evidence-based treatment for the disorder, the treatment is more palliative than curative. Unlike tics, the hair-pulling tends to be covert, and, once initiated, described as enjoyable and difficult to stop. Accordingly, treatment requires addressing the immediate reward that comes from expression of the symptoms (Abramowitz & Jacoby, 2015).

Excoriation disorder is a more recent condition defined in the DSM-5. This condition is comparable in nature and symptom expression to nonsuicidal self-injury, and it is unclear whether it shares etiological features with OCD (McKay & Andover, 2012). Given the nature of nonsuicidal self-injury, this problem should be prioritized over obsessive-compulsive symptoms (Andover & Morris, 2014).

Etiology and Theoretical Underpinnings of Treatment

The underlying mechanisms that lead to OCD are diverse, with no single model viewed as the dominant etiological framework. Several different routes for symptom development have been investigated, falling in two broad categories: neurobiological and learning/psychosocial.

Neurobiological Models

Fear circuitry models of neurobiological onset have been developed for OCD. There have been several different circuit models hypothesized (Rauch & Jenike, 1998); most of the current investigations rely on a single circuit model with the basal ganglia serving a central role in controlling repetitive behaviors, with pathways through the orbitofrontal cortex, ventromedial caudate, globus pallidius and substantia nigra, and mediodorsal thalamus (Abramowitz, Taylor, & McKay, 2009). Support for dysfunction in parts of this circuit has been observed in the literature, notably the right orbitofrontal cortex, portions of the thalamic nucleus, and parts of the caudate (i.e., Shaw et al., 2015). However, connectivity involving other brain regions has been observed, notably the insula (Bernstein et al., 2016) and thalamic functioning generally (Boedhoe et al., 2017).

Pediatric acute onset neuropsychiatric syndrome (PANS) is a specific clinical presentation of the disorder that may support a link to brain structures in the fear circuit. A small body of research has suggested that PANS is a result of inflammation in the basal ganglia following infection with streptococcal virus (for a review, see Williams & Swedo, 2015). Prior research has suggested a link between OCD and other choreas (i.e., Huntington's or Sydenham's choreas; Fibbe et al., 2012).

Learning/Psychosocial Models

As with the neurobiological models of OCD, there are not yet satisfactory learning/psychosocial conceptualizations of the disorder. To this date, the foundation of the learning model for OCD derives from Mowrer's two-factor theory of fear learning (Mowrer, 1960). Specifically, the feared stimuli are learned through classical conditioning, and avoidance is maintained through negative reinforcement. This account is a challenge for three major reasons. First, most people with OCD do not have a clear learning history for the feared stimuli. Second, many OCD sufferers shift their primary feared stimuli with no clear learning that served to eliminate the prior feared stimuli. And finally, on the occasions when a specific traumatic learning event is described, it precedes the onset of symptoms by a long duration (see Abramowitz, Taylor, & McKay, 2007 for detailed critique of learning models).

More recent conceptualizations have emphasized cognitive deficits, such as working memory, organization strategy, reality monitoring, or cognitive inhibition. These models have had mixed support in adults (Abramovitch & Cooperman, 2015), and the literature in children is too limited at this point to draw meaningful conclusions. A separate recent review showed that there are broad deficits in executive functioning in OCD (Snyder et al., 2015), but how this impacts OCD as compared to other conditions marked by extensive cognitive impairment has yet to be described.

In addition to the cognitive deficit models, there is also the cognitive belief model (i.e., Salkovskis, 1985). This model suggested that the person with OCD makes specific appraisals of thoughts regarding the degree of responsibility one has for outcomes following the appearance of unwanted ideas or images. This leads to a range of core belief domains that are considered central to later ritualistic behavior designed to alleviate the intrusive images and ideas. This conceptualization of OCD has generated considerable research, but comparably little has been conducted with children. Further, the available research in adults has not established a strong unique and specific link between the hypothesized cognitive domains and either obsessions or compulsions (i.e., Kim et al., 2016; McKay et al., 2014; Taylor, et al., 2006).

A potential reason for the lack of a clear and empirically supported model of OCD is due to its wide heterogeneity. As noted earlier, symptoms range from symmetry and ordering to intrusive ideas of harm and sexuality to fears of contamination. There have been conceptualizations of etiology put forth that are specific to symptom manifestations (e.g., disgust in contamination fear; McKay & Moretz, 2009), but these have not accumulated sufficient support to serve as stand-alone models of conceptualization. Interestingly, although as of yet there are no dominant perspectives on the etiology of OCD, the treatment developed for the condition is efficacious.

Theoretical Basis for Treatment

The most efficacious and well-developed treatment for OCD in children is exposure with response prevention (ERP). This is typically administered as part of a broader cognitive-behavioral treatment program. Although the aforementioned models of etiology have varied empirical support, these still serve as the basis for the underlying theory guiding treatment, in addition to conceptualizations of information processing that occur as part of exposure generally.

Foa and Kozak (1986) describe the theoretical basis for exposure that remains dominant to this day. Specifically, it was suggested that an essential ingredient of treatment was presentation of the stimuli in sufficient intensity that the neural structures associated with fear were engaged, but not in so much intensity that new learning would be impeded. This means that treatment, when properly implemented, involves provoking fear and awaiting habituation, then moving to more advanced feared stimuli.

The approach described has some inherent challenges in implementation. First, many children are reluctant to engage in the necessary levels of fear provocation to make therapy viable. Second, many therapists are reticent to cause the kind of in-session distress necessary for fidelity with the theoretical model. As a result of strict adherence to the theoretical model, some investigators have noted that dropout in ERP therapy, across all ages, is high, with some estimates as high as 40% (Eddy et al., 2004). As a consequence, many clinicians have reluctance to conduct exposure for fear of possibly harming clients or causing premature termination (Richard & Gloster, 2006). Indeed, so significant is this concern among clinicians that at least one treatment guide emphasized the potential of complete therapeutic success employing solely cognitive methods without any exposure procedures (Wilhelm & Steketee, 2006).

More recently it has been suggested that engagement of the neural structures associated with fear learning is not an essential ingredient of exposure. Instead, it has been suggested that merely engaging in behaviors that are counter to those associated with fear prompts new learning that can overcome the anxiety response. This model is broadly described as the inhibitory learning model (i.e., Abramowitz, 2013; Craske et al., 2014). This approach to exposure emphasizes a wide range of tactics designed to ensure new learning occurs around the otherwise feared stimulus. This includes, but is not limited to: changing expectancies, labeling emotional experiences associated with the feared stimulus, changing contexts for stimulus exposure, and removal of safety signals. As will be discussed below, the existing evidence-based treatment approaches for childhood OCD largely have adhered to the inhibitory learning model, even if only implicitly.

Brief Overview of Evidence-Based Treatments

Treatment studies for OCD demonstrate support for cognitive-behavior therapy (CBT) with ERP accompanied by pharmacotherapy for severe cases (Abramowitz, Whiteside, & Deacon, 2005). The American Psychological Association formed their first Task Force for evaluating evidence-based practice in psychology (EBPP) in 1992 and since then have disseminated several guidelines (e.g., American Psychological Association, 1995, 2002, 2006) outlining evaluation criteria, includ-ing strength of empirical evidence and clinical utility of any psychological inter-vention. American Psychological Association Division 53 (The Society for Clinical Child and Adolescent Psychology) established a Task Force to identify and disseminate information on specific evidence-based treatments (EBTs) for youth mental health disorders. Division 53 utilizes guidelines set forth by Chambless and colleagues (1998) to categorize psychological treatments by their research support with five levels ranging from "well-established" (Level 1) to "does not work" (Level 5). Cognitive-behavior therapy with ERP meets the definition of "probably efficacious treatment" (Level 2) for youth with OCD (Freeman et al., 2014). Probably efficacious treatments have strong research sup-port but have not yet exhibited efficacy in two between-group experiments conducted by independent teams, a requirement of well-established treatments (Chambless et al., 1998). Additionally, the Anxiety and Depression Association of America (ADAA), not affiliated with the APA, lists CBT with ERP alone or in combination with SSRIs as first-line psychotherapy treatments for pediatric OCD (ADAA, 2017). These designations by Division 53 and ADAA are promising for the treatment of childhood and adolescent OCD.

At this point, the only evidence-based approach to treatment for childhood OCD is CBT, specifically ERP. Controlled treatment trials have been conducted comparing ERP to waitlist control groups, credible attention control groups, pill placebo, and active medication. Collectively, ERP has been shown to be superior to these varied control groups, typically with large effect sizes favoring the approach, and with generally durable outcomes at up to nine-month follow-up (Franklin et al., 2015). However, it should be noted that, although this finding is encouraging, it is based on research conducted over a limited time (15 years) and a comparably small number of highly controlled studies (14 trials). Prior meta-analyses of all treatment trials have suggested comparably large effect sizes (i.e., Abramowitz, Whiteside, & Deacon, 2005). What follows is a general description of treatment procedures that are broadly described as CBT in nature, with particular emphasis on ERP given its observed efficacy. It is important to note, however, that considerable additional research is warranted given the comparably limited number of controlled investigations.

Although the evidence favors ERP, some investigations include evaluation of cognitive therapy that targets core beliefs associated with OCD. These cognitive domains include: inflated responsibility, overimportance of thoughts, need to control thoughts, overestimation of threat, perfectionism, and intolerance of uncertainty. As noted previously, these domains are not specific or unique to OCD, but nonetheless can serve as potent contributors to obsessional experiences and compulsive behaviors. By way of example, in some cases with obsessions about harming others, the mere occurrence of the thought could increase the likelihood that the feared imagery would become real, illustrating overimportance of thoughts, specifically thought–action fusion (Rachman et al., 1996). Children with symptoms like this might further fear thinking about other people, especially friends and loved ones, since they could be the object of unwanted harmful thoughts, illustrating overestimation of threat. These domains can serve as the basis for later cognitive intervention (i.e., disputation), or can be used as part of ERP interventions as will be shown below.

Components of Evidence-Based Treatments

There are three broad components of evidence-based treatment for childhood OCD: psychoeducation, hierarchy development, and ERP.

Psychoeducation

Given the broad disabling nature of OCD, psychoeducation about the disorder and scope of impairment is essential before initiating treatment. As part of this education process, involvement of key family members is standard. In order to ensure comprehension, information regarding OCD must be presented in developmentally appropriate terms for the child, and in clear form to parents or caregivers. This can include illustrations with analogous situations that the child can relate to readily (e.g., cartoon animals that have repetitive behaviors and depictions of reasons for this). In some instances ancillary reading material can be offered, such as children's books on OCD (see, e.g., Moritz, 2011).

The education process at this early stage of treatment typically also involves depiction of other disorders that are distinct from OCD. This is important for parents and caregivers since there is a wealth of information on a wide range of conditions that could be ruled out. Parents and caregivers benefit from understanding the difference between obsessions and normal anxious thoughts, such as worry. So a parent might be instructed that obsessions are senseless and impossible intrusive images and ideas, whereas worries might be exaggerated concerns (i.e., excessive concerns over grades or friendships). Also useful is helping parents and caregivers understand the distinction between obsessions and ruminations (i.e., excessive thoughts about prior events). This helps to ensure that parents avoid overpathologizing their child as well as recognize other potential problems that could be the subject of other interventions.

In addition to covering the nature of the disorder, the psychoeducation portion covers the conceptualization of treatment. This portion is critical since clients are more likely to fully participate in treatment when they understand the rationale for treatment and have clear expectations for duration of possible discomfort and anticipated outcome (Skarphedinsson & Weidle, 2018). In protocol-driven treatment of OCD, the psychoeducation portion typically encompasses one to two sessions.

Hierarchy Development

Before initiating ERP, a hierarchy of feared stimuli must be developed. This is the basis for treatment development, and sets the stage for how ERP-based exercises are implemented. Wolpe (1990), in his seminal text on behavior therapy, noted the importance of the hierarchy for ensuring that progress through treatment was manageable for clients. For many clients, providing a rationale for the hierarchy can be couched in terms associated with activities in their everyday environment. For example, a child who is involved in athletics might better understand the hierarchy based on concepts of skill development in their chosen sport. Another child might better appreciate concepts based on increasing academic demands in a subject as comparable to how treatment will progress for OCD.

In hierarchy development, the clinician must prioritize which symptoms will be the focus of intervention, and design hierarchies around those first. By targeting the symptoms that likely cause the greatest disability, and providing relief relatively early in treatment, then this could lead to greater engagement in treatment for higher items on the hierarchy, as well as for other symptoms that are not the primary focus of treatment but that nonetheless cause interference.

Finally, clinicians might consider viewing the hierarchy development portion of treatment as a phenomenological exercise. That is, it will be necessary to try to view the world from the child's perspective. To illustrate, if the child is presenting with contamination fear, the clinician might need to ask herself what life would be like to have those symptoms. What situations would cause problems in everyday life? By asking oneself this question, it sets the occasion to enquire about feared situations that might be easier or harder for the child as the clinician develops a detailed hierarchy (see McKay, 2018a for a discussion of hierarchy development).

Exposure with Response Prevention

Once a hierarchy has been developed, treatment with ERP may begin. Typically, therapists begin with items on the hierarchy that the child will clearly be successful in managing. This will further increase the credibility of the therapist and build confidence for the child as more advanced aspects of the hierarchy are approached. It is here that the theoretical distinctions in how ERP is conducted become clearer. In most treatment models for children, successfully engaging in exposure is reinforced, often by a caregiver as well as within session by the therapist. This is consistent with the inhibitory learning model, where new learning is rewarded. It is also common for clinicians implementing ERP with children to do so in ways that are substantially different from how the child encounters the stimulus situations in the real world (such as through humor or cartoons). Doing so shifts the expectations of the child from the stimuli being solely fear provoking to one producing other emotional states (see McKay, 2018b for methods for implementing ERP).

Exposure with response prevention is used to target specific obsessions and compulsions. During these exposures the child experiences stimuli that typically trigger anxiety and obsessions and is given strategies to help them not engage in compulsions. These exercises are also performed as homework between sessions with oversight from parents. If the child reports a reduction in obsessions and compulsions in relation to a stimulus, exposures during session follow a hierarchy until the most anxiety-provoking stimuli are addressed. For example, the Pediatric OCD Treatment Study (POTS) led by March and Foa (POTS Team, 2004) utilized a treatment that included 14 one-hour sessions in 12 weeks focused on psychoeducation, cognitive training, mapping OCD, exposure with response prevention, and relapse prevention and generalization training. Sessions occurred once per week except during the first two weeks when sessions occurred twice per week. Patients in this study were randomly assigned to receive CBT alone, sertraline alone, combined CBT and sertraline, or placebo. Results demonstrated the greatest support for treatment of pediatric OCD with combined CBT and sertraline (POTS Team, 2004). However, the remission rate for combined CBT and sertraline did not differ from that for CBT administered without sertraline indicating that either treatment is appropriate for children with treatment decisions made on a case-by-case basis. It is important to note that CBT collectively includes teaching appropriate behaviors and effective problem-solving skills, while challenging maladaptive thoughts. This approach is not well examined in childhood OCD.

Role of Parents in Treatment

Parents are often involved in their child's obsessions and compulsions, and may end up reinforcing compulsions by offering reassurance or modifying their parental behavior (e.g., helping children wash their hands excessively, reassuring children of safety, or serving food in a specific way). Children with families that reinforce their compulsions are more likely to have poor treatment outcome (Flessner et al., 2011; Lavell et al., 2016). Parenting style can also affect trajectory of OCD symptoms. For instance, children with OCD tend to have more dominant parents who are less encouraging of their independence (Waters & Barrett, 2000). Children with an immediate family member with OCD have poorer treatment outcomes than those without affected family members (Garcia et al., 2010), which is notable since OCD and anxiety disorders tend to co-occur in families. Thus, parental psychopathology, family relationships, and pediatric OCD symptoms should be assessed and integrated into the treatment plan. Parents should also be included in treatment strategies for their children and be provided psychoeducation for why treatment techniques may be beneficial. Parents often find it difficult to have neutral or detached responses while their children engage in ritualistic behaviors; however, parental involvement is critical to eliminating reinforcement for obsessive or compulsive symptoms.

Labouliere and colleagues (2014) created a treatment program where parents facilitate the completion of between-session exercises outside of the clinic. Parent training in this protocol involves psychoeducation to teach parents that outbursts are common in children with OCD, that compulsions are used to relieve distress caused by obsessions, and that the cycle of reinforcement and parent accommodation may make obsessive-compulsive behavior worse. Parents are also taught how exposure therapy works (i.e., by extinguishing the anxious response to stimuli through habituation) and how new adaptive responses are formed. Parents learn to positively reinforce noncompulsive, adaptive, and independent behavior and to ignore compulsions. Parents can help children focus less on compulsions by drawing their attention to other fun activities. Additionally, parents are encouraged not to accommodate their child's compulsions and to ignore or redirect to a positive activity when compulsions arise. This strategy of including parent training in CBT with ERP may improve treatment outcomes by enhancing homework compliance.

Other Variables Influencing Treatment

Assessment

Unlike other conditions, where there is known reactivity and treatment benefits from assessment, there is little comparable effect in the case of OCD, either in young children using a parent interview measure (Cook et al., 2015) or in adolescents using a self-report scale (Fernandez de la Cruz et al., 2013). This aspect of the condition has not been widely examined, however.

Comorbidity

In addition to its considerable heterogeneity, OCD frequently presents with comorbid psychiatric problems. In general, additional disorders such as anxiety or mood disturbance interfere with implementation of evidence-based interventions for the disorder. However, many individuals suffering from OCD also show a specific cognitive error referred to as overvalued ideation (OVI) (for conceptual discussion, see Kozak & Foa, 1994). Children who show an increased level of conviction for the reasonableness of their compulsions or the risks of their intrusive ideas could be considered to potentially have OVI as a complicating factor in their OCD. However, OVI is more difficult to assess in children than in adults, and its role in treatment is only hypothesized as a poor prognostic sign (McKay et al., 2009).

Recent research has focused on specific adjustments to evidence-based treatment employing ERP with autism spectrum disorder (i.e., Storch et al., 2015, in relation to anxiety disorders broadly). This line of work is still in early development. The preliminary findings thus far suggest that good outcome can be obtained with modified protocols that address socialization and other specific features of autism spectrum disorder as well as target repetitive behaviors and intrusive ideas associated with OCD.

An additional complicating factor in treatment is comorbid depression (Lavell et al., 2016). However, this has not been consistently observed (i.e., Rudy et al., 2014). The role of depression as a complicating factor in treatment has been examined extensively in adult OCD (Keeley et al., 2008), but has received comparably less attention in children. At this point, it should be considered a potential limiting factor in treatment deserving of clinical care.

Demographics

Research on demographic factors that influence treatment has been underexamined in childhood OCD. Of the limited research that has been conducted, gender has been found to predict treatment outcome, with males having worse outcomes. However, this finding has been inconsistent, with some work demonstrating a significant gender effect (Lavell et al., 2016), and others finding no difference (Rudy et al., 2014). This finding is comparable to demographic differences observed in adult samples. An important caveat to this should be highlighted, namely that research on OCD generally has undersampled diverse populations (Williams et al., 2010), greatly limiting the generalizations that can be made about treatment, and hence also limiting the degree demographic variables can be understood as complicating factors in treatment.

Medication

Pharmacotherapy for childhood OCD principally involves serotonin reuptake inhibitors (SRIs). This class of medications has been found, in systematic and controlled research, to produce medium effect sizes for obsessions and compulsions. Further, in a small series of studies comparing CBT to CBT plus SSRI, the addition of pharmacotherapy produced minimal additional gains (see Ivarsson et al., 2015). What is not well known is how prior medication history might influence CBT treatment. It was observed in the POTS trial that it was difficult to recruit children with OCD who had no prior medication history (see Franklin et al., 2015). This issue warrants additional investigation.

Tic-Related Specifier

Tic disorders frequently co-occur with OCD, or can accompany a case of PANS onset OCD, with some investigators characterizing this as a possible subtype of OCD (Eichstedt & Arnold, 2001). One potential explanation offered for the complications in the comorbid tic subtype is the potential presence of PANS (Leckman et al., 2011).

In such cases, additional evidence-based treatment for tics should be applied to manage the full gamut of symptoms. It is beyond the scope of this chapter to cover etiology and treatment for tics (see Chapter 6, Wellen & Himle, this volume), but briefly these are considered neurological impulses that the person experiences as under "pseudocontrol." That is, someone suffering from tics can prevent the occurrence briefly, but will also experience an increasing urge to express the tic under these circumstances (see Ricketts et al., in press).

The major efficacious ingredient of treatment for tics is habit reversal. Developed by Azrin and Peterson (1990), the original approach involved identifying major motor actions associated with the tic, and training the child in producing an incompatible motoric action. For example, if the urge was to swing the arm upward, the child would be trained to move the arm in the opposite direction when the urge arose. Since the time of the first trial for the procedure, it has been shown that the best practice for habit reversal entails two major components. The first is awareness training, where the child is taught to monitor the specific situations where the tics are most likely to occur, and the specific physical sensations associated with the tic. This is based on the observation that most tics are automatic responses, and bringing these into conscious awareness increases the likelihood that habit reversal exercises will be effective. The second portion entails practice in engaging in a muscle tensing response when the urge to produce the tic occurs. This has the beneficial effect of allowing children to engage in habit reversal in highly covert ways (i.e., pressing the toes downward within one's shoes; clenching a fist slightly) (see Capriotti & Woods, 2013). Quantitative reviews show that habit reversal is associated with large effect sizes at the end of treatment and at follow-up (McGuire et al., 2014) (see also Chapter 6, Wellen & Himle, this volume).

Conclusion

The accumulated evidence supports the application of CBT, specifically ERP, in the treatment of childhood OCD. In recognition of the heterogeneity of symptom presentation, the application of ERP can also be highly varied. Additionally, involvement of family members in treatment is essential for efficacious outcome owing to accommodation of symptoms that occurs in the households of affected children. Finally, tic disorders are frequently comorbid to OCD in children, which necessitates additional intervention in conjunction with ERP. With careful clinical case conceptualization employing the available approaches to OCD, clinicians are well positioned to provide significant relief to affected children.

Useful Resources

- *Cognitive-Behavioral Treatment of Childhood OCD*, John Piacentini, Audra Langley, and Tami Roblek, Oxford University Press, 2007
- *The Clinician's Guide to Cognitive-Behavioral Therapy for Childhood Obsessive-Compulsive Disorder*, Eric A. Storch, Joseph F. McGuire, and Dean McKay, Academic Press, 2018
- International Obsessive-Compulsive Disorder Foundation (IOCDF) children's resource page: https://kids.iocdf.org/
- "Understand the Facts" page of the Anxiety and Depression Association of America, Obsessive-Compulsive Disorder: www.adaa.org/understanding-anxiety/obsessive-compulsive-disorder-ocd
- Association for Behavioral and Cognitive Therapies "Fact Sheets": www.abct.org/Information/?m=mInformation&fa=fs_OBSESSIVE_COMPULSIVE
- Tourette's Association of America at www.tourette.org/

References

Abramovitch, A., & Cooperman, A. (2015). The cognitive neuropsychology of obsessive-compulsive disorder: A critical review. *Journal of Obsessive-Compulsive and Related Disorders, 5,* 24–36. http://dx.doi.org/10.1016/j.jocrd.2015.01.002

Abramowitz, J. S. (2013). The practice of exposure therapy: Relevance of cognitive-behavioral theory and extinction theory. *Behavior Therapy, 44,* 548–558.

Abramowitz, J. S., & Jacoby, R. J. (2015). Obsessive-compulsive and related disorders: A critical review of the new diagnostic class. *Annual Review of Clinical Psychology, 11,* 165–186.

Abramowitz, J. S., Storch, E. A., McKay, D., Taylor, S., & Asmundson, G. J. G. (2009). The obsessive-compulsive spectrum: A critical review. In D. McKay, J. S. Abramowitz, S. Taylor, & G. J. G. Asmundson (eds.), *Current perspectives on anxiety disorders: Implications for DSM-V and beyond* (pp. 329–352). New York: Springer.

Abramowitz, J. S., Taylor, S., & McKay, D. (2007). Psychological theories of obsessive-compulsive disorder. In E. A. Storch, G. R. Geffken, & T. K. Murphy (eds.), *Handbook of child and adolescent obsessive-compulsive disorder* (pp. 100–129). Mahwah, NJ: Erlbaum.

Abramowitz, J. S., Taylor, S., & McKay, D. (2009). Obsessive-compulsive disorder. *Lancet, 374,* 491–499.

Abramowitz, J. S., Whiteside, S. P., & Deacon, B. J. (2005). The effectiveness of treatment for pediatric obsessive-compulsive disorder: A meta-analysis. *Behavior Therapy, 36*(1), 55–63. doi:10.1016/S0005-7894(05)80054–1

American Psychological Association. (1995). *Template for developing guidelines: Interventions for mental disorders and psychosocial aspects of physical disorders.* Washington, DC: American Psychological Association.

American Psychological Association. (2002). Criteria for evaluating treatment guidelines. *American Psychologist, 57,* 1052–1059.

American Psychological Association. (2006). Evidence-based practice in psychology. *American Psychologist, 61*(4), 271–285.

American Psychiatric Association. (2013). *Diagnostic and statistical manual of mental disorders.* 5th edn. Washington, DC: American Psychiatric Association.

Andover, M. S., & Morris, B. W. (2014). Suicidal and nonsuicidal self-injury in the obsessive-compulsive spectrum. In E. A. Storch & D. McKay (eds.), *Obsessive-compulsive disorder and its spectrum: A life-span approach* (pp. 241–259). Washington, DC: American Psychological Association.

Anxiety and Depression Association of America (ADAA). (2017). Clinical practice review of OCD. Washington, DC: ADAA. https://adaa.org/resources-professionals/practice-guidelines-ocd

Azrin, N. H., & Peterson, A. L. (1990). Treatment of Tourette Syndrome by habit reversal: A waiting-list control group comparison. *Behavior Therapy, 21,* 305–318.

Bernstein, G. A., Mueller, B. A., Schreiner, M. W., Campbell, S. M., Regan, E. K., Nelson, P. M., Houri, A. K., . . . & Cullen, K. R. (2016). Abnormal striatal resting-state functional connectivity in adolescents with obsessive-compulsive disorder. *Psychiatry Research: Neuroimaging, 247,* 49–56.

Boedhoe, P. S. W., Schmaal, L., Abe, Y., Ameis, S. H., Arnold, P. D., Batistuzzo, M. C., Benedetti, F., . . . & van den Heuvel, O. A. (2017). Distinct subcortical volume alterations in pediatric and adult OCD: A worldwide meta- and mega-analysis. *American Journal of Psychiatry, 174,* 60–70.

Capriotti, M. R., & Woods, D. W. (2013). Cognitive-behavioral treatment for tics. In D. Martino & J. F. Leckman (eds.), *Tourette Syndrome* (pp. 503–523). New York: Oxford University Press.

Chambless, D. L., Baker, M. J., Baucom, D. H., Beutler, L. E., Calhoun, K. S., Crits-Cristoph, P., et al. (1998). Update on empirically validated therapies, II. *The Clinical Psychologist, 51*(1), 3–16.

Chorpita, B. F., & Weisz, J. R. (2009). *Match-ADTC: Modular approach to therapy for children with anxiety, depression, trauma, or conduct problems.* Satellite Beach, FL: PracticeWise.

Cook, N. E., Freeman, J. B., Garcia, A. M., Sapyta, J. J., & Franklin, M. E. (2015). Assessment of obsessive compulsive disorder in young children: Psychometric properties of the Children's Yale-Brown Obsessive Compulsive Scale. *Journal of Psychopathology and Behavioral Assessment, 37*, 432–441.

Craske, M. G., Treanor, M., Conway, C. C., Zbozinek, T., & Vervliet, B. (2014). Maximizing exposure therapy: An inhibitory learning approach. *Behaviour Research and Therapy, 58*, 10–23. doi:10.1016/j.brat.2014.04.006

Eddy, K. T., Dutra, L., Bradley, R., & Westen, D. (2004). A multidimensional meta-analysis of psychotherapy and pharmacotherapy for obsessive-compulsive disorder. *Clinical Psychology Review, 24*, 1011–1030.

Eichstedt, J. A., & Arnold, S. L. (2001). Childhood-onset obsessive-compulsive disorder: A tic-related subtype of OCD? *Clinical Psychology Review, 21*, 137–157.

Fernandez de la Cruz, L., Micali, N., Roberts, S., Turner, C., Nakatani, E., Heyman, I., & Mataix-Cols, D. (2013). Are the symptoms of obsessive-compulsive disorder temporally stable in children/adolescents? A prospective naturalistic study. *Psychiatry Research, 209*, 196–201.

Ferrão, Y. A., Euripedes, M., & Stein, D. J. (2009). Tourette's syndrome, trichotillomania, and obsessive-compulsive disorder: How closely are they related. *Psychiatry Research, 170*, 32–42.

Fibbe, L. A., Cath, D. C., van den Heuvel, O. A., Veltman, D. J., Tijssen, M. A. J., & van Balkom, A. J. L. M. (2012). Relationship between movement disorders and obsessive-compulsive disorder: Beyond the obsessive-compulsive-tic phenotype: A systematic review. *Journal of Neurology, Neurosurgery & Psychiatry, 83*, 646–654.

Fireman, B., Koran, L. M., Leventhal, J. L., & Jacobson, A. (2001). The prevalence of clinically recognized obsessive-compulsive disorder in a large health maintenance organization. *The American Journal of Psychiatry, 158*(11), 1904–1910.

Flament, M. F., Rapoport, J. L., Zaremba Berg, C., Sceery, W., Whitaker, A., Davies, M., . . . & Shaffer, D. (1988). Obsessive compulsive disorder in adolescence: An epidemiological study. *Journal of the American Academy of Child & Adolescent Psychiatry, 27*(6), 764–771.

Flessner, C. A., Freeman, J. B., Sapyta, J., Garcia, A., Franklin, M. E., March, J. S., & Foa, E. (2011). Predictors of parental accommodation in pediatric obsessive-compulsive disorder: Findings from the pediatric obsessive-compulsive disorder treatment study (POTS) trial. *Journal of the American Academy of Child & Adolescent Psychiatry, 50*(7), 716–725.

Foa, E. B., & Kozak, M. J. (1986). Emotional processing of fear: Exposure to corrective information. *Psychological Bulletin, 99*, 20–35.

Franklin, M. S., Dingfelder, H. E., Freeman, J. B., Ivarsson, T., Heyman, I., Sookman, D., McKay, D., Storch, E. A., & March, J. (2015). Cognitive behavioral therapy for pediatric obsessive-compulsive disorder: Empirical review and clinical recommendations. *Psychiatry Research, 227*, 78–92.

Freeman, J., Garcia, A., Frank, H., Benito, K., Conelea, C., Walther, M., & Edmunds, J. (2014). Evidence base update for psychosocial treatments for pediatric obsessive-compulsive disorder.

Journal of Clinical Child & Adolescent Psychology, *43*(1), 7–26. doi:10.1080/15374416.2013.804386

Garcia, A. M., Sapyta, J. J., Moore, P. S., Freeman, J. B., Franklin, M. E., March, J. S., & Foa, E. B. (2010). Predictors and moderators of treatment outcome in the pediatric obsessive compulsive treatment study (POTS I). *Journal of the American Academy of Child & Adolescent Psychiatry*, *49*(10), 1024–1033.

Geller, D., Biederman, J., Jones, J., Park, K., Schwartz, S., Shapiro, S., & Coffey, B. (1998). Is juvenile obsessive-compulsive disorder a developmental subtype of the disorder? A review of the pediatric literature. *Journal of the American Academy of Child & Adolescent Psychiatry*, *37*(4), 420–427. doi:10.1097/00004583–199804000-00020

Gryczkowski, M., & Whiteside, S. P. H. (2014). Nature and treatment of pediatric obsessive-compulsive disorder. In E. A. Storch & D. McKay (eds.), *Obsessive compulsive disorder and its spectrum: A life-span approach*. Washington, DC: American Psychological Association.

Hanna, G. L. (1995). Demographic and clinical features of obsessive-compulsive disorder in children and adolescents. *Journal of the American Academy of Child & Adolescent Psychiatry*, *34*(1), 19–27.

Heyman, I., Fombonne, E., Simmons, H., Ford, T., Meltzer, H., & Goodman, R. (2001). Prevalence of obsessive-compulsive disorder in the British nationwide survey of child mental health. *The British Journal of Psychiatry*, *179*(4), 324–329. doi:10.1192/bjp.179.4.324

Højgaard, D. R. M. A., Mortensen, E. L., Ivarsson, T., Skarphedinsson, G., Nissen, J. B., Valderhaug, R., Dahl, K., ... & Thomsen, P. H. (2017). Structure and clinical correlates of obsessive-compulsive disorder in a large sample of children and adolescents: A factor analytic study across five nations. *European Child & Adolescent Psychiatry*, *26*, 281–291.

Horwath, E., & Weissman, M. M. (2000). The epidemiology and cross-national presentation of obsessive-compulsive disorder. *Psychiatric Clinics of North America*, *23*(3), 493–507. doi:10.1016/S0193-953X(05)70176–3

Houghton, D. C., Maas, J., Twohig, M. P., Saunder, S. M., Compton, S. N., Neal-Barnett, A. M., Franklin, M. E., & Woods, D. W. (2016). Comorbidity and quality of life in adults with hair pulling disorder. *Psychiatry Research*, *239*, 12–19.

Ivarsson, T., Skarphedinsson, G., Kornor, H., Axelsdottir, B., Biedilae, S., Heyman, I., Asbahr, F., ... & March, J. (2015). The place of and evidence for serotonin reuptake inhibitors (SRIs) for obsessive compulsive disorder (OCD) in children and adolescents: Views based on a systematic review and meta-analysis. *Psychiatry Research*, *227*, 93–103.

Karno, M., Golding, J. M., Sorenson, S. B., & Burnam, M. A. (1988). The epidemiology of obsessive-compulsive disorder in five US communities. *Archives of General Psychiatry*, *45*(12), 1094–1099.

Keeley, M. L., Storch, E. A., Merlo, L. J., & Geffken, G. R. (2008). Clinical predictors of response to cognitive-behavioral therapy for obsessive-compulsive disorder. *Clinical Psychology Review*, *28*, 118–130.

Kim, S. K., McKay, D., Taylor, S., Tolin, D., Olatunji, B. O., Timpano, K., & Abramowitz, J. S. (2016). The structure of obsessive-compulsive symptoms and beliefs: A correspondence and biplot analysis. *Journal of Anxiety Disorders*, *38*, 79–87.

Kozak, M. J., & Foa, E. B. (1994). Obsessions, overvalued ideas, and delusions in obsessive-compulsive disorder. *Behaviour Research and Therapy*, *32*, 343–353.

Labouliere, C. D., Arnold, E. B., Storch, E. A., & Lewin, A. B. (2014). Family-based cognitive-behavioral treatment for a preschooler with obsessive-compulsive disorder. *Clinical Case Studies*, *13*(1), 37–51. doi:10.1177/1534650113504985

Lavell, C. H., Farrell, L. J., Waters, A. M., & Cadman, J. (2016). Predictors of treatment response to group cognitive behavioural therapy for pediatric obsessive-compulsive disorder. *Psychiatry Research, 245*, 186–193.

Leckman, J. F., King, R. A., Gilbert, D. L., Coffey, B. J., Singer, H. S., Dure, L. S., Grantz, H., . . . & Kaplan, E. L. (2011). Streptococcal upper respiratory tract infections and exacerbations of tic and obsessive-compulsive symptoms: A prospective longitudinal study. *Journal of the American Academy of Child & Adolescent Psychiatry, 50*, 108–118.

Markarian, Y., Larson, M. J., Aldea, M. A., Baldwin, S. A., Good, D., Berkeljon, A., . . . & McKay, D. (2010). Multiple pathways to functional impairment in obsessive-compulsive disorder. *Clinical Psychology Review, 30*, 78–88.

McGuire, J. F., Piacentini, J., Brennan, E. A., Lewin, A. B., Murphy, T. K., Small, B. J., & Storch, E. A. (2014). A meta-analysis of behavior therapy for Tourette syndrome. *Journal of Psychiatric Research, 50*, 106–112.

McKay, D. (2018a). Developing exposure hierarchies. In E. A. Storch, J. McGuire, & D. McKay (eds.), *Clinicians' guide to cognitive-behavioral therapy for childhood obsessive-compulsive disorder* (pp. 75–88). Amsterdam: Academic Press.

McKay, D. (2018b). Developing and implementing exposure treatment in youth obsessive-compulsive symptoms. In E. A. Storch, J. McGuire, & D. McKay (eds.), *Clinicians' guide to cognitive-behavioral therapy for childhood obsessive-compulsive disorder* (pp. 89–104). Amsterdam: Academic Press.

McKay, D., Abramowitz, J. S., Calamari, J. E., Kyrios, M., Radomsky, A., Sookman, D., . . . & Wilhelm, S. (2004). A critical evaluation of obsessive-compulsive disorder subtypes: Symptoms versus mechanisms. *Clinical Psychology Review, 24*(3), 283–313. doi:10.1016/j.cpr.2004.04.003

McKay, D., & Andover, M. (2012). Should nonsuicidal self-injury be a putative obsessive-compulsive related condition? A critical appraisal. *Behavior Modification, 36*, 3–17.

McKay, D., Kim, S. K., Taylor, S., Abramowitz, J. S., Tolin, D., Coles, M., Timpano, K. R., & Olatunji, B. (2014). An examination of obsessive-compulsive symptoms and dimensions using Profile Analysis via Multidimensional Scaling (PAMS). *Journal of Anxiety Disorders, 28*, 352–357.

McKay, D. & Moretz, M. W. (2009). The intersection of disgust and contamination fear. In B. O. Olatunji & D. McKay (eds.), *Disgust and its disorders* (pp. 211–227). Washington, DC: American Psychological Association Press.

McKay, D., Storch, E. A., Nelson, B., Morales, M., & Moretz, M. W. (2009). Obsessive-compulsive disorder in children and adolescents: Treating difficult cases. In D. McKay & E. A. Storch (eds.), *Cognitive-behavior therapy for children: Treating complex and refractory cases* (pp. 81–113). New York: Springer.

Micali, N., Heyman, I., Perez, M., Hilton, K., Nakatani, E., Turner, C., & Mataix-Cols, D. (2010). Long-term outcomes of obsessive-compulsive disorder: Follow-up of 142 children and adolescents. *The British Journal of Psychiatry, 197*(2), 128–134. doi:10.1192/bjp.bp.109.075317

Moritz, E. K. (2011). *Blink, blink, clop, clop, why do we do things we can't stop?* Ridgefield, CT: Weston Press.

Mowrer, O. H. (1960). *Learning theory and behavior.* New York: Wiley.

The Pediatric OCD Treatment Study Team (POTS). (2004). Cognitive-behavior therapy, sertraline, and their combination for children and adolescents with obsessive-compulsive disorder:

The Pediatric OCD Treatment Study (POTS) randomized controlled trial. *JAMA*, *292*(16), 1969–1976. doi:10.1001/jama.292.16.1969

Rachman, S., Shafran, R., Mitchell, D., Trant, J., & Teachman, B. (1996). How to remain neutral: An experimental analysis of neutralization. *Behaviour Research and Therapy*, *34*, 889–898.

Rauch S. L., & Jenike, M. A. (1998). Neurobiologic models of obsessive-compulsive disorder. In M. A. Jenike, L. Baer, & W. E. Minichiello (eds.), *Obsessive-compulsive disorders: Practical management* (pp. 222–253). St. Louis, MO: Mosby.

Rettew, D. C., Swedo, S. E., Leonard, H. L., Lenane, M. C., & Rapoport, J. L. (1992). Obsessions and compulsions across time in 79 children and adolescents with obsessive-compulsive disorder. *Journal of the American Academy of Child & Adolescent Psychiatry*, *31*, 1050.

Richard, D. C. S., & Gloster, A. T. (2006). Exposure therapy has a public relations problem: A dearth of litigation amid a wealth of concern. In D. C. S. Richard & D. L. Lauterbach (eds.), *Handbook of exposure therapies* (pp. 409–425). Amsterdam: Academic Press.

Ricketts, E. J., McGuire, J. F., Chang, S., Bose, D., Rasch, M. M., Woods, D. W., Specht, M. W., . . ., & Piacentini, J. (in press). Benchmarking treatment response in Tourette's disorder: Psychometric evaluation and signal detection analysis of the parent tic questionnaire. *Behavior Therapy*.

Roswell, M., & Francis, S. E. (2015). OCD subtypes: Which, if any, are valid? *Clinical Psychology: Science and Practice*, *22*, 414–435.

Rudy, B. M., Lewin, A. B., Geffken, G. R., Murphy, T. K., & Storch, E. A. (2014). Predictors of treatment response to intensive cognitive-behavioral therapy for pediatric obsessive-compulsive disorder. *Psychiatry Research*, *220*, 433–440.

Ruscio, A. M., Stein, D. J., Chiu, W. T., & Kessler, R. C. (2010). The epidemiology of obsessive-compulsive disorder in the National Comorbidity Survey Replication. *Molecular Psychiatry*, *15*(1), 53–63.

Salkovskis, P. M. (1985). Obsessive-compulsive problems: A cognitive-behavioral analysis. *Behaviour Research and Therapy*, *23*, 571–583.

Scahill, L., Riddle, M. A., McSwiggin-Hardin, M., Ort, S. I., King, R. A., Goodman, W. K., Cicchetti, D., & Leckman, J. F. (1997). Children's Yale-Brown Obsessive-Compulsive Scale: Reliability and validity. *Journal of the American Academy of Child & Adolescent Psychiatry*, *36*, 844–852.

Shaw, P., Sharp, W., Sudre, G., Wharton, A., Greenstein, D., Raznahan, A., Evans, A., . . . & Rapoport, J. (2015). Subcortical and cortical morphological anomalies as an endophenotype in obsessive-compulsive disorder. *Molecular Psychiatry*, *20*, 224–231.

Skarphedinsson, G., & Weidle, B. (2018). Psychoeducation for children, parents, and family members about obsessive-compulsive disorder and cognitive-behavior therapy. In E. A. Storch, J. McGuire, & D. McKay (eds.), *Clinicians' guide to cognitive-behavioral therapy for childhood obsessive-compulsive disorder*. Amsterdam: Academic Press.

Snorrason, I., Belleau, E. L., & Woods, D. W. (2012). How related are hair pulling disorder (trichotillomania) and skin picking disorder? A review of evidence for comorbidity, similarities and shared etiology. *Clinical Psychology Review*, *32*, 618–629.

Snyder, H. R., Kaiser, R. H., Warren, S. L., & Heller, W. (2015). Obsessive compulsive disorder is associated with broad impairments in executive function: A meta-analysis. *Clinical Psychological Science*, *3*, 301–330. doi:10.1177/2167702614534210

Storch, E. A., Lewin, A. B., Collier, A. B., Arnold, E., de Nadai, A. S., Dane, B. F., Nadeau, J. M., . . . & Murphy, T. K. (2015). A randomized controlled trial of cognitive-behavioral therapy versus treatment as usual for adolescents with autism spectrum disorders and comorbid anxiety. *Depression and Anxiety, 32*, 174–181.

Storch, E. A., Merlo, L. J., Bloss, C. S., Geffken, G. R., Jacob, M. L., Murphy, T. K., & Goodman, W. K. (2008). Symptom dimensions and cognitive-behavioural therapy outcome for pediatric obsessive-compulsive disorder. *Acta Psychiatrica Scandinavica, 117*, 67–75.

Taylor, S. (2011). Early versus late onset obsessive-compulsive disorder: Evidence for distinct subtypes. *Clinical Psychology Review, 31*(7), 1083–1100. doi:10.1016/j.cpr.2011.06.007

Taylor, S., Abramowitz, J., McKay, D., Calamari, J., Sookman, D., Kyrios, M., Wilhelm, S., & Carmin, C. (2006). Do dysfunctional beliefs play a role in all types of obsessive-compulsive disorder? *Journal of Anxiety Disorders, 20*, 85–97.

Valleni-Basile, L. A., Garrison, C. Z., Jackson, K. L., Waller, J. L., McKeown, R. E., Addy, C. L., & Cuffe, S. P. (1994). Frequency of obsessive-compulsive disorder in a community sample of young adolescents. *Journal of the American Academy of Child & Adolescent Psychiatry, 33*(6), 782–791. doi:10.1097/00004583–199407000-00002

Waters, T. L., & Barrett, P. M. (2000). The role of the family in childhood obsessive-compulsive disorder. *Clinical Child and Family Psychology Review, 3*(3), 173–184. doi:10.1023/a:1009551325629

Wilhelm, S., & Steketee, G. (2006). *Cognitive therapy for obsessive-compulsive disorder*. Oakland, CA: New Harbinger.

Williams, K. A. & Swedo, S. E. (2015). Post-infectious autoimmune disorders: Sydenham's chorea, PANDAS and beyond. *Brain Research, 1617*, 144–154.

Williams, M., Powers, M., Yun, Y. G., & Foa, E. B. (2010). Minority participation in randomized controlled trials for obsessive-compulsive disorder. *Journal of Anxiety Disorders, 24*, 171–177.

Wolpe, J. (1990). *The practice of behavior therapy*. 4th edn. Elmsford, NY: Pergamon.

World Health Organization (WHO). (2005). Mental health: Facing the challenges, building solutions. Report from the WHO European Ministerial Conference, Helsinki, January 12–15. WHO Regional Office for Europe.

12

Trauma and Attachment

Monique LeBlanc, Megan Lilly, Whitney Rostad, and Brittany Babycos

Approximately two-thirds of children and adolescents in the United States are exposed to traumatic events, including child maltreatment, witnessed violence, peer victimization, natural disasters, traumatic death, medical trauma, and accidents (Copeland et al., 2007; Costello et al., 2002; McLaughlin et al., 2013). The *Diagnostic and Statistical Manual of Mental Disorders* (DSM-5; American Psychiatric Association [APA], 2013) delineates five disorders as trauma- and stressor-related disorders: posttraumatic stress disorder (PTSD), acute stress disorder, adjustment disorder, reactive attachment disorder (RAD), and disinhibited social engagement disorder (DSED). Traumatic stressors, wherein children experience or witness actual or threatened death, serious injury, sexual violence, or learn about the experience of a loved one, are necessary for a diagnosis of acute stress disorder and PTSD, while nontraumatic stressors are associated with adjustment disorder. Severe early trauma, specifically pathological caregiving or unusually inconsistent caregivers during early childhood, are diagnostic criteria for RAD and DSED (APA, 2013). Many children exposed to traumatic events do not evidence clinically significant difficulties; however, a small, yet nontrivial, subset meets diagnostic criteria for one of these disorders (Copeland et al., 2007), requiring treatment.

Children with PTSD experience painful recall of the traumatic event, often in the form of nightmares, flashbacks, and repetitive play and thoughts (APA, 2013; Copeland et al., 2007). They attempt to avoid and suppress painful thoughts and memories, as well as the situations that trigger them, and thus experience increased arousal, manifesting itself in sleep difficulties, irritability, and anxious behavior. Youth with PTSD often have negative cognitions, such as negative beliefs about the self or the world, including blaming oneself or others, as well as behavioral changes, such as less interest in play and/or social withdrawal. Similar to PTSD, the most common symptoms of acute stress disorder associated with impairment are intrusive, distressing memories and/or dreams. Due to the time criteria of acute stress disorder, youth with this disorder rarely present to treatment (Kassam-Adams et al., 2012).

Concerning adjustment disorder, the DSM-5 does not delineate a specific set of symptoms for the diagnosis; youth can present with internalizing or externalizing symptomology. Importantly, suicidal ideation is a common symptom for children and adolescents diagnosed with an adjustment disorder (Casey & Bailey, 2011). Most evidence-based treatments for traumatic stress focus upon these diagnoses or key symptomology.

The experience of a single traumatic event has been linked to acute and posttraumatic stress symptoms (i.e., re-experiencing, avoidance, and hyperarousal; Jonkman et al., 2013). However, chronic interpersonal trauma has been associated with more diffuse problems in regulating affect, attachment, and behavior (e.g., aggressive behavior, poor impulse control, attention deficits, and anger management), in addition to traditional PTSD symptoms (i.e., re-experiencing, hyperarousal, and avoidance; Cook et al., 2005; Jonkman et al., 2013; Milot et al., 2010). Children exposed to chronic traumatic events, particularly interpersonal trauma (i.e., child maltreatment), are more likely to suffer more profound and pervasive developmental deficits across various areas of functioning compared to children exposed to a single traumatic event, and, thus, are often referred to as experiencing "complex trauma" (Cook et al., 2005; van der Kolk, 2009).

Etiology and Theoretical Underpinnings of Treatment

The main objective of evidence-based treatment for children exhibiting symptoms of traumatic stress is to provide youth with the skills necessary to help them confront and make sense of traumatic experiences, and manage trauma stressors without relying on avoidant strategies (Cohen, Mannarino, & Deblinger, 2012; Deblinger & Heflin, 1996; Foa et al., 2009). Innocuous environmental reminders of past traumatic events automatically activate memories and negative emotions associated with those experiences. Since dysregulated affect, behaviors, physiology, and cognitions are learned or conditioned, cognitive-behavioral approaches theorize that they can be unlearned or extinguished through exposure techniques. Similarly, cognitive distortions, such as inaccurate or unhelpful thoughts about the traumatic event, can be corrected through cognitive and contextualizing techniques (Foa et al., 2009). Moreover, childhood exposure to traumatic events appears to be associated with alterations in physiology, including higher resting pulse rates, as well as brain function and structure, including smaller intracranial volume and corpus collosi (Cohen, Mannarino, & Deblinger, 2012; Milani, 2017). These alterations may contribute to the maintenance of trauma symptoms; research is ongoing concerning the psychobiological effects of evidence-based treatment (Cohen, Mannarino, & Deblinger, 2012).

Historically, behavior therapy for trauma exposure was based upon Mowrer's two-factor learning theory (1960). The associations between fear and other aversive emotions and trauma-related cues are acquired through classical conditioning and then maintained through operant conditioning, particularly negative reinforcement (Deblinger & Heflin, 1996). The associations between the trauma-related cues, both internal and external, and negative emotions are not allowed to extinguish, maintaining symptoms over time. Therefore, exposure-based techniques of cognitive-behavioral therapy (CBT) provide opportunities for youth to extinguish the association between trauma-related cues and aversive emotions. Cognitive theories also informed the development of evidence-based treatment (Foa & Rothbaum, 1998). Simplistically, cognitive theories posit that emotions, behaviors, and thoughts are interrelated and the negative interpretations of events can lead to maladaptive emotions and behaviors. These faulty interpretations are identified, challenged, and corrected through cognitive restructuring techniques.

Reactive Attachment and Disinhibited Social Engagement

RAD and DSED are two attachment-related disorders whose diagnostic criteria were recently modified for the DSM-5. Children with RAD demonstrate limited positive affect and social responsiveness, do not seek comfort when distressed, and, in general, do not exhibit a preference for the caregiver toward whom they should direct attachment behavior. Conversely, children with DSED nonselectively approach and seek comfort from any potential caregivers (including peers), are overly social with a limited understanding of personal boundaries, and do not demonstrate developmentally appropriate wariness of strangers (APA, 2013; Zeanah & Gleason, 2015).

Little high-quality research exists concerning treatments for RAD and DSED (Zeanah & Gleason, 2015). Because these diagnoses often occur within the caregiving system, such as among children who have experienced chronic maltreatment and are now in institutional care, interventions grounded in attachment theory have typically focused on improving the caregiver–child relationship, which is hypothesized to enhance attachment security and reduce the detrimental effects of trauma. Attachment security is facilitated by caregivers who are emotionally available and respond sensitively and appropriately to the child's needs, and, thus, interventions for children with attachment disorders and other attachment problems as a result of chronic interpersonal trauma would target caregiver availability, responsiveness, and sensitivity (Zeanah & Gleason, 2015). Zeanah and colleagues (2016) identified promising treatments based in attachment theory; however, they cautioned that these studies involved infants/toddlers with attachment difficulties, but not children with RAD or DSED.

Cognitive and behavioral deficits are proposed to contribute to the restricted attachment or disinhibition and violation of social boundaries exhibited by children with RAD or DSED; therefore, approaches that target these problems may be helpful, in addition to an enhanced caregiving environment (Zeanah & Gleason, 2015). One case study was conducted using behavioral parent training targeting behavioral deficits and excesses in a young child diagnosed with RAD (Buckner et al., 2008). Behavioral parent training, discussed in Chapter 17 of this book, resulted in fewer inappropriate attachment relations, more positive peer interactions, and increased compliance in a school-aged child with RAD. Although this is promising finding, more research is clearly needed.

Brief Overview of Evidence-Based Treatments

Three forms of cognitive-behavioral therapy (CBT) for traumatic stress have been identified as well-established treatments (Dorsey et al., 2016), using the *Journal of Clinical Child & Adolescent Psychology* evidence-based evaluation criteria (Southam-Gerow & Prinstein, 2014). These are individual CBT with parent involvement, individual CBT, and group CBT. The most widely studied version of individual CBT with parent involvement is trauma-focused CBT (TF-CBT; Deblinger & Heflin, 1996), which has consistently demonstrated effectiveness in reducing posttraumatic stress symptoms, internalizing behavior, and externalizing behavior among youth exposed to trauma (Dorsey et al., 2016; Silverman et al., 2008). While there is considerable evidence of the efficacy of TF-CBT with children exposed to a single traumatic event, increasing evidence suggests that, with a few adaptations, it can also benefit children who have experienced complex, or chronic interpersonal trauma (Cohen, Mannarino, Kliethermes, & Murray, 2012). TF-CBT includes children and parents in individual and conjoint structured sessions. The initial sessions focus on teaching coping skills (e.g., affect modulation, relaxation). The following sessions focus on trauma narrative and processing and in vivo mastery of trauma reminders with gradual exposure embedded through all sessions (Cohen, Berliner, & Mannarino, 2010; Dorsey, Briggs, & Woods, 2011). Later sessions include both parents and children in joint activities and focus on establishing safety plans for the future. Parents are involved throughout with some content focused specifically on behavioral parent training techniques, such as contingency management, targeting the children's emotional and behavioral regulation skills (Cohen, Berliner, & Mannarino, 2010).

Individual CBT without parent involvement, examined in both randomized controlled trials and open trials, was the second intervention determined to be a well-established treatment (Dorsey et al., 2016). Individual CBT includes adaptations of adult treatments, such as Prolonged Exposure for Adolescents (PE-A; Foa et al., 2013) and CBT packages developed specifically for youth (e.g., Shirk et al., 2014). Individual CBT treatments vary in their duration, as well as emphasis on different components of treatment. For example, some forms of individual CBT rely heavily on exposure-based techniques, while others utilize a multiple component approach similar to TF-CBT.

Lastly, group CBT was determined to be a well-established treatment (Dorsey et al., 2016) with Cognitive-Behavioral Interventions for Children in Schools (CBITS; Kataoka et al., 2003) as the most widely researched variant (Cohen & AACAP, 2010). CBITS consists of ten group sessions, as well as one to three individual sessions; additionally, CBITS has one teacher and two optional parent psychoeducation sessions. CBITS is similar to TF-CBT as components include psychoeducation, relaxation, cognitive restructuring, and exposure, but differs with inclusion of social problem-solving. Group content is presented didactically and practiced through age-appropriate examples and games (Kataoka et al., 2003).

Components of Evidence-Based Treatments

Psychoeducation

This component involves providing information to the child regarding trauma and its overall functional impact (Cohen, Mannarino, & Deblinger, 2006). Normalizing the experience of exposure to traumatic events may help reduce feelings of isolation or abnormality for children and their families (Cohen, Mannarino, & Deblinger, 2006). Given the broad range of possible traumatic events, it may also be helpful to provide specific base rate statistics for exposure to the child's particular traumatic experience. This would be followed with information regarding symptoms of PTSD and avoidance associated with trauma reminders. Handouts and worksheets may be beneficial to aid in discussion and can be adapted across developmental levels, and to fit exposure to a particular traumatic experience. For example, cartoons or picture books can be used with younger children to supplement the discussion of common symptoms of PTSD (Neugebauer et al., 1999; Scheeringa et al., 2010). In addition, psychoeducation includes a thorough explanation of the components and structure of CBT and current empirical support in order to convey a message of hope for the future. Psychoeducation is considered an ongoing process throughout treatment, as additional information may be necessary depending on a child's particular trauma history. For example, developmentally appropriate education about sexual health and body safety may be beneficial for children with a history of sexual abuse (e.g., Deblinger & Heflin, 1996).

Relaxation

Progressive muscle relaxation and focused breathing are two of the primary interventions which have been found effective for reducing distress in the moment (Cohen, Mannarino, & Deblinger, 2006). Progressive muscle relaxation involves tensing and relaxing targeted muscle groups and helps the child develop awareness of their capacity to exert control over personal physical reactions (Goldfried & Davison, 1976; Ollendick & Cerny, 1981). Focused breathing involves teaching the child to take deep-diaphragmatic breaths to lower their level of arousal. Teaching these skills focuses less on ensuring mastery of any particular technique, and more on helping youth develop a set of skills that can be implemented across settings. Also, skill acquisition means ensuring that the child understands what is being taught, and can implement it effectively. Based on the developmental level of the child, it may be beneficial to use creative techniques (e.g., blowing out the candles on a birthday cake, filling up a balloon) to enhance engagement. A number of additional strategies such as yoga, mindfulness, and distraction (e.g., watching TV, playing games, texting, listening to music) may be helpful for reducing distress in specific situations (Cohen, Mannarino, & Deblinger, 2006). However, overuse of distraction techniques may inhibit practice of more effective strategies; therefore, these should be discouraged as the child becomes more adept at implementing other forms of relaxation. Finally, it is important to allocate enough time in session to allow for modeling and practice of the skills. Particular care would be taken when working with children who have experienced complex trauma, as they may require additional time before engaging these skills effectively across situations (Cohen, Mannarino, Kliethermes, & Murray, 2012).

Affect Modulation

Youth may require varying degrees of intervention regarding affective education. Generally, the goal is to increase their ability to identify their feelings with a diverse affective vocabulary that is connected to an appropriate emotional expression (Cohen, Mannarino, & Deblinger, 2006). There are a number of different methods available (e.g., pictures, games, modeling, feelings faces) for teaching children how to recognize and understand emotional expression. Next, children are instructed to rate their feelings at various intensities by using subjective units of distress (SUDS) or a feelings thermometer. Following a traumatic experience, some youth may have developed biases toward perception of negative emotions from others and modification strategies are incorporated for correction (Cohen, Mannarino, & Deblinger, 2012), generally through cognitive strategies discussed below.

Imaginal Exposure

To facilitate processing of the child's traumatic experience, they are encouraged to develop a narrative that incorporates their feelings and cognitions about what occurred (Cohen, Mannarino, & Deblinger, 2006). Initially, the therapist collaboratively engages with the child in a discussion of the traumatic event in order to construct a stimulus hierarchy. The child's traumatic experience is divided into multiple component parts, which are then ranked based on the intensity of feelings they elicit or their SUDS. Alternatively, some children may benefit from using a temporal sequence rather than hierarchical levels of increasing distress. For youth with complex trauma, it is often more appropriate for them to select a common theme of experiences and feelings rather than particular occurrences (Cohen, Mannarino, Kliethermes, & Murray, 2012). Each component piece of the traumatic experience becomes a separate imaginal exposure that will be addressed across multiple treatment sessions.

During subsequent sessions, the therapist encourages the child to focus on one specific narrative moment from the hierarchy. This can be accomplished through a variety of methods (e.g., writing, poem, song) based on the individual preference of the child. For young children, drawing images associated with the traumatic experience is an effective technique for exposure (Scheeringa et al., 2010; Steele & Kuban, 2011). Regardless of method, the child is gradually encouraged to incorporate discussion of affective sensations and cognitions about the experience. Some children may be reluctant to engage in the narrative exposure and small rewards can be provided as incentives for their effort (Cohen, Mannarino, & Deblinger, 2006). The therapist identifies the child's inaccurate cognitions as they occur, with particular attention taken to address overgeneralizing beliefs, which have been shown to produce worse treatment outcomes (Ready et al., 2015). Overgeneralizing beliefs are more global, exaggerated cognitions concerning the impact of trauma on the child's life (e.g., "The world is dangerous, so I must never let my guard down"). Socratic or guided questioning may be useful to facilitate collaboration regarding maladaptive cognitions. Accommodation, or more balanced cognitions concerning trauma (e.g., "I have a scar on my heart, but it's healing"), has been shown to moderate overgeneralization during treatment (Ready et al., 2015). Whereas an additional goal of the narrative exposure is to aid the child in finding context and perspective regarding their traumatic experience, practicing accommodation may facilitate more adaptive responses.

Although no harm has been associated with the use of exposure-based techniques, a significant minority of children report hesitance concerning the trauma narrative portion (Salloum et al., 2015) and many therapists report they are reluctant to administer it (Borntrager et al., 2013). Dismantling research involving children lags behind that of adults (Nixon, Sterk, & Pearce, 2012), but recent studies have examined CBT with and without the trauma narrative portion. Deblinger and colleagues (2011) found that CBT with and without the trauma narrative resulted in posttraumatic stress symptom improvements; however, inclusion of the trauma narrative was associated with greater reduction in children's general anxiety and abuse-related fear and parents' abuse-related distress. However, differences between groups did not continue at six- and 12-month follow-ups in that children in both conditions evidenced overall significant improvements (Mannarino et al., 2012). Mannarino and colleagues cautioned that the trauma narrative may be particularly important in eliciting the dysfunctional abuse-related cognitions, thereby important for treatment outcome, but others note that the effectiveness of cognitive therapy alone allows clinicians necessary flexibility (Nixon, Sterk, & Pearce, 2012).

In Vivo Exposure

Children may have developed generalized avoidance of certain trauma reminders and in vivo exposure can be used to overcome these fear responses (Cohen, Mannarino, & Deblinger, 2006). Before conducting in vivo exposures with children who have been traumatized, it is important to conduct a thorough assessment regarding the danger-ousness of a particular stimulus. Only innocuous trauma reminders should be selected for exposure, as desensitizing the child to adaptive danger cues may make them vulnerable to actual future threat. Once a stimulus has been selected, the therapist collaboratively develops a hierarchy of triggers that interfere with the child's daily functioning (Cohen, Mannarino, & Deblinger, 2006). Following the development of the hierarchy, exposures for overcoming trauma reminders generally follow the same exposure principles developed for use in traditional CBT (Kendall, 1990). In vivo exposures may increase the child's potential ability to generalize their skills and overcome avoidance outside of the therapy session; however, unlike with in-session imaginal exposures, the therapist is not available to facilitate accommodation of cognitive and affective processes. Despite these challenges, in vivo exposures may be considered particularly warranted for trauma reminders that are overly impairing in the child's daily life (Cohen, Mannarino, & Deblinger, 2006).

Cognitive Coping

The goal of cognitive coping is to help the youth identify and change maladaptive cognitions regarding their traumatic experience (Cohen, Mannarino, & Deblinger, 2006). Children often hold excessively negative assumptions about the trauma (e.g., self-blame) and subsequently overgeneralize abstract ideas and beliefs across global contexts. Research suggests that high levels of overgeneralized thinking predict less symptom improvement in treatment (Ready et al., 2015). Therefore, the therapist encourages the youth to identify patterns of negative thinking and develop more accurate reappraisals. Initially, as the child is developing more adaptive cognitive strategies, it is important to focus the practice exercises on everyday situations and problems rather than on the cognitions associated with the traumatic experience (Cohen & Mannarino, 2008). By practicing with everyday stressors, children can more easily learn to recognize concrete and factual details without the additive affective dysregulation that is associated with their trauma reminders. During trauma narrative sessions, the therapist facilitates reattribution to reduce maladaptive cognitions regarding responsibility and overgeneralizing dissimilar events. A child who has successfully learned to utilize cognitive coping strategies will be able to successfully account for a particular situation or extenuating circumstance rather than apply broad generalizations across contexts and locations (Ready et al., 2015).

Safety Skills/Safety Planning

Through a collaborative process, the therapist works with the youth to create a concrete and developmentally appropriate behavioral plan regarding future safety (Cohen, Mannarino, & Deblinger, 2006). First, a thorough assessment is conducted in order to identify the child's particular needs regarding the nature and severity of their past traumas and any ongoing threats or concerns in their current living situation (Cohen, Mannarino, & Murray, 2011). Examples of skills training could range from specific strategies for dealing with bullying or drug refusal to awareness of safety regarding fire hazards and natural disasters. The therapist takes care to ensure that the child does not believe they may be responsible for their traumatic experience because they did not have the skills being taught.

Skills training generally is adapted to the developmental and cognitive level of the youth and must account for the environmental and community resources available to a particular family. For youth living in areas of ongoing community violence, the therapist helps the family recognize safe routes to and from school or other locations they frequent, as well as any relatives or specific safe locations that could serve as a haven in case of an unexpected incidence of violence (Cohen, Mannarino, Kliethermes, & Murray, 2012). Addressing safety is essential for youth who are experiencing ongoing trauma or who are engaged in dangerous (e.g., self-injury, substance abuse) or high-risk behaviors (Cohen, Mannarino, & Deblinger, 2012; Cohen, Mannarino, Kliethermes, & Murray, 2012). For younger children who are developmentally more reliant on adult availability for protection, the therapist assists in identifying other safe adults who are accessible in particular locations. In addition, younger children may require a more concrete behavioral intervention with rewards and consequences for practicing their skills outside of therapy (Cohen, Mannarino, & Deblinger, 2012).

Social Problem-Solving

Some forms of CBT for traumatic stress include social problem-solving components. Social problem-solving refers to "real-world" problem-solving (D'Zurilla, 1986). Youth are taught specific problem-solving steps, particularly problem identification, solution generation, identification of pros and cons, selection/implementation, and evaluation. Children engage in practicing these during the session and throughout homework. Practice involves both trauma-related social concerns, such as disclosing to others, as well as more general social difficulties, such as conflict with peers (Cohen, Mannarino, & Deblinger, 2006).

Role of Parents in Treatment

Traumatic events have the potential to disturb the child's psychosocial development and family environment (Cohen, Mannarino, & Deblinger, 2012). Therefore, including parents in the treatment of PTSD in children is often recommended so that they may provide support, reinforce learned skills, facilitate active coping, and learn effective parenting strategies for behavioral dysregulation (Foa et al., 2009). Moreover, parental factors during treatment, such as emotional support, avoidance, and child blame, are associated with children's treatment outcome (Yasinski et al., 2016); these factors may need to be targeted during treatment to ensure the best outcome. In support, a review of EBT for childhood disorders concluded that CBT with parent involvement reached Level 1 or the "best support" (Chorpita et al., 2011) in the treatment of traumatic stress. Nonetheless, individual CBT without significant parental involvement has been identified as an efficacious treatment, obtaining Level 2 or "good support" in the same review of EBT for childhood disorders and, as discussed previously, Dorsey and colleagues (2016) identified CBT without parent involvement as a well-established treatment.

Although more research is needed, parent participation may be necessary when parents are the source of the trauma exposure (Dorsey et al., 2016). For instance, child maltreatment often occurs within the context of the caregiving relationship, in which the caregiver is the source of both comfort and fear. This may increase the child's risk for experiencing chronic and severe states of stress and can have a profoundly deleterious impact on socioemotional and behavioral functioning and development (Milot et al., 2010).

Parental functioning, particularly maternal depressive symptoms (Nixon, Sterk, & Pearce, 2012) and parental emotional support (Yasinski et al., 2016), were associated with treatment outcome in children, providing further support for inclusion of parents when possible. Concerning emotional support, when parents voiced more statements of child blame and were more avoidant of issues related to the trauma during therapy, children evidenced more negative outcome in the months following treatment completion (Yasinski et al., 2016). Contrarily, maternal symptoms of posttraumatic stress did not moderate children's response to treatment (Nixon, Sterk, & Pearce, 2012).

Other Factors Influencing Treatment

Assessment

Screening for exposure to a variety of traumatic events is an integral part of any mental health assessment in that children and families often do not report exposure to trauma without direct questioning (National Child Traumatic Stress Network, 2004). Upon identification of a child's history of exposure to traumatic events, assessment focuses upon the presence and severity of symptoms of traumatic stress, anxiety, depression, and behavioral problems, as well as parental support and psychopathology. Secondary adversity related to the trauma is also assessed (Cohen, Mannarino, & Deblinger, 2012). Ideally, information from the child, caregivers, teachers, and other involved adults would be gathered. Following commencement of treatment, the pace at which treatment components are implemented is informed by regular monitoring of the child's symptoms, level of parental support, and treatment adherence. Although treatment involves reducing avoidance of trauma-related cues, the need for school accommodations while therapy progresses would be assessed (Cohen & AACAP, 2010).

Comorbidity

Youth who exhibit clinically significant symptoms of traumatic stress often present with other internalizing and externalizing behavior problems. CBT for traumatic stress has been found to alleviate comorbid symptoms of depression, anxiety, and behavioral difficulties without major modifications (de Arellano et al., 2014; Trask, Walsh, & DiLillo, 2011). However, children and adolescents who have experienced complex trauma may require more attention to the coping skills and safety components of treatment. As discussed earlier, modifications to in vivo and imaginal exposure components are often necessary (Cohen, Mannarino, Kliethermes, & Murray, 2012). Additionally, some youth exhibit comorbid DSM-5 disorders, with major depressive disorder, attention-deficit/hyperactivity disorder (ADHD), anxiety disorders, and substance abuse as the most common comorbid disorders. When comorbid diagnoses are present, CBT for traumatic stress may need to be augmented with other evidence-based treatments when CBT for traumatic stress alone does not ameliorate these difficulties or when comorbidity significantly impairs treatment implementation (Cohen & AACAP, 2010).

Demographics

A meta-analysis examining outcomes associated with sexual abuse treatment found that research studies with a higher proportion of older children and boys had more favorable treatment outcomes (Trask, Walsh, & DiLillo, 2011). Salloum and Overstreet (2008) also found that younger girls had less symptom improvement, but other studies have not found differential outcome by gender or age (Dorsey et al., 2016). Recent modifications to TF-CBT for young children are promising (Salloum et al., 2014). Ethnicity was not associated with differential outcome (Trask, Walsh, & DiLillo, 2011). In support, both TF-CBT and CBITS have demonstrated efficacy in diverse samples (Dorsey et al., 2016; Huey & Polo, 2008).

Medication

Medication may be efficacious in reducing select symptoms of posttraumatic stress in youth; however, the overall evidence is weak as there are few randomized controlled trials involving children. It has been recommended that medication is only used under select conditions, such as when evidence-based therapy is unavailable or the child presents with significant comorbidity or treatment-resistant symptoms (Huemer, Greenberg, & Steiner, 2017).

Treatment Duration

One factor influencing the effectiveness of treatment is duration, as a meta-analysis focusing on child sexual abuse treatment found support for dose effects, with longer treatments associated with better outcomes (Trask, Walsh, & DiLillo, 2011). Nonetheless, some children have been identified as "early responders" with significant and sustained improvement after only four sessions (Wamser-Nanney, Scheeringa, & Weems, 2014), although more research is needed to identify predictors of early response.

Expressed Dysfunctional Cognitions

Dysfunctional cognitions expressed during therapy by youth (Ready et al., 2015) were associated with decreased treatment success for children receiving TF-CBT following sexual abuse. Children who expressed more statements reflecting overgeneralization evidenced less improvement following TF-CBT, while those who voiced more statements reflecting accommodation had greater symptom improvement (Ready et al., 2015).

Conclusion

Individually administered and group CBT have been found to be efficacious for the treatment of symptoms of posttraumatic stress in children and adolescents. These evidence-based treatments generally include psychoeducation, anxiety management strategies, such as relaxation, exposure, cognitive coping, safety planning, and social problem-solving. Exposure may involve imaginal and/or in vivo techniques. Evidence-based treatments for traumatic stress differ in their level of parental involvement. Parental factors, such as emotional support and child blame, appear to be associated with treatment outcome in children, and parental participation may be important when parents are the source of trauma exposure. Nonetheless, individual CBT without parental involvement has also been identified as an efficacious treatment. As with all psychological disorders, careful assessment is key to successful treatment planning, as well as consideration of comorbidity.

Useful Resources

- Free online training in TF-CBT for clinicians is offered by the Medical University of South Carolina, National Crime Victims Research and Treatment Center at www.musc.edu/tfcbt
- The National Child Traumatic Stress Network has many useful resources (www.nctsn.org), including a Child Welfare Trauma Training Toolkit that details how welfare staff can serve children who have experienced trauma.

- CBITS is designed for delivery in a school setting and has been adapted for use with low-literacy groups, children in foster care, and Spanish-speaking populations. Information regarding CBITS training and implementation can be located at www.cbitsprogram.org. A recent modification, Support for Students Exposed to Trauma, was designed to be used by teachers and school counselors (https://ssetprogram.org).
- A description of TF-CBT for children of Latino descent can be found in *Trauma-Focused CBT for Children and Adolescents: Treatment Applications* by Judith A. Cohen, Anthony P. Mannarino, and Esther Deblinger, Guilford Press, 2012.
- Parent-led, therapist-assisted, trauma-focused cognitive-behavior therapy (PTA-TF-CBT) was designed for preschool children who have experienced trauma or have been diagnosed with PTSD and may be a cost-effective alternative to TF-CBT. More information regarding PTA-TF-CBT can be found in the parent workbook, *Stepping Together*, by Salloum and Storch.
- A large summary of findings from federal reviews of research studies and program evaluations of evidence-based treatments for children exposed to violence can be found in the book *Evidence-Based Practices for Children Exposed to Violence: A Selection from Federal Databases by the US Department of Justice* at https://nccadv.org/images/pdfs/CEDVFEDERALEvidence-Based-Practices-Matrix_2011.pdf
- Other resources regarding evidence-based treatments for childhood trauma include the following groups and their websites:
- The California Evidence-Based Clearinghouse for Child Welfare (CEBC) at www.cebc4cw.org/
- The National Registry of Evidence-Based Programs and Practices (NREPP) at www.nrepp .samhsa.gov
- The Virginia Child Protection Newsletter (VCPN) at https://psychweb.chbs.jmu.edu/Graysojh

References

American Psychiatric Association. (2013). *Diagnostic and statistical manual of mental disorders.* 5th edn. Washington, DC: American Psychiatric Association.

Borntrager, C., Chorpita, B. F., Higa-McMillan, C. K., Daleiden, E. L., & Starace, N. (2013). Usual care for trauma-exposed youth: Are clinician-reported therapy techniques evidence-based? *Children and Youth Services Review, 35*(1), 133–141. doi:10.1016/j.childyouth.2012.09.018

Buckner, J. D., Lopez, C., Dunkel, S., & Joiner, T. E. (2008). Behavior management training for the treatment of reactive attachment disorder. *Child Maltreatment, 13*(3), 289–297. doi:10.1177/1077559508318396

Casey, P., & Bailey, S. (2011). Adjustment disorders: The state of the art. *World Psychiatry, 10*, 11–18. doi:10.1002/j.2051-5545.2011.tb00003.x

Chorpita, B. F., Daleiden, E. L., Ebesutani, C., Young, J., Becker, K. D., Nakamura, B. J., ... & Smith, R. L. (2011). Evidence-based treatments for children and adolescents: An updated review of indicators of efficacy and effectiveness. *Clinical Psychology: Science and Practice, 18*(2), 154–172. doi:10.1111/j.1468-2850.2011.01247.x

Cohen, J. A., & AACAP Work Group on Quality Issues. (2010). Practice parameter for the assessment and treatment of children and adolescents with posttraumatic stress disorder. *Journal of the American Academy of Child & Adolescent Psychiatry, 49*(4), 414–430. doi:10.1016/j.jaac.2009.12.020

Cohen, J. A., Berliner, L., & Mannarino, A. (2010). Trauma focused CBT for children with co-occurring trauma and behavior problems. *Child Abuse & Neglect*, *34*(4), 215–224. doi:10.1016/j.chiabu.2009.12.003

Cohen, J. A., & Mannarino, A. P. (2008). Trauma-focused cognitive behavioural therapy for children and parents. *Child and Adolescent Mental Health*, *13*(4), 158–162. doi:10.1111/j.1475-3588.2008.00502.x

Cohen, J. A., Mannarino, A. P., & Deblinger, E. (2006). *Treating trauma and traumatic grief in children and adolescents*. New York: Guilford Press.

Cohen, J. A., Mannarino, A. P., & Deblinger, E. (2012). *Trauma-focused CBT for children and adolescents: Treatment applications*. New York: Guilford Press.

Cohen, J. A., Mannarino, A. P., Kliethermes, M., & Murray, L. A. (2012). Trauma-focused CBT for youth with complex trauma. *Child Abuse & Neglect*, *36*(6), 528–541. doi:10.1016/j.chiabu.2012.03.007

Cohen, J. A., Mannarino, A. P., & Murray, L. K. (2011). Trauma-focused CBT for youth who experience ongoing traumas. *Child Abuse & Neglect*, *35*(8), 637–646. doi:10.1016%2Fj.chiabu.2011.05.002

Cook, A. P., Spinazzola, J. P., Ford, J. P., Lanktree, C. P., Blaustein, M. P., Cloitre, M. P., . . . & van der Kolk, B. M. D. (2005). Complex trauma in children and adolescents. *Psychiatric Annals*, *35*(5), 390–398.

Copeland, W. E., Keeler, G., Angold, A., & Costello, E. J. (2007). Traumatic events and posttraumatic stress in childhood. *Archives of General Psychiatry*, *64*(5), 577–584. doi:10.1001/archpsyc.64.5.577

Costello, E. J., Erkanli, A., Fairbank, J. A., & Angold, A. (2002). The prevalence of potentially traumatic events in childhood and adolescence. *Journal of Traumatic Stress*, *15*(2), 99–112. doi:10.1023/A:1014851823163

de Arellano, M. A. R., Lyman, D. R., Jobe-Shields, L., George, P., Dougherty, R. H., Daniels, A. S., . . . & Delphin-Rittmon, M. E. (2014). Trauma-focused cognitive behavioral therapy: Assessing the evidence. *Psychiatric Services*, *65*(5), 591–602. doi:10.1176/appi.ps.201300255

Deblinger, E., & Heflin, A. H. (1996). *Treating sexually abused children and their nonoffending parents: A cognitive behavioral approach*. Thousand Oaks, CA: Sage Publications.

Deblinger, E., Mannarino, A. P., Cohen, J. A., Runyon, M. K., & Steer, R. A. (2011). Trauma-focused cognitive behavioral therapy for children: Impact of the trauma narrative and treatment length. *Depression and Anxiety*, *28*(1), 67–75.

Dorsey, S., Briggs, E. C., & Woods, B. A. (2011). Cognitive-behavioral treatment for posttraumatic stress disorder in children and adolescents. *Child and Adolescent Psychiatric Clinics of North America*, *20*(2), 255–269. doi:10.1016/j.chc.2011.01.006

Dorsey, S., McLaughlin, K. A., Kerns, S. E., Harrison, J. P., Lambert, H. K., Briggs, E. C., . . . & Amaya-Jackson, L. (2016). Evidence base update for psychosocial treatments for children and adolescents exposed to traumatic events. *Journal of Clinical Child & Adolescent Psychology*, *46*(3), 1–28. doi:10.1080/15374416.2016.1220309

D'Zurilla, T. J. (1986). *Problem-solving therapy: A social competence approach to clinical intervention*. New York: Springer.

Foa, E. B., Keane, T. M., Friedman, M. J., & Cohen, J. A. (2009). Cognitive-behavioral therapy for children and adolescents. In E. B. Foa, T. M. Keane, M. J. Frieman, & J. A. Cohen (eds.), *Effective treatments for PTSD: Practice guidelines from the International Society for Traumatic Stress Studies* (pp. 223–244). New York: Guilford Press.

Foa, E. B., McLean, C. P., Capaldi, S., & Rosenfield, D. (2013). Prolonged exposure vs supportive counseling for sexual abuse-related PTSD in adolescent girls: A randomized clinical trial. *JAMA*, *310*(24), 2650–2657. doi:10.1001/jama.2013.282829

Foa, E. B., & Rothbaum, B. A. (1998). *Treating the trauma of rape: Cognitive behavioral therapy for PTSD*. New York: Guilford Press.

Goldfried, M. R., & Davison, G. R. (1976). *Clinical behavior therapy*. New York: Holt, Rinehart, & Winston.

Huemer, J., Greenberg, M., & Steiner, H. (2017). Pharmacological treatment for children and adolescents with trauma-related disorders. In M. A. Landolt, M. Cloitre, & U. Schnyder (eds.), *Evidence-based treatments for trauma related disorders in children and adolescents* (pp. 385–401). Cham, Switzerland: Springer International Publishing. doi:10.1007/978-3-319-46138-0_18

Huey Jr., S. J., & Polo, A. J. (2008). Evidence-based psychosocial treatments for ethnic minority youth. *Journal of Clinical Child & Adolescent Psychology*, *37*(1), 262–301. doi:10.1080/15374410701820174

Jonkman, C. S., Verlinden, E., Bolle, E. A., Boer, F., & Lindauer, R. J. (2013). Traumatic stress symptomatology after child maltreatment and single traumatic events: Different profiles. *Journal of Traumatic Stress*, *26*(2), 225–232. doi:10.1002/jts.21792

Kassam-Adams, N., Palmieri, P. A., Rork, K., Delahanty, D. L., Kenardy, J., Kohser, K. L., . . . & McGrath, C. (2012). Acute stress symptoms in children: Results from an international data archive. *Journal of the American Academy of Child & Adolescent Psychiatry*, *51*(8), 812–820. doi.: 10.1016/j.jaac.2012.05.013

Kataoka, S. H., Stein, B. D., Jaycox, L. H., Wong, M., Escudero, P., Tu, W., . . . & Fink, A. (2003). A school-based mental health program for traumatized Latino immigrant children. *Journal of the American Academy of Child & Adolescent Psychiatry*, *42*(3), 311–318. doi:10.1097/00004583-200303000-00011

Kendall, P. C. (1990). *Coping cat manual*. Ardmore, PA: Workbook Publishing.

Mannarino, A. P., Cohen, J. A., Deblinger, E., Runyon, M. K., & Steer, R. A. (2012). Trauma-focused cognitive-behavioral therapy for children: Sustained impact of treatment 6 and 12 months later. *Child Maltreatment*, *17*(3), 231–241. doi:10.1177/1077559512451787

McLaughlin, K. A., Koenen, K. C., Hill, E. D., Petukhova, M., Sampson, N. A., Zaslavsky, A. M., & Kessler, R. C. (2013). Trauma exposure and posttraumatic stress disorder in a national sample of adolescents. *Journal of the American Academy of Child & Adolescent Psychiatry*, *52*(8), 815–830. doi:10.1016/j.jaac.2013.05.011

Milani, A. C., Hoffmann, E. V., Fossaluza, V., Jackowski, A. P., & Mello, M. F. (2017). Does pediatric post-traumatic stress disorder alter the brain? Systematic review and meta-analysis of structural and functional magnetic resonance imaging studies. *Psychiatry and Clinical Neurosciences*, *71*(3), 154–169. doi:10.1111/pcn.12473

Milot, T., Ethier, L. S., St-Laurent, D., & Provost, M. A. (2010). The role of trauma symptoms in the development of behavioral problems in maltreated preschoolers. *Child Abuse & Neglect*, *34*(4), 225–234. doi:10.1016/j.chiabu.2009.07.006

Mowrer, O. (1960). *Learning theory and behavior*. Hoboken, NJ: Wiley.

National Child Traumatic Stress Network, Child Sexual Abuse Task Force and Research & Practice Core. (2004). *How to implement trauma-focused cognitive behavioral therapy*. Durham, NC and Los Angeles, CA: National Center for Child Traumatic Stress.

Neugebauer, R., Wasserman, G. A., Fisher, P. W., Kline, J., Geller, P. A., & Miller, L. S. (1999). Darryl, a cartoon-based measure of cardinal posttraumatic stress symptoms in school-age children. *American Journal of Public Health, 89*, 758–761.

Nixon, R. D., Sterk, J., & Pearce, A. (2012). A randomized trial of cognitive behavior therapy and cognitive therapy for children with posttraumatic stress disorder following single-incident trauma. *Journal of Abnormal Child Psychology, 40*, 327–337. doi:10.1007/s10802-011-9566-7

Ollendick, T. H., & Cerny, J. A. (1981). *Clinical behavior therapy with children*. New York: Plenum Press.

Ready, C. B., Hayes, A. M., Yasinski, C. W., Webb, C., Gallop, R., Deblinger, E., & Laurenceau, J. P. (2015). Overgeneralized beliefs, accommodation, and treatment outcome in youth receiving trauma-focused cognitive behavioral therapy for childhood trauma. *Behavior Therapy, 46*(5), 671–688. doi:10.1016/j.beth.2015.03.004

Salloum, A., Dorsey, C. S., Swaidan, V. R., & Storch, E. A. (2015). Parents' and children's perception of parent-led trauma-focused cognitive behavioral therapy. *Child Abuse & Neglect, 40*(2), 12–23. doi:10.1016/j.chiabu.2014.11.018.

Salloum, A., & Overstreet, S. (2008). Evaluation of individual and group grief and trauma interventions for children post disaster. *Journal of Clinical Child & Adolescent Psychology, 37*(3), 495–507. doi:10.1080/15374410802148194

Salloum, A., Scheeringa, M. S., Cohen, J. A., & Storch, E. A. (2014). Development of stepped care trauma-focused cognitive-behavioral therapy for young children. *Cognitive and Behavioral Practice, 21*(1), 97–108. doi:10.1016/j.cbpra.2013.07.004

Scheeringa, M. S., Weems, C. F., Cohen, J. A., Amaya-Jackson, L., & Guthrie, D. (2010). Trauma-focused cognitive-behavioral therapy for posttraumatic stress disorder in three through six year-old children: A randomized clinical trial. *Journal of Child Psychology and Psychiatry, 52*, 853–860. doi:10.1111/j.1469-7610.2010.02354.x

Shirk, S. R., DePrince, A. P., Crisostomo, P. S., & Labus, J. (2014). Cognitive behavioral therapy for depressed adolescents exposed to interpersonal trauma: An initial effectiveness trial. *Psychotherapy, 51*(1), 167–179. doi:10.1037/a0034845

Silverman, W. K., Ortiz, C. D., Viswesvaran, C., Burns, B. J., Kolko, D. J., Putnam, F. W., & Amaya-Jackson, L. (2008). Evidence-based psychosocial treatments for children and adolescents exposed to traumatic events. *Journal of Clinical Child & Adolescent Psychology, 37*(1), 156–183. doi:10.1080/15374410701818293

Southam-Gerow, M. A., & Prinstein, M. J. (2014). Evidence base updates: The evolution of the evaluation of psychological treatments for children and adolescents. *Journal of Clinical Child & Adolescent Psychology, 43*(1), 1–6. doi:10.1080/15374416.2013.855128

Steele, W., & Kuban, C. (2011). Using drawing in short-term trauma resolution. In C. A. Malchiodi (ed.), *The clinical handbook of art therapy* (pp. 162–174). New York: Guilford Press.

Trask, E. V., Walsh, K., & DiLillo, D. (2011). Treatment effects for common outcomes of child sexual abuse: A current meta-analysis. *Aggression and Violent Behavior, 16*(1), 6–19. doi:10.1016/j.avb.2010.10.001

van der Kolk, B. A. (2009). Developmental trauma disorder: Towards a rational diagnosis for chronically traumatized children. *Praxis Der Kinderpsychologie und Kinderpsychiatrie, 58*(8), 572–586. doi:10.13109/prkk.2009.58.8.572

Wamser-Nanney, R., Scheeringa, M. S., & Weems, C. F. (2014). Early treatment response in children and adolescents receiving CBT for trauma. *Journal of Pediatric Psychology, 41*(1), 128–137. doi:10.1093/jpepsy/jsu096

Yasinski, C., Hayes, A. M., Ready, C. B., Cummings, J. A., Berman, I. S., McCauley, T., ... & Deblinger, E. (2016). In-session caregiver behavior predicts symptom change in youth receiving trauma-focused cognitive behavioral therapy (TF-CBT). *Journal of Consulting and Clinical Psychology, 84*, 1066–1077. doi:10.1037/ccp0000147

Zeanah, C. H., Chesher, T., Boris, N. W., & the AACAP Committee on Quality Issues. (2016). Practice parameter for the assessment and treatment of children and adolescents with reactive attachment disorder and disinhibited social engagement disorder. *Journal of the American Academy of Child & Adolescent Psychiatry, 55*(11), 990–1003. doi:10.1016/j.jaac.2016.08.004

Zeanah, C. H., & Gleason, M. M. (2015). Annual research review: Attachment disorders in early childhood – clinical presentation, causes, correlates, and treatment. *Journal of Child Psychology and Psychiatry, 56*(3), 207–222. doi:10.1111/jcpp.12347

13

Feeding

Peter A. Girolami and John Borgen

Estimates of pediatric feeding disorders vary, as there is no commonly agreed upon definition of maladaptive feeding behaviors (Benjasuwantep, Chaithirayanon, & Eiamudomkan, 2013). For the purposes of this chapter, pediatric feeding disorders are identified as a child not feeding in a developmental or age-typical manner, including failure to eat a sufficient amount or variety of foods (Piazza, 2008). Atypical feeding behaviors include variable caloric intake, poor growth, severe nutrient deficits, and hospitalizations (Piazza, Milnes, & Shalev, 2015). In addition to adverse health and growth consequences, behaviors that are often included in definitions of pediatric feeding disorders include food refusal, self-feeding deficits, improper pacing (i.e., eating too fast or slow), and vomiting and rumination (Kozlowski et al., 2015). Food refusal can result in the refusal to consume any food by mouth, or be partial, where a child has a diet that is limited on one or many aspects of the food (e.g., food group, taste). Food refusal behavior can take many forms, including disruptive vocalizations, turning the head away, pushing food away, aggression, and covering the mouth (González, Rubio, & Taylor, 2014). A child can refuse food based on any aspect of the food or the mealtime environment, including taste, texture, food group, brand, utensil, color, food presentation, feeder present, and setting, among many others (Marí-Bauset et al., 2014). Additionally, treatment goals for children admitted to intensive pediatric feeding programs often include the child participating in meals at school and in the community (e.g., restaurants, picnics).

Estimates of point prevalence of picky eating range from 13% to 22% in typically developing populations at ages from two to 11 years-old, and a duration of over two years for 40% of those identified with feeding problems (Mascola, Bryson, & Agras, 2010). Overall, prevalence of pediatric feeding disorders in typically developing children ranges from 18% to 50%. Prevalence of pediatric feeding disorders ranges from 33% to 100% in populations diagnosed with an intellectual or developmental disability (Matson & Kuhn, 2001; Williams, Field, & Seiverling, 2010), and 46% to 89% in children diagnosed with autism spectrum disorder (ASD; Ledford & Gast,

2006; Berlin et al., 2011; Nadon et al., 2011). Lastly, in a meta-analysis William G. Sharp and colleagues (2013) concluded that children diagnosed with ASD are five times more likely than those not diagnosed with ASD to have a feeding problem.

Etiology and Theoretical Underpinnings of Treatment

Behavioral processes are often implicated in the development of pediatric feeding disorders. For example, if feeding is correlated with a painful or frightening event (e.g., choking, aspiration) a child may be reluctant to consume the food associated with the event. Additionally, when a child refuses to eat a certain type of food, the child's caregiver will often remove that food and replace it with a food they have previously observed the child to have willingly consumed. Over time, through negative reinforcement (i.e., removal of a nonpreferred food), and positive reinforce-ment (i.e., providing a preferred food) a child may go from being a "picky eater" to not consuming any fruits or vegetables (Borrero et al., 2010). Food refusal may increase in rate and magnitude as they become more effective in inducing caregivers to remove a nonpreferred food and replace it with a preferred food. Additionally, caregivers may at times initially refuse to remove the nonpreferred food, but relent when food refusal occurs at too high of a rate or magnitude for them to tolerate, in turn, shaping further increases the rate and magnitude of food refusal. Also, food refusal may occasion additional stress in caregiver or familial relationships, increasing the likelihood of food refusal to persist (Curtin et al., 2015).

Illnesses and other physiological processes may initiate or exacerbate pediatric feeding disorders as well. For other children there may be a physical abnormality or illness that makes swallowing difficult or painful for some time, or the interruption of oral feeding due to medical procedures. Interruption in oral feeding due to an illness or physical abnormality may necessitate the need for a nasogastronomy tube (ng-tube), j-tube, or gastronomy-tube (g-tube) to ensure the child continues to receive adequate calories and nutrition to maintain growth. During this time children may come to prefer tube feedings to oral feedings due to decreased effort when consuming food or lack of exposure to oral feeding. Unpleasant physiological sensations when consuming food (e.g., pain when swallowing) may decrease oral feeding. Illnesses and unpleasant physiological sensations may be idiosyncratic or difficult to detect. Indeed, some illnesses (e.g., eosinophilic esophagitis) may relapse and remit without a child com-municating their discomfort to caregivers or medical professionals.

Williams, Field, and Seiverling (2010) surveyed 38 studies of pediatric feeding disorder treatments, and found 212 of 218 participants had some sort of medical issue. Of those identified as having a medical issue, 55% had a gastrointestinal disorder and 62% had a non-gastrointestinal disorder. Specifically, 83% of a sample of children admitted to an intensive pediatric feeding disorder program were diagnosed with gastrointestinal reflux (Greer et al., 2008), and 53% of a sample of 234 in another study (Williams, Riegel, & Kerwin, 2009). Non-gastrointestinal medical issues are also often reported, including 64% of the sample in Greer et al. (2008). Due to the frequent comorbidity of gastrointestinal and non-gastrointestinal medical issues, interdisciplinary teams including physicians, dieticians, and occupational therapists are often necessary to safely treat pediatric feeding disorders (Sharp et al., 2017).

Brief Overview of Evidence-Based Treatments

Treatments to address pediatric feeding disorders have included behavior analytic treatments, and other treatments based on other disciplines in psychology. Treatments based on applied behavior analysis (ABA) have received the most empirical support. Numerous recent reviews (Lukens & Silverman, 2014; Marshall et al., 2015; Volkert & Piazza, 2012) have found extensive empirical support for multiple ABA-based treatments discussed below. Other treatments have received minimal support, including cognitive-behavioral therapy, nutritional treatment, oral motor treatment, and sequential-oral-sensory (SOS) therapy. However, a direct comparison of SOS and ABA therapy conducted by Peterson, Piazza, and Volkert (2016) found no increases in accepting and swallowing food after at least 1,020 minutes of SOS therapy, but over an 80% increase in acceptance and swallowing after as little as 65 minutes of ABA therapy. Also, ABA-based treatments range from manualized time-limited treatments (Sharp et al., 2016) to intensive, interdisciplinary programs (Sharp et al., 2017).

Numerous behavioral interventions for pediatric disorders range from more intensive treatments focused on increasing food acceptance and decreasing food refusal, to less intensive treatments focused on increasing feeding-related skills (e.g., self-feeding, chewing). The review of the empirical research base by Volkert and Piazza (2012) identified escape extinction, differential reinforcement of alternative behavior, and physical guidance of self-feeding to be well established. The behavioral treatments discussed below are separated into treatments focused on increasing food acceptance and decreasing food refusal, and those focused on increasing other skills related to feeding. Also, ABA-based feeding treatments are rarely implemented individually. Most often treatment involves multiple components that includes two or more of the treatments discussed below.

Assessment of pediatric feeding disorders must be conducted before treatment to identify the functions of food refusal, possible physiological processes that contribute to food refusal, and environmental variables that maintain food refusal. First, assessment by an interdisciplinary team is completed to determine if the child is safe to feed orally, nutritional deficits, and other physiological factors. Oral motor and self-feeding skills are assessed by a speech-language pathologist and/or an occupational therapist. Second, a caregiver interview and caregiver report measures are completed to broadly survey variables that may maintain food refusal and to provide a history of the pediatric feeding disorder. Third, a mealtime observation or home baseline session is conducted to directly observe the strategies the caregiver uses to try and get the child to accept bites, and decrease food refusal. Last, functional analyses and other data-based behavioral assessments may be implemented if necessary to directly assess functions of the food refusal and environmental variables that may maintain food refusal (Piazza, Fisher, et al., 2003).

Components of Evidence-Based Treatments

Increasing Food Acceptance and Decreasing Food Refusal

Escape Extinction. One of the earliest, and most replicated behavioral treatments is escape extinction (O'Brien, Bugle, & Azrin, 1972; Volkert & Piazza, 2012), where food is presented in front of a child and not withdrawn until a child accepts the food or the session duration elapses (Patel et al., 2002). As described above, descriptive and functional analyses indicate caregivers often remove a nonpreferred food contingent on food refusal. Escape extinction terminates this contingency, and thus the child's food refusal no longer produces the desired effect. Escape extinction is rarely implemented independent of other treatments, and is often combined with differential reinforcement of alternative behavior where the child is provided praise or other reinforcers contingent on accepting the food into their mouth (Patel et al., 2002; Piazza, Patel, et al., 2003). Furthermore, as escape extinction also functions as positive punishment (i.e., an aversive stimulus is put in front of the child to decrease food refusal), it may occasion behaviors that are side effects of punishment (e.g., aggression, elopement, emotional responding) (Catania, 2012).

Escape extinction is commonly implemented in one of two methods: nonremoval of spoon and physical guidance. Nonremoval of spoon can be implemented in a stationary spoon or full nonremoval of spoon format. In stationary spoon presentations, the food is presented approximately one inch in front of the child's upper lip. Regardless of food refusal, the spoon remains in the position where it was initially presented. While stationary spoon discontinues the removal of food based on refusal, children often respond to stationary spoon presentations with passive refusal (e.g., leaning back, sitting quietly). When stationary spoon presentations do not lead to an increase in acceptance, nonremoval of spoon presentations are conducted. During these presentations the bite is presented on a spoon to the child's upper lip. Instead of remaining stationary, the feeder keeps the bite at the child's upper lip if they turn their head, move their head away, or attempt to push the bite away (Rubio, Borrero, & Taylor, 2015). With both methods the feeder waits until the child begins to open their mouth before attempting to deposit the food in their mouth.

Physical guidance may be warranted if acceptance of food does not increase after implementation of escape extinction. With all physical guidance procedures the goal is not to overcome a child's active physical resistance, but to augment a nonremoval of spoon procedure with additional prompting. A finger prompt, where a feeder runs their index finger along the upper gum line to gently separate the lips, has been demonstrated to increase acceptance when escape extinction alone was not sufficient (Borrero et al., 2013). Another option is a jaw prompt, where gentle pressure on the jaw guides the mouth to open (Ahearn et al., 1996). Additionally, lower texture food may be placed on a Nuk® brush to increase acceptance by depositing the bite in the child's cheek or on their tongue (Kadey, Roane, Diaz, & McCarthy, 2013; Rubio, Borrero, & Taylor, 2015). Lastly, as is the case with severe behaviors (e.g., aggression, self-injurious behavior), it may be necessary for additional therapists to block food refusal (e.g., pushing spoon away, covering mouth) if the feeder is not able to keep the spoon at the child's upper lip. During blocking, a therapist stands behind the child and holds their arms above the child's arms so that a child is blocked from food refusal behaviors. The therapist does not hold down the child in any way, and is removed from sessions as soon as the feeder is able to implement escape extinction by themselves (Wilkins et al., 2014).

Along with refusal to accept a bite of food into the mouth, children may engage in other behaviors once the food is deposited. First, the child may spit (i.e., expel) the food out of their mouth. Multiple treatments to decrease expelling include re-presentation of expelled bites, and using a chin prompt. Re-presentation of expelled food, but not saliva or emesis, involves scooping up expelled food as quickly as possible and presenting the bite again on a spoon or Nuk® brush (Girolami, Boscoe, & Roscoe, 2007). A chin prompt, where the forefinger is placed under the chin and the thumb underneath the lower lip with gentle upward pressure, can augment re-presentation by facilitating closing the mouth instead of expelling food (Wilkins et al., 2011). Packing, defined as the child holding the bite in their mouth without swallowing the bite, has also been successfully treated using a chaser, and flipped spoon swallow facilitation. Also, lowering the texture of food to a pureed texture has been demonstrated to decrease packing (Patel et al., 2005). A liquid or solid that is consistently consumed by the child is presented immediately after a packed bite in a chaser procedure to decrease packing (Vaz et al., 2012). Flipped spoon swallow facilitation collects the packed bite and deposits the bite on the back of the tongue while placing gentle downward pressure and dragging the spoon forward along the tongue (Volkert et al., 2011). Swallow facilitation can be implemented with a Nuk® brush, but the flipped spoon swallow facilitation has the advantage of using a utensil that is used in typical meals. Lastly, children may engage in bouts of emesis even after having swallowed the food to escape the nonpreferred food.

Antecedent Treatments. Antecedent treatments include manipulations to the mealtime environment, the presentation of food, or to instructions given during meals to maximize the likelihood that a child will accept bites of food. Demand fading is an antecedent strategy where the child is initially instructed to accept and swallow foods that they already consume, but over time the volume, variety, or other aspects of food are systematically increased to work toward treatment goals. For instance, a child that consumes only pureed fruits would first be asked to eat one bite of pureed fruit during a session, then increase by one bite per session to five bites, and then be presented four bites of pureed fruit and one bite of pureed vegetable. Demand fading can be an alternative to escape extinction in some cases, although in others the child may continue to refuse nonpreferred foods and escape extinction will be necessary. Demand fading has been demonstrated to be effective in increasing meal volume and food variety (Freeman & Piazza, 1998), number of bites per meal (Najdowski et al., 2003), and amount of food on the spoon (Kerwin et al., 1995).

Stimulus fading treatments gradually change the properties of food or utensils to transition from one food to another or one utensil to another. For example, a child that drinks fruit juice but not water would be initially presented a cup of 100% juice. Next, they would receive 90% fruit juice and 10% water. The child then accepts more and more dilute fruit juice/water mixtures until they accept water alone. Stimulus fading has been utilized to, among many studies, transition from lower textured food to higher textures (Shore et al., 1998), from spoon to cup drinking (Groff et al., 2011), and from chocolate milk to plain milk (Tiger & Hanley, 2006). Other manipulations to food that augment stimulus fading treatments include presenting a nonpreferred food and a preferred food simultaneously (i.e., side by side or one on top of the other) (Ahearn, 2003), or blending the two foods together (Mueller et al., 2004). Sequential presentation may also be effective, but did not increase compliance as quickly as simultaneous presentation in a comparison (Piazza et al., 2002).

High-probability instructional sequence (high-p) is an antecedent-based treatment targeting compliance to instructions instead of changes to food or the feeding environment. Based on the work of Mace et al. (1988), a high-p sequence rapidly issues instructions that the child is likely to comply with (e.g., touch your nose, give me five) before issuing an instruction the child is less likely to comply with (e.g., eating a nonpreferred food). The high-p sequence alone increased acceptance in one study (Patel et al., 2007), and with other components in other studies (Dawson et al., 2003; Penrod, Gardella, & Fernand, 2012). Still, the high-p sequence is unlikely to increase acceptance if the food is too aversive or requires too much effort to eat.

Consequence Treatments. Among the simplest and least restrictive treatments to increase food acceptance, and indirectly decrease food refusal, are providing positive or negative reinforcement for food acceptance. Positive reinforcement in the form of praise, access to a video or toy, or by utilizing a token economy has been demonstrated to increase acceptance (Casey et al., 2006). However, positive reinforcement alone is often not sufficient to increase acceptance, and acceptance only increases after escape extinction is implemented (Piazza, Patel, et al., 2003; Seiverling, Kokitus, & Williams, 2012). Negative reinforcement could be utilized by allowing the child to leave the meal (i.e., the aversive situation) once they have accepted and swallowed all the food presented to them, or to take breaks from the meal contingent on a sufficient rate of acceptance (Voulgarakis & Forte, 2015).

Instead of providing reinforcement contingent on a behavior, noncontingent reinforcement provides access to preferred items and/or activities throughout the meal. Noncontingent reinforcement either makes the mealtime environment more pleasant for the child, or discontinues a previously learned food refusal/reinforcement contingency. Noncontingent reinforcement has increased acceptance when implemented alone (Wilder, Normand, & Atwell, 2005), but other studies found it to only be effective when implemented with escape extinction (Reed et al., 2004).

Punishment procedures may be used in the treatment of pediatric feeding disorders, but are only implemented after less restrictive treatments have not produced increases in acceptance or in cases of medical necessity. Response cost – the removal of a token or preferred item contingent on a behavior – reduced food refusal in one study (Kahng, Tarbox, & Wilke, 2001). Another study deposited an avoidance food (i.e., an aversive food with an unpleasant taste) in the mouth of a child when the child did not self-feed within a specified time (Vaz, Volkert, & Piazza, 2011). Again, as with escape extinction, punishment-based procedures may lead to the child experiencing meals as an unpleasant event, or occasion behaviors secondary to punishment.

Skill Development Treatments

Unlike with treatments for food acceptance and swallowing, which typically only require the child to move pureed food to the back of their mouth and swallow, treatments to develop skills require long behavior chains that may include behaviors which the child does not possess the skill to successfully complete. For chewing, the child must hold the bite on their molars, chew while moving the lower jaw vertically and horizontally, and detect when the food is sufficiently masticated to swallow. A child feeding themselves must be able to scoop or otherwise pick up a bite, keep the food on the utensil or in their fingers, and deposit the bite in their mouth. Consuming liquids requires holding liquid in the mouth and swallowing without coughing, expelling, or aspirating for children fed by feeders. For children that are self-feeding they also must pick up the cup, bring it to their mouth, and deposit the liquid in their mouth without spilling.

Chewing. Treatments to increase the efficiency of a child's chewing have centered on prompting strategies to facilitate and instruct chewing, and assistive equipment to assist in the transition to chewing regular texture foods. Many published chewing treatments utilize verbal or physical prompting, along with differential reinforcement, to increase rate and efficiency of chewing. Verbal prompting and differential reinforcement have been shown to produce increases in chewing and swallowing (Shore, LeBlanc, & Simmons, 1999). Physical placement of a bite on the molars using a chewing tube, along with differential reinforcement, have been shown to increase chewing by minimizing the effort and skill involved in chewing (Kadey, Roane, Diaz, & Merrow, 2013). Modeling efficient chewing, along with differential reinforcement, have been effective for some children (Butterfield & Parson, 1973). Lastly, texture fading, starting with softer, easier-to-chew foods and systematically increasing to more difficult foods, has been demonstrated to increase chewing for some children (Sheppard, 2008). Still, treatments to increase the rate and efficiency of chewing often encounter obstacles, such as noncompliance to verbal instructions and prompts, swallowing foods before they are sufficiently masticated (and putting the child at risk of choking or aspiration), and use of nonchewing behavior to masticate softer regular textured foods (e.g., tongue mashing).

Self-Feeding. Physical guidance of self-feeding is a prompting-based treatment with strong empirical support (Volkert & Piazza, 2012). During physical guidance a feeder uses the minimal amount of assistance necessary to assist the child in scooping, bringing the bite to their mouth, and depositing the bite. As the child develops skill and becomes more efficient the physical guidance is decreased, and verbal prompts replace physical guidance. Ultimately, verbal prompts are also faded so that the child self-feeds without any instruction. Depending on the child's skill they may initially self-feed a limited number of bites by themselves, and the number of self-fed bites per meal is systematically increased as data warrants. Also, some foods are more difficult to self-feed than others, and thus easier foods are typically introduced before more difficult foods (e.g., pudding versus chicken noodle soup). Additionally, differential reinforcement alone (Peterson, Volkert, & Zeleny, 2015) and demand fading with negative reinforcement (Rivas et al., 2014) have also produced increases in self-feeding.

Swallowing Liquids. Treatments to increase the acceptance and swallowing of liquids span the gamut from escape extinction and representation of expelled liquid, to prompting and fading strategies to increase acceptance or self-feeding. A cut-out cup is used during escape extinction so that the child's nose does not prevent the liquid from contacting the lips and mouth (Milnes & Piazza, 2013). Otherwise the procedure mirrors escape extinction with solids as the cup remains at the upper lip until the child begins to open their mouth to accept the liquid. Some children do not accept liquids from a cup at the beginning of treatment, and a stimulus fading treatment is utilized. A spoon to cup (Groff et al., 2011) and a syringe to cup (Groff et al., 2014) fading procedure has received empirical support. Also, when starting with liquids a small amount of liquid is typically presented (e.g., 1/8 oz.) so that it minimizes the amount of effort and likelihood of coughing when swallowing the liquid (Patel et al., 2001). Lastly, physical guidance and fading of guidance and instructions are effective in increasing self-feeding of liquids (Collins et al., 1991).

Role of Parents in Treatment

A key consideration in treatments for pediatric feeding disorders is the ability to teach parents or other caregivers to implement an effective behavioral protocol (i.e., step-by-step instructions) with good fidelity (see the Side-Bar Box for more on this).

Continuum of Care in Treatment of Pediatric Feeding Disorders

Regardless of the severity of pediatric feeding disorders at intake, the ultimate goal of pediatric feeding disorder programs is to facilitate children eating in an age-typical manner, and participate in meals at home and in the community. For some children, this may require minimal education for caregivers about the functions of food refusal. For others the treatment process may take many years to arrive at the ultimate goal. During intake interviews caregivers are asked for treatment goals that would be the most meaningful for them. These goals may range from accepting any food orally, to no longer having to do time-consuming food preparation, to a child eating at any fast food restaurant (i.e., no longer demonstrating food selectivity by fast food brand). Caregivers are observed feeding the child before treatment not only to assess the functions of food refusal, but also to provide therapists with information about what a typical family meal may look like post-treatment. Throughout treatment caregivers are consulted to identify new foods to introduce into the child's diet, but also to discuss treatment components. When possible, other professionals that work with a child (e.g., school personnel, occupational therapists) are consulted to assess if it is feasible for them to implement protocols and to train them if possible. Before discharge from intensive feeding programs children are transitioned to the least restrictive setting (if possible), and meals are conducted in the community and in the home to facilitate generalization and maintenance of treatment gains. Caregivers observe sessions throughout treatment, and are often gradually faded in to the treatment room during caregiver training. This ensures that caregivers are able to master small increments of a treatment protocol instead of learning the whole protocol at once, and that any differences in the child's behavior are likely due to the presence of the caregiver. Therapists provide feedback while a caregiver is implementing a protocol, and may feed meals to give caregivers a break from the caregiver training process. At discharge from intensive pediatric feeding programs caregivers are provided with a written treatment protocol and other training materials that may include videos demonstrating the treatment protocol. Therapists check in with caregivers by email and phone post-discharge to assist caregivers with any resurgence of food refusal or novel behaviors that did not occur during treatment. Follow-up clinic appointments and other consultation by the interdisciplinary team are completed to continue to monitor medical conditions. Also, recommendations regarding the volume of food to be fed in meals, and the transition from tube to oral feedings is provided. Some children may benefit from multiple intensive pediatric feeding program admissions. For instance, the first admission may focus on getting acceptance of foods and liquids orally, and the second may focus on developing age-typical feeding skills such as chewing and self-feeding. Independent of the rate and magnitude of food refusal, caregivers are instructed to reach out to the pediatric feeding disorder program their child participated in if problems arise, or if all is going well.

Two methods of caregiver training are utilized to promote generalization of treatment gains to the home. Therapists can develop a protocol consisting of multiple components with caregivers not present, demonstrate its effectiveness, and then bring the parents back in to be trained on the protocol. Treatment can be caregiver-conducted, where parents are taught to conduct assessment and treatment and then treatment protocols are altered based off of observations of the caregiver's and child's behavior. Caregiver training may be conducted in clinic, in the community, and in the home. Also, group-based caregiver training and training of other professionals (e.g., school personnel) has been conducted.

Training caregivers on pre-developed written protocols is typically augmented with verbal instructions, modeling, rehearsals, and post-session feedback among others. Mueller et al. (2003) evaluated the contributions of training components including verbal instructions, modeling, and rehearsal. They found verbal instruction alone to be insufficient for caregivers, but when combined with another component parents implemented the protocol with a high level of fidelity. Pangborn, Borrero, and Borrero (2013) utilized a sequential multicomponent training package consisting of observation, protocol review, video review, modeling, role-play, and immediate feedback, and demonstrated high levels of treatment protocol fidelity by trained caregivers. Further, the study evidenced caregivers' ability to learn in individual components, and thus have training packages tailored for them. Generalization and maintenance of high levels of treatment integrity have been also observed in the home, and at follow-up (Aclan & Taylor, 2017). Najdowski et al. (2003) trained a caregiver to conduct functional analysis and implement a standard treatment package including escape extinction and differential reinforcement as components. While measures of treatment fidelity were not taken, the treatment was successful in increasing acceptance and decreasing food refusal. Also, caregiver trainings include a manual-based treatment delivered in a group setting (Sharp, Burrell, & Jaquess, 2014).

Other Variables Influencing Treatment

Assessment

A sequence of coughing, gagging, and then emesis is often observed in children admitted to intensive pediatric feeding disorders programs (Dieter, Borrero, & Ibanez, 2015). As such, data are taken on these three behaviors throughout treatment, and intervention to decrease coughing and gagging is warranted for some children to prevent emesis. Coughing is also a precursor to choking and aspiration, thus coughing and other clinical signs of aspiration (e.g., turning red, grimacing) are monitored in case immediate intervention is necessary. Modified barium swallow studies are conducted when risk of aspiration is suspected, and medical clearance for safety of oral feeding is necessary before initiating treatment for pediatric feeding disorders.

Comorbidity

Medical conditions may be present at the time of treatment, and require management or alteration to treatment packages. Constipation may cause gastrointestinal discomfort, and reduce the motivation to consume more food. Children admitted to intensive pediatric feeding disorder programs at times demonstrate volume sensitivity in that consuming too much food may induce vomiting. Also, co-occurring medical conditions (e.g., eosinophilic esophagitis, gastrointestinal reflux disease) may make oral feeding uncomfortable or painful.

Demographics

Cultural considerations are also important to integrate into treatment for pediatric feeding disorders. Foods the family typically eats at home are often introduced during treatment, sometimes at lower textures, to facilitate generalization and maintenance or increase in acceptance and swallowing of food. Foods associated with holidays, and foods eaten in the community, are also introduced during treatment. Cultural considerations with food preparation (e.g., Kosher food preparation) are also respected during treatment in intensive pediatric feeding disorder programs. Lastly, some families prefer electronic devices not to be permitted at the table during meals, so the use of videos as a tangible is either minimized or eliminated during treatment.

Medication

Medications are not typically used as a primary intervention for pediatric feeding disorders; they may be used to help treat related medical conditions which may contribute to the development or maintenance of the feeding problem (e.g., medications for gastroesophageal reflux or constipation).

Conclusion

Parents commonly deal with the picky eating of their children, and sometimes the extreme variations of this behavior begin to significantly interfere with the child's functioning, thus qualifying as a pediatric feeding disorder. Limited food intake can cause health problems as well as frustration for both parents and their children. Etiology can be both biological (e.g., illnesses, physical abnormalities) and environmental (e.g., escape from nonpreferred foods, access to preferred foods). Research-supported treatments include behavioral techniques related to decreasing food refusal behaviors, increasing food acceptance behaviors, and building behavioral skills related to feeding. Parents are often effective collaborators when it comes to providing the interventions.

References

Aclan, M. D., & Taylor, R. S. (2017). An evaluation of a caregiver training protocol on the generalization and maintenance of successful pediatric feeding interventions. *Behavioral Interventions*, *32*, 182–189. doi:10.1002/bin.1468

Ahearn, W. H. (2003). Using simultaneous presentation to increase vegetable consumption in a mildly selective child with autism. *Journal of Applied Behavior Analysis*, *36*, 361–365. doi:10.1901/jaba.2003.36–361

Ahearn, W. H., Kerwin, M. E., Eicher, P. S., Shantz, J., & Swearingin, W. (1996). An alternating treatments comparison of two intensive interventions for food refusal. *Journal of Applied Behavior Analysis*, *29*, 321–332. doi:10.1901/jaba.1996.29–321

Benjasuwantep, B., Chaithirayanon, S., & Eiamudomkan, M. (2013). Feeding problems in healthy young children: Prevalence, related factors and feeding practices. *Pediatric Reports*, *5*, E10. doi:10.4081/pr.2013.e10

Berlin, K. S., Lobato, D. J., Pinkos, B., Cerezo, C. S., & LeLeiko, N. S. (2011). Patterns of medical and developmental comorbidities among children presenting with feeding problems: A latent class analysis. *Journal of Developmental & Behavioral Pediatrics*, *32*(1), 41–47.

Borrero, C. S., Woods, J. N., Borrero, J. C., Masler, E. A., & Lesser, A. D. (2010). Descriptive analyses of pediatric food refusal and acceptance. *Journal of Applied Behavior Analysis*, *43*, 71–88. doi:10.1901/jaba.2010.43–71

Borrero, C. S. W., Schlereth, G. J., Rubio, E. K., & Taylor, T. (2013). A comparison of two physical guidance procedures in the treatment of pediatric food refusal. *Behavioral Interventions*, *28*, 261–280. doi:10.1002/bin.1373

Butterfield, W. H., & Parson, R. (1973). Modeling and shaping by parents to develop chewing behavior in their retarded child. *Journal of Behavior Therapy and Experimental Psychiatry*, *4*, 285–287. doi:http://dx.doi.org/10.1016/0005–7916(73)90090–6

Casey, S. D., Cooper-Brown, L. J., Wacker, D. P., & Rankin, B. E. (2006). The use of descriptive analysis to identify and manipulate schedules of reinforcement in the treatment of food refusal. *Journal of Behavioral Education*, *15*, 39–50. doi:10.1007/s10864-005–9001-7

Catania, A. C. (2012). *Learning*. 5th edn. New York: Sloan.

Collins, B. C., Gast, D. L., Wolery, M., Holcombe, A., & Leatherby, J. G. (1991). Using constant time delay to teach self-feeding to young students with severe/profound handicaps: Evidence of limited effectiveness. *Journal of Developmental and Physical Disabilities, 3,* 157–179. doi:10.1007/bf01045931

Curtin, C., Hubbard, K., Anderson, S. E., Mick, E., Must, A., & Bandini, L. G. (2015). Food selectivity, mealtime behavior problems, spousal stress, and family food choices in children with and without autism spectrum disorder. *Journal of Autism and Developmental Disorders, 45,* 3308–3315.

Dawson, J. E., Piazza, C. C., Sevin, B. M., Gulotta, C. S., Lerman, D., & Kelley, M. L. (2003). Use of the high-probability instructional sequence and escape extinction in a child with food refusal. *Journal of Applied Behavior Analysis, 36,* 105–108. doi:10.1901/jaba.2003.36-105

Dieter, D., Borrero, C. S. W., & Ibanez, V. (2015). Descriptive and lag-sequential analyses of emesis related to pediatric feeding disorders. Paper presented at the 41st Annual Convention of the Association for Behavior Analysis International, May 24, Antonio, TX.

Freeman, K. A., & Piazza, C. C. (1998). Combining stimulus fading, reinforcement, and extinction to treat food refusal. *Journal of Applied Behavior Analysis, 31,* 691–694. doi:10.1901/jaba.1998.31-691

Girolami, P. A., Boscoe, J. H., & Roscoe, N. (2007). Decreasing expulsions by a child with a feeding disorder: Using a brush to present and re-present food. *Journal of Applied Behavior Analysis, 40,* 749–753. doi:10.1901/jaba.2007.749-753

González, M. L., Rubio, E. K., & Taylor, T. (2014). Inappropriate mealtime behavior: The effects of noncontingent access to preferred tangibles on responding in functional analyses. *Research in Developmental Disabilities, 35,* 3655–3664.

Greer, A. J., Gulotta, C. S., Masler, E. A., & Laud, R. B. (2008). Caregiver stress and outcomes of children with pediatric feeding disorders treated in an intensive interdisciplinary program. *Journal of Pediatric Psychology, 33,* 612–620. doi:10.1093/jpepsy/jsm116

Groff, R. A., Piazza, C. C., Volkert, V. M., & Jostad, C. M. (2014). Syringe fading as treatment for feeding refusal. *Journal of Applied Behavior Analysis, 47,* 834–839. doi:10.1002/jaba.162

Groff, R. A., Piazza, C. C., Zeleny, J. R., & Dempsey, J. R. (2011). Spoon-to-cup fading as treatment for cup drinking in a child with intestinal failure. *Journal of Applied Behavior Analysis, 44,* 949–954. doi:10.1901/jaba.2011.44-949

Kadey, H. J., Roane, H. S., Diaz, J. C., & McCarthy, C. M. (2013). Using a Nuk® brush to increase acceptance of solids and liquids for two children diagnosed with autism. *Research in Autism Spectrum Disorders, 7,* 1461–1480. doi:http://dx.doi.org/10.1016/j.rasd.2013.07.017

Kadey, H. J., Roane, H. S., Diaz, J. C., & Merrow, J. M. (2013). An evaluation of chewing and swallowing for a child diagnosed with autism. *Journal of Developmental and Physical Disabilities, 25,* 343–354. doi:10.1007/s10882-012-9313-1

Kahng, S., Tarbox, J., & Wilke, A. E. (2001). Use of a multicomponent treatment for food refusal. *Journal of Applied Behavior Analysis, 34,* 93–96. doi:10.1901/jaba.2001.34-93

Kerwin, M. E., Ahearn, W. H., Eicher, P. S., & Burd, D. M. (1995). The costs of eating: A behavioral economic analysis of food refusal. *Journal of Applied Behavior Analysis, 28,* 245–260. doi:10.1901/jaba.1995.28-245

Kozlowski, A. M., Taylor, T., González, M. L., & Girolami, P. A. (2015). Feeding disorders. In J. L. Matson and M. L. Matson (eds.), *Comorbid conditions in individuals with intellectual disabilities* (pp. 109–143). Cham: Springer.

Ledford, J. R., & Gast, D. L. (2006). Feeding problems in children with autism spectrum disorders: A review. *Focus on Autism and Other Developmental Disabilities, 21*(3), 153–166.

Lukens, C. T., & Silverman, A. H. (2014). Systematic review of psychological interventions for pediatric feeding problems. *Journal of Pediatric Psychology*, *39*, 903–917. doi:10.1093/jpepsy/jsu040

Mace, F. C., Hock, M. L., Lalli, J. S., West, B. J., Belfiore, P., Pinter, E., & Brown, D. K. (1988). Behavioral momentum in the treatment of noncompliance. *Journal of Applied Behavior Analysis*, *21*, 123–141. doi:10.1901/jaba.1988.21–123

Marí-Bauset, S., Zazpe, I., Mari-Sanchis, A., Llopis-González, A., & Morales-Suárez-Varela, M. (2014). Food selectivity in autism spectrum disorders: A systematic review. *Journal of Child Neurology*, *29*, 1554–1561.

Marshall, J., Ware, R., Ziviani, J., Hill, R. J., & Dodrill, P. (2015). Efficacy of interventions to improve feeding difficulties in children with autism spectrum disorders: A systematic review and meta-analysis. *Child: Care, Health and Development*, *41*, 278–302. doi:10.1111/cch.12157

Mascola, A. J., Bryson, S. W., & Agras, W. S. (2010). Picky eating during childhood: A longitudinal study to age 11 years. *Eating Behaviors*, *11*, 253–257.

Matson, J. L., & Kuhn, D. E. (2001). Identifying feeding problems in mentally retarded persons: Development and reliability of the screening tool of feeding problems (STEP). *Research in Developmental Disabilities*, *22*(2), 165–172.

Milnes, S. M., & Piazza, C. C. (2013). Intensive treatment of pediatric feeding disorders. In D. D. Reed, F. D. DiGennaro Reed, & J. K. Luiselli (eds.), *Handbook of crisis intervention and developmental disabilities* (pp. 393–408). New York: Springer New York.

Mueller, M. M., Piazza, C. C., Moore, J. W., Kelley, M. E., Bethke, S. A., Pruett, A. E., . . . & Layer, S. A. (2003). Training parents to implement pediatric feeding protocols. *Journal of Applied Behavior Analysis*, *36*, 545–562. doi:10.1901/jaba.2003.36–545

Mueller, M. M., Piazza, C. C., Patel, M. R., Kelley, M. E., & Pruett, A. (2004). Increasing variety of foods consumed by blending nonpreferred foods into preferred foods. *Journal of Applied Behavior Analysis*, *37*, 159–170. doi:10.1901/jaba.2004.37–159

Nadon, G., Feldman, D. E., Dunn, W., & Gisel, E. (2011). Mealtime problems in children with autism spectrum disorder and their typically developing siblings: A comparison study. *Autism*, *15*(1), 98–113.

Najdowski, A. C., Wallace, M. D., Doney, J. K., & Ghezzi, P. M. (2003). Parental assessment and treatment of food selectivity in natural settings. *Journal of Applied Behavior Analysis*, *36*, 383–386. doi:10.1901/jaba.2003.36–383

O'Brien, F., Bugle, C., & Azrin, N. H. (1972). Training and maintaining a retarded child's proper eating. *Journal of Applied Behavior Analysis*, *5*, 67–72. doi:10.1901/jaba.1972.5–67

Pangborn, M. M., Borrero, C. S. W., & Borrero, J. C. (2013). Sequential application of caregiver training to implement pediatric feeding disorder protocols. *Behavioral Interventions*, *28*, 107–130. doi:10.1002/bin.1356

Patel, M., Reed, G. K., Piazza, C. C., Mueller, M., Bachmeyer, M. H., & Layer, S. A. (2007). Use of a high-probability instructional sequence to increase compliance to feeding demands in the absence of escape extinction. *Behavioral Interventions*, *22*, 305–310. doi:10.1002/bin.251

Patel, M. R., Piazza, C. C., Kelly, M. L., Ochsner, C. A., & Santana, C. M. (2001). Using a fading procedure to increase fluid consumption in a child with feeding problems. *Journal of Applied Behavior Analysis*, *34*, 357–360. doi:10.1901/jaba.2001.34–357

Patel, M. R., Piazza, C. C., Layer, S. A., Coleman, R., & Swartzwelder, D. M. (2005). A systematic evaluation of food textures to decrease packing and increase oral intake in children with pediatric feeding disorders. *Journal of Applied Behavior Analysis*, *38*, 89–100. doi:10.1901/jaba.2005.161–02

Patel, M. R., Piazza, C. C., Martinez, C. J., Volkert, V. M., & Santana, C. M. (2002). An evaluation of two differential reinforcement procedures with escape extinction to treat food refusal. *Journal of Applied Behavior Analysis, 35*, 363–374. doi:10.1901/jaba.2002.35–363

Penrod, B., Gardella, L., & Fernand, J. (2012). An evaluation of a progressive high-probability instructional sequence combined with low-probability demand fading in the treatment of food selectivity. *Journal of Applied Behavior Analysis, 45*, 527–537. doi:10.1901/jaba.2012.45–527

Peterson, K. M., Piazza, C. C., & Volkert, V. M. (2016). A comparison of a modified sequential oral sensory approach to an applied behavior-analytic approach in the treatment of food selectivity in children with autism spectrum disorder. *Journal of Applied Behavior Analysis, 49*(3), 485–511.

Peterson, K. M., Volkert, V. M., & Zeleny, J. R. (2015). Increasing self-drinking for children with feeding disorders. *Journal of Applied Behavior Analysis, 48*, 436–441. doi:10.1002/jaba.210

Piazza, C. C. (2008). Feeding disorders and behavior: What have we learned? *Developmental Disabilities Research Reviews, 14*, 174–181. doi:10.1002/ddrr.22

Piazza, C. C., Fisher, W. W., Brown, K. A., Shore, B. A., Patel, M. R., Katz, R. M., . . . & Blakely-Smith, A. (2003). Functional analysis of inappropriate mealtime behaviors. *Journal of Applied Behavior Analysis, 36*, 187–204. doi:10.1901/jaba.2003.36–187

Piazza, C. C., Milnes, S. M., & Shalev, R. A. (2015). A behavior-analytic approach to the assessment and treatment of pediatric feeding disorders. *Clinical and Organizational Applications of Applied Behavior Analysis, 69*.

Piazza, C. C., Patel, M. R., Gulotta, C. S., Sevin, B. M., & Layer, S. A. (2003). On the relative contributions of positive reinforcement and escape extinction in the treatment of food refusal. *Journal of Applied Behavior Analysis, 36*, 309–324. doi:10.1901/jaba.2003.36–309

Piazza, C. C., Patel, M. R., Santana, C. M., Goh, H.-L., Delia, M. D., & Lancaster, B. M. (2002). An evaluation of simultaneous and sequential presentation of preferred and nonpreferred food to treat food selectivity. *Journal of Applied Behavior Analysis, 35*, 259–270. doi:10.1901/jaba.2002.35–259

Reed, G. K., Piazza, C. C., Patel, M. R., Layer, S. A., Bachmeyer, M. H., Bethke, S. D., & Gutshall, K. A. (2004). On the relative contributions of noncontingent reinforcement and escape extinction in the treatment of food refusal. *Journal of Applied Behavior Analysis, 37*, 27–42. doi:10.1901/jaba.2004.37–27

Rivas, K. M., Piazza, C. C., Roane, H. S., Volkert, V. M., Stewart, V., Kadey, H. J., & Groff, R. A. (2014). Analysis of self-feeding in children with feeding disorders. *Journal of Applied Behavior Analysis, 47*, 710–722. doi:10.1002/jaba.170

Rubio, E. K., Borrero, C. S. W., & Taylor, T. (2015). Use of a side deposit to increase consumption in children with food refusal. *Behavioral Interventions, 30*, 231–246. doi:10.1002/bin.1404

Seiverling, L., Kokitus, A., & Williams, K. (2012). A clinical demonstration of a treatment package for food selectivity. *The Behavior Analyst Today, 13*, 11. doi:10.1037/h0100719

Sharp, W. G., Berry, R. C., McCracken, C., Nuhu, N. N., Marvel, E., Saulnier, C. A., . . . & Jaquess, D. L. (2013). Feeding problems and nutrient intake in children with autism spectrum disorders: A meta-analysis and comprehensive review of the literature. *Journal of Autism and Developmental Disorders, 43*(9), 2159–2173. doi:10.1007/s10803-013–1771-5

Sharp, W. G., Burrell, T. L., & Jaquess, D. L. (2014). The Autism MEAL Plan: A parent-training curriculum to manage eating aversions and low intake among children with autism. *Autism, 18*, 712–722. doi:doi:10.1177/1362361313489190

Sharp, W. G., Stubbs, K. H., Adams, H., Wells, B. M., Lesack, R. S., Criado, K. K., . . . & Scahill, L. D. (2016). Intensive, manual-based intervention for pediatric feeding disorders: Results from a randomized pilot trial. *Journal of Pediatric Gastroenterology and Nutrition*, *62*, 658–663. doi:10.1097/mpg.0000000000001043

Sharp, W. G., Volkert, V. M., Scahill, L., McCracken, C. E., & McElhanon, B. (2017). A systematic review and meta-analysis of intensive multidisciplinary intervention for pediatric feeding disorders: How standard is the standard of care? *The Journal of Pediatrics*, *181*, 116–124.e114. doi:10.1016/j.jpeds.2016.10.002

Sheppard, J. J. (2008). Using motor learning approaches for treating swallowing and feeding disorders: A review. *Language, Speech, and Hearing Services in Schools*, *39*, 227–236. doi:10.1044/0161–1461(2008/022)

Shore, B. A., Babbitt, R. L., Williams, K. E., Coe, D. A., & Snyder, A. (1998). Use of texture fading in the treatment of food selectivity. *Journal of Applied Behavior Analysis*, *31*, 621–633. doi:10.1901/jaba.1998.31–621

Shore, B. A., LeBlanc, D., & Simmons, J. (1999). Reduction of unsafe eating in a patient with esophageal stricture. *Journal of Applied Behavior Analysis*, *32*, 225–228. doi:10.1901/jaba.1999.32–225

Tiger, J. H., & Hanley, G. P. (2006). Using reinforcer pairing and fading to increase the milk consumption of a preschool child. *Journal of Applied Behavior Analysis*, *39*, 399–403. doi:10.1901/jaba.2006.6–06

Vaz, P. C. M., Piazza, C. C., Stewart, V., Volkert, V. M., Groff, R. A., & Patel, M. R. (2012). Using a chaser to decrease packing in children with feeding disorders. *Journal of Applied Behavior Analysis*, *45*, 97–105. doi:10.1901/jaba.2012.45–97

Vaz, P. C. M., Volkert, V. M., & Piazza, C. C. (2011). Using negative reinforcement to increase self-feeding in a child with food selectivity. *Journal of Applied Behavior Analysis*, *44*, 915–920. doi:10.1901/jaba.2011.44–915

Volkert, V. M., & Piazza, C. C. (2012). Pediatric feeding disorders. In P. Sturmey and M. Hersen (eds.), *Handbook of evidence-based practice in clinical psychology*. Hoboken, NJ: John Wiley & Sons, Inc.

Volkert, V. M., Vaz, P. C. M., Piazza, C. C., Frese, J., & Barnett, L. (2011). Using a flipped spoon to decrease packing in children with feeding disorders. *Journal of Applied Behavior Analysis*, *44*(3), 617–621. doi:10.1901/jaba.2011.44–617

Voulgarakis, H., & Forte, S. (2015). Escape extinction and negative reinforcement in the treatment of pediatric feeding disorders: A single case analysis. *Behavior Analysis in Practice*, *8*, 212–214. doi:10.1007/s40617-015–0086-8

Wilder, D. A., Normand, M., & Atwell, J. (2005). Noncontingent reinforcement as treatment for food refusal and associated self-injury. *Journal of Applied Behavior Analysis*, *38*, 549–553. doi:10.1901/jaba.2005.132–04

Wilkins, J. W., Piazza, C. C., Groff, R. A., & Vaz, P. C. M. (2011). Chin prompt plus re-presentation as treatment for expulsion in children with feeding disorders. *Journal of Applied Behavior Analysis*, *44*(3), 513–522. doi:10.1901/jaba.2011.44–513

Wilkins, J. W., Piazza, C. C., Groff, R. A., Volkert, V. M., Kozisek, J. M., & Milnes, S. M. (2014). Utensil manipulation during initial treatment of pediatric feeding problems. *Journal of Applied Behavior Analysis*, *47*(4), 694–709. doi:10.1002/jaba.169

Williams, K. E., Field, D. G., & Seiverling, L. (2010). Food refusal in children: A review of the literature. *Research in Developmental Disabilities*, *31*, 625–633.

Williams, K. E., Riegel, K., & Kerwin, M. L. (2009). Feeding disorder of infancy or early childhood: How often is it seen in feeding programs? *Children's Health Care*, *38*, 123–136. doi:10.1080/02739610902813302

14

Eating

*Emily C. Stefano, Brooke L. Bennett, Frances Bozsik, Danae L. Hudson,
and Brooke L. Whisenhunt*

Eating disorders (EDs) are characterized by maladaptive eating behaviors, body image disturbance, and dysfunctional attempts to control weight and shape. The *Diagnostic and Statistical Manual of Mental Disorders*, 5th edition (DSM-5; American Psychiatric Association, 2013) includes three primary eating disorders: anorexia nervosa, bulimia nervosa, and binge eating disorder. Twelve-month prevalence rates for these disorders among adolescents are 0.2%, 0.6%, and 0.9%, respectively (Swanson, Crow, & Le Grange, 2011), and median age of onset ranges from 12 to 18 years of age (Favaro et al., 2009; Swanson, Crow, & Le Grange, 2011). However, recent findings have indicated an increase in prevalence rates and a decrease in age of onset for eating disorders (Favaro et al., 2009; Hudson et al., 2007), underscoring the importance of evidence-based treatments for eating disorder pathology, particularly among adolescents and children.

Anorexia nervosa (AN) is characterized by extreme caloric restriction resulting in significant weight loss or, in children and adolescents, a failure to make expected weight gains (i.e., a body mass index [BMI] lower than the 5th percentile). Intense fear of weight gain is present and, among younger patients, may be better evidenced by behaviors that interfere with weight gain (e.g., increased exercise or fasting) rather than explicit expression of fear of fatness (Eddy, Murray, & LeGrange, 2015). Other key features of AN include an overevaluation of weight and shape, a disturbance in the perception of weight and shape, and persistent lack of recognition of the ramifications of a low weight status. AN is associated with serious physical outcomes because of starvation and malnutrition (e.g., pubertal delay/interruption and bone mass reduction).

Bulimia nervosa (BN) is marked by repeated binge eating episodes in which an objectively large amount of food is eaten within a relatively short period of time (i.e., two hours or less) and accompanied by a sense of loss of control over eating. Typically, after the binge episode, the individual attempts to "compensate" for the excessive intake of calories. Compensatory behaviors can include self-induced vomiting, fasting, excessive exercise, or misusing medications such as laxatives, diuretics, or diet pills. Similar to AN, individuals with BN endorse body image disturbances and intense fear of weight gain. However, individuals with BN often remain within the normal or overweight range due to some calorie absorption during binge eating episodes. Medical concerns associated with BN include cardiac arrhythmias, dental erosion, esophageal tears, and gastric rupture.

Binge eating disorder (BED) is also depicted by recurrent episodes of binge eating. However, unlike BN, individuals with BED do not regularly engage in compensatory behaviors and, therefore, are likely to be or become overweight. During binge eating episodes, the individual may feel uncomfortably full, eat rapidly, or eat in the absence of hunger. Eating may occur in isolation due to embarrassment or guilt, and a feeling of disgust with oneself often follows the binge episode. Among younger individuals with BED, it is important to note the amount and context of food consumption for a binge eating episode is different than the increased intake of food commonly spurred by growth in children and adolescents. Increased food consumption may occur periodically among children due to greater physical activity or growth. Therefore, the experience of a lack of control over eating may be the best diagnostic indicator of a binge episode within this population (Shomaker et al., 2010).

The DSM-5 also includes other specified feeding and eating disorder (OSFED) category. This category encompasses eating disturbances that cause significant distress or interfere with functioning but do not fit the specific diagnostic criteria for the aforementioned eating disorders. This category includes symptom profiles similar to AN in individuals at or above a normal weight, symptoms of BN in which the occurrences of binge eating and compensatory behaviors do not meet the frequency criterion, recurrent purging without binge eating, and consistently eating a significant amount of one's total calories after dinner or during the night. Research suggests OSFED and subthreshold ED pathology are much more prevalent among adolescents and adults compared to AN, BN, or BED, and many individuals within these categories show similar levels of significant psychological distress and impairment (Eddy et al., 2008; Hudson et al., 2007; Rockert, Kaplan, & Olmsted, 2007; Schmidt et al., 2008; Swanson, Crow, & Le Grange, 2011; Turner, Bryant-Waugh, & Peveler, 2010). The research suggests evidence-based treatment approaches are likely effective for treating individuals within subclinical ED categories, and individuals within these categories should receive further consideration in clinical and research settings (Le Grange & Loeb, 2007; Schapman-Williams, Lock, & Couturier, 2006).

Borderline Personality Disorder

Studies have suggested that up to 58% of individuals with eating disorders also meet diagnostic criteria for a personality disorder (Cassin & von Ranson, 2005). Borderline personality disorder (BPD) is one of the most common personality disorders among adolescents and adults who engage in binge eating behavior (Cassin & von Ranson, 2005). BPD is characterized by a pervasive pattern of instability in emotional regulation, interpersonal relationships, impulse control, and self-image (APA, 2013). The individual may engage in frantic efforts to avoid real or imagined abandonment from others, display intense and inappropriate emotional responses, and engage in impulsive and self-damaging behavior. BPD can cause significant and chronic impairment; individuals may routinely seek psychotherapy for their distress (Zimmerman, Rothschild, & Chelminski, 2005). While ED symptomology and severity do not notably differ between eating disorder patients with and without BPD, ED patients with BPD are more likely to report significant histories of abuse, trauma, self-injury, suicidal gestures, and volatile interpersonal relationships (Zittel Conklin & Westin, 2005). This clinical complexity may significantly affect progress and recovery among individuals seeking eating disorder treatment. Indeed, patients with BPD who also sought treatment for an ED were more likely to "migrate" to other ED diagnoses and presentations during the following decade (Zanarini et al., 2010).

Dialectical behaviorial therapy (DBT) is an empirically supported psychotherapy for BPD among adolescents and adults (Koerner & Linehan, 2000; Panos et al., 2013). Developed by Marsha M. Linehan, DBT is a modified form of cognitive-behavioral therapy that focuses on emotional and cognitive regulation, distress tolerance, coping skills, and interpersonal functioning (Lynch et al., 2007). Current treatment research suggests that DBT is effective for patients with co-occurring BPD and binge eating disorder or bulimia nervosa (Chen et al., 2008; Kröger et al., 2010; Salbach-Andrae et al., 2008). However, further research is needed to better establish its effectiveness, particularly for use with adolescents with co-occurring EDs and BPD. For additional information about BPD and DBT, see Koerner (2012).

Etiology and Theoretical Underpinnings of Treatment

The etiology of eating disorders is multifaceted (Rikani et al., 2013), and while many etiological theories have been proposed and investigated, an integrative "biopsychosocial model" may best capture the various etiological factors. Biological factors have focused on the role of genetics and serotonin dysregulation (Polivy & Herman, 2002). Psychological factors related to the etiology of eating disorders include many cognitive, behavioral, and personality influences, such as clinical perfectionism, persistent negative affect, emotional dysregulation, low self-esteem, and overevaluation of weight and shape as a measure of self-worth (Stice, 2002; Stice et al., 2017). Lastly, sociocultural factors have been increasingly of focus as an etiological mechanism for eating disorders, specifically repeated exposure to the "thin-ideal" standard of beauty in the media and weight-related teasing among adolescent peers (Stice et al., 2017).

Currently, there are two primary evidence-based treatments for EDs in children and adolescents: family-based treatment (FBT) and cognitive-behavioral therapy (CBT). While both treatments are effective in addressing ED symptoms, the theoretical underpinnings that guide each treatment have some substantive differences including beliefs about the maintaining factors of the eating disorder, and the roles of the patient, family, and therapist in treatment.

FBT is based on the notion that the adolescent is embedded within the family structure and best understood through the relationships with their family members. Assessment and treatment focus on the family unit and direct parental involvement in therapy is considered essential to the patient's treatment progress and success (Lock, 2011; Lock & Le Grange, 2015). The FBT model considers the ED as "separate" from the individual. Consequently, the patient is encouraged to externalize the disorder, a practice borrowed from narrative therapy (White & Epston, 1990). The goal of this externalization, or separation from the disorder, is to remove the blame and judgment of the eating disorder from the child and the parents. Time is not spent investigating the cause or development of the ED, but rather on finding solutions to reduce symptom severity (Lock, 2015).

Within the FBT framework, the therapist adopts a collaborative, yet neutral, stance. FBT borrows the idea of neutrality from Milan's systemic family therapy (Boscolo et al., 1987). This approach views the family as a homeostatic system. It is assumed that direct pressure for change unbalances the family system and is therefore met with counterpressure from the family as they attempt to reinstate balance (Boscolo et al., 1987). To avoid this outcome, the FBT therapist resists taking the expert role and instead defers to the parents' expertise regarding their child. One exception to this neutrality is the therapist's stance that weight gain and return to normal eating are immediate, nonnegotiable requirements of treatment (Lock, 2011).

FBT assumes the ED has impaired the child's ability to function at the appropriate developmental level (Lock & Le Grange, 2015). Therefore, the very ill child cannot be responsible for making decisions regarding their own eating and wellbeing. Parents are placed in an executive role and asked to assert temporary control over their child's eating until the severity of the eating disorder has lessened and the child begins to act in a more developmentally appropriate manner (Lock, 2011).

The CBT model asserts that an individual's beliefs, perceptions, and automatic thoughts influence their emotional and behavioral reactions. Individuals can learn to identify and evaluate automatic thoughts and reframe their thinking to more accurately reflect reality (Beck, 1967). CBT emphasizes the independence of the individual. That is, the patient is encouraged to assume responsibility for their thoughts, emotions, and behavior and to become the driving force behind their progress in treatment (Beck, 1967; Waller et al., 2007). Additionally, CBT for eating disorders takes the stance that behavior must not be dependent on emotions and, regardless of how they may feel at the time, the patient must choose to participate in treatment, complete their homework, and engage in behavioral experiments (Vitousek, Watson, & Wilson, 1998).

A key principle of CBT is a collaborative relationship and strong therapeutic alliance between the therapist and patient. Eating disorders are notoriously difficult to treat; patients often present as ambivalent or resistant to change due to their extreme concerns over control and weight (Vitousek, Watson, & Wilson, 1998). In order for the therapist and patient to overcome the barriers associated with ED treatment, a strong alliance between patient and therapist is essential.

The most recent version of CBT for both adolescents and adults with eating disorders utilizes a transdiagnostic approach, which asserts that emphasis on the specific diagnosis (i.e., AN, BN, and BED) is not necessary due to the significant overlap between the development, mechanisms, and presentations of each disorder (Fairburn, Cooper, & Shafran, 2003; Fairburn et al., 2008). For example, a fundamental characteristic of both AN and BN is the overvaluation and disturbed perception of weight and shape (APA, 2013), a feature which must be addressed in treatment regardless of the diagnosis or treatment approach. CBT also assumes that the majority of patients with EDs share underlying characteristics, such as low self-esteem (Fairburn, 2008; Fairburn et al., 2008). Furthermore, it is common for body mass index (BMI) and compensatory behaviors to change over time, therefore altering the specific ED diagnosis. Despite this diagnostic fluidity, the underlying principles of CBT remain the same, supporting the move toward transdiagnostic treatments (Fairburn, Cooper, & Shafran, 2003).

Brief Overview of Evidence-Based Treatments

Family-Based Treatment

Manualized family-based treatment packages have been developed and examined specifically for both anorexia nervosa (FBT-AN; Lock & Le Grange, 2015) and bulimia nervosa (FBT-BN; Le Grange & Lock, 2007). The FBT approach is designed for adolescents or children younger than 18 years of age and living at home with parents or consistent caregivers. Treatment typically lasts one year and involves between 15 and 20 joint sessions with the patient, family, and therapist (Le Grange & Lock, 2007; Lock & Le Grange, 2015).

Both FBT-AN and FBT-BN consist of three phases of treatment with considerable overlap. Phase I primarily focuses on weight gain, regular eating, and the impact of the adolescent's ED on family dynamics. Parents are encouraged to absolve themselves of blame for the occurrence of their child's ED and engage in active problem-solving to address disordered eating behaviors. In FBT-AN, Phase I is largely concentrated on the goal of weight restoration, while FBT-BN is focused on interrupting and ending the cycle of bingeing and purging.

Phase II occurs after the patient has met the parents' demands for increased or regular food intake, resulting in weight gain or stabilization. At this time, disordered eating behaviors have significantly decreased, and family dynamics typically improve as a result. Throughout Phase II, control over the patient's eating and exercise is slowly transitioned from the parents back to the adolescent. Additionally, family issues related to the ED beyond weight restoration or bingeing and purging are addressed.

Phase III begins once the patient's weight is stable or within normal range and disordered eating behaviors have subsided. The primary goal during this phase is the establishment of a healthy relationship between the patient and parents. The therapist may aid the family in recognizing adolescent issues that are independent of the patient's ED and in helping establish appropriate family boundaries between all parties. Finally, relapse prevention and treatment termination are addressed.

Cognitive-Behavior Therapy

Outpatient CBT for eating disorders typically takes place over the course of six months and includes 15 to 20 sessions with the patient (Fairburn, 2008). The majority of sessions are conducted individually with the adolescent, with parental involvement on an *as needed* basis to facilitate the child's recovery.

As CBT is primarily concerned with the cognitive and behavioral processes that maintain the patient's ED pathology, the patient and therapist jointly create a "formulation," or set of hypotheses, at the beginning of treatment. The personalized case formulation informs the development of treatment targets and provides the patient with insight into the underlying mechanisms of the disorder. This increased understanding, paired with motivation-enhancing strategies, engages the patient in treatment and provides an important sense of control over the processes of their disordered eating.

Early stages of treatment focus on weight restoration or weight stabilization and rely heavily on in-session weighing, meal planning, self-monitoring, and psychoeducation. The return to regular eating and the reduction of other disordered eating behaviors (e.g., overexercising, purging) are identified early in treatment as they are considered problematic behaviors that maintain the ED mindset. After weight has stabilized and disordered eating behaviors have reduced, the therapist and patient review progress and focus on more complex patient-specific treatment goals. These objectives are often identified during the joint formulation at the beginning of treatment, and typically include the patient's overevaluation of weight and shape, low self-esteem, perfectionism, difficulties with interpersonal functioning, and/or poor mood regulation strategies. Finally, relapse prevention strategies and treatment termination are discussed.

Overall Level of Research Support

FBT is one of the most extensively investigated approaches for treating EDs in children and adolescents. Though the literature is mixed regarding BN and BED, recent meta-analyses support FBT as the first-line treatment for adolescent AN (Lock, 2011, 2015). A review by Couturier, Kimber, and Szatmari (2013) found that although there were no post-treatment differences between FBT and individual therapy for adolescents with AN, FBT yielded superior remission rates and benefits when measured at the six- to 12-month follow-up. One potential explanation for the extended benefits of FBT involved the notion that those who participated in FBT had substantial external support from parents and family after the treatment had ended, while those in individual treatment may not have had the same post-treatment support (Couturier, Kimber, & Szatmari, 2013).

Currently, there is support for CBT as an effective treatment for BN and subclinical disordered eating within adolescent populations (Dalle Grave et al., 2015; Lock, 2015; Wilfley, Kolko, & Kass, 2011; Wilson & Sysko, 2006). Schmidt and colleagues (2008) reported that CBT with guided self-care had superior treatment outcomes compared to family therapy, including more rapid symptom reduction and greater acceptability among adolescents. Additionally, some research has suggested that CBT may provide a more cost-effective alternative for adolescents without access to the significant family support required by FBT (Dalle Grave et al., 2014; Schmidt et al., 2007). Research on the most effective treatment specific to adolescents with BED is less established (Wilson, 2005), which may be due to the very recent addition of BED as a formal eating disorder diagnosis in the DSM-5 (APA, 2013). A review by Brownley et al. (2007) identified both individual and group CBT as evidence-based treatments for adults with binge eating, and it is possible these results may generalize to adolescent populations, though further research is needed.

A systematic review by Hay (2013) called for future research in adolescent ED treatments to include controlled comparisons between novel and existing treatments. Additionally, treatment research for adolescent EDs should include diverse participants representing individuals from ethnic minority populations, varying weight statuses, and those exhibiting comorbid psychological disorders (Couturier, Kimber, & Szatmari, 2013; Hay, 2013).

Components of Evidence-Based Treatments

Medical Evaluation and Consultation

Due to the serious health consequences associated with eating disorders, all evidence-based treatments strongly encourage an initial medical evaluation to determine if the patient is medically appropriate for outpatient treatment. A medical evaluation can help provide diagnostic clarification, underscore the danger and severity of the ED to the patient and family, and potentially provide motivating information about impending physical health ramifications if the disordered eating persists (Lock & Le Grange, 2015). For more severely symptomatic and underweight patients, ongoing medical evaluations and treatment are often necessary.

A medical evaluation for an adolescent with an ED typically involves a complete physical examination that includes: checking for signs of malnutrition, tooth erosion, esophageal tears, bone density, cardiac arrhythmia, and organ functioning. Additionally, patients should obtain comprehensive laboratory tests, such as a complete blood count, basic metabolic panel that includes electrolytes, thyroid functioning, and other hormone levels (Fairburn, 2008; Le Grange & Lock, 2007; Waller et al., 2007).

Addressing Ambivalence and Motivation to Change

In both adolescent and adult populations, eating disorders have a relatively poor prognosis with high rates of relapse and low rates of full recovery (Grilo, Masheb, & Crosby, 2012; Herzog et al., 1999; Löwe et al., 2001; Strober, Freeman, & Morrell, 1997). Longitudinal and follow-up studies have identified early onset and chronicity of illness to be important contributors to poorer prognoses (Lewinsohn, Striegel-Moore, & Seeley, 2000; Morgan, Purgold, & Welbourne, 1983; Steinhausen, 2002). Particularly for child and adolescent patients, EBTs for eating disorders and their supporting research underscore the importance of both early intervention and achieving early change in treatment, which have been identified as robust predictors of immediate and long-term treatment success (Doyle et al., 2010; Fairburn et al., 2004; Le Grange et al., 2008; Le Grange & Loeb, 2007).

A common obstacle to early engagement in treatment is the ambivalence patients often feel about recovery (Geller, Cockell, & Drab, 2001). The patient's and family's motivation to engage in therapy should be assessed in conjunction with other ED symptoms (Geller et al., 2008) as it is an important factor for achieving early change in treatment (Le Grange & Lock, 2007; Lock & Le Grange, 2015). As early as possible, therapists should convey the gravity and seriousness of this illness to both the patient and family and validate the understandable concern parents will have for their child's health and safety. By conveying the severity of the illness in a noncritical manner to the patient and family, they may understand the importance of early change and more readily engage in treatment. Before effectively employing strategies to enhance motivation, therapists should make an effort to understand the ambivalent nature of EDs in that patients are likely to be unwilling or hesitant to change certain behaviors. Many patients with EDs are fearful of altering their food intake due to their intense concern about gaining weight. Specifically addressing readiness to change dietary restriction has been found to be an important predictor in overall treatment outcome in ED patients (Geller et al., 2004).

Psychoeducation

There are many misconceptions and harmful myths about eating, weight control, and the development and course of eating disorders. Patients with EDs are typically well informed regarding methods of weight control, regardless of the efficacy of the approach (Boutelle et al., 2002; Neumark-Sztainer et al., 2002), whereas parents are often lacking in knowledge and report a desire for more education about the etiology, symptoms, and treatment of EDs (Kopec-Schrader et al., 1993).

EBTs focus on psychoeducation heavily during the early stages of therapy. The therapist provides empirically based information to help the patient and family understand the mechanisms behind the eating disorder (e.g., creating a joint case formulation) and distinguish healthy and unhealthy eating and weight control behaviors. For example, many patients with disordered eating use laxatives in an attempt to lose or maintain their weight (Turner et al., 2000). A study by Bo-Linn and colleagues (1983) indicated that large doses of laxatives have a very minimal effect on absorption of calories after a binge episode and little to no effect on true weight gain or weight loss. Sharing this empirically based information with patients may result in an immediate reduction of their misuse of laxatives due to the understanding that they are not effective for weight loss and prolonged misuse can have serious health ramifications. Geist and colleagues (2000) found that both family-based therapy and family group psychoeducation for adolescents with AN yielded similar positive outcomes in weight restoration, highlighting the importance of psychoeducation in treatment.

Weight Restoration and Stabilization

Eating disorder behavior, specifically extreme caloric restriction and compensatory behaviors (e.g., self-induced vomiting, laxative abuse, excessive exercise), can result in devastating physical harm and psychological impairment. The primary psychological effects of starvation can include intense preoccupation with food, impulsive behavior, irritability, poor concentration, ritualistic eating behavior, and binge eating (Polivy, 1996; Schocken, Holloway, & Powers, 1989). Prolonged physical effects of starvation can inhibit normal physical development and growth, which is of immediate and serious concern in children and adolescents (Golden, 1994; Modan-Moses et al., 2003). These effects of starvation are likely to impact both the patient's overall functioning and their ability to engage in treatment (Fairburn, 2008). Therefore, a nearly universal component of evidence-based treatment of adolescent EDs is an immediate and persistent emphasis on weight restoration and stabilization (Fairburn, 2008; Lock & Le Grange, 2015). Patients with BN, BED, or subthreshold symptoms of AN may not require weight restoration but are likely to require weight stabilization (Le Grange & Lock, 2007).

The importance of restoring and stabilizing weight is typically discussed during the first treatment session; the therapist should convey to the patient and family the severe ramifications of being underweight or engaging in extreme calorie restriction. Both FBT and CBT endorse in-session weighing and calculating a series of weight goals for the patient if needed. For older adolescents, weight goals may be appropriately guided by BMI. However, due to the individual variability in development, it may be more appropriate to use growth charts, such as those provided by the Centers for Disease Control and Prevention, as a marker of healthy weight gain progression (CDC, 2015). The therapist should chart the patient's weight weekly, but review only the general trends with the patient and parents. It is generally not beneficial to share specific weights with the patient and clinical judgment should be used in sharing weight information with parents.

As therapists may not have sufficient understanding of nutrition, it is often necessary to consult with a registered dietician or pediatrician with experience in adolescent EDs, particularly when working with underweight patients (Le Grange & Lock, 2007). Weight restoration and stabilization are primarily achieved through regular eating and, when needed, significantly increased calorie consumption. Treatment approaches differ in their placement of responsibility for weight restoration and regular eating, but it is generally agreed that parents should be involved in meal planning and preparing dinner based on the patient's age and developmental stage.

Self-Monitoring

EBTs for adolescent EDs place a common emphasis on the importance of ongoing self-monitoring of food intake and associated eating behaviors (Fairburn, 2008; Le Grange & Lock, 2007; Lock & Le Grange, 2015). Dependent upon the patient's age or developmental stage, either the patient or parents are asked to maintain a record of the child's daily food intake. Adolescents who engage in bingeing and purging are also encouraged to keep a record of binge eating episodes and instances of purging or other compensatory behaviors that include time and location of the event, the amount and type of food consumed, and associated thoughts or emotions.

Consistent self-monitoring is beneficial because it requires the patient and/or parent to take responsibility for monitoring and assessing the disordered eating outside of therapy sessions, which can improve the patient's sense of autonomy or alleviate the parents' feelings of loss of control over their child's deteriorating health (Fairburn, 2008; Lock & Le Grange, 2015). Additionally, self-monitoring provides rich data that can be used to identify patterns and draw conclusions about changes in the patient's weight and inform future meal and treatment planning (Waller et al., 2007).

Addressing Maintaining Factors

EBTs for EDs focus on identifying and changing the factors that are currently maintaining the eating disorder rather than etiological causes. Fairburn (2008) equates an eating disorder to a house of cards: "If one wants to bring down the house, the key structural cards need to be identified and removed, and then the house will fall down" (2008, p. 47). For example, binge eating and subsequent compensatory behaviors often occur in response to extreme dietary restriction and rigid dietary rules (Fairburn, Cooper, & Shafran, 2003; Steiger, Lehoux, & Gauvin, 1999). By implementing regular eating and adequate food intake, binge eating episodes are likely to decrease in frequency and the perceived need to compensate for binge episodes will also be removed (Fairburn, 2008).

A core maintaining factor of eating disorders is an overvaluation of weight and shape (APA, 2013). In other words, the patient considers their weight and shape to be the utmost important aspect of their self-worth. All EBTs encompass strategies to identify and address low self-esteem while expanding other potential areas of self-worth and identity. Clinical perfectionism, distress intolerance, emotional dysregulation, and poor interpersonal functioning are also considered maintaining factors for EDs (Fairburn, Cooper, & Shafran, 2003), and are incorporated in EBTs.

Relapse Prevention

Late stage ED treatment includes a discussion of and planning for relapse prevention. The therapist, patient, and family discuss methods to ensure that progress is maintained even after treatment ends. In order to minimize the risk of relapse, the patient and family are encouraged to be proactive and stay attuned to the return of disordered eating behaviors and the mechanisms that were previously maintaining the eating disorder, such as frequent body checking, rigid dietary rules, or unhealthy weight control behaviors (Fairburn, 2008; Le Grange & Lock, 2007). Additionally, potential high-risk, upcoming eating- and weight-related events are identified (e.g., weight loss due to an illness, binge eating episode, holidays or parties involving large amounts of food); the therapist assists the patient and family in creating a plan to manage during these events and minimize subsequent risk of relapse.

Role of Parents in Treatment

Though EBTs differ on the centrality of the family's role, the inclusion of family in the treatment of adolescent and childhood EDs is considered essential (Le Grange et al., 2010). By involving the parents in treatment and keeping them informed of their child's progress, family members can become an indispensable resource for recovery and support. On a practical level, parental responsibility and consent are required for their child to engage in any type of medical or psychological treatment for their ED.

Additionally, a patient cannot be viewed in isolation from their family environment. Parents and other family members have a major influence and are an integral part of the child's environment. Parents can assist in monitoring and addressing problematic ED behaviors by altering the home environment (e.g., removing the bathroom scale or mirrors if the patient is excessively body checking). Parents are also primarily responsible for purchasing food and preparing meals, requiring them to have significant involvement in the child's meal planning in treatment (Fairburn, 2008; Le Grange & Lock, 2007). Family members can help the child adhere to a regular eating schedule and introduce avoided foods through their preparation of meals.

While parental involvement is necessary and typically constructive, at times it may also pose a hindrance to treatment progress. Evidence suggests persistent appearance-focused and weight control comments by family members, a critical family environment, and coercive parental control can perpetuate feelings of body dissatisfaction and disordered eating among child and adolescent family members (Haworth-Hoeppner, 2000; Kluck, 2010). Furthermore, parental criticism has been shown to hinder the family's ability to remain in treatment and therefore would need to be addressed in treatment (Eisler et al., 2000; Le Grange et al., 1992). For families exhibiting high levels of parental criticism, research suggests that treatment outcomes improve when sessions are primarily conducted separately with the child and parents rather than conjointly (Eisler et al., 2000; Lock & Le Grange, 2015).

The extent of parental involvement and role in the recovery process varies by the chosen evidence-based approach. FBT requires parents to play a direct and active role in their child's treatment (Le Grange et al., 2010; Lock, 2011). Parents are advised that they may have to miss work or other planned activities in order to regularly attend their child's treatment sessions and that this level of commitment is a requirement of FBT. In the first phase of FBT, parents are asked to assert complete control over their child's eating and food-based decisions (Lock & Le Grange, 2015). Once the severity of the eating disorder has decreased and significant weight gain has occurred the parents gradually relinquish control over eating back to their child while helping them make decisions consistent with recovery (Lock & Le Grange, 2015).

CBT with adult eating disorder populations almost exclusively consists of individual sessions between the patient and therapist. However, when working with children and adolescents, it is necessary to modify the treatment protocol to appropriately involve parents (Fairburn, 2008). The amount and frequency of information that is shared with caregivers vary based on the age, development, and risk of the patient, with the exception of any instance in which the child is in imminent risk or danger (Waller et al., 2007). Unlike FBT, proponents of individual treatment argue that emphasizing parental control over the patient's eating and weight-related behaviors may undermine crucial issues in adolescent development, such as the desire for autonomy and independence from parents (Le Grange et al., 2010). Therefore, the role of parents in CBT can vary depending on the patient's developmental stage and the collaborative decision between the therapist, patient, and parents regarding the best course of action. By facilitating an environment that promotes attitudes and behaviors consistent with what the patient is learning in therapy, parents can support CBT throughout treatment, relapse prevention, and long after therapy has terminated (Waller et al., 2007).

Other Variables Influencing Treatment

Assessment

Conducting a thorough and accurate eating disorder assessment can be challenging, particularly with adolescent patients who are often brought to treatment at the insistence of their parents or family members. Behaviors and other symptoms may be underreported, minimized, or purposefully hidden, in an effort to conceal and maintain the eating disorder. The clinician should make substantial effort to establish rapport with both the adolescent patient and the family in order to achieve a valid assessment (Lock & Le Grange, 2015). Whenever possible, it is beneficial for the clinician to conduct both separate and joint assessments with the patient and their parents (Fairburn, 2008).

Comorbidity

Adolescents with EDs have high rates of comorbidity with other psychological disorders, including mood disorders, social anxiety, obsessive-compulsive disorder, substance use disorders, and childhood behavioral disorders. This additional psychopathology is likely to complicate treatment adherence and outcome (Grilo, White, & Masheb, 2009; Herzog, Nussbaum, & Marmor, 1996; Swanson, Crow, & Le Grange, 2011). Lock and Le Grange (2015) note that in many patients, it can be difficult to distinguish between premorbid symptomology and impairment directly resulting from the disordered eating behaviors (e.g., mood dysregulation as a result of starvation). Secondary impairment may be passively resolved after ED symptoms have diminished (Le Grange & Lock, 2007). However, the therapist should take care to address the patient's distress due to a comorbid illness, particularly if symptoms are impacting the patient's ability to engage in treatment.

Demographics

Historically, epidemiological research has suggested that EDs were most prevalent among high socioeconomic status, White female adolescents. However, recent findings indicate that maladaptive weight control behaviors and eating disturbances also occur among male adolescents and racial minority groups (Walcott, Pratt, & Patel, 2003). While eating disorder diagnostic criteria remain the same regardless of gender or race, it is important to note that clinical presentations may vary based on demographic variables. For example, male adolescent patients may be less likely to endorse preoccupation with shape and weight control and report more concern about their upper body and muscularity compared to their female counterparts (Walcott, Pratt, & Patel, 2003). Additionally, unique risk factors, assessment considerations, and treatment barriers exist among ethnic minority groups. Kempa and Thomas (2000) provide a review of culturally sensitive considerations for assessment and treatment of EDs among minority populations. For example, the authors noted that some cultural groups might view mental health concerns as shameful or stigmatizing. These individuals are more likely to report somatic complaints when presenting for treatment, and it may be premature to immediately delve into the psychological aspects of therapy before first addressing the bodily complaints and providing psychoeducational treatment (Kempa & Thomas, 2000).

Medication

Current research indicates that existing pharmacological interventions are largely ineffective in treating both the medical consequences and psychological symptoms of AN (e.g., Lock, 2010). There is some evidence for select pharmacotherapy for treating BN and BED. Specifically, selective serotonin reuptake inhibitors (SSRIs), such as fluoxetine and sertraline, have shown some effectiveness in reducing the frequency of binge eating behavior when compared to a placebo (McElroy et al., 2012). Additionally, anticonvulsant medications, such as topiramate, have shown some effectiveness in suppressing appetite and subsequently reducing binge eating frequency among patients with BN and BED (Marazziti et al., 2012). However, the long-term effectiveness of these medications for binge eating is unknown (Iacovino et al., 2012). Research suggests that medication does not yield better treatment outcomes for EDs compared to psychotherapy alone nor does it increase effectiveness of psychotherapy when used in conjunction (Hay & Claudino, 2010; Iacovino et al., 2012).

Low Weight Status and Starvation

Patients who have persistently maintained a low weight status may be especially resistant to engaging in treatment. These patients may have limited motivation to change their eating behaviors because their underweight status is consistent with their overevaluation of thinness and is often perceived as a measure of their self-control and will power (Fairburn, 2008; Vitousek, Watson, & Wilson, 1998). Furthermore, the psychological and physical effects of prolonged starvation will likely impact the patient's ability to remain focused and engaged in treatment. EBTs attempt to mitigate starvation effects and resistance to refeeding through motivational strategies, psychoeducation, and a heavy emphasis on increased food intake during the early stages of treatment.

Patients of very low weight status may eventually become too ill to be safely treated outside of an inpatient hospital setting. Financial cost and logistical issues alone may become barriers to continuing treatment (Le Grange & Lock, 2007). Additionally, a hospitalization during treatment may cause significant demoralization for the family, therapist, and patient (Gowers et al., 2000). If immediate hospitalization is necessary, Lock and Le Grange (2007) suggest framing the abrupt hospitalization as further evidence of the severity of the disorder, underscoring the importance of continued engagement in treatment.

Obesity

While most children with obesity do not have eating disorders, studies suggest children with binge eating disorder or subclinical episodic overeating are at significant risk for obesity and associated health effects in later adolescence and adulthood (Decaluwé & Braet, 2003; Neumark-Sztainer et al., 2006). For an adolescent with obesity and binge eating disorder, the patient and caregivers may wrongly label weight loss as the primary treatment goal rather than addressing the disordered eating behaviors (Thompson & Smolak, 2001). Dietary restriction and preoccupation with weight loss have been shown to maintain and exacerbate weight gain among over-weight or obese populations (Stice, 2002). Therefore, it is important for the clinician to be cognizant of any ongoing or underreported weight loss behaviors that may have adverse effects on treatment progress. In many cases, the patient will naturally lose weight over time in treatment due to the reduction of binge eating and the restoration of regular eating (Fairburn, 2008).

Other focuses of adolescent obesity treatment involve family-based interventions that include behavioral strategies and modifications to dietary and physical activities (Altman & Wilfley, 2014). Family involvement and support is considered essential. Parents can directly modify the food environment at home and can be extremely important models of healthy lifestyle choices. Their importance in their child's obesity treatment is reflected in the finding that "parent-only" behavioral treatments for obesity have yielded similarly successful treatment outcomes as family-based therapy that involves both the child and parents (Altman & Wilfley, 2014).

Suicide and Self-Injurious Behavior

Rates of suicidal ideation and attempts are significantly elevated in adolescents with eating disorders, including those with subthreshold symptoms (Sansone & Levitt, 2002; Swanson, Crow, & Le Grange, 2011). Due to its high prevalence, it is critical for the therapist to conduct comprehensive risk assessments throughout treatment. If a patient becomes actively suicidal, it is necessary to cease treatment focused on disordered eating until the crisis has been managed and suicidal ideation has diminished.

Sansone and Levitt (2002) have found similarly high prevalence rates of self-injurious, but nonlethal, behavior (e.g., cutting or burning oneself, skin picking) among adolescents with EDs. These behaviors are often extremely upsetting to the parents and can disrupt the focus and engagement in treatment sessions. If persistent self-injury significantly interrupts treatment, the therapist may need to utilize additional evidence-based approaches to address these behaviors, such as dialectical behavioral therapy (DBT; Linehan, 1987; Ougrin et al., 2015), before continuing treatment of the eating disorder.

Conclusion

Eating disorders are complex and often resistant to treatment. However, evidence-based treatments exist. Current findings suggest FBT is the best-supported treatment for adolescent AN and CBT for adolescent BN and subclinical eating disorders. While these treatment approaches stem from differing theoretical underpinnings, they share common evidence-based components and procedures, including an emphasis on early weight restoration and stabilization, psychoeducation, self-monitoring, and parental and family involvement. It is also important to consider factors that may complicate eating disorder treatment, such as comorbid psychological and medical problems. As eating disorders become increasingly prevalent in adolescent and child populations, continued exploration of evidence-based treatments for eating problems becomes essential.

Useful Resources

Articles

- Myra Altman and Denise E. Wilfley (2014). Evidence update on the treatment of overweight and obesity in children and adolescents. *Journal of Clinical Child & Adolescent Psychology, 4*, 521–537
- Maureen L. Kempa and Anita Jones Thomas (2000). Culturally sensitive assessment and treatment of eating disorders. *Eating Disorders, 8*, 17–30
- James Lock and Daniel Le Grange (2005). Family-based treatment of eating disorders. *International Journal of Eating Disorders, 37*, S64–S67

Books

- *Cognitive Behavior Therapy and Eating Disorders* by Christopher G. Fairburn, Guilford Press, 2008
- *Doing Dialectical Behavior Therapy: A Practical Guide* by Kelly Koerner, Guildford Press, 2012
- *Treating Bulimia in Adolescents: A Family-Based Approach*, by James Lock and Daniel Le Grange, Guilford Press, 2007.
- *Treatment Manual for Anorexia Nervosa: A Family-Based Approach* by James Lock and Daniel Le Grange, Guildford Press, 2015

References

Altman, M., & Wilfley, D. E. (2014). Evidence update on the treatment of overweight and obesity in children and adolescents. *Journal of Clinical Child & Adolescent Psychology*, *4*, 521–537.

American Psychiatric Association. (2013). *Diagnostic and statistical manual of mental disorders.* 5th edn. Washington, DC: American Psychiatric Association.

Beck, A. T. (1967). *Depression: Clinical, experimental, and theoretical aspects.* New York: Hoeber. Republished as *Depression: Causes and treatment.* Philadelphia: University of Pennsylvania Press.

Bo-Linn, G. W., Santa Ana, C. A., Morawski, S. G., & Fordtran, J. S. (1983). Purging and calorie absorption in bulimic patients and normal women. *Annals of Internal Medicine*, *99*, 14–17.

Boscolo, L., Cecchin, G., Hoffman, L., & Penn, P. (1987). *Milan systemic family therapy: Theoretical and practical aspects.* New York: Basic Books.

Boutelle, K., Neumark-Sztainer, D., Story, M., & Resnick, M. (2002). Weight control behaviors among obese, overweight, and nonoverweight adolescents. *Journal of Pediatric Psychology*, *27*, 531–540.

Brownley, K. A., Berkman, N. D., Sedway, J. A., Lohr, K. N., & Bulik, C. M. (2007). Binge eating disorder treatment: A systematic review of randomized controlled trials. *International Journal of Eating Disorders*, *40*, 337–348.

Cassin, S. E., & von Ranson, K. M. (2005). Personality and eating disorders: A decade in review. *Clinical Psychology Review*, *25*, 895–916.

Centers for Disease Control and Prevention (CDC). (2015). *About child and teen BMI.* www.cdc.gov/healthyweight/assessing/bmi/childrens_bmi/about_childrens_bmi.html

Chen, E. Y., Matthews, L., Allen, C., Kuo, J. R., & Linehan, M. M. (2008). Dialectical behavior therapy for clients with binge-eating disorder or bulimia nervosa and borderline personality disorder. *International Journal of Eating Disorders*, *41*, 505–512.

Couturier, J., Kimber, M., & Szatmari, P. (2013). Efficacy of family-based treatment for adolescents with eating disorders: A systemic review and meta-analysis. *International Journal of Eating Disorders*, *46*, 3–11.

Dalle Grave, R., Calugi, S., Doll, H. A., & Fairburn, C. G. (2014). Enhanced cognitive behaviour therapy for adolescents with anorexia nervosa: An alternative to family therapy? *Behaviour Research*, *51*, R9–R12.

Dalle Grave, R., Calugi, S., Sartirana, M., & Fairburn, C. G. (2015). Transdiagnostic cognitive behaviour therapy for adolescents with an eating disorder who are not underweight. *Behaviour Research and Therapy*, *73*, 79–82.

Decaluwé, V., & Braet, C. (2003). Prevalence of binge-eating disorder in obese children and adolescents seeking weight-loss treatment. *International Journal of Obesity*, *27*, 404–409.

Doyle, P. M., Le Grange, D., Loeb, K., Doyle, A. C., & Crosby, R. D. (2010). Early response to family-based treatment for adolescent anorexia nervosa. *International Journal of Eating Disorders*, *43*, 659–662.

Eddy, K. T., Doyle, A. C., Hoste, R. R., Herzog, D. B., & Le Grange, D. (2008). Eating disorder not otherwise specified in adolescents. *Journal of the American Academy of Child & Adolescent Psychiatry*, *47*, 156–164.

Eddy, K. T., Murray, B. B., & Le Grange, D. (2015). Eating and feeding disorders. In Dulcan, M. K. (ed.), *Dulcan's textbook of child and adolescent psychiatry* (pp. 435–460). Arlington, VA: American Psychiatric Association Publishing.

Eisler, I., Dare, C., Hodes, M., Russell, G., Dodge, E., & Le Grange, D. (2000). Family therapy for adolescent anorexia nervosa: The results of a controlled comparison of two family interventions. *Journal of Child Psychology and Psychiatry*, *41*, 727–736.

Fairburn, C. G. (2008). *Cognitive behavior therapy and eating disorders*. New York: Guilford Press.

Fairburn, C. G., Agras, W. S., Walsh, B. T., Wilson, G. T., & Stice, E. (2004). Prediction of outcome in bulimia nervosa by early change in treatment. *American Journal of Psychiatry*, *161*, 2322–2324.

Fairburn, C. G., Cooper, Z., & Shafran, R. (2003). Cognitive behaviour therapy for eating disorders: A "transdiagnostic" theory and treatment. *Behaviour Research and Therapy*, *41*, 509–528.

Fairburn, C. G., Cooper, Z., Shafran, R., & Wilson, T.G. (2008). Eating disorders: A transdiagnostic protocol. In D. H. Barlow (ed.), *Clinical handbook of psychological disorders: A step-by-step treatment manual*. 4th edn (pp. 578–614). New York: Guilford Press.

Favaro, A., Caregaro, L., Tenconi, E., Bosello, R., & Santonastaso, P. (2009). Time trends in age at onset of anorexia nervosa and bulimia nervosa. *The Journal of Clinical Psychiatry*, *70*, 1715–1721.

Geist, R., Heinmaa, M., Stephens, D., Davis, R., & Katzman, D. K. (2000). Comparison of family therapy and family group psychoeducation in adolescents with anorexia nervosa. *The Canadian Journal of Psychiatry*, *45*, 173–178.

Geller, J., Brown, K. E., Zaitsoff, S. L., Menna, R., Bates, M. E., & Dunn, E. C. (2008). Assessing readiness for change in adolescents with eating disorders. *Psychological Assessment*, *20*, 63–69.

Geller, J., Cockell, S. J., & Drab, D. L. (2001). Assessing readiness for change in the eating disorders: The psychometric properties of the readiness and motivation interview. *Psychological Assessment*, *13*, 189–198.

Geller, J., Drab-Hudson, D. L., Whisenhunt, B. L., & Srikameswaran, S. (2004). Readiness to change dietary restriction predicts outcomes in the eating disorders. *Eating Disorders*, *12*, 209–224.

Golden, M. H. N. (1994). Is complete catch-up possible for stunted malnourished children? *European Journal of Clinical Nutrition*, *48*, 58–71.

Gowers, S. G., Weetman, J., Shore, A., Hossain, F., & Elvins, R. (2000). Impact of hospitalisation on the outcome of adolescent anorexia nervosa. *The British Journal of Psychiatry*, *176*, 138–141.

Grilo, C. M., Masheb, R. M., & Crosby, R. D. (2012). Predictors and moderators of response to cognitive behavioral therapy and medication for the treatment of binge eating disorder. *Journal of Consulting and Clinical Psychology, 80,* 897–906.

Grilo, C. M., White, M. A., & Masheb, R. M. (2009). DSM-IV psychiatric disorder comorbidity and its correlates in binge eating disorder. *International Journal of Eating Disorders, 42,* 228–234.

Haworth-Hoeppner, S. (2000). The critical shapes of body image: The role of culture and family in the production of eating disorders. *Journal of Marriage and Family, 62,* 212–227.

Hay, P. (2013). A systemic review of evidence for psychological treatments in eating disorders: 2005–2012. *International Journal of Eating Disorders, 46,* 462–469.

Hay, P., & Claudino, A. M. (2010). Evidence-based treatment for the eating disorders. In W. Stewart Agras (ed.),*The Oxford handbook of eating disorders* (pp. 453–479). Oxford: Oxford University Press.

Herzog, D. B., Dorer, D. J., Keel, P. K., Selwyn, S. E., Ekeblad, E. R., Flores, A. T., ... & Keller, M. B. (1999). Recovery and relapse in anorexia and bulimia nervosa: A 7.5-year follow-up study. *Journal of the American Academy of Child & Adolescent Psychiatry, 38,* 829–837.

Herzog, D. B., Nussbaum, K. M., & Marmor, A. K. (1996). Comorbidity and outcome in eating disorders. *Psychiatric Clinics of North America, 19,* 843–859.

Hudson, J. I., Hiripi, E., Pope, H. G., & Kessler, R. C. (2007). The prevalence and correlates of eating disorders in the National Comorbidity Survey Replication. *Biological Psychiatry, 61,* 348–358.

Iacovino, J. M., Gredysa, D. M., Altman, M., & Wilfley, D. E. (2012). Psychological treatments for binge eating disorder. *Current Psychiatry Reports, 14,* 432–446.

Kempa, M. L., & Thomas, A. J. (2000). Culturally sensitive assessment and treatment of eating disorders. *Eating Disorders, 8,* 17–30.

Kluck, A. S. (2010). Family influence on disordered eating: The role of body image dissatisfaction. *Body Image, 7,* 8–14.

Koerner, K. (2012). *Doing dialectical behavior therapy: A practical guide.* New York: Guildford Press.

Koerner, K., & Linehan, M. M. (2000). Research on dialectical behavior therapy for patients with borderline personality disorder. *Psychiatric Clinics, 23*(1), 151–167.

Kopec-Schrader, E. M., Marden, K., Rey, J. M., Touyz, S. W., & Beumont, P. J. V. (1993). Parental evaluation of treatment outcome and satisfaction with an inpatient program for eating disorders. *Australian and New Zealand Journal of Psychiatry, 27,* 264–269.

Kröger, C., Schweiger, U., Sipos, V., Kliem, S., Arnold, R., Schunert, T., & Reinecker, H. (2010). Dialectical behaviour therapy and an added cognitive behavioural treatment module for eating disorders in women with borderline personality disorder and anorexia nervosa or bulimia nervosa who failed to respond to previous treatments. An open trial with a 15-month follow-up. *Journal of Behavior Therapy and Experimental Psychiatry, 41,* 381–388.

Le Grange, D., Doyle, P., Crosby, R. D., & Chen, E. (2008). Early response to treatment in adolescent bulimia nervosa. *International Journal of Eating Disorders, 41,* 755–757.

Le Grange, D., Eisler, I., Dare, C., & Russell, G. F. (1992). Evaluation of family treatments in adolescent anorexia nervosa: A pilot study. *International Journal of Eating Disorders, 12,* 347–357.

Le Grange, D., & Lock, J. (2007). *Treating bulimia in adolescents: A family-based approach.* New York: Guilford Press.

Le Grange, D., Lock, J., Loeb, K., & Nicholls, D. (2010). Academy for eating disorders position paper: The role of the family in eating disorders. *International Journal of Eating Disorders*, *43*, 1–5.

Le Grange, D., & Loeb, K. L. (2007). Early identification and treatment of eating disorders: Prodome to syndrome. *Early Intervention in Psychiatry*, *1*, 27–39.

Lewinsohn, P. M., Striegel-Moore, R. H., & Seeley, J. R. (2000). Epidemiology and natural course of eating disorders in young women from adolescence to young adulthood. *Journal of the American Academy of Child & Adolescent Psychiatry*, *39*, 1284–1292.

Linehan, M. M. (1987). Dialectical behavioral therapy: A cognitive behavioral approach to parasuicide. *Journal of Personality Disorders*, *1*, 328–333.

Lock, J. (2010). Treatment of adolescent eating disorders: Progress and challenges. *Minerva Psichiatrica*, *51*, 207–216.

Lock, J. (2011). Evaluation of family treatment models for eating disorders. *Current Opinion in Psychiatry*, *24*, 274–279.

Lock, J. (2015). An update on evidence-based psychosocial treatments for eating disorders in children and adolescents. *Journal of Clinical Child & Adolescent Psychology*, *44*, 707–721.

Lock, J., & Le Grange, D. (2015). *Treatment manual for anorexia nervosa: A family-based approach*. New York: Guilford Publications.

Löwe, B., Zipfel, S., Buchholz, C., Dupont, Y., Reas, D. L., & Herzog, W. (2001). Long-term outcome of anorexia nervosa in a prospective 21-year follow-up study. *Psychological Medicine*, *31*, 881–890.

Lynch, T. R., Trost, W. T., Salsman, N., & Linehan, M. M. (2007). Dialectical behavior therapy for borderline personality disorder. *Annual Review of Clinical Psychology*, *3*, 181–205.

Marazziti, D., Corsi, M., Baroni, S., Consoli, G., & Catena-Dell'Osso, M. (2012). Latest advancements in the pharmacological treatment of binge eating disorder. *European Review of Medical and Pharmacological Sciences*, *16*, 2102–2107.

McElroy, S. L., Guerdjikova, A. I., Mori, N., & O'Melia, A. M. (2012). Current pharmacotherapy options for bulimia nervosa and binge eating disorder. *Expert Opinion on Pharmacotherapy*, *13*, 2015–2026.

Modan-Moses, D., Yaroslavsky, A., Novikov, I., Segev, S., Toledano, A., Miterany, E., & Stein, D. (2003). Stunting of growth as a major feature of anorexia nervosa in male adolescents. *Pediatrics*, *111*, 270–276.

Morgan, H. G., Purgold, J., & Welbourne, J. (1983). Management and outcome in anorexia nervosa: A standardized prognostic study. *The British Journal of Psychiatry*, *143*, 282–287.

Neumark-Sztainer, D., Story, M., Hannan, P. J., Perry, C. L., & Irving, L. M. (2002). Weight-related concerns and behaviors among overweight and nonoverweight adolescents: Implications for preventing weight-related disorders. *Archives of Pediatrics & Adolescent Medicine*, *156*, 171–178.

Neumark-Sztainer, D., Wall, M., Guo, J., Story, M., Haines, J., & Eisenberg, M. (2006). Obesity, disordered eating, and eating disorders in a longitudinal study of adolescents: How do dieters fare 5 years later? *Journal of the American Dietetic Association*, *106*, 559–568.

Ougrin, D., Tranah, T., Stahl, D., Moran, P., & Asarnow, J. R. (2015). Therapeutic interventions for suicide attempts and self-harm in adolescents: Systematic review and meta-analysis. *Journal of the American Academy of Child & Adolescent Psychiatry*, *54*, 97–107.

Panos, P. T., Jackson, J. W., Hasan, O., & Panos, A. (2014). Meta-analysis and systematic review assessing the efficacy of dialectical behavior therapy (DBT). *Research on Social Work Practice*, *24*, 213–223.

Polivy, J. (1996). Psychological consequences of food restriction. *Journal of the American Dietetic Association*, *96*, 589–592.

Polivy, J., & Herman, C. P. (2002). Causes of eating disorders. *Annual Review of Psychology*, *53*, 187–213.

Rikani, A. A., Choudhry, Z., Choudhry, A. M., Ikram, H., Asghar, M. W., Kajal, D., ... & Mobassarah, N. J. (2013). A critique of the literature on etiology of eating disorders. *Annals of Neurosciences*, *20*, 157–161.

Rockert, W., Kaplan, A. S., & Olmsted, M. P. (2007). Eating disorder not otherwise specified: The view from a tertiary care treatment center. *International Journal of Eating Disorders*, *40*, S99–S103.

Salbach-Andrae, H., Bohnekamp, I., Pfeiffer, E., Lehmkuhl, U., & Miller, A. L. (2008). Dialectical behavior therapy of anorexia and bulimia nervosa among adolescents: A case series. *Cognitive and Behavioral Practice*, *15*, 415–425.

Sansone, R. A., & Levitt, J. L. (2002). Self-harm behaviors among those with eating disorders: An overview. *Eating Disorders*, *10*, 205–213.

Schapman-Williams, A. M., Lock, J., & Couturier, J. (2006). Cognitive-behavioral therapy for adolescents with binge eating syndromes: A case series. *International Journal of Eating Disorders*, *39*, 252–255.

Schmidt, U., Lee, S., Perkins, S., Eisler, I., Treasure, J., Beecham, J., ... & Johnson-Sabine, E. (2008). Do adolescents with eating disorder not otherwise specified or full-syndrome bulimia nervosa differ in clinical severity, comorbidity, risk factors, treatment outcome or cost? *International Journal of Eating Disorders*, *41*, 498–504.

Schocken, D. D., Holloway, J. D., & Powers, P. S. (1989). Weight loss and the heart: Effects of anorexia nervosa and starvation. *Archives of Internal Medicine*, *149*, 877–881.

Shomaker, L. B., Tanofsky-Kraff, M., Elliott, C., Wolkoff, L. E., Columbo, K. M., Ranzenhofer, L. M., ... & Yanovski, J. A. (2010). Salience of loss of control for pediatric binge episodes: Does size really matter? *International Journal of Eating Disorders*, *43*, 707–716.

Steiger, H., Lehoux, P. M., & Gauvin, L. (1999). Impulsivity, dietary control and the urge to binge in bulimic syndromes. *International Journal of Eating Disorders*, *26*, 261–274.

Steinhausen, H. C. (2002). The outcome of anorexia nervosa in the 20th century. *American Journal of Psychiatry*, *159*, 1284–1293.

Stice, E. (2002). Risk and maintenance factors for eating pathology: A meta-analytic review. *Psychological Bulletin*, *128*, 825–848.

Stice, E., Gau, J. M., Rohde, P., & Shaw, H. (2017). Risk factors that predict future onset of each DSM-5 eating disorder: Predictive specificity in high-risk adolescent females. *Journal of Abnormal Psychology*, *126*, 38–51.

Strober, M., Freeman, R., & Morrell, W. (1997). The long-term course of severe anorexia nervosa in adolescents: Survival analysis of recovery, relapse, and outcome predictors over 10–15 years in a prospective study. *International Journal of Eating Disorders*, *22*, 339–360.

Swanson, S. A., Crow, S. J., & Le Grange, D. (2011). Prevalence and correlates of eating disorders in adolescents: Results from the National Comorbidity Survey Replication–Adolescent Supplement. *Archives of General Psychiatry*, *68*, 714–723.

Thompson, J. K., & Smolak, L. (eds.) (2001). *Body image, eating disorders, and obesity in youth: Assessment, prevention, and treatment*. Washington, DC: American Psychological Association.

Turner, H., Bryant-Waugh, R., & Peveler, R. (2010). The clinical features of EDNOS: Relationship to mood, health status and general functioning. *Eating Behaviors, 11*, 127–130.

Turner, J., Batik, M., Palmer, L. J., Forbes, D., & McDermott, B. M. (2000). Detection and importance of laxative use in adolescents with anorexia nervosa. *Journal of the American Academy of Child & Adolescent Psychiatry, 39*, 378–385.

Vitousek, K. M., Watson, S., & Wilson, T. G. (1998). Enhancing motivation for change in treatment-resistant eating disorders. *Clinical Psychology Review, 4*, 391–420.

Walcott, D. D., Pratt, H. D., & Patel, D. R. (2003). Adolescents and eating disorders: Gender, racial, ethnic, sociocultural, and socioeconomic issues. *Journal of Adolescent Research, 18*, 223–243.

Waller, G., Cordery, H., Corstorphine, E., Hinrichsen, H., Lawson, R., Mountford, V., & Russell, K. (2007). *Cognitive behavioral therapy for eating disorders: A comprehensive treatment guide*. Cambridge: Cambridge University Press.

White, M., & Epston, D. (1990). *Narrative means to therapeutic ends*. New York: W.W. Norton & Company.

Wilfley, D. E., Kolko, R. P., & Kass, A. E. (2011). Cognitive-behavioral therapy for weight management and eating disorders in children and adolescents. *Child and Adolescent Psychiatric Clinics of North America, 20*, 271–285.

Wilson, G. T. (2005). Psychological treatment of eating disorders. *Annual Review of Clinical Psychology, 1*, 439–465.

Wilson, G. T., & Sysko, R. (2006). Cognitive-behavioural therapy for adolescents with bulimia nervosa. *European Eating Disorders Review, 14*, 8–16.

Zanarini, M. C., Reichman, C. A., Frankenburg, F. R., Reich, D. B., & Fitzmaurice, G. (2010). The course of eating disorders in patients with borderline personality disorder: A 10-year follow-up study. *International Journal of Eating Disorders, 43*, 226–232.

Zimmerman, M., Rothschild, L., & Chelminski, I. (2005). The prevalence of DSM-IV personality disorders in psychiatric outpatients. *American Journal of Psychiatry, 162*, 1911–1918.

Zittel Conklin, C., & Westen, D. (2005). Borderline personality disorder in clinical practice. *American Journal of Psychiatry, 162*, 867–875.

15

Toileting

Michael I. Axelrod

This chapter discusses the evidence-based treatment of nocturnal enuresis (NE) and functional encopresis (FE), elimination disorders common in childhood and adolescence. Although physiological features highlight each disorder, a combination of medical, psychological, and behavioral research supports a biobehavioral approach to assessment, conceptualization, and intervention. The purpose of this chapter is to provide an evidence-based perspective on the treatment of elimination disorders.

The *Diagnostic and Statistical Manual of Mental Disorders*, 5th edition (DSM-5; American Psychiatric Association [APA], 2013) defines enuresis as repeated voiding of urine, accidental or on purpose, into clothing or the bed, at least twice a week for three consecutive months, in children older than five years of age. The voiding of urine cannot be a result of the physiological effects of a substance or another medical condition (e.g., diabetes, urinary tract infection). Enuresis is presented either nocturnally, diurnally, or mixed, although NE is by far the most frequent type (Friman, 2008). The DSM-5 also identifies two courses: primary and secondary. Primary enuresis includes those individuals who never established urinary continence. Secondary enuresis develops only after urinary continence has been established and typically emerges between five and eight years. According to the DSM-5, symptoms of enuresis spontaneously remit in approximately 5–10% of cases suggesting some children achieve nighttime continence without ever receiving treatment.

NE is reportedly one of the most frequent referrals in primary care pediatrics and prevalence data suggest it is a common and potentially enduring problem (Friman, 2008). For example, bedwetting has been reported in approximately 33% of five-year-old children, 25% of six-year-old boys and 17% of six-year-old girls, 10% of seven-year-old children, and 7% of 11-year-olds (Buckley, Lapitan, & the Epidemiology Committee of the Fourth International Consultation on Incontinence, 2010; Byrd et al., 1996; Friman, 2008). Furthermore, bedwetting at subclinical levels (e.g., several times per month) has been reported in as many as 20% of first-graders (Butler & Heron, 2008). Although not common, adolescent bedwetting does occur in approximately 1–3% of the population (see Axelrod, Tornehl, & Fontanini-Axelrod, 2014).

FE involves the repeated passage of feces, voluntary or involuntary, in inappropriate places (e.g., clothing) at least once a month over at least three consecutive months for children with a chronological age of at least four years (APA, 2013). The passage of feces cannot be as a result of the physiological effects of a substance (e.g., laxative) or a general medication condition, except when the condition involves constipation. The DSM-5 specifies two subtypes: encopresis *with constipation and incontinence overflow* (called retentive encopresis [RE]) often involves feces that are poorly formed, with accidents occurring most often during the day (Axelrod, Tornehl, Simpson, Lamoureux, & Fontanini-Axelrod, 2015). Encopresis *without constipation and incontinence overflow* (called nonretentive encopresis) often involves fecal matter that is normally formed (e.g., tubular) and left in conspicuous locations (Axelrod et al., 2015). RE makes up the overwhelming majority of cases and most of the research on encopresis involves children with a history of constipation (Christopherson & Friman, 2010). Accordingly, the majority of this chapter related to encopresis will focus on RE.

RE is diagnosed in 1.5–7.5% of all children and adolescents (Axelrod et al., 2015). Encopresis and constipation make up approximately 5% of all primary care pediatric referrals, 4% of all pediatric psychiatry referrals, and 30% of all pediatric gastroenterology referrals (see Axelrod et al., 2015; Christopherson & Friman, 2010). Up to one-third of school-aged children experience constipation during a given year, with 35% of girls and 55% of boys who have constipation having problems associated with encopresis (McGrath, Mellon, & Murphy, 2000). Unlike NE, which has high spontaneous remission rates, problems with constipation and FE often persist into adolescence despite attempts at treatment (Axelrod et al., 2015). In fact, almost two-thirds of children treated for constipation continue to experience problems into adolescence (Staiano et al., 1994; Sutphen et al., 1995).

Etiology and Theoretical Underpinnings of Treatment

There are several explanations as to NE's etiology. The most commonly cited etiologies are briefly discussed below. However, the reader should keep in mind that multiple etiologies are likely responsible for NE and that combinations of causal variables will likely differ from child to child. In addition, the bladder clearly plays a role in NE and it is important to understand the physiology of the bladder in order to speak with some authority on NE. However, such a discussion is beyond the scope of this chapter and readers are referred to other sources for easy-to-understand explanations (e.g., Ferrara et al., 2008; Friman & Jones, 1998).

NE appears to run in families. For example, von Gontard, Heron, and Joinson (2011), examining a very large sample of children and parents, found that a seven-year-old child was 3.63 times more likely to be diagnosed with NE when a maternal history of NE was present and 1.85 times more likely to be diagnosed when a paternal history of NE was present. Maturational delays might be partially responsible for NE in children as there is a noted correlation between NE and bone growth, build, and the development of secondary sex characteristics (Fergusson, Horwood, & Sannon, 1986). Friman (2008) noted there are many possible pathophysiological explanations for NE including urinary tract infections (UTIs), diabetes, and bladder instability. There also exists a relationship between NE and functional bladder capacity (Troup & Hodson, 1971). Finally, there is growing evidence that slowness to arouse from sleep may increase the probability that a child might experience problems with NE (see Yeung, Diao, & Sreedhar, 2008).

Regarding encopresis, achieving successful outcomes requires treatment that initially targets functional constipation or constipation that is not directly related to an underlying physiological and anatomic condition (termed organic constipation, which is most often associated with hypothyroidism, spinal cord abnormalities, cerebral palsy, and motility disorders such as Hirschsprung's disease) (Axelrod et al., 2015). Understanding functional constipation requires some knowledge of the alimentary tract, although a thorough discussion of the relevant physiology is beyond the scope of this chapter and readers are referred to other sources for additional detail (e.g., Christopherson & Friman, 2010). Briefly, fecal impaction is a consequence of insufficient intake of fluids and fiber, reduced colonic motility, and increased time between bowel movements resulting in dry or hard stools. When passed, these stools are uncomfortable and often painful for the child. Children experiencing painful bowel movements are likely to avoid having future bowel movements or refuse to use the toilet (Friman, 2008). This learned resistance or avoidance is a central feature of why RE persists in many children. Furthermore, not being able to voluntarily control the external sphincter during defecation will lead to uncontrollable passage of feces (Axelrod et al., 2015). This is likely why children with RE report losing the urge to defecate over time.

Steps to Encouraging Successful Toilet Training

It is common for parents to struggle with toilet training. This Side-Bar Box includes some general steps to encourage successful toilet training.

1. Assess for physical readiness signs (e.g., child recognizes urge, child is dry for two- to three-hour periods during the day, child has adequate motor skills to pull down pants).
2. Assess for cognitive readiness signs (e.g., child understands urges are followed by trips to the bathroom).
3. Assess for behavioral readiness signs (e.g., child is able to follow instructions).

4. Parent can act as a model for child (e.g., sits on toilet, washes hands).
5. Set out "potty chair" so child can become familiar with the chair and accustomed to sitting on the chair (e.g., child might watch TV or read while sitting on the chair).
6. Increase fluid intake. The child will have many more opportunities to practice appropriate toileting skills if her bladder is kept full.
7. Practice appropriate toileting behavior even when the child does not have to use the toilet. State to the child, "it's time to use the potty," and guide him to the potty chair. Include instruction and practice in appropriate hygiene tasks (e.g., wiping, washing hands).
8. Transition the child from diapers to underwear.
9. Schedule brief (e.g., one to two minutes) toilet sits across the day. Take advantage of knowing when the child is most likely to have a bowel movement by requiring a toilet sit at those times. The parent might move to a dense schedule (i.e., schedule sits more frequently across the day) should accidents occur.
10. Develop a reward system that delivers reinforcers (e.g., social attention, tangible, edible, activity) contingent on appropriate toileting behavior.
11. Consider using an overcorrection procedure when the child has an accident. Have the child demonstrate the steps of using the toilet with a doll first and then practice the steps themselves following an accident. This strategy, however, can generate resistance and upset in children and parents might be tempted to use overcorrection punitively.

Notes: (a) empirical, peer-reviewed research comparing different toilet training approaches is sparse; (b) despite limited empirical research, current toilet training guidelines in North America recommend a child-centered approach that begins only when the child expresses interest in using the toilet; and (c) Azrin and Foxx's (1974) approach using principles of applied behavior analysis has demonstrated effectiveness for individuals with developmental and intellectual disabilities (see Kiddoo et al., 2006).

Brief Overview of Evidence-Based Treatments

Urine Alarm for Nocturnal Enuresis

There is consensus in the literature that the urine alarm is the most effective treatment for NE (see Friman, 2008; Invie & Axelrod, 2011). For example, Shepard, Poler, and Grabman (2016), in their exhaustive review of the literature, found the urine alarm to be a well-established treatment using intervention review criteria provided by Southam-Gerow and Prinstein (2014) for the *Journal of Clinical Child &*

Adolescent Psychology. Glazener, Evans, and Peto (2005), examining 53 studies involving over 2,800 children, found the urine alarm was superior to no treatment at reducing the number of wet nights and was more effective than medication over the entire course of treatment. Overall, controlled clinical evaluations have found that the urine alarm's success rate (defined as complete cessation of bedwetting) is between 65% and 75% after 5–12 weeks of treatment (Friman, 2008). Furthermore, the urine alarm has produced the most successful long-term follow-up outcomes (i.e., lowest relapse rates) when compared with other treatments including medication (Ahmed et al., 2013; Kiddoo, 2012).

The urine alarm is a moisture sensitive device triggered when a small-voltage electrical circuit becomes closed when wet. Most urine alarms are either placed under the bottom bedsheet (i.e., bed device) or attached to the child's underwear or pajamas. The bed device involves a thin cloth placed between two thin aluminum sheets. Urine collects in the cloth after passing through perforations in the top aluminum sheet, closing the circuit and setting off the alarm. The pajama device uses a small alligator-like clip attached to the child's underwear or pajamas. The alarm itself is attached to the child's pajamas or clothes near the shoulder. The device is activated when the underwear or pajamas become wet thus closing the circuit. The activated alarm sets off a signal that theoretically is strong enough to wake the child (e.g., buzzer, light, vibration). Evidence identifying the most effective type of alarm is not currently available (Glazener, Evans, & Peto, 2005). Common urine alarm protocols require the child to wake when alerted, stop urinating at that moment, finish urinating in the toilet, and return to bed. Parents might be alerted before their child when an auditory alarm is used (Friman, 2008). In this case, the parent would wake the child and direct him through the protocol's steps.

The urine alarm's mechanism of action was originally described by Mowrer and Mowrer (1938) using a classical conditioning paradigm. They proposed the alarm as the unconditioned stimulus, bladder distention as the conditioned stimulus, and wakening as the conditioned response, reasoning that wakening becomes a conditioned response to bladder distention through repeated associations with the alarm over time. However, Lovibond (1964) suggested a negative reinforcement paradigm (i.e., operant conditioning) where the alarm is an aversive stimulus the child learns to avoid through increased awareness of urinary demand, sphincter contraction (muscular control that restricts the flow of urine), and wakening. More recently, Friman and Jones (1998) also endorsed an avoidance paradigm by noting that the alarm's aversive qualities strengthen the responses required (i.e., awareness, muscular control, wakening) to avoid it.

Research on parental acceptability (i.e., degree to which parents find the treatment acceptable, effective, and easy to implement) of the urine alarm is limited but positive. For example, Axelrod, Tornehl, and Fontanini-Axelrod (2014) found that parents were highly satisfied with a treatment protocol consisting of the urine alarm plus reward contingent on dry nights. Specifically, parents noted that the treatment proto-col was effective (which the data confirmed) and easy to implement, and that their children were compliant with the treatment's procedures.

Behavioral Intervention for Retentive Encopresis

Shepard, Poler, and Grabman (2016), following their comprehensive review of the research, concluded that a combination of behavioral and medical intervention was most effective for the treatment of RE. Specifically, they found enhanced toilet training, a comprehensive behavioral intervention that targets appropriate toileting behavior, plus medical components was *probably efficacious* according to review criteria provided by Southam-Gerow and Prinstein (2014). Medical intervention typically involved initial disimpaction of the colon and laxative therapy to increase and maintain bowel regularity. Behavioral components generally included scheduled toilet sits and rewards for bowel movements in the toilet. In an earlier review of the literature, McGrath, Mellon, and Murphy (2000) found that comprehensive medical treatments that failed to include behavioral components did not produce favorable outcomes. More recently, Brazzelli and colleagues (2011) found in their review that treatment comprised of behavioral interventions plus laxative therapy was more effective than treatment involving laxative therapy alone.

Several specific studies highlight the value and importance of a comprehensive approach that includes both medical and behavioral treatment. Stark and colleagues (1997) investigated the efficacy of a group-based comprehensive treatment protocol with 59 children who had previously been unsuccessful with standard medical care. They reported that 86% of children stopped having fecal accidents after only nine weeks of treatment. Moreover, these children did not require follow-up for relapse. Borowitz et al. (2002) randomly assigned children with RE to an intensive medical intervention (i.e., colonic disimpaction using enemas and laxative therapy), biofeed-back, or a comprehensive treatment consisting of medical and behavioral interven-tion. All three groups decreased fecal accidents and increased bowel movements in the toilet after three, six, and 12 months of treatment. However, improvement rates were higher for children in the comprehensive treatment group. Furthermore, results were achieved quicker using fewer laxatives. Finally, Ritterband and colleagues (2003) employed a novel approach by combining standard medical care with an internet-based toilet training program involving behavioral components. Children participating in the internet-based treatment had fewer fecal accidents, more bowel movements in the toilet, and more unprompted toilet sits than children receiving the non-internet-based treatment.

Similar to NE, evidence of parental acceptability of a combined RE treatment protocol is limited but positive. Steege and Harper (1989) reported that parents of an 11-year-old boy treated for RE with behavior interventions and laxative therapy found the treatment acceptable and appropriate for the home setting. Axelrod and Fontanini-Axelrod (2012) reported high levels of parental acceptability including ease of procedural implementation for an RE treatment protocol also consisting of behavioral interventions and laxative therapy. It is largely unknown whether positive parental feedback is a function of treatment acceptability, ease of implementation, improvements, or some combination. However, these preliminary findings are encouraging especially given the degree of parental involvement required for successful treatment implementation and complexity of the condition.

Components of Evidence-Based Treatments

Behavioral Intervention for Nocturnal Enuresis

The following section describes a broad range of strategies that have been used alone or in combination with the urine alarm. Two comprehensive treatments for NE, dry-bed training (DBT) and full spectrum home training (FSHT), combine elements of these strategies with the urine alarm. According to Shepard, Ploer, and Grabman's (2016) review of the literature, DBT is a *well-established* treatment and FSHT is *probably efficacious*. However, the degree of evidence varies substantially for each of these components, which should be considered when selecting interventions to augment the urine alarm.

Retention Control Training (RCT). RCT is based on the notion that children with NE have smaller functional bladder capacities than their peers. RCT involves drinking extra fluids (e.g., 16 oz. of water) and then delaying urination for as long as possible in an attempt to expand the functional capacity of the bladder. In theory, lengthening the interval of urinations will increase the volume of daytime urinations and, consequently, the interval between urinary urges at night (Friman, 2008). Progress is assessed by tracking the amount of time the child is able to delay daytime urinations and how much urine is produced. Parents are encouraged to schedule RCT sessions at regular times and at least several hours prior to bedtime. Research on RCT alone or with the urine alarm is sparse. Friman mentioned two studies suggesting RCT was successful in as many as 50% of cases. However, following their review of the literature, the National Clinical Guideline Centre (2010) stated that RCT or other strategies requiring the child to withhold urination during the day do not lead to reductions in the frequency of bedwetting when implemented by themselves. They also noted that it is difficult to determine the relative effectiveness of RCT when used as part of a larger treatment package. More recently, Shepard, Poler, and Grabman (2016) concluded in their review of the literature that RCT fails to add beneficial effects to the urine alarm.

Lifting. Traditionally, lifting has been used by parents to manage NE. The procedure involves waking the child during the night, walking the child to the toilet, and then returning the child to bed. As an intervention, van Dommelen and colleagues (2009) found lifting to be more effective than a reward system alone or a control. However, lifting was not compared against the urine alarm and the dropout rates for the treatment were higher than the other conditions, suggesting lifting may have low acceptability among parents. Consequently, practice parameters recommend lifting not be used as a treatment for NE (see National Clinical Guideline Centre, 2010).

Overlearning. Overlearning is a simple procedure whereby the child drinks extra fluids just before bedtime. Theoretically similar to RCT, overlearning posits that children with NE benefit from having to control the muscles that restrict the flow of urine at nighttime when the bladder is full. According to Friman (2008), overlearning aids in the maintenance of improvements made using the urine alarm but should only be used when a predetermined dryness criterion has been achieved (e.g., seven consecutive dry nights). Research on the use of overlearning is positive, as relapse rates tend to be lower when overlearning is added to the urine alarm (see Glazener, Evans, & Peto, 2005).

Responsibility Training. Several authors suggest having the child take responsibility for household chores associated with accidents (see Axelrod, Tornehl, & Fontanini-Axelrod, 2014; Friman, 2008, Houts & Liebert, 1985). Younger children might be required to place wet bedding and clothing in a laundry basket, while older children might be expected to actually launder the wet bedding and clothing. These recommendations encourage independence and responsibility in the toileting routine, and should not be used by parents as punishment for urinary accidents. Conceptually, responsibility training is a natural consequential event that follows an undesirable response (i.e., urinary accident). Furthermore, it is logically sequenced within a comprehensive treatment protocol, thus making it a common recommendation by practitioners. However, research specific to responsibility training's effectiveness does not exist. Rather, the strategy is typically mentioned only as part of a study's procedures and not specifically evaluated by investigators (e.g., Axelrod, Tornehl, & Fontanini-Axelrod, 2014).

Contingent Rewards. Reward systems implemented as part of an NE treatment protocol generally involve the delivery of a reinforcer following a dry night (i.e., desired response). Contingent rewards alone do not treat NE directly and are unlikely to improve nighttime continence. However, reward systems have been evaluated in multicomponent treatment protocols (e.g., Axelrod, Tornehl, & Fontanini-Axelrod, 2014) and recommended by several authors as a mechanism to enhance outcomes (e.g., Friman, 2008; Friman & Jones, 1998; Invie & Axelrod, 2011). Axelrod and colleagues used a simple reward system to improve children's response to the urine alarm. All children demonstrated modest improvement when using the urine alarm alone but failed to achieve full nighttime continence after nine to 11 weeks of treatment. A reward system for dry nights was added to the urine alarm resulting in full nighttime continence for all children within one to two weeks. In a slightly different twist, Ruckstuhl and Friman (2003) combined the urine alarm with an incentive system that had children earn small rewards contingent on successively smaller urine stains. They found this combination to effectively improve nighttime continence for children who initially had infrequent dry nights.

It is uncertain how contingent rewards contribute to the overall improvements made by children with NE. Both Axelrod, Tornehl, and Fontanini-Axelrod (2014) and Ruckstuhl and Friman (2003) speculated that the reward systems enhanced children's motivation to stay with treatment when discouraged by unfavorable results. As a result, contingent rewards might be indicated when dry nights are infrequent or a child becomes unmotivated to continue with treatment. However, practitioners should note that children failing to achieve dry nights might also become discouraged because they are not earning rewards or being successful.

Behavioral Intervention for Retentive Encopresis

The literature generally identifies four major components of a comprehensive, evidence-based treatment protocol for RE: (1) education about RE and demystification; (2) disimpaction of the colon; (3) increasing and maintaining regularity of bowel movements; and (4) behavioral interventions to encourage appropriate toileting behavior. Each component is discussed below.

Education and Demystification. Practitioners should initially consider introducing parents, children, and others (e.g., daycare providers, school staff) to RE's diagnostic criteria, etiological formulations, and evidence-based treatment approaches. Regarding etiological formulations, education should focus on the physiological causes of RE as well as the role constipation, diet and fluid intake, and learning-based resistance to toileting play in RE. Such an explanation is important, as adults sometimes blame, punish, or shame children who have frequent fecal accidents (Campbell, Cox, & Borowitz, 2009). Furthermore, the terms "lazy," "purposeful," and "defiant" are often used to describe children with RE (Christopherson & Wassom, 2013). The demystification of RE can help parents and others working with the child to better understand the recommended course of treatment.

Because RE is often erroneously attributed to psychopathological explanations and frequently cited as a symptom of sexual abuse, parents and professionals (e.g., educators, mental health providers) should be aware of the pathophysiology of RE. Inappropriate or harmful first-line treatments, such as punitive disciplinary procedures, are more likely to be avoided when parents and professionals are educated about an evidence-based conceptualization of RE (Axelrod et al., 2015). Parents and others working with the child are also encouraged to maintain a positive and supportive environment during treatment. Finally, practitioners should discuss with parents the importance of maintaining strong treatment fidelity in order to increase success and avoid potential medical complications. This is especially important given that treatment noncompliance has been identified as a source of ongoing problems with constipation and RE (Steege & Harper, 1989).

Disimpaction of the Colon. Bowel evacuation is the second component of treatment. Without some form of "cleanout" procedure, maintaining regular bowel movements is virtually impossible and successful progress is unlikely (Christopherson & Wassom, 2013). Relief from fecal impaction is most often accomplished through the use of enemas, rectal suppositories, or laxatives (Campbell, Cox, & Borowitz, 2009; Friman, 2008). No randomized controlled studies have compared methods of disimpaction. Rectal enemas and suppositories are rapid but generally invasive and can be traumatic for the child and family. Laxatives given orally are less invasive but are slow to take effect and might not lead to full bowel evacuation. Manual fecal extraction is recommended in extreme cases where the impaction is causing acute pain or might immediately lead to medical complications (Araghizadeh, 2005). Any bowel evacuation procedure should be overseen by a qualified physician.

Increasing and Maintaining Bowel Regularity. Sustaining complete disimpaction of the bowel and increasing the regularity of bowel movements are the primary goals following bowel evacuation (Campbell, Cox, & Borowitz, 2009; Friman & Jones, 1998). Most RE treatment protocols use osmotic laxatives (e.g., polyethylene glycol, magnesium hydroxide), which aid in fluid retention within the colon resulting in distention and encouraging colonic peristalsis (see Axelrod, Tornehl, & Fontanini-Axelrod, 2016; Borowitz et al., 2002). Stool softeners, such as mineral oil, are sometimes prescribed for children with RE (Axelrod et al., 2015). Both medications help prevent the build-up of stool in the colon discouraging the reoccurrence of constipation (Campbell, Cox, & Borowitz, 2009). Furthermore, having stool pass more easily through the lower digestive tract might help the colon and rectum return to more normal functioning (Christopherson & Wassom, 2013). Similar to disimpaction, a physician should direct the use of laxatives or stool softeners.

Practitioners should look for regularity of bowel movements as a sign that disimpaction was successful and that fecal matter is passing adequately through the colon. Research suggests that the average child will have between three bowel movements per week to up to three bowel movements per day (see van der Berg, Benninga, & DiLorenzo, 2006). In addition, stools should be well-formed, solid, and appropriately colored. Again, bowel movements that are small, dry, and hard (e.g., pebble-like) are consistent with constipation.

Dietary changes are often used as an adjunctive to laxatives or stool softeners in maintaining the regularity of bowel movements. Furthermore, practice parameters almost always recommend the intake of fiber and healthy, nondairy fluids (see Friman, 2008). Fiber improves colonic motility and fluids aid in hydration reducing the need of the colon to absorb fluid from waste, both of which make it easier to pass stools. Other suggested dietary changes include decreasing consumption of dairy products and highly processed foods. Research on dietary changes to improve colonic motility and decrease constipation in children is limited, although there is some evidence that dietary fiber supplements improve regularity in pediatric populations (Castillejo et al., 2006). However, literature on the treatment of childhood constipation suggests that aggressive intervention (i.e., disimpaction plus laxative therapy) corresponds most often with success and that dietary changes alone are not likely to improve the condition (Borowitz et al., 2005).

Encouraging Appropriate Toileting Behavior. Behavioral interventions should be implemented concurrently with the use of laxatives or stool softeners. The literature generally recommends some combination of the following: (1) teaching the child proper defecation dynamics including how to sit on the toilet and strain appropriately when attempting to pass stool; (2) conducting brief (e.g., one to three minutes), regularly scheduled toilet sits at least several times per day; (3) using praise and encouragement for complying with the toilet sits, which might be aversive to some children; and (4) using rewards contingent on successful bowel movements in the toilet (see Campbell, Cox, & Borowitz, 2009; Christopherson & Wassom, 2013; Friman, 2008; Ritterband et al., 2003).

Research comparing different toilet sit lengths and schedules is nonexistent. Furthermore, large-scale controlled trials often fail to provide sufficient detail regarding toilet sit procedures to establish evidence-based practice recommendations. However, single case design studies can provide some guidance for practitioners. For example, Axelrod, Tornhel, and Fontanini-Axelrod (2016) demonstrated the efficacy of a toilet training plus laxative therapy protocol for two adolescents, both with co-occurring autism and intellectual disability, that involved two-minute toilet sits every 15 minutes across the entire day. The authors also implemented individualized reward systems involving reinforcing tangible items and activities contingent on bowel movements in the toilet, and a clean-up procedure that included taking off soiled clothing, cleaning soiled skin, washing hands, putting on clean clothing, and laundering soiled clothing. Similar to responsibility training described above, the clean-up procedure encourages independence and adds effort to undesirable responses (i.e., fecal accidents) without punishing the child.

Role of Parents in Treatment

Parents play a significant role in the treatment of their child's elimination disorder. Specifically, parents are called on to provide practitioners with valuable clinical information during the assessment, assist the child in most treatment components, closely track progress, and communicate with the child's medical team. For NE, parents are needed to help with the urine alarm (e.g., clip the device into the child's pajamas), initiate a reward system, and require responsibilities associated with accidents (e.g., laundering wet bedding). In addition, parents might be called to wake the child when an auditory alarm is used and guide the child through the remainder of the treatment protocol. While parents are likely to be involved in most aspects of treatment, children frequently become more independent with specific components as they establish routines around the intervention protocol and experience success. In these cases, ensuring the child's compliance with treatment might become a parent's primary duty.

Parents are likely to be more involved in the treatment of RE, given the complexity of the condition and intervention protocol. Bowel evacuation using enemas, rectal suppositories, or laxatives is likely to be initiated by the parent, although in some extreme cases initial disimpaction of the colon is conducted by medical professionals. Ongoing maintenance of bowel regularity using laxatives will also likely be managed by the parent. Finally, parents will be needed to encourage appropriate toileting behavior by prompting toilet sits and implementing a reward system. To ensure successful outcomes, parental consistency with both NE and RE treatment protocols is needed.

Other Variables Influencing Treatment

Assessment

Any formal evaluation of enuresis or encopresis should be conducted by a physician or other qualified healthcare professional. In addition to a physical examination, assessment should address the possible pathognomonic nature of the presenting problems (i.e., signs or symptoms characteristic of a particular disease), previous attempts at treatment, and parent and child motivation. Screening for behavior, emotional, and/or psychological problems might be helpful in understanding the problem and crafting a comprehensive treatment plan. For encopresis specifically, assessment should always include determining the degree to which constipation is implicated as a cause for the fecal soiling.

Comorbidity

Generally speaking, children with elimination disorders do not have comorbid psychological disorders (APA, 2013). However, emerging research is finding that children with attention-deficit/hyperactivity disorder (ADHD) are slightly more likely than their non-ADHD peers to develop enuresis or encopresis (Mellon et al., 2013). Common medical comorbidities for enuresis include constipation, urinary tract infections, obstructive sleep apnea, dysfunctional voiding, and obesity (Baird, Seehusen, & Bode, 2014). For encopresis, urinary problems are more frequent in children with constipation (van der Berg, Benninga, & DiLorenzo, 2006).

Demographics

Elimination disorders are more common in males and younger children (APA, 2013). Despite common misconceptions, socioeconomic factors including poverty are not associated with either enuresis or encopresis (van der Berg, Benninga, & DiLorenzo, 2006; Shreeram et al., 2009).

Medication

Because medication is so often prescribed for NE and has demonstrated efficacy, a brief discussion of pharmacological interventions is warranted. Antidiuretics (e.g., desmopressin [DDAVP]) and imipramine, a tricyclic antidepressant, are the most frequently prescribed medications to treat bedwetting (Friman, 2008). Imipramine's mechanism of action is largely unknown, although it appears to reduce nighttime urine output (Hunsballe et al., 1997). DDAVP concentrates urine thus decreasing its volume and reducing pressure within the bladder (Friman & Jones, 1998). Because of imipramine's side effects (e.g., cardiotoxic effects of overdose), DDAVP has become the medication of choice for NE.

Research on medication to treat NE is mixed. For example, Schulman, Stokes, and Salzman (2001) demonstrated that DDAVP produced statistically significant reductions in episodes of bedwetting after ten weeks when compared to a placebo control. They also found that DDAVP's effects were rather immediate, which is consistent with previous studies. However, other research suggests that less than 25% of children prescribed DDAVP show improvements and relapse rates are exceptionally high for those children taking DDAVP (Invie & Axelrod, 2011). For example, Ahmed and colleagues (2013) found that relapse rates were higher (66%) for those children prescribed DDAVP compared with children using the urine alarm (17%). Accordingly, practice parameters for the treatment of bedwetting recommend the urine alarm by itself initially but that DDAVP could become an adjunct should the urine alarm fail to produce sufficient results or an immediate treatment response is necessary (Friman, 2008).

Medical intervention for RE or chronic constipation typically involves two distinct phases. First, bowel evacuation must occur to ensure the colon is no longer impacted with fecal matter. Disimpaction of the colon is most often achieved through the use of enemas, rectal suppositories, or laxatives (Campbell, Cox, & Borowitz, 2009; Friman, 2008). Second, osmotic laxatives or stool softeners are most often used to increase and maintain bowel regularity (see Axelrod, Tornhel, & Fontanini-Axelrod, 2016; Axelrod et al., 2015). Children presenting with chronic constipation are often on laxatives for months to years, especially when the laxative is used for maintenance (Pashankar, 2005). However, research has found that behavioral interventions, such as those described in this chapter, implemented in conjunction with laxatives have the effect of decreasing the duration children are on laxatives (Axelrod, Tornhel, & Fontanini-Axelrod, 2016; Borowitz et al., 2002).

Nonretentive Encopresis

Nonretentive encopresis, or encopresis without constipation, accounts for a very small percentage of FE cases (e.g., less than 10%) and, as a result, has not been studied as extensively as RE (Kuhn, Marcus, & Pitner, 1999). Consequently, large-scale clinical trials are missing from the literature and evidence-based treatment protocols have yet to be established. Moreover, effective strategies have been difficult to identify because of the complexity of this problem. The remainder of this section offers assessment and treatment recommendations based on the limited literature.

Friman (2008) noted that concerns other than soiling, such as emotional and behavioral problems, are frequently present in this subgroup of children. Identifying these commonly co-occurring problems through a comprehensive psychological evaluation is a good initial step when treating nonretentive encopresis. For example, parent behavior management training is recommended in cases where noncompliance and aggression are salient features of the child's behavioral profile. An evaluation of the antecedent and consequent events that might be present during toileting is also suggested. There may be environmental variables occurring before (e.g., prompts to use the toilet) or following (e.g., social attention) appropriate or inappropriate defecation that could aid in treatment plan development. In these cases, practitioners might consider the problem from a functional analytic perspective and identify reinforcing contingencies that might be encouraging appropriate toileting behavior or maintaining soiling.

The very limited literature suggests practitioners utilize a behavioral approach to treating nonretentive encopresis. Although medical intervention (e.g., laxative therapy) might be necessary when the child is withholding stools, a toileting training protocol similar to the treatment protocol indicated for RE is recommended (Kuhn, Marcus, & Pitner, 1999). Appropriate toileting behavior can be established using frequent and brief toilet sits coupled with a reward system contingent on compliance with toilet sits and/or successful bowel movements in the toilet (Boles, Roberts, & Vernberg, 2008). For those children who refuse or are afraid to use the toilet, Kuhn and colleagues recommended a shaping procedure whereby the parent initiates the process by modeling sitting on the toilet (with clothes on) followed by the parent and child playing games or reading near or in the bathroom. This gradually shifts to eventually the child sitting on the toilet. Behaviorally specific praise or tangible rewards are provided contingent on the child complying with each shaping step. As Kuhn and colleagues noted, however, rewarding clean pants might lead to the withholding of bowel movements, which could result in constipation, or hiding of soiled clothing. Furthermore, rewarding the absence of accidents does not encourage appropriate toileting behavior.

Conclusion

Empirically based, peer-reviewed research on treatments that combine appropriate medical intervention (e.g., laxative therapy) with behavioral approaches to learning and behavior change (e.g., reward systems) have been highlighted in this chapter. Because elimination disorders might have medically oriented complications (e.g., pathophysiological explanations for nighttime incontinence, perforated bowel in cases of chronic and severe constipation), practitioners are advised to adopt a "go no further" dictum before proceeding and first refer children to a physician for a medical evaluation. Collaboration between the practitioner, parents, and the child's physician is likely to improve outcomes. In addition, understanding the role relevant physiology plays in the development of elimination disorders can assist practitioners in conceptualizing the problem for parents and others from an evidence-based perspective, which may also improve outcomes.

Useful Resources

- *Elimination Disorders in Children and Adolescents* by Edward R. Christopherson and Patrick C. Friman, Hogrefe Publishing, 2010
- *Elimination Disorders: Evidence-Based Treatment for Enuresis and Encopresis* by Thomas M. Reimers, Momentum Press, 2016
- University of Virginia School of Medicine, Department of Pediatrics website on Encopresis: https://med.virginia.edu/pediatrics/about/clinical-and-patient-services/patient-tutorials/chronic-constipation-encopresis/about-encopresis/
- Mayo Clinic website on Enuresis: www.mayoclinic.org/diseases-conditions/bed-wetting/basics/definition/con-20015089

References

Ahmed, A. A., Amin, M. M., Ali, M. M., & Shalaby, E. A. (2013). Efficacy of an enuresis alarm, desmopressin, and combination therapy in the treatment of Saudi children with primary mono-symptomatic nocturnal enuresis. *Korean Journal of Urology, 54,* 783–790.

American Psychiatric Association. (2013). *Diagnostic and statistical manual of mental disorders.* 5th edn. Washington, DC: American Psychiatric Association.

Araghizadeh, F. (2005). Fecal impaction. *Clinics in Colon and Rectal Surgery, 18,* 116–119.

Axelrod, M. I., & Fontanini-Axelrod, A. (2012, May). Implementing an incentive system as part of a treatment package for elimination disorders. Paper presented at the Bi-Annual Conference of the Midwest Society of Pediatric Psychology, Milwaukee, WI.

Axelrod, M. I., Tornehl, C., & Fontanini-Axelrod, A. (2014). Enhanced response using a multicomponent urine alarm treatment for nocturnal enuresis. *Journal for Specialists in Pediatric Nursing*, *19*, 172–183.

Axelrod, M. I., Tornehl, M., & Fontanini-Axelrod, A. (2016). Co-occurring autism and intellectual disability: A treatment for encopresis using a behavioral intervention plus laxative across settings. *Clinical Practice in Pediatric Psychology*, *4*, 1–10.

Axelrod, M. I., Tornehl, M., Simpson, J. N., Lamoureux, E. A., & Axelrod-Fontanini, A. (2015). A review of encopresis for the school psychologist: Definition, developmental course, prevalence, etiological formulations, and assessment. *WSPA Sentinel*, *14*, 16–19.

Azrin, N. H., & Foxx, R. M. (1974). *Toilet training in less than a day*. New York: Simon & Schuster.

Baird, D. C., Seehusen, D. A., & Bode, D. V. (2014). Enuresis in children: A case-based approach. *American Family Physician*, *90*, 560–568.

Boles, R. E., Roberts, M. C., & Vernberg, E. M. (2008). Treating non-retentive encopresis with rewarded scheduled toilet sits. *Behavior Analysis in Practice*, *1*, 68–72.

Borowitz, S. M., Cox, D. J., Kovachez, B., Ritterband, L. M., Sheen, J., & Sutphen, J. (2005). Treatment of childhood constipation by primary care physicians: Efficacy and predictors of outcome. *Pediatrics*, *115*, 873–877.

Borowitz, S. M., Cox, D. J., Sutphan, J. L., & Kovatchez, B. (2002). Treatment of childhood encopresis: A randomized trial comparing three treatment protocols. *Journal of Pediatric Gastroenterology and Nutrition*, *34*, 378–384.

Brazzelli, M., Griffiths, P. V., Cody, D., & Tappin, D. (2011). Behavioural and cognitive intervention with or without other treatments for the management of faecal incontinence in children. *Cochrane Database of Systematic Reviews*, *12*, 1–69.

Buckley, B. S., Lapitan, M. C. M., & the Epidemiology Committee of the Fourth International Consultation on Incontinence. (2010). Prevalence of urinary incontinence in men, women, and children – current evidence: Findings of the fourth international consultation on incontinence. *Urology*, *76*, 265–271.

Butler, R. J., & Heron, J. (2008). The prevalence of infrequent bedwetting and nocturnal enuresis in childhood: A large British cohort. *Scandinavian Journal of Urology and Nephrology*, *42*, 257–264.

Byrd, R. S., Weitzman, M., Lanphear, N. E., & Auinger, P. (1996). Bed-wetting in U.S. children: Epidemiology and related behavior problems. *Pediatrics*, *98*, 414–419.

Campbell, L. K., Cox, D. J., & Borowitz, S. M. (2009). Elimination disorders: Enuresis and encopresis. In M. C. Roberts & R. G. Steele (eds.), *Handbook of pediatric psychology*. 4th edn (pp. 481–490). New York: Guilford Press.

Castillejo, G., Bulló, M., Anguera, A., Escibano, J., & Salas-Salvadó, J. (2006). A controlled, randomized, double-blind trial to evaluate the effect of a supplement of cocoa husk that is rich in dietary fiber on colonic transit time in constipated pediatric patients. *Pediatrics*, *118*(3), 641–648.

Christopherson, E. R., & Friman, P. C. (2010). *Elimination disorders in children and adolescents*. Cambridge, MA: Hogrefe Publishing.

Christopherson, E. R., & Wassom, M. (2013). Managing encopresis in the pediatric setting. *American Academy of Pediatrics: Section on Developmental and Behavioral Pediatrics Newsletter, Fall 2013*.

Fergusson, D. M., Horwood, L. J., & Sannon, F. T. (1986). Factors related to the age of attainment of nocturnal bladder control: An 8-year longitudinal study. *Pediatrics*, *78*, 884–890.

Ferrara, P., Gatto, A., Vitelli, O., Romano, V., Del Bufalo, F., Romaniello, L., & Ruggiero, A. (2008). Nocturnal enuresis in children: A review of the literature. *Current Pediatric Reviews, 4,* 120–131.

Friman, P. C. (2008). Evidence-based therapies for enuresis and encopresis. In R. G. Steele, T. D. Elkin, & M. C. Roberts (eds.), *Handbook of evidence-based therapies for children and adolescents: Bridging science and practice* (pp. 311–333). New York: Springer.

Friman, P. C., & Jones, K. M. (1998). Elimination disorders in children. In T. S. Watson & F. M. Gresham (eds.), *Handbook of child behavior therapy* (pp. 239–260). New York: Plenum Press.

Glazener, C. M., Evans, J. H., & Peto, R. E. (2005). Alarm interventions for nocturnal enuresis in children. *Cochrane Database of Systematic Reviews, 2,* 1–106.

Houts, A. C., & Liebert, R. M. (1985). *Bedwetting: A guide for parents.* Springfield, IL: Thomas.

Hunsballe, J. M., Rittig, S., Pedersen, E. B., Olesen, O. V., & Djurhuus, J. C. (1997). Single dose imipramine reduces nocturnal urine output in patients with nocturnal enuresis and nocturnal polyuria. *Journal of Urology, 158,* 830–836.

Invie, B., & Axelrod M. I. (2011). School psychologist as parent health resource: A review of nocturnal enuresis. *WSPA Sentinel, 11,* 22–24.

Kiddoo, D. A. (2012). Nocturnal enuresis. *Canadian Medical Association Journal, 184,* 908–911.

Kiddoo, D., Klassen, T. P., Lang, M. E., Friesen, C., Russell, K., Spooner, C., & Vandermeer, B. (2006). The effectiveness of different methods of toilet training for bowel and bladder control. Evidence Report/Technical Assessment No. 147. (Prepared by the University of Alberta Evidence-based Practice Center, under contract number 290–02-0023.)

Kuhn, B. R., Marcus, B. A., & Pitner, S. L. (1999). Treatment guidelines for primary nonretentive encopresis and stool toileting refusal. *American Family Physician, 59,* 2171–2178.

Lovibond, S. H. (1964). *Conditioning and enuresis.* Oxford: Pergamon Press.

McGrath, M. L., Mellon, M. M., & Murphy, L. (2000). Empirically supported treatments in pediatric psychology: Constipation and encopresis. *Journal of Pediatric Psychology, 25,* 225–254.

Mellon, M. W., Natchev, B. E., Katusic, S. K., Colligan, R. C., Weaver, A. L., Voigt, R. G., & Barbaresi, W. J. (2013). Incidence of enuresis and encopresis among children with attention deficit hyperactivity disorder in a population-based birth cohort. *Academic Pediatrics, 13,* 322–327.

Mowrer, O. H., & Mowrer, W. M. (1938). Enuresis: A method for its study and treatment. *American Journal of Orthopsychiatry, 8,* 436–459.

National Clinical Guideline Centre. (2010). *Nocturnal enuresis: The management of bedwetting in children and young people.* London: National Clinical Guideline Centre.

Pashankar, D. S. (2005). Childhood constipation: Evaluation and management. *Clinics in Colon and Rectal Surgery, 18,* 120–127.

Ritterband, L. M., Cox, D. J., Walker, L. S., Kovatchev, B., McKnight, L., Patel, K., Borowitz, S., & Sutphen, J. (2003). An internet intervention as adjunctive therapy for pediatric encopresis. *Journal of Consulting and Clinical Psychology, 71,* 910–917.

Ruckstuhl, L. E., & Friman, P.C. (2003, May). Evaluating the effectiveness of the vibrating urine alarm: A study of effectiveness and social validity. Paper presented at the 29th Annual Convention of the Association for Behavior Analysis, San Francisco, CA.

Schulman, S. L., Stokes, A., & Salzman, P. M. (2001). The efficacy and safety of oral desmopressin in children with primary nocturnal enuresis. *Journal of Urology, 166,* 2427–2431.

Shepard, J. A., Poler, J. E., & Grabman, J. H. (2016). Evidence-based psychosocial treatments for pediatric elimination disorders. *Journal of Clinical Child & Adolescent Psychology.* Advance online publication. http://dx.doi.org/10.1080/15374416.2016.1247356

Shreeram, S., He, J., Kaladjian, A., Brothers, A., & Merikangas, K. R. (2009). Prevalence of enuresis with attention deficit/hyperactivity disorder among U.S. children: Results from a nationally representative study. *Journal of the American Academy of Child & Adolescent Psychiatry, 48,* 35–41.

Southam-Gerow, M. A., & Prinstein, M. J. (2014). Evidence based update: The evolution of the evaluation of psychological treatments for children and adolescents. *Journal of Clinical Child & Adolescent Psychology, 43,* 1–6.

Staiano, A., Andreotti, M. R., Greco, L., Basile, P., & Auricchio, S. (1994). Long-term follow-up of children with chronic idiopathic constipation. *Digestive Diseases and Sciences, 39,* 561–564.

Stark, L. J., Opipari, L. C., Donaldson, D. L., Danovsky, M. B., Rasile, D. A., & DelSanto, A. F. (1997). Evaluation of a standard protocol for retentive encopresis: A replication. *Journal of Pediatric Psychology, 22,* 619–633.

Steege, M. W., & Harper, D. C. (1989). Enhancing the management of secondary encopresis by assessing acceptability of treatment: A case study. *Journal of Behavior Therapy and Experimental Psychiatry, 20,* 333–341.

Sutphen, J. L., Borowitz, S. M., Hutchinson, R. L., & Cox, D. J. (1995). Long-term follow-up of medically treated childhood constipation. *Clinical Pediatrics, 34,* 576–580.

Troup, C. W., & Hodgson, N. B. (1971). Nocturnal functional bladder capacity in enuretic children. *Journal of Urology, 105,* 129–132.

van der Berg, M. M., Benninga, M. A., & DiLorenzo, C. (2006). Epidemiology of childhood constipation: A systematic review. *American Journal of Gastroenterology, 101,* 2401–2409.

van Dommelen, P., Kamphuis, M., van Leerdam, F. J., de Wilde, J. A., Rijpstra, A., Campagne, A. E., & Verkerk, P. H. (2009). The short- and long-term effects of simple behavioral interventions for nocturnal enuresis in young children: A randomized controlled trial. *Journal of Pediatrics, 154,* 662–666.

von Gontard, A., Heron, J., & Joinson, C. (2011). Family history of nocturnal enuresis and urinary incontinence. *Journal of Urology, 185,* 2303–2307.

Yeung, C. K., Diao, M., & Sreedhar, B. (2008). Cortical arousal in children with severe enuresis. *New England Journal of Medicine, 358,* 2414–2415.

16

Sleep

Bieke D. Puncochar and Sarah Morsbach Honaker

Sleep is a basic need thought to aid in restoring the body and improving our mental functions, while also protecting us from overstimulation (e.g., Cirelli & Tononi, 2008; Mignot, 2008). The impact of insufficient or low quality sleep has been thoroughly documented in the literature and includes impairment in cognitive, emotional, behavioral, and physical functioning (Beebe, 2011). Research suggests that approximately 25% of children (Owens, 2008) experience some form of sleep problem, and that these problems may persist if not addressed (Lam, Hiscock, & Wake, 2003).

One of the most common sleep disorders in children is insomnia, with estimated prevalence rates of 20–30% (Mindell et al., 2006). According to the 3rd edition of the *International Classification of Sleep Disorders* (American Academy of Sleep Medicine, 2004), insomnia presents with one or more of the following symptoms: difficulties with initiation or maintenance of sleep, early waking, a need for the presence of a caregiver to fall asleep, or bedtime resistance. In the *Diagnostic and Statistical Manual of Mental Disorders*, 5th edition (DSM-5), the latter symptom is not included among the diagnostic criteria for insomnia. For both classification systems, difficulties are associated with daytime symptoms and cannot be explained by a lack of adequate sleep opportunity. While insomnia symptoms may present at any point during development, infants and toddlers often experience difficulties with falling asleep independently and sleeping through the night, while common sleep complaints in preschoolers and school-aged children revolve around bedtime resistance and nighttime fears. Older children and adolescents, in turn, are more likely to experience sleep onset issues due to anxiety about being able to fall asleep or a misalignment between when they feel sleepy and when they try to fall asleep.

Insomnia in children and adolescents has been associated with numerous negative sequelae affecting both the child and the family. Children with insomnia are more likely to experience externalizing and internalizing difficulties (Gruber et al., 2012), impaired cognitive functioning (Sadeh, Gruber, & Raviv, 2003), academic difficulties (de Carvalho et al., 2013), illness (e.g., common cold; Cohen et al., 2009), and injury

(Hiscock, Canterford, et al., 2007). Negative consequences for families include parental stress (Byars, Yeomans-Maldonado, & Noll, 2011), maternal depression (Lam, Hiscock, & Wake, 2003), and overall poorer caregiver physical and mental health (Bayer et al., 2007).

Problems transitioning to bed, falling asleep, and staying asleep can be caused by a variety of factors. These include poor sleep hygiene, inconsistent or developmentally inappropriate bed and wake times, limit-setting issues, problematic sleep associations, nighttime fears, nightmares, and excessive arousal or mentation at bedtime. Comorbid psychiatric (Ivanenko, Crabtree, & Gozal, 2004), medical (Lewandowski, Ward, & Palermo, 2011), and sleep disorders (Mohri et al., 2008) can also cause or exacerbate insomnia symptoms. Encouragingly, most behavioral sleep problems can be effectively treated with psychological interventions (Kuhn & Elliott, 2003). Though psychological intervention for insomnia and other sleep disturbances is often referred to as *behavioral* sleep intervention, treatments derive from a variety of theoretical foundations.

Etiology and Theoretical Underpinnings of Treatment

Physiology of Sleep

Sleep and wakefulness are biologically regulated. Thus, it is important to understand basic sleep processes in order to maximize the efficacy of psychological interventions. Specifically, sleep is regulated via two interconnected processes: Process S and Process C. Process S refers to the homeostatic pressure to sleep, which involves the build-up of sleep-promoting "somnogens" and increases the longer we are awake. Problematic sleep habits such as late afternoon naps can disrupt Process S, making it difficult for a child to fall asleep at a regular bedtime. Process C, or the circadian wake-promoting rhythm, fluctuates reliably throughout the day (and night) and is entrained by "zeitgebers" such as light exposure and the timing of meals and other routines. Process C produces predictable peaks and drops in alertness during the day, and it contributes to sleep maintenance as sleep pressure lessens the longer we are asleep. If a child has a bedtime that is not aligned with her circadian rhythm, she may struggle to fall asleep at bedtime and/or have difficulty waking the next morning.

Behaviorism

Many of the most common interventions for behavioral sleep problems have their roots in behaviorism. A guiding principle is that behavior is seen as learned through classical or operational conditioning. Classical conditioning involves repeatedly pairing a neutral stimulus ("conditioned stimulus") with an environmental stimulus ("unconditioned stimulus" that produces an automatic response) until the neutral stimulus produces this automatic response in the absence of the environmental stimulus. A sleep onset association is a classic example of conditioning in insomnia. If parental assistance is needed to facilitate sleep onset at bedtime (e.g., rocking, nursing), it is more likely to also be needed to help children return to sleep after normal, brief nighttime awakenings. Through extinction and relearning of sleep onset associations, children can be taught to fall asleep and return to sleep without the need for parental intervention throughout the night.

Operant conditioning involves the shaping of behavior through its consequences. Behavioral sleep interventions that rely on operant conditioning typically involve shifting the balance from incidental reinforcement of unwanted behavior (e.g., providing a child with extra attention and one-on-one time with a parent when she repeatedly leaves the bed) to intentional reinforcement of wanted behavior (e.g., by offering verbal and other rewards for staying in bed).

Cognitive Psychology

In addition to behavioral concepts, cognitively based interventions can be highly relevant in the treatment of childhood sleep problems. Some children experience pre-sleep arousal, or mental and/or physiological arousal at bedtime. Cognitive and, to a lesser extent, physiologic arousal have been associated with insomnia in children (Gregory et al., 2008) and adolescents (Noone et al., 2014). Arousal can also be present following night wakings, resulting in difficulty returning to sleep. Both relaxation training and cognitive therapy are thought to promote sleep by reducing arousal and promoting a more relaxed state. Some children or adolescents may present with sleep-specific negative cognitions or beliefs, such as a worry that they will not achieve sufficient sleep and will function poorly the next day, which can contribute to increased arousal. Treatment strategies such as cognitive restructuring or structured worry time seek to reduce cognitive arousal around bedtime.

Nightmares

A nightmare can be described as a vivid dream with frightening content that may result in an awakening. Upon awakening, children typically remember their dream, and they often seek comfort from a caregiver. Nightmares most frequently occur during the last third of the night, when REM sleep is most prominent. In contrast, parasomnias (e.g., sleep terrors, sleep walking, and sleep talking) are most prevalent during the first third of the night (i.e., when more slow-wave sleep occurs), generally do not result in an awakening, and are typically not remembered by the child. While nightmares are common, severe and recurrent presentations may negatively impact sleep due to resistance to bedtime and fears about falling asleep or returning to sleep.

Nightmares are more prevalent in children who do not obtain sufficient sleep, so an important initial intervention involves ensuring adequate sleep opportunity. Anxiety, stress, and trauma are often associated with increased nightmare frequency as well, and they may have to be addressed first or simultaneously. When children suffer from recurrent nightmares, imagery rehearsal therapy (IRT) may be indicated. IRT has strong empirical support in adults (e.g., Krakow & Zadra, 2006) and one uncontrolled study supporting its efficacy in adolescents (Krakow, 2011). With IRT, children are instructed to bring to mind as many aspects of their recurrent nightmares as possible, including associated physical sensations, and create new, more positive endings to their dreams. They are then encouraged to frequently retell or reimagine their altered dreams while awake and rewrite any nightmares they experience at night. Simard and Nielsen (2009) found that asking children to draw their nightmare, in addition to using IRT, helped reduce nightmare-related distress.

Brief Overview of Evidence-Based Treatments

Several studies support the efficacy of behavioral sleep intervention programs, with the majority focusing on treatment for infants and toddlers. Using the GRADE system (Guyatt et al., 2011) to classify the strength of the evidence, Meltzer and Mindell (2014) concluded that there is moderate evidence for the efficacy of treatments for young children and low evidence for older children, adolescents, and children of all ages with special needs. While most infant and toddler intervention studies are conceptualized as providing support for a single treatment component (extinction), these programs often involve at least one other treatment component, such as setting an appropriate bedtime, adding a bedtime routine, and parental education.

Components of Evidence-Based Treatments

Components of evidence-based treatments for behavioral sleep disturbances in young children, school-aged children, and adolescents are described below. Specific components were selected for inclusion because they have been evaluated independently and found to be efficacious (e.g., bedtime routine, bedtime pass), were frequently included in the packaged treatments described above, or are commonly used in clinical practice.

Addressing Problematic Sleep Habits

Treatment of insomnia and other behavioral sleep disturbances should be targeted toward addressing the cause(s) of these problems, which often differ for individual children. Problematic sleep habits are often associated with sleep onset difficulties, and removal of such habits through parent and child psychoeducation regarding appropriate sleep hygiene is considered an essential first step in the treatment of sleep issues (Owens & Mindell, 2011). Studies on adult insomnia, however, strongly suggest that sleep hygiene alone is often not sufficient (Morgenthaler et al., 2006), and this is likely also the case for pediatric insomnia. One sleep hygiene recommendation with strong empirical support is the avoidance of electronic screens after bedtime (Allen et al., 2016). The normal darkness-related secretion of melatonin in the evening that helps us feel more tired is thought to be suppressed by the blue-spectrum light emitted by electronic screens (e.g., Wood et al., 2013). In addition, access to electronic media before and after bedtime has been repeatedly associated with insomnia symptoms and shorter sleep duration (Cain & Gradisar, 2010). While a common recommendation is to avoid electronic screens for an hour before bed, at this time there is not sufficient support for this recommendation (Allen et al., 2016). For a review of sleep hygiene recommendations, see Allen and colleagues (2016).

Sleep Scheduling

In addition to sleep hygiene, an important initial component of behavioral sleep treatments involves sleep scheduling. Having a consistent bedtime and wake time, selecting an optimal bedtime, and restricting sleep have all been found to be helpful in reducing sleep problems, particularly difficulties with sleep onset (Mindell & Owens, 2015).

Consistent Bedtime and Wake Time. Variable bedtimes and wake times can affect both Processes C and S. Since our circadian system (Process C) is entrained by exposure to light, variability in wake time (i.e., variable timing of exposure to light) can alter the circadian timing system. Sleep pressure (Process S) is largely dependent on the amount of time that has passed since the last sleep period. These processes together can explain why significant oversleep on a Sunday morning is likely to result in difficulty falling asleep on Sunday evening: fewer hours since the last sleep period results in a lower sleep pressure, and later exposure to morning light causes a circadian delay. Combined circadian misalignment and reduced sleep pressure can contribute to notable difficulties with sleep onset. Many children and adolescents have variable bedtimes and wake times during the week versus the weekend, which can result in sleep onset difficulties (Biggs et al., 2011). Treatment in such cases often starts with implementation of a consistent bedtime and wake time (e.g., Malow et al., 2014). Daytime naps can also disrupt the build-up of somnogens and result in reduced sleepiness at bedtime, which is why naps in children over age five are typically discouraged if there are sleep onset difficulties.

Optimal Timing of Bedtime. Alignment between a child's sleep schedule and the child's natural circadian rhythm will increase the likelihood of a quick sleep onset. Most children experience a peak in alertness approximately two hours before their circadian bedtime. If placed in bed during this "forbidden zone," they will likely have considerable difficulty with sleep onset. Optimal bedtimes vary across development: while young children often have a tendency toward an advanced circadian phase (i.e., tendency for earlier sleep onset and wake times, compared to adults), adolescents tend to have a delayed circadian phase (i.e., tendency for later sleep onset and wake times, compared to adults). For prepubescent children, a bedtime of 9:00 p.m. or earlier has been associated with fewer behavioral sleep difficulties (Mindell, Meltzer, et al., 2009). During adolescence, the timing of the dim light melatonin onset (DLMO), a marker of circadian phase that usually occurs approximately two hours before sleep onset, is delayed as a result of hormonal changes. This circadian delay often manifests as difficulty falling asleep early enough to achieve sufficient sleep on week nights, particularly for adolescents with early morning school start times. As a result, many adolescents experience significant sleep deficits and associated daytime consequences (Carskadon, 2011). In the case of misalignment between when children or adolescents naturally feel tired and their bedtime, the bedtime fading strategy (see below) may be helpful.

Bedtime Fading and Sleep Restriction. Bedtime fading involves temporarily delaying a child's bedtime to more closely approximate the time that he typically falls asleep. For example, a child who goes to bed at 9:00 p.m. and falls asleep at 10:30 p.m. most nights may temporarily use a 10:00 p.m. bedtime. A typical protocol involves fading the bedtime earlier at a rate of 15 to 30 minutes after three consecutive days with a sleep onset latency of 30 minutes or less. Bedtime fading has not been evaluated as an independent approach, but it is often recommended by clinicians (Honaker & Meltzer, 2014) and included in packaged treatments (e.g., Paine & Gradisar, 2011).

A related approach is sleep restriction, which is typically used in the treatment of adult insomnia and is efficacious as an independent intervention (Morgenthaler et al., 2006). While it has not been evaluated independently in adolescents or school-aged children, it is often employed as part of packaged interventions for this age group (e.g., Schlarb et al., 2016). While keeping children up until they seem sleepy is a form of sleep restriction, a structured sleep restriction protocol restricts time in bed to reflect an individual's average sleep duration plus 30 minutes. As with bedtime fading, restricting time in bed and sleep opportunity is thought to facilitate sleep onset and maintenance through an increase in sleep pressure (Process S) as well as conditioning. As a result of this recommendation, less time is spent in bed awake, which, over time, results in a conditioned response between the bed and bedroom and feelings of sleepiness (see Conditioning Sleepiness section below). Sleep restriction and bedtime fading approaches are often not recommended in children ages three and under, as young children who are sleep restricted may become overtired and have even greater difficulty settling to sleep (Honaker & Meltzer, 2014).

Conditioning Sleepiness

As discussed above, certain responses can become classically conditioned through repeated pairing. Individuals with insomnia often experience an association between their bed and arousal, whereas those who sleep well often associate their bed with a relaxed state. In the treatment of sleep difficulties, classical conditioning plays an important role. Strategies such as a consistent bedtime routine and stimulus control are thought to help strengthen the association between bed and a relaxed state conducive to sleep.

Bedtime Routine. A consistent, predictable bedtime routine can help children transition to bed and may facilitate better sleep onset by conditioning sleepiness, serving as a zeitgeber for the circadian timing system, and minimizing negative parent–child interactions around bedtime. Ideally, this short routine (e.g., 20 to 30 minutes) includes a few calm activities (e.g., take shower, put on pajamas, brush teeth, read a book). Several observational studies have shown a relationship between a consistent bedtime routine and better sleep in children (e.g., Hale et al., 2011). There also appears to be a dose-dependent relationship between the consistency of a bedtime routine (e.g., number of nights per week) and positive sleep outcomes (e.g., quick sleep onset latency; Mindell et al., 2015) Additionally, an RCT evaluating a bedtime routine as an independent intervention in young children (ages seven to 36 months) found that children randomized to receive a bedtime routine fell asleep more quickly and had fewer night wakings (Mindell, Telofski, et al., 2009) compared to children on a waitlist. For younger children or children with special needs, a visual bedtime schedule is thought to promote successful implementation (Malow et al., 2014).

Stimulus Control. Stimulus control is empirically supported as an independent approach in the treatment of adult insomnia (Morgenthaler et al., 2006), though it has not been evaluated independently in children. Often part of packaged interventions in adolescent insomnia treatment, stimulus control instructions involve asking an individual to (1) avoid spending time in bed aside from when trying to sleep and (2) get out of bed for brief periods if unable to fall asleep. The goal of this approach is to strengthen the association between the bed and feelings of sleepiness. This approach is thought to reduce the experience of "conditioned arousal" or arousal associated with the bed and bedroom due to repeated time spent in bed awake feeling frustrated or worried.

Addressing Problematic Sleep Associations

Beginning in infancy, children learn to associate certain conditions with falling asleep. Positive sleep onset associations are conditions that facilitate sleep onset but do not require parental involvement (e.g., a "lovey" or other transitional object). Negative sleep onset associations, on the other hand, are often parent-dependent conditions (e.g., being rocked or nursed to sleep) that can interfere with a baby's ability to learn to fall asleep independently and return to sleep independently following normative nighttime awakenings. For negative or problematic sleep associations, extinction approaches are typically recommended (Honaker & Meltzer, 2014), though such approaches can vary widely in their implementation.

Extinction Approaches with Infants and Toddlers. Within the extinction paradigm, several different techniques (e.g., standard and graduated extinction, standard extinction after parental fading, and gradual parental weaning) are efficacious in infants and toddlers, without support for any one approach as superior to another (Mindell et al., 2006). Thus, selecting an approach is often a clinical decision based on parental preference and child temperament. Most approaches have been studied in young children (e.g., three years and below). In its most basic form, standard extinction, sometimes called unmodified extinction, involves placing a child in bed "drowsy but awake," and allowing the child to fall asleep independently by ceasing interactions with her until the child falls asleep. Graduated extinction allows parents to check on their child during this process, though without soothing her back to sleep. Checks can be employed using a fixed schedule (e.g., every five minutes), a variable schedule (e.g., increasing the number of minutes between checks), or as needed (e.g., when a parent feels the need). It is recommended that parental checks are brief and noncontingent on the child's behaviors (e.g., increased escalation) to avoid accidental positive reinforcement of such behaviors. Parental fading (Sadeh, 1994) consists of sleeping in the child's bedroom (without interacting with the child) for one week before implementing a standard extinction paradigm. Using this strategy, the child can learn to fall asleep independently without simultaneously experiencing separation anxiety. In one study, France and Blampied (2005) demonstrated that this strategy resulted in less crying and fewer nighttime awakenings than unmodified extinction, rendering parental fading a "promising intervention" (Kuhn & Elliott, 2003). Blunden also found a very gradual weaning strategy to be effective, which included a very gradual wean of parental presence with parental soothing in response to child crying (Blunden, 2011).

Many parents express concerns about the perceived negative impact of extinction paradigms on their child's wellbeing or the parent–child relationship. Research to date does not suggest any adverse effects associated with an infant extinction paradigm either in the short term (Gradisar et al., 2016) or up to six years later (Price et al., 2012). In fact, extinction-based interventions for sleep are robustly associated with improvements in both child and family functioning (Mindell et al., 2006). While extensive research supports extinction approaches, it is important to note that these interventions often also involve setting an age-appropriate bedtime and implementing a bedtime routine, both of which could be considered additional interventions. Furthermore, the majority of studies evaluating extinction for sleep in young children have been conducted in Caucasian families with above average educational attainment (Jameyfield et al., 2016).

Extinction Approaches with Preschoolers and School-Aged Children. Gradually weaning parental presence is a related extinction-based approach used frequently with older children who struggle with independent sleep. This strategy may be implemented to target negative sleep onset associations or nighttime fears and consists of gradually increasing the physical distance between the child and the parent at bedtime. If a child is used to falling asleep in her parents' bed, for example, a first step may be for a parent to sleep in the bed with the child in the child's bedroom and later on the floor next to the child's bed. As treatment progresses and the child falls asleep easily in the new arrangement, the parent may sit in a chair in the room with the child at bedtime until she falls asleep. Over the course of several days or even weeks, the distance between the child's bed and the parent's chair is increased, until the parent is no longer in the child's bedroom. While the empirical support for extinction-based approaches to encourage independent sleep onset in infants is strong, the gradual weaning method for older children is mainly based on clinical experience (e.g., Meltzer & Crabtree, 2015).

The Excuse-Me Drill (Kuhn, 2011) is another strategy to promote independent sleep in children who are accustomed to sleeping with a parent or having a parent in the room at sleep onset. Though found to be efficacious in small, uncontrolled studies (Kuhn, Floress, & Newcomb, 2008), this approach has limited support at this time. However, the approach is based on the principles of behaviorism. The Excuse-Me Drill may be used in children who refuse to stay in bed, are anxious about being in bed alone, or have parent-related sleep onset associations. In short, this treatment component consists of the parent putting a child to bed and then excusing himself for a few moments to complete a task (e.g., I have to go wash my hands, turn on the dishwasher) before returning to the bedroom. Departures are initially brief (e.g., a few seconds), but become progressively longer as the child becomes increasingly comfortable with staying alone in the bedroom.

Alternatively, parents may use the checking method, which consists of checking on their child after a predetermined time interval. Over time, or over the course of the night, the duration of this interval is extended. This method is similar to the gradual extinction paradigm with the addition that the child receives a reward and praise for staying in bed between checks. In both scenarios, it is important to explain to parents that their return to the bedroom may not be contingent on the child's behaviors (e.g., calling out), to avoid positively reinforcing such behaviors. In addition, to foster trust between parents and children, it is important that the parent return to the bedroom when he said he would. In the event the child is asleep upon the parent's return, he may leave an object (e.g., marble) on the child's nightstand to document his checking on the child.

Positive Reinforcement

Difficulties with starting the bedtime routine or going to bed may be addressed through the use of a token economy behavior management system. Reinforcers could be provided for a range of desired behaviors, such as completing steps of the bedtime routine, getting into bed, or staying in bed. One limitation to the use of tangible rewards is the inherent delay between the target behavior (e.g., compliance at bedtime) and the reward (e.g., a prize the next morning). Praise is a powerful positive reinforcer as well, and it is recommended that parents use praise to further encourage their children's cooperation. For children who are able to delay gratification, a fun variation is the use of the "Sleep Fairy," who leaves treats for children who follow tailored sleep rules. In a small study with four young children, the use of a social story about the Sleep Fairy along with positive reinforcement for appropriate bedtime behavior resulted in reductions in disruptive bedtime behavior (Burke, Kuhn, & Peterson, 2004).

The Bedtime Pass

For children with frequent "curtain calls," or bids for parental attention after bedtime, the bedtime pass is a helpful intervention. In this intervention, the child receives one or more special passes or tokens that can be exchanged for allowed departures from bed or parental interactions (e.g., a glass of water, an extra hug). Parents are instructed to respond in a very neutral, brief, and consistent manner to any requests that are made after the bedtime pass has been surrendered. This strategy has been shown to reduce the frequency of bedtime resistance and shorten average time to quiet (e.g., Moore et al., 2007). It can also be very helpful for encouraging children with nighttime fears to remain in bed and thereby overcome their fears through gradual exposure (see more in next section). The use of a reward the next morning for retaining one or more passes is used frequently in clinical practice, though may be not necessary and was not included in studies evaluating this intervention.

Addressing Fears and Worries

The cognitive-behavioral literature for the treatment of anxiety typically relies on the use of gradual exposure with response prevention in addition to cognitive coping strategies. The treatment of nighttime fears is based on these principles as well. It is important to note that there are few studies examining treatment of nighttime fears, specifically. Yet many of the strategies below are used clinically and based on well-established principles.

The content of children's fears and worries changes as they grow older. While separation anxiety tends to be more prevalent in very young children, fears involving fantasy (e.g., monsters) occur most commonly in preschool and young school-aged children. Older children and adolescents tend to have fears around real dangers, such as crime or natural disasters. Fears of the dark may be addressed behaviorally by having children spend increasing lengths of time in the dark (i.e., exposure therapy). Games that include hiding or finding an object in the dark with a flashlight are deemed an effective strategy of exposure therapy (e.g., Mikulas & Coffman, 1989). A cognitive approach for helping children manage scary thoughts (e.g., thoughts about monsters or bad guys) involves repeated mental exposure by intentionally talking and thinking about the scary thoughts (e.g., "chewing on the thoughts") until they lose their potency (e.g., March & Mullen, 1998). Coping self-talk (Gordon et al., 2007), such as making brave self-statements, has also been found beneficial for targeting nighttime fears. Another cognitive approach to nighttime fears involves the use of fantasy. "Monster Spray" or a dream catcher have been used to target fears associated with monsters or nightmares respectively. Kushnir and Sadeh (2012) found that children ages four to six years experienced reduced fears and improved sleep in response to being provided with a stuffed animal that was said to either protect them or need their protection, with no differences in effectiveness between the two approaches. In a study by Muris, Verweij, and Meesters (2003), children ages four to six years were told a story about a child whose fears of a monster disappeared after he drew the monster and wrote it a letter indicating he was no longer afraid of it. Imitating the strategies mentioned in the story resulted in a significant reduction in fears in these children, compared to waitlist controls.

Many children struggle to fall asleep because they worry about what has happened during the day or what might happen the next day. Scheduling designated "worry times" (i.e., times during which the child is encouraged to talk, write, or think about all the things that might otherwise keep her up at night), outside the bedroom and separated in time from bedtime, can be a powerful strategy for addressing worries and eliminating them from the bedroom. Children and adolescents are further instructed to stop engaging with any residual worry thoughts after "worry time" is over, especially when lying in bed, and postpone thinking about them until the next scheduled worry time. This treatment component has been associated with reductions in anxiety (Jellesma, Verkuil, & Brosschot, 2009), which are expected to facilitate sleep onset. Older children and adolescents may develop worries about not being able to fall asleep when desired, resulting in difficulties with sleep onset or maintenance. This fear can be directly targeted with cognitive therapy, an approach with independent efficacy for adult insomnia (Harvey et al., 2014) that is also included frequently in packaged interventions with adolescents (e.g., Bootzin & Stevens, 2005). In the adult literature, cognitive therapy involves examining and challenging dysfunctional beliefs about sleep and insomnia (e.g., Morgenthaler et al., 2006). The impact of poor sleep on daytime functioning is often significantly exaggerated (e.g., "If I don't get more than six hours of sleep, I will definitely fail the exam tomorrow"), and cognitive restructuring aims to result in more reality-based estimates of poor sleep (e.g., "I have completed exams without notable problems in the past after a poor night's sleep, so I will probably be okay tomorrow"). People may also engage in maladaptive sleep-related behaviors (e.g., daytime napping) due to specific beliefs (e.g., "I need to nap to make up for poor night-time sleep, so I can study"). Psychoeducation about factors that impact the sleep–wake cycle as well as behavioral experiments aimed to test some of these beliefs can help target maladaptive beliefs and behaviors. An RCT comparing treatment approaches for adult insomnia found that cognitive therapy independently was effective but less so than a combined cognitive-behavioral therapy (Harvey et al., 2014).

Arousal Reduction and Relaxation

Problems with sleep initiation can be caused by difficulties transitioning from daytime mental and physical activity levels to those that are conducive to falling asleep. Therefore, scheduled wind down time prior to initiation of the bedtime routine can be an important component of treatment for sleep onset difficulties. During this time, children are encouraged to engage in calming, pleasant activities (e.g., reading, drawing, doing puzzles) that do not involve electronics (see earlier note about electronics and melatonin). It can also be helpful to engage in relaxation strategies. In the adult literature, relaxation strategies have been found to be an effective intervention strategy for insomnia (Means et al., 2000). Strategies commonly used in adult relaxation for insomnia include progressive muscle relaxation, mindfulness, and diaphragmatic breathing. Relaxation strategies are considered efficacious in the treatment of a variety of mental health conditions (Chorpita et al., 2011), though they have not been evaluated independently for pediatric insomnia.

Role of Parents in Treatment

Limit-setting difficulties at bedtime (e.g., stalling, refusing to go to bed, not staying in bed) or following night wakings are fairly common, presenting in 10–30% of toddlers and preschoolers and 15% of four- to ten-year-olds (Mindell & Owens, 2015), and may result in reduced sleep duration. In addressing these issues, in-depth assessment of the function of behavioral issues at bedtime is an essential first step that guides the selection of treatment strategies. Some children exhibit bedtime resistance due to nighttime fears, while other children present with behavioral difficulties throughout the day that affect their bedtime behavior. Other children refuse to go to bed because they do not feel tired or have trouble falling asleep. A number of strategies can be used to promote consistent limits around sleep.

Strengthening parental limit-setting skills and improving children's cooperation is typically based on operant conditioning principles and is described in more detail in the following chapter. Parents can more effectively set limits through the use of positive reinforcement (e.g., praise, attention, rewards) for appropriate behavior and consistent, firm, and calm responding to inappropriate behavior. In addition, most strategies aimed at improving compliance and limiting unwanted behaviors involve relationship building (e.g., "special time" between the child and parent). We are not aware of any studies evaluating parent training (to promote limit-setting) as an independent approach to addressing behavioral sleep issues. Yet, this approach is recommended in clinical practice (Honaker & Meltzer, 2014) and is an integral component of successfully implementing other behavioral sleep strategies (e.g., gradual wean, consistent bedtime).

Other Variables Influencing Treatment

Assessment

The most widely used assessment tool in behavioral sleep medicine is the sleep diary (e.g., consensus sleep diary described in Carney et al., 2012), which typically contains information (provided by the child or parent) about the time the child got in bed, turned the lights off, fell asleep, woke up at night, woke up in the morning, and got out of bed. Based on this information, various sleep parameters such as sleep efficiency (i.e., time asleep divided by time in bed), sleep onset latency, duration and frequency of wakings after sleep onset (WASOs) can be calculated, which help guide sleep scheduling. Actigraphy, which estimates sleep parameters based on movement, is another highly informative and validated (Meltzer et al., 2012) tool in behavioral sleep medicine. For a review of pediatric sleep questionnaires, see Lewandowski, Toliver-Sokol, & Palermo (2011).

Comorbidity

Treatment begins only after underlying or comorbid disorders have been properly considered. Insomnia can be caused by an underlying condition (e.g., obstructive sleep apnea, restless legs syndrome, pain), and treatment of the underlying condition may resolve the presenting insomnia complaint. However, treating comorbid conditions (e.g., depression) often does not fully resolve insomnia, particularly if conditioned arousal has developed. The relationship between insomnia and other comorbid conditions may be complex, requiring clinical judgment about whether to treat one condition first or to address both simultaneously.

Regarding primary sleep disorders, it is recommended that clinicians consistently assess for symptoms of sleep disordered breathing, as obstructive sleep apnea can cause frequent night wakings and impaired daytime functioning. Restless legs syndrome can cause sleep onset insomnia, as leg discomfort and/or the urge to move can inhibit a relaxed state (Mohri et al., 2008). Screening instruments for sleep apnea (Chervin et al., 2000) and restless legs syndrome (Arbuckle et al., 2010) are available.

Sleep difficulties are more prevalent in children and adolescents with psychiatric diagnoses (Alfano & Gamble, 2009). In turn, poor sleep has been shown to worsen symptom presentation in these disorders. For a review of comorbid sleep and psychiatric disorders, see Ivanenko, Crabtree, and Gozal (2004). Careful assessment of these conditions and medications, and collaboration with prescribing physicians, is deemed essential.

Finally, a wide range of medical complaints and diseases as well as medications used to address them can contribute to or cause sleep difficulties. It is therefore important to obtain a good medical history of the child or adolescent, understand the role of medical issues (e.g., pain), and address such issues if possible. However, the presence of a medical condition is not necessarily a contraindication for behavioral treatment for insomnia. In adults, cognitive-behavioral therapy for insomnia (CBT-I) has been found to be effective in treatment of insomnia in patients with multiple medical and psychiatric issues (Morgenthaler et al., 2006). CBT-I also has efficacy in treating adolescents with comorbid insomnia and pain disorders (Palermo et al., 2016).

Demographics

Because presenting sleep problems in children change as they mature, age and development are important factors in determining which treatment is most effective. We are not aware of any evidence advising treatment modifications based on sex or ethnicity. Of note, many of the studies examining the efficacy of behavioral sleep intervention in young children either did not report sample demographics or used samples that were predominantly Caucasian and had higher maternal educational attainment (Jameyfield et al., 2016).

Medication

At the present time, there are no US Food and Drug Administration-approved sleep medications for children and adolescents. Nevertheless, medications are commonly prescribed for sleep issues in the young (Owens, Rosen, & Mindell, 2003).

In addition, over-the-counter medications, such as supplemental melatonin, are commonly used to treat sleep problems. While there is growing evidence for the use of this hormone as a hypnotic or phase shifter, particularly in special needs populations (e.g., Malow, Adkins, & McGrew, 2012), there are large individual differences in the quality and composition of over-the-counter melatonin (Erland & Saxena, 2017), and caution is warranted.

Conclusion

Many multicomponent behavioral sleep intervention programs are efficacious in improving sleep outcomes, particularly in young children but also in school-aged children and adolescents. Additionally, there is independent efficacy for several treatment components, such as a bedtime routine and the bedtime pass program. However, there are a number of interventions that are used frequently in clinical practice and incorporated into packaged interventions, yet have limited or no support as an independent intervention. This supports the need for additional clinical research to better ascertain the efficacy of several interventions as recommended treatment components. Also needed is further guidance about the target ages and clinical presentations for specific interventions. Nonetheless, the wealth of evidence convincingly supports the use of behavioral sleep intervention as an effective tool to improve children's sleep and overall functioning.

Useful Resources

- *A Clinical Guide to Pediatric Sleep: Diagnosis and Management of Sleep Problems* by Jodi A. Mindell and Judith A. Owens, Lippincott Williams & Wilkins, 2015
- *Pediatric Sleep Problems: A Clinician's Guide to Behavioral Interventions* by Lisa J. Meltzer and Valerie McLaughlin Crabtree, American Psychological Association, 2015
- *Behavioral Treatments for Sleep Disorders: A Comprehensive Primer of Behavioral Sleep Medicine Interventions* edited by Michael L. Perlis, Mark Aloia, and Brett Kuhn, Academic Press, 2010

References

Alfano, C. A., & Gamble, A. L. (2009). The role of sleep in childhood psychiatric disorders. *Child Youth Care Forum*, *38*(6), 327–340. http://doi.org/10.1007/s10566-009–9081-y

Allen, S. L., Howlett, M. D., Coulombe, J. A., & Corkum, P. V. (2016). ABCs of SLEEPING: A review of the evidence behind pediatric sleep practice recommendations. *Sleep Medicine Reviews*, *29*, 1–14. http://doi.org/10.1016/j.smrv.2015.08.006

American Academy of Sleep Medicine. (2014). *International classification of sleep disorders – third edition* (ICSD-3). Darien, IL: American Academy of Sleep Medicine.

Arbuckle, R., Abetz, L., Durmer, J. S., Ivanenko, A., Owens, J. A., Croenlein, J., ... & Picchietti, D. L. (2010). Development of the Pediatric Restless Legs Syndrome Severity Scale (P-RLS-SS)©: A patient-reported outcome measure of pediatric RLS symptoms and impact. *Sleep Medicine*, *11*(9), 897–906. http://doi.org/10.1016/j.sleep.2010.03.016

Bayer, J. K., Hiscock, H., Hampton, A., & Wake, M. (2007). Sleep problems in young infants and maternal mental and physical health. *Journal of Paediatrics and Child Health*, *43*(1–2), 66–73. http://doi.org/10.1111/j.1440–1754.2007.01005.x

Beebe, D. W. (2011). Cognitive, behavioral, and functional consequences of inadequate sleep in children and adolescents. *Pediatric Clinics of North America*, *58*(3), 649–665. http://doi.org/10.1016/j.pcl.2011.03.002

Biggs, S. N., Lushington, K., van den Heuvel, C. J., Martin, A. J., & Kennedy, J. D. (2011). Inconsistent sleep schedules and daytime behavioral difficulties in school-aged children. *Sleep Medicine*, 12(8), 780–786. http://doi.org/10.1016/j.sleep.2011.03.017

Blunden, S. (2011). Behavioural treatments to encourage solo sleeping in pre-school children: An alternative to controlled crying. *Journal of Child Health Care*, *15*(2), 107–117. http://doi.org/10.1177/1367493510397623

Bootzin, R. R., & Stevens, S. J. (2005). Adolescents, substance abuse, and the treatment of insomnia and daytime sleepiness. *Clinical Psychology Review*, *25*(5), 629–644.

Burke, R. V., Kuhn, B. R., & Peterson, J. L. (2004). Brief report: A "storybook" ending to children's bedtime problems – the use of a rewarding social story to reduce bedtime resistance and frequent night waking. *Journal of Pediatric Psychology*, *29*(5), 389–396. http://jpepsy.oxfordjournals.org/content/29/5/389.full.pdf

Byars, K. C., Yeomans-Maldonado, G., & Noll, J. G. (2011). Parental functioning and pediatric sleep disturbance: An examination of factors associated with parenting stress in children clinically referred for evaluation of insomnia. *Sleep Medicine*, *12*(9), 898–905. http://doi.org/10.1016/j.sleep.2011.05.002

Cain, N., & Gradisar, M. (2010). Electronic media use and sleep in school-aged children and adolescents: A review. *Sleep Medicine*, *11*(8), 735–742.

Carney, C. E., Buysse, D. J., Ancoli-Israel, S., Edinger, J. D., Krystal, A. D., Lichstein, K. L., & Morin, C. M. (2012). The consensus sleep diary: Standardizing prospective sleep self-monitoring. *Sleep*, *35*(2), 287–302.

Carskadon, M. A. (2011). Sleep in adolescents: The perfect storm. *Pediatric Clinics of North America*, *58*(3), 637–647. http://doi.org/10.1016/j.pcl.2011.03.003

Chervin, R. D., Hedger, K., Dillon, J. E., & Pituch, K. J. (2000). Pediatric sleep questionnaire (PSQ): Validity and reliability of scales for sleep-disordered breathing, snoring, sleepiness, and behavioral problems. *Sleep Medicine*, *1*(1), 21–32.

Chorpita, B. F., Daleiden, E. L., Ebesutani, C., Young, J., Becker, K. D., Nakamura, B. J., ... & Starace, N. (2011). Evidence-based treatments for children and adolescents: An updated review of indicators of efficacy and effectiveness. *Clinical Psychology: Science and Practice*, *18*, 154–172.

Cirelli, C., & Tononi, G. (2008). Is sleep essential? *PLoS Biology*, *6*(8), e216.

Cohen, S., Doyle, W. J., Alper, C. M., Janicki-Deverts, D., & Turner, R. B. (2009). Sleep habits and susceptibility to the common cold. *Archives of Internal Medicine*, *169*(1), 62–67.

de Carvalho, L. B. C., do Prado, L. B. F., Ferrreira, V. R., da Rocha Figueiredo, M. B., Jung, A., de Morais, J. F., & do Prado, G. F. (2013). Symptoms of sleep disorders and objective academic performance. *Sleep Medicine*, *14*(9), 872–876.

Erland, L. A., & Saxena, P. K. (2017). Melatonin natural health products and supplements: Presence of serotonin and significant variability of melatonin content. *Journal of Clinical Sleep Medicine, 13*(2), 275–281.

France, K. G., & Blampied, N. M. (2005). Modifications of systematic ignoring in the management of infant sleep disturbance: Efficacy and infant distress. *Child & Family Behavior Therapy, 27*(1), 1–16.

Gordon, J., King, N. J., Gullone, E., Muris, P., & Ollendick, T. H. (2007). Treatment of children's nighttime fears: The need for a modern randomised controlled trial. *Clinical Psychology Review, 27*(1), 98–113.

Gradisar, M., Jackson, K., Spurrier, N. J., Gibson, J., Whitham, J., Williams, A. S., ... & Wilkins, D. (2016). Behavioral interventions for infant sleep problems: A randomized controlled trial. *Pediatrics, 137*(6), 477–492. http://doi.org/10.1542/peds.2015-1486

Gregory, A. M., Willis, T. A., Wiggs, L., & Harvey, A. G. (2008). Presleep arousal and sleep disturbances in children. *Sleep, 31*(12), 1745–1747. www.ncbi.nlm.nih.gov/pmc/articles/PMC2603482/pdf/aasm.31.12.1745.pdf

Gruber, R., Cassoff, J., Frenette, S., Wiebe, S., & Carrier, J. (2012). Impact of sleep extension and restriction on children's emotional lability and impulsivity. *Pediatrics, 130*(5), e1155–e1161.

Guyatt, G., Oxman, A. D., Akl, E. A., Kunz, R., Vist, G., Brozek, J., ... & Schunemann, H. J. (2011). GRADE guidelines: 1. *Journal of Clinical Epidemiology, 64*, 383–394.

Hale, L., Berger, L. M., LeBourgeois, M. K., & Brooks-Gunn, J. (2011). A longitudinal study of preschoolers' language-based bedtime routines, sleep duration, and well-being. *Journal of Family Psychology, 25*(3), 423–433. http://doi.org/10.1037/a0023564

Harvey, A. G., Bélanger, L., Talbot, L., Eidelman, P., Beaulieu-Bonneau, S., Fortier-Brochu, É., ... & Mérette, C. (2014). Comparative efficacy of behavior therapy, cognitive therapy, and cognitive behavior therapy for chronic insomnia: A randomized controlled trial. *Journal of Consulting and Clinical Psychology, 82*(4), 670–683.

Hiscock, H., Canterford, L., Ukoumunne, O. C., & Wake, M. (2007). Adverse associations of sleep problems in Australian preschoolers: National population study. *Pediatrics, 119*(1), 86–93. http://doi.org/10.1542/peds.2006-1757

Honaker, S. M., & Meltzer, L. J. (2014). Bedtime problems and night wakings in young children: An update of the evidence. *Paediatric Respiratory Reviews, 15*(4), 333–339. http://doi.org/10.1016/j.prrv.2014.04.011

Ivanenko, A., Crabtree, V. M., & Gozal, D. (2004). Sleep in children with psychiatric disorders. *Pediatric Clinics of North America, 51*(1), 51–68. www.ncbi.nlm.nih.gov/entrez/query.fcgi?cmd=Retrieve&db=PubMed&dopt=Citation&list_uids=15008582

Jameyfield, B., Honaker, S., Drozd, H., & Schwichtenberg, A. (2016, June). Inclusion of diverse samples in pediatric behavioral sleep intervention studies. Paper presented at the Annual Meeting of the Associated Professional Sleep Societies, LLC, Denver, CO.

Jellesma, F. C., Verkuil, B., & Brosschot, J. F. (2009). Postponing worrisome thoughts in children: The effects of a postponement intervention on perseverative thoughts, emotions and somatic complaints. *Social Science & Medicine, 69*(2), 278–284.

Krakow, B. (2011). Imagery rehearsal therapy for adolescents. In M. L. Perlis, M. S. Aloia, & B. R. Kuhn (eds.), *Behavioral treatments for sleep disorders: A comprehensive primer of behavioral sleep medicine interventions* (pp. 299–310). London: Academic Press.

Krakow, B., & Zadra, A. (2006). Clinical management of chronic nightmares: Imagery rehearsal therapy. *Behavioral Sleep Medicine, 4*(1), 45–70.

Kuhn, B. R. (2011). The Excuse-Me Drill: A behavioral protocol to promote independent sleep initiation skills and reduce bedtime problems in young children. In M. L. Perlis, M. S. Aloia, & B. R. Kuhn (eds.), *Behavioral treatments for sleep disorders: A comprehensive primer of behavioral sleep medicine interventions* (pp. 299–310). London: Academic Press.

Kuhn, B. R., & Elliott, A. J. (2003). Treatment efficacy in behavioral pediatric sleep medicine. *Journal of Psychosomatic Research, 54*(6), 587–597. www.ncbi.nlm.nih.gov/pubmed/12781314

Kuhn, B. R., Floress, M. T., & Newcomb, T. C. (2008, November). Strategic attention for children's sleep-compatible behaviors: Treatment outcome and acceptability of the "excuse-me drill." Presented at the Annual Meeting of the Association for Behavioral and Cognitive Therapies, Orlando, FL.

Kushnir, J., & Sadeh, A. (2012). Assessment of brief interventions for nighttime fears in preschool children. *European Journal of Pediatrics, 171*(1), 67–75.

Lam, P., Hiscock, H., & Wake, M. (2003). Outcomes of infant sleep problems: A longitudinal study of sleep, behavior, and maternal well-being. *Pediatrics, 111*(3), e203. http://pediatrics.aappublications.org/content/111/3/e203.full.pdf

Lewandowski, A. S., Toliver-Sokol, M., & Palermo, T. M. (2011). Evidence-based review of subjective pediatric sleep measures. *Journal of Pediatric Psychology, (36)*7, 780–793.

Lewandowski, A. S., Ward, T. M., & Palermo, T. M. (2011). Sleep problems in children and adolescents with common medical conditions. *Pediatric Clinics of North America, 58*(3), 699–713. http://doi.org/10.1016/j.pcl.2011.03.012

Malow, B., Adkins, K. W., McGrew, S. G., et al. (2012). Melatonin for sleep in children with autism: A controlled trial examining dose, tolerability, and outcomes. *Journal of Autism Developmental Disorders, 42*, 1729–1737. doi:10.1007/s10803-011–1418-3

Malow, B. A., Adkins, K. W., Reynolds, A., Weiss, S. K., Loh, A., Fawkes, D., . . . & Clemons, T. (2014). Parent-based sleep education for children with autism spectrum disorders. *Journal of Autism and Developmental Disorders, 44*(1), 216–228. http://doi.org/10.1007/s10803-013-1866-z

March, J. S. & Mullen, K. M. (1998). *OCD in children and adolescents: A cognitive-behavioral treatment manual*. New York: Guilford Press.

Means, M. K., Lichstein, K. L., Epperson, M. T., & Johnson, C. T. (2000). Relaxation therapy for insomnia: Nighttime and daytime effects. *Behaviour Research and Therapy, 38*(7), 665–678.

Meltzer, L. J., & Crabtree, V. M. (2015). *Pediatric sleep problems: A clinician's guide to behavioral interventions*. Washington, DC: American Psychological Association.

Meltzer, L. J., & Mindell, J. A. (2014). Systematic review and meta-analysis of behavioral interventions for pediatric insomnia. *Journal of Pediatric Psychology, 39*(8), 932–948.

Meltzer, L. J., Montgomery-Downs, H. E., Insana, S. P., & Walsh, C. M. (2012). Use of actigraphy for assessment in pediatric sleep research. *Sleep Medicine Reviews, 16*(5), 463–475.

Mignot, E. (2008). Why we sleep: The temporal organization of recovery. *PLoS Biology, 6*(4), e106.

Mikulas, W. L., & Coffman, M. F. (1989). Home-based treatment of children's fear of the dark. In C. E. Schaefer & J. M. Briesmeister (eds.), *Handbook of parent training: Parents as co-therapists for children's behavior problems* (pp. 179–202). Wiley series on personality processes. Oxford: John Wiley & Sons.

Mindell, J. A., Kuhn, B., Lewin, D. S., Meltzer, L. J., & Sadeh, A. (2006). Behavioral treatment of bedtime problems and night wakings in infants and young children. *Sleep, 29*(10), 1263–1276.

Mindell, J. A., Li, A. M., Sadeh, A., Kwon, R., & Goh, D. Y. T. (2015). Bedtime routines for young children: A dose-dependent association with sleep outcomes. *Sleep*, *38*(5), 717–722. http://doi.org/10.5665/sleep.4662

Mindell, J. A., Meltzer, L. J., Carskadon, M. A., & Chervin, R. D. (2009). Developmental aspects of sleep hygiene: Findings from the 2004 National Sleep Foundation Sleep in America Poll. *Sleep Medicine*, *10*(7), 771–779.

Mindell, J. A., & Owens, J. A. (2015). *A clinical guide to pediatric sleep: Diagnosis and management of sleep problems*. Philadelphia, PA: Lippincott Williams & Wilkins.

Mindell, J. A., Telofski, L. S., Wiegand, B., & Kurtz, E. S. (2009). A nightly bedtime routine: Impact on sleep in young children and maternal mood. *Sleep*, *32*(5), 599–606.

Mohri, I., Kato-Nishimura, K., Kagitani-Shimono, K., Tachibana, N., Ozono, K., & Taniike, M. (2008). Restless legs syndrome – Possible unrecognized cause for insomnia and irritability in children. *No To Hattatsu*, *40*(6), 473–477.

Moore, B. A., Friman, P. C., Fruzzetti, A. E., & MacAleese, K. (2007). Brief report: Evaluating the bedtime pass program for child resistance to bedtime – A randomized, controlled trial. *Journal of Pediatric Psychology*, *32*(3), 283–287.

Morgenthaler, T., Kramer, M., Alessi, C., Friedman, L., Boehlecke, B., Brown, T., . . . & American Academy of Sleep (2006). Practice parameters for the psychological and behavioral treatment of insomnia: An update. An American academy of sleep medicine report. *Sleep*, *29*(11), 1415–1419.

Muris, P., Verweij, C., & Meesters, C. (2003). The "Anti-monster Letter" as a simple therapeutic tool for reducing night-time fears in young children. *Behaviour Change*, *20*(4), 200–207.

Noone, D. M., Willis, T. A., Cox, J., Harkness, F., Ogilvie, J., Forbes, E., . . . & Gregory, A. M. (2014). Catastrophizing and poor sleep quality in early adolescent females. *Behavioral Sleep Medicine*, *12*(1), 41–52. http://doi.org/10.1080/15402002.2013.764528

Owens, J. (2008). Classification and epidemiology of childhood sleep disorders. *Primary Care: Clinics in Office Practice*, *35*(3), 533–546. http://doi.org/10.1016/j.pop.2008.06.003

Owens, J. A., & Mindell, J. A. (2011). Pediatric insomnia. *Pediatric Clinics of North America*, *58*(3), 555–569. http://doi.org/10.1016/j.pcl.2011.03.011

Owens, J. A., Rosen, C. L., & Mindell, J. A. (2003). Medication use in the treatment of pediatric insomnia: Results of a survey of community-based pediatricians. *Pediatrics*, 111(5 Pt 1), e628–35. www.ncbi.nlm.nih.gov/entrez/query.fcgi?cmd=Retrieve&db =PubMed& dopt=Citation&list_uids=12728122

Paine, S., & Gradisar, M. (2011). A randomised controlled trial of cognitive-behaviour therapy for behavioural insomnia of childhood in school-aged children. *Behaviour Research and Therapy*, *49*(6), 379–388.

Palermo, T. M., Bromberg, M. H., Beals-Erickson, S., Law, E. F., Durkin, L., Noel, M., & Chen, M. (2016). Development and initial feasibility testing of brief cognitive-behavioral therapy for insomnia in adolescents with comorbid conditions, *Clinical Practice in Pediatric Psychology*, *4*(2), 214–226.

Price, A. M., Wake, M., Ukoumunne, O. C., & Hiscock, H. (2012). Five-year follow-up of harms and benefits of behavioral infant sleep intervention: Randomized trial. *Pediatrics*, *130*(4), 643–651.

Sadeh, A. (1994). Assessment of intervention for infant night waking: Parental reports and activity-based home monitoring. *Journal of Consulting and Clinical Psychology*, *62*, 63–68.

Sadeh, A., Gruber, R., & Raviv, A. (2003). The effects of sleep restriction and extension on school-age children: What a difference an hour makes. *Child Development*, *74*(2), 444–455.

Schlarb, A. A., Bihlmaier, I., Velten-Schurian, K., Poets, C. F., & Hautzinger, M. (2016). Short- and long-term effects of CBT-I in groups of children suffering from chronic insomnia: The KiSS program. *Behavioral Sleep Medicine*, 1–21.

Simard, V., & Nielsen, T. (2009). Adaptation of imagery rehearsal therapy for nightmares in children: A brief report. *Psychotherapy: Theory, Research, Practice, Training*, 46(4), 492.

Wood, B., Rea, M. S., Plitnick, B., & Figueiro, M. G. (2013). Light level and duration of exposure determine the impact of self-luminous tablets on melatonin suppression. *Applied Ergonomics*, 44, 237–240.

17

Disruptive Behavior and Conduct

Ann F. Garland

Disruptive behavior and conduct problems are cited as the most common reasons for children to be referred to public mental health care (Garland et al., 2001; Lochman et al., 2011). This may not be surprising given that these types of problems are most troublesome to the adults who care for children (e.g., parents and teachers). Disruptive behavior and conduct problems include aggression, defiance, violation of rules and/or other people's rights, destruction of property, bullying, and other delinquent, disobedient, and hostile behavior. These problems are sometimes referred to as "externalizing" problems because they are observable and are exhibited toward others, as contrasted to "internalizing" problems reflecting internal psychological experiences which can be less obvious to the external observer, such as anxiety or depressed mood.

Disruptive behavior and conduct problems reflect a lack of developmentally appropriate self-control of emotions and behavior. The developmental context is important to consider in that some behaviors which are normative at one age (e.g., occasional temper tantrums at age two) are not developmentally appropriate for older youth. Likewise, the two primary diagnoses from the *Diagnostic and Statistical Manual* (DSM-5; American Psychiatric Association, 2013) within this broad problem category are generally associated with different age groups. The first, oppositional defiant disorder (ODD), is often diagnosed in childhood (as opposed to adolescence) and is characterized by a consistent pattern of disobedient, defiant, and hostile behavior toward parents or other authority figures lasting at least six months. Children diagnosed with ODD are often described as arguing with adults, deliberately annoying others, blaming others, refusing to comply with rules or requests, losing their temper, and being easily annoyed. Estimates suggest that approximately 3% of youth in the United States are diagnosed with ODD and it is more common in boys (www.samhsa.gov/disorders/mental).

The second major DSM-5 diagnosis in this category, conduct disorder (CD), is characterized by a pattern of behavior which violates social norms or other people's rights (APA, 2013). This can include (a) aggressive behavior threatening or harming people or animals (e.g., bullying, fighting); (b) property destruction (e.g., vandalism, fire-setting); (c) deceitfulness or theft (e.g., lying, shop-lifting); and (d) other serious violation of rules or laws (e.g., truancy, running away from home). CD can be diagnosed among youth at any age, but it is more common in teenagers. When diagnosed with an onset before age ten there is a greater risk of poor long-term outcomes (Lochman et al., 2011). Estimates suggest a national lifetime prevalence of 8.5% in the United States (www.samhsa.gov/disorders/mental).

Research on the development of aggressive behavior in children suggests that it can be multidetermined with risk factors ranging from the child's genetic make-up, temperament, and social cognitive style (i.e., the way they interpret social situations), to their community context and social peers, and their caregivers' parenting style. Some children may be predisposed to aggressive behavior which may be exacerbated by community and/or peer influences or harsh or neglectful parenting. In addition, research suggests that children with these types of behavior problems often exhibit a pattern of distorted thinking whereby they interpret social situations in a hostile way and respond accordingly. These children may be less likely to attend to nonhostile cues and may judge aggressive behavior positively, expecting aggressive behavior to be the most effective response (Dodge, 2006; Lochman et al., 2011). The interventions discussed below are intended to address these etiological features of disruptive and conduct disorders.

Etiology and Theoretical Underpinnings of Treatment

As described more fully in the next sections, there are two major classes of effective treatment for children with disruptive behavior and/or conduct problems. These are: (1) behavioral parent training models wherein caregivers (hereinafter all those in a parenting role will be referred to as parents) learn new parenting strategies to change their child's behavior; and (2) child skill-building treatments wherein children learn skills to improve their anger management and social interactions. Both of these types of interventions are based in social learning theory, and the most effective parent training approaches also incorporate family systems theory (McCart & Sheidow, 2016).

Social learning theory focuses on how individuals learn and/or change behavior based on observation, imitation, and modeling; it represents an expansion of traditional learning theory, which established how behavior is shaped by differential reinforcement (i.e., consequences) (Bandura, 1986). Behavioral parent training applies social learning theory by teaching and coaching parents to monitor their child's behavior carefully and to clearly and consistently respond with either positive reinforcement for positive behaviors (e.g., attention and praise for cooperative behavior) or negative consequences for negative behavior (e.g., withdrawing attention and ignoring "annoying" behaviors or punishing negative behaviors). The most effective parent training interventions implement this behavioral training approach within a family systems theoretical framework which posits that a family member's behavior problems are actually a reflection of dysfunctional relationships within the family. The family systems perspective adds appreciation for the importance of attending to the quality of the family members' attachments and alliances and the communication patterns within the family. It also acknowledges how family members' roles can often maintain problems. In family systems theory, an individual's problems are actually attributed to a problem in the system, as opposed to a problem within the individual (Hoffman, 1981).

Child skill-building treatments are also based largely on social learning theory as applied through cognitive-behavioral therapy (CBT) interventions. These treatments target children and adolescents directly (individually or in groups) and are aimed at educating the youth about their thoughts, emotions, and behaviors. Decades of research has demonstrated that aggressive behavior problems are often associated with a "hostile attribution bias" whereby children are more likely to perceive social situations as potentially threatening, and are thus more likely to behave aggressively (Dodge, 2006). The goal of treatment is to change these dysfunctional interpretations and responses. Child skill-building treatments include a focus on learning and implementing improved social skills and communication skills to supplant the aggressive, oppositional, or deviant responses that led these youth into treatment. The treatments include techniques described below to help children build more positive social skills and developmentally appropriate emotion regulation skills (i.e., the ability to manage emotions).

Intermittent Explosive Disorder and Fire-Setting

Intermittent explosive disorder (IED) is a condition characterized by dangerous, violent, or rageful behavior that cannot be explained by another diagnosis or medical problem and that is disproportionate to the situation. The prevalence and causes are not well understood, but one estimate suggests a lifetime incidence as high as 5–7% (Kessler et al., 2006). The average onset of the disorder is age 13 for males and 19 for females, thus it is rare in young children. Treatment recommendations include CBT to address anger management and coping, as well as psychopharmacology to reduce impulsivity and aggression, but there is limited research on efficacy. The disorder is somewhat controversial as it has been used to "explain" violent and/or illegal behavior.

Another particularly concerning problem related to disruptive and conduct problems is fire-setting, also called pyromania. Pyromania is classified as an impulse control disorder in which individuals fail to resist the impulse or compulsion to start fires. These individuals may have a fascination with fire and fire-related interests. They often also have other antisocial tendencies and significant anger. This is a low prevalence disorder, but one with severe potential consequences. Risk factors can include early trauma, parental neglect, early experiences of fire-setting, and peer pressure. Treatments include CBT strategies such as problem-solving skill training, cognitive restructuring, anger management, and response prevention. Behavioral parent training and fire safety education are also recommended for childhood effective treatment of fire-setting. Successful treatment may be very challenging as one study found a greater than 50% recidivism rate in fire-setting (Kolko et al., 2001).

Brief Overview of Evidence-Based Treatments

Some of the treatment models with the strongest evidence of positive impact for youth with severe disruptive and conduct problems incorporate behavioral parent training, family therapy, and child CBT skill-building components. McCart and Sheidow (2016) conducted an extensive review of treatments for adolescents with these problems and identified two treatment packages meeting the most rigorous criteria as well-established treatments, namely Multisystemic therapy (MST; Henggeler et al., 2009) and Treatment Foster Care Oregon (TFCO; Chamberlain 2003). Both of these treatments are intensive, home-based, multicomponent interventions targeting parents and youth; they have demonstrated strong effectiveness with adolescents whose behavior problems are severe enough to involve the juvenile justice system.

Several additional treatments were classified as "probably efficacious" for adolescents with disruptive and conduct problems, including additional multicomponent programs, such as Functional Family Therapy (Sexton & Turner, 2010); and youth-focused treatments, such as Aggression Replacement Training + Positive Peer Culture (Leeman, Gibbs, & Fuller, 1993) and Solution-Focused Group Program (Shin, 2009). Many additional treatments were classified as possibly efficacious.

A recently updated review of treatments for children age 12 and younger identified two types of treatment as well established; these were group parent behavior therapy and individual parent behavior therapy (Kaminski & Claussen, 2017). The treatment programs within these two treatment types included Incredible Years (Webster-Stratton & Reid, 2003), Positive Parenting Program (Triple P; Sanders, 1999), Parent Management Treatment – Oregon Model (Ogden & Hagen, 2008), and Parent–Child Interaction Therapy (PCIT; Brinkmeyer & Eyberg, 2003).

An additional 13 types of treatment were classified as "probably efficacious." These included a variety of variations of group and individual behavior therapy for children and/or parents, some including teacher training. Behaviorally oriented treatments predominated as contrasted to other types of treatment (Kaminski & Claussen, 2017). Details regarding treatment models mentioned in this section are available at the websites listed in the Useful Resources section at the end of this chapter.

Components of Evidence-Based Treatments

As noted above, there are many different individual treatment models which have demonstrated efficacy and effectiveness for children and adolescents with disruptive and conduct problems and there are core treatment components which are common across these multiple individual treatments (Garland et al., 2008). These common components include techniques a therapist uses, and content or skills the therapist addresses with children and families. Garland and colleagues (Garland, Hurlburt, & Hawley, 2006; Garland et al., 2008) were among the early proponents of a common components approach to identifying and implementing evidence-based practices. First we conducted a study to dissect the eight most well-established individual evidence-based psychosocial treatments for children (ages four to 13 years) with disruptive behavior problems to identify core elements of each individual treatment. Multiple raters reviewed treatment materials for each of the eight treatments and then elements that were found in a majority of treatments were labeled as common elements. The initial list of common core elements was distributed to a panel of national experts who endorsed its validity. The resulting set of common elements included (a) therapeutic content components (i.e., what a therapist addresses in therapy) and (b) treatment technique components (i.e., strategies a therapist uses to address the content). These components can be delivered to parents, children, or both (Garland et al., 2008).

This method of identifying core common elements of evidence-based treatments is only a first step in identifying treatment components that may be the essential "active ingredients" in evidence-based practice for this clinical problem area. In other words, just because treatment elements are common across multiple evidence-based treatment models does not necessarily mean that these elements are the essential active ingredients responsible for the effectiveness of the treatment. Dismantling studies which can rigorously test the unique impact of treatment components are needed to confirm the active ingredients of treatment. However, short of that, Garland and colleagues (2008) have speculated that the common elements (components) of evidence-based practices are a reasonable set of elements to examine as potential important treatment components. In subsequent research, Garland and colleagues (2014) demonstrated that families who received treatment that was more consistent with some of the common elements of evidence-based practice also demonstrated greater positive outcomes.

Other research teams have used different research methods to identify common components of evidence-based treatment for children and adolescents with disruptive behaviors and conduct problems. For example, Kaminski and colleagues (2008) conducted a meta-analysis and identified treatment components associated with effectiveness of parent behavioral training interventions. In addition, Lochman and colleagues (2011) conducted a comprehensive review of cognitive-behavioral therapy for disruptive behaviors in children and adolescents and they identified the treatment elements included in the evidence-based models. Chorpita, Daleiden, and Weisz (2005) also list the practice elements derived from their distillation and matching model of identifying practice elements of evidence-based practice for specific clinical populations. In sum, research teams have used a variety of methods to identify and highlight the treatment components that are common to evidence-based practice for this clinical population and these are incorporated in Table 1 below. Each of these components is described subsequently.

Table 1: *Content Components of Evidence-Based Practice for Youth with Disruptive Behavior and Conduct Problems*

Youth-Focused	Parent-Focused
(1) Education about emotions	(1) Improving parent–child relationship quality
(2) Anger management	(2) Social learning concepts: principles of differential reinforcement
(3) Perspective taking / Cognitive restructuring	(3) Consistent discipline: use of time-outs and consequences
(4) Problem-solving skill building	(4) Stress management
	(5) Improving family communication
	(6) Minimizing peer influence

(Sources for Table 1 include: Garland et al., 2008; Kaminski et al., 2008; Lochman et al., 2011; McCart & Sheidow, 2016)

Table 1 lists therapeutic content and/or skills that therapists may address in treatment, but therapists use a variety of different techniques to deliver these content components. In evidence-based practice, therapists use techniques such as psychoeducation, skill modeling (e.g., demonstrating through enactment or through use of toys or characters), role-playing (e.g., behavioral rehearsal), coaching, reinforcement or limit-setting (e.g., praising or correcting), and homework assignments and follow-up (Garland et al., 2008). Research on parent training interventions has demonstrated that the active skill-building techniques such as role-playing with coaching feedback appear to be associated with the most successful treatment, as contrasted to relying on imparting information exclusively (Kaminski et al., 2008).

Youth-Focused Skill-Building Treatments

Education About Emotions. Prior to working on changing emotional responses, CBT-based interventions educate children about emotions. This often includes helping children to recognize emotions in themselves and others, and helping them to learn labels to use when talking about emotions. Young children often lack the ability to differentiate types of emotions and they often have a limited vocabulary to describe emotions. For example, children may experience emotions as feeling good versus feeling bad, but their ability to distinguish and describe the distinction between "bad" feelings of anger, fear, worry, sadness, etc. may not be as well developed. Therapists can use photos or drawings of facial expressions depicting different emotional states to help children differentiate, describe, and label emotions.

Children are also taught to recognize physiological experiences associated with different emotions so they can identify early "warning signs" of their emotional responses. This focus on bodily sensations can be very important with children who may not be as ready to engage in psychotherapy when it is entirely based on talking about emotions as abstract phenomena. Grounding a discussion of emotions in how it feels in your body (e.g., muscles tightening, face reddening, stomach hurting) may engage a child more effectively. Education about emotions can also include teaching children to more accurately assess and respond to the intensity of the emotion as a first step in attempting to prevent a rapid escalation in emotional outbursts.

Anger Management. Once children have greater awareness of their emotions and an improved ability to label them and identify physiological sensations signaling different emotions, the next step is to help them to regulate or manage their emotions in a more socially and developmentally appropriate way. Teaching strategies to control anger, in particular, is essential to CBT-based interventions for this group of children and youth (Lochman et al., 2011). Anger management strategies addressed in treatment include techniques to calm, distract, or deflect anger-arousing situations, as described below.

Therapists may start with very basic calming skills such as deep-breathing exercises. Relaxation training is a common approach to anger management and may include "guided imagery" exercises where the client is trained to distract and calm themselves with peaceful imagined scenes. To be effective, these imagery exercises must be personalized to the individual. For example, one person's ideal relaxation image may be the experience of floating in a pool whereas another person's ideal relaxation image may involve climbing mountains and enjoying the view from atop a high peak. Either of these images could be anxiety provoking to others. In guided imagery, therapists coach clients on how to imagine themselves in their unique ideal scene, including imagining the sensory experiences associated with the scene (e.g., sounds, sights, physical sensations). Clients are encouraged to practice the imagery outside of therapy sessions, with the goal that clients will be able to use this skill independently over time to calm themselves. Sometimes therapists use aids such as tape recordings to facilitate guided imagery. There is an ever-expanding proliferation of apps and online resources for guided imagery and relaxation skills.

Therapists may also help clients learn to relax themselves through an exercise known as "progressive muscle relaxation." Clients are taught to tense and release muscle groups in their body progressing from their feet up through the body to the head and face. The goal is to empower the client to feel as if they can discard anger (or other negative emotions such as anxiety) as they release muscle tension. Like guided imagery, this exercise is initially led by the therapist with the goal of the client ultimately being able to use the strategy independently and aids such as recordings or apps are often used.

Anger management is also addressed through social practice or role-playing. This can be done individually with a therapist initially modeling constructive anger management skills and then coaching the child to practice these skills in a role-play.

Specific exercises might look like this: the therapist plays the role of a child on the playground who says something rude to the client, like "Why are you so slow?" The therapist may then model a variety of verbal or behavioral responses to demonstrate a range of potential responses. The therapist and child may also generate likely consequences of these potential responses. The client is then coached to work on responses that are most likely to prevent further escalation of anger and aggression. These might include use of a calming self-statement (e.g., "I'm not going to let him get to me this time"), behavioral strategies such as ignoring and walking away, and/or communication strategies that may diffuse the situation (e.g., use of humor as a distraction). These approaches are most likely to be effective when they are personalized to the child's unique personality and context and when children are involved in generating the potential coping strategies and statements that fit for them.

Anger management skill building can also be addressed in group treatment where clients practice communication and social problem-solving skills with each other, while being coached by a therapist. This may provide the best "in vivo" training for children to practice more constructive social skills. Another alternative for children who may be reluctant to participate in role-plays is to use toys or puppets to enact the role-plays. Regardless of the format, evidence-based therapy models advise a progressive escalation in the potential anger arousal of the role-play situations to incrementally build anger management skills (Lochman et al., 2011). Anger management is a common focus of psychotherapy and the strategies summarized above are found in many evidence-based treatments (Garland et al., 2008; Lochman et al., 2011).

Perspective-Taking as a Type of Cognitive Restructuring. Given that children with disruptive behaviors and conduct problems tend to misinterpret other people's intentions as potentially threatening even in benign or ambiguous situations (i.e., the youths have a hostile attribution bias; Dodge, 2006), therapists work with these children to change these "automatic" thoughts and behavioral responses. Therapists work to help clients challenge their usual patterns of thoughts and actions (e.g., the hostile attributions leading to aggressive responses) and to teach them to generate alternative, nonhostile interpretations of social behavior. Therapists may use role-plays to help clients to experience an ambiguous situation from multiple perspectives and explore alternative interpretations of other people's intentions. These kinds of perspective-taking exercises can also help to build empathy skills whereby children improve their ability to imagine how others may be feeling in a situation.

Problem-Solving Skill Building. In addition to the anger management and perspective-taking skills that therapists teach children, most evidence-based treatment models include some variation of training on general problem-solving strategies, or, specifically, social problem-solving strategies. The goal is to teach children a step-by-step problem-solving approach which they can ultimately apply across a wide variety of interpersonal situations (e.g., peer or sibling conflict, conflict with parents or other authority figures). This treatment component is usually introduced after children have gained some ability to manage their anger well enough to actually attempt to solve a problem (Lochman et al., 2011).

Alan Kazdin (2003) developed one of the early problem-solving skills training approaches and there is a great deal of research to support its efficacy with children who have conduct problems. In his model, children are taught the following five basic steps of problem-solving: (1) identify the problem, (2) list possible solutions, (3) evaluate the possible solutions (in terms of likely consequences, etc.), (4) choose one solution, and (5) try it and evaluate the outcome.

Like the other skill-building activities reviewed so far, therapists use a variety of techniques to help children gain these skills, including psychoeducation, skill modeling, and role-playing practice with corrective feedback. Homework assignments are used to try to generalize the skill building beyond the confines of the therapy session and children are encouraged to evaluate how well the approach worked in their real-life situations. Therapists are trained to positively reinforce children's efforts to use these steps within and outside of therapy sessions (e.g., with specific praise or other tangible rewards). There is some evidence that including the parents and teachers in the exercises will help to reinforce the skill-building impact.

There are a variety of other problem-solving or social problem-solving approaches, but all share a focus on improving children's understanding of the chain of Antecedents–Behavior–Consequences (Lochman et al., 2011). An important goal is to help children recognize that different behavioral choices will result in different consequences. The evidence-based Coping Power intervention for children with disruptive and conduct problems includes a model similar to the Kazdin model, but it is simplified into three primary steps: Problem Identification, Choices, and Consequences (Lochman et al., 2011). Children often learn this approach in a group setting and practice it using role-plays, story writing, and even creation of a video portraying effective problem-solving.

Parent-Focused Behavioral Treatments

Improving Parent–Child Relationship Quality. Many of the parent management training interventions emphasize the importance of empowering parents with improved disciplinary skills (as described below). However, prior to focusing on discipline, some interventions include treatment components designed to improve the attachment bond and quality of the parent–child relationship, which can often be particularly negative by the time children with disruptive behavior and their parents present for treatment. The goal is to increase positive parenting skills and warmth in the parent–child relationship as a foundation for the subsequent disciplinary emphasis (Brinkmeyer & Eyberg, 2003).

Therapists work with parents to increase their positive interactions with their child by paying more attention to positive behaviors, intentionally seeking out pleasant activities, showing an interest in the child's favorite topics and strengths, etc. One evidence-based treatment program called Parent–Child Interaction Therapy (PCIT; Brinkmeyer & Eyberg, 2003) teaches parents to play with their children in more constructive ways through an exercise called Child-Directed Interaction. Parents are coached to avoid giving commands, asking questions, or criticizing the child's choices in play. Instead, parents are guided by the acronym PRIDE to emphasize: Praise, Reflect, Imitate, Describe, and Enjoyment. While this particular model is intended for young children, the goal of improving the quality of the relationship or the emotional bond between parent and child through more positive interactions and "special time" together is common in evidence-based treatments (Lochman et al., 2011).

A meta-analysis designed to identify critical elements of effective parent management interventions identified increasing positive parent–child interactions as a particularly significant treatment element associated with positive outcomes (Kaminski et al., 2008).

Social Learning Concepts: Principles of Differential Reinforcement. Behavioral parent training is based largely on the principles of learning theory as applied to parenting practices. Using psychoeducation, therapists help parents recognize how behavior can be predicted and how it is influenced by consequences. Parents are taught to identify and monitor their child's positive and negative behaviors through the Antecedents–Behaviors–Consequences "lens." Therapists work with parents to be more alert to positive behaviors and to deliver positive consequences (e.g., positive reinforcement such as attention and praise for helping out a sibling). Therapists often work with parents to develop a reward chart for use at home, or a "token economy" system whereby children earn points for positive behaviors and lose points for negative behaviors with the ultimate goal of gaining a larger reward (e.g., a special activity, privilege, or desired "prize"). To be effective, these interventions need to be individualized to the specific reward preferences of the child or teen and the parent needs to be very clear and explicit about the behavior that is being rewarded or punished.

Given that parental attention can be very reinforcing for children even if that attention is not positive, parents are taught to withdraw their attention from their child's mildly "annoying" behaviors. A classic pattern can evolve whereby children exhibit annoying behavior such as whining in an effort to get their parents' attention. Parents can inadvertently reinforce this behavior by then interacting with the child and even if the parents are expressing annoyance, the child's behavior has captured the parents' attention and thus has been reinforced. Learning how to ignore minor behavior disruptions is an important component of parent training. Parents are forewarned that when they initially implement this strategy, a child's demands for attention through annoying behavior may escalate as they are seeking the usual parental attention response, but this strategy is often effective in reducing annoying behaviors in the long-term (Lochman et al., 2011). Therapists use psychoeducation, modeling, role-playing, and review of homework assignments to help parents gain these skills.

Consistent Discipline: Use of Time-Outs and Consequences. Research has demonstrated that parenting practices such as particularly harsh discipline, as well as nonresponse or neglectful discipline, are associated with children's aggressive behavior (Lochman et al., 2011). Therefore, one of the goals of parent training is to empower parents with new, more constructive disciplinary strategies and to encourage parents to be consistent and clear in their disciplinary practices. Therapists work with the parents to evaluate the types of discipline they have used in the past and to explore their openness to alternative methods. One of the issues that often arises is the use of corporal punishment (e.g., spanking); many therapists use psychoeducation, attempting to persuade parents about the risks (e.g., increased aggression) and ineffectiveness of corporal punishment. These discussions require sensitivity regarding potential cultural and historical differences in child-rearing norms.

One of the common disciplinary techniques included in evidence-based approaches with children is the "time-out." Parents learn a step-by-step approach to placing their child in a time-out if the child does not comply with a request. Parents of older children and teens are encouraged to use punishment strategies such as the loss of desired privileges, objects, or activities. Therapists will use modeling and role-playing to help parents learn to practice these skills. The overriding goal is to improve the parents' repertoire of effective, age-appropriate, and ethical discipline strategies.

A meta-analysis designed to identify critical elements of effective parent management interventions identified teaching time-out and the importance of consistent discipline as a particularly significant treatment component associated with positive outcomes (Kaminski et al., 2008).

Stress Management. Therapists often work with parents to help them reduce their own stress in order to be able to work more effectively on their parenting practices. Therapists may help parents learn relaxation techniques, or identify the activities they find stress relieving and help to find more opportunities to pursue these activities. Peer support groups can also be stress relieving for parents as they can share their challenges with other parents who are similarly stressed and thus feel less alone. Intensive, multicomponent treatment programs also include explicit attention to a wide variety of potential parent and family needs that are causing stress, such as housing, financial, vocational, legal, marital, or health issues.

Improving Family Communication. In order to improve the quality of parent–child relationships and the consistency of discipline practices, parents often need to learn how to communicate more effectively. Communication training may include psychoeducation about age-appropriate expectations (e.g., teaching parents that long, nuanced explanations about behavior expectations are not appropriate for toddlers). In addition, communication training may include a focus on how parents can help children to recognize and describe their emotions (see the first component in child treatment section). Kaminski and colleagues' (2008) meta-analysis of parent training approaches reported that teaching parents to improve their emotional communication skills was associated with more positive outcomes.

Communication training for parents also addresses how parents make requests or, when necessary, commands, to their children. Through therapist modeling and role-playing, parents learn to be clear and concise. Clarity in rule-setting and follow-through is emphasized to build consistency in expectations for children and teens.

Communication training is also a major focus of functional family therapy approaches which seek to build new patterns of family behavior with the ultimate goal of shifting the dysfunctional family relationships which were maintaining the behavior problems (McCart & Sheidow, 2016).

Minimizing Peer Influence. Given that association with other youth with conduct behavior problems is a significant risk factor for future conduct problems, some of the effective interventions for these youths explicitly seek to limit the teen's exposure to other "deviant" youth (McCart & Sheidow, 2016). These interventions aim to engage the youth in more prosocial peer activities and school performance while disengaging from deviant peers (e.g., delinquent youth). The goal is to empower the parents to enforce limit-setting around peer activities and to improve the youth's prosocial skills and problem-solving (as described above).

Role of Parents in Treatment

Parents clearly have an essential role in effective treatment for disruptive behavior and conduct problems. Many of these interventions rely on parents to "collect data" about their child's or adolescent's behavior, noting the circumstances surrounding positive or negative behaviors, as well as the frequency and duration of targeted behaviors. Parents are viewed as partners in these interventions, which are sometimes called "parent-mediated" treatments, referring to the fact that the therapist works directly with the parent, who is the agent or mechanism to impact the desired changes in child or adolescent behavior. As noted above, the goal is to empower parents with more effective parenting skills. The majority of the well-researched treatments for adolescents with disruptive and conduct problems include parents (McCart & Sheidow, 2016) and both of the two treatment groups identified as well-established for children age 12 and under are parent behavioral training interventions (Kaminski & Claussen, 2017).

Given the research indicating that children who have experienced harsh, inconsistent, or neglectful parenting are at increased risk for these disruptive and conduct problems, many of the evidence-based interventions are designed to help parents increase the consistency of constructive disciplinary strategies (and also decrease ineffective disciplinary techniques). In addition, as noted above, some of the interventions are intended to improve parents' ability to build more positive relationships with their children.

Other Variables Influencing Treatment

Assessment

Accurate assessment of the environmental and social context, frequency, severity, and functional impairment impact of disruptive and conduct behaviors is essential given that most of these behaviors (defiance, aggression) are within normative developmental expectations at different ages. In other words, almost every child or adolescent will exhibit some of these behaviors, so it is important to assess for severity and frequency, as well as impairment in functioning related to the disruptive and conduct problems. In addition, as noted throughout the chapter, assessment of parenting behaviors and family relationships is also important in understanding how problems may have developed and how they are maintained in the family system.

Comorbidity

Disruptive behavior and conduct problems can co-occur with a variety of other behavioral/mental health problems and/or developmental disorders. Attention-deficit/hyperactivity disorders (ADHD) may co-occur or present somewhat similarly with impulsivity as a common feature. Alternatively, youth with disruptive and conduct problems may also be experiencing anxiety or mood symptoms that can be "masked" by the troublesome externalizing behaviors which are more obvious to others. It can be a surprise sometimes to parents or other adults to learn that youth with conduct problems are also frequently depressed and/or anxious. In addition, one of the distinguishing symptoms of depression in youth, as compared to adults, is irritability which can be exhibited as oppositionality and defiance.

Demographics

Many studies have attempted to identify family demographic factors associated with treatment effectiveness and most have not found any significant variables (McCart & Sheidow, 2016). However, a large meta-analysis of 71 studies indicated that CBT treatments were more effective for adolescents compared to young children (McCart, Priester, & Davies, 2006). Another study of 40 CBT treatments indicated that children with moderately severe behavior problems are more likely to benefit from treatment compared to children with severe or mild problems, and children without a history of violent behavior also seem to benefit more from treatment (Sukhodolsky, Kassinove,

& Gorman, 2004). There is no consistent evidence regarding gender differences in childhood treatment effectiveness (Kaminski & Claussen, 2017).

There is limited evidence of significant potential differences in treatment effectiveness by race/ethnicity of the youth or family (Kaminski & Claussen, 2017). Many of the treatments described in this chapter have been tested with relatively diverse samples and some of them have demonstrated equivalent overall outcomes with Caucasian youth/families and youth/families of color (Huey & Polo, 2008; Ollendick et al., 2016). However, there is some evidence of race/ethnic differences in engagement in treatment (e.g., sustained attendance and participation) and cultural factors are likely to impact families' receptivity to certain types of interventions; thus some cultural tailoring of interventions may be warranted (Lau, 2006).

Medication

There is a moderately strong overlap in children with ADHD and oppositional defiant disorder and there is evidence that medication treatment for the ADHD (e.g., psychostimulants) can have positive effects on impulsive behavior. In addition, children with severe disruptive and conduct problems sometimes receive atypical antipsychotic medication to reduce aggression and impulsivity (Turgay, 2009). Limited research suggests this may be helpful for some, but long-term safety is relatively unknown and some concerns regarding health risks have been raised (Loy et al., 2012).

Treatment Techniques

Treatment techniques that emphasize actual behavior change and skill building appear to be more impactful than exclusive reliance on education about emotions (Sukhodolsky, Kassinove, & Gorman, 2004). This finding is consistent with another meta-analytic study of parent training treatments which found that actual skill-building techniques were associated with more positive outcomes (Kaminski et al., 2008).

Multimodal Approaches

Studies indicate that multimodal approaches which combine CBT skill building for children with behavioral parent training may be more effective than singular approaches (Lochman et al., 2011).

Conclusion

Disruptive behavior and conduct disorders are among the most common of mental health problems. Left untreated, or ineffectively treated, the long-term negative impacts of such problems can result in devastating social, academic, family, and potentially legal consequences. However, there is reason for optimism because many treatment approaches have demonstrated significant positive effects for children, adolescents, and their families. These approaches target improvements in parenting behaviors and youths' social and emotional skills. By skillfully utilizing the treatment components reviewed in this chapter, a therapist can help a child and family relieve years of antagonism and frustration, to build more positive relationships and a brighter future.

Useful Resources

Web-based resources providing more information about effective treatment for children and adolescents with disruptive behavior and conduct disorders are listed below. General sites for information on promising practices:

- General information about evidence-based treatment for families and professionals: www.effectivechildtherapy.org
- Resource for healthy youth development programs: www.blueprintsprograms.com/
- California Evidence-Based Clearinghouse for Child Welfare: www.cebc4cw.org/

Websites for specific programs:

- Anger Coping/Coping Power: www.copingpower.com/
- Parent–Child Interaction Therapy (PCIT): www.pcit.org/
- Problem-Solving Skills Training: yaleparentingcenter.yale.edu
- Multisystemic Therapy: www.mstservices.com/
- Parent Management Training – Oregon Model: www.isii.net/index.html
- Incredible Years: http://incredibleyears.com/
- Triple P (Positive Parenting Program): www.triplep-parenting.com/us-en/triple-p/

References

American Psychiatric Association (APA). (2013). *Diagnostic and statistical manual of mental disorders*. 5th edn. Washington, DC: American Psychiatric Association.

Bandura, A. (1986). *Social foundations of thought and action: A social cognitive theory*. Engelwood Cliffs, NJ: Prentice-Hall.

Brinkmeyer, M. Y., & Eyberg, S. M. (2003). Parent–child interaction therapy for oppositional children. In A. E. Kazdin & J. R. Weisz (eds.), *Evidence-based psychotherapies for children and adolescents* (pp. 204–223). New York: Guilford Press.

Chamberlain, P. (2003). *Treating chronic juvenile offenders: Advances made through the Oregon Multidimensional Treatment Foster Care Model*. Washington, DC: American Psychological Association.

Chorpita, B. F., Daleiden, E. L., & Weisz, J. R. (2005). Identifying and selecting the common elements of evidence based interventions: A distillation and matching model. *Mental Health Services Research*, 7, 5–20. PMID:15832690

Dodge, K. A. (2006). Translational science in action: Hostile attributional style and the development of aggressive behavior problems. *Developmental Psychopathology*, *18*(3), 791–814.

Garland, A. F., Accurso, E. C., Haine-Schlagel, R., Brookman-Frazee, L., Roesch, S., & Zhang, J. J. (2014). Searching for elements of evidence-based practices in children's usual care and examining their impact. *Journal of Clinical Child & Adolescent Psychology*, *43*, 201–215. doi:10.1080/15374416.2013.869750

Garland, A. F., Hawley, K. M. Brookman-Frazee, L. I., & Hurlburt, M. (2008). Identifying common elements of evidence-based psychosocial treatments for children's disruptive behavior problems. *Journal of the American Academy of Child & Adolescent Psychiatry*, *47*, 505–514.

Garland, A. F., Hough, R., McCabe, K., Yeh, M., Wood, P., & Aarons, G. (2001). Prevalence of psychiatric disorders for youths in public sectors of care. *Journal of the American Academy of Child & Adolescent Psychiatry*, *40*, 409–418.

Garland, A. F., Hurlburt, M. S., & Hawley, K. M. (2006). Examining psychotherapy processes in a services research context. *Clinical Psychology: Science and Practice*, *13*, 30–46.

Henggeler, S. W., Schoenwald, S. K., Borduin, C. M., Rowland, M. D., & Cunningham, P. B. (2009). *Multisystemic therapy for antisocial behavior in children and adolescents*. 2nd edn. New York: Guilford Press.

Hoffman, L. (1981). *Foundations of family therapy: A conceptual framework for systems change*. New York: Basic Books.

Huey, S. J., & Polo, A. J. (2008). Evidence-based psychosocial treatments for ethnic minority youth. *Journal of Clinical Child & Adolescent Psychology*, *37*, 262–301.

Kaminski, J. W., & Claussen, A. H. (2017). Evidence base update for psychosocial treatments for disruptive behaviors in children. *Journal of Clinical Child & Adolescent Psychology*, *46*(4). doi:10.1080/15374416.2017.1310044

Kaminski, J. W., Valle, L. A., Filene, J. H., & Boyle, C. L. (2008). A meta-analytic review of components associated with parent training program effectiveness. *Journal of Abnormal Child Psychology*, *36*, 567–589.

Kazdin, A. E. (2003). Problem-solving skills training and parent management training for conduct disorder. In A. E. Kazdin & J. R. Weisz (eds.). *Evidence-based psychotherapies for children and adolescents* (pp. 241–262). New York: Guilford Press.

Kessler, R. C., Coccaro, E. F., Fava, M., Jaeger, S., Jin, R., & Walters, E. (2006). The prevalence and correlates of DSM-IV intermittent explosive disorder in the National Comorbidity Survey Replication. *Archives of General Psychiatry*, *63*(6), 669–678.

Kolko, D. J., Day, B. T., Bridge, J. A., & Kazdin, A. E. (2001). Two-year prediction of children's fire-setting in clinically referred and nonreferred samples. *Journal of Child Psychology and Psychiatry*, *42*(3), 371–380. doi:10.1111/1469–7610.00730

Lau, A. S. (2006). Making the case for selective and directed cultural adaptations of evidence-based treatments: Examples from parent training. *Clinical Psychology: Science and Practice*, *13*, 295–310.

Leeman, L. W., Gibbs, J. C., & Fuller, D. (1993). Evaluation of a multicomponent group treatment program for juvenile delinquents. *Aggressive Behavior*, *19*(4), 281–292. doi:10.1002/(ISSN)1098–2337.

Lochman, J. E., Powell, N. P., Boxmeyer, C. L., & Jimenez-Camargo, L. (2011). Cognitive-behavioural therapy for externalizing disorders in children and adolescents. *Child Adolescent Psychiatric Clinics of North America*, *20*, 305–218.

Loy, J. H., Merry, S. N., Hetrick, S. E., & Stasiak, K. (2012). Atypical antipsychotics for disruptive behaviour disorders in children and youths. Cochrane Database of Systematic Reviews 2012, Issue 9. Art. No.: CD008559.

McCart, M. R., Priester, P. E., Davies, W. H., et al. (2006). Differential effectiveness of behavioral parent training and cognitive-behavioral therapy for antisocial youth: A meta-analysis. *Journal of Abnormal Child Psychology, 34*(4), 527–543.

McCart, M. R., & Sheidow, A. J. (2016). Evidence-based psychosocial treatments for adolescents with disruptive behavior. *Journal of Clinical Child & Adolescent Psychology, 49*(5), 529–563. doi:10.1018/15374416.2016.1146990

Ogden, T., & Hagen, K. A. (2008). Treatment effectiveness of parent management training in Norway: A randomized controlled trial of children with conduct problems. *Journal of Consulting and Clinical Psychology, 76*(4), 607–621. doi:10. 1037/0022-006X.76.4.607

Ollendick, T. H., Greene, R. W., Austin, K. E., Fraire, M. G., Halldorsdottir, T., Allen, K. B. . . . & Wolff, J. C. (2016). Parent management training and collaborative & proactive solutions: A randomized control trial for oppositional youth. *Journal of Clinical Child & Adolescent Psychology, 45*(5), 591–604. doi:10.1080/158374416.2015.1004681

Sanders, M. R. (1999). Triple P-positive parenting program: Towards an empirically validated multilevel parenting and family support strategy for the prevention of behavior and emotional problems in children. *Clinical Child and Family Psychology Review, 2*, 71–90.

Sexton, T., & Turner, C. W. (2010). The effectiveness of functional family therapy for youth with behavioral problems in a community practice setting. *Journal of Family Psychology, 24*(3), 339–348. doi:10.1037/a0019406

Shin, S. K. (2009). Effects of a solution-focused program on the reduction of aggressiveness and the improvement of social readjustment for Korean youth probationers. *Journal of Social Service Research, 35*(3), 274–284, doi:10.1080/01488370902901079

Sukhodolsky, D. G., Kassinove, H., & Gorman, B. S. (2004). Cognitive-behavioural therapy for anger in children and adolescents: A meta-analysis. *Aggression and Violent Behavior, 3*, 247–269.

Turgay, A. (2009). Psychopharmacological treatment of oppositional defiant disorder. *CNS Drugs, 23*(1), 1–17.

Webster-Stratton, C., & Reid, M. (2003). The Incredible Years parents, teachers, and children training series: A multifaceted treatment approach for young children with conduct problems. In A. E. Kazdin & J. R. Weisz (eds.), *Evidence-based psychotherapies for children and adolescents* (pp. 224–240). New York: Guilford Press.

18

Substance Use

Molly Bobek, Nicole Piazza, Tiffany John, Jacqueline Horan Fisher,
and Aaron Hogue

Substantial research indicates that substance use is highly prevalent among adolescents in the United States. Among twelfth-graders surveyed annually, 64% have used alcohol, 45% have used marijuana, 38% have used cigarettes, and 49% have used other illicit drugs (Johnston et al., 2016). Concerningly, the Substance Abuse and Mental Health Services Administration (SAMHSA, 2007) estimates that nationwide ~125,000 adolescents enroll in outpatient substance use treatment each year; however, this is only 9.1% of the youth who are deemed in need of such services (Haughwout et al., 2016; Johnston et al., 2016).

While adolescent experimentation with alcohol and drugs is considered to be developmentally normative behavior, research shows that those who begin using at an early age are at greater risk for developing a substance use disorder (SUD; SAMHSA, 2013) and are also at risk for other emotional and behavioral problems (The National Center on Addiction and Substance Abuse, 2011). In particular, adolescents who use substances demonstrate increased risk for internalizing and externalizing problems, attention-deficit/hyperactivity disorder, oppositional defiant disorder, and conduct problems (Chan, Dennis, & Funk, 2008). About 60% of youth involved in the juvenile justice system are in need of SUD treatment (Young, Dembo, & Henderson, 2007). In addition, adolescents with SUDs are more likely to sustain injuries due to accidents, overdose, suicide, and violent crime (Keyes, Brady, & Li, 2015; Wong et al., 2013).

Etiology and Theoretical Underpinnings of Treatment

It is widely accepted that adolescent substance use (ASU) is likely influenced by a host of intersecting risk, promotive, and protective factors (e.g., Cleveland et al., 2008). Two prevailing theoretical models – biopsychosocial and dual-process – are particularly relevant in considering the appropriateness of differing models of evidence-based treatment for ASU. From a biopsychosocial perspective, ASU is the result of interactions between biological (e.g., genetics, pubertal changes), psychological (e.g., personality, motivations, expectancies), and social (e.g., peer affiliations, familial substance use, parenting practices) factors (see Griffiths, 2005 for a review). Alternatively, the dual-process model identifies ASU as the result of an interplay between distinct cognitive processes – relatively automatic (i.e., impulsive) processes and relatively controlled (i.e., reflective) processes (see Wiers et al., 2007 for a review). Both of these models are relevant to treatment planning and can be useful in identifying optimal treatment approaches.

Brief Overview of Evidence-Based Treatments

As detailed in a number of published reviews and meta-analyses (Becker & Curry, 2008; Hogue et al., 2014; Tanner-Smith, Wilson, & Lipsy, 2013; Waldron & Turner,

Gambling Disorder

Gambling disorder is considered a substance-related and addictive disorder and is diagnosed using the DSM-5. Like substance abuse, adolescent gambling is important to consider in a neurodevelopmental context, as this period is a time of higher levels of risk-taking and impulsivity (Wilber & Potenza, 2006). Participation in gambling follows a similar trajectory to ASU behavior, with involvement in gambling observed to increase progressively during the adolescent years and peak in early adulthood (St-Pierre & Derevensky, 2016). Recent research represents a shift in thinking of gambling as mainly an adult activity, showing that a significant percentage of adolescents participate in gambling as a form of recreation, and that it may, in fact, be higher among youth than adults (Winters & Stinchfield, 2012), although youth are less likely to be identified as needing treatment for problem gambling (Wilber & Potenza, 2006).

Youth gambling behavior occurs across a continuum, with complete abstinence at one extreme through social or recreational gambling with problem/pathological/disordered gambling at the other extreme (St-Pierre & Derevensky, 2016). Untreated disordered gambling among youths often occurs with multiple negative consequences, such as concurrent smoking, alcohol, and illegal drug use (Weinberger et al., 2015), as well as academic difficulties, poor or disrupted family relationships, delinquency and future criminal behavior, mental health and psychiatric issues, and suicidal ideation and behaviors (St-Pierre & Derevensky, 2016).

Although a small number of gambling assessment instruments for youth have been developed (Winters & Stinchfield, 2012) and some case studies have been published, there are no current treatments considered to be best practices or evidence-based for adolescent gambling. Although research is only recently gaining traction, given the similar trajectory and co-occurrence with SUD and other disorders, opportunities do exist and should be utilized to prevent and treat adolescent gambling. Screening, prevention, intervention, and consideration of novel treatment services are important steps in ensuring gambling behavior does not progress to addiction.

2008), the theoretical treatment approaches with the highest evidence base for out-patient treatment of ASU are cognitive-behavioral therapy (CBT) and ecological and behavioral family therapy (FT).

Cognitive-Behavioral Therapy

With origins in cognitive psychotherapy, social learning theory, and behavior therapy, CBT reduces ASU by helping adolescents monitor thoughts and feelings, alter faulty thinking patterns and manage behavioral responses, identify triggers, and develop communication and problem-solving strategies (Kendall, 2012). Although not studied as often as family therapy, CBT has been studied more consistently in methodologically strong trials (Becker & Curry, 2008).

Other forms of treatment for ASU exist and have demonstrated effectiveness, but do not yet meet this highest standard. These include motivational interviewing, motivation enhancement therapy, and drug counseling (see Useful Resources at the end of this chapter for where to find information on these other approaches; Hogue et al., 2014). Here we focus on the specific core components of the treatments meeting the highest standard of care – family-based treatment (FBT) and cognitive-behavioral therapy (CBT). Chorpita and Daleiden's 2009 core components distillation project defines core components as specific strategies that are common among successful treatments.

Family Therapy

Family-based approaches aim to reduce ASU and corresponding problem behaviors by addressing family risk factors, including poor family communication, cohesiveness, and problem-solving. FT is rooted in the notion that the family unit has the most significant and longest-lasting influence on youth development (Winters et al., 2014). It is the most widely researched outpatient behavioral treatment and has consistently been shown to be more effective across diverse samples of adolescents with SUDs (Baldwin et al., 2012; Tanner-Smith, Wilson, & Lipsey, 2013) and for those exhibiting disruptive behavior (Baldwin et al., 2012; Chorpita et al., 2011; McCart & Sheidow, 2016) and internalizing and externalizing symptoms (Hogue & Liddle, 2009).

Components of Evidence-Based Treatments

Cognitive-Behavioral Therapy

In contrast to earlier concerns about the efficacy of CBT for ASU, Waldron and Kaminer (2004) conducted a review of randomized clinical trials (RCTs) and demonstrated that both individual and group CBT can lead to significant and clinically meaningfully reductions in ASU. CBT endeavors to reduce ASU by blending cognitive strategies, which aim to identify and change distorted thinking, with behavioral strategies to learn coping, communication, problem-solving, and substance refusal skills (Kendall, 2012).

Establishing a Working Relationship. The first core component for ASU is establishing a working relationship with the adolescent and caregiver(s). For the therapist, the primary goal is to ensure that the youth and family are interested in returning for a second session after the first. The therapist focuses on engaging the client in productive discussion, maintaining client interest in the therapeutic process, and ensuring therapy is an equally shared collaboration. During the therapeutic process, the therapist does not assume that they already know better than the adolescent and abstains from providing solutions or making decisions for the adolescent. Beginning in the first session, therapist and client work jointly to set goals and a course of treatment, and this collaboration is continued throughout all points of therapy (Sudhir, 2015). Effectively engaging the adolescent in order to build a working relationship can include engagement exercises designed to build rapport and creative assessment of problems, including a molar assessment of problematic behavior. This intervention is not dissimilar from a core component of FBT for ASU: family engagement.

Drug Monitoring and Harm Reduction. The second core component of CBT for ASU is drug use monitoring and harm reduction, a nonjudgmental analysis of drug use behavior, also known as a functional analysis or chain analysis, to meaningfully support the teen in understanding the significance and implications of their use. There are two main purposes for functional analysis: one is to help an adolescent recognize triggers for use; the second is to identify both positive and negative consequences of use (Carroll & Onken, 2005). The therapist's goal in this process is to help the youth understand how external variables (i.e., settings, people, events) may contribute to use and identify ways to meet needs in other and more positive ways. Harm reduction includes interventions by the therapist to impart the ability to the teen to moderate their use and to teach effective use of refusal skills when around substance using peers. Harm reduction and moderated use training teach adolescents to identify high-risk situations, defined as situations and/or states of mind in which the adolescent is most vulnerable to drug use, and prepare to utilize the behavioral and cognitive skills learned in therapy when triggers and cravings occur. Refusal training teaches adolescents to refuse alcohol or drugs assertively, and is particularly important for resisting peer pressure.

Behavioral Skills Training. The third core component of CBT for ASU is behavioral skills training. Behavioral skills training is a part of all CBT, not just for ASU. These skills can generally be thought of as addressing interpersonal, emotion regulation, organizational, and problem-solving deficits (McHugh, Hearon, & Otto, 2010). Some of the specific behavioral skills that are part of CBT for ASU include the therapist teaching skills in communication, decision making, problem-solving, and anger management; role-playing use of these skills; and relaxation techniques. In particular, relaxation and other stress reduction techniques can support the adolescent in coping with thoughts and emotions that substance use may have mediated historically, as well as the difficulties prompted by a reduction in their substance use. Decision-making and problem-solving techniques are important lifelong skills that can not only help adolescents handle real-world problems without relying on alcohol and drugs as a harmful coping skill, but can also increase self-efficacy and self-esteem. Therapists help adolescents break down problems into smaller and more manageable steps. Opportunities for clients to practice the skills learned in therapy and to receive corrective feedback are the most important factor in the success of cognitive-behavioral skills training and increase the odds that adolescents will use these skills in everyday life (Sharma, Mehta, & Dhawan, 2015). Use of role-plays during sessions helps adolescents test new skills in a safe environment. Therapists should also process the role-play with the adolescent in order to provide positive feedback, constructive criticism, and work through potential roadblocks (Sampl & Kadden, 2002).

Cognitive Therapy Techniques. The fourth core component of CBT for ASU is cognitive therapy techniques, again an essential part of all CBT. CBT for ASU includes cognitive monitoring and change strategies. Therapists teach teens to monitor and enhance the way they talk to themselves (their "self-talk," or use of positive statements to counteract negative ones) and to become aware of how cognitions influence behavior and emotions, and vice versa. In most cases, adolescent clients are not fully aware of the strong connection between distorted thinking and the unwelcome feelings and behaviors that follow. Cognitive interventions include any question, observation, or statement directed at either specific thoughts, or more global thinking habits, of the teen. The therapist's primary goal, therefore, is to identify and explore the client's underlying cognitions. Therapists ask their teen clients to consider other possibilities, view things in a new light, or reason things out before jumping to conclusions. Change strategies include challenging these thoughts and cognitive restructuring. Cognitive restructuring is a two-step process that includes pointing out how negative thought patterns and triggers identified during the functional analysis have led to use in the past and teaching the adolescent positive ways to respond to these triggers (Godley et al., 2001). Therapists may also help teens become aware of negative and unrealistic beliefs and practice positive self-statements.

Increasing Prosocial Behavior. The fifth and last core component for CBT for ASU is increasing prosocial behavior. Typically, adolescents in treatment for SUD have social and recreational lives based around the use of alcohol or drugs. Youth may find it challenging to make drug-free friends and find sober activities. Therapists can help adolescents understand that everyone wants to have fun, but there are alternatives to drug use in which the adolescent can engage (Godley et al., 2002). The therapist's aim is to support the teen in searching for new, positive recreational outlets that are incompatible with substance use. This therapeutic technique is supported by the notion that teens can create a drug-free lifestyle that is so rewarding that they would not want to return to drug use because of the potential to lose all that they have achieved (e.g., improved family relationships, new friends, fun activities). Therapist techniques include introducing the topic of prosocial activities to youth and family, helping the adolescent to identify activities to try out, and using systematic encouragement (brainstorming, role-playing, and feedback) to help the adolescent maintain their commitment to trying activities he or she has identified.

Family-Based Treatment

Substantial research on the effectiveness of FBT has been consolidated into several comprehensive reviews that support its use in addressing a range of adolescent clinical outcomes (Chorpita & Daleiden, 2009; Hogue et al., 2014; Waldron & Turner, 2008). However, in Chorpita and Daleiden's (2009) distillation project, including 322 RCTs, FBT could only be distilled to one element, family therapy, underscoring the need for further elucidation of core components. In understanding more meaningfully the EBT core components for FBT, it is important to understand how the packages, or the different forms of manualized family therapies, are described and classified. The five major categories of FBT are behavioral, systems, functional, ecological, and educational, and are derived based on the focus of the intervention for ASU; that is, whether the focus is within and/or outside the system of the family (Becker & Curry, 2008). Hogue and colleagues' (2014) review identified ecological family therapy as the approach most supported by evidence. Manualized models of evidence-based ecological family therapy include multidimensional family therapy (MDFT), multisystemic therapy (MST), brief strategic family therapy (BSFT), and functional family therapy (FFT). While these models differ in the specific nature of their interventions and increased adherence to the therapeutic techniques within model, all are associated with improved clinical outcomes (Robbins et al., 2011).

Across fidelity outcome studies of manualized family therapy for ASU, common treatment techniques have emerged as meaningful mechanisms for change, but information on core components is lacking. However, a randomized trial that evaluated nonmanualized family therapy in a community setting demonstrated that there is value in therapist utilization of these core components of family therapy even in usual care settings (i.e., individual sessions; Hogue et al., 2015). Understanding the common treatment strategies of these manualized FT models can maximize treatment efficacy and improve the way that EBTs are adopted in general clinical practice; therefore, the mechanisms that reliably predict clinical gains within each model have been identified in the literature (Kazdin & Nock, 2003). Moreover, these techniques are represented in several assessment measures, making these tools ideal foundations for establishing core components:

- *Therapist Behavior Rating Scale*: Describes and assesses techniques that are universal within the FT approach (e.g., coach family interactions; improve communication and attachment) and that predict long-term improvement in family functioning as well as decreases in adolescent symptoms (Hogue et al., 1998, 2004).
- *Videotape Rating Checklist*: Captures classic emphases of the FT approach (e.g., joining, enactments, reframing, and restructuring interventions) that are associated with sequence-specific effects on treatment engagement, family relationships, and adolescent symptoms (Hervis & Robbins, 2015; Robbins et al., 2011).
- *Therapist Adherence Rating Scale*: Defines vital family interventions (e.g., minimizing parents' blaming attributions, and reframing negative behaviors) that have been associated with improved outcomes (Alexander et al., 1989; Ozechowki & Waldron, 2016).

The process of identifying core components of FT is underway by the authors of this chapter and began by examining these observational fidelity scales for three prominent manualized models (MDFT, BSFT, FFT). The core components derived by this exploration are thematic clinical strategies that are (1) common across all three models, (2) theoretically important and relevant to the FT approach, and (3) embodied by multiple items from all three scales. This process has yielded four core components: Family Engagement, Relational Reframing, Family Behavior Change, and Family Restructuring.

Family Engagement. This component incorporates interventions that simultaneously aim to build the relationship between the therapist and all family members and encourage family members' investment in treatment goals and involvement in therapy. Therapists trained in family engagement interventions view engagement as a process influenced by the family, the therapist, the interactions between them, and the social context (Cunningham & Henggeler, 1999). Engagement difficulties are natural experiences that are systemic, and are expected and meant to be explored rather than characterized as "resistance" (Liddle, 1995). Family engagement interventions are invariably specified by manualized FT models as taking place during the early part of treatment and include building balanced alliances with teens, parents, and siblings. The goal of family engagement in ASU treatment is to support family members in identifying therapy as a benefit to the adolescent, their SUD, their family relationships, and any other challenges that are identified in the engagement process. Family engagement therapeutic techniques also aim to establish therapist credibility and value to family members. It is vital that the therapist convey acceptance, curiosity, and a nonjudgmental attitude in order to build the rapport that categorizes effective family engagement.

Relational Reframing. This component consists of therapeutic techniques designed to move away from individual and intrapsychic ways of defining problems and generating solutions, and toward a systemic conceptualization focused on relational processes. Relational reframing techniques include keeping a relational focus, educating family members on behaviors that are a part of normative adolescent development, and selling family members on a more positive view of a behavior or relationship. Family members are often motivated to make systemic changes by understanding their problems differently. Put another way, relational reframing prepares family members to effect change in their relationships. These interventions also aim to remove pathological descriptions and attributions for behaviors, specifically removing overly pathological ways of describing ASU. For example, a parent's angry outburst might be reframed by a therapist as an expression of worry and fear of loss of control, and a teen's increase in time away from the home might be reframed as a search for autonomy and independence. While a family might initially experience ASU as evidence of a teen's individual frailty or pathology, relational reframing can create an organizing theme for the family through which to understand ASU, and then can link each person's behavior to that theme.

In understanding the third and fourth core components of FT for ASU, it is useful to consider the mechanisms of change as defined by early family therapists: the theory of first- and second-order change (Davey et al., 2011; Nichols & Schwartz, 1991). As defined by pioneering family therapists, first-order change consists of family cycles of interactions altering at the behavioral level only, such that therapists endeavor to bring about observable shifts in actions. In second-order change, therapists target underlying beliefs, premises, or family rules; it is hoped that changes in these latent processes will then prompt behavior change (Watzlawick & Weakland, 1977). Family members may be instructed on using more effective communication strategies to decrease arguments about an adolescent's drug use (first order); or, they may explore and then repair relationship ruptures that have created interpersonal distance and conflict (and perhaps led to the ASU itself), which would, in turn, decrease their arguing (second order). The clinical outcome is the same, but the processes for change are fundamentally different. As implied, it is also a recursive process in which one type of change can beget another.

Family Behavior Change. This component constitutes first-order change. Therapists employing therapeutic techniques that address family behavior change aim to teach new, concrete skills to all family members and encourage individual behavior change that will allow for improved family relationships. A key feature of this core component, which is in fact true of all the core components, is that *all* family members, not just the substance using adolescent, can benefit from changing their behavior, and that *all* family members need new skills in order to be able to do so. Therapists actively teach general skills and specific skills, such as assertive communication, and often assign homework to support skill retention and generalizability. These new skills and behaviors are then positively reinforced and coached, for the individual as well as the entire family. Family behavior change can be implemented with the whole family at once, or therapists can encourage change and teach skills working with subsystems or in meetings with individuals within the family. While individuals are often encouraged to make changes, the goal for the change is to make improvements for the entire family. For example, an adolescent may be taught to use mindfulness-based stress reduction techniques, instead of substances, in the presence of their siblings and parents, who are also invited to explore the pros and cons of their own substance use and utilize the stress reduction technique, with the goal of all family members changing the behavior of problematic use.

Family Restructuring. This component constitutes second-order change, that is, change in the way the family system is governed. The premise of advocating for second-order change is that therapists must create a context for change and must work to change premises and assumptions, rather than behaviors, as endeavoring to change behavior alone is insufficient (Atkinson & Heath 1990). Family restructuring interventions aim to prompt shifts in attachment and emotional processes between family members. For ASU, such interventions can include: focusing on process and relationship functions, bringing mindfulness to the present moment and nonverbal exchanges, realigning boundaries, and justifying the importance of new skills. In family restructuring, parents and teens are also encouraged to develop insight into predominant cycles of relational interactions, and how these cycles are linked to observable behaviors. If a parent and teen have developed a cycle of interaction in which they only engage when there is a violation of rules and then a consequence to enforce, and thus there is a premise that connection equates conflict, a therapist would want to highlight this dynamic with the family, justify the skill of developing new ways to connect with one another, and explore other unexpressed negative emotions outside of the parent–teen interactions. Therapists can also move toward family restructuring by highlighting strengths in the family system and enhancing the positive connections that exist within the family.

Role of Parents in Treatment

The family system has emerged as a vital component and target of ASU treatment. Youth from complex, blended families often experience significant stressors, and therefore identification of family members – including both biological family members and those incorporated into the family unit by choice – is an important element of treatment. That is, ASU treatment should honor the group of people whom the target adolescent defines as part of their family unit and identify ways in which these family members can be engaged in treatment to support recovery (SAMHSA, 2015).

Maladaptive family environments including those characterized by familial substance use, poor parenting practices and family management, unhealthy attitudes toward drug use, and weak family bonds have consistently been correlated with ASU (Clark, 2004; Fisher et al., in press; Olsson et al., 2003; Wood et al., 2004). Therefore, current literature advocates for involving family in treatment to transform problematic family relationships and provide caregivers with tools and skills for better parenting practices and confidence. Research suggests that involving caregivers and families in this way supports treatment engagement for youth and reduces ASU (Bertrand et al., 2013; Henderson et al., 2009; Velleman, Templeton, & Copello, 2005).

Research has identified several specific aspects of family relationships that interact with individual youth characteristics to produce ASU risk, including family structure, cohesion, communication, management, attitudes, and behavior monitoring, as well as parental supervision and influences (Velleman, Templeton, & Copello, 2005). Therefore, adolescent treatment includes caregiver involvement to impart: (1) parenting skill to support development of family cohesion, appropriate supervision, and conflict resolution; (2) substance use psychoeducation to ensure understanding of the genetic cycle of addiction and the importance of modeling appropriate behavior and attitudes; and (3) quality communication skills (Vellemen, Templeton, & Copello, 2005). Apart from providing moral and emotional support, caregivers also play a crucial role in functional treatment aspects including scheduling and attending appointments and providing transportation.

A first step in treatment planning includes gaining an understanding of how barriers to treatment may hinder family involvement. Common barriers include denial, poor family motivation, prior negative treatment experiences, parental substance use and/or mental health disorders; and cultural differences (Suveg et al., 2006; SAMHSA, 2004). Caregivers also may experience difficulty in balancing employment, childcare, and transportation. Strategies for addressing potential barriers start with a careful, family-specific assessment to identify factors that may impede treatment engagement. Then treatment can progress to include identification of family-focused and relevant treatment goals, provision of psychoeducation, validation of the thoughts and feelings of all family members, and acknowledgment of parenting stress and burden. Open and frequent communication on the therapist's part, as well as flexibility in scheduling, are well-documented strategies for fostering family engagement in treatment (SAMHSA, 2004).

Other Factors Influencing Treatment

Assessment

Assessment is an integral aspect of ASU treatment to identify the level of problem severity and appropriate level of care, define needed services, and provide appropriate referrals. Lack of a thorough assessment undermines the development of a treatment and recovery plan tailored to the individual needs of each adolescent. The most important elements of effective assessment for ASU include: (1) the use of a standardized, evidence-based ASU assessment interview (see Alcohol and Drug Abuse Institute online database, in Useful Resources below, for a list of standardized instruments); (2) implementation of services and interventions appropriate for presenting problems; (3) comprehensive assessment of co-occurring problems, assets, and resources; (4) reassessment throughout treatment to monitor progress.

Comorbidity

Up to 75% of youth with a SUD suffer from a comorbid mental health (MH) condition (e.g., conduct disorders, attention-deficit/hyperactivity disorder, and depression; Deas & Thomas, 2002), requiring more complex clinical care. Research suggests that youth with co-occurring disorders have more severe substance use patterns, higher levels of pre-treatment problem behaviors, and poorer treatment outcomes. Specifically, youth with comorbid MH conditions are more likely to experience early treatment dropout, fewer reductions in problem behaviors, and post-treatment drug use compared to youth with SUD alone (Grella, 2001; Waldron & Turner, 2008). Emerging literature and practice recommendations highlight the need for comprehensive MH screening, assessment, and treatment congruent to ASU treatment for youth to promote positive treatment outcomes and development across contexts (New York State Office of Mental Health & Office of Substance Abuse and Mental Health Services Administration, 2009; Whitmore, Sakai, & Riggs, 2010).

Demographics

Research suggests that ASU treatment that is culturally informed and youth guided achieves more successful engagement, retention, and clinical outcomes for adolescents (Drug Strategies, 2003). The target youth should be at the center of the treatment team, with service delivery informed by the distinct developmental stage, life experiences, sexuality, gender identity, religion, and culture of each adolescent and their family as these factors impact how youth respond to different interventions and treatment modalities (Griner & Smith, 2006; SAMHSA, 2015).

ASU treatment should also acknowledge and address disparities in access to treatment and recovery supports across different ethnic and racial groups. For example, research suggests that minority adolescents may be less likely to receive ASU treatment, especially black and Hispanic youth (Cummings, Wen, & Druss, 2011) and that when they do attain access to the treatment system they are less likely to receive services with an ASU treatment professional or in a residential setting (Perron et al., 2009). Moreover, research indicates that minority youth exhibit lower retention and treatment completion rates (Campbell, Weisner, & Sterling, 2006; Shillington & Clapp, 2003), particularly Black and Hispanic youth (Saloner, Carson, & Cook, 2014). Finally, ASU treatment providers should be aware that the efficacy of existing evidence-based practices may not be generalizable beyond samples of White adolescents. For ethnic minority youth, research fails to identify a well-established set of evidence-based treatments for ASU, though MDFT (Liddle et al., 2004) was deemed probably efficacious for drug abusing ethnic minority youth (Huey & Polo, 2008). For a full review of evidence-based practices across presenting problems for ethnic minority youth, see Huey and Polo (2008).

Medication

Medication-assisted treatment (MAT) is the use of medication, in combination with behavioral therapies and counseling, to reduce substance use, risk for overdose, withdrawal symptoms, and relapse prevention and maintenance (Lee et al., 2015). While research and practice exemplifies the effectiveness of MAT for adult alcohol and opioid use disorders over and above traditional behavioral treatments alone (SAMHSA, 2011; World Health Organization [WHO], 2009), MAT for youth is seldom available even for the more severe cases of youth SUD. This is partly due to limited research investigating the effectiveness, risk, and long-term impact of common addiction medications for youth (e.g., methadone, naltrexone, buprenorphine). Currently, the only addiction medication approved by the FDA to treat adolescents is buprenorphine for opioid use disorder, which is only approved for adolescents 16 years and older (Kampman & Jarvis, 2015). Therefore, in the face of rising opioid use among adolescents, ASU treatment providers are more limited in addressing withdrawal from dependence as well as maintenance needed for relapse prevention, which leads to ASU treatment attrition, relapse, and poor clinical outcomes (Sharma et al., 2016).

Conclusion

As described above, we have ample ways to understand, screen, assess, diagnose, and treat adolescent substance use and substance use disorders. Despite these advances in our field, there exists a disturbing treatment gap. Over 90% of adolescents who meet SUD diagnostic criteria do not receive appropriate treatment (Center for Behavioral Health Statistics and Quality, 2015). This gap makes it apparent that evidence-based assessment and treatment services are not reaching the intended population. Information from the National Household Survey on Drug Use and Health (US Department of Health and Human Services, 2002) indicates that the most significant barriers to seeking treatment include beliefs that treatment can't help and lack of knowledge about where to seek treatment. The impact on both young lives and the public health of unmet treatment need is tremendously meaningful (Hogue et al., 2014). In order to reduce barriers and increase access to treatment, our field needs to identify how to develop novel ways to improve dissemination and implementation of evidence-based services, and reach out in direct and accessible ways to adolescents and families.

Useful Resources

Additional resources should be consulted for further information on evidence-based treatment for ASU:

- For information on *validated screening/assessment tools*, the Alcohol and Drug Abuse Institute instrument is available and updated regularly: http://lib.adai.washington.edu/instruments/

- For *prevalence rates and trends of ASU*, see the annual survey data from Monitoring the Future: www.drugabuse.gov/news-events/news-releases/2016/12/teen-substance-use-shows-promising-decline
- For more information on *risks associated with ASU*, see the White Paper produced by The National Center on Addiction and Substance Abuse (2011).
- For a summary of the *biospsychosocial model of ASU*, see Wiers and colleagues (2007).
- For a summary of the *dual-process model of ASU*, see Griffiths (2005).
- For *reviews and meta-analyses of EBTs*, see Becker and Curry (2008), Waldron and Turner (2008), Hogue and colleagues (2014), and Tanner-Smith and colleagues (2013).
- For more information on *culturally informed treatment*, see *Treatment Improvement Protocol 59, Improving Cultural Competence*: https://store.samhsa.gov/shin/content/SMA14-4849/SMA14-4849.pdf
- For more information on *MAT for youth*, see the American Academy of Pediatrics' policy statement: www.aap.org/en-us/Documents/cosup_pcsso_webinar5_1-pager.pdf

References

Alcohol and Drug Abuse Institute. (2015). Substance use screening & assessment instruments database. Seattle, WA: University of Washington.

Alexander, J. F., Waldron, H. B., Barton, C., & Mas, C. H. (1989). Minimizing blaming attributions and behaviors in delinquent families. *Journal of Consulting and Clinical Psychology, 57*, 19–24.

American Academy of Pediatrics, Committee on Substance Use and Prevention. (2016). Medication-assisted treatment of adolescents. http://pediatrics.aappublications.org/content/early/2016/08/18/peds.2016–1893

Atkinson, B. J., & Heath, A. W. (1990). Further thoughts on second-order family therapy – This time it's personal. *Family Process, 29*(2), 145–155.

Baldwin, S. A., Christian, S., Berkeljon, A., & Shadish, W. R. (2012). The effects of family therapies for adolescent delinquency and substance abuse: A meta-analysis. *Journal of Marital and Family Therapy, 38*, 281–304.

Becker, S., & Curry, J. F. (2008). Outpatient interventions for adolescent substance abuse: A quality of evidence review. *Journal of Consulting and Clinical Psychology, 76*(4), 531–543.

Bertrand, K., Richer, I., Brunelle, N., Beaudoin, I., Lemieux, A., & Ménard, J. M. (2013). Substance abuse treatment for adolescents: How are family factors related to substance use change? *Journal of Psychoactive Drugs, 45*(1), 28–38.

Campbell, C. I., Weisner, C., & Sterling, S. (2006). Adolescents entering chemical dependency treatment in private managed care: Ethnic differences in treatment initiation and retention. *Journal of Adolescent Health, 38*(4), 343–350.

Carroll, K. M., & Onken, L. S. (2005). Behavioral therapies for drug abuse. *American Journal of Psychiatry, 162*(8), 1452–1460.

Center for Behavioral Health Statistics and Quality. (2015).Behavioral health trends in the United States: Results from the 2014 National Survey on Drug Use and Health (HHS Publication No. SMA 15–4927, NSDUH Series H-50). Rockville, MD: Substance Abuse and Mental Health Services Administration.

Chan, Y. F., Dennis, M. L., & Funk, R. R. (2008). Prevalence and comorbidity of major internalizing and externalizing problems among adolescents and adults presenting to substance abuse treatment. *Journal of Substance Abuse Treatment, 35*(1), 14–24.

Clark, D. (2004). The natural history of adolescent alcohol use disorders. *Addiction, 99*(s2), 5–22.

Chorpita, B. F., & Daleiden, E. L. (2009). Mapping evidence-based treatments for children and adolescents: Application of the distillation and matching model to 615 treatments from 322 randomized trials. *Journal of Consulting and Clinical Psychology, 77*, 566–579.

Chorpita, B. F., Daleiden, E., Ebesutani, C., Young, J. Becker, K., … & Starace, N. (2011). Evidence-based treatments for children and adolescents: An updated review of indicators of efficacy and effectiveness. *Clinical Psychology: Science and Practice, 18*, 154–172.

Cleveland, M. J., Feinberg, M. E., Bontempo, D. E., & Greenberg, M. T. (2008). The role of risk and protective factors in substance use across adolescence. *Journal of Adolescent Health, 43*(2), 157–164.

Cummings, J. R., Wen, H., & Druss, B. G. (2011). Racial/ethnic differences in treatment for substance use disorders among U.S. adolescents. *Journal of the American Academy of Child & Adolescent Psychiatry, 50*(12), 1265–1274.

Cunningham, P. B., & Henggeler, S. W. (1999). Engaging multiproblem families in treatment: Lessons learned throughout the development of multisystemic therapy. *Family Process, 38*(3), 265–281.

Davey, M., Duncan, T., Kissil, K., Davey, A., & Fish, L. S. (2011). Second-order change in marriage and family therapy: A web-based modified Delphi study. *American Journal of Family Therapy, 39*, 100–111.

Deas, D., & Thomas, S. (2002). Comorbid psychiatric factors contributing to adolescent alcohol and other drug use. *Alcohol Research and Health, 26*(2), 116–121.

Drug Strategies. (2003). *Treating teens: A guide to adolescent drug programs*. Washington, DC: Drug Strategies.

Fisher, J., Becker, S., Bobek, M., & Hogue, A. (in press). Substance-related and addictive disorders. In T. H. Ollendick, S. W. White, & B. A. White (eds.), *The Oxford handbook of clinical child and adolescent psychology*. Oxford: Oxford University Press.

Godley, S. H., Meyers, R. J., Smith, J. E., Karvinen, T., Titus, J. C., Godley, M. D., … & Kelberg, P. (2001). *The adolescent community reinforcement approach for adolescent cannabis users*. Volume 4 of the Cannabis Youth Treatment (CYT) manual series. Rockville, MD: Center for Substance Abuse Treatment, Substance Abuse and Mental Health Services Administration.

Grella, C. E. (2001). Drug treatment outcomes for adolescents with comorbid mental and substance use disorders. *Journal of Nervous and Mental Disease, 189*(6), 384–392.

Griffiths, M. (2005). A "components" model of addiction within a biopsychosocial framework. *Journal of Substance Use, 10*(4), 191–197.

Griner, D., & Smith, T. B. (2006). Culturally adapted mental health intervention: A meta-analytic review. *Psychotherapy: Theory, Research, Practice, Training, 43*(4), 531–548.

Haughwout, S. P., Harford, T. C., Castle, I. J. P., & Grant, B. F. (2016). Treatment utilization among adolescent substance users: Findings from the 2002 to 2013 National Survey on Drug use and Health. *Alcoholism: Clinical and Experimental Research, 40*(8), 1717–1727.

Henderson, C. E., Rowe, C. L., Dakof, G. A., Hawes, S. W., & Liddle, H. A. (2009). Parenting practices as mediators of treatment effects in an early-intervention trial of multidimensional family therapy. *The American Journal of Drug and Alcohol Abuse, 35*, 220–226.

Hervis, O. E., & Robbins, M. S. (2015). *Brief strategic family therapy videotape rating checklist*. Miami, FL: Family Therapy Training Institute of Miami.

Hogue, A., Dauber, S., Henderson, C. E., Bobek, M., Johnson, C., Lichvar, E., & Morgenstern, J. (2015). Randomized trial of family therapy versus nonfamily treatment for adolescent behavior problems in usual care. *Journal of Clinical Child & Adolescent Psychology*, *44*(6), 954–969.

Hogue, A., Henderson, C. E., Ozechowski, T. J., & Robbins, M. S. (2014). Evidence base on outpatient behavioral treatments for adolescent substance use: Updates and recommendations 2007–2013. *Journal of Clinical Child & Adolescent Psychology*, *43*, 697–720.

Hogue, A., & Liddle, H. A. (2009). Family-based treatment for adolescent substance abuse: Controlled trials and new horizons in service research. *Journal of Family Therapy*, *31*, 126–154.

Hogue, A., Liddle, H. A., Dauber, S., & Samuolis, J. (2004). Linking session focus to treatment outcome in evidence-based treatments for adolescent substance abuse. *Psychotherapy: Theory, Research, Practice, Training*, *41*, 83–96.

Hogue, A., Liddle, H. A., Rowe, C. L., Turner, R. M., Dakof, G. A., & LaPann, K. (1998). Treatment adherence and differentiation in individual versus family therapy for adolescent substance abuse. *Journal of Counseling Psychology*, *45*, 104–114.

Huey, S. J., & Polo, A. J. (2008). Evidence-based psychosocial treatments for ethnic minority youth. *Journal of Clinical Child & Adolescent Psychology*, *37*(1), 262–301.

Johnston, L., O'Malley, P., Bachman, J., & Schulenberg, J. (2016). Monitoring the future National Survey results on drug use, 1975–2015: Overview, key findings on adolescent drug use. www .monitoringthefuture.org/pubs/monographs/mtf-overview2015.pdf

Kampman, K., & Jarvis, M. (2015). American Society of Addiction Medicine (ASAM) National Practice Guidelines for the use of medications in the treatment of addiction involving opioid use. *Journal of Addiction Medicine*, *9*(5), 358–368.

Kazdin, A. E., & Nock, M. K. (2003). Delineating mechanisms of change in child and adolescent therapy: Methodological issues and research recommendations. *Journal of Child Psychology and Psychiatry*, *44*(8), 1116–1129.

Keyes, K. M., Brady, J. E., & Li, G. (2015). Effects of minimum legal drinking age on alcohol and marijuana use: Evidence from toxicological testing data for fatally injured drivers aged 16 to 25 years. *Injury Epidemiology*, *2*(1), 1.

Kendall, P. C. (ed.) (2012). *Child and adolescent therapy: Cognitive-behavioral procedures*. 4th edn. New York: Guilford Press.

Lee, J., Kresina, T. F., Campopiano, M., Lubran, R., & Clark, H. W. (2015). Use of pharmacotherapies in the treatment of alcohol use disorders and opioid dependence in primary care. *BioMed Research International*, 2015.

Liddle, H. A. (1995). Conceptual and clinical dimensions of multidimensional multisystems engagement strategy in family-based adolescent treatment. *Psychotherapy*, *32*, 39–58.

Liddle, H. A., Rowe, C. L., Dakof, G. A., Ungaro, R. A., & Henderson, C. E. (2004). Early intervention for adolescent substance abuse: Pretreatment to posttreatment outcomes of a randomized clinical trial comparing multidimensional family therapy and peer group treatment. *Journal of Psychoactive Drugs*, *36*, 49–63.

McCart, M. R., & Sheidow, A. J. (2016). Evidence-based psychosocial treatments for adolescents with disruptive behavior. *Journal of Clinical Child & Adolescent Psychology*, *45*(5), 1–35.

McHugh, R. K., Hearon, B. A., & Otto, M. W. (2010). Cognitive behavioral therapy for substance use disorders. *Psychiatric Clinics of North America*, *33*(3), 511–525.

The National Center on Addiction and Substance Abuse. (2011). *Adolescent substance use: America's #1 public health problem*. New York: The National Center on Addiction and Substance Abuse. www.centeronaddiction.org/addiction-research/reports/adolescent-

New York State Office of Mental Health & Office of Substance Abuse and Mental Health Services Administration. (2009). Task force on co-occurring disorders, subcommittee on youth and adolescents final report. New York: Author.

Nichols, M. P., & Schwartz, R. C. (1991). *Family therapy: Concepts and methods.* 2nd edn. Boston: Allyn & Bacon.

Olsson, C., Coffey, C., Bond., L., Toumbourou, J., & Patton, G. (2003). Family risk factors for cannabis use: A population based survey of Australian secondary school students. *Drug and Alcohol Review*, *22*, 143–152.

Ozechowski, T. J., & Waldron, H. B, (2016). Functional Family Therapy Therapist Adherence Rating Scale. Oregon Research Institute (instrument available from the authors).

Perron, B. E., Mowbray, O. P., Glass, J. E., Delva, J., Vaughn, M. G., & Howard, M. O. (2009). Differences in service utilization and barriers among Blacks, Hispanics, and Whites with drug use disorders. *Substance Abuse Treatment, Prevention, and Policy*, *4*(1), 1.

Robbins, M. S., Feaster, D. J., Horigian, V. E., Puccinelli, M. J., Henderson, C. E., & Szapocznik, J. (2011). Therapist adherence in Brief Strategic Family Therapy for adolescent drug abusers. *Journal of Consulting and Clinical Psychology*, *79*, 43–53.

Saloner, B., Carson, N., & Cook, B. L. (2014). Explaining racial/ethnic differences in adolescent substance abuse treatment completion in the United States: A decomposition analysis. *Journal of Adolescent Health*, *54*(6), 646–653.

Sampl, S., & Kadden, R. (2002). *Motivational Enhancement Therapy and Cognitive Behavioral Therapy for adolescent cannabis users: 5 sessions.* Volume 1 of the Cannabis Youth Treatment (CYT) manual series, 158 pp. Rockville, MD: Center for Substance Abuse Treatment, Substance Abuse and Mental Health Services Administration. www.samhsa.gov/csat/csat.htm

Sharma, B., Bruner, A., Barnett, G., & Fishman, M. (2016). Opioid use disorders. *Child and Adolescent Psychiatric Clinics of North America*, *25*(3), 473–487.

Sharma, R., Mehta, M., & Dhawan, A. (2015). Treatment of substance-abusing adolescents. In M. Mehta and R. Sagar (eds.), *A practical approach to cognitive behaviour therapy for adolescents* (pp. 331–361). New Delhi: Springer India.

Shillington, A. M., & Clapp, J. D. (2003). Adolescents in public substance abuse treatment programs: The impacts of sex and race on referrals and outcomes. *Journal of Child & Adolescent Substance Abuse*, *12*(4), 69–91.

St-Pierre, R., & Derevensky, J. L. (2016). Youth gambling behavior: Novel approaches to prevention and intervention. *Current Addiction Reports*, *3*(2), 157–165.

Substance Abuse and Mental Health Services Administration (SAMHSA). (2004). Treatment Improvement Protocol (TIP) Series, No. 39. Center for Substance Abuse Treatment. Rockville, MD: Center for Substance Abuse Treatment.

Substance Abuse and Mental Health Services Administration (SAMHSA). (2007). The OAS Report: A day in the life of American adolescents: Substance use facts. Rockville, MD: Government Printing Services.

Substance Abuse and Mental Health Services Administration (SAMHSA). (2011). Medication-assisted treatment for opioid addiction: Facts for families and friends. www.ct.gov/dmhas/lib/dmhas/publications/MAT-InfoFamilyFriends.pdf

Substance Abuse and Mental Health Services Administration (SAMHSA). (2013). Results from the 2012 National Survey on Drug Use and Health: Summary of National Findings. NSDUH Series H-46, HHS Publication No. (SMA) 13–4795. Rockville, MD: Government Printing Services.

Substance Abuse and Mental Health Service Administration (SAMHSA). (2015). Treatment Improvement Protocol (TIP) Series, No. 59: Improving Cultural Competence. Center for Substance Abuse Treatment. Rockville, MD: Government Printing Services.

Sudhir, P. M. (2015). Cognitive behavior therapy with adolescents. In A. Mehta & R. Sagar (eds.), *A practical approach to cognitive behavior therapy for adolescents* (pp. 21–42). New Delhi: Springer India.

Suveg, C. S., Roblek, T. L., Robin, J., Krain, A., Aschenbrand, S., & Ginsburg, G. S. (2006). Parental involvement when conducting cognitive-behavioral therapy for children with anxiety disorders. *Journal of Cognitive Psychotherapy*, *20*, 287–299.

Tanner-Smith, E. E., Wilson, S. J., & Lipsey, M. W. (2013). The comparative effectiveness of outpatient treatment for adolescent substance abuse: A meta-analysis. *Journal of Substance Abuse Treatment*, *44*(2), 145–158.

US Department of Health and Human Services. (2002). National Household Survey on Drug Use and Health. www.datafiles.samhsa.gov/study/national-survey-drug-use-and-health-nsduh-2002-2014-nid16959

Velleman, R. D. B., Templeton, L. J., & Copello, A. G. (2005). The role of the family in preventing and intervening with substance use and misuse: A comprehensive review of family interventions, with a focus on young people. *Drug and Alcohol Review*, *24*, 93–109.

Waldron, H. B., & Kaminer, Y. (2004). On the learning curve: The emerging evidence supporting cognitive-behavioral therapies for adolescent substance abuse. *Addiction*, *99*, 93–105.

Waldron, H. B., & Turner, C. W. (2008). Evidence-based psychosocial treatments for adolescent substance abuse. *Journal of Clinical Child & Adolescent Psychology*, *37*(1), 238–261.

Watzlawick, P., & Weakland, J. H. (1977). *The interactional view*. New York: Norton.

Weinberger, A. H., Franco, C. A., Hoff, R. A., Pilver, C., Steinberg, M. A., Rugle, L., ... & Potenza, M. N. (2015). Cigarette smoking, problem-gambling severity, and health behaviors in high-school students. *Addictive Behaviors Reports*, *1*, 40–48.

Whitmore, E. A., Sakai, J., & Riggs, P. D. (2010). *Practice guidelines for adolescents with co-occurring substance use and psychiatric disorders*. Denver, CO: School of Medicine, University of Colorado Denver.

Wiers, R., Bartholow, B. D., van den Wildenberg, E., Thush, C., Engels, R. C., Sher, K. J., ... & Stacy, A. W. (2007). Automatic and controlled processes and the development of addictive behaviors in adolescents: A review and a model. *Pharmacology, Biochemistry and Behavior*, *86*(2), 263–283.

Wilber, M. K., & Potenza, M. N. (2006). Adolescent gambling: Research and clinical implications. *Psychiatry (Edgmont)*, *3*(10), 40.

Winters, K. C., & Stinchfield, R. D. (2012). Youth gambling: Prevalence, risk and protective factors and clinical issues. In *Increasing the odds: A series dedicated to understanding gambling disorders. Vol. 7: What clinicians need to know about gambling disorders* (pp. 14–25). Beverly, MA: The National Center for Responsible Gambling.

Winters, K. C., Tanner-Smith, E. E., Bresani, E., & Meyers, K. (2014). Current advances in the treatment of adolescent drug use. *Adolescent Health, Medicine and Therapeutics*, *5*, 199.

Wong, S. S., Zhou, B., Goebert, D., & Hishinuma, E. S. (2013). The risk of adolescent suicide across patterns of drug use: A nationally representative study of high school students in the United States from 1999 to 2009. *Social Psychiatry and Psychiatric Epidemiology*, *48*(10), 1611–1620.

Wood, M. D., Read J. P., Mitchell R. E., & Brand, N. H. (2004). Do parents still matter? Parent and peer influences on alcohol involvement among recent high school graduates. *Psychology of Addictive Behaviours, 18*(1), 19–30.

World Health Organization (WHO). Dept. of Mental Health, Substance Abuse, World Health Organization, International Narcotics Control Board, United Nations Office on Drugs, & Crime. (2009). *Guidelines for the psychosocially assisted pharmacological treatment of opioid dependence.* Geneva: World Health Organization.

Young, D. W., Dembo, R., & Henderson, C. E. (2007). A national survey of substance abuse treatment for juvenile offenders. *Journal of Substance Abuse Treatment, 32*(3), 255–266.

19

Therapy Relationships and Relational Elements

Stephen R. Shirk

Child and adolescent therapy occurs in the context of a relationship. With the rise of manual-guided therapies, relational processes such as alliance, cohesion, and empathy have been overshadowed by illumination of specific treatment procedures. To date, efforts to identify common elements have focused on procedural elements shared by empirically supported treatments for specific child disorders (see Chorpita & Daleiden, 2009). Of course, the assumption that specific technical procedures primarily account for therapeutic change is not without controversy (Ahn & Wampold, 2001). For example, a meta-analysis of *comparative* child and adolescent outcome studies for four common conditions (i.e., attention-deficit/hyperactivity disorder, depression, anxiety, and conduct disorder) produced effect sizes that varied widely but that were relatively small when aggregated across diverse treatment methods (Miller, Wampold, & Varhely, 2008). However, the aim of this chapter is not to re-litigate the specific versus common factors debate. Instead, this chapter functions as a reminder that technical procedures that populate treatment manuals are implemented through dyadic or group interactions and that the character and quality of these interactions can have an important bearing on treatment outcomes. To this end, the primary aim of this chapter is to identify common *relational* elements that contribute to outcomes in child and adolescent therapy.

What Are Common Relational Elements?

Dating to the work of Rogers (1957) characteristics of the therapeutic relationship such as empathy and positive regard were viewed as necessary and sufficient conditions for emotional and behavioral change. This view has evolved over time with therapy researchers distinguishing between relational elements as *change processes* that *directly* contribute to outcome, and as *facilitating processes* that *indirectly* contribute to outcome by promoting other active, therapeutic ingredients (Shirk & Russell, 1996). When conceptualized as change processes, relational elements are on par with other common elements such as cognitive restructuring or time-out; they are posited as mechanisms that directly influence the outcome of therapy. When conceptualized as facilitating processes the effects of relational processes on outcome are indirect; they are mediated by other therapy procedures or components, by other treatment processes. For example, empathy could be viewed as a change process, as an active component of therapy that directly promotes change, or as a facilitating process that increases involvement in other treatment components such as coping skills training.

Where, then, to begin the search for common relational elements? The Task Force on Evidence-Based Therapy Relationships, sponsored by the American Psychological Association, conducted a broad-band review and evaluation of relationship processes and their association with treatment outcomes (Norcross & Wampold, 2011). The Task Force produced over a dozen meta-analyses of associations between candidate, relationship variables, and treatment outcomes and identified a set of six relational elements as "demonstratively effective" (Norcross & Wampold, 2011). The majority of analyses focused on adult therapy; only the review of alliance in youth therapy exclusively focused on children and adolescents (Shirk, Karver, & Brown, 2011).

A comprehensive meta-analysis of relationship variables in child and adolescent therapy showed that most of the relational elements highlighted by the Task Force have received very limited attention in the youth literature (Karver et al., 2006), Further, a review of the literature since the publication of this meta-analysis uncovered little change. Instead, research on relationship variables in youth therapy has coalesced around two primary constructs: alliance and treatment involvement. These relational elements will be the focus of this chapter.

It is important to note that the evidence supporting relational elements differs from evidence supporting treatments. Specifically, evidence consists of predictive associations between relationship variables and treatment outcomes. Effects are gauged by the magnitude of correlations averaged across studies and represented as the effect size r. Clearly, causation cannot be inferred from correlations but associations are necessary for causal inferences and inferences are strengthened when temporal order is clear. Nevertheless, such evidence is not equivalent to results from controlled experiments such as randomized clinical trials. Yet, it is critical to remember that clinical trials almost always evaluate complex treatment packages composed of multiple treatment elements. The dearth of dismantling studies aimed at isolating active components makes it difficult to precisely assess which elements are responsible for change (Shirk, Jungbluth, & Karver, 2010). As a result, evidence for common elements is ultimately correlational insofar as causal inferences depend on the co-occurrence of specific elements across varied efficacious treatment packages (and presumably not in those that are not efficacious). Although distillation is an important first step in efforts to identify active ingredients of therapy, it is not equivalent to results based on experimental manipulation of treatment components. In a similar manner, correlational data will be regarded as an important first step in identifying relational elements.

Review of Relational Elements in Child and Adolescent Therapy

Alliance in Individual Child and Adolescent Therapy

Early psychodynamic and client-centered child therapists underscored the importance of the therapy relationship as pivotal for successful treatment (Shirk & Russell, 1996). In this early work, the distinction between alliance as a change process and a facilitating process can be discerned (Shirk & Saiz, 1992). For play therapists the curative components of therapy resided in the permissive and affirming therapy relationship. In contrast, psychoanalytic, and, later, cognitive-behavioral theorists viewed the alliance as a catalyst for promoting active participation in core treatment tasks (Freud, 1946; Kendall, 1991).

Alliance as Relational Element. Recent studies of the therapeutic alliance in child and adolescent therapy have drawn heavily from Bordin's (1979) transtheoretical model of alliance. According to Bordin (1979), the alliance consists of three inter-related features: bond, tasks, and goals. "Bond" refers to the emotional quality of the therapy relationship, the valence of the relationship between client and therapist. Essentially, bond involves a sense of being on the same side, united as part of a team. "Task" in Bordin's model concerns *agreements* about the methods of therapy, such as to what degree the client and therapist are on the same page about the focus and activities of therapy. Finally, "goals" refer to *agreements* about the aims of therapy, such as to what degree the client and therapist share a common purpose or set of goals. One critical question, then, is whether the adult construct of alliance fits with children's experience of the therapy relationship. It is certainly possible that other features might be far more salient to children (e.g., friendliness, trustworthiness, and helpfulness) than explicit agreements about tasks and goals (Shirk, Karver, & Brown, 2011; Shirk & Saiz, 1992). Nevertheless, Bordin's multidimensional framework has been the starting point for operational definitions of the alliance in youth therapy. However, recent factor analyses of youth alliance scales suggest that these dimensions are not differentiated by children and that a unidimensional structure (positive versus negative alliance) provides a better fit to the data (Accurso, Hawley, & Garland, 2013; Ormhaug, Shirk, & Wentzel-Larsen, 2015).

Relations Between Alliance and Outcome in Individual Youth Therapy. An initial meta-analysis of associations between relationship variables and treatment outcomes in child and adolescent therapy revealed a small overall correlation of 0.24 (Shirk & Karver, 2003). Although consistent with results from the adult alliance literature, few studies in this sample actually assessed the alliance and only one evaluated alliance–outcome relations prospectively (Eltz, Shirk, & Sarlin, 1995). In the intervening years, three independent meta-analyses have evaluated alliance–outcome relations in child and adolescent treatment (Karver et al., 2006; McLeod, 2011; Shirk, Karver, & Brown, 2011). Two of these meta-analyses examined prospective alliance–outcome relations in individual therapy either for the full sample (Shirk, Karver, & Brown, 2011) or for a subsample of included studies (McLeod, 2011). Based on a sample of nine studies that met these criteria, McLeod (2011) reported a weighted mean correlation of 0.14. Drawing on a slightly larger sample of 16 studies, Shirk, Karver, and Brown (2011) found a somewhat larger association with a mean $r = 0.22$. Taken together, these results reveal a relatively small, but reliable, prospective association between alliance and outcome. By way of comparison, these effects translate into the more familiar treatment effect size, d, as 0.28 and 0.45, respectively. Thus, the likely estimate ranges somewhere between a small and medium effect. Additional analyses highlighted the common character of this association with only small variations in effects across age groups, treatment methods, and disorders (Shirk, Karver, & Brown, 2011).

Of particular relevance to the search for common elements is the role of alliance in treatments of known efficacy. One indicator is the mean association between alliance and outcome in behavioral and cognitive-behavioral therapies. In this subset of studies, the weighted mean correlation is 0.25 (Shirk, Karver, & Brown, 2011). Findings from several randomized, controlled trials published after these meta-analyses are consistent with this finding. For example, results from an effectiveness trial comparing trauma-focused cognitive-behavioral therapy (TF-CBT) and treatment-as-usual (TAU) showed that alliance significantly predicted outcome in the more effective TF-CBT condition but not in TAU. Similarly, child, parent, and therapist reported alliance has been shown to significantly predict symptom reduction in CBT for pediatric obsessive-compulsive disorder (Keeley et al., 2011). Alliance, then, remains predictive of outcome in treatments with active procedural elements.

One important difference between child and adult therapy involves the role of parents. Parents typically are treatment gatekeepers. Decisions about need for treatment, type of treatment, and duration of treatment are made largely by parents. Equally important, parents often participate in treatment itself. Meta-analytic results indicate a significant association between parent–therapist alliance and outcome in youth therapy with a mean correlation of 0.21 (Shirk, Karver, & Brown, 2011). This result is based on studies of both child-focused and parent-focused treatments. Research on the alliance in parent management training, an important parent-focused intervention, has consistently produced significant associations between parent alliance and child outcomes (Kazdin & Whitley, 2006; Kazdin, Whitley, & Marciano, 2006), although a recent study of parent management training showed therapist fidelity to be a better predictor of outcome than parent alliance, which actually predicted lower levels of child behavior change (Hukkelberg & Ogden, 2013).

In an important study of child and parent alliance in usual clinical care, Hawley and Weisz (2005) found that child-reported alliance was a better predictor of symptom changes than parent-reported alliance. However, consistent with the view of parents as treatment gatekeepers, parent alliance was related to fewer cancellations, no shows, and greater therapist–parent consensus on termination. A similar pattern of findings was obtained by Acurrso, Hawley, and Garland (2013), who found that more positive parent alliance predicted less dropout, a greater number of sessions attended, and higher levels of treatment satisfaction. Parent alliance, then, appears to be critically important for treatment engagement and retention. Early dropout and sporadic attendance are likely to compromise even the most efficacious treatments.

Mechanisms of Action. Alliance has been conceptualized as a change process – an active element in therapy that directly affects outcomes – and as a facilitating process – a catalyst that promotes the effects of other active elements. As a change process, direct associations between alliance and outcome are expected, whereas indirect or mediated relations are posited when alliance is viewed as a facilitating process. The vast majority of alliance–outcome studies has examined direct, unmediated associations consistent with alliance as a change process. A common account for this direct link is that the therapeutic relationship itself has corrective properties; that is, the experience of a close relationship characterized by acceptance, support, and empathy prompts emotional and behavioral change (Shirk & Russell, 1996). Although clinically appealing, this view lacks adequate conceptual specificity for understanding mechanisms of change. It is possible that the therapeutic alliance, like other close relationships, directly impacts arousal and reactivity, but this effect has not been demonstrated in a therapy relationship (Coan & Maresh, 2014).

When alliance is viewed as a facilitating process it is assumed that the alliance promotes involvement in active components – common elements – of therapy. The development of a positive, collaborative relationship enhances client participation in therapy tasks, especially those tasks that may be challenging, such as prolonged exposure. Alliance, then, is connected to outcome through client involvement in active elements. This view of alliance has roots in both psychodynamic and behavioral traditions (Shirk & Saiz, 1992), but mediated alliance effects have not been evaluated in the child and adolescent literature.

Of course, for the alliance to be either a change or facilitating process it must be demonstrated that the alliance is not merely the consequence of early symptom change or a marker for other pre-treatment characteristics (e.g., attachment style or social skills) that might impact outcome. Recent studies are beginning to clarify these issues (Kazdin & Durbin, 2012; Labouliere et al., 2015) but further study is needed.

Alliance-Building Strategies. Given the potential contribution of alliance to outcome, how is a positive working relationship established? Although many treatment manuals recommend attending to alliance formation, remarkably few studies have examined this issue with children and adolescents. Instead, therapists are typically advised to provide a warm, friendly relationship with few behavioral specifics. In a study of therapist alliance-building behaviors in CBT for child anxiety, Creed and Kendall (2005) examined 11 behaviors across the first three sessions as predictors of subsequent alliance. Three therapist behaviors emerged as predictors of early child-reported alliance. Therapist collaborative behavior positively predicted early alliance. Collaboration refers to both language use, using words like "us" and "we" frequently as well as describing and designing activities in a collaborative manner. In contrast, *pushing the child to talk* and *finding common ground* (e.g., "Oh, I like baseball, too") negatively predicted early child-reported alliance. Collaboration and *not being overly formal* positively predicted therapist-rated alliance later in treatment. Although this study represents an important first empirical effort to identify therapist behaviors that contribute to child alliance, the absence of a measure of initial alliance or resistance makes it difficult to know if these therapist behaviors are cause or consequence of initial child presentation. For example, children who initially present as cooperative might elicit higher rates of collaborative behaviors from therapists. In addition, it is instructive to consider behaviors that did not predict child alliance. Surprisingly, common clinically recommended behaviors such as playfulness, encouragement, and validation did not predict stronger alliances although limited variability might account for the lack of associations. In a study involving child anxiety and depression, McLeod and Weisz (2005) found associations between alliance and specific intervention strategies. Therapists' greater use of CBT strategies predicted stronger child alliances. This finding is interesting in that it suggests that technical elements are interconnected with relational elements. In this context, Kendall and colleagues (2009) examined the impact of a challenging treatment component – in-session exposure – on child alliance. Using latent growth curve analyses, they found alliance growth to be steep early in treatment and then slow or flatten over time. Importantly, this trajectory was evident in treatments that included or did not include in-session exposure. Thus, in contrast to clinical expectations in-session exposure did not undermine alliance.

Although alliance formation with adolescents has been described as especially difficult in the clinical literature, few studies have addressed this process. In an initial study, Karver and colleagues (2008) examined associations between therapist engagement strategies and alliance among adolescents who were depressed and had made a suicide attempt. Three clusters of therapist behaviors coded during the first two sessions were used as predictors of adolescent-reported and observationally coded alliance at session three. Two positive clusters of rapport strategies were assessed, one involving the social-emotional aspects of therapy (e.g., explores experience, expresses support, and uses socialization strategies), and the other involving structural aspects of therapy (e.g., presents a collaborative approach, presents treatment model, formulates goals). In addition, one negative cluster was also measured which involved therapist lapses (e.g., criticizes, fails to acknowledge expressed emotion). In the CBT condition, more extensive rapport-building strategies predicted more positive adolescent-reported alliance at session three (a similar trend emerged for observed alliance). Higher rates of therapist lapses in session two strongly predicted both self-reported and observed alliance at session three. This pattern also was found in the nondirective, supportive therapy condition. When the three clusters were considered simultaneously, only session two therapist lapses significantly predicted alliance. These results suggest that therapists need to consider strategies that promote alliance formation and guard against lapses that undermine it. Of course, causal direction cannot be established with these findings; it is possible that difficult adolescents elicit negative therapist behaviors.

Building on these results, Russell, Shirk, and Jungbluth (2008) examined patterns in therapist alliance-building behaviors over the course of the first session of CBT for adolescent depression. Based on an analysis of 16 therapist behaviors coded across ten-minute segments, four underlying factors were identified. The first involved highly structured presentation of the treatment model combined with low exploration of the adolescent's experience. Given that the factors were extracted over time, this factor represents oscillation between socialization and experiential (eliciting information and focusing on experiences) behaviors over time. One might view this factor as efforts to personalize treatment. The second factor included items reflecting therapist responsiveness (e.g., eliciting thoughts and feelings, providing support, restructuring cognitions). The third involved therapist lapses and the fourth included motivational behaviors (e.g., explores motivations, sets positive expectations for treatment). Factors showed different patterns of prominence over the course of the first session. Factor one showed a U-shaped pattern consistent with the notion that therapists provide higher structure at the beginning and end of the first session as they lay out the treatment model and then assign initial homework. In contrast, therapist responsiveness and motivational behaviors increased sharply during the middle part of the first session. The growth in both therapist responsiveness and motivation-focused behaviors accounted for significant variance in therapist-rated alliance following session three. Further, variance in adolescent-reported alliance was associated with greater therapist approximation of the U-shaped trend for personal socialization. One of the most important findings to emerge from this study is that patterns of therapist behavior were better predictors of subsequent alliance than average scores on individual items or factors. Thus, both the content and timing of therapist strategies appear to be important for alliance formation.

Alliance in Family Therapy

Given that multiple individuals are seen conjointly in family therapy, the character and complexity of the alliance differs from individual therapy. In addition to the "identified patient's" alliance with the therapist, each family member develops their own relationship with the therapist. Minimally then, the alliance in family therapy must account for multiple relationships either as the sum of individual alliances or as *patterns* of alliances (Friedlander et al., 2011). Family therapists have long recognized that family properties emerge from the interactions among individual family members (Minuchin, 1974). Consequently, constructs such as structure, cohesion, and boundaries represent emergent characteristics of the whole rather than the sum of individual parts. Similarly, the alliance in family therapy might not be most adequately conceptualized as the sum of individual alliances (Pinsof & Catherall, 1986). Instead, a conceptual model that accounts for the structure of alliances or the overall character of the family's alliance has been proposed (Pinsof, Horvath, & Greenberg, 1994). Unfortunately, measures of alliance in family therapy have not always captured these emergent qualities (Friedlander et al., 2011). Instead, parent, target patient, or therapist perspectives often are used to assess family alliance. As in individual therapy, Bordin's (1979) transtheoretical model of bonds, tasks, and goals has informed the *content* of many family alliance measures.

Relations Between Alliance and Outcome in Family Therapy. Two meta-analyses of alliance–outcome relations in family therapy have produced mixed results. One yielded a small to moderate mean correlation of 0.27 (Friedlander et al., 2011), whereas the other (McLeod, 2011) revealed a nonsignificant mean correlation of 0.05. The difference in effect sizes appears to be due to the exclusions of studies that evaluated retention/continuation as an outcome in the McLeod (2011) meta-analysis; such studies were included by Friedlander and colleagues (2011).

A similar pattern emerges when alliance–outcome relations in evidence-based family therapies are considered. The contribution of alliance to outcome has been evaluated in multidimensional family therapy (MDFT; Liddle et al., 2009), a well-established treatment for adolescent substance use and externalizing problems (Liddle, 2016; Waldron & Turner, 2008). Four studies evaluated alliance–outcome relations in MDFT. Two of these studies examined the association between observed family alliance and treatment retention (Robbins et al., 2008; Shelef & Diamond, 2008). Both studies revealed medium effects ($r = 0.36$ and $r = 0.41$). In contrast, two studies that examined alliance and problem outcomes (Hogue et al., 2006; Shelef et al., 2005) yielded mixed results ($r = 0.05$ and $r = 0.24$). These results suggest that alliance in MDFT is a better predictor of family retention than symptom outcomes. Two studies of alliance in functional family therapy (FFT), an empirically supported family-based treatment for externalizing problems, also produced small to moderate associations between alliance and treatment continuation/completion (Flicker et al.,

2008; Robbins et al., 2003). Taken together, the alliance appears to be an important buffer against premature dropout in these family treatments.

Mechanisms of Action. The preponderance of evidence suggests that the primary contribution of alliance in family therapy is its role in treatment retention. The absence of a robust literature comparing outcomes for treatment completers versus treatment dropouts makes the magnitude of this contribution difficult to assess. To the degree that early dropout portends poorer outcomes the alliance appears to impact outcome *indirectly* by offsetting premature termination. A strong alliance appears to promote increased exposure to active treatment elements in family therapy.

Family Alliance-Building Strategies. Given the importance of the alliance for treatment continuation, are there therapist behaviors or strategies that promote family alliance formation? Despite extensive clinical discussion of engagement strategies, the empirical literature is quite thin. In a series of early studies, Szapocznik and colleagues (Santisteban et al., 1996; Szapocznik et al., 1988) developed an explicit engagement intervention based on core structural and strategic therapy principles. From the point of initial contact with referred families, therapists immediately focused on exploring family patterns and offering family-based reframes for presenting problems. Results from two randomized trials showed that the engagement intervention produced higher rates of initial engagement and better retention than standard family therapy without the engagement intervention (Santisteban et al., 1996). Although results from these studies indicate that very early therapist strategies can impact initial attendance and continuation, family alliance was not assessed in these studies.

In a study of engagement and alliance in MDFT, Diamond and colleagues (1999) examined therapists' alliance-building behaviors in MDFT with adolescents who abused substances. The extensiveness of specific therapist behaviors was compared to two alliance groups: those that started with poor alliances and remained poor, and those that started out poor and improved across sessions. Results indicated that therapists attended to adolescents' experiences, presented themselves as the adolescent's ally, and focused on developing meaningful goals more extensively in improved than nonimproved alliance cases. Although this small, exploratory study actually addressed alliance *building* by examining cases with initially poor alliances, the study only assessed adolescents' alliances and not family alliance per se. Given the importance of alliance for retention in family therapy, additional studies of alliance-building strategies are sorely needed.

Client Involvement in Therapy

Closely related to the construct of alliance is client involvement. Client involvement refers to the level of active participation in the therapy process (O'Malley, Suh, & Strupp, 1983). In this respect, client involvement appears to overlap with the task collaboration dimension of the alliance. Rather than reflecting an *agreement* about tasks, involvement refers to behavioral engagement in therapy processes and procedures. Tasks vary markedly across types of therapy (e.g., participating in exposure, problem-solving, emotion expression, or symbolic play), and involvement reflects the degree to which the client is actively participating or collaborating in these activities. Although the early literature on child involvement included a wide range of measures (Karver et al., 2006), in recent years the focus has shifted to observations of overall session involvement (Chu & Kendall, 2004) marked by specific behavioral indicators (child elaborates, child spontaneously brings up topic) or to the coding of participation in specific therapy tasks (e.g., participation in cognitive restructuring activity; Shirk et al., 2013).

Relations Between Client Involvement and Outcome. In their meta-analysis of relationship factors in child and adolescent therapy, Karver et al. (2006) found a small to moderate, weighted mean correlation, $r = 0.27$, between measures of involvement and treatment outcomes. Given the varied treatments included (e.g., psychodynamic, cognitive-behavioral, treatment-as-usual, family therapy) and the broad range of treated problems (e.g., self-control, externalizing, emotional, mixed problems) it is tempting to conclude that involvement is a transtheoretical *and* transdiagnostic relational element. Across treatments, problems, and settings, level of client involvement appears to be a consistent predictor of outcome. From a clinical perspective, promoting active participation in therapy is a pivotal task regardless of treatment content.

A number of studies have evaluated client involvement in evidence-based therapies for children and adolescents. In a series of studies Chu and colleagues (Chu & Kendall, 2004, 2009) evaluated the contribution of client involvement to outcome in CBT for child anxiety. To assess client involvement the *Client Involvement Rating Scale (CIRS)* was used (Chu & Kendall, 1999). This scale includes six items, four indicating positive involvement (e.g., child shows enthusiasm in therapy-related tasks), and two negative (e.g., child is withdrawn or passive). Two ten-minute segments from early and late therapy sessions are coded to index child involvement. In a sample of children between the ages of eight and 13, all diagnosed with anxiety disorders, Chu and Kendall found that involvement at mid-treatment in CBT positively predicted treatment gains, though early involvement did not. Importantly, involvement was not related to client demographic or diagnostic characteristics, suggesting that level of involvement is, at least partially, an emergent process in the therapy relationship. In fact, in a subsequent study, Chu and Kendall (2009) found that observed therapist flexibility, that is, the degree to which therapists customized manual-based CBT content, predicted level of child involvement at mid-treatment. More recently, Hudson and colleagues (2014) evaluated changes in child involvement and therapist flexibility over the course of CBT for child and early adolescent anxiety. Data were derived from multiple randomized, clinical trials. Using latent growth modeling, small but somewhat inconsistent associations were found between positive treatment gains and positive changes in child involvement. Results suggested that therapists who maintained high levels of involvement produced better outcomes. As in the prior study, level of therapist flexibility was associated with child involvement; however, change in these variables was not connected.

Two studies have examined the link between *adolescent* involvement in CBT and treatment outcome. In the first, Karver et al. (2008) evaluated client involvement with the patient participation subscale of the *Vanderbilt Psychotherapy Scales* (O'Malley, Suh, & Strupp, 1983). Coding was anchored to specific therapeutic tasks as outlined by the treatment manual (e.g., problem-solving). A ten-minute segment of interaction was coded from the point of task introduction. In the initial study, involvement was assessed in both CBT and client-centered therapy for adolescents experiencing depression. Client involvement was strongly associated with symptom reduction in the CBT condition but not in client-centered therapy. Given the small sample size, the association was not statistically reliable despite its magnitude. In a second study, Shirk and colleagues (2013) examined links among client involvement in cognitive restructuring, changes in cognitive distortions, and reductions in depressive symptoms. Although changes in cognitive distortions predicted changes in depressive symptoms, client involvement did not predict changes in distortions or symptoms. It is possible that observation of involvement in a single, albeit important, therapy task was too narrow to capture variation in adolescent involvement. Although anchoring involvement observations to core components has advantages, involvement in a range of tasks is likely to provide a better index of client involvement.

Mechanisms of Action. Active involvement, in contrast to passive exposure, is assumed to result in (a) greater encoding of therapy content and concepts, (b) increased probability of skill acquisition and strengthening, and (c) greater likelihood of integrated activation of cognitive, emotional, and behavioral systems. As in other learning contexts, active involvement promotes sustained attention, application, and elaboration of relevant material. Although observation of a model (mere exposure) can be sufficient to produce behavior change, active behavioral rehearsal with feedback is more likely to strengthen acquisition. Alternatively, increased involvement in the case of graded exposure provides more opportunities to unlearn behavioral patterns and emotional reactions.

To a great degree, the central question concerns *involvement in what?* Results showing links between involvement and outcome across widely divergent forms of therapy suggest the answer is, whatever the active ingredients might be. However, children can be actively involved in puppet play or board games without therapeutic benefit. In fact, one might expect that involvement would be a relatively weak predictor of outcome in treatments with no known active ingredients. This is not to say that play therapy, for example, is inert. Rather therapist warmth, support, and empathy might constitute active ingredients in nondirective child therapy. In contrast, in treatments with known active components, variations in client involvement should be strongly related to variations in outcomes. In a comparative RCT, this is precisely what emerged. Client involvement showed a sizable relation with outcome in the CBT condition, but virtually no association in nondirective supportive therapy (Karver et al., 2006). Client involvement should matter most in the context of common elements, that is, treatment procedures derived from therapies of known efficacy.

Given the importance of client involvement, *how* do therapists promote engagement in child and adolescent therapy? As noted, therapist flexibility is associated with client involvement, at least in the treatment of child anxiety. As Kendall and colleagues (2009) have observed, there are many ways to present the core content of manuals while maintaining fidelity. Rigid adherence to content and examples is unlikely to be engaging. Instead, personalizing content to fit a child's interests and preferred activities is important. For example, emotion identification, a common component of emotion regulation procedures, can be delivered through downloading scenes from the internet, making collages from magazines, or by playing emotional charades. In essence, the therapist's task is to "breathe life into the therapy manual" by making treatment tasks stimulating (Kendall et al., 1999). Again, depending on the child's developmental level, therapists can use action figures in play or a simulated radio talk show to present and practice problem-solving steps. Manuals represent a way to operationalize treatment principles and procedures; the therapist's job is to embed these principles into customized activities that promote child involvement.

Many treatment protocols include the use of rewards to promote client involvement. Commonly, positive reinforcement is used for homework completion between sessions. For example, *Coping Cat* (Kendall, Podell, & Gosch, 2010) explicitly recommends the use of STIC (Show That I Can) charts, which emphasize child mastery and serve as a basis for rewarding homework completion. Similar strategies can be applied to in-session involvement ranging from systematic use of verbal praise to earning points toward special activities (e.g., going for an ice cream). Some therapists effectively use free play time at the end of sessions to promote child involvement in treatment tasks. Although the use of in-session rewards for involvement has not been systematically evaluated, the use of contingent reinforcement for increasing targeted behavior has a robust evidence base.

Finally, emerging evidence suggests that therapist initial engagement strategies are associated with subsequent client involvement. Jungbluth and Shirk (2009) evaluated therapist engagement behaviors in CBT for adolescents experiencing depression. Initial level of adolescent resistance at the start of therapy was assessed. After controlling for initial adolescent resistance, nearly 40% of the variance in adolescent involvement in sessions four and eight was explained by therapist behaviors in session one. Specifically, higher levels of adolescent involvement were associated with greater therapist attention to adolescent experiences, more exploration of adolescent motivation, and lower levels of therapist-provided structure in session one.

The negative association between initial therapist structuring and subsequent adolescent involvement is somewhat surprising. However, intercorrelations among therapist behaviors indicated that low structure was associated with higher levels of eliciting adolescent experience. This pattern might set the stage for adolescent involvement by encouraging adolescent verbal participation from the start of treatment. Therapists who structured the first session by talking about the treatment model and the nature of depression might have inadvertently cast the adolescent in a receptive, rather than active role.

Relational Elements in Therapy with Adults

The search for common elements has focused on treatment procedures that populate variants of efficacious child therapies. Relational elements refer to features of the therapeutic relationship that contribute to positive outcomes. Research on adult therapy has identified several relational elements including group cohesion, empathy, collecting client feedback, and alliance across individual adult, youth, and family therapy (Norcross & Wampold, 2011). Research on relationship processes in the youth treatment literature has focused primarily on alliance and client involvement.

Conclusion

The search for common elements in child and adolescent therapy has focused on the identification of treatment procedures that are shared across multiple efficacious therapies (Chorpita, Deleiden, & Weisz, 2005). However, psychological therapies do not occur in a vacuum. Rather, they are implemented in the context of a relationship. Relational elements refer to relationship processes that cut across therapeutic approaches and contribute to outcome, either directly or indirectly. This review of potential relational elements provides solid, but modest, support for a direct association with outcome for two elements – alliance in individual child and adolescent therapy and client involvement – and mixed support for one – alliance in family therapy. That there has been limited research on other relational elements found to contribute to outcome in adult therapy makes it difficult to assess their role in child and adolescent therapy. Constructs such as group cohesion, empathy, and positive regard are prominent in the theoretical literature, but understudied in the empirical literature.

In the past, relational features and technical components were often pitted against each other in terms of their contribution. Growing evidence indicates that relational elements like alliance and involvement contribute to outcome in evidence-based therapies. Consequently, the integration of relational and common elements is essential for effective child and adolescent therapy.

Useful Resources

- *Elusive Alliance: Treatment Engagement with High-Risk Adolescents* edited by David Castro-Blanco and Marc S. Karver, American Psychological Association, 2010
- *Psychotherapy Relationships that Work* edited by John C. Norcross, Oxford University Press, 2011

References

Accurso, E. C., Hawley, K. M., & Garland, A. F. (2013). Psychometric properties of the Therapeutic Alliance Scale for Caregivers and Parents. *Psychological Assessment, 25*(1), 244.

Ahn, H. N., & Wampold, B. E. (2001). Where oh where are the specific ingredients? A meta-analysis of component studies in counseling and psychotherapy. *Journal of Counseling Psychology, 48*(3), 251.

Bordin, E. S. (1979). The generalizability of the psychoanalytic concept of the working alliance. *Psychotherapy: Theory, Research, & Practice, 16*(3), 252.

Chorpita, B. F., & Daleiden, E. L. (2009). Mapping evidence-based treatments for children and adolescents: Application of the distillation and matching model to 615 treatments from 322 randomized trials. *Journal of Consulting and Clinical Psychology, 77*, 566–579.

Chorpita, B. F., Daleiden, E. L., & Weisz, J. R. (2005). Identifying and selecting the common elements of evidence based interventions: A distillation and matching model. *Mental Health Services Research, 7*(1), 5–20.

Chu, B. C., & Kendall, P. C. (1999). Child Involvement Rating Scale (CIRS): Scoring manual. Unpublished coding manual.

Chu, B. C., & Kendall, P. C. (2004). Positive association of child involvement and treatment outcome within a manual-based cognitive-behavioral treatment for children with anxiety. *Journal of Consulting and Clinical Psychology, 72*(5), 821.

Chu, B. C., & Kendall, P. C. (2009). Therapist responsiveness to child engagement: Flexibility within manual-based CBT for anxious youth. *Journal of Clinical Psychology, 65*(7), 736–754.

Coan, J. A., & Maresh, E. L. (2014). Social baseline theory and the social regulation of emotion. In J. Gross (ed.), *The handbook of emotion regulation*. 2nd edn (pp. 221–238). New York: Guilford Press.

Creed, T. A., & Kendall, P. C. (2005). Therapist alliance-building behavior within a cognitive-behavioral treatment for anxiety in youth. *Journal of Consulting and Clinical Psychology, 73*(3), 498.

Diamond, G. M., Liddle, H. A., Hogue, A., & Dakof, G. A. (1999). Alliance-building interventions with adolescents in family therapy: A process study. *Psychotherapy: Theory, Research, Practice, Training, 36*(4), 355.

Eltz, M. J., Shirk, S. R., & Sarlin, N. (1995). Alliance formation and treatment outcome among maltreated adolescents. *Child Abuse & Neglect, 19*(4), 419–431.

Flicker, S. M., Turner, C. W., Waldron, H. B., Ozechowski, T. J., & Brody, J. L. (2008). Ethnic background, therapeutic alliance, and treatment retention in functional family therapy with adolescents who abuse substances. *Journal of Family Psychology*, 22, 167–170.

Freud, A. (1946). *The psycho-analytical treatment of children*. Oxford: Imago Publishing Co.

Friedlander, M. L., Escudero, V., Heatherington, L., and Diamond, G. M. (2011). Alliance in couple and family therapy. *Psychotherapy*, *48*(1), 25.

Hawley, K. M., & Weisz, J. R. (2005). Youth versus parent working alliance in usual clinical care: Distinctive associations with retention, satisfaction, and treatment outcome. *Journal of Clinical Child & Adolescent Psychology*, *34*(1), 117–128.

Hogue, A., Dauber, S., Stambaugh, L. F., Cecero, J. J., & Liddle, H. A. (2006). Early therapeutic alliance and treatment outcome in individual and family therapy for adolescent behavior problems. *Journal of Consulting and Clinical Psychology*, 74, 121–129.

Hudson, J. L., Kendall, P. C., Chu, B. C., Gosch, E., Martin, E., Taylor, A., & Knight, A. (2014). Child involvement, alliance, and therapist flexibility: Process variables in cognitive-behavioural therapy for anxiety disorders in childhood. *Behaviour Research and Therapy*, *52*, 1–8.

Hukkelberg, S. S., and Ogden, T. (2013). Working alliance and treatment fidelity as predictors of externalizing problem behaviors in parent management training. *Journal of Consulting and Clinical Psychology*, *81*(6), 1010.

Jungbluth, N. J., & Shirk, S. R. (2009). Therapist strategies for building involvement in cognitive-behavioral therapy for adolescent depression. *Journal of Consulting and Clinical Psychology*, *77*(6), 1179.

Karver, M. S., Handelsman, J. B., Fields, S., & Bickman, L. (2006). Meta-analysis of therapeutic relationship variables in youth and family therapy: The evidence for different relationship variables in the child and adolescent treatment outcome literature. *Clinical Psychology Review*, *26*(1), 50–65.

Karver, M., Shirk, S., Handelsman, J. B., Fields, S., Crisp, H., Gudmundsen, G., & McMakin, D. (2008). Relationship processes in youth psychotherapy: Measuring alliance, alliance-building behaviors, and client involvement. *Journal of Emotional and Behavioral Disorders*, *16*, 15–28.

Kazdin, A. E., & Durbin, K. A. (2012). Predictors of child–therapist alliance in cognitive behavioral treatment of children referred for oppositional and antisocial behavior.*Psychotherapy*, *49*(2), 202.

Kazdin, A. E., & Whitley, M. K. (2006). Pretreatment social relations, therapeutic alliance, and improvements in parenting practices in parent management training. *Journal of Consulting and Clinical Psychology*, *74*(2), 346.

Kazdin, A. E., Whitley, M., & Marciano, P. L. (2006). Child–therapist and parent–therapist alliance and therapeutic change in the treatment of children referred for oppositional, aggressive, and antisocial behavior. *Journal of Child Psychology and Psychiatry*, *47*(5), 436–445.

Keeley, M. L., Geffken, G. R., Ricketts, E., McNamara, J. P., & Storch, E. A. (2011). The therapeutic alliance in the cognitive behavioral treatment of pediatric obsessive-compulsive disorder. *Journal of Anxiety Disorders*, *25*(7), 855–863.

Kendall, P. C. (1991). *Child and adolescent therapy: Cognitive-behavioral procedures*. New York: Guilford Press.

Kendall, P. C., Comer, J. S., Marker, C. D., Creed, T. A., Puliafico, A. C., Hughes, A. A., . . . & Hudson, J. (2009). In-session exposure tasks and therapeutic alliance across the treatment of childhood anxiety disorders. *Journal of Consulting and Clinical Psychology*, *77*(3), 517–525.

Kendall, P. C., Podell, J., Gosch, E. A., & Behr, R. (2010). *The coping cat: Parent companion*. Ardmore, PA: Workbook Publishing.

Labouliere, C. D., Reyes, J. P., Shirk, S., & Karver, M. (2017). Therapeutic alliance with depressed adolescents: Predictor or outcome? Disentangling temporal confounds to understand early improvement. *Journal of Clinical Child & Adolescent Psychology, 46*(4), 600–610.

Liddle, H. A. (2016). Multidimensional family therapy: Evidence base for transdiagnostic treatment outcomes, change mechanisms, and implementation in community settings. *Family Process, 55*(3), 558–576.

Liddle, H. A., Rowe, C. L., Dakof, G. A., Henderson, C. E., & Greenbaum, P. E. (2009). Multidimensional family therapy for young adolescent substance abuse: Twelve-month outcomes of a randomized controlled trial. *Journal of Consulting and Clinical Psychology, 77*(1), 12.

McLeod, B. D. (2011). Relation of the alliance with outcomes in youth psychotherapy: A meta-analysis. *Clinical Psychology Review, 31*(4), 603–616.

McLeod, B. D., & Weisz, J. R. (2005). The therapy process observational coding system-alliance scale: Measure characteristics and prediction of outcome in usual clinical practice. *Journal of Consulting and Clinical Psychology, 73*(2), 323.

Miller, S., Wampold, B., & Varhely, K. (2008). Direct comparisons of treatment modalities for youth disorders: A meta-analysis. *Psychotherapy Research, 18*(1), 5–14.

Minuchin, S. (1974). *Families and family therapy.* Cambridge, MA: Harvard University Press.

Norcross, J. C., & Wampold, B. E. (2011). Evidence-based therapy relationships: Research conclusions and clinical practices. *Psychotherapy, 48*(1), 98.

O'Malley, S. S., Suh, C. S., & Strupp, H. H. (1983). The Vanderbilt Psychotherapy Process Scale: A report on the scale development and a process-outcome study. *Journal of Consulting and Clinical Psychology, 51*(4), 581–586.

Ormhaug, S. M., Shirk, S. R., & Wentzel-Larsen, T. (2015). Therapist and client perspectives on the alliance in the treatment of traumatized adolescents. *European Journal of Psychotraumatology, 6.*

Pinsof, W. M., & Catherall, D. R. (1986). The integrative psychotherapy alliance: Family, couple and individual therapy scales. *Journal of Marital and Family Therapy, 12*(2), 137–151.

Pinsof, W. M., Horvath, A. O., & Greenberg, L. S. (1994). An integrative systems perspective on the therapeutic alliance: Theoretical, clinical, and research implications. In A. O. Horvath (ed.), *The working alliance: Theory, research, and practice* (pp. 173–195). New York: Wiley.

Robbins, M. S., Mayorga, C. C., Mitrani, V. B., Szapocznik, J., Turner, C. W., & Alexander, J. F. (2008). Adolescent and parent alliances with therapists in brief strategic family therapy with drug-using Hispanic adolescents. *Journal of Marital and Family Therapy, 34,* 316–328.

Robbins, M. S., Turner, C. W., Alexander, J. F., & Perez, G. A. (2003). Alliance and dropout in family therapy for adolescents with behavior problems: Individual and systemic effects. *Journal of Family Psychology, 17,* 534–544.

Rogers, C. R. (1957). The necessary and sufficient conditions of therapeutic personality change. *Journal of Consulting Psychology, 21*(2), 95.

Russell, R., Shirk, S., & Jungbluth, N. (2008). First-session pathways to the working alliance in cognitive-behavioral therapy for adolescent depression. *Psychotherapy Research, 18*(1), 15–27.

Santisteban, D. A., Szapocznik, J., Perez-Vidal, A., Kurtines, W. M., Murray, E. J., & LaPerriere, A. (1996). Efficacy of intervention for engaging youth and families into treatment and some variables that may contribute to differential effectiveness. *Journal of Family Psychology, 10*(1), 35.

Shelef, K., & Diamond, G. M. (2008). Short form of the revised Vanderbilt Therapeutic Alliance Scale: Development, reliability, and validity. *Psychotherapy Research, 18*(4), 433–443.

Shelef, K., Diamond, G. M., Diamond, G. S., & Liddle, H. A. (2005). Adolescent and parent alliance and treatment outcome in multidimensional family therapy. *Journal of Consulting and Clinical Psychology, 73*, 689–698.

Shirk, S., Jungbluth, N., & Karver, M. (2012). Change processes and active components. In P. C. Kendall (ed.), *Child and adolescent therapy: Cognitive-behavioral procedures* (pp. 471–498). New York: Guilford Press.

Shirk, S. R., Crisostomo, P. S., Jungbluth, N., & Gudmundsen, G. R. (2013). Cognitive mechanisms of change in CBT for adolescent depression: Associations among client involvement, cognitive distortions, and treatment outcome. *International Journal of Cognitive Therapy, 6*(4), 311–324.

Shirk, S. R., & Karver, M. (2003). Prediction of treatment outcome from relationship variables in child and adolescent therapy: A meta-analytic review. *Journal of Consulting and Clinical Psychology, 71*(3), 452.

Shirk, S. R., Karver, M. S., & Brown, R. (2011). The alliance in child and adolescent psychotherapy. *Psychotherapy, 48*(1), 17.

Shirk, S. R., & Russell, R. L. (1996). *Change processes in child psychotherapy: Revitalizing treatment and research*. New York: Guilford Press.

Shirk, S. R., & Saiz, C. C. (1992). Clinical, empirical, and developmental perspectives on the therapeutic relationship in child psychotherapy. *Development and Psychopathology, 4*(4), 713–728.

Szapocznik, J., Perez-Vidal, A., Brickman, A. L., Foote, F. H., Santisteban, D., Hervis, O., & Kurtines, W. M. (1988). Engaging adolescent drug abusers and their families in treatment: A strategic structural systems approach. *Journal of Consulting and Clinical Psychology, 56*(4), 552.

Waldron, H. B., & Turner, C. W. (2008). Evidence-based psychosocial treatments for adolescent substance abuse. *Journal of Clinical Child & Adolescent Psychology, 37*(1), 238–261.

20

Closing the Research to Practice Gap

Amy Altszuler, Stephen Hupp, and William E. Pelham Jr.

As described in the companion book, *Pseudoscience in Child and Adolescent Psychotherapy* (Hupp, 2019), pseudoscientific psychotherapy practices for youth are continuing to proliferate. Fortunately, recent decades have also witnessed an explosion of research aiming to improve mental health outcomes for children and adolescents. Over 750 manualized treatment protocols, targeting a wide range of youth-focused mental health conditions, have been evaluated in hundreds of randomized trials (Chorpita et al., 2011), and many of these treatments are now classified as "well-established" according to evidence-based treatment (EBT) guidelines put forth by leading organizations (e.g., Southam-Gerow & Prinstein, 2014). Yet, the United States continues to be faced with an enormous mental health burden. For example, approximately one-third of adolescents in the United States experience severe impairment due to a mental health condition over their lifetimes, but only about a third of these youth receive treatment, with even lower rates among ethnic/racial minorities (Merikangas et al., 2010, 2011). While improving access to care remains a top priority, past research demonstrates that providing more treatment through a comprehensive continuum of care often does not lead to better outcomes (Bickman et al., 2000), highlighting the need to focus on the content and quality of care provided.

Most youth are treated in community-based settings, where the average effect of treatment is zero (The National Advisory Mental Health Council, 2001; Weisz & Jensen, 2001). That is, on average, youth treated in usual care settings commonly do not get better with treatment (Garland et al., 2012). In contrast, EBTs yield effect sizes in the moderate to large range, significantly outperforming usual care (Chorpita et al., 2011; Weisz et al., 2013). A major reason for this disparity is that EBTs, and, more broadly, evidence-based practices, are seldom used in community-based settings (Garland, Bickman, & Chorpita, 2010). Further, when components of EBTs are used in usual care, they are rarely delivered with the intensity or comprehensiveness recommended by the literature (Garland, Brookman-Frazee, et al., 2010). For example, Garland, Bickman, and Chorpita (2010) conducted an observational study of usual care practices for youth with externalizing behavior problems and found that many components that are associated with large effect sizes, such as parent skill practice, were delivered in less than 10% of sessions and were almost never delivered with high intensity.

While the efficacy of youth-focused treatments has been demonstrated in multiple research settings, the effectiveness of EBTs in usual care settings has received much less attention. This is problematic given that university-based clinics, in which the majority of randomized trials are conducted, vary from usual care settings in a number of important ways (Chorpita et al., 2002; Southam-Gerow, Ringeisen, & Sherrill, 2006). That is, compared to youth who are included in clinical trials, youth treated in usual care settings tend to be more ethnically and racially diverse, come from families with fewer economic resources, have more comorbid conditions, and experience more psychosocial stressors (Ehrenreich-May et al., 2011; Southam-Gerow et al., 2008). Therefore, therapy in usual care tends to focus on multiple problems, whereas EBTs are typically focused around one specific problem area (Weisz et al., 2015). This poses a challenge to usual care organizations, who must decide which of the many available EBTs in which to train providers with varying backgrounds. On the contrary, therapists in research studies are typically graduate students or masters-level clinicians who are supervised by doctoral-level psychologists and who receive many hours of focused training on a particular protocol prior to its implementation (Weisz et al., 2013). Training in EBTs is further complicated by the funding structure of usual care systems. While clinical trials are typically supported through grant funding devoted to demonstrating efficacy of a particular treatment, usual care organizations often rely on a combination of private and public funds that must be spread across multiple priorities (Schoenwald et al., 2008). In sum, relative to research settings, usual care organizations are tasked with serving a needier and more complex population with fewer resources.

Given the many differences between the conditions under which EBTs are tested and the usual care settings in which they are disseminated, it is unsurprising that many clinicians are hesitant regarding the use of evidence-based approaches. Often cited reasons for disliking EBTs include difficulty individualizing treatments to complex client populations, client resistance to treatment approach, and irrelevance of the research supporting EBTs (Jensen-Doss et al., 2009; Nelson & Steele, 2008; Nelson, Steele, & Mize, 2006).

Clinician factors that positively predict use of EBTs include training in and knowledge of EBTs; positive attitudes towards EBTs and clinical research; and holding a behavioral, cognitive, or cognitive-behavioral theoretical orientation (Jensen-Doss et al., 2009; Karekla, Lundgren, & Forsyth, 2004; Nakamura, Higa-McMillan, et al., 2011; Nelson & Steele, 2007, 2008). The organizational culture of service-providing agencies also plays an important role, with clinicians from more open and supportive agencies reporting greater use of EBTs (Aarons et al., 2012; Nelson & Steele, 2007).

Agency heads must also worry about affording EBTs as the name-brand versions can be quite costly, and although generic equivalents are often free and available they are sometimes not accepted by state or local funding agencies that do not understand the underlying basis for the interventions. All dissemination and implementation efforts should keep these factors in mind.

Key Organizations Emphasizing Evidence-Based Practice

In this last Side-Bar Box, a few organizations and their websites deserve special recognition. These organizations are immensely useful for professionals and parents because they describe evidence-based approaches and also identify how to find practitioners experienced in their use. First, the website of Association for Behavioral and Cognitive Therapies (ABCT; abct.org) contains extremely useful information related to both adults and youth, and the organization holds a yearly convention. Second, the Society for Clinical Child and Adolescent Psychology (SCCAP; Division 53 of the American Psychological Association) has also been a leader in disseminating information about evidence-based practices specifically geared for intervention with youth. The affiliated websites (clinicalchildpsychology.org & effectivechildtherapy.org) also contain a treasure trove of information. The SCCAP co-sponsors a National Conference in Clinical Child and Adolescent Psychology, and most recently they have partnered with the Center for Children and Families at Florida International University to provide continuing education for professionals and informational videos for parents through a new not-for-profit website – indices4kids.com (Kuriyan et al., 2017). Overall, both of these organizations have been instrumental in moving the evidence-based ball forward.

Efforts to Close the Research to Practice Gap

National calls to improve access to quality mental health services for youth, such as the Surgeon General's Conference on Children's Mental Health (Satcher, 2000), have led to increased scrutiny of traditional methods for evaluating treatment practices and have given rise to dissemination and implementation research within child and adolescent psychology (Schoenwald & Hoagwood, 2001). Dissemination and implementation research broadly aims to understand how to: (1) disseminate knowledge regarding evidence-based practices, and (2) effectively implement interventions in usual care settings (National Institute of Mental Health, 2015). Whereas traditional models of treatment evaluation emphasize demonstrating what works best for most under ideal conditions, dissemination and implementation models attempt to account for the many factors that impact services in usual care settings (e.g., complex presenting problems, overburdened clinicians) to understand what works best for whom under what conditions (Shoham & Insel, 2011). As the dissemination and implementation field grows, two major models for addressing the research to practice gap have emerged: (1) working toward scaling up evidence-based systems of care in which youth and their families receive quality mental health care in usual care settings (Chorpita, Daleiden, & Collins, 2013), and (2) expanding the current individual psychotherapy paradigm to include broader and less expensive models for treatment delivery to improve access to mental health services across the broad spectrum of youth requiring care (Chorpita & Daleiden, 2014; Kazdin & Blase, 2011).

Chorpita and colleagues (2013) have conducted extensive work on the multiple components that make up an evidence-based care model. These efforts have led to the development of Managing and Adapting Practice (MAP), a system for applying evidence-based care that has been successfully adopted in two state-wide systems and one county-wide system in the United States (Nakamura, Chorpita, et al., 2011; Southam-Gerow et al., 2014). A major tenet of the MAP system is "doing more with what we know," and significant progress has been made toward making the extant research literature more accessible and relevant to usual care clinicians (Chorpita & Daleiden, 2014). For example, the PracticeWise Evidence-Based Services Database matches client characteristics with EBTs to help clinicians choose an initial treatment plan (e.g., cognitive-behavioral therapy for anxiety, behavioral parent training for disruptive behavior problems) (Chorpita et al., 2011; Chorpita, Daleiden, & Collins, 2013). Further, this team has worked to identify the specific treatment procedures and techniques that are common among the hundreds of available EBTs. This work has resulted in a list of "common elements" (e.g., problem-solving, relaxation) that are most likely to produce clinical change (Chorpita, Becker, & Daleiden, 2007). Synthesizing the literature in this way allows usual care clinicians, who often have little time to prepare treatment plans, to quickly access the information most pertinent to making meaningful clinical change.

Expanding on the common elements approach, Chorpita and Weisz developed a modular treatment protocol (MATCH; Weisz et al., 2012), which restructures the key components of manualized EBTs for youth anxiety, depression, trauma, and conduct problems into stand-alone modules that teach a specific skill (e.g., praise) or strategy (e.g., cognitive restructuring). These modules are accompanied by decision trees that guide clinicians in charting the course of treatment based on individual client factors (e.g., presenting concerns, progress in treatment). MATCH has been shown to outperform both standard EBTs and usual care in community mental health settings (Chorpita, Weisz, et al., 2013; Weisz et al., 2012). Further, clinicians viewed MATCH as more acceptable than standard EBTs, citing more flexibility to personalize treatment and increase involvement in clinical decision making (Borntrager et al., 2009; Weisz et al., 2012).

Other research teams have also been working to improve the flexibility with which EBTs can be implemented across presenting problems through the development of transdiagnostic protocols. These approaches target underlying factors that are common across multiple mental health problems (e.g., maladaptive cognitions, poor problem-solving skills), and have been shown to effectively reduce both internalizing and externalizing problems in youth (Ehrenreich et al., 2009; Weisz et al., 2017). In addition to demonstrating effectiveness and acceptability, transdiagnostic protocols minimize the need for usual care organizations to provide trainings in multiple EBTs targeting individual presenting problems. Efforts to repackage EBTs in ways that increase clinician and organization acceptability are important given that both clinician attitude and organizational climate predict increased use of evidence-based approaches in usual care (Jensen-Doss et al., 2009; Nakamura, Higa-McMillan, et al., 2011; Nelson & Steele, 2008).

Another key component of evidence-based systems of care is effective intervention implementation. While treatment outcomes research has traditionally evaluated how one manualized treatment protocol impacts outcomes on a group level, clinical practice requires providers to evaluate whether interventions are effectively serving their clients and to change course if a client is nonresponsive to recommended treatments. Measurement feedback systems are useful tools that facilitate the collection and analysis of client assessment data to inform clinicians how their treatments are working in real time (Bickman, 2008). Research supports that increased use of measurement feedback systems leads to improved youth outcomes; however, clinician implementation of measurement feedback systems has been variable, highlighting the need for further research identifying barriers to consistent implementation (Bickman et al., 2011; Lyon et al., 2017). While measurement feedback systems inform clinicians when they are getting off course, they do not tell clinicians where to go next. Results from randomized controlled trials (RCTs), the current gold standard method for evaluating interventions (Chambless & Ollendick, 2001), do a similarly poor job of guiding clinicians on how to proceed in treatment when things do not go as planned.

Fortunately, recent advancements in research methodology have allowed us to begin to rigorously evaluate interventions that more closely approximate clinical practice (Almirall & Chronis-Tuscano, 2016; Collins, Murphy, & Strecher, 2007). Specifically, by allowing for multiple randomizations to several treatment protocols, adaptive designs can shed light on the most effective and efficient treatment algorithms for youth. For example, Pelham and colleagues (2016) used an adaptive design to evaluate the most effective sequencing and dosing of the two existing EBTs for youth with attention-deficit/hyperactivity disorder (ADHD) – behavioral intervention and stimulant medication (Evans, Owens, & Bunford, 2014). Findings from this study suggest that initiating treatment with eight sessions of group behavioral parent training and a school-based daily report card, rather than stimulant medication, produces better outcomes after a year of treatment compared to starting with stimulant medication. Further, this behavioral-first approach is the more cost-effective of the two approaches for youth with ADHD (Page et al., 2016; Pelham et al., 2016). Future research using adaptive designs will allow us to continue to identify the most effective treatment algorithms for youth, which can help reduce the amount of time youth spend in treatment and facilitate efficient allocation of resources (Sherrill, 2016).

Expanding the ways in which mental health services are delivered is another top priority in dissemination and implementation research. The current predominate delivery model for psychotherapy services is to treat one youth or family at a time, which is a costly and time-intensive model that limits the impact of services on mental health burden (Kazdin & Blase, 2011). While this level of intensity is certainly indicated in a number of cases, applying a public health framework to mental health services, in which the level of care intensifies with the level of need, can help reach a larger number of youth and their families (Atkins & Frazier, 2011). The Triple P – Positive Parenting Program is an Australia-based example of a comprehensive tiered approach used to treat youth behavior problems, in which Tier 1 (lowest intensity) involves nationwide media campaigns to increase knowledge of positive parenting (e.g., television programming, newspaper articles), and Tier 5 (highest intensity) involves intensive individual or group parent training sessions (Sanders, 2012). Relatedly, in the study cited above, Pelham and colleagues found that one-third of those families that received group BPT (16 families per group) did not require further treatment, and of those that needed additional, individual sessions, only 2+ additional sessions on average were required. This dramatic reduction in the intensity of the behavioral treatment resulted in the lower cost of the psychosocial treatment relative to medication, a result not reported previously. The United States has also seen increased efforts to expand models of delivery to reach those with mental health needs more efficiently and in a cost-effective manner (Yates, 2011).

The availability of telehealth-based interventions such as videoconferencing has increased substantially in recent years, and these interventions have been shown to be effective in improving a range of youth outcomes (Nelson & Patton, 2016) and in cutting treatment-related costs (Hedman, Ljótsson, & Lindefors, 2012). Research supports that other cost-saving interventions such as telephone-based therapy and computer-assisted interventions effectively reduce youth mental health problems, including disruptive behavior problems and anxiety (Khanna & Kendall, 2010; McGrath et al., 2011). Several smartphone applications have also come on board, but more research is needed to support their effectiveness (Grist, Porter, & Stallard, 2017). In addition to technology-based solutions, research has examined the effectiveness of offering mental health services outside of traditional clinic or hospital settings to increase the reach of services. Several programs have successfully leveraged the natural settings in which children and families typically spend time, including pediatrician's offices, schools, and afterschool programs (Atkins, Shernoff, & Frazier, 2015; Frazier et al., 2012; Njoroge et al., 2016). Further, research supports that programs delivered by nontraditional providers (e.g., parents, laypersons), either alone or in combination with mental health professionals, are acceptable to families and improve parent-perceived support; however, more research is needed to evaluate the impact of such programs on youth's functioning (Hoagwood et al., 2010).

Conclusion

Historically, research and practice in clinical child and adolescent psychology have taken two relatively disparate paths. Research on best practices was typically conducted with a sample of carefully selected participants who were treated by clinicians with extensive training in the particular treatment protocol being implemented, and the protocol was determined to be effective if most participants improved. Whereas this approach has provided the field with valuable information regarding practices that can be effective under ideal circumstances, it has provided little information on how to make these approaches effective under typical circumstances, in which clinicians with varying training backgrounds are required to treat youth with multiple problems and evaluate how interventions are working on an individual level.

Fortunately, growing concern regarding the mental health burden and advancements in research methodology have allowed the field to shift toward conducting research that better addresses how to improve youth outcomes in routine clinical practice. Recent years have witnessed impressive efforts to modify existing evidence-based intervention and assessment practices to make them more accessible and relevant to usual care settings, and to expand models of care to more efficiently target youth in need. Future work that continues to consider the factors that impact usual care practice, including those relevant to individual clients (e.g., racial/ethnic background, treatment preferences, comorbidity), clinicians (e.g., training, theoretical orientation, clinical decision making), and organizations (e.g., resources, attitudes toward evidence-based practices) is imperative for closing the research to practice gap. As research and clinical practice become more fully integrated (e.g., Almirall & Toscano, 2016), we expect to see reductions in the enormous mental health burden facing our nation.

References

Aarons, G. A., Glisson, C., Green, P. D., Hoagwood, K., Kelleher, K. J., Landsverk, J. A., ... & Schoenwald, S. (2012). The organizational social context of mental health services and clinician attitudes toward evidence-based practice: A United States national study. *Implementation Science, 7*, 56. http://doi.org/10.1186/1748-5908-7-56

Almirall, D., & Chronis-Tuscano, A. (2016). Adaptive interventions in child and adolescent mental health. *Journal of Clinical Child & Adolescent Psychology, 45*(4), 383–395. http://doi.org/10.1080/15374416.2016.1152555

Atkins, M. S., & Frazier, S. L. (2011). Expanding the toolkit or changing the paradigm: Are we ready for a public health approach to mental health? *Perspectives on Psychological Science, 6*(5), 483–487. http://doi.org/10.1177/1745691611416996

Atkins, M. S., Shernoff, E. S., & Frazier, S. L. (2015). Redesigning community mental health services for urban children: Supporting schooling to promote mental health. *Journal of Consulting and Clinical Psychology, 83*(5), 839–852. https://doi.org/10.1177/1745691611416996

Bickman, L. (2008). A measurement feedback system (MFS) is necessary to improve mental health outcomes. *Journal of the American Academy of Child & Adolescent Psychiatry, 47*(10), 1114–1119. https://doi.org/10.1097/CHI.0b013e3181825af8

Bickman, L., Kelley, S. D., Breda, C., de Andrade, A. R., & Riemer, M. (2011). Effects of routine feedback to clinicians on mental health outcomes of youths: Results of a randomized trial. *Psychiatric Services, 62*(12), 1423–1429. http://doi.org/10.1176/appi.ps.002052011

Bickman, L., Lambert, E. W., Andrade, A. R., & Penaloza, R. V. (2000). The Fort Bragg continuum of care for children and adolescents: Mental health outcomes over 5 years. *Journal of Consulting and Clinical Psychology, 68*(4), 710–716.

Borntrager, C., Chorpita, B., Higa-McMillan, C., & Weisz, J. (2009). Provider attitudes toward evidence-based practices: Are the concerns with the evidence or with the manuals? *Psychiatric Services, 60*(5). http://doi.org/10.1176/appi.ps.60.5.677

Chambless, D. L., & Ollendick, T. H. (2001). Empirically supported psychological interventions: Controversies and evidence. *Annual Review of Psychology, 52*, 685–716.

Chorpita, B. F., Angeles, L., Daleiden, E. L., & Phillips, L. (2011). Evidence-based treatments for children and adolescents: An updated review of indicators of efficacy and effectiveness. *Clinical Psychology: Science and Practice, 18*, 154–172.

Chorpita, B. F., Becker, K. D., & Daleiden, E. L. (2007). Understanding the common elements of evidence-based practice: Misconceptions and clinical examples. *Journal of the American Academy of Child & Adolescent Psychiatry, 46*(5), 647–652. http://doi.org/10.1097/chi.0b013e318033ff71

Chorpita, B. F., & Daleiden, E. L. (2014). Doing more with what we know: Introduction to the Special Issue. *Journal of Clinical Child & Adolescent Psychology, 43*(2), 143–144. http://doi.org/10.1080/15374416.2013.869751

Chorpita, B. F., Daleiden, E. L., & Collins, K. S. (2013). Managing and adapting practice: A system for applying evidence in clinical care with youth and families. *Clinical Social Work Journal.* Advance online publication. http://doi.org/10.1007/s10615-013-0460-3

Chorpita, B. F., Weisz, J. R., Daleiden, E. L., Schoenwald, S. K., Palinkas, L. A., Miranda, J., . . . & Gibbons, R. D. (2013). Long-term outcomes for the Child STEPs randomized effectiveness trial: A comparison of modular and standard treatment designs with usual care. *Journal of Consulting and Clinical Psychology, 81*(6), 999–1009. http://doi.org/10.1037/a0034200

Chorpita, B. F., Yim, L. M., Donkervoet, J. C., Arensdorf, A., Amundsen, M. J., McGee, C., . . . & Morelli, P. (2002). Toward large-scale implementation of empirically supported treatments for children: A review and observations by the Hawaii Empirical Basis to Services Task Force. *Clinical Psychology: Science and Practice, 9*(2), 165–190.

Collins, L. M., Murphy, S. A., & Strecher, V. (2007). The Multiphase Optimization Strategy (MOST) and the Sequential Multiple Assignment Randomized Trial (SMART): New methods for more potent eHealth interventions. *American Journal of Preventive Medicine, 32* (Supplement 5), S112–S118.

Ehrenreich, J. T., Goldstein, C. M., Wright, L. R., & Barlow, D. H. (2009). Development of a Unified Protocol for the Treatment of Emotional Disorders in Youth. *Child & Family Behavior Therapy, 31*(1), 20–37. https://doi.org/10.1080/07317100802701228

Ehrenreich-May, J., Southam-Gerow, M. A., Hourigan, S. E., Wright, L. R., Pincus, D. B., & Weisz, J. R. (2011). Characteristics of anxious and depressed youth seen in two different clinical contexts. *Administration and Policy in Mental Health and Mental Health Services Research*, *38*(5), 398–411. http://doi.org/10.1007/s10488-010-0328-6

Evans, S. W., Owens, J. S., & Bunford, N. (2014). Evidence-based psychosocial treatments for children and adolescents with attention-deficit/hyperactivity disorder. *Journal of Clinical Child & Adolescent Psychology*, *43*, 527–551. http://doi.org/10.1080/15374410701820117

Frazier, S. L., Chacko, A., Van Gessel, C., O'Boyle, C., & Pelham, W. E. (2012). The Summer Treatment Program meets the South Side of Chicago: Bridging science and service in urban after-school programs. *Child and Adolescent Mental Health*, *17*(2), 86–92. http://doi.org/10.1111/j.1475-3588.2011.00614.x

Garland, A. F., Bickman, L., & Chorpita, B. F. (2010). Change what? Identifying quality improvement targets by investigating usual mental health care. *Administration and Policy in Mental Health and Mental Health Services Research*, *37*(1–2), 15–26. http://doi.org/10.1007/s10488-010-0279-y

Garland, A. F., Brookman-Frazee, L., Hurlburt, M., Accurso, E. C., Zoffness, R., Haine, R. A., & Ganger, W. (2010). Mental health care for children with disruptive behavior problems: A view inside therapists' offices. *Psychiatric Services*, *61*(8), 788–795. https://doi.org/10.1176/ps.2010.61.8.788

Garland, A. F., Haine-Schlagel, R., Brookman-Frazee, L., Baker-Ericzen, M., Trask, E., & Fawley-King, K. (2012). Improving community-based mental health care for children: Translating knowledge into action. *Administration and Policy in Mental Health and Mental Health Services Research*. http://doi.org/10.1007/s10488-012-0450-8

Grist, R., Porter, J., & Stallard, P. (2017). Mental health mobile apps for preadolescents and adolescents: A systematic review. *Journal of Medical Internet Research*, *19*(5), e176.

Hedman, E., Ljótsson, B., & Lindefors, N. (2012). Cognitive behavior therapy via the Internet: A systematic review of applications, clinical efficacy and cost–effectiveness. *Expert Review of Pharmacoeconomics & Outcomes Research*, *12*(6), 745–764.

Hoagwood, K. E., Cavaleri, M. A., Olin, S. S., Burns, B. J., Slaton, E., Gruttadaro, D., & Hughes, R. (2010). Family support in children's mental health: A review and synthesis. *Clinical Child and Family Psychology Review*, *13*(1), 1–45. http://doi.org/10.1007/s10567-009-0060-5

Hupp, S. (2019). *Pseudoscience in child and adolescent psychotherapy: Skeptical guide for therapists and parents*. Cambridge, UK: Cambridge University Press.

Jensen-Doss, A., Hawley, K. M., Lopez, M., & Osterberg, L. D. (2009). Using evidence-based treatments: The experiences of youth providers working under a mandate. *Professional Psychology: Research and Practice*, *40*(4), 417–424. http://doi.org/10.1037/a0014690

Karekla, M., Lundgren, J. D., & Forsyth, J. P. (2004). A survey of graduate training in empirically supported and manualized treatments: A preliminary report. *Cognitive and Behavioral Practice*, *11*(2), 230–242. http://doi.org/10.1016/S1077-7229(04)80034-8

Kazdin, A. E., & Blase, S. L. (2011). Rebooting psychotherapy research and practice to reduce the burden of mental illness. *Perspectives on Psychological Science*, *6*(1), 21–37. http://doi.org/10.1177/1745691610393527

Khanna, M. S., & Kendall, P. C. (2010). Computer-assisted cognitive behavioral therapy for child anxiety: Results of a randomized clinical trial. *Journal of Consulting and Clinical Psychology*, *78*(5), 737–745. http://doi.org/10.1037/a0019739

Kuriyan, A. B., Altszuler, A. R., Comer, J. S., & Pelham Jr., W. E. (2017). Disseminating evidence-based practices for child and adolescent mental health: A web-based initiative. *Evidence-Based Practice in Child and Adolescent Mental Health*, *2*(1), 54–67.

Lyon, A. R., Pullmann, M. D., Whitaker, K., Ludwig, K., Wasse, J. K., & McCauley, E. (2017). A digital feedback system to support implementation of measurement-based care by school-based mental health clinicians. *Journal of Clinical Child & Adolescent Psychology*, 1–12. http://doi.org/10.1080/15374416.2017.1280808

McGrath, P. J., Lingley-Pottie, P., Thurston, C., MacLean, C., Cunningham, C., Waschbusch, D. A., ... & Chaplin, W. (2011). Telephone-based mental health interventions for child disruptive behavior or anxiety disorders: Randomized trials and overall analysis. *Journal of the American Academy of Child & Adolescent Psychiatry*, 50(11), 1162–1172. http://doi.org/10.1016/j.jaac.2011.07.013

Merikangas, K., Jian-ping, H., Burstein, M., Swanson, S., Avenevoli, S., Lihong, C., ... & Swendsen, J. (2010). Lifetime prevalence of mental disorders in US adolescents: Results from the National Comorbidity Study – Adolescent Supplement. *Journal of the American Academy of Child & Adolescent Psychiatry*, 49(10), 980–989. https://doi.org/10.1016/j.jaac.2010.05.017

Merikangas, K. R., He, J., Burstein, M. E., Avenevoli, S., Case, B., Georgiades, K., ... & Olfson, M. (2011). Service utilization for lifetime mental disorders in U.S. adolescents: Results of the National Comorbidity Survey – Adolescent Supplement (NCS-A). *Journal of the American Academy of Child & Adolescent Psychiatry*, 50(1), 32–45. https://doi.org/10.1016/j.jaac.2010.10.006

Nakamura, B. J., Chorpita, B. F., Hirsch, M., Daleiden, E., Slavin, L., Amundson, M. J., ... & Vorsino, W. M. (2011). Large-scale implementation of evidence-based treatments for children 10 years later: Hawaii's evidence-based services initiative in children's mental health. *Clinical Psychology: Science and Practice*, 18(1), 24–35. http://doi.org/10.1111/j.1468-2850.2010.01231.x

Nakamura, B. J., Higa-McMillan, C. K., Okamura, K. H., & Shimabukuro, S. (2011). Knowledge of and attitudes towards evidence-based practices in community child mental health practitioners. *Administration and Policy in Mental Health and Mental Health Services Research*, 38(4), 287–300. http://doi.org/10.1007/s10488-011-0351-2

The National Advisory Mental Health Council Workgroup on Child and Adolescent Mental Health Intervention Development and Deployment. (2001). *Blueprint for change: Research on child and adolescent mental health*. Washington, DC: National Institute of Mental Health. www.nimh.nih.gov/about/advisory-boards-and-groups/namhc/reports/blueprint-for-change-research-on-child-and-adolescent-mental-health.shtml#ch-vi-a

National Institute of Mental Health. (2015). *National Institute of Mental Health Strategic Plan for Research*. Bethesda, MD: National Institute of Mental Health. www.nimh.nih.gov/about/strategic-planning-reports/nimh_strategicplanforresearch_508compliant_corrected_final_149979.pdf

Nelson, E.-L., & Patton, S. (2016). Using videoconferencing to deliver individual therapy and pediatric psychology interventions with children and adolescents. *Journal of Child and Adolescent Psychopharmacology*, 26(3), 212–220. http://doi.org/10.1089/cap.2015.0021

Nelson, T. D., & Steele, R. G. (2007). Predictors of practitioner self-reported use of evidence-based practices: Practitioner training, clinical setting, and attitudes toward research. *Administration and Policy in Mental Health and Mental Health Services Research*, 34(4), 319–330. http://doi.org/10.1007/s10488-006-0111-x

Nelson, T. D., & Steele, R. G. (2008). Influences on practitioner treatment selection: Best research evidence and other considerations. *Journal of Behavioral Health Services and Research*, 35(2), 170–178. http://doi.org/10.1007/s11414-007-9089-8

Nelson, T. D., Steele, R. G., & Mize, J. A. (2006). Practitioner attitudes toward evidence-based practice: Themes and challenges. *Administration and Policy in Mental Health and Mental Health Services Research, 33*(3), 398–409. http://doi.org/10.1007/s10488-006-0044-4

Njoroge, W. F. M., Hostutler, C. A., Schwartz, B. S., & Mautone, J. A. (2016). Integrated behavioral health in pediatric primary care. *Current Psychiatry Reports, 18*(12), 106. http://doi .org/10.1007/s11920-016-0745-7

Page, T. F., Pelham III, W. E., Fabiano, G. A., Greiner, A. R., Gnagy, E. M., Hart, K. C., . . . & Pelham Jr., W. E. (2016). Comparative cost analysis of sequential, adaptive, behavioral, pharmacological, and combined treatments for childhood ADHD. *Journal of Clinical Child & Adolescent Psychology, 45*(4), 416–5427. http://doi.org/10.1080/15374416.2015.1055859

Pelham, W. E., Jr., Fabiano, G. A., Waxmonsky, J. G., Greiner, A. R., Gnagy, E. M., Pelham III, W. E., . . . & Murphy, S. A. (2016). Treatment sequencing for childhood ADHD: A multiple-randomization study of adaptive medication and behavioral interventions. *Journal of Clinical Child & Adolescent Psychology, 45*(4), 396–415. http://doi.org/10.1080/15374416.2015 .1105138

Sanders, M. R. (2012). Development, evaluation, and multinational dissemination of the Triple P–Positive Parenting Program. *Annual Review of Clinical Psychology, 8,* 345–379. http://doi.org /10.1146/annurev-clinpsy-032511-143104

Satcher, D. (2000). *Mental health: A report of the Surgeon General.* Rockville, MD: U.S. Department of Health and Human Services.

Schoenwald, S. K., Chapman, J. E., Kelleher, K., Hoagwood, K. E., Landsverk, J., Stevens, J., . . . & The Research Network on Youth Mental Health. (2008). A survey of the infrastructure for children's mental health services: Implications for the implementation of empirically supported treatments (ESTs). *Administration and Policy in Mental Health, 35,* 84–97. http://doi.org/10 .1007/s10488-007-0147-6

Schoenwald, S. K., & Hoagwood, K. (2001). Effectiveness, transportability, and dissemination of interventions: What matters when? *Psychiatric Services, 52*(9), 1190–1197.

Sherrill, J. T. (2016). Adaptive treatment strategies in youth mental health: A commentary on advantages, challenges, and potential directions. *Journal of Clinical Child & Adolescent Psychology, 45*(4), 522–527. http://doi.org/10.1080/15374416.2016.1169539

Shoham, V., & Insel, T. R. (2011). Rebooting for whom? Portfolios, technology, and personalized intervention. *Perspectives on Psychological Science, 6*(5), 478–482. http://doi.org/10.1177 /1745691611418526

Southam-Gerow, M. A., Chorpita, B. F., Miller, L. M., & Gleacher, A. A. (2008). Are children with anxiety disorders privately referred to a university clinic like those referred from the public mental health system? *Administration and Policy in Mental Health and Mental Health Services Research, 35*(3), 168–180. http://doi.org/10.1007/s10488-007-0154-7

Southam-Gerow, M. A., Daleiden, E. L., Chorpita, B. F., Bae, C., Mitchell, C., Faye, M., & Alba, M. (2014). MAPping Los Angeles County: Taking an evidence-informed model of mental health care to scale. *Journal of Clinical Child & Adolescent Psychology, 43*(2), 190–200. http:// doi.org/10.1080/15374416.2013.833098

Southam-Gerow, M. A., & Prinstein, M. J. (2014). Evidence base updates: The evolution of the evaluation of psychological treatments for children and adolescents. *Journal of Clinical Child & Adolescent Psychology, 43*(1), 1–6. http://doi.org/10.1080/15374416.2013.855128

Southam-Gerow, M. A., Ringeisen, H. L., & Sherrill, J. T. (2006). Integrating interventions and services research: Progress and prospects. *Clinical Psychology: Science and Practice, 13*(1), 1–8. http://doi.org/10.1111/j.1468-2850.2006.00001.x

Weisz, J., Bearman, S. K., Santucci, L. C., & Jensen-Doss, A. (2017). Initial test of a principle-guided approach to transdiagnostic psychotherapy with children and adolescents. *Journal of Clinical Child & Adolescent Psychology, 46*(1), 44–58. http://doi.org/10.1080/15374416.2016.1163708

Weisz, J. R., Chorpita, B. F., Palinkas, L. A., Schoenwald, S. K., Miranda, J., Bearman, S. K., . . . & Gibbons, R. D. (2012). Testing standard and modular designs for psychotherapy treating depression, anxiety, and conduct problems in youth: A randomized effectiveness trial. *Archives of General Psychiatry, 69*(3), 274–282. http://doi.org/10.1001/archgenpsychiatry.2011.147

Weisz, J. R., & Jensen, A. L. (2001). Child and adolescent psychotherapy in research and practice contexts: Review of the evidence and suggestions for improving the field. *European Child & Adolescent Psychiatry, 10* (Supplement 1), I12–I18. http://doi.org/10.1007/s007870170003

Weisz, J. R., Krumholz, L. S., Santucci, L., Thomassin, K., & Ng, M. Y. (2015). Shrinking the gap between research and practice: Tailoring and testing youth psychotherapies in clinical care contexts. *Annual Review of Clinical Psychology, 11*, 139–163. http://doi.org/10.1146/annurev-clinpsy-032814-112820

Weisz, J. R., Kuppens, S., Eckshtain, D., Ugueto, A. M., Hawley, K. M., & Jensen-Doss, A. (2013). Performance of evidence-based youth psychotherapies compared with usual clinical care: A multilevel meta-analysis. *JAMA Psychiatry, 70*(7), 750–761. http://doi.org/10.1001/jamapsychiatry.2013.1176

Yates, B. T. (2011). Delivery systems can determine therapy cost, and effectiveness, more than type of therapy. *Perspectives on Psychological Science, 6*(5), 498–502. http://doi.org/10.1177/1745691611416994

Index